soluzioni

A Practical Grammar of
Contemporary Italian

Second Edition

soluzioni

A Practical Grammar of
Contemporary Italian

Second Edition

Denise De Rôme

HODDER
EDUCATION
AN HACHETTE UK COMPANY

Orders: please contact Bookpoint Ltd, 130 Milton Park, Abingdon, Oxon OX14 4SB. Telephone: (44) 01235 827720. Fax: (44) 01235 400454. Lines are open from 9.00 to 5.00, Monday to Saturday, with a 24-hour message answering service. You can also order through our website www.hoddereducation.co.uk.

If you have any comments to make about this, or any of our other titles, please send them to educationenquiries@hodder.co.uk

British Library Cataloguing in Publication Data
A catalogue record for this title is available from the British Library

ISBN: 978 1444 10125 6

First Edition Published 2003
This Edition Published 2010
Impression number   10 9 8 7 6 5 4 3 2 1
Year   2014, 2013, 2012, 2011, 2010

Hachette UK's policy is to use papers that are natural, renewable and recyclable products and made from wood grown in sustainable forests. The logging and manufacturing processes are expected to conform to the environmental regulations of the country of origin.

Cover photo from © Maxim Tupikov/iStockphoto.com.
Typeset by MPS Limited (A Macmillan Company).
Printed in Malta for Hodder Education, an Hachette UK Company, 338 Euston Road, London NW1 3BH

Contents

Acknowledgments

The author and publisher would like to thank the following for permission to use copyright material from the works listed:

Simonetta Agnello Hornby and Giangiacomo Feltrinelli Editore, Milano for: *Boccamurata*, 2007

Niccolò Ammaniti and Giulio Einaudi Editore, SpA, Torino for: *Io non ho paura*, 2001

The Estate of Italo Calvino and Arnoldo Mondadori Editore SpA, Milano for: *Marcovaldo, ovvero le stagioni in città*, 1963

Andrea Camilleri and Arnoldo Mondadori Editore SpA, Milano for: 'Il mio debito con Simenon' *in Racconti quotidiani*, 2007

Lara Cardella and Arnoldo Mondadori Editore SpA, Milano for: *Volevo i pantaloni*, 1989

Umberto Eco and RCS Libri/Bompiani for: *Il nome della rosa*, 1980.

Carlo Lapucci and Arnoldo Mondadori Editore SpA, Milano for:'La novella dell'enigma' in *Fiabe Toscane*, 1984

The Estate of Carlo Levi and Giulio Einaudi Editore SpA, Torino for: *Cristo si è fermato a Eboli*, 1945

The Estate of Primo Levi and Giulio Einaudi Editore SpA, Torino for: 'Titanio' in *Il sistema periodico*, 1975 and *Se non ora, quando?*, 1982

The Estate of Cesare Pavese and Giulio Einaudi Editore SpA, Torino for: 'L'eremita' in *La casa in collina e altri racconti*, 1967

The Estate of Fabrizia Ramondino and Giulio Einaudi Editore SpA, Torino for: *Althénopis*, 1981

The Estate of Gianni Rodari and Edizioni EL for: 'Un giocattolo per Natale' in *Il gioco dei quattro cantoni*, 1980

The Editorial board of *Focus* and Gruner+Jahr/Mondadori SpA for: 'Amici in rete' and 'Se non ci fosse la luna', May 2009

Rosario Gambera for his review of Leonardo Sciascia, *Una storia semplice*, 2009 in Jazz al Nero, http://jazzalnero.blogspot.com

---

The author would also like to thank Paola Tite for all her help on the first edition of **Soluzioni**

The author and publisher would like to thank Umberto Eco and RCS Libri/Bompiani for permission to publish. Copyright RCS LibriS.p.A/Bompiani 1980.

Introduction

This is a revised, updated and expanded edition of *Soluzioni*, so even if you have previously consulted it, do read this introduction before you start, as it will help you get the most out of the new features.

Soluzioni is a grammar book for the committed learner. It is designed to improve your understanding of how the Italian language works so that you can learn to communicate with confidence. It takes you from basic to intermediate/advanced level and provides answers to the most frequently asked questions, as well as devoting space to points not always covered in traditional teaching grammars.

No formal knowledge of either English or Italian grammar is taken for granted and all essential terminology is clearly explained. Considerable emphasis is placed on giving you the opportunity to consolidate and practise what you learn, so all the grammar explanations are followed by exercises with answers. You also have the opportunity for additional practice by completing further specially designed interactive exercises on the internet and by consulting the weblinks on www.hodderplus.co.uk/languages

Using *Soluzioni*

Soluzioni is a reference book, so the list of contents does not dictate the order you read it in. This means that you need to familiarise yourself with the special features of the book in order to make the most of all the information it contains.

- All essential grammatical terms are explained: you will find the key ones at the beginning of each chapter and additional ones are explained in more depth in the Glossary at the end.
- The explanations are presented in easy-to-follow tabular form, and are specially designed with difficulties of English speaking learners in mind. There are tips to help you with points which sometimes confuse the learner. These are signposted with the symbol ⚠.
- Levels of difficulty are shown throughout the book. Each main heading within a chapter is signposted with one of three symbols. ◎ indicates core language, ✚ indicates more advanced language, while ◎/✚ signposts a mixture of the two. In this case the more advanced points are individually shown next to the relevant subsections. The same signposting system applies to the exercises.
- You will find lots of examples. They present the language Italians use in daily conversation and writing, and cover a wide range of essential contemporary vocabulary, all with English translations.
- There are plenty of exercises in each unit, so you can consolidate and practise what you learn at every stage: there is a key at the back with the answers.
- Exercises are supplemented by authentic material from contemporary Italian media and literature covering a wide variety of topics and text types: this will help you place the grammar in context and see it in action. Each text is accompanied by short exercises and a few of them provide special opportunity for extensive revision.
- For further revision there are over 160 exercises which you can complete online at www.hodderplus.co.uk/languages. They are best done once you have completed an entire chapter, as they are designed to refresh your memory and extend your knowledge.
- Information is easy to find, as there is a comprehensive Index which you can consult under both English and Italian headings without knowing all the grammatical terms.

- In addition, for quick reference there is a verb Appendix with three tables covering all the important information in a rapidly accessible form.
- There are also numerous cross-references in the text to help you check and consolidate what you learn.

Language and grammar

Although most languages have a more or less standard body of grammar which is taught, in reality there are acceptable 'deviations' from this. In any language what is 'acceptable' grammar may vary considerably. This is most obvious in the difference between the grammar of the spoken and written language and is particularly true of Italian, where regional dialects have had a strong influence. (As late as the early 1950s it is estimated that at least two-thirds of the Italian population habitually spoke regional dialects to family and friends rather than standard Italian.) Learners of Italian therefore need to be aware that there are regional differences and variations, both of grammar and vocabulary, many of which are equally acceptable or 'correct'.

Soluzioni focuses on standard Italian grammar and explains it from the point of view of the English learner, contrasting the different structures of the two languages. It presents the most useful and common language patterns and does not try to account for all possible contexts and all varieties of Italian. However, you will find that the numerous examples and exercises in the book expose you to the way the Italian language is used today.

Learners' tools

Apart from getting the most out of your grammar book, you should seriously consider paying attention to how to use a dictionary. You may not wish to read this right now, but do consult it at some stage for useful tips.

Types of dictionaries

The main types you might consider using are:
- Bilingual (English–Italian; Italian–English)
- Italian monolingual (Italian words explained in Italian)
- Italian synonyms (Italian words explained and similar words given, sometimes with opposites).

Whatever the dictionary, there are usually four kinds of information which tend to be provided:

- spelling ● meaning ● grammar ● pronunciation

Essential abbreviations

Get to know your dictionary: learning to use one effectively is an important language learning skill. No two dictionaries are alike, so familiarise yourself with the one you are using in order to make the most of the information it contains. Begin by understanding the abbreviations – **abbreviazioni**. There is usually a table at the front. This may seem time-consuming, but the effort pays off. The most basic abbreviations include: *agg*. adjective; *art*. article; *avv*. adverb; *f.* feminine; *intr*. intransitive; *inv*. invariable; *m.* masculine; *sost*. or *s.* noun (from *sostantivo*); *tr*. transitive; *v.* verb. So if you come across *s. m. inv*. you will know the word is an invariable masculine noun; if you encounter *v.t.* you will know that it refers to a transitive verb. Finally, two abbreviations can help you avoid embarrassment: *gerg*. slang – and especially *volg*. vulgar.

Trying out a monolingual dictionary

Most learners begin with a bilingual dictionary, but as you progress you may find it rewarding to consult a monolingual dictionary; the definitions provided by a bilingual dictionary may not be detailed enough, whereas a monolingual dictionary will provide more information. You will also find that on the whole the grammatical information in a monolingual dictionary is more complete – for example, when it comes to irregular or controversial plurals.

Finally, bear in mind that it takes time to learn a language, so persevere and enjoy it. The key is to use it as much as you can: take every opportunity to listen to Italian and to read whenever possible. Even if you cannot go to Italy, you can make giant strides at home by using the internet or watching Italian satellite TV. You can also attend a class and try out your Italian in shops and restaurants. I hope you will find *Soluzioni* a clear and useful guide along the way to success. **Buona fortuna!**

Denise De Rôme

1 Nouns

Nouns (**i sostantivi**) are words for naming people, animals, places, things and abstractions such as emotions and ideas. *Anna, dog, Rome, car, anger* and *justice* are all nouns. In Italian, nouns have a gender: they are either masculine or feminine and most of them have a different form for the singular and the plural.

Nouns are often used with articles – words for *the* and for *a/an*. In this chapter the examples are given with definite articles – words for *the* – but these are not translated.

◎ 1.1 Regular nouns

Regular nouns follow a common and predictable pattern depending on their gender (masculine or feminine) and on their number (singular or plural). The gender and number of nouns are very important. This is because in Italian they affect the form of other words, such as articles or adjectives. Compare: **Il ragazzo alto** *the tall boy* and **la ragazza alta** *the tall girl*. In English the article *the* and the adjective *tall* remain the same, but in Italian there are different forms for *the* (**il** and **la**), and for *tall* (**alto** and **alta**), because they depend on the gender and number of the all-important nouns, **ragazzo** and **ragazza**.

(See Chapter 2 for articles and Chapter 3.1 (d), pp. 37–8 for more on number and agreement.)

(a) Nouns ending in -o

Most regular nouns ending in **-o** are masculine and form their plural in **-i**.

Sing. ➡ plural	Examples	Explanations
-o/-io ➡ -i	il treno ➡ i treni *train/s* lo sconto ➡ gli sconti *discount/s* l'aereo ➡ gli aerei *plane/s*	In the plural **-i** replaces **-o**. If the final **-i** of the singular is stressed, the plural ends in **-ii**.
	il cucchiaio ➡ i cucchiai *spoon/s* il figlio ➡ i figli *son/s/children* lo zio (stressed **-i**) ➡ gli zii *uncle/s*	
Exceptions	**But:** il dio ➡ gli dei *god/s* il tempio ➡ i templi *temple/s* l'uomo ➡ gli uomini *man/men* **And note the feminine noun:** la mano ➡ le mani *hand/s*	There are a few important exceptions.
-go ➡ -ghi	l'albergo ➡ gli alberghi *hotel/s* il catalogo ➡ i cataloghi *catalogue/s* il dialogo ➡ i dialoghi *dialogue/s* il gergo ➡ i gerghi *slang/s* il lago ➡ i laghi *lake/s* **But:** l'asparago ➡ gli asparagi	**-ghi** is the most common **-go** plural. An **-h** is needed before **-i** to keep the hard sound of the singular.
-ologo ➡ ologi/ ghi (people only)	il biologo ➡ i biologi *biologist/s* lo psicologo ➡ gli psicologi *pyschologist/s* il sociologo ➡ i sociologi *sociologist/s*	These mostly have **-gi** plurals but **-ghi** endings are sometimes preferred.

Consonant or stressed vowel before **-co** **-co ➡ -chi**	il bo**sc**o ➡ i boschi *wood/s* l'ele**n**co ➡ gli elenchi *list/s* il ta**cc**o ➡ i tacchi *heel/s* il tu**r**co ➡ i turchi *Turk/s* **But:** il po**r**co ➡ i porci *pig/s*	If **-co** is preceded by a consonant or by a stressed vowel, the plural is normally **-chi**.
	il bu**c**o ➡ i buchi *hole/s* il cu**o**co ➡ i cuochi *cook/s* il fi**c**o ➡ i fichi *fig/s* il fu**o**co ➡ i fuochi *fire/s* l'**e**co (m. or f.) ➡ gli echi (m.) *echo/es* **But:** l'a**m**ico ➡ gli amici *friend/s* il gr**e**co ➡ i greci *Greek/s* il nem**i**co ➡ i nemici *enemy/ies*	There are significant exceptions.
Unstressed vowel before **-co** **-co ➡ -ci**	il fa**r**maco ➡ i farmaci *medicine/s* il m**e**dico ➡ i medici *doctor/s* il si**n**daco ➡ i sindaci *mayor/s* **But:** lo st**o**maco ➡ gli stomachi *stomach/s*	When the first, not the last vowel in the word is stressed, the plural is **-ci**.

(b) Nouns ending in -*a*

Most regular nouns ending in -**a** are feminine and form their plural in -**e**.

Sing. ➡ plural	Examples	Explanations
-a ➡ -e	la casa ➡ le case *house/s* l'idea ➡ le idee *idea/s* la galleria ➡ le gallerie *gallery/ies, tunnel/s* **But:** l'ala ➡ le ali *wing/s* l'arma ➡ le armi *weapon/s*	In the plural **-e** replaces **-a**.
-ca ➡ che **-ga ➡ ghe**	l'amica ➡ le amiche *friend/s* la giacca ➡ le giacche *jacket/s* la collega ➡ le colleghe *colleague/s* la paga ➡ le paghe *pay (packet/s)*	An **-h** is inserted before **-e** to keep the hard sound.
Consonant + **-cia ➡ ce** **-gia ➡ ge**	l'ara**n**cia ➡ le arance *orange/s* la pelli**c**cia ➡ le pellicce *fur coat/s* la pio**g**gia ➡ le piogge *rain/s* la spia**g**gia ➡ le spiagge *beach/es*	The -**i** is usually dropped from the plural.
Vowel + **-cia ➡ cie** **-gia ➡ gie**	la bu**g**ia ➡ le bugie *lie/s* la farma**c**ia ➡ le farmacie *chemist/s* (stressed final -**i**) la cili**e**gia *cherry* ➡ le ciliegie *cherry/ies* la vali**g**ia ➡ le valigie *suitcase/s*	The -**i** is normally kept. The plural is sometimes made without the -**i** but never if it is stressed, e.g. **ciliege** but not **buge**.

(c) Nouns ending in -e

Nouns ending in -e can be masculine or feminine and form their plural in -i.

Sing. ➡ plural	Examples	Explanations
-e ➡ -i	il padre ➡ i padri *father/s* il leone ➡ i leoni *lion/s* ***But:*** il bue ➡ i buoi *ox/ oxen* la madre ➡ le madri *mother/s* la tigre ➡ le tigri *tiger/s*	The masculine and feminine forms differ only in the use of the articles.

 Esercizi

1 You're setting up house. Say what you need, beginning, 'Ho bisogno di …' and make each noun plural.

lampada • letto • armadio • tavolo • sedia • poltrona • tendina • specchio • tappeto

2 Now say what you need to bring for the picnic, beginning 'Abbiamo bisogno di …'

piatto • coltello • forchetta • cucchiaio • bicchiere • tazza • scodella • tovagliolo

3 You're buying fruit and vegetables. Draw up your shopping list by making the nouns plural.

lattuga • asparago • fungo • peperone • fico • albicocca • limone • pesca • arancia • ciliegia

✚ 4 The following nouns all refer to people. Four of them form their plural in **-ci** and four in **-chi**. Which is which?

greco • polacco • idraulico • medico • cuoco • tedesco • parroco • turco

✚ 5 All except two of the following nouns form their plural in **-gi**. Which two end in **-ghi**?

archeologo • biologo • chirurgo • dermatologo • drammaturgo • psicologo • sociologo

(d) The gender of nouns ending in -e

⚠ **Attenti!** When you come across a new word ending in **-e,** learn its gender, not just the meaning. When the noun refers to a person, e.g. il padre *father*, la madre, *mother*, gender can be easy to determine. It's worth noting that some -e nouns can be either masculine or feminine: il/la cantante *singer*, il/la complice *accomplice*, l'interprete (m. & f.) *interpreter*, l'ospite (m. & f.) *guest,* il/la superstite *survivor,* il/la testimone *witness.*

It is especially important to learn the gender of **-e** nouns which begin with a vowel, since there is only one singular article, l', for both feminine and masculine words. It can help to repeat the plurals to yourself, as the articles differ: l'eroe, **gli** eroi (m.) *hero/es* but, l'uniforme, **le** uniformi (f.) *uniform/s.* In addition, it will help to learn the gender patterns of some common **-e** endings. These are given below.

Masculine gender patterns

Endings	Examples	Explanations
-ame -iere **-ile -one** **-ore -tore**	il pollame *poultry* il quartiere *district* il cortile *courtyard* il balcone *balcony* il cuore *heart* il pattinatore *male skater* ***But:*** la fame *hunger*, la bile *bile*, la canzone *song*	There are very few exceptions.
-ale	l'animale *animal* il capitale *capital (sum)* il giornale *newspaper* l'ospedale *hospital* il segnale *sign* il canale *canal TV channel* ***But:*** la cattedrale *cathedral* la capitale *capital city* la spirale *spiral* la vocale *vowel*	Mostly masculine, but some common nouns are feminine.

| -ante
-ente | l'atlante *atlas* l'elefante *elephant* il gigante *giant*
il pulsante *push button*
But: la consonante *consonant* la stampante *printer*
l'ambiente *environment* il continente *continent*
il dente *tooth* l'incidente *accident*
But: la corrente *current* la gente *people* la mente *mind* | Mostly masculine,
but some common
nouns are feminine. |

Feminine gender patterns

Endings	Examples	Explanations
-gione -sione **-zione -trice** **-udine**	la ragione *reason* la tensione *tension* la stazione *station* la pittrice *painter* l'abitudine (f.) *habit* la gratitudine *gratitude*	There are no exceptions.

Take care with the following patterns, as some common nouns are masculine.

-ione	l'alluvione (f.) *flood* la comunione *communion* l'opinione (f.) *opinion* la riunione *meeting* l'unione (f.) *union* **But:** il campione *champion/sample* il lampione *lamp post/ street light* il milione *million* il rione *district*	More likely to be feminine but note the exceptions.
-ine	la grandine *hail* l'immagine (f.) *picture/image* l'indagine (f.) *enquiry* l'origine (f.) *origin* la ruggine *rust* **But:** l'argine (m.) *river bank* il cardine *hinge* il confine *border* il fulmine *lightning* l'ordine (m.) *order* il margine *margin* il pettine *comb*	Mostly feminine but some common nouns are masculine.

Masculine and feminine gender patterns

-ice	**masculine:** il codice *code* il giudice *judge* l'indice *index/index finger* il pollice *thumb* **But:** il/la complice *accomplice*	**-ice** nouns are m. if the stress falls before the ending and f. if the stress is on the final **-i.**
	feminine: l'appendice *appendix* la cornice *frame* la narice *nostril* la pattinatrice *woman skater* la radice *root*	

◎/✚ Esercizi

6 Group the following nouns into masculine or feminine, using the endings as a guide.

abitudine • amore • animale • appendice • atlante • azione • elefante • esame • immagine • incidente • indagine • infermiere • opinione • ordine • origine • unione

✚ 7 Now establish the gender of the following: some are irregular, so beware. Make sure you know what they mean.

(a) consonante	vocale	**(d)** alluvione	ambiente		
(b) temporale	monsone	**(e)** appendice	indice		
(c) fulmine	grandine	**(f)** dente	mente	pollice	

◎/✚ 1.2 Irregular nouns

Although irregular nouns do not follow the predictable patterns shown in the previous sections, their forms are governed by clear rules.

(a) Irregular nouns ending in -*a*

Masculine and feminine

Many nouns denoting people end in **a** and are masculine as well as feminine.

Singular ➡ plurals	Explanations
✎ i giornalisti (m.) il/la giornalista (m. and f.)　　　*journalist/s* ◀ le giornaliste (f.)	There is one singular form but different singular articles (**il** or **la** and **l'** for m. and f. nouns beginning with a vowel).
Further examples: l'autista ➡ gli/le autiste *driver/s* il/la pianista ➡ i/pianisti/le pianiste *pianist/s* lo/la specialista ➡ gli specialisti/ le specialiste *specialist/s*	The two plurals are regularly formed, with m. and f. endings in **-i** and **-e** respectively.
l'atleta ➡ gli atleti/le atlete *athlete/s* il/la belga ➡ i belgi/le belghe *Belgian/s* il/la collega ➡ i colleghi/ le colleghe *colleague/s* il pilota ➡ i piloti/le pilote *pilot/s,(motor) racing driver/s* il pirata ➡ i pirati/le pirate *pirate/s* lo/la psichiatra ➡ gli psichiatri/le psichiatre *psychiatrist/s*	

Masculine

Singular ➡ plurals	Explanations
-a ➡ **-i** il clima ➡ i climi *climate/s*	Many masculine nouns in **-ma, -ta, -ca, -ita** and **-ida** have a regular plural in **-i**.
Further examples: l'aroma ➡ gli aromi *aroma/s* il diploma ➡ i diplomi *diploma/s* l'enigma ➡ gli enigmi *enigma/s* il fantasma ➡ i fantasmi *ghost/s* il panorama i panorami *view/s* il problema ➡ i problemi *problem/s* il programma ➡ i programmi *programme/s* il sistema ➡ i sistemi *system/s* lo sperma ➡ gli spermi *sperm/s* lo stratega ➡ gli stateghi *strategist/s* il pianeta ➡ i pianeti *planet/s* il poeta ➡ i poeti *poet/s* il duca ➡ i duchi *duke/s* il parassita ➡ i parassiti *parasite/s* il pesticida ➡ i pesticidi *pesticide/s*	A few are invariable (see next section).

 Attenti! Many nouns ending in -**ma** and -**ta** are regular feminine nouns, e.g. la cometa/le comete *comet/s,* la firma/le firme *signature/s,* la lacrima/le lacrime *tear/s,* la porta/le porte *door/s,* la salma/le salme *corpse/es,* la trama/le trame *plot/s.*

(b) Invariable nouns

Invariable nouns have the same singular and plural forms except for the article, and have a variety of different endings. Here are some common examples.

Masculine

Endings	Examples	Explanations
-a	il/i cinema *cinema/s* il/i cobra *cobra* il/i delta *delta/s* il/i gorilla *gorilla/s* il/i koala *koala bear/s* il/i panda *panda/s* il/i vaglia *money order/s*	Some common invariable nouns in **-a** are of foreign origin.

-è -é **-ò** **-ì**	il/i caffè *coffee/s* il karatè *karate* il/i soufflé *soufflé/s* il/i comò *chest of drawers* il/i falò *bonfire/s* il/i lunedì *Monday/s* il/i tassì *taxi/s* ***But:*** la pipì *wee*	This is quite a small group.
One syllable	lo/gli gnu *gnu/s* il/i re *king/s* il/i tè *tea/s* lo/gli sci *ski/s* ***But:*** la/le gru *crane/s*	Nouns of one syllable are mostly masculine.

Feminine

Endings	Examples	Explanations
-à	l'attività/le attività *activity/ies* la/le città *town/s* l'età/le età *age/s* la/le società *society/ies* ***But:*** il/i papà *Daddy* lo/gli scià *Shah* il/i sofà *sofa*	This is a very large group.
-o	l'auto/le auto *car/s* la/le biro *biro/s* la/le foto *photo/s* la/le moto *motorbike/s* la/le radio *radio/s*	Many are shortened nouns, e.g. l'automobile ➡ l'auto. A few invariable nouns in **o** are masculine.
	il/i frigo *fridge/s* il/i lavabo *wash basin/s* il/i video lo/gli stereo ***Note:*** il/i bancomat *cash dispenser/s* (from **banco automatico**)	
-i	l'analisi/le analisi *analysis/ses* la/le crisi *crisis/es* la/le diagnosi *diagnosis/es* l'eclissi/le eclissi *eclipse/s* l'ipotesi/le ipotesi *hypothesis/es* la/le metropoli *metropolis/es* l'oasi/le oasi *oasis/es* la/le tesi *thesis/es*	Feminine nouns in **-i** are generally of Greek origin – the masculine ones below are not. A few invariable nouns in **-i** are masculine.
	l'alibi/gli alibi *alibi/s* il/i brindisi *toast/s* (*drink*) il/i bisturi *scalpel/s* il/i safari *safari/s*	
-ie	la/le serie *series* la/le specie *type/s, species* ***But:*** la moglie le mogli *wife/wives* la superficie le superfici *surface/s*	A small group. Note the important exceptions.

Masculine and feminine

-ù	il/i bambù *bamboo/s* l'emù/gli emù *emus/s* il/i menù *menu/es* il/i ragù *meat sauce/s* il/i tabù *taboo/s*	The genders of nouns in **-ù** must be learned.
	la gioventù *youth* la/le tivù *TV/s* la/le tribù *tribe/s* la/le virtù *virtue/s*	

Foreign nouns

Masculine foreign nouns are more numerous than feminine ones.

Masculine	l'AIDS (*no plural*) l'/gli autobus *bus/es* il/i blog il/i compact disc/CD il/i computer il/i film il/i flashback il/gli hacker il/i modem il/i pacemaker il/i rapper il/i record l'/gli sms *text message/s* lo/gli sport il/i takeover	**Ending in a consonant** Most end in a consonant, but some end in a vowel.
	il/i database l'/gli euro il/i file il/i mascara/a il/i mouse il software il/i single *unmarried person/s* il reggae	**Ending in a vowel**

| Feminine | la/le brioche (*a kind of croissant*) l'/le élite la/le hit-parade la moquette (*fitted carpet*) l'/le overdose la/le routine la/le toilette la/le roulotte *caravan* | **Ending in a vowel** Most end in a vowel, but a few end in a consonant. |
| | la/le chat room l'/le e-mail la/le jeep la/le holding la/le hostess la/le reception | **Ending in a consonant** |

◎/✚ Esercizi

1 The following are all people. Make them plural, giving two plurals where necessary and including appropriate definite articles.

atleta • collega • ginnasta • tennista • pilota • pediatra • poeta

2 Make these plural nouns singular.

le analisi • le crisi • i dilemmi • i diplomi • le mogli • i problemi • i programmi • i sistemi

3 The following nouns all relate to the natural world. Identify their gender and make each one plural, including appropriate definite articles.

clima • cometa • delta • eclissi • oasi • pianeta

4 Sort the nouns below into masculine and feminine.

auto • foto • frigo • moto • stereo • video

✚ **5** Words for the workplace. Give their gender. Which is the odd one out?

computer • cursore • database • email • fax • file • software • mouse • modem

✚ 1.3 Compound nouns

Compound nouns are common in Italian. They are made up of two or more separate words combined as one and are nearly always masculine. There are complicated rules for forming their plurals, so it is easier to learn them individually, always referring to a dictionary. Italians themselves may vary in their use of compound plurals and so occasionally do dictionaries! Below are some general guidelines.

The formation of plurals

Regular plural	il grattacielo/i *skyscraper/s* il/i passaporto/i *passport/s* il/i portafoglio/i *wallet/s* il/i reggiseno/i *bra/s* il/i capoluogo/ghi *capital town/s* la/le calzamaglia/e *tights*	Either: verb + a singular m. noun or: two nouns of the same gender.
Invariable	l'/gli apriscatole *tin opener/s* il/i portamonete *purse/es* lo/gli stuzzicadenti *toothpick/s* la/le lavastoviglie *dishwasher/s* il/i battiscopa *skirting board/s* il/i cavalcavia *flyover/s*	The most common noun of this type consists of a verb + a plural or a f. singular noun.
	l'/gli aspirapolvere *vacuum cleaner/s* il/la/i/le portavoce *spokesperson/s* lo/gli spazzaneve *snowplough/s* il/la/i/le senzatetto *homeless person/s* il/i dopobarba *aftershave/s* il/i fuorilegge *outlaw/s*	Also common is a verb or preposition + an uncountable noun (e.g. **polvere**) or a noun which is not normally plural in the context (e.g. **tetto**).

A few nouns are made up of two separate words: the first word forms its plural regularly, the second is invariable, e.g. **l'asilo nido/gli asili nido** *nursery/s;* **la conferenza stampa/le**

conferenze stampa *press conference/s*, **il bambino soldato/i bambini soldato** *boy/child soldier/s*; **la ragazza madre/le ragazze madre** *single mother/s*.
   But: **il conto corrente/i conti correnti** *current account/s*.

✚ Esercizi

1 Make the following gadgets plural.

l'accendisigaro • l'apribottiglie • l'aspirapolvere • il cavatappi • il portacenere • il portasapone lo stuzzicadenti • il tagliaerba • il tritacarne (*mincer*) • il tritadocumenti (*shredder*), • il tritarifiuti (*waste disposal unit*)

2 Group these nouns into those with a regular plural ending and those that are invariable.

il portachiavi • il portafoglio • il portamonete • il/la portavoce

il doposcuola • il dopobarba • il senzatetto • il sottotitolo

✚ 1.4 Defective nouns

Very few nouns are truly defective, i.e. possessing only a singular or only a plural form. However, many are used defectively, either mainly in the singular or mainly in the plural.

In Italian and English their use occasionally coincides in the plural form, e.g. **le forbici** *scissors*, **gli occhiali** *glasses*, **i vestiti** *clothes*, but as can be seen from the table below, this is not often the case.

Italian plural, English singular	gli affari *business* i bagagli *luggage* i capelli *hair* i compiti *homework* i consigli *advice* le dimissioni *resignation* le informazioni *information* i lavori di casa *housework* i (mass) media *(mass) media* i mobili *furniture* le notizie *news* le nozze *wedding* le posate *cutlery* i progressi *progress* i soldi *money* gli spaghetti *spaghetti* gli spiccioli *change* gli spinaci *spinach* le stoviglie *crockery*
Italian singular, English plural	il pigiama *pyjamas* la roba *things/stuff* l'uva *grapes*

 Attenti! Remember to use (i) a plural verb when the Italian noun is plural and (ii) a singular verb when it is singular:
   (i) Come vanno gli affari? *How is business?* Sono consigli inutili. *It is useless advice.*
   (ii) La tua roba è pesante. *Your things are heavy.* L'uva è buonissima. *The grapes are delicious.*

✚ Esercizio

1 Express the following in Italian.

(a) *The luggage is here.*

(b) *I need information.*

(c) *He has too much money.*

(d) *The media must be independent.*

(e) *I have no change.*

(f) *Are they seedless grapes?* (**senza semi**)

(g) *Are your pyjamas new?*

(h) *The news is good.*

✚ 1.5 Collective nouns

Collective nouns are used to refer to people, animals or things as a group.

Collective nouns	l'esercito *army* la famiglia *family* la gente *people* il governo *government* il partito *party* la polizia *police* il popolo *people*	Italian collective nouns are generally used with a singular verb.
	e.g. Il governo è stato sconfitto *The government was/were defeated* Il popolo norvegese ha votato a favore dell'UE *The Norwegian people have voted for the EU*	

Numerical collectives	un centinaio *about a hundred* la maggioranza *the majority* un migliaio *about a thousand*	In English the preference is for a plural verb. When there is a clear reference to plural subjects, plural agreements are also possible in Italian.
	e.g. La maggioranza della Camera ha votato a favore *The majority of the Chamber have/has voted in favour* **But:** La maggioranza degli inquilini ha/hanno protestato *The majority of the tenants have protested*	

For the use of singular or plural verbs with percentages, fractions and other collective numbers, see Chapter 17, Numerals and units of measurement, p. 233 and pp. 235–6. For **la maggior parte** *most*, see Chapter 12, Indefinites, p. 173.

✦ Esercizio

1 Choose the appropriate verb(s) to complete the sentences in Italian.

    (a) Il popolo danese **era/erano** contro la UE (*The Danish people were against the EU.*)

    (b) **C'è/Ci** sono troppa gente qui. (*There are too many people here.*)

    (c) **È arrivato/Sono arrivati** un centinaio di ospiti. (*A hundred or so guests have arrived.*)

    (d) La maggioranza dei prigionieri **è stata/sono stati** torturati. (*The majority of the prisoners were tortured.*)

◎/✦ 1.6 More on gender

The gender of nouns in Italian is important because it affects both form and meaning. It affects the form of articles, pronouns, adjectives and participles. In addition, a different gender can give the same word a different meaning. Gender needs to be learned, as even in the case of nouns referring to people, it is not always possible to predict.

(a) The gender of nouns referring to people

Most nouns referring to people are either masculine or feminine according to the sex of the person and many have separate, though similar, forms:

    il cugino/la cugina *cousin*, l'infermiere (m.)/l'infermiera (f.) *nurse*, il nuotatore/la nuotatrice *swimmer*, il padrone/la padrona *owner*, il nipote/la nipote *nephew*, *niece* lo studente/la studentessa *student*.

Some nouns, however, have a single gender for both men and women.

Single-gender nouns

Feminine only	la guida *guide* la guardia *guard* l'icona *icon* la persona *person* la sentinella *sentry, guard* la spia *spy* la star *star* la vittima *victim*	These are some of the most common. Note that the adjectives are always feminine.
	e.g. Guy Burgess è stato/Mata Hari è stata una spia famosa	

Masculine only	il braccio destro *right-hand man* il fantasma *ghost* il monarca *monarch* il sosia *double* il mezzosoprano *mezzosoprano* il contralto *contralto* **But:** il/la soprano *soprano* (**la** is more common)	These can refer to either sex, apart from the singers. **Sosia, contralto, mezzosoprano** and **soprano** are invariable.
	e.g. Pino/Pina è diventato/a il mio braccio destro È diventata un mezzosoprano famoso È una soprano giovanissima	
Masculine for most professions	l'architetto *architect* l'avvocato *lawyer* il designer *designer* il ministro *minister* il redattore *editor* e.g. Mia zia è un noto avvocato (*Not* avvocatessa) Giulia è diventata capo redattore (*Not* redattrice)	Nowadays the masculine form is usually preferred for women as well as men even where feminine forms exist.

◎/✚ Esercizi

1 The following nouns are all masculine, although most of them can refer to both men and women. Which two refer only to women?

architetto • capo • contralto • direttore • ministro • presidente • medico • mezzosoprano

2 The nouns below are all feminine but most of them can refer to men as well. Spot the two that refer only to women.

comparsa • guardia • guida • icona • levatrice • persona • regina • spia • star • vittima

✚ 3 Complete the following sentences making the correct agreement of adjectives and participles.

(a) Maria è diventato/a un architetto molto bravo/a.

(b) Mio figlio è diventato/a una guida molto conosciuto/a.

(c) James Bond, l'agente 007, è una spia famoso/a inventato/a da Ian Fleming.

(d) Le vittime più tragici/tragiche sono stati/e i bambini.

◎/✚ (b) The gender of geographical names

The gender of geographical names is important, as this affects the use of other parts of speech such as the agreement of adjectives and the article used with the prepositions **di, da, a, su** and **in**. (See Chapter 2, pp. 27–9.)

Masculine geographical names	seas	l'Atlantico lo Jonio il Mediterraneo **But:** la Manica *the Channel*
	rivers	il Po il Tevere il Tamigi *the Thames* **But:** la Senna *the Seine* la Loira *the Loire*
	mountains	gli Appennini l'Everest i Pirenei il Monte Bianco il Gran Sasso l'Himalaia **But:** le Alpi le Ande le Dolomiti
	lakes	il Garda il Trasimeno
Feminine geographical names	continents	l'Africa l'Europa
	towns	Londra Milano Parigi **But:** il Cairo il Pireo *Piraeus*
	islands	la Sicilia le Canarie **But:** il Madagascar

Regions and countries can be masculine or feminine. There are no clear-cut rules governing their gender.

Feminine and masculine geographical names	f. regions	la Toscana le Marche la Cornovaglia *Cornwall*
	m. regions	il Friuli il Lazio il Piemonte gli Abruzzi lo Yorkshire il Texas
	f. countries	l'Arabia Saudita l'Australia la Francia la Germania l'Inghilterra l'Irlanda l'Italia la Nuova Zelanda la Scozia la Spagna la Svizzera
	m. countries	il Belgio il Bengala il Brasile il Canada il Galles il Guatamala il Pakistan lo Sri Lanka il Sudafrica ***and:*** Israele (see p. 28)

 Attenti! When you come across the name of a new country or region, learn its gender as well, since this is not always easy to predict from the endings. Most countries ending in **-a,** such as la Nigeria, la Somalia and l'Uganda, are feminine, but some are masculine: e.g. il Botswana, il Kenya, lo Zambia. Note that countries ending in a consonant or in **-e** tend to be masculine: e.g. l'Afghanistan, l'Iraq , il Kuwait, il Nepal, il Cile, lo Zimbabwe.

For practice with geographical names, see pp. 29–30.

◎/✚ (c) Gender and meaning

The gender of similar or related words can cause confusion. Sometimes the difference in meaning resulting from a different gender is slight, but at times it makes a big difference.

Different gender: different meaning

Many nouns with quite different meanings are identical in form apart from the article.

il boa *boa constrictor*	la boa *buoy*	il capitale *capital (funds)*	la capitale *capital (city)*
il fine *aim*	la fine *end, aim*	il fronte *front (war)*	la fronte *forehead*
il lama *llama, lama*	la lama *blade*	il morale *morale*	la morale *moral*

Others are almost identical in form.

il banco *counter, desk*	la banca *bank*	il bilancio *budget, toll*	la bilancia *scales, balance*
il cappello *hat*	la cappella *chapel*	il cartello *sign(post)*	la cartella *file, briefcase*
il manico *handle*	la manica *sleeve*	il mostro *monster*	la mostra *exhibition*
il partito *party (political)*	la partita *match (game)*	il pasto *meal*	la pasta *pasta, cake*
il soffitto *ceiling*	la soffitta *attic*	il testo *text*	la testa *head*

◎ Different gender: related meaning

Some nouns differ in gender but have closely related meanings.

Masculine: the plant	Feminine: the fruit/produce
il ciliegio *cherry tree* il melo *apple tree* il pero *pear tree* il cioccolato *chocolate* il fico *fig tree* il limone *lemon tree* il mandarino *mandarin tree*	la ciliegia *cherry* la mela *apple* la pera *pear* la cioccolata *eating/drinking chocolate* ***But:*** il fico *fig* il limone *lemon* il mandarino *mandarine*

The following nouns with two singular forms and one plural also have closely related meanings.

Two singular forms – m. and f.	One m. plural
il frutto *a (piece of) fruit/fruit (of labour)* la frutta *type of fruit/fruit (in general)*	i frutti *individual fruits*
il legno *wood* la legna *firewood*	i legni *types of wood, woodwind (orchestra)*

◎/✚ Plural gender changes: related meanings

Some masculine nouns have two plurals, masculine and feminine, which are related in meaning. The most common plural is usually feminine, while the masculine plural usually – but not always – expresses the figurative (non-literal) meaning. Here are the most common.

Masculine singular	Feminine plural	Masculine plural
il braccio	le braccia *arms*	i bracci *arms of chair, lake, cross,* etc.
il ciglio	le ciglia *eyelashes*	i cigli *edges* (of road/ditch)
il dito	le dita *fingers* (of the hand)	i diti *individual fingers*
il gesto	le gesta *exploits*	i gesti *gestures*
il grido	le grida *cry, cries*	i gridi *cries* (of animals)
il labbro	le labbra *lips*	i labbri *rim, edge* (of cup, jug, wound)
il membro	le membra *member, limbs* (of body)	i membri *members* (of family, club, etc.)
il muro	le mura *city/castle/house walls*	i muri *individual walls*
l'osso	le ossa *bones* (of the body)	gli ossi *individual bones* (of dead animals)
l'urlo	le urla *yell/s, roar* (of crowd)	gli urli *yells* (of an individual)
il ginocchio	le ginocchia *knee/s* (both knees)	i ginocchi *individual knees*
il lenzuolo	le lenzuola *sheet/s* (a pair of sheets)	i lenzuoli *separate sheets*

The following masculine nouns have an irregular feminine plural ending in **-a,** but there is no change in meaning except in the case of the numbers, where the shift is very slight.

Masculine singular	Feminine plural
il miglio *mile*	le miglia *miles*
il paio *pair*	le paia *pairs*
il riso *laugh*	le risa *laughs*
l'uovo *egg*	le uova *eggs*
il centinaio *about 100*	le centinaia *hundreds*
il migliaio *about 1000*	le migliaia *thousands*

◎/✚ Different gender: same or similar meaning

Occasionally a difference in gender has little significant impact on the meaning, although in practice the different nouns are rarely interchangeable in all contexts. The use of gender with the following words may depend on the speaker's regional origin or on individual preference.

il mattino/la mattina *morning*	**La mattina** is the general word for morning, e.g. **Mi alzo presto la mattina** *I get up early in the morning.* However, these are often interchangeable: **Mi alzo alle sette di mattino/mattina** *I get up at seven in the morning.*
l'orecchio/l'orecchia *ear*	It is more common to use **orecchio**, but the feminine is used in some regions. Both m. and f. plural forms are used with no change in meaning, but the feminine **orecchie** is more common.

il tavolo/la tavola *table* ✚	**Tavolo** usually refers to the item of furniture with a practical use: a table in a restaurant, an ironing board (**tavolo da stiro,** etc.). **Tavola** has a wider range of meanings, e.g. **sedersi a tavola** *to sit down to eat,* **apparecchiare la tavola** *to lay the table.*
terrazzo/terrazza ✚	**Terrazzo** is a terrace of cultivated land or a balcony, while **terrazza** is larger, often a roof terrace.

◎/✚ Esercizi

4 Complete the following sentences in Italian by making the nouns given plural, including an appropriate article if necessary.

    (a) Mi fanno male (orecchio).

    (b) Ho comprato una dozzina di (uovo).

    (c) Il calzolaio fabbricava tante (paio) di scarpe.

    (d) Il giornalaio vendeva (migliaio) di giornali.

    (e) Il fioraio vende (centinaio) di fiori al giorno.

5 The following are trees; give the names of their fruits.

    l'arancio • il fico • il pesco • il mandorlo • l'olivo

6 Make these parts of the body plural. Which is the odd one out?

    il braccio • il ciglio • il dito • il ginocchio • il labbro • la mano

✚ **7** Complete the sentences by putting the words in brackets into Italian, choosing the word with the correct gender.

    (a) È (*il/la fine*) dell'anno scolastico.

    (b) Gli manca (*il/lacapitale*) per comprare la ditta.

    (c) (*Il/la capitale*) dell'Australia non è Sydney.

    (d) Non hanno capito (*il/la morale*) della favola.

    (e) Sono senza soldi, devo andare in (*banco/banca*).

    (f) Devo far riparare (*il manico/la manica*) della borsa.

    (g) Il maestro era già (*nel buco/nella buca*) dell'orchestra.

    (h) Ho prenotato (*un tavolo/una tavola*) per le otto.

✚ **8** Read the following text about Africa, paying particular attention to the geographical names and the words in bold, then answer the questions below.

L'Africa è il terzo continente per **estensione** dopo l'Asia e le Americhe. La sua **superficie** rappresenta il 20,2% delle terre emerse del **pianeta**; i suoi **abitanti** costituiscono un settimo della popolazione mondiale. È attraversata dall'**equatore** e caratterizzata da una grande **varietà** di **climi**. Lo stato più grande del continente è il Sudan mentre quello più piccolo sono le Seychelles, un **arcipelago** al largo della costa orientale.* Lo stato più piccolo sulla terraferma* è invece il Gambia.

Le montagne più alte dell'Africa sono il Ruwenzori (5110 m di **altitudine**), il Kilimangiaro (5895 m di altitudine) e il Monte Kenya (5199 m di altitudine). Il principale fiume africano è il Nilo che attraversa l'Africa nord-orientale e quando raggiunge il Mediterraneo sfocia con un'ampia foce a **delta**.*

Una lunga catena di **laghi** corre lungo la Rift Valley, ai **confini tra** il Congo, l'Uganda, la Tanzania, il Burundi e il Ruanda: i più importanti sono il Lago Vittoria e il Lago Tanganica.

(Wikipedia)

orientale *eastern* • terraferma *mainland* • sfocia ... delta *flows into a wide delta*

    (a) Identify the gender of: **estensione, equatore, abitante, altitudine.**

    (b) Give the gender and singular of: **climi, laghi, confini.**

    (c) Give the gender and plural of: **pianeta, varietà, arcipelago, superficie, delta.**

    (d) Of the eight countries mentioned, name the two feminine ones.

2 Articles

Articles (**gli articoli**) can be definite, indefinite, prepositional or partitive. In English there is one definite article, *the*, and there are two indefinite articles, *a/an*. Prepositional articles are combinations of prepositions with the definite article, e.g. *on the, to the*, etc. and they have special forms in Italian. Partitive articles correspond to *some/any* and also have special forms in Italian.

◎ 2.1 The indefinite article

There are four indefinite articles in Italian: two masculine and two feminine. They can be used before singular nouns, e.g. *a dog, an animal*, and sometimes before an accompanying adjective, e.g. *a big dog, a tiny animal*. In Italian their form depends on the gender and spelling of the noun or adjective which follows.

(a) Indefinite articles: masculine and feminine forms

The form of the article depends on the gender, number and spelling of the following word.

un (m.)	un amico *a friend* un impermeabile *a raincoat* un negozio *a shop* un operaio *a worker* un signore *a man* un treno *a train*	Used before most consonants and all vowels.
uno (m.)	uno sbaglio *a mistake* uno sconto a *discount* uno straniero *a foreigner* uno psicologo *a pyschologist* uno zio *an uncle* uno yogurt *a yoghurt* uno gnomo *a gnome* uno xilofono *a xylophone* uno chalet *a chalet*	Used before **s** + consonant, **ps, z, y, gn, x,** and a few French words beginning with **ch.**
una (f.)	una casa *a house* una straniera a *foreigner* una zia *an aunt* una psichiatra *a pyschiatrist*	Used before all consonants.
un' (f.)	un'amica *a friend* un'elezione *an election* un'idea *an idea* un'operaia *a worker* un'uniforme *a uniform*	Used before all vowels.

⚠ **Attenti!** Indefinite articles used with nouns beginning with a vowel sound the same but actually differ in the masculine and feminine form: **un** amico (m.) but **un'**amica (f.) *friend*, **un** infermiere (m.) but **un'**infermiera (f.) *nurse*.

◎ Esercizi

1 You're a busy cook. Say what you've made, beginning, 'Ho fatto un/uno/una/un' ...'
frullato di frutta • arrosto • insalata • zabaglione • zuppa inglese • spezzatino • sugo di pomodoro

2 **Un** or **uno**? The nouns below are all masculine and refer to people. Which require **un** and which **uno**?
studente • scienziato • signore • spettatore • soldato • sacerdote • psichiatra • pediatra • profugo • produttore • psicologo • poliziotto

3 Un or **un'**? These nouns all begin with a vowel. Which require **un** and which require **un'**?

amico	elicottero	inchiesta	offerta	uccello
amica	enciclopedia	ingresso	ombrello	ufficio
appartamento	estate	isola	operaio	uniforme
automobile	etto	ispettore	opinione	uscita

◎ Indefinite articles before adjectives

The form of the indefinite article may change when it comes before an adjective.

un ➡ uno	**un** castello ➡ **uno** splendido castello *a splendid castle*	When an indefinite article is directly followed by an adjective rather
uno ➡ un	**uno** studente ➡ **un** ottimo studente *an excellent student*	than by a noun, its form depends on the gender and initial letter(s) of the adjective, not the noun. The
una ➡ un'	**una** casa ➡ **un'**immensa casa *an immense house*	same noun may therefore require a different article if it is preceded by
un' ➡ una	**un'**idea ➡ **una** buona idea *a good idea*	an adjective.

◎ Esercizio

4 Describe these people and places by using an appropriate indefinite article.

(a) È — signora elegante. È — elegante signora spagnola.

(b) È — chef famoso. È — famoso chef francese.

(c) È — palazzo strano. È — strano palazzo barocco.

(d) È — isola meravigliosa. È — meravigliosa isola mediterranea.

(b) Some uses of the indefinite article

The indefinite article is used much as the English *a/an*, but there are some important cases in which it is omitted.

Omission of the indefinite article

Occupation, status or religion	Sono ingegnere *I am an engineer* Mia zia è vedova *My aunt is a widow* Sandro è diventato buddista *Sandro has become a Buddist* **But:** È **un** ingegnere <u>molto bravo</u> *He is an excellent engineer*	No article is required unless an adjective or adjectival phrase is used.
Exclamations	Che peccato! *What **a** shame/pity!* Che bella ragazza! *What **a** beautiful girl!*	No article with exclamations.

◎ Esercizio

5 Complete the following sentences, inserting an indefinite article where necessary. Then translate into English.

(a) Sono — medico. (d) Sono — studente.

(b) È — bravo medico. (e) È — cattolica tua zia?

(c) È — studente che studia tanto. (f) Mia zia è — cattolica molto tradizionale.

◎ 2.2 The definite article

The definite article in Italian has four singular forms and three plural forms, all of which correspond to *the* in English. Like indefinite articles, they come before a noun and sometimes before an adjective. Their form depends on the gender, number and initial letter(s) of the following word.

(a) The definite article: masculine and feminine forms
Singular ➡ plural

il ➡ i **(m.)**	il bambino ➡ i bambini *the child, children* il sugo ➡ i sughi *the sauce/s*	Used before most consonants.
l' ➡ gli **(m.)**	l'amico ➡ gli amici *the friend/s* l'esercizio ➡ gli esercizi *the exercise/s*	Used before vowels.
lo ➡ gli **(m.)**	lo sciopero ➡ gli scioperi *the strike/s* lo psichiatra ➡ gli psichiatri *the pyschiatris/s* lo zoo ➡ gli zoo *the zoo/s* lo yacht ➡ gli yacht *the yacht/s* lo gnocco ➡ gli gnocchi *the gnoccho/i* lo xilofono ➡ gli xilofoni *the xylophone/s* lo chef ➡ gli chef *the chef/s*	Used before **s**+ consonant, **ps, z, y, gn, x** and a few words beginning with **ch** (usually of French origin).
la ➡ le **(f.)**	la bicicletta ➡ le biciclette *the bicycle/s* la scuola ➡ le scuole *the school/s* la zanzara ➡ le zanzare the *mosquitoe/s*	Used before all consonants.
l' ➡ le **(f.)**	l'amica ➡ le amiche *the friend/s* l'opinione ➡ le opinioni *the opinion/s* l'università ➡ le università *the university/ies*	Used before all vowels.

 Attenti! Singular masculine and feminine definite articles used before a vowel are the same, but the plural articles differ: l'amico, l'amica *but:* **gli** amici, **le** amiche; l'infermiere, l'infermiera, *but:* **gli** infermieri, **le** infermiere.

◎ Esercizi

1 Name some of the contents of the bathroom, using the singular definite article.
asciugamano • carta igienica • dentifricio • sapone • shampoo • spugna • rasoio

2 The following nouns refer to animals. Give their singular definite articles.
gnu • scimmia • scoiattolo • serpente • struzzo • yak • zanzara

3 Give the definite article for the signs of the zodiac, beginning with 'zodiac' itself.
zodiaco • Capricorno • Acquario • Pesci • Ariete • Toro • Gemelli • Cancro
Leone • Vergine • Bilancia • Scorpione • Sagittario

4 Say you would like to see these different types of shoe, using the plural definite articles.
Begin, 'Mi fa vedere i/le …'
l'espadrille (f) • il mocassino • la pantofola • il sandalo • la scarpa da tennis
lo scarpone • lo stivale • lo zoccolo

5 Give the definite article for the following: which do you consider the odd one out?
antisemitismo • intolleranza • razzismo • sessismo • xenofobia

Definite articles before adjectives

The form of definite articles may change when placed before an adjective.

il ➡ l'/lo **l' ➡ il/lo** **lo ➡ il/l'** **i ➡ gli** **gli ➡ i**	**il** giorno ➡ **l'**ultimo giorno ➡ **lo** stesso giorno *the day ➡ the last/the same day* **l'**esercizio ➡ **il** seguente esercizio ➡ **lo** stesso esercizio *the exercise ➡ the next/the same exercise* **lo** stipendio ➡ **il** mio stipendio ➡ **l'**ultimo stipendio *the salary ➡ my/the last salary* **i** bambini ➡ **gli** altri bambini *the children ➡ the other children* **gli** zii ➡ **i** vecchi zii *the uncles (and aunts) ➡ the old uncles (and aunts)*	When a definite article is directly followed by an adjective rather than by a noun, its form depends on the gender and initial letter(s) of the adjective, not the noun. This means the same noun may require a different article if it is preceded by an adjective.
la ➡ l' **l' ➡ la**	**la** scuola ➡ **l'**enorme scuola *the school ➡ the enormous school* **l'**opinione ➡ **la** mia opinione *the opinion ➡ my opinion*	

◎ Esercizio

6 Use the appropriate definite article with the following phrases.

    (a) ... edificio grande   ... grande edificio moderno

    (b) ... palazzo stupendo   ... stupendo palazzo rinascimentale

    (c) ... messaggio urgente   ... urgente messaggio telefonico

    (d) ... invito strano   ... strano invito illegibile

(b) Some uses of the definite article

In Italian, as in English, the definite article is used to refer to something known or specific.

A specific or known thing	Mi piace la camicia verde *I like the green shirt* I bambini sono stanchi *The children are tired* È il gatto di Nina *It's Nina's cat* (the cat of Nina)	Definite articles indicate a specific or known thing, person or creature.

In Italian the use of the definite article often does not coincide with the English. Here are some of the most important cases.

Plural nouns used in a general sense	Mi piacciono **i** bambini *I like children* **I** volontari non sono pagati *Volunteers are not paid* **Gli** animali selvatici sono pericolosi *Wild animals are dangerous* **But:** I leoni sono animali selvatici *Lions are wild animals* Lavorano come volontari *They work as volunteers*	When plural nouns indicate a general category, the article is used unless the noun comes after **essere** or **come**.
Specific categories	**L'**ossigeno è un gas *Oxygen is a gas* **Lo** zucchero fa ingrassare *Sugar makes you fat* **L'**Aids e **la** tubercolosi sono molto diffusi *Aids and tuberculosis are very widespread* **Il** tennis fa bene *Tennis is good for you* È arrivata **la** primavera *Spring has arrived* **But:** Ho comprato zucchero, burro e olio	Categories such as substances and materials, food, diseases, sports and seasons are all used with the definite article unless part of a list. (See partitive articles p. 31.)
	Il gatto è un animale domestico *The cat is a domestic animal* **La** tigre è una specie minacciata *The tiger is a threatened species*	Singular nouns can indicate a category, as in English.

Abstract nouns	**L'**arte è la mia materia preferita *Art is my favourite subject* **La** gelosia è un brutto vizio *Jealousy is an ugly vice* Mi piace **l'**insegnamento *I like teaching*	Abstract nouns refer to things which are not physical entities.
Languages	Studiano **il** tedesco *They are studying German* Non capisco **il** cinese *I don't understand Chinese* Parla tedesco *He speaks German* Ha studiato inglese alle medie *He has studied English in middle school* ***But:*** Parla bene/perfettamente **il** tedesco *She/he speaks German well/perfectly*	Used to name a language. Not normally used with **parlare** or when referring to a school subject. With an adverb, e.g. **bene,** the article is more commonly used.
Proper names with titles	C'è **la** dottoressa Poli? *Is Dr Poli in?* **I** signori Velli sono partiti *Mr and Mrs Velli have left* Buongiorno, dottoressa Poli *Good morning, Dr Poli* Come sta, signor Velli? *How are you, Mr Velli?*	Used with titles when talking <u>about</u> a person. No article when talking directly **to** a person.

In Italian, unlike English, the definite article is also required in the following cases relating to time and place.

Telling the time	Sono **le** undici *It's eleven o'clock* È partito **all'** una *He left at one*	The time of day requires a definite article. See also p. 26.
Time of day Days of the week	**La** mattina mi alzo presto e **la** sera mi corico tardi *In the morning I get up early and in the evening I go to bed late* **La** domenica mi riposo *On Sundays I rest* **Il** martedì mattina vado in palestra *On Tuesday mornings I go to the gym **But:*** Domenica vado al cinema *On Sunday I'm going to the cinema* È partito martedì mattina *He left on Tuesday morning*	The article is used only to express habitual action (i.e. where 'every' is implied).
Years and dates	**Il** 1321 è la data della sua nascita *1321 is the year of his birth* È nato **il** 25 aprile 1945 *He was born on 25 April 1945* Si sposeranno sabato 16 giugno *They will get married on Saturday 16 June*	The article is used with years unless the date precedes it. It is used with dates unless the day of the week is included.
Continents, countries, regions and groups of islands	**L'**Europa non è unita *Europe is not united* **L'**America confina con **il** Messico *America borders on Mexico* **La** Sardegna e **il** Piemonte sono regioni italiane *Sardinia and Piedmont are Italian regions* **La** Corsica fa parte della Francia *Corsica is part of France* **Le** Canarie appartengono alla Spagna *The Canaries belong to Spain*	Exceptions are **Israele** *Israel,* and most countries which are islands, e.g. Cuba, Haiti, Malta. Islands which are regions mostly require the article: **la Sicilia**. See also pp. 27–8.
Mountains, volcanoes, lakes, rivers and seas	**il** Monte Bianco *Mont Blanc* **il** Vesuvio *Vesuvius* **il** Lago Maggiore *Lake Maggiore* **il** Po *the Po* **il** Tamigi *the Thames* **il** Mediterrraneo *the Mediterranean*	For rivers and seas only, the use of the article coincides with English.

In Italian the definite article is used with possessives and expressions with **fare**.

With possessive adjectives and pronouns	Mi piace **il tuo** iPhone *I like **your** iPhone* Qual è **il mio** biglietto? *Which is **my** ticket?* Questo non è **il tuo** *This isn't **yours*** Qual è **il nostro**? *Which is **ours**?*	The article is nearly always used. For exceptions see Possessives pp. 34–40.
Some expressions with **fare**	Fa **il** medico *He is a̲ doctor* Vorrebbe fare **l'**infermiera *She would like to be a̲ nurse* Sta facendo **il** bagno *He is having a̲ bath* Bisogna fare **il** biglietto *You have to buy a̲ ticket*	**Fare** takes the definite article before the name of many professions and in some set expressions. Others include **fare la doccia** *to shower*, **farsi la barba** *to (have a) shave*.

For further uses of the definite article, see pp. 23–5.

◎ Esercizi

7 Insert a definite article where appropriate and then translate each sentence into English.

(a) Cani sono animali fedeli.

(b) Cani che abbiamo visto erano adorabili.

(c) In Italia bambini vanno a scuola a sei anni.

(d) Ieri bambini erano stanchi.

(e) Guerra risolve poco.

(f) Guerra nei Balcani è stata una tragedia.

8 Give the Italian equivalent of the following.

(a) *I don't like tea but I love coffee.*

(b) *I love tennis but I don't like football.*

(c) *I hate winter but I love spring.*

(d) *Life is beautiful.*

(e) *Time flies.* (**volare**)

(f) *Work is necessary.*

9 Insert a definite article where necessary.

(a) Mi piace italiano.

(b) Parli greco? – No, ma parlo bene spagnolo.

(c) Al liceo studio tedesco e inglese.

(d) Dottor Binni, le presento signor Giusti.

10 When? Complete the following sentences by translating the English phrases into Italian.

(a) Vado a teatro (*on Friday*).

(b) Vado in palestra (*on Tuesdays*).

(c) (*In the evening*) non bevo mai caffè.

(d) Siamo arrivati (*on 5 February 1993*).

(e) Partono (*on Monday 10 June*).

(f) Ci vediamo (*on 27 May*).

11 Insert a definite article where necessary.

(a) Gran Bretagna è un'isola.

(b) Messico confina con Stati Uniti.

(c) Cuba e Haiti non sono paesi ricchi.

(d) Sardegna e Sicilia sono isole e regioni italiane.

12 In which sentences is there an article missing? Supply the correct one.

(a) Dammi tuo libro.

(b) Mi presti la tua penna?

(c) Avete visto mio cappotto?

(d) Questa è la tua giacca e questa è la mia.

13 Express the following in Italian. The first part has been done.

(a) *I am a doctor.*   Faccio …

(b) *Maria is having a bath.*   Maria sta facendo …

(c) *I need to have a shower.*   Ho bisogno di …

(d) *I haven't bought a/my ticket.*   Non ho fatto …

◎ (c) Omission of the definite article

Towns and most single islands	Roma, Torino, Firenze e Napoli sono città italiane Capri, Lampedusa e Lipari sono isole italiane **But:** Mi affascina **la** <u>vecchia</u> Torino *Old Turin fascinates me* **Note the names of the following towns and islands:** l'Aia (*the Hague*) l'Aquila il Cairo l'Havana la Mecca il Pireo (*Piraeus*) l'isola del Giglio l'isola d'Elba/l'Elba	No articles are used with towns and most single islands (as opposed to groups of islands) unless they are modified by an adjective or adjectival phrase or are part of the name itself.
Expressions with **a** and **in**	Vado **a** casa (mia) *I'm going home* Ci vediamo **a** scuola *See you at school* **But:** Si trova vicino **alla** casa <u>di Mario</u> *It is near Mario's house*	The article is usually omitted with certain expressions of place and time requiring **a** and **in** unless they are modified by an adjective or adjectival phrase. See also Prepositional articles pp. 27–28 and Prepositions, p. 197.
	Ci vediamo **in** centro *I'll see you in town* È nato/arriva **in** autunno *He was born/he is coming in the autumn* **But:** Si trova **nel** centro <u>storico</u> *It is in the historic centre* È nato **nell'**autunno <u>del 1948</u> *He was born in the autumn of 1948* Arriva **l'**autunno <u>prossimo</u> *He's coming next autumn*	
Possessives + singular family members	Questo è mio fratello *This is my brother* Questa è mia moglie *This is my wife* **But:** Questo è **il** mio fratel<u>lino</u> *This is my little brother* Questa è **la** mia sorella <u>più grande</u> *This is my big/older/est sister* Gina è **la** sorella <u>di mio marito</u> *Gina is my husband's sister*	No article for singular family members unless modified by a diminutive, a descriptive adjective or phrase. For more details see Possessives pp. 135–36.

◎ Esercizio

14 Decide which of the underlined nouns require a definite article and insert them where necessary, remembering to join them to any prepositions.

(a) <u>Roma</u> è una bella città.

(b) <u>Aia</u> si trova in <u>Olanda</u>.

(c) <u>Lipari</u> è un'isola affascinante.

(d) Mi ha fatto vedere <u>Parigi</u> di Sartre e Camus.

(e) Oggi Gianni non è andato a <u>scuola</u>.

(f) Studia a <u>scuola</u> di <u>suo fratello</u>.

(g) Siamo arrivati <u>primavera</u> dell'anno scorso.

(h) Siamo arrivati in <u>primavera</u>.

✚ (d) Further uses of the definite article

In most of the following cases the Italian article is used where in English there is none.

Proper names: institutions, clubs and famous people	**La** Fiat è stata fondata a Torino *Fiat was founded in Turin.* **La** Juventus e **il** Milan sono in serie A *Juventus and Milan are in the Premier League*	**La** is used with companies, but both **il** and **la** are used with clubs. They are best learned individually.

	La Loren e la Callas sono famose *Sophia Loren and Maria Callas are famous* Il Petrarca e il Boccaccio sono scrittori del Trecento *Petrarch and Boccaccio are 14th-century writers* **But:** Dante fu un grande poeta *Dante was a great poet*	The article must be used with surnames of famous women. With masculine surnames it is optional. The article cannot be used with Dante, Leonardo, Michelangelo or Raffaello, as these are not surnames.
Approximation	Avrà tra **gli** 11 e **i** 13 anni *He must be between 11 and 13* Erano tutti ragazzi sotto **i** 10 anni *They were all boys under 10* La temperatura si aggira **sui** 30 gradi *The temperature is around 30°* Partiamo fra **un** 35 minuti *We're leaving in about 35 minutes/35 minutes or so* Si trova a **un** 200 chilometri da qui *It's about 200 km from here/200km or so from here*	The definite article + a preposition is used for age and temperature. The indefinite article is used colloquially to express approximate time, distance and quantity.
Percentages and fractions	Gli sconti online sono **del** 25 per cento *The discounts online are 25 per cent* Nonostante la diffusione della banda larga, più **della metà** dei toscani non naviga in Internet *Despite the spread of broadband, more than half of Tuscans do not use the internet*	Percentages are used with the definite article, as is the fraction **metà** (see pp. 235–6). In these examples they are combined with **di** as prepositional articles.

✚ Esercizio

15 Insert definite articles as appropriate.

(a) Olivetti, Pirelli e Fiat sono famose società italiane.

(b) Juventus è in testa alla serie A.

(c) Leonardo e Michelangelo erano grandi artisti.

(d) Petrarca e Leopardi erano grandi poeti.

(e) Morante e Ginzburg sono note scrittrici italiane.

(f) Giuseppe Verdi è morto fra 86 e 87 anni, credo.

◎/✚ 2.3 Special uses of the definite and indefinite article

In Italian the definite article is often used to express an English possessive. It may also express the indefinite or the partitive, *any*.

Definite articles with the body, clothing and personal belongings

Italian definite article, English possessive	Ha **gli** occhi azzurri *His eyes are blue (He's got blue eyes)* Hanno **i** capelli biondi *Their hair is blond (They've got blond hair)*	Description of parts of the body require the definite article.
	Mi sto lavando **le** mani *I'm washing my hands* Mi sono rotto **il** braccio *I broke my arm* Mettiti **le** scarpe *Put on your shoes*	✚ When reflexive verbs are used with parts of the body and clothing the definite article is used. See also p. 139.
	Ho perso **l'**ombrello *I've lost my umbrella* Hai **la** patente? *Have you got your driving licence?/Can you drive?* Parte con **il** marito *She is leaving with her husband*	✚ The Italian definite article expresses an English possessive when the ownership of the object is obvious.

+ Definite articles with familiar objects

| Italian definite article, English indefinite article: a, any | Non ho **la** macchina
*I haven't got **a** car*
Hai **la** TV satellite?
Have you got (a) satellite TV? | The Italian definite article often expresses an English indefinite, *a,* when it is used with the names of familiar things. |
| | **Il** burro non c'è *There's no butter*
Il sapone c'è? *Is there any soap?* | The definite article can express *no* or *any* when you refer to something you expect to be there. See also p. 32. |

Definite and indefinite articles: illness and ailments

On the whole, the use of the Italian articles does not correspond to the English.

Italian definite article, English indefinite article or no article	Ho **la** febbre/**la** tosse/**il** raffreddore/ **l'**emicrania *I've got a temperature/a cough/a cold/a migraine* Ho **la** pressione alta/**la** diarrea/**l'**influenza *I've got high blood pressure/diarrhoea/'flu.* ***But also:*** Ho **un** raffreddore	Illnesses mostly require a <u>definite</u> article in Italian. **Raffreddore** may be used with **un**.
	Ho mal di gola/di denti/di testa/d'orecchio/ di pancia/di schiena *I've got a sore throat/a tooth/head/ear/stomach/back ache*	Aches and pains require no article in Italian.
Indefinite article for Italian and English	Ho **un** terribile mal di testa *I've got an awful headache* Ho **un** brutto raffreddore *I've got a bad cold*	If the above ailments are modified the indefinite article is used.

For the use of the articles with numbers, see pp. 232–3 and pp. 235–6. For the use of the article in expressions involving the Italian equivalents of *most*, and *all*, see Indefinites p. 170 and pp. 172–3.

◎/+ **Esercizi**

1 Describe this man and his condition by using the definite article where appropriate. Give English equivalents.

   (a) Ha capelli biondi, occhi azzurri, pelle chiara e orecchie a sventola.

   (b) Ha raffreddore e mal di gola ma non ha tosse.

   (c) Purtroppo si è rotto gamba!

+ 2 Where possible substitute the underlined words with an appropriate definite article.

   (a) Arriva domani con <u>sua</u> moglie.

   (b) Non ho <u>un</u> Blackberry e nemmeno <u>un</u> iPhone.

   (c) <u>I miei</u> figli vanno alla partita con <u>il loro</u> zio.

   (d) Hai dimenticato <u>i tuoi</u> occhiali?

◎ **2.4 The prepositional article**

Prepositional articles are formed by combining the prepositions **a**, **da**, **di**, **in** and **su** with the definite article to form one word. With the preposition **con** the combination is optional and much less common.

(a) Forms and uses of prepositional articles

	Masculine definite articles					Feminine definite articles		
	il	**lo**	**l'**	**i**	**gli**	**la**	**l'**	**le**
a	al	allo	all'	ai	agli	alla	all'	alle
da	dal	dallo	dall'	dai	dagli	dalla	dall'	dalle
di	del	dello	dell'	dei	degli	della	dell'	delle
in	nel	nello	nell'	nei	negli	nella	nell'	nelle
su	sul	sullo	sull'	sui	sugli	sulla	sull'	sulle
con	col	collo	coll'	coi	cogli	colla	coll'	colle

Italian prepositional articles generally express two English words in one: a preposition and a definite article, e.g. *from the, of the, on the*. They are required when a preposition is used before a definite article followed by a noun or adjective; their form depends on the number, gender and spelling of that noun or adjective.

in + **il** cassetto **su** + **la** vecchia scrivania	La chiave non è **nel** cassetto, è **sulla** vecchia scrivania *The key isn't **in the** drawer, it's **on the** old desk*
a + **l'**entrata **di** + **il** luna-park	Ci vediamo **all'**entrata **del** luna-park *We'll meet **at the** entrance **of the** funfair*

As with all articles, the form of prepositional articles is determined by the number and gender of the word immediately following. Compare these examples.

in + **il** parco **in** + **lo** stesso parco	I bambini giocano sempre **nel** parco *The children always play **in the** park* I bambini giocano sempre **nello** stesso parco *The children always play **in the** same park*
da + **i** cinesi **da** + **gli** antichi cinesi	I fuochi d'artificio sono stati inventati **dai** cinesi *Fireworks were invented **by the** Chinese* I fuochi d'artificio sono stati inventati **dagli** antichi cinesi *Fireworks were invented **by the** ancient Chinese*

 Attenti! When the use of the definite article in Italian and English does not coincide, it is less easy to spot the need for a prepositional article.

In the following examples there are no definite articles in the English, but they are required in Italian.

di + **i** miei amici	La casa **dei** miei amici è bellissima *My friends' house is beautiful* (the house **of** my friends)
di + **la** mia macchina	Il motore **della** mia macchina è rotto *My car motor is broken* (the motor **of** my car)
da + **le** nove/**a** + **le** cinque **da** + **la** A/**a** + **la** Z	Lavoro **dalle** nove fino **alle** cinque *I work **from** nine **until** five* Idee pratiche **dall'**A **alla** Z *Practical ideas **from** A **to** Z*

If you need to, take another look at pp. 20–2 to brush up on the use of the definite article. For the omission of prepositional articles see geographical names, pp. 27–9.

◎ Esercizi

1 Provide the correct form of the appropriate prepositional article.

   (a) **To the** … Say where you are going, using **a** and a definite article. Begin, 'Vado …'
      il mercato • l'aeroporto • lo stadio • la stazione

   (b) **In the** … Say where these items are, using **in** and the definite article. Begin, 'La carta è …'
      la carta (il cassetto) • i biscotti (l'armadio) • la lampada (lo studio) • le matite (la scatola)

   (c) **On the** … Say what these items are on.
      il pane (il tavolo) • la chiave (l'armadietto) • il dizionario (lo scaffale) • la penna (la scrivania)

   (d) **From the** … What can be seen from these places? Begin, 'Dai/dalle, etc. … si vede …'
      i giardini (la casa) • gli scalini (la fontana) • le montagne (la pianura)

2 Complete these extracts from an Italian guide to the Highlands by supplying the correct form of the prepositional article where required.

> **Centro visitatori (1** di) **distilleria (2** di) **Talisker**
> L'unica distilleria (**3** di) isola di Skye, situata in una zona di grande bellezza naturale (**4** su) riva (**5** di) Loch Harport. Aperta tutto l'anno (**6** da) lunedì (**7** a) venerdì, (**8** da) 9.30 (**9** a) 16.30.
> **Centro visitatori (10** di) **distilleria (11** di) **Oban**
> Costruita (**12** in) 1794, la nostra favolosa ubicazione (**13** in) centro (**14** di) città ci rende una (**15** di) distillerie più interessanti (**16** di) Scozia. Aperta tutta l'anno (**17** da) lunedì (**18** a) venerdì. (**19** Da) dicembre (**20** a) febbraio ore limitate (**21** di) apertura. Ingresso (**22** a) pagamento.

3 Provide the correct form of the prepositional article to complete each sentence and then translate into English. There is one sentence where the prepositional article is not required.

   (a) La baby sitter (di) i miei figli è greca.

   (b) La porta (di) la macchina è chiusa?

   (c) La ragazza (di) mio figlio è molto gentile.

   (d) Il gatto dorme (in) lo studio.

   (e) Mi piace lavorare (in) il mio studio.

◎/✚ (b) Further uses of prepositional articles: geographical names

The use of definite articles and prepositional articles with geographical names differs in English and Italian. (For the definite article see pp. 20–2.) In Italian it depends largely on the category of the geographical place.

Continents, countries and regions

Use of the articles with *in*: saying *in* and *to*

È nato **in** Australia/Gran Bretagna/Sicilia *He was born in Australia/Great Britain/Sicily* Andiamo **in** Canada/Piemonte *We are going to Canada/Piedmont* ***But:*** Andrò **nell'**Australia <u>del nord</u> *I'll go to northern Australia* Passerò le ferie **nella** Sicilia <u>orientale</u> *I will spend my holidays in eastern Sicily* Abito **nei** Paesi Bassi/**nelle** Marche/**nel** Regno Unito *I live in the Netherlands/the Marches/the UK*	**No prepositional articles.** Used with continents, countries, regions, (including islands which are regions, e.g. Sicily), **in** means both *to* and *in*. The article is omitted unless the place name is modified by an adjective, is plural or is a masculine compound name such as **il Regno Unito**.

Sono nato **in/nel** Belgio *I was born in Belgium* Sono nato **nel** Veneto *I was born in the Veneto* Ho una casa **nel** Molise/Texas *I have a house in the Molise/Texas*	**Exceptions.** The article may be used with some masculine countries and regions even when they are not modified.

Articles with other prepositions: *a, da, di* and *su*

Ha intenzione di viaggiare **dall'**Australia fino **all'**Africa *He intends to travel from Australia to Africa* Arriva **dal** Sudafrica/**dal** Trentino/**dalla** Corsica *He is arriving from South Africa/Trentino/Corsica* La capitale **del** Galles è Cardiff *The capital of Wales is Cardiff* Il capoluogo **della** Sicilia è Palermo *The (regional) capital of Sicily is Palermo* Ho bisogno di informazioni **sulla** Sardegna *I need some information on Sardinia*	**Prepositional articles are required** with continents, countries and regions (including regional islands, e.g. Corsica). The exception is **in,** where the article is usually omitted (see table above).
È partito **da** Israele/Cuba *He left from Israel/Cuba* La capitale **di** Haiti è Port au Prince *The capital of Haiti is Port au Prince*	**No prepositional articles** because Israel and most countries which are islands require no article. See p. 21.

✚ Omission of the article with *di*

La capitale **d'**Italia, le capitali **d'**Europa, etc. Luigi XIV, re **di** Francia, Elisabetta **d'**Inghilterra, il Granduca **di** Toscana, Cosimo I ***But:*** Ferdinando II **delle** Due Sicilie La capitale **dell'**Italia <u>unita</u>, le capitali **dell'**Europa <u>centrale</u> Paola **del** Belgio, Carlo, Principe **del** Galles	**Di** is mostly used with an article but is often omitted with **Italia** and **Europa** or after a noble title + a singular place name. If the place name is plural, modified by an adjective or is masculine, the article is mostly used.

◎/✚ Towns, single islands and groups of islands

Use of the articles with *a*: saying 'to' and 'in'

È nato **a**/Andrà **a** Firenze *He was born in/He'll go to Florence* Siamo andati **a** Capri, **a** Lipari, **a** Lampedusa, e **a** Malta *We went to Capri, Lipari, Lampedusa and Malta* Abitano **a** Creta/**a** Cuba *They live in Crete/in Cuba* ***But:*** Lavoro **al** Cairo/**all'**Aia/**all'**Elba *I work in Cairo/in the Hague/in Elba* È nato **nella** Berlino <u>degli Anni venti</u> *He was born in the Berlin of the 1920s* Ha lavorato per anni **nella** Cuba <u>di Castro</u> *He worked for years in Castro's Cuba*	**No prepositional articles** with towns and single islands. Both *to* and *in* are expressed by **a.** It only combines with the article when it is part of the name, or when the place name is modified. Note that when these places are modified, **in** + definite article is used.

✚ With groups of islands, note that **in**, rather than **a**, is sometimes used to express *in*.

Andiamo **alle** Canarie/**alle** Eolie *We are going to the Canaries/to the Aeolian islands* Andrò **all'**Isola di Man/**all'**isola d'Elba* *I'll go to the Isle of Man/to Elba* Ho trovato un paradiso terrestre **alle/nelle** Seychelles *I've found a paradise on earth in the Seychelles* Abita **nelle** Eolie, a Lipari *He lives in the Aeolian islands on Lipari* Ho passato il Capodanno **nelle** Canarie, a Lanzarote *I spent the New Year in the Canaries, in Lanzarote* Abita **nell'/sull'**Isola di Man/**nell'/sull'**isola d'Elba *She lives on the Isle of Man/on Elba*	**Prepositional articles are required** with groups of islands and islands where **isola** is part of the name. * Sometimes just **l'Elba** (see previous table). **a** + definite article = *to* and sometimes *in*. **in** + definite article = *in* or *on*. **su** + definite article is also used for *on*.

Articles with other prepositions: *da, di, su*

L'aereo è partito **da** Cuba *The plane left from Cuba* Le fontane **di** Roma sono belle *Rome's fountains are beautiful* Scrive libri **su** Creta *He writes books on/about Crete* ***But:*** Scrive libri **sulla** Creta <u>antica</u> *He writes books on/about ancient Crete*	**Towns and single islands: mostly no articles.** The same rules as above apply, i.e. no articles unless modified or part of the name itself.
Dalle Tremiti fino a Termoli il viaggio è breve *It is a short journey from the Tremiti islands to Termoli* Mi hanno parlato per ore **delle** Maldive/**dell'**Isola d'Elba *They talked to me for hours about the Maldives/Elba* Vorrei delle informazioni **sulle** Eolie/**sulle** Tremiti *I would like some information on/about the Tremiti islands/the Aeolian islands*	**Groups of islands** and islands where **isola** is part of the name always require articles.

For the gender of geographical names, see Nouns, pp. 13–4.

◎/✚ **Esercizi**

4 Fill in the boxes using an appropriate form of **in** or **a**.

VADO ... *(to)*	Roma		VIVIAMO ... *(in)*	Boston
	Capri			Il Cairo
	l'Isola d'Elba			Lampedusa
	Le Tremiti			Malta
	Cipro			le Eolie

5

VADO ... *(to)*	Inghilterra		LAVORIAMO ... *(in)*	Europa
	Paesi Bassi			Italia
	Asia			Italia meridionale
	Toscana			Sardegna
	Sicilia			Emilia Romagna

6 Use prepositional articles where appropriate.

    (a) Passo sempre le ferie (in) Francia, (in) Francia del sud.
    (b) Io lavoro (in) Gran Bretagna.
    (c) Carlo è nato (in) Regno Unito.

7 Combine **in** and **di** with the definite article where necessary.

    (a) Torino è (in) Piemonte. È il capoluogo (di) Piemonte.

    (b) L'Aquila è (in) Abruzzi. È il capoluogo (di) Abruzzi.

    (c) Cagliari è (in) Sardegna. È il capoluogo (di) Sardegna.

8 Combine **di** with the definite article where necessary.

    (a) La capitale (di) Scozia è Edinburgo.   **(d)** La capitale (di) Canada è Ottawa.

    (b) La capitale (di) Italia è Roma.   **(e)** La capitale (di) Cuba è l'Avana.

    (c) La capitale (di) Israele è Gerusalemme.   **(f)** La capitale (di) Filippine è Manila.

✚ **9** Complete these sentences by using each of the words given once. There are two spaces too many.

    il   le   la   in   da   dall'   dell'   della   della

    (a) — Cipro è situata a sud — Turchia. (*Cyprus is situated south of Turkey.*)

    (b) —Ci sono molti libri e guide — isola d'Elba. (*There are lots of books and guides about Elba.*)

    (c) — Sicilia non è lontana — Africa. (*Sicily is not far from Africa.*)

    (d) — Bratislava è — Slovakia, ma non è lontana — Vienna. (*Bratislava is in Slovakia but is not far from Vienna.*)

    (e) — Eolie sono al largo — Sicilia. (*The Aeolian islands are off the coast of Sicily.*)

    (f) —Canada occupa la parte nord — America settentrionale. (*Canada occupies the northern part of North America.*)

✚ **10** Give the Italian equivalent of the English.

    (a) *Fiona lives on the island of Skye.*   **(e)** *Alistair is going to the Hebrides.*

    (b) *Donald lives in the Orkneys.* (**Le Orcadi**)   (**Le Ebridi**)

    (c) *Alberto lives in Capri.*   **(f)** *Sandra is going to Cuba.*

    (d) *Barbara is going to the Isle of Man.*

✚ **11** Chose the appropriate form of **di**.

    (a) Il futuro re di/dell'Inghilterra è Carlo, Principe di/del Galles.

    (b) Carlo Alberto di/della Savoia abdicò nel 1849.

    (c) Nel 1861 Vittorio Emanuele II, re di/della Sardegna, fu proclamato Re d'/dell'Italia.

◎ ## 2.5 The partitive article

(a) Forms and uses of the partitive article

Partitive articles express *some*, *any* and are formed by combining **di** and the definite article. (See p. 26.)

Masculine partitive articles		Feminine partitive articles	
di + il	**del** pane	**di + la**	**della** carta
di + lo	**dello** zucchero	**di + l'**	**dell'**acqua
di + l'	**dell'**olio		
di + i	**dei** pantaloni	**di + le**	**delle** matite
di + gli	**degli** amici		

In Italian there is no distinction between *some* for statements and *any* for questions. Both *some* and *any* are expressed by **di** plus the definite article.

Expressing *some*	Mi serve **dell'**olio d'oliva *I need some olive oil* Ho comprato **dei** libri inglesi *I bought some English books*
Expressing *any*	Ti serve **dell'**olio d'oliva? *Do you need any olive oil?* Hai comprato **dei** libri inglesi? *Did you buy any English books?*

Omission of the partitive article

There is no partitive article in the following four cases:

Non hanno bambini *They don't have any children/ They have no children* Non hai cugini? *Don't you have any cousins?*	In negative sentences, unlike in English, there is no partitive article. See p. 32 for alternatives.
Hai fratelli? *Have you got any brothers or sisters?* Hanno amici o no? *Have they got (any) friends or not?* Mi servono viti, non chiodi *I need (some) screws, not nails*	If the noun is emphasised or contrasted there is no partitive article, unlike in English.
Ho comprato pane, burro e marmellata *I bought bread, butter and jam*	In both Italian and English there are no partitive articles in lists.
Ho bisogno di scarpe nuove *I need (some) new shoes* Invece di soldi mi ha mandato un regalo *Instead of money he sent me a present*	To avoid repetition of **di** there are no partitive articles with some constructions taking **di**, such as **aver bisogno di** *to need* and **invece di** *instead of*.

For other ways of saying *some/any* and for other partitive expressions, see pp. 32–3.

◎ Esercizi

1 In the second sentence, provide the correct form of the partitive article **di**.

(a) Ad Arezzo ho visto **degli** affreschi meravigliosi. Ho visto … meravigliosi affreschi del Cinquecento.

(b) A Firenze ho visto **dei** dipinti eccezionali. Ho visto … incredibili dipinti del Seicento.

(c) A Dresden ho visto **della** porcellana antica. Ho visto … antica porcellana settecentesca.

2 Use the correct partitive article to complete the following, leaving blank where necessary. Give the English equivalents.

(a) Mi dà … caffè macinato?

(b) Avete … pasta fresca?

(c) Devo comprare … camicie nuove.

(d) Ho comprato … pantaloni neri.

(e) Mi ha prestato … scarponi da sci.

(f) Mi serve … sciroppo per la tosse.

(g) Ho bisogno … aspirina.

(h) Non ho … fratelli.

(i) Devo comprare … olio, … aceto, … sale e … pepe.

(j) Volevo … mandarini, non … arance.

◎/✚ 2.6 Partitive expressions and their alternatives

Partitive articles (see above) are often replaced by other words and expressions, such as **un po' di** and **alcuni/e**.

Below are some common alternatives to **del, della**, etc.

'Some' and 'any'

un po' di a bit/a little of/ some/a few	Vorrei **un po' di** formaggio *I would like some/a bit of cheese* **Or:** Vorrei **del** formaggio È rimasta **un po' di** pasta? *Is there any/a bit of pasta left?* **Or:** È rimasta **della** pasta?	**un po' di** is commonly used with uncountable nouns. (See below.) When used with countable nouns (e.g. **formaggi, pesche**), **un po' di** is fairly colloquial. See below for countable nouns.
	Ho comprato **un po' di** formaggi francesi *I bought some/a few French cheeses* **Or:** Ho comprato **dei** formaggi francesi Mi sono portato **un po' di** pesche *I brought along some/a few peaches* **Or:** Mi sono portato **delle** pesche	

Negatives: 'not … any', 'no'

Partitive articles are not used in negative expressions. (See p. 31.) The following are common alternatives.

essere senza (to be without) not … any/ no …	Siamo senza pane *We haven't got any bread* **Or:** Non abbiamo pane Sono senza soldi *I've got no money* **Or:** Non ho soldi	**Essere senza** is commonly used in speech instead of **non** + the noun without the article. See p. 31.
mancare (to be lacking) There isn't/ aren't any … There is/are no …	Manca il sapone *There isn't any soap/There is no soap* **Or:** Non c'è sapone/Il sapone non c'è Mancano gli asciugamani? *Aren't there any towels?* **Or:** Non ci sono asciugamani?/Gli asciugamani non ci sono?	Note that with **mancare** a definite article is used. The expression implies that you expect the item to be there.
niente *no, not any*	Niente pane oggi? *Is there is no/Isn't there any bread today?* **Or:** Non c'è pane oggi? Niente lezioni domani *There are no/There aren't any lessons tomorrow* **Or:** Non ci sono lezioni domani	**Niente** is colloquially used to mean *there is/there are no/not any*, and can be followed by countable or uncountable nouns.

Alcuni/e and qualche

These both mean *some* or *a few*, but unlike the expressions above, they cannot be used with uncountable nouns such as **pane, benzina**, etc. They are only used with countable nouns, i.e. nouns referring to objects and people that can be counted.

alcuni some/a few	Mi ha dato **alcuni** suggerimenti *He has given me some/a few suggestions* **Or:** Mi ha dato **dei** suggerimenti Ho comprato **alcune** riviste *I have bought some/a few magazines* **Or:** Ho comprato **delle** riviste	Note that **alcuni/e** is not generally used in questions and cannot be expressed by *any*.
qualche some/ a few/ any + singular noun only	Mi ha dato **qualche** suggerimento *He has given me a few suggestions/the odd suggestion* **Or:** Mi ha dato **dei** suggerimenti Hai comprato **qualche** rivista? *Have you bought any magazines?* **Or:** Hai comprato **delle** riviste? Non c'è **qualche** altra soluzione? *Aren't there any other solutions?/Is there no other solution?* **Or:** Non ci sono altre soluzioni?	**Qualche** usually has a plural meaning but is followed by the singular form of a countable noun only (i.e. you cannot say 'Hai comprato qualche pane?') It is used in negative questions, but not in negative statements, where **nessuno/a** is used. See below.

✚ Emphatic negatives: *nessuno/a* and *alcuno/a*

Like **alcuni/e** and **qualche** these are mainly used with countable nouns only.

| **nessuno/a**
not any,
no (at all) | Non ho fatto **nessuno** sbaglio
I didn't make a single mistake/any
mistakes (at all)
Non c'è **nessun'**(altra) alternativa?
Is there absolutely no alternative?
Are there absolutely no (other)
alternatives?
Or: Non ci sono (altre) alternative? | In negative statements and questions
nessuno/a, used with <u>singular</u> nouns
only, is an emphatic alternative to
omitting the partitive. |
| **alcuno/a**
not any,
no ...
whatsoever/
at all | Non c'è **alcun'**alternativa
There is no alternative whatsoever
Non c'è **alcun** dubbio?
Is there is no doubt whatsoever/at all? | **Alcuno/a** is used instead of
nessuno/a for emphasis. |

For more on **qualche**, see p. 168 and for **alcuni/e** see pp. 163 and 171. For more on **nessuno**, see pp. 163, 169 and pp. 187–8.

◎/✚ **Esercizi**

1 Find an alternative way in Italian of expressing each sentence below.

    (a) Mi dà dello zucchero?   **(d)** Non abbiamo burro.

    (b) Mi porti dell'acqua frizzante?   **(e)** Non ho soldi.

    (c) Mi dà dei fagiolini?   **(f)** Non ci sono lenzuola.

2 Find alternatives for these sentences with approximately the same meaning. There is sometimes more than one possibility.

    (a) Ho delle lettere da scrivere.   **(c)** Avete degli impegni per domani?

    (b) Ho dei dubbi da chiarire.   **(d)** Hai degli articoli da leggere?

✚ **3** Now rewrite these sentences to mean approximately the same. There may be more than one possibility.

    (a) Non ha nessun valore.   **(d)** Non c'è nessun problema.

    (b) Non ho alcuna voglia di farlo   **(e)** Non ci sono alternative.

    (c) Non ci sono altre possibilità?   **(f)** Lo ha fatto senza nessuna ragione.

✚ **4** Read the short magazine article on drinking amongst minors and answer the questions.

In Italia un ragazzino su cinque inizia a bere già **tra gli 11 e i 15 anni** (1). Lo afferma la Consulta nazionale **sull'alcol** (2). **Il 19.5% dei minori** (3) di questa fascia di età* dichiara di aver bevuto birra, vino o superalcolici nonoostante il divieto di somministrazione* di bevande alcoliche **ai minori** (4) di 16 anni. Anche tra **i ragazzi** (5) di 16-17 anni il consumo di alcolici è diffuso: uno su due beve e **l'8% dei maschi** (6) lo fa tutti i giorni. Non solo, **l'Italia** (7) presenta l'età più bassa in Europa per quanto riguarda* il primo contatto con **le bevande alcoliche** (8): la media è 12.2 anni, contro **i 14.6 dell'Europa** (9). Subito dopo vengono **l'Irlanda e l'Austria** (10) con 12,7 anni.

(Di Tutto, 31 ottobre 2008)

> • di questa fascia di età *in this age group* • il divieto di somministrazione *the ban on supplying* • per quanto riguarda *as far as (the first contact) is concerned*

   (a) Give the English equivalent of the nouns and phrases in bold.

   (b) Give the Italian equivalent of the following: *In Italy about 12 per cent of children between the ages of 11 and 15 drink alcohol.*

✚ 5 Now read the following from the same magazine about guidelines for treating flu.

L'influenza? Poche cure,* arriva e se ne va da sola.* È una delle regole contenute nelle linee guida diffuse* dall'Istituto superiore di sanità. **Niente** omeopatia, antibiotici o terapie alternative, spiegano i medici. Non servono. Le persone sane si rimettono in piedi nel giro di* **qualche** giorno. Per bimbi e anziani invece, è sempre consigliabile il vaccino (che è gratuito).

   • cure *treatments* • se ne va da sola *it goes away by itself* • diffuse *handed out*
   • nel giro di *in the space of*

   (a) Is it possible to substitute **nessun** for **niente** in the text?

   (b) Find another way of saying **qualche giorno** in Italian.

   (c) Give the Italian equivalent of the following: *Doctors say there are no treatments for flu but vaccination is always advisable for children and old people.*

3 Descriptive adjectives

Descriptive adjectives (**gli aggettivi qualificativi**) are words which modify or qualify nouns and pronouns by providing more information about them, e.g. *a **tall** boy*, *an **important** book*, *a **white** one*, *those **new** ones*.

3.1 Regular adjectives

In Italian, adjectives change their form to agree in number and gender with the noun or pronoun they qualify.

In dictionaries adjectives are listed in their masculine singular form, and it is this form which is used to identify the group to which an adjective belongs.

There are three main regular groups with endings in -**o**, in -**e** and in -**a**.

(a) Adjectives ending in -o: forms and agreements

These -**o** adjectives have four different vowel endings, which depend on the number and gender of the noun or pronoun they qualify. When used with regular masculine nouns in -**o** and regular feminine nouns in -**a**, the adjective and noun endings match.

In the plural, -**i** replaces -**o**. Note that if the ending is -**eo**, the -**e** is always retained in the plural.

	Masculine Singular -o ➡ -i Plural	Feminine Singular -a ➡ -e Plural
italiano	un ragazzo **italiano** ➡ ragazzi **italiani** *Italian boy/s*	una ragazza **italiana** ➡ ragazze **italiane** *Italian girl/s*
europeo	un conflitto **europeo** ➡ conflitti **europei** *European conflict/s*	una guerra **europea** ➡ guerre **europee** *European war/s*

If the ending is -**io**, the -**i** is nearly always dropped in the masculine plural unless it is stressed in speech (as in **pio**).

vecchio **but:** **pio**	un palazzo **vecchio** ➡ palazzi **vecchi** *old apartment block/s* un animo **pio** ➡ animi **pii** *pious soul/s*	una casa **vecchia** ➡ case **vecchie** *old house/s* una donna **pia** ➡ donne **pie** *pious woman/women*	

 Attenti! Making adjectives agree with a noun does not always mean matching up identical endings. This is because you match up the gender and number of the adjectives and nouns, not the endings themselves.

Consider the following:

-**e** nouns + -**o** adjectives

Masculine	Feminine
un cantant**e** italian**o** ➡ cantant**i** italian**i** *Italian singer/s* (m.) un paes**e** europe**o** ➡ paes**i** europe**i** *European country/ies*	una cantant**e** italian**a** ➡ cantant**i** italian**e** *Italian singer/s* (f.) una nazion**e** europe**a** ➡ nazion**i** europe**e** *European nation/s*

Irregular nouns + -o adjectives

| un problema complicato ➡ problemi complicati
complicated problem/s | una mano pulita ➡ mani pulite
clean hand/s |
| un film straniero ➡ film stranieri
foreign film/s | un'analisi dettagliata ➡ analisi dettagliate
detailed analysis/es |

See also pp. 37–38 for more on agreements.

More -o adjectives: spelling changes with endings in -cio, -gio, -co and -go

Endings in -**cio** and -**gio**. In the masculine plural the -**i** is always dropped. In the feminine plural the -**i** is optional unless a consonant precedes the endings, as in **liscio** and **saggio.**

	Masculine **Singular -o ➡ -i Plural**	**Feminine** **Singular -a ➡ -e Plural**
sudicio	un vestito sudicio ➡ vestiti sudici *dirty dress/es*	una gonna sudicia ➡ gonne sudicie/sudice *dirty skirt/s*
grigio	un cappotto grigio ➡ cappotti grigi *grey coat/s*	una sciarpa grigia ➡ sciarpe grigie/grige *grey scarve/s*
liscio	un tessuto liscio ➡ tessuti lisci *smooth material/s*	una pietra liscia ➡ pietre lisce *smooth stone/s*
saggio	un commento saggio ➡ commenti saggi *wise comment/s*	una donna saggia ➡ donne sagge *wise woman/women*

Endings in -**co** and -**go**. If the ending is preceded by a consonant or a stressed vowel, an -**h** in both masculine and feminine plurals is required.

bianco	un piatto bianco ➡ piatti bianchi *white plates*	una tazza bianca ➡ tazze bianche *white cups*
lungo	un articolo lungo ➡ articoli lunghi *long article/s*	una storia lunga ➡ storie lunghe *long story/ies*
antico	un orologio antico ➡ orologi antichi *old/antique clock/s*	una chiesa antica ➡ chiese antiche *old/ancient church/es*
sacrilego	un atto sacrilego ➡ atti sacrileghi *sacrilegious act/s* ***But:** greco ➡ greci*	un'idea sacrilega ➡ idee sacrileghe *sacrilegious idea/s*

Unstressed vowel + -**co**. If the vowel before -**co** is unstressed, the masculine plural is usually -**ci** but the feminine plural always requires an -**h**.

| **comico** | un attore comico ➡ attori comici
comic actor/s | una scena comica ➡ scene comiche
comic scene/s |
| **simpatico** | un amico simpatico ➡ amici simpatici
nice friend/s (m.) | un'amica simpatica ➡
amiche simpatiche *nice friend/s* (f.) |

◎ Esercizi

1 Using first the masculine noun, then the feminine one, make the necessary agreements with the adjectives, then make them plural:

    (a) un appartamento/una stanza: **spazioso ma scuro**

    (b) un armadio/una cucina: **vecchio ma pulito**

    (c) uno studente/una studentessa: **pigro ma simpatico**

    (d) un signore/una signora: **ricco e stupido**

    (e) un panorama/una città: **grigio e brutto**

    (f) un programma/un'analisi: **lungo e noisoso**

2 Using the adjectives given, make the necessary agreements with each noun, then make the nouns and adjectives plural.

    (a) Ho perso un fazzoletto/una camicia: **bianco/sudicio.**

    (b) Sono andato al cinema con un amico/un'amica: **turco/greco.**

    (c) Ho comprato un melone/una pera: **fresco/marcio.**

    (d) È un parco/una piazza: **pubblico/antico.**

    (e) Mi sembra un discorso/una decisione: **saggio/necessario.**

    (f) Secondo il giudice l'autista/la cantante era: **stanco/ubriaco.**

(b) Adjectives ending in -e: forms and agreements

Many adjectives end in **-e** and have two forms only: a singular and a plural.

	Singular -e ➡ -i Plural	Explanations
giovane **felice**	il ragazz**o**/la ragazz**a** **giovane** ➡ i ragazzi/le ragazze **giovani** *young boy/s/girl/s* il bambin**o**/la bambin**a** **felice** ➡ i bambini/le bambine **felici** *happy child/children* (m. and f.)	The masculine and feminine forms of the adjectives are identical except for the article. They will not necessarily match the noun endings (see (d) below).

A few **-e** adjectives such as **marrone** are invariable.

(c) Adjectives ending in -a: forms and agreements

Adjectives ending in **-a** are often also nouns. They end mostly in **-ista,** with a few in **-asta,** **-ida**, **-ita** and **-ota.** They have one singular form but two plurals.

egoista	il fratello/la sorella **egoista**	➢ i fratell**i** **egoisti** *selfish brother/s/sister/s* ➢ le sorell**e** **egoiste**	The singular m. and f. adjectives are identical except for the articles, but the plural adjectives have a masculine ending in **-i** and a feminine ending in **-e**.
entusiasta	l'amico/l'amica **entusiasta**	➢ gli amic**i** **entusiasti** *enthusiastic friend/s* (m./f.) ➢ le amich**e** **entusiaste**	

(d) Summary of agreements

Remember that adjectival endings depend on the group of the adjective and the form of the noun (singular/plural/m./f.), so the noun and adjective endings are not necessarily identical.

Masculine agreements

	m. noun	-o adjective	-e adjective	-a adjective
Singular Plural	**il ragazzo** **i ragazzi**	alto alti	giovane giovani	ipocrita ipocriti
Singular Plural	**lo scrittore** **gli scrittori**	anziano anziani	interessante interessanti	razzista razzisti
Singular Plural	**il collega** **i colleghi**	simpatico simpatici	gentile gentili	entusiasta entusiasti
Singular Plural	**il film** **i film**	bello belli	triste tristi	sessista sessisti

Feminine agreements

	f. noun	-o adjective	-e adjective	-a adjective
Singular Plural	**la ragazza** **le ragazze**	alta alte	giovane giovani	ipocrita ipocrite
Singular Plural	**la scrittrice** **le scrittrici**	anziana anziane	interessante interessanti	razzista razziste
Singular Plural	**la collega** **le colleghe**	simpatica simpatiche	gentile gentili	entusiasta entusiaste
Singular Plural	**la città** **le città**	bella belle	importante importanti	cosmopolita cosmopolite

 Attenti! If two or more nouns of different gender are qualified by a single adjective, the adjective is masculine plural:

La casa e il giardino sono **stupendi.**

And of course if the adjective is invariable it does not change:

La maglia e i pantaloni sono **blu**.

◎/✛ Esercizi

3 Here is how three different people see the same individuals. Complete the descriptions by making the necessary agreements. Which person is there clear disagreement about?

(a)	È una collega	depresso	lunatico	squilibrato
(b)	Sua sorella, Cinzia, è	aggressivo	sensibile	dolce
(c)	Il professore è	timido	pedante	conformista
(d)	I miei cugini sono	vanitoso	ignorante	egoista
(e)	Le mie zie sono	colto	intelligente	cosmopolita
(f)	Gina e Franco sono	bravo	simpatico	gentile

✛ **4** Use each of the following adjectives once in the sentences below, making the appropriate agreements.

antisemita • arabo • astronomico • avvincente (*gripping*) • cristiano • ebreo • felice e contento • grave • preoccupante • prolungato • stanco morto • umano • xenofoba

(a) Per fortuna l'esame è andato benissimo, quindi Franco e Giula sono —.

(b) È una storia — che si legge d'un fiato. (*that you can't put down*)

(c) Con questi prezzi —, tutti dicono che la crisi è molto —.

(d) Dopo i ritardi — dei voli le ragazze erano —.

(e) Al 'Festival della Coesistenza' hanno cantato artiste —, — e —.

(f) Il Commissario per i Diritti — ha espresso la sua preoccupazione per la tendenza — che porta a ad atti violenti contro gli immigrati.

(g) Secondo lo studioso dell'Olocausto, il sondaggio ha rivelato l'esistenza di un sentimento — molto —.

(e) Some special -o and -e adjectives: *bello, buono, santo* and *grande*

These adjectives are all regular in form except when they precede nouns.

Bello

The forms of **bello** change before singular and plural nouns to resemble those of the definite article.

Masculine and feminine singular		Masculine and feminine plural	
il l' lo	un **bel** palazzo *a lovely block of flats* un **bell'**appartamento *a lovely flat* un **bello** studio *a beautiful study*	i gli	dei **bei** palazzi dei **begli** appartamenti dei **begli** studi
l' la	una **bell'**isola or: una bella isola *a beautiful island* una bella stanza *a lovely room* (no change)	le	delle belle isole delle belle stanze

Buono

The forms of **buono** change only before a singular noun to resemble those of the indefinite article.

Masculine singular		Feminine singular	
un un uno	un **buon** libro *a good book* un **buon** ospedale *a good hospital* un **buono** sconto *a good discount*	un' una	una **buon'**idea *a good idea* **or:** una buona idea una buona pizza *a good pizza* (no change)

The plurals **buoni** (m.) and **buone** (f.) are regular in form whatever the position of the noun: **libri buoni** or **buoni libri**; **idee buone** or **buone idee**.

Santo

The adjective **santo** is regular in form except when it means *saint* and precedes a singular masculine Christian name or a feminine Christian name beginning with a vowel.

Masculine singular		Feminine singular	
Before a vowel	**Sant'**Andrea	Before a vowel	**Sant'**Elisabetta
Before most consonants	**San** Giorgio **San** Severo **San** Zeno	Before all consonants: no change	Santa Lucia Santa Sabina
Before *s*+ consonant	**Santo** Stefano		

Before other singular nouns, **santo** means *holy, blessed* or *saintly* and is regular in form, e.g. **Il Santo Padre**, *the Holy Father* (the Pope); **la Santa Bibbia**, *the Holy Bible*. The plurals **santi** and **sante** are regular in form whatever their position, e.g. **i Santi Apostoli**, *the Holy Apostles*; **le Scale Sante**, *the Holy Stairs*. See p. 45 for more on the position of **santo**.

Grande

Grande may change its spelling before some singular nouns, but these changes are slight and optional. They depend on the initial letter of the following word.

		Masculine and feminine singular nouns
Before a vowel	**grande** or **grand'**	un **grande/grand'**appartamento *a large apartment* una **grande/grand'**isola *a large island*
Before most consonants	**grande** or **gran** (more common)	un **grande/gran** palazzo *a large apartment block* una **grande/gran** confusione *a great commotion*
Before *s* + consonant and *z*	**grande** (no change)	un **grande** studio *a large study* un **grande** zaino *a large rucksack*

The plural **grandi** never changes, whatever its position: **palazzi grandi** or **grandi palazzi**, **isole grandi** or **grandi isole**, **appartamenti grandi** or **grandi appartamenti**.

Special meanings of gran

Gran has come to have meanings of its own.

La Gran Bretagna *Great Britain* Il Gran San Bernardo *The Great St Bernard (Pass)* Ho una gran voglia di uscire *I'm desperate/really keen to go out* C'è un gran freddo *It's freezing cold* È un gran bugiardo *He's such a liar/a total liar* Non è gran che *It's not up to much/no great shakes*	**Gran** is most commonly used with masculine or feminine geographical names meaning *great*, or as an intensifier in emphatic phrases.

For more on the position of **grande**, see p. 45.

◎ Esercizi

5 Complete the sentences using the appropriate form of **bello**.
- **(a)** Ho scoperto un posto molto bello: un — posto di villeggiatura.
- **(b)** Ho trovato un appartamento molto bello: un — appartamento spazioso.
- **(c)** Ho affittato una stanza veramente bella: una — stanza luminosa.
- **(d)** Ho visto dei sandali molto belli: dei — sandali di cuoio.
- **(e)** Ho comprato degli armadi molto belli: dei — armadi di mogano. (*mahogany*)

6 Insert the correct forms of **buono** to complete these sentences.
- **(a)** Il dolce è veramente buono: è un — dolce di cioccolato.
- **(b)** Lo zabaglione è veramente buono: è un — zabaglione leggero.
- **(c)** L'insalata è molto buona: è una — insalata mista.
- **(d)** I biscotti sono molto buoni: sono dei — biscotti casalinghi.
- **(e)** Le tagliatelle sono proprio buone: sono delle — tagliatelle fatte in casa.

7 Use **santo** correctly in these sentences.
- **(a)** Il santo patrono della Scozia è — Andrea, non — Giorgio!
- **(b)** — Agata è la santa patrona del nostro paese. (*village*)

(c) A Roma tante chiese sono dedicate a — Pietro ma nessuna a — Zeno.

(d) La chiesa di — Spirito a Firenze è famosa.

(e) Le Scale — si trovano nella chiesa romana di — Giovanni in Laterano.

8 In the following sentences, provide alternative forms of **grande** where possible.

(a) È veramente un grande peccato.

(b) È stato un errore grande.

(c) Ho comprato un grande armadio.

(d) Mi ha fatto una grande impressione.

(e) Ho sempre avuto piedi grandi.

(f) Adjectival phrases

Adjectival phrases perform the same function as descriptive adjectives and are invariable.

un albergo di lusso *a luxury hotel* un compagno di scuola *a school friend* orecchini di valore *valuable earrings* una camicia a righe/a quadretti *a striped/checked shirt* una torta al limone/alla fragola *a lemon/strawberry cake* occhiali da sole *sunglasses* un insegnante in gamba *a great teacher* una maglia in lana leggera *a light wool top* un abito da sera di seta *a silk evening dress*	The most common adjectival phrases are made up of **di** + a noun and a few are composed of **a**, **da** or **in** + a noun. Adjectival phrases follow the noun or sometimes another adjectival phrase.

(g) Adjectives and pronouns

Agreements

When adjectives qualify pronouns they agree in number and gender with the noun the pronoun refers to.

La tua è **bella,** la mia no. (la camera) *Yours is lovely, mine isn't*	Possessive pronouns: *mine, yours*, etc.
Questi qua sono troppo **cari** (i libri) *These ones are too expensive* Quella **nera** non mi piace (la borsa) *I don't like the (that) black one* Quelle **lunghe** mi piacciono di più (le collane) *I like the (those) long ones best*	Demonstrative pronouns: *this, that,* etc. For the use of **quello** + adjective, see p. 142.
Sono tutte **simpatiche** (le insegnanti) *They are all nice* Alcuni sono veramente **brutti** (appartamenti) *Some are really ugly*	Indefinite pronouns: *some, others, few, many*, etc.
Lui (Giorgio) è **italiano** ma lei (Angela) è **tedesca.** *He is Italian but she is German.* Lei è **contenta**, signora? *Are you pleased, Madam?* Lei è **soddisfattto**, signore? *Are you satisfied, Sir?*	Subject pronouns: *I, you, he, she*, etc. Note that with **Lei**, the formal *you*, the m. form of the adjective is used for a man and the f. form for a woman.

Pronoun + *di* + adjective

Adjectives are often used after some common pronouns, always preceded by **di**.

Ho mangiato qualcosa **di strano** *I ate something strange* Non è niente/nulla **di grave** *It's nothing serious* Che cosa c'è **di nuovo**? *What's new?/Is there anything new?* Che cosa fai **di bello**? *What are you doing (that's nice)?* Quello che c'è **di buono** è la sua onestà *What's good/The good thing is his honesty*	The pronouns **qualcosa/ qualche cosa** *something*, **niente/nulla** *nothing*, **che cosa? che? cosa?** *what?* and **quello che** *what* all require a masculine singular agreement.
Non ho fatto niente **di male** *I haven't done anything wrong* Ha fatto qualcosa **di peggio** *He did something worse*	The adverbs **male** and **peggio** can also be similarly used.

◎ Esercizio

9 Complete the Italian sentences with an appropriate adjective using the English version as a guide.

(a)	Che cosa fai — oggi?	*Are you doing anything nice today?*
(b)	Vorrei bere qualcosa di —.	*I would like to drink something hot.*
(c)	Non hanno fatto niente di.	*They haven't done anything wrong.*
(d)	Non danno nulla — al cinema stasera.	*They aren't showing anything good at the cinema tonight.*
(e)	Che cosa c'è — in tutto questo?	*What's extraordinary in all this?*
(f)	Quello che c'è — è la sua indifferenza.	*What's odd is his/her indifference.*

◎/✚ 3.2 Irregular adjectives

(a) Invariable adjectives

The adjectives in the following categories are invariable, i.e. do not change their form.

la musica folk/pop/rock *folk/pop/rock music* una moda gay/sexy/liberty *a gay/sexy/art nouveau fashion* una signora snob *a snobbish woman* l'italiano standard *standard Italian* l'ingresso gratis *free entry*	**Foreign adjectives**
la maglia/i pantaloni beige/blu *the beige/blue jumper* i cappelli lilla/rosa/viola *the lilac/pink/violet hats* la borsa/i calzini nocciola/crema *the light brown/cream bag/socks* il cappotto/gli zoccoli marrone *the brown coat/clogs* la camicetta/i guanti arancione *the orange blouse/gloves*	**Colours of foreign origin** or derived from plants The plurals **marroni, arancioni** also exist.
una maglia verde scuro/blu marino *a dark green/navy jumper* degli occhi grigio chiaro *light grey eyes* delle sciarpe verde smeraldo *emerald green scarves* ***But:*** delle giacche grigioverdi *grey-green jackets* la squadra bianconera *the black and white team* (Juventus)	**Compound colours** If the colour is a single word it often agrees with the accompanying noun.
Dieci è un numero **pari** *Ten is an even number* Tre è un numero **dispari** *Three is an odd number* È una ragazza **perbene** *She is a respectable girl* Ho mangiato pollo/carne **arrosto** *I ate roast chicken/meat*	**Other invariable adjectives** These are the most common.

◎ Esercizio

1 What did you come across at the flea market? Give the Italian equivalent of the English adjectives given, making any necessary agreements. Begin, 'Ho visto …'

(a) una lampada (*art nouveau*)

(b) tappeti (*multicoloured*)

(c) delle riviste (*gay*)

(d) dei pappagalli (*emerald green*)

(e) dei pantaloni (*grey-green*)

(f) un parasole (*purple*)

(g) dei vestitini (*sexy*)

(h) un boa con piume (*pink*)

✦ (b) Compound adjectives

Compound adjectives are usually made up of a prefix followed by another adjective and sometimes a noun.

Adjectives with prefixes: e.g. **bio, extra, super, stra, mezzo**	Una sostanza biogradabile ➡ sostanze biodegradabili *biodegradable substances* Un paese extraeuropeo ➡ paesi extraeuropei *non-European countries* una donna straricca *a mega-rich woman* una bottiglia mezza/o vuota *a half-full bottle*	These mostly have regular endings. When **mezzo** is used, the ending may, optionally, remain the same.
Anti + adjective	un rifugio antiaereo ➡ rifugi antiaerei *air raid shelter/s* un'idea anticonformistica ➡ idee anticonformistiche *non-conformist idea/s* un pregiudizio antifemminista ➡ pregiudizi antifemministi *antifeminist prejudice/s* un libro antisemita ➡ libri antisemiti *antisemitic book/s*	Many compound adjectives are formed of **anti** plus an adjective (which can sometimes also be a noun). These have regular endings.
Anti + noun	uno shampoo antiforfora *an antidandruff shampoo* dispositivi antifurto *antitheft devices* gli scudi antimissile *antimissile shields* le mine antipersona *landmines*	When a compound adjective is formed of **anti** plus a noun which cannot also be used as an adjective, it usually has an invariable ending.
Hyphenated adjectives	la chiesa greco-ortodossa *the Greek Orthodox church* una ragazza italo-americana *an Italian-American girl* progressi tecnico-scientifici *technical and scientific progress* **But:** partiti marxisti-leninisti *Marxist-Leninist parties*	In hyphenated adjectives, only the second part changes to agree with the noun. Some are written as one word: **socioeconomico, anglosassone.**

✦ Esercizio

2 Invariable or regular? Complete the sentences using one of the adjectives given below.

antiaereo • antidroga • antigienico • antinucleare • antipersona • angloamericano • russo-afgano

(a) I centri — curano i tossicodipendenti.

(b) A Hiroshima ci sono state delle manfestazioni —.

(c) I rifugi — non servono a molto contro le esplosioni nucleari.

(d) La guerra — ha rovinato l'Afganistan.

(e) Nel luglio del 1943, le truppe — sono sbarcate in Sicilia.

(f) La Croce Rossa ha organizzato una giornata di studio contro le mine —.

(g) Il Comune ha lanciato una campagna di sensibilizzazione contro l'abitudine — di sputare per terra.

◎/✛ 3.3 The position of single adjectives

In English adjectives generally come before the noun, but in Italian their position varies depending on their function.

(a) After the noun: specifying adjectives

The majority of Italian descriptive adjectives follow the noun when they have a specifying function – i.e. when they pinpoint specific characteristics or distinguishing features of the noun. These adjectives can be grouped as shown below. For a summary of the position of adjectives, see pp. 345–6.

1. Adjectives denoting a category: (often derived from a noun, **televisione, mondo**, etc.)	lo schermo televisivo *the TV screen* la guerra mondiale *the world war* una crisi nazionale *a national crisis* uno sperimento scientifico *a scientific experiment* un elenco telefonico *a telephone directory* un cane di razza *a pedigree dog*
2. Nationality or origin Religion Ideology	una donna tedesca *a German woman* un ragazzo napoletano *a Neapolitan boy* una chiesa protestante *a Protestant church* il partito socialista *the socialist party*
3. Colour, shape, design, material	un vestito rosso *a red dress* una scatola rettangolare *a rectangular box* una camicetta a righe *a striped blouse* un cappotto di lana *a woollen coat* una strada polverosa *a dusty road*
4. Adjectives derived from a past participle usually ending in **-ato, -ito, -uto**. Some adjectives ending in **-ante** or **-ente** derived from a present participle	uno straccio bagnato *a wet rag* un fazzoletto pulito *a clean handkerchief* una sedia rotta *a broken chair* una società tollerante *a tolerant society* la squadra vincente *the wining team* acqua bollente *boiling water*
5. Adjectives with a suffix such as **-ino** or **-etto**	un cagnolino piccolino *a tiny puppy* un bambino furbetto *a crafty child*
6. Adjectives used with an adverb, e.g. **molto** *very*, **abbastanza** *quite*, **piuttosto** *rather*, **troppo** *too*, **poco** *little*	una ragazza molto bella *a very beautiful girl* un film abbastanza interessante *quite an interesting film* un viaggio piuttosto lungo *a rather long journey* una città poco consociuta *a little-known town*
7. Adjectival phrases: usually part of categories 1, 2 and 3 above	un paese di montagna *a mountain village* una storia d'amore *a love story* una porta di vetro *a glass door*

◎ Esercizio

1 Who or what did you see at the airport? Use the English version as a guide and complete these descriptions, placing the adjectives given below in an appropriate position and making the correct agreements.

americano • annoiato • buddista • di seta • giallo • indiano • molto grande
• piccolino • sorridente • strano • triangolare • ubriaco

(a)	dei soldati	*some American soldiers*
(b)	un gruppo di suore	*a group of smiling nuns*
(c)	dei bambini	*some bored children*
(d)	dei giovani	*some drunken youths*
(e)	un monaco con la veste	*a Buddhist monk in a yellow robe*
(f)	una signora con il sari	*an Indian lady in a silk sari*
(g)	una donna con un cappello	*a weird woman in a triangular hat*
(h)	un gatto in una gabbia	*a tiny cat in a very large cage*

✛ (b) Before or after the noun: specifying and generic adjectives

Most Italian adjectives can go either before or after the noun depending on their function:
(i) specifying or restrictive and (ii) 'generic'. The latter refers to adjectives used for descriptive, rhetorical or metaphorical purposes. Adjectives whose meaning is fairly broad are most likely to be used in both ways in different contexts and therefore to have flexible positions. Some of the most common are: **anziano, bello, brutto, buono, cattivo, giovane, grande, lungo, nuovo, piacevole, piccolo, simpatico, strano**. They are used before the noun for generic, subjective description and after it to pinpoint and identify specific characteristics, especially when choice, contrast or particular emphasis is implied.

Generic description: subjective Before noun	Specifying function: objective After noun
È un **grande** amico *He is a great friend*	Mi dà una birra **grande**? *Can I have a large beer?*
C'era una **lunga** fila *There was a long queue*	Ho scelto la gonna **lunga** *I chose the long skirt*
Mi sono comprato delle **belle** scarpe *I bought myself some lovely shoes*	Mettiti le scarpe **belle** stasera *Put on your good/best shoes tonight*
È una **buona** soluzione *It's a good solution*	Hai trovato la soluzione **buona** *You've found the right/a good solution*
L'olio di ricino ha un **cattivo** sapore *Castor oil has a horrible taste*	Quel vino ha un sapore **cattivo**, l'altro no *This wine tastes horrible, the other one doesn't*
Hai sentito la **nuova** teoria di Carlo? *Have you heard Carlo's new (latest) theory?*	Mi sembra una teoria **nuova** *It strikes me as a new (novel/original) theory*

The same distinction above applies to **santo**. Generic function: **la Santa Messa** *Holy Mass*, **una santa vita** *a holy/saintly life*, **santo cielo/Dio!** *Good heavens!* **Tutto il santo giorno** *the whole (blessed) day long*.
Specifying function: **il Venerdì Santo**, *Good Friday*, **lo Spirito Santo** *the Holy Spirit/Ghost*, **la Settimana Santa** *Holy Week*, **la Terra Santa** *the Holy Land*.

◎/✚ (c) Position and changes in meaning

The meaning of the adjectives in section (b) above is not significantly modified by their position. However, the meaning of some common adjectives is affected by position. The following are some of the most frequently used.

Before the noun	Meaning	After the noun	Meaning
gli **antichi** romani	*The ancient Romans*	un orologio **antico**	*an old/antique clock*
un **alto** ufficiale	*a high-ranking officer*	un ragazzo **alto**	*a tall boy*
l'**alta** Italia	*Northern Italy*	un muro **alto**	*a high wall*
la **bassa** Italia	*Southern Italy*	un uomo **basso**	*a short man*
il **basso** Po	*the lower Po*	un voto **basso**	*a low mark*
un **caro** amico	*a dear friend*	un albergo **caro**	*an expensive/dear hotel*
certe notizie	*certain/some news*	notizie **certe**	*definite/reliable news*
un **discreto** risultato	*quite a good result*	un prezzo **discreto**	*a reasonable/moderate price*
una **discreta** età	*a considerable age*	una domanda **discreta**	*a discrete question*
diversi libri	*several books*	libri **diversi**	*different books*
una **leggera** ferita	*a slight wound*	una borsa **leggera**	*a light bag*
il **massimo** rispetto	*the utmost respect*	la velocità **massima**	*the maximum speed*
un **povero** uomo	*a poor/unfortunate man*	un uomo **povero**	*a poor man* (financially)
lo **stesso** ragazzo	*the same boy*	il ragazzo **stesso**	*the boy himself*
una **semplice** domanda	*just a question*	una domanda **semplice**	*an easy question*
l'**unica** occasione	*the only opportunity*	un'occasione **unica**	*a unique opportunity*
l'**unico** figlio	*the only child*	figlio **unico**	*an only child* (i.e.unique)
varie volte	*several times*	un paesaggio **vario**	*a varied landscape*
un **vecchio** amico	*an old/longstanding friend*	un amico **vecchio**	*an old friend* (in years)

From the list above it is possible to see that when used in a non-literal sense, or when quantity is involved, many of the adjectives tend to precede the noun. On the other hand, the adjectives generally follow the noun when identifying its distinguishing features. These rules of position are not watertight and are best learned through use or by consulting a dictionary.

◎/✚ Esercizi

2 Look at these pairs of sentences. Mark each sentence D or S according to whether the adjective is used for general description or for precise specification.

(a) In centro c'è una grande piazza.
Ci vediamo nella piazza grande.

(b) È un film bello, ma deprimente.
Mi piace: è un bel film.

(c) Come! Ti sei comprato un nuovo vestito?
Mettitti il vestito nuovo stasera.

(d) Mi fa vedere quel vaso strano?
Ha avuto una strana reazione.

(e) È una brutta giornata.
È una sedia brutta, ma comoda.

(f) Abito in un piccolo paese in montagna.
Non abito in città, abito in un paese piccolo.

3 Complete the sentences below using the adjectives given and placing them appropriately, either before or after the nouns.

(a) Due — buste — e tre — buste — per piacere.
(grande, piccolo)

Two large envelopes and three small envelopes, please.

(b) Un — caffè — in una — tazza — per piacere.
(lungo, grande)

A weak coffee in a large cup, please.

(c) Prendo il — caffè — per piacere e un — tè —.
(solito, freddo)

I'll have my/the usual coffee please and a cold tea.

4 Give the Italian equivalent of the sentences below, taking care to place the adjectives correctly.

(a) *She is a dear friend.* (caro)
I bought an expensive jacket.

(c) *I talked to the same manager.* (stesso)
I talked to the manger himself.

(b) *There are several solutions.* (diverso)
There are different solutions.

(d) *I admire her; she is a unique woman.* (unico)
She is the only woman for me.

✚ 5 Use each of the adjectives given twice, and place them correctly in the sentences. Use the English as a guide.

semplice • vari

(a) È un — ristorante — ma al tempo stesso raffinato.

It's a simple restaurant but at the same time it's refined.

(b) Non è un — ristorante —, è un tempio della gastronomia.

It's not just a restaurant, it's a temple of gastronomy.

(c) Di recente ho visto — film — sul Risorgimento.

I've recently seen several films about Italian Unification.

(d) È una lista delle recensioni recenti di — film —.

It's a list of recent reviews of various/ miscellaneous films.

✚ 3.4 The position of multiple adjectives

Broadly speaking, the rules governing the position of a single adjective also apply to several adjectives.

(a) Several adjectives after the noun

When several adjectives are used with a noun, they may vary in descriptive importance.

Adjectives of equal descriptive importance

Any two Italian adjectives of equal descriptive importance usually follow the noun and are separated by **e**. If there are more than two adjectives, the first ones are separated by a comma and the last two by **e**.

Noun + two or more adjectives (specifying or generic)	una signora snella e piccolina *a slim, petite woman* un impiegato onesto e fedele *an honest, faithful employee* un vino corposo e fruttato *a full-bodied, fruity wine*	The English adjectives are separated by a comma unless there are three or more adjectives or two or more colours. Note that 'black and white' is 'white and black' in Italian.
	una bandiera rossa, bianca e verde *a red, white and green flag* una sciarpa azzurra e gialla *a blue and yellow scarf* un vestito bianco e nero *a black and white dress*	
Variable position	una signora giovane e simpatica *a nice young woman* un attentato sanguinoso e tragico *a tragic, bloody bomb attack*	Generic adjectives may also go before the noun. See the lists on pp. 45–6.

Adjectives of different descriptive importance

When Italian adjectives are of different descriptive importance, the one which most closely defines the noun immediately comes after it, directly followed by the other one. The first adjective specifies a type or category and the next adds subordinate, related information.

Noun + specifying adjectives	aqua minerale naturale *still mineral water* un vino bianco frizzante *a sparkling white wine* un impiegato statale corrotto *a corrupt state official*	The Italian adjectives are usually in reverse order to the English.
Noun + specifying and generic adjectives: variable position	un film poliziesco banale *a banal detective film* un vino biologico squisito *a delicious organic wine* un corso d'inglese noioso *a boring English course* scarpe nere nuove *new black shoes* una vacanza estiva piacevole *a pleasant summer holiday* una guerra mondiale lunga e tragica *a long and tragic world war* conflitti etnici e religiosi sanguinosi *bloody ethnic and religious conflicts*	Generic adjectives – **banale**, **squisito**, etc. (not specifying adjectives) – may also go before the noun. See table (b) p. 49 and pp. 345–6.
Adjectival phrases	una camicetta di seta rossa *a red silk blouse*/una camicetta rossa di seta *a red blouse of silk* un pantalone di velluto verde scuro *dark green corduroy trousers*/un pantalone verde scuro di velluto *dark green trousers of corduroy* ***Invariable positions:*** il primo presidente nero d'America *the first American black president* un abito da sera di seta *a silk evening dress* una maglia in lana leggera a coste *a ribbed light woollen top* mezzi di comunicazione di massa *means of mass communication*	With another adjective the position of an adjectival phrase may be flexible (see first two examples opposite), depending on which of the two most closely specifies the noun. If there are two adjectival phrases, the most specific one goes first.

✛ Esercizi

1 Describe some of your wardrobe using the adjectives given.

(a)	guanti	nero, di pelle	*black leather gloves*
(b)	un golf	verde, di cachemire	*a green cashmere sweater*
(c)	una camicetta	bianco, nero, di cotone	*a black and white cotton blouse*
(d)	una giacca	nero, giallo, verde a quadretti	*a black, yellow and green checked jacket*

2 Give the Italian for the following.

(a) *a French airline company*

(b) *an irregular masculine noun*

(c) *the European Economic Community*

(d) *a valuable gold bracelet* (**braccialetto**)

(e) *a Russian nuclear power station* (**impianto**)

(f) *a vintage Italian wine* (**invecchiato**)

(g) *quite a complicated technical problem*

(h) *a brilliant political speech* (**geniale**)

3 Explain some of the things you did last week, using the adjectives given.

(a)	*I went out with some extremely nice school friends.*	simpaticissimo, di scuola
(b)	*I saw a boring historical documentary.*	noioso, storico
(c)	*I went to a really wonderful rock concert.*	meraviglioso, rock
(d)	*I met a very interesting Canadian couple.*	canadese, interessante
(e)	*I bought a pair of stunning red shoes.*	rosso, stupendo

(b) Adjectives before and after the noun

It is common for many generic adjectives to precede the noun and for specifying ones to follow.

Generic adjectives + specifying adjectives: general description	Porta delle **nuove** scarpe **rosse** e **vecchi** pantaloni **neri** *She is wearing new red shoes and old black trousers* Ho conosciuto una **giovane** coppia **gallese** *I met a young Welsh couple* Sono tornati da una **piacevole** vacanza **estiva** *They have returned from a pleasant summer holiday*	Many common adjectives have a general descriptive function as well as a specifying or emphatic one. They very often precede the noun.
Generic adjectives + specifying adjectives: value judgements	Ho visto un **banale** film **poliziesco**, non perdere tempo a vederlo *I saw a banal detective film, don't waste time watching it* Produce uno **squisito** vino **biologico** che mi piace da morire *He produces an exquisite organic wine to die for/ which I absolutely love* Quel **noioso** corso **d'inglese** è una perdita di tempo *That boring English course is a waste of time*	Other generic adjectives involving value judgements precede the noun when they have a subjective, emotive force. See table 1, p. 48 for an alternative position and a more objective, specifying emphasis.
Generic adjectives used together	una **bella** casa **grande** *a lovely big house* un **grande** albergo **nuovo** *a large new hotel* un **nuovo** attentato **sanguinoso** *another/a new bloody bomb attack* un **gentile** signore **anziano** *a kind, elderly man*	When one or more generic adjectives are used together, the most specific one usually follows the noun.

✚ Esercizi

4 Describe where some of your friends and acquaintances live placing one of the adjectives before the noun. In two cases there is a second possibility. Begin, 'Abita in …'

    (a) un bungalow (moderno, piccolo)   **(d)** una stanza (affittato, piccolino)

    (b) un quartiere (di Roma, vecchio)   **(e)** un attico (antico, stupendo)

    (c) una casa (bello, grande)   **(f)** una villa (rinascimentale, enorme)

5 Complete the sentences by giving the Italian equivalent of the English. Place the adjectives before or after the nouns according to whether you believe they have equal or different descriptive importance. You may need to refer to the tables on pp. 47–8 as well as to the table above.

    (a) Tiziana era bellissima, con — capelli — e — occhi — . (*long, dark hair and big blue eyes*)

    (b) Stanno cercando una — donna — dai — capelli — . (*a young woman with long dark hair*)

    (c) È stata una — decisione — . (*an absurd bureaucratic decision*)

    (d) Non si può mica accettare quell' — decisione — ! (*that absurd bureaucratic decision*)

    (e) È stato un — disastro — . (*a terrible, completely unforeseen ecological disaster*) (inatteso)

    (f) I profughi vivono in — condizioni — . (*very disadvantaged social and economic conditions*) (svantaggiato)

(c) Several adjectives before the noun

More than one adjective before the noun is common only in literary language, in travel literature and in the stereotyped set phrases to be found in some journalism or in the language of advertising. It is not common in spoken Italian.

Lo scrittore abbandonò la sua **grande e vecchia** dimora
The writer abandoned his large, ancient dwelling
Non si dimenticherà il **sanguinoso e tragico** attentato di Firenze
The bloody, tragic bomb attack in Florence will not be forgotten
Si possono ammirare le **placide e austere** abbazie benedettine
One can admire the quiet, austere Benedictine abbeys
È un **avvincente e imprevedibile** black comedy, in onda dal 15 novembre
It is a gripping, unpredictable black comedy, out from 15 November

---

In spoken Italian several adjectives may occasionally be used before the noun, but only when there is a particularly subjective or emotive focus.

> È proprio una **giovane e simpatica** signora. *She's a really nice young woman.*

> È veramente un **caro e bravo** ragazzo. *He really is a dear, good boy.*

✦ 3.5 Expressing 'good and 'bad': notes on meaning

(a) *Bello, buono* and *bravo*: 'good'

The following are broad guidelines to the use of these common adjectives whose meanings overlap. For further examples consult an Italian monolingual dictionary. Like most common adjectives, these adjectives tend to precede the noun for general description and follow it when specifying or restricting the meaning. (See examples on p. 45.) They are more commonly found before the noun.

bello and **buono**	È una **bella** casa *It is a beautiful/lovely house* È un **buona** casa editrice *It is a good publishing house* È un **bel** lavoro *It's a great/good job* (i.e. *impressive/looks good*) È un **buon** lavoro *It's a great/good job* (i.e. *well done or worthwhile*) È un **bel** romanzo *It's a great/good novel* (i.e. *enjoyable*) È un **buon** romanzo *It's a good novel* (i.e. *well written*)	**Bello** defines visual or aural beauty, what is aesthetic, pleasant or impressive. **Buono** defines what is physically good, e.g. to taste or smell, and what is morally good or worthwhile. It can convey the idea of something well done.
bravo and **buono**	È un **bravo** ragazzo *He is a good boy* (i.e. *well behaved, moral*) È un ragazzo **bravo** *He is a clever boy* È un ragazzo buono *He is a good-natured/kind boy* È un **bravo** insegnante *or, more emphatic*: È un insegnante **bravo** *He's a good teacher* (i.e. *skilled and clever*) È un **buon** insegnante *He is a good teacher*	Both often used for describing people. **Bravo** defines skill, cleverness and (good) behaviour. **Buono** tends to describe inherent qualities, e.g. good nature. It can also be used instead of **bravo** to mean experienced/ skilled.
Well done! Good!	**Bravo!** Hai fatto un buon lavoro *Good!/Well done! You've done a good job* Domani arriverò presto. – **Bene** *Tomorrow I'll arrive early. – Good*	**Bravo** is used as a compliment. Note that the adverb **bene** (well), not the adjective **buono**, is used to express pleasure and approval.

✦ Esercizio

1 Bello, bravo or **buono**? Select the most appropriate adjective for *good* and complete the sentences by giving the Italian equivalent of the English phrases. You may find that you can use more than one adjective.

(a) *It's a good painting.*
È un dipinto magnifico.

(e) *It's a good novel.*
È un romanzo originale.

(b) *It's a good wine.*
È un vino stagionato.

(f) *They are good children.*
Sono bambini educati.

(c) *He's a good cook.*
È un cuoco geniale.

(g) *He is a good person.*
Aiuta sempre gli altri.

(d) *It's a good textbook.*
È un libro di testo utile.

(h) *He's a good student.*
Che studia tanto.

(b) *Brutto* and *cattivo*: 'bad'

Brutto *ugly/bad* and **cattivo** *bad* are sometimes but not always interchangeable. The following are broad guidelines to their use. Like other adjectives, **brutto** and **cattivo** tend to precede the noun for general description and follow it for particular specification. (See examples on p. 45.) They are more commonly found before the noun.

cattivo	Non è un **cattivo** ragazzo *He's not a naughty/badly behaved boy* È di **cattivo** umore *He's in a bad mood* È un **cattivo** insegnante *He's a bad teacher* È una persona veramente **cattiva** *He/She is a really bad/nasty person* Che **cattivo** odore/sapore! *What a horrible smell/taste!* Quel pesce è **cattivo** *That fish is bad/off*	Can describe behaviour, skill and morals as well as what is physically bad, e.g. taste and smell.
brutto	È una **brutta** città industriale *It's an ugly industrial town* Ha un **brutto** naso *He has an ugly nose* Che **brutta** giornata! *What a horrible day!* Ho fatto un **brutto** viaggio *I had a terrible journey* Ho un **brutto** mal di testa *I've got a bad headache*	Used when the emphasis is on physical unpleasantness or ugliness, but not taste or smell (see **cattivo** above).
brutto and cattivo	una **brutta/cattiva** abitudine *a bad habit* una **brutta/cattiva** impressione *a bad impression* **brutto/cattivo** tempo *bad weather* un **brutto/cattivo** voto *a bad mark*	Both used to convey the idea of something bad or unpleasant in many different contexts.

✦ Esercizi

2 Give the Italian equivalent of the following, choosing either **brutto** or **cattivo.** In some instances either is possible.

(a) *It's an ugly painting.*

(e) *The weather is bad.*

(i) *He's a bad student.*

(b) *It's a horrible wine.*

(f) *It's a bad textbook.*

(j) *It's a bad essay.* (**saggio**)

(c) *He's a terrible cook.*

(g) *It's a bad novel.*

(k) *She's a bad mother.*

(d) *He's a nasty person.*

(h) *They are naughty children.*

(l) *He's an ugly man.*

3 Finally, give the Italian version of the film ***The Good, the Bad and the Ugly***, but be aware that the Italians say, 'The Good, the Ugly, the Bad.'

◎/+ **3.6 Further uses of adjectives**

(a) Adjectives used as nouns

Most adjectives used as nouns are masculine singular and preceded by the masculine definite article.

Il bello è che non ho dovuto pagare *The good thing/best bit/joke is I didn't have to pay* Ha fatto tutto **il possibile** *He did everything possible* **Il peggio** è che ho perso la ricevuta *The worst thing is I've lost the receipt* L'inflazione è oltre **l'immaginabile** *The inflation is unimaginable* Non chiedere **l'impossibile** *Don't ask for the impossible* Devi fare **del** tuo **meglio** *You must do your best* Qual è il segreto per avere **la meglio** sugli inglesi? *What is the secret of getting the better of the English?*	Some adjectives used as nouns express abstract concepts. Note the use of **la** in the expression **avere la meglio su (di) qlcu.**, *to get the better of someone.*
È **un ambizioso/un'ambiziosa** *He is an ambitious man/She's an ambitious woman* Odiano **i ricchi** *They hate rich people/the rich* **I pentiti** hanno paura *The (ex-terrorist/mafia) informers are afraid* **I neri** sono stati sconfitti *The fascists were defeated* Hanno vinto **gli azzurri** *The Italian team won*	Some adjectives used as nouns describe people or groups of people.

For adjectives used as adverbs, see p. 54–5.

◎ Esercizio

1 Give the English equivalent of the following.

    (a) Abbiamo fatto il possibile per aiutarlo.

    (b) Il bello è che alla fine mi hanno fatto uno sconto.

    (c) Il peggio è che le banche sono chiuse.

    (d) Nei vecchi film western i buoni vincono sempre i cattivi.

(b) Adjectives with impersonal expressions and imperatives

The masculine plural form of adjectives is normally used with impersonal constructions because these mostly refer to an indeterminate number and gender of people.

Impersonal phrases + infinitive	Bisogna sempre essere **onesti** *One/You must always be honest* Non è il caso di essere **offesi** *There's no need to be offended* Basta stare **zitti** *All you have to do is keep quiet*
The impersonal **si**: plural adjective but singular verb	Quando si è **malati**, si è spesso **depressi** *When one is ill, one is often depressed* Se si sta **attenti**, si sente il mare *If you pay attention, you can hear the sea.* (See also p. 325.)

Note that, even where there is no explicit impersonal structure, the masculine plural adjective is used if it refers to an indeterminate group of people. Note in addition that the plural adjective is also used as part of the **voi** imperative when addressing an indeterminate audience/ readership.

Implicit impersonal form	La pillola che rende **intelligenti** non esiste *A pill that makes you intelligent does not exist*
Imperatives	**Attenti**! *Watch out! Be careful!* **Zitti**! *Be quiet!* (Short for **State attenti/zitti**)

✚ Esercizio

2 Complete the sentences, making the correct adjectival agreements.

(a) Non è il caso di essere (scortese). *There's no need to be rude.*

(b) Per rimanere (giovane) bisogna essere (ottimista). *To stay young you have to be optimistic.*

(c) Si vive più (sano) se si pratica uno sport. *You live more healthily if you practise a sport.*

(d) È peggio essere (sordo) che (cieco). *It's worse being deaf than blind.*

(e) L'Internet è sempre utile per tenersi (aggiornato). *The internet is always useful to keep up to date.*

 For adjectives used with prepositions and dependent infinitives, e.g. **soddisfatto di** *satisfied with*, **interessato a** *interested in,* see pp. 208–9.

3 The following is from a recent novel set in the south of Italy by Niccolò Ammaniti. In this extract he describes the tiny hamlet of Aqua Traverse as it is today and as it used to be. Read the description, then answer the questions.

Oggi Aqua Traverse è una frazione* di Lucignano. A metà degli anni Ottanta un geometra* ha costruito due lunghe schiere* di villette di cemento armato. Dei cubi con le finestre circolari, le ringhiere* azzurre e i tondini* d'acciaio che spuntano* dal tetto. Poi sono arrivati una Coop e un bar tabacchi. E una strada asfaltata a due corsie* che corre dritta come una pista d'atterraggio fino a Lucignano.

Nel 1978 Aqua Traverse invece era così piccola che non era niente. Un borgo di campagna, lo chiamerebbero oggi su una rivista di viaggi. ...

C'era la villa di Salvatore, che chiamavamo il Palazzo. Un casone costruito nell'Ottocento, lungo e grigio e con un grande portico di pietra e un cortile interno con una palma. E c'erano altre quattro case. Non per modo di dire. Quattro case in tutto. Quattro misere case di pietra e malta* con il tetto di tegole* e le finestre piccole. ... Due case da una parte, due dall'altra. E una strada, sterrata* e piena di buchi, al centro. Non c'era una piazza. Non c'erano vicoli. C'erano però due panchine sotto una pergola di uva fragola e una fontanella che aveva il rubinetto con la chiave per non sprecare l'aqua. Tutto intorno i campi di grano.

L'unica cosa che si era guadagnata quel posto dimenticato da Dio e dagli uomini era un bel cartello blu con scritto in maiuscolo AQUA TRAVERSE.

(Niccolò Ammaniti, *Io non ho paura*, Einaudi, 2001)

> una frazione *sub-district* • un geometra *surveyor* • schiere *rows* • ringhiere *railings*
> • tondini d'acciaio *steel rods to reinforce the concrete* • spuntano *stick up* • corsie *lanes*
> • malta *mortar* • di tegole *tiled* • sterrata *unpaved, of beaten earth, dirt*

(a) In paragraphs 1 and 2, identify six adjectival phrases and the other adjectives.

(b) In paragraph 3, pick out one or two nouns qualified by two adjectives of the same descriptive importance.

(c) Find the Italian equivalent in the text for: *two long rows of small concrete villas*; *a large stone portico*; *four miserable stone and mortar houses*; *a beautiful blue signpost*.

(d) The new and the old road are described: **una strada asfaltata a due corsie**; and **una strada, sterrata e piena di buchi.** Find English equivalents.

(e) Are the majority of adjectives in the description specifying or generally descriptive (generic)? What effect does this have?

4 Adverbs

Adverbs (**gli avverbi**) pepper our speech and writing and yet they are often neglected. They are important invariable words with a wide variety of uses. For example, they answer such questions as *how? when? where? why? to what extent?* They provide more information about verbs – e.g. *He eats **slowly*** – but they also modify adjectives, other adverbs or even a whole sentence: *It's **quite** difficult. He speaks **really** well. I **usually** get up at seven.*

◎ 4.1 The forms of adverbs

Adverbs are varied in form and many are linked to other parts of speech, such as adjectives.

(a) Adverbs derived from descriptive adjectives

Most adverbs derived from adjectives are adverbs of manner (see p. 56) and have a characteristic **-mente** ending, which usually corresponds to the English *-ly*.

Regular adverbs derived from adjectives ending in **-o**	rapido (rapida) *rapid* ➡ rapidamente *rapidly* lento (lenta) *slow* ➡ lentamente *slowly* ***But:*** leggero *slight* leggermente *slightly* benevolo *benevolent* benevolmente *benevolently* violento *violent* violentemente *violently*	**-mente** is added to the feminine singular form of **-o** adjectives. There are some exeptions which have to be learned.
Regular adverbs derived from adjectives ending in **-e**	prudente *prudent* ➡ prudentemente *prudently* semplice *simple* ➡ semplicemente *simply*	**-mente** is added to the singular form of **-e** adjectives.
	facile *easy* ➡ facilmente *easily* naturale *natural* ➡ naturalmente *naturally* particolare *particular* ➡ particolarmente *particularly* regolare *regular* ➡ regolarmente *regularly* ***But:*** folle *mad* follemente *madly* mediocre *mediocre* mediocremente *in a mediocre way*	If the adjective ends in **-le** or **-re**, the **-e** is dropped before **-mente** unless preceded by a consonant.

Some common adverbs are very different in form from the adjectives they are derived from.

Irregular adverbs derived from adjectives	buono *good* ➡ bene *well* cattivo *bad* ➡ male *badly* migliore *better/best* ➡ meglio *better/best* peggiore *worse/worst* ➡ peggio *worse/worst*	These forms have to be learned.

Other adjectives used as adverbs do not change their form at all.

Adjectives used as adverbs: **forte, lontano, piano, sodo, svelto, vicino, veloce**	Maria vive **lontano** *Maria lives far away* Piove **forte** *It is raining hard* Aldo e Mario lavorano **sodo** *Aldo and Mario work hard* Camminiamo troppo **svelto**? *Are we walking too fast?*	These are some of the adjectives most commonly used as adverbs. They are normally invariable.

An Italian descriptive adjective used as an adverb may occasionally agree with the subject when it refers to both the subject and the verb.

La ragazza lo guardò, **indignata**.   *The girl looked at him indignantly.*
Di solito arrivano **puntuali**.   *They usually arrive punctually.*

A few adverbs derived from adjectives have two forms: an adjectival form and a -**mente** form.

Two adverbial forms, e.g. **chiaro/chiaramente** **forte/fortemente** **giusto/giustamente** **veloce/velocemente**	È bene parlarsi **chiaro** *It's as well to speak frankly/plainly* Cerca di esprimerti più **chiaramente** *Try and express yourself more clearly* Parli troppo **forte** *You're speaking too loudly* Sono rimasti **fortemente** impressionati *They were deeply shocked*	There is sometimes a shift in meaning. For the -**mente** forms, see also pp. 64 and 63.

For other adverbs derived from adjectives, see **molto**, **tanto**, etc., pp. 56–57.

(b) Other parts of speech used as adverbs

Many adverbs borrow their form from other parts of speech, e.g. prepositions or indefinite adjectives and pronouns.

Prepositions, e.g. **dentro, fuori, sotto, sopra**	Vera è andata **dentro** *Vera went inside* Mangiamo **fuori** *Let's eat outside*	These adverbs are identical to the prepositions and, like the prepositions, are always invariable.
Indefinites, e.g. **molto, poco, tanto, troppo** ⚠	Angela mangia **molto** *Angela eats a lot* Susi dorme **troppo** *Susi sleeps too much*	The masculine singular forms only of indefinite adjectives and pronouns are used. See pp. 56–7.

(c) Other adverbial forms

Adverbs of independent formation	abbastanza *quite/enough* almeno *at least* così *so* forse *perhaps* già *already* ieri *yesterday* piuttosto *fairly* qui *here* volentieri *gladly/willingly*	Many adverbs have forms of their own and are not derived from other parts of speech.
Adverbial phrases	all'improvviso *suddenly* a lungo *for a long time/at length* con attenzione *attentively* con cura *carefully* con entusiasmo *enthusiastically* del tutto *completely* di solito *usually* di rado *rarely* in gran parte *mostly/largely* in fretta *quickly/in a hurry* per caso *by chance/accidentally* per sbaglio *by mistake* senza entusiasmo *unenthusiastically*	Most adverbial phrases consist of **a, con, in, di, per, senza** + noun or adjective. Others begin with **in modo** or **in maniera** (more formal) followed by an adjective (feminine, in the case of **in maniera**). A few are differently formed, for example, by two adverbs together.
	in modo strano *strangely* in maniera vergognosa *shamefully* ogni tanto *occasionally/now and again* per lo più *mostly* poco a poco *gradually* su per giù *approximately*	

◎/✦ Esercizi

1 Describe the actions below by transforming the adjectives given into adverbs.

(a)	Ha risposto	**onesto**		**(e)**	Gioca	**buono**
(b)	Ha parlato	**breve**		**(f)**	Parla	**cattivo**
(c)	Mi ha salutato	**cordiale**		**(g)**	Si sente	**migliore**
(d)	Rideva	**volgare**		**(h)**	È andato	**peggiore**

2 Identify and translate the adverbs and adverbial phrases; what do you think the proverb in (f) means?

(a) Giorgio corre **veloce**.

(b) È una notizia **del tutto inaspettata**.

(c) Mi guardava **fisso**.

(d) Sono partiti **tutti quanti all'improvviso**.

(e) Ti voglio **così bene**.

(f) Chi va **piano** va **sano** e va **lontano**.

✦ **3** Identify the **verb, adjective** or **other adverb** which the adverbs and adverbial phrases above modify.

✦ **4** (a) Which of the words in bold below are not used as adverbs?

(b) Which two adverbs below do not modify a verb?

(i) Studia **poco**

(ii) Non fuma **molto**

(iii) Abita **lontano**

(iv) Abita in una città **lontana**

(v) Mettilo **dentro**

(vi) C'è **poco** vento

(vii) Suona **tanto** male

(viii) È **troppo** caro

(ix) Hanno vissuto **felici e contenti**

◎/✦ **4.2 Different types of adverbs and their uses**

There are four main categories: manner; quantity and degree; time and frequency; place.

(a) Adverbs of manner, quantity and degree: main uses

Adverbs of manner answer the question: *how?* Adverbs of quantity or degree explain how much and to what extent.

Adverbs of manner	Lo ha punito **severamente** *He punished him severely* Lo abbiamo fatto **apposta** *We did it on purpose* Andiamo **insieme**? *Shall we go together?*
Adverbs of quantity and degree	Lavoro **poco** *I don't work much* Ti sento **appena** *I can hardly hear you* È **piuttosto** difficile *It's quite/rather difficult*

Typical adverbs of quantity and degree include:

abbastanza *quite/fairly, enough*	così *so*	poco *not very, not much/a lot*
almeno *at least*	meno *less*	quasi *almost/nearly*
altrettanto *just as much*	molto *very*	tanto *so, so much*
ancora *some more*	parecchio *a lot*	troppo *too, too much*
appena *not quite/barely, hardly*	più *more*	
circa *about*	piuttosto *quite/rather a lot*	

⚠ **Attenti!** Don't mix up adverbs and adjectives. Many adverbs of quantity can also be indefinite adjectives, e.g. **molto, poco, tanto, troppo, parecchio, altrettanto.** To distinguish adverbs from adjectives, remember that adverbs do not change their form and they normally modify verbs, adjectives or other adverbs. Adjectives modify nouns and change their form to agree with them. Compare:

Adverbial use: no agreement	Marina è **molto** stanca/triste *Maria is very tired/sad* Lucia lavora **tanto** bene/rapidamente *Lucia works so well/quickly*	**Molto** is an adverb modifying the adjectives **stanca/triste**, not **Maria**. **Tanto** is an adverb modifying the adverbs **bene/rapidamente**, not **Lucia**.
Adjectival use: agreement	Carla ha **molta** pazienza *Carla has a lot of patience* I bambini hanno **pochi/tanti** compiti *The children have little/so much homework*	Here **molto, tanto** are adjectives which modify the nouns **pazienza, compiti**. They agree in number and gender with those nouns.

◎ Esercizio

1 Complete the sentences using the appropriate forms of **molto** and **tanto**. Make sure you spot the adjectives.

    (a) Maria è — stanca.   *Maria is very tired.*

    (b) Giuliana legge — la sera.   *Giuliana reads a lot in the evening.*

    (c) Anna ha — amiche.   *Anna has many/lots of friends.*

    (d) Paolo ha — voglia di uscire.   *Paola very much wants to go out.*
        (lit. *has much desire*)

    (e) I tuoi amici sono — simpatici.   *Your friends are so nice.*

    (f) Luciana lavora —.   *Luciana works so much/such a lot.*

    (g) Silvano ha — amici.   *Silvana has so many/such a lot of friends.*

    (h) Hanno — fame la sera.   *They are so hungry in the evening.*
        (lit. *have so much hunger*)

(b) Adverbs of manner, quantity and degree: position

There are few hard and fast rules regarding the position of adverbs. The ones that follow apply to the most standard, neutral positions and take no account of variations in style.

After the verb and before adjectives and other adverbs	Sta dormendo La lezione è stata Mi è piaciuto Vai	**tranquillamente** **insolitamente** **parecchio** **troppo**	noiosa forte	*He is sleeping peacefully* *The lesson was unusually boring* *I liked it a lot* *You are going too fast*
Before a direct noun object: this is not always the case in English	Parla Hai chiuso Non aiuta Mi è piaciuto	**perfettamente** **bene** **abbastanza** **molto**	italiano la porta? i genitori il concerto	*He speaks Italian perfectly* *Have you closed the door properly?* *He doesn't help his parents enough* *I liked the concert a lot*

Adverbial phrases or long adverbs may follow the direct object:

    Ha aperto la porta pian piano.   *He opened the door very quietly.*

    Ha vinto il premio inaspettatamente.   *He won the prize unexpectedly.*

◎ Esercizio

2 Rewrite the Italian sentences using the adverbs given, to make them equivalent to the English.

(a)	Giocano a calcio. (bene)	*They play football well.*
(b)	Suona la chitarra. (molto)	*He plays the guitar a lot.*
(c)	Amava i gatti. (tanto)	*She loved cats so much.*
(d)	Mi è piaciuto quel film. (parecchio)	*I liked that film quite a lot.*
(e)	Ha sbattuto la porta. (forte)	*He slammed the door hard.*
(f)	La minestra non è calda. (abbastanza)	*The soup is not hot enough.*
(g)	Mio cugino capisce i cani. (benissimo)	*My cousin understands dogs extremely well.*

✚ (c) Adverbs of manner, quantity and degree: position and change of meaning

The position of some adverbs can depend on their meaning.

Ha aperto **appena** la finestra *He barely/only just opened the window* Ha **appena** aperto la finestra/Aveva **appena** aperto la finestra *He has just opened the window/He had just opened the window*	As an adverb of manner meaning *only just*, **appena** follows the verb. As an adverb of time, in compound tenses it comes between the auxiliary and the past participle.
Gli piace **molto** giocare a tennis *He likes playing tennis a lot* (He is very fond of playing tennis) Gli piace giocare **molto** a tennis *He likes to play tennis a lot* (i.e. often) Vorrei **tanto** mangiare adesso *I would so much like to eat now* Vorrei mangiare **tanto** *I would like to eat a great deal/such a lot*	When a verb such as **piacere** or **volere** is followed by an infinitive, adverbs of quantity such as **molto** or **tanto** follow either the main verb or the infinitive verb, depending on which one it refers to.

✚ Esercizio

3 Place the adverbs appropriately so that the Italian is equivalent to the English.

(a)	Siamo arrivati. (appena)	*We have just arrived.*
(b)	Ti sento. (appena)	*I can hardly hear you.*
(c)	Sono le due.	*It's barely two o'clock.*
(d)	Ho fatto in tempo per prendere il treno. (appena)	*I was only just in time to catch the train.*
(e)	Gli piace mangiare. (molto)	*He likes to eat a lot.*
(f)	Mi piacerebbe mangiare adesso. (molto)	*I would very much like to eat now.*

(d) Adverbs of time, frequency and place: main uses

Adverbs of time answer the question: *when*? Adverbs of frequency tell you how often and adverbs of place tell you where.

Adverbs of time and frequency	Partiamo **adesso** *We're leaving now* Ci vediamo **spesso** *We often see each other* Il treno è arrivato **in orario** *The train arrived on time*
Adverbs of place	Il pane è **qui** *The bread is here* Mettilo **là** *Put it there* Siediti **dietro** *Sit behind/in the back* Non lo trovo **da nessuna parte** *I can't find it anywhere*

Typical adverbs of time and frequency

adesso/ora *now*	fino a *until*	poi *then, next later*
allora *then, at that time*	finora *until now/so far*	presto *early/soon*
ancora *still, again*	fra *in*	prima *first*
appena *just*	fra poco *soon*	qualche volta *sometimes*
a volte *at times/sometimes*	già *already, yet*	raramente *rarely, not often*
di nuovo *again*	ieri *yesterday*	sempre *always*
di rado *rarely*	non … mai *never*	spesso *often*
domani *tomorrow*	oggi *today*	subito *at once*
dopo *after(wards)*	ogni tanto *occasionally*	tardi *late*
fa *ago*	ormai *by now*	

Typical adverbs of place

altrove *elsewhere*	fino a *as far as*	quaggiù *down here*
avanti *on/forward*	indietro *back*	quassù *up here*
dappertutto *everywhere*	laggiù *down there*	qui/qua[2] *here*
davanti *in front*	lassù *up there*	via *away*
dietro *behind*	lì/lá[1] *there*	

[1] **lì** and **là** are also almost synonymous, though **lì** indicates somewhere slightly more precise and often closer. [2] **qui** and **qua** are virtually synonymous, though **qui** may suggest somewhere closer and more precise.

◎ **Esercizio**

4 Identify the adverbs of frequency in the list of adverbs of time and frequency above.

◎/✚ **(e) Adverbs of time, frequency and place: position**

In Italian as in English, the position of adverbs of time is particularly variable and often depends on style, emphasis and context. The same adverb can have several positions. The main ones are as follows.

Beginning and ending a sentence	Che cosa fai **domani**? **Domani** vado a Firenze. *What are you doing tomorrow?* *Tomorrow I'm going to Florence* Cosa fai **qui**? **Qui** cosa fai? *What are you doing here?*
Directly after the verb	Vai **oggi** a Firenze? No, vado **domani** a Firenze. *Are you going to Florence today? No, I'm going to Florence tomorrow/It's tomorrow I'm going to Florence* Rimani **qui** stasera? *Are you staying here tonight?* No, stasera vado **via** *No, tonight I'm going away/leaving*

Given the variety of positions in both languages, the following examples focus on generally accepted standard usage, rather than on all possible permutations.

As in English, if an adverb modifies a sentence it usually goes at the beginning or the end.

Beginning and ending a sentence: time, frequency and place	**Qualche volta** esco con mia sorella/Esco con mia sorella, **qualche volta** *Sometimes I go out with my sister/I go out with my sister sometimes* **Qui** fa molto caldo/Fa molto caldo **qui** *Here it's very hot/It's very hot here*	Especially common with **adesso, dopo, ogni tanto, quà, là**.

Otherwise, the most common position for adverbs of time, frequency and place is after the verb.

| After the verb | Arriverò **tardi/fra poco**
I'll arrive late/soon
Non studio **mai** a casa
I never study at home
Lavoro **sempre** per lui
I always work for him
È venuto **spesso** a trovarmi
He has often come to see me
Devo partire **subito/ora**
I have to leave right away/now
Piove **dapperttutto** in Italia
It's raining everywhere in Italy
Stanno giocando **lassù**
They are playing up there | Adverbs of time, frequency and place also follow compound tenses and verb + infinitive except in the case of **sempre, ancora, già** and **mai**. These come between the auxiliary and participle, or verb and dependent infinitive. |
| **✚** Special position for **sempre, ancora, già** and **mai** | Ho **sempre** lavorato per lui
I have always worked for him
Non ho **mai** mangiato la carne
I have never eaten meat
Sta **ancora** giocando con Enrico
He is still playing with Enrico
Devi **già** partire? *Must you leave already/yet?* | See also p. 66 and pp. 67–8 for **ancora**, p. 66 for **gia** and pp. 187–8 for **mai**. |

 Attenti! You may have noticed, from some of the examples above, that in English adverbs of frequency tend to *precede* the verb, so take care when using **sempre, spesso** and **raramente**, especially when using a direct noun object: in Italian you literally say, 'I read often the paper' or 'I close always the gate', etc.

| **✚** Adverbs of frequency: Italian and English may differ | Leggo **spesso** il giornale
*I **often** read the paper*
Ho letto **spesso** il giornale
*I have **often** read the paper*
Vedo **raramente** mia sorella
*I **rarely** see my sister*
Ho visto **raramente** mia sorella
*I have **rarely** seen my sister*
Chiudo **sempre** il cancello
*I **always** close the gate*
But: Ho **sempre** chiuso il cancello
*I have **always** closed the gate* | In simple tenses these adverbs of frequency nearly always follow the verb and precede a direct noun object. However, in compound tenses the position of **sempre** can coincide with the English. |
| Italian and English coincide | Leggilo **spesso** *Read it often*
Preferisco vederla **raramente**
I prefer to see her rarely
Devi **sempre** chiuderlo
You must always close it | Note also that the adverb position coincides in Italian and English when direct object pronouns are attached to an infinitive or imperative. |

Note also that Italian and English may differ when an adverb of place such as **via** or **indietro** is an integral part of a verb, e.g. **buttare via** *to throw away* – see the following table.

| ✚ Adverbs of place: Italian and English may differ | Hai buttato via **le bottiglie**? *Have you thrown the bottles away?/Have you thrown away the bottles?*
But: Devi buttar**li** via
You must throw them away
Devi mandare indietro **il pacco**
You have to send the parcel back/send back the parcel
But: Ho dimenticato di mandar**lo** indietro
I've forgotten to send it back
And note:
Perché non metti i bagagli **lì sopra**?/Perché non metti **lì sopra** i bagagli?
Why don't you put the luggage up there? | In English the adverb of place can be separated from the verb. This is not possible in Italian unless there is an object pronoun attached to the verb.

However, when not linked to a verb, the position of adverbs of place is flexible. |

 Attenti! Adverbs commonly follow the verb, but when they are linked to a construction with two verbs, the one they follow may make a difference to the meaning.

| ✚ Different position, change in meaning or emphasis | Gli piace **spesso** giocare a tennis
He often likes playing tennis
Gli piace giocare **spesso** a tennis
He likes to play tennis often
Bisogna **sempre** chiudere il cancello
You must always close the gate
Bisogna chiudere **sempre** il cancello
You must close the gate at all times | With a verb followed by an infinitive, the position of these adverbs (especially **spesso** and **sempre**) is flexible: they follow either the main verb or the infinitive, depending on which one they specifically refer to. |

For changes of meaning with a change of position, see also **appena**, p. 58 and **ancora**, pp. 67–8.

◎/✚ Esercizi

5 Say how often the following happen by correctly placing the adverbs given to complete the sentences.

(a) Vedo mia sorella. (spesso)

(b) Andiamo al cinema. (qualche volta)

(c) Lando esce. (raramente)

(d) Non beve la birra. (mai)

(e) Si alzano presto. (sempre)

(f) Mangiamo gli spaghetti. (ogni tanto)

6 Now place the adverbs given in the following sentences.

(a) Siamo arrivati ieri sera. (tardi)

(b) Hanno mangiato al ristorante. (spesso)

(c) Ha nevicato in Inghilterra. (dappertutto)

(d) Devi chiamare tuo fratello (spesso)

(e) Ha dimenticato le chiavi. (sempre)

(f) Dovresti chiudere le finestre. (sempre)

(g) Sono uscito con lui. (raramente)

(h) Non ho bevuto la birra. (mai)

7 Give the Italian equivalent of the English, taking care to place the adverbs of frequency correctly.

(a) *I always do the shopping.*

(b) *We occasionally eat out.*

(c) *We sometimes go to the theatre.*

(d) *I rarely watch TV.*

✚ **8** Complete (a)–(e) by placing in each sentence the adverb of time or frequency given. You must use the adverb twice each time. Give English equivalents.

(a) Marco è a Roma. Sta studiando. (ancora *still*).

(b) Davide frequenta l'università? Ha dato gli esami? (già *yet/already*)

(c) Studi in biblioteca? Devi studiare in bibioteca? (sempre *always*)

(d) Suo marito non aiuta in casa. Non ha aiutato in vita sua. (mai *never*)

(e) Usciamo la sera. Siamo usciti la sera. (spesso *often*)

✚ 9 Use the adverbs in brackets twice in each sentence, paying attention to their position.

    (a) Hai portato i piatti? Li hai portati? (dentro)

    (b) Potresti portare i documenti? Portali. (indietro)

    (c) Frequentiamo i corsi serali. Abbiamo deciso di frequentarli. (spesso)

    (d) Aiuta il fratello. Fa male ad aiutarlo. (raramente)

✚ **10** Spot the difference: give the English equivalent of the following.

    (a) Bisogna sempre tenere la porta chiusa.   Bisogna tenere la porta sempre chiusa.

    (b) Mi piace spesso giocare a calcio.   Mi piace giocare a calcio spesso.

    (c) Non conviene sempre dire la verità.   Non conviene dire sempre la verità.

◎/✚ 4.3 Other adverbs and their uses

There are five main categories: affirmation; doubt and possibility; viewpoint; focus; intensifiers.

(a) Adverbs of affirmation

Vieni ? – **Sì/Certo/Sicuro** *Are you coming?* – **Yes/Of course/Definitely** Dobbiamo aiutare – **Appunto**, ma come? *We have to help* – **Precisely/Quite**, *but how?* Arriva alle cinque, allora – **Esatto** *So he's arriving at five* – **That's right** Ti chiamerò **senz'altro** *I'll definitely call you*	These adverbs and adverbial phrases express agreement in varying ways. The English equivalents depend to a large extent on context.

Other adverbs of affirmation include:

certamente *certainly*   di sicuro/sicuro/sicuramente *definitely/certainly*

come no? *but of course/why not?*   indubbiamente/senza dubbio *undoubtedly*

d'accordo *agreed/alright*   volentieri *gladly/it's a pleasure*

davero *really*

(b) Adverbs of doubt and possibility

Forse verrà stasera ***Perhaps/maybe*** *he'll come this evening* Tornerò presto, **probabilmente** domani *I'll come back soon,* ***probably*** *tomorrow* Vieni? – **Può darsi** *Are you coming?* – ***Maybe/Perhaps/I might*** Hai voglia di venire? – **Quasi quasi**, ma prima devo chiamare Rita *Do you feel like coming?* ***I don't mind if I do/I might just do that***, *but first I must call Rita* Ci vediamo presto, **magari** domani *We'll see each other soon,* ***possibly/maybe*** *tomorrow* Se c'è sciopero possiamo **magari** andare in macchina *If there's a strike we* ***could maybe*** *go by car* Se l'aereo è troppo caro possiamo **eventualmente** prendere l'aereo *If the plane is too expensive we* ***might possibly/could perhaps*** *take the train*	These all convey degrees of uncertainty. **Può darsi** + **che** is used with the subjunctive (p. 300).

Esercizio

1 Use the adverbs below in place of the English ones and complete the sentences.

appunto • certo • come no? • d'accordo • esatto • magari • può darsi • senz'altro

    (a) È molto difficile! – (*Exactly*), te l'avevo detto.

    (b) Siete pronti? – (*Of course*), arriviamo subito.

    (c) Se sei libera domani possiamo (*maybe*) andare al cinema.

    (d) Venite domani? – (*We might/maybe*), se non piove.

    (e) L'appuntamento è per giovedì, vero? – (*That's right*), per giovedì alle dieci.

    (f) Vieni martedì? – (*Definitely*), ma ti chiamerò prima.

    (g) Ci vediamo più tardi. – (*Alright*), alle due allora.

    (h) Posso accompagnarvi? – (*But of course*), ci fa piacere.

(c) Comment and viewpoint adverbs

Sinceramente, non vale la pena di andarci It **honestly** isn't worth going **Francamente** non mi dispiace *Frankly I don't mind* **Ovviamente** viene anche lui *Obviously he's coming too* **Psicologicamente** è rimasto un bambino *Psychologically he's still a child* **Economicamente** è stato un disastro ***Economically** it was a disaster* **But:** La amava sinceramente *He sincerely/genuinely loved her* (adverb of manner)	Used for comment on what is being said, to express value judgements, or to specify a viewpoint. They usually modify a whole sentence, but if they are used as adverbs of manner, they directly follow the verb.

✛ (d) Focus adverbs

Mi ha **perfino** scritto *He **even** wrote to me* Costa **solo** 50 euro *It **only** costs 50 euros* Vado **anche** a Torino *I'm going to Turin **as well*** Ti piacerebbe **davvero**? *Would you **really** like it?* Lo ha lasciato **proprio** davanti alla porta *He left it **right** in front of the door* Me l'ha detto **proprio** prima di partire *He told me **just** before he left* Non capisco **proprio** *I **simply/just** don't understand* **Sul serio**, mi hanno dato il posto ***Seriously/honestly,** they gave me the job*	These adverbs focus on and emphasise a particular word or phrase.

Some focus adverbs can also be intensifiers. See next section. For more on **solo** and **anche**, see pp. 69–70.

◎/✛ Esercizi

2 Put your own slant on things and complete the sentences below using the English as a guideline.

    (a) Ha perso la chiave.   *unfortunately*

    (b) Non si è fatto male.   *luckily*

    (c) Non capiscono niente.   *obviously/clearly*

    (d) Lo trovo antipatico.   *frankly*

    (e) Non mi sembra necessario.   *honestly*

✦ **3** Now choose one or more of the adverbs below to complete the sentences.
davvero • solo • perfino/persino • proprio

(a)	Non ho capito niente.	*really*
(b)	È lui!	*really/definitely*
(c)	È quello che cercavo.	*exactly/just*
(d)	Mi ha prestato dei soldi.	*even*
(e)	Lo troverai davanti alla porta.	*right/just*
(f)	È un gioco.	*only*

✦ (e) Intensifiers

These are mostly used to modify adjectives and other adverbs rather than verbs. They intensify the meaning of adjectives and other adverbs and are all close in meaning.

Intensifiers with adjectives and adverbs	Mi sento **proprio** male *I feel really/ absolutely awful* È **proprio** impossibile *It is quite/really/just/ totally impossible* È **davvero** interessante *It is truly interesting* Canta **davvero** bene *He sings really well* È **assolutamente** impossibile *It is absolutely/utterly impossible* È **addirittura** assurdo *It's actually/ absolutely/quite simply absurd*	The adverb used depends on the collocation, i.e. which adverbs and adjectives are normally found together. If in doubt, use **proprio**.
	È **completamente** falso *It is totally/completely untrue* La tua idea è **decisamente** originale *Your idea is distinctly original* Sei **incredibilmente** testardo *You are incredibly stubborn* Sono ragazzi **spaventosamente** viziati *They are horrifically/dreadfully spoilt children*	Some adverbs of manner can be used as intensifiers.

Other common intensifiers are also adverbs of quantity. Note that **tutto** agrees with the adjective it modifies.

tutto: adjective used as intensifier	Maria è tornata **tutta** bagnata *Maria came back all wet/totally soaked* Era **tutta** orgogliosa, aveva vinto la gara *She was really/extremely proud, she had won the competition* Sei **tutto** sudato, Mario *You're all/really sweaty, Mario* Sono **tutti** eccitati *They are all/really excited*	With plural subjects the meaning may be ambiguous, as in English, e.g. the last sentence can also mean *All of them are excited.*
così tanto	Ti amo **così tanto** *I love you so, so much/I'm crazy about you* Perché stai **così tanto** nel bagno? *Why do you spend such an age in the bathroom?* Come hai fatto a dimagrire **così tanto**? *How have you managed to lose such a huge amount of weight?*	The adverbs **così** and **tanto** are often placed together for emphasis.

In Italian a noun may be used as an intensifier before an adjective to express added emotion.

| Other adverbial intensifiers: **di** + Italian noun + adjective | È di una bellezza straordinaria
*She is **extraordinarily** beautiful*
È di una volgarità sorprendente
*He is **surprisingly** vulgar*
Sono di un'ignoranza paurosa
*They are **frighteningly** ignorant*
Fa un freddo incredibile
*It is **incredibly/unbelievably** cold* | Note that the English equivalent is an adverb + adjective. |

Other adverbs. (i) For adverbs of negation, e.g. **neanche** *not even*, **per nulla**, *not in the least*, see Negatives pp. 187–8. (ii) For connecting adverbs, e.g. **invece** *instead, on the other hand*, see pp. 217–8. (iii) For interrogative adverbs, e.g. **come**? *how?*, **quando**? *when?*, **dove**? *where?* see Interrogatives pp. 147–9.

✚ Esercizi

4 Intensify your statements by using **addirittura** or **proprio** in the sentences below. In one sentence, either will do. Give English equivalents.

    (a) Mi ha insultato!   **(b)** Sono matti!   **(c)** Non è possibile!   **(d)** È assurdo!

5 Form adverbs of manner from the adjectives below and use them as intensifiers in the sentences given.

eccessivo • eccezionale • forte • terribile

    (a) Suonava (*exceptionally*) bene il flauto.

    (b) La lezione è stata (*terribly*) noiosa.

    (c) Lo trovo (*excessively*) sensibile. (*sensitive*)

    (d) È stato (*extremely/greatly/strongly*) influenzato dal padre.

6 Below, Italian adjectives are used adverbially as intensifiers. Give the English equivalents of these sentences.

    (a) Fa un caldo incredibile.

    (b) È un ragazzo di un'intelligenza eccezionale.

    (c) Quel film è di una stupidità deprimente.

    (d) Quell'uomo è di un'ignoranza spaventosa.

    (e) La bambina era tutta triste: aveva perso il gattino.

    (f) Perché te la prendi così tanto? (**prendersela** *to be offended*)

4.4 Further uses of adverbs

(a) More on adverbs of time and quantity

In ritardo/tardi; in anticipo/presto

⚠ **Attenti!** In Italian there is more than one way of saying *late* and *early*.

| *late*
(for an appointment) | Sei **in ritardo**, abbiamo già mangiato
You're late, we've already eaten
Il treno è **in ritardo di** dieci minuti
The train is ten minutes late
È arrivato **con** un quarto d'ora **di ritardo**
He arrived a quarter of an hour late | Used when a timetable is directly or indirectly implied.
in ritardo means *with delay*.
di ritardo is used to be specific about how late. |

early (for an appointment)	Arriva sempre a scuola **in anticipo** *He always arrives at school early* L'aereo è **in anticipo di** dieci minuti *The plane is 10 minutes early* Il treno è arrivato **con un anticipo di** cinque minuti *The train arrived five minutes early*	**in anticipo** means *ahead of the appointed time/in advance*. **con un anticipo di** is used to be specific about how early.
late (in general)	Ceniamo sempre **tardi** *We always have supper late* È troppo **tardi** per andare al cinema *It's too late to go to the cinema*	When the meaning is more general, **tardi** and **presto** are used.
early (in general)	Preferisco partire presto per non perdere il treno *I prefer to leave early so I don't miss the train* È un po' presto per pranzare *It's a bit early to have lunch*	

◎ Esercizio

1 Complete the sentences using the Italian equivalent of the English.

(a) Sei *(late)*, abbiamo finito di cenare.

(b) Sei *(early)*, non sono ancora pronto.

(c) È un po' *(late)*, perché non usciamo domani?

(d) È troppo *(early)* per partire.

(e) L'aereo arriva *(an hour late)*.

(f) Gli ospiti sono arrivati *(ten minutes early)*.

The negative forms of *ancora?* and *già?*

Attenti! The negative of **ancora** (*again, still*) is **non ... più** (*not again, not any more*).

ancora ➡ non ... più = *again ➡ not again* **or:** *still ➡ not any more*	Ti ha chiamato **ancora**? *Has he rung you **again**?* No, **non** mi ha **più** chiamato *No, he hasn't rung me **again*** Giochi **ancora** a tennis? *Do you **still** play tennis?* No, **non** gioco **più** a tennis *No, I don't play tennis any more*

And the negative of **già?** (*yet?*) is **non ... ancora** or **non ... finora** (*not yet, not so far*).

già? ➡ non ... ancora/ancora ... non = *yet? ➡ not yet/still not* **già? ➡ non ... finora/finora ... non** = *yet? ➡ not (as) yet/so far*	Ti ha **già** chiamato? *Has he rung you **yet**?* No, **non ancora**. **Non** mi ha **ancora** chiamato *No, **not yet**. He **hasn't** called me **yet*** No, **ancora non** ha chiamato *No, he **still hasn't** called (yet)* Hanno chiamato? No, **finora non** hanno chiamato *Have they rung? No, **as yet/so far** they haven't rung*

The difference between **non ancora/ancora non** and **non finora/finora non** is very slight. For more on **ancora**, see pp. 67–8.

◎ Esercizio

2 Answer these questions negatively by giving the Italian equivalent of the English.

(a) Lo hai visto ancora/di nuovo? — *No, I haven't seen him again.*

(b) Vuoi provare ancora/di nuovo? — *No, I don't want to try again/any more.*

(c) Hai già rifatto il letto? — *No, I haven't made the bed yet.*

(d) Ti ha già scritto? — *No, he hasn't written yet.*

(e) Sono già arrivati?   *No, they still haven't arrived/they haven't arrived yet.*

(f) Non hai ancora avuto notizie?   *No, I haven't had any news so far/as yet.*

◎/✚ *Sempre* and *ancora*

Sempre and **ancora** have several meanings. These depend on the context, the tense they are used in or on their position.

sempre: *always*	Lavoro **sempre** la mattina *I always work in the morning* Ho sempre lavorato di sera *I have always worked in the evening* Non lavoravo **sempre** tardi *I didn't always use to work late* Non farò **sempre** lo stesso lavoro *I won't always do the same job*	The main meaning of **sempre** in all tenses is *always*.
✚ **sempre:** *still*	Hai cambiato lavoro? No, faccio **sempre** lo stesso lavoro *Have you changed jobs? No, I still do the same job* Quest'anno dove andrete in vacanza? Mah, penso che andremo **sempre** nello stesso posto *Where will you go on holiday this year? Well, I expect we'll still be going to the same place* Aveva cambiato idea? No, era **sempre** della stessa idea *Had he changed his mind? No, he was still of the same opinion*	In the affirmative present, future and imperfect only, **sempre** can also mean *still*. The key word is usually **stesso**. If in doubt, use **ancora** for *still*.

✚ Esercizio

3 Give the meaning of **sempre** in the following sentences.

(a) Il giovedì arriva sempre in ritardo.

(b) La mattina andava sempre a messa.

(c) Ti amerò sempre.

(d) Abiti sempre nella stessa strada?

(e) Mi ha detto che lavorava sempre per la stessa ditta.

(f) Domani avremo sempre le stesse difficoltà.

(g) Non prendo sempre il caffè la mattina.

(h) Non lavorava sempre a casa.

Ancora is the most common way of expressing *still*.

ancora: *still*	È **ancora** malato *He is still ill* A mezzanotte saremo **ancora** in piedi *We will still be up at midnight* Era **ancora** a letto *He was still in bed*	**Ancora** is used in the present, future and imperfect only, including the present and imperfect continuous. It follows a simple tense, but
	Stiamo **ancora** facendo colazione *We're still having breakfast* Devo **ancora** fare i compiti *I've still got to do my homework* Hai **ancora** voglia di uscire? *Do you still feel like going out?* Ti voglio **ancora** bene *I still love you*	comes between: an auxiliary and a present participle; a modal verb and a dependent infinitive; or in the middle of a verb phrase, e.g. **aver voglia di**.

| ✚ ancora: *again* | Dimmi **ancora** com'è andato *Tell me again how it went*
 Proverò **ancora**, se vuoi *I'll try again if you want*
 Te lo spiego **ancora**? *Shall I explain it to you again?* | **Ancora** is one way of expressing *again* (often with **una volta**), although there are more common alternatives (see table below). Used in all tenses, it tends to follow the complete verb, but this is not a hard-and-fast rule. |
| | Hai voglia di uscire **ancora**? *Do you feel like going out again?*
 Mi piacerebbe incontrarlo **ancora** (una volta) *I'd like to meet him (once) again* | |

 Attenti! The position of **ancora** can be the key to determining the meaning. Compare:

Hai ancora voglia di uscire?   Hai voglia di uscire ancora?
Do you still want to go out?   *Do you want to go out again?*
Spero ancora di vederla.   Spero di vederla ancora.
I still hope to see her.   *I hope to see her again.*
Sta ancora giocando con Enrico.   Sta giocando ancora con Enrico.
He is still playing with Enrico.   *He is playing with Enrico again.*

Ancora can be an adverb of quantity.

| ancora:
 (some)
 more | Ne vuoi **ancora**? *Do you want some more?*
 Ci sono **ancora** tre fette *There are three more slices*
 Puoi rimanere **ancora** una settimana/ un po' *You can stay another week/a bit longer*
 Sono rimasto **ancora** 15 giorni *I stayed two more/another two weeks* | As an adverb of quantity, **ancora** usually follows the complete verb in all constructions and comes before the amount referred to. |

◎/✚ Esercizi

4 *More*. Provide Italian equivalents to the English, using **ancora**.

(a) *Would you like some more?*

(b) *Can you give me four more slices?*

(c) *I'm staying ten more days.*

(d) *I would like to stay a bit longer.*

5 Give the Italian equivalent of the following.

(a) *Is he still asleep?*   (c) *Gianni, will you still go to Milan?*

(b) *Is Paolo still out?*   (d) *He still had to go to the bank.*
      (**doveva andare**)

✚ **6** *Still or again*? Say which meaning of **ancora** is used in each sentence below. Its position is the clue.

(a) Mi piace ancora suonare la tromba.   (d) Devo parlargli ancora domani

(b) Mi piacerebbe vederlo ancora.   (e) Hai ancora voglia di uscire?

(c) Devo ancora rifare i letti.   (f) Hai voglia di uscire ancora?

Alternatives to *ancora*

Ancora is often not the most natural way of expressing *again*.

again: **di nuovo, un'altra volta**	Te lo spiego **di nuovo/un'altra volta**, allora? *Shall I explain it to you again, then?* Sì, mi piacerebbe sentirlo **di nuovo/un'altra volta** *Yes, I would like to hear it again*	**Di nuovo** is a very common expression for *again*. **Un'altra volta** also means *another time*.
Verbs beginning with **ri-**	Si è risposata *She got married again* Non lo rifare! *Don't do it/that again!* Bisogna riprovare *We'll have to try again* Ricominciamo? *Shall we start again/do it again?*	There are many verbs with the prefix **–ri**, which expresses the idea of *again*.

more: **altro**	Ne vuoi un **altro** po'? *Do you want a bit more?* Mi ha dato **altri** cinquanta euro *He gave me fifty more euros* Rimango **altre** tre settimane/**un'altra** settimana *I'm staying three more weeks/another week*	An alternative to **ancora** as an adverb of quantity is the indefinite adjective **altro**, which must agree with any accompanying noun.

For **altro**, see also Chapter 12, Indefinites, pp. 171–2.

◎ Esercizi

7 Rewrite the sentences without using **ancora** for *again*. There is more than one possibility.

    (a) Mi si è bloccato il computer!   *My computer's crashed again!*

    (b) Ho perso le chiavi dell'ufficio.   *I've lost the office keys again!*

    (c) Mi si è rotta la stampante.   *My printer's broken again!*

8 The following things have to be redone. Produce Italian equivalents of the English, using appropriate verbs to express *again*.

    (a) Il fax non è arrivato. – *Shall I send it again?*

    (b) È stato bocciato. – *He'll have to take the exam again.* (**dare l'esame**)

    (c) Il mio compito è andato male. – *You'll have to do it again.*

9 *Again*. Rewrite the sentences in Exercise 8 above using **altro**.

10 *More*. Rewrite the sentences in Exercise 4, p. 68, using **altro** instead of **ancora**.

✚ (b) More on intensifiers

Using *anche* and *solo*

Different positions of **anche** and **solo** may affect the meaning.

anche: *also, too, as well*	Ho **anche** parlato con Maria *I also spoke to Maria* (i.e. in addition to the other things I did) Ho parlato **anche** con Maria *I also spoke to Maria/I spoke to Maria as well/ too* (in addition to speaking to other people) **Anch'**io ho parlato con Maria *I also spoke to Maria/I too spoke to Maria* (I spoke, as well as others)	**Anche** must be placed before the word or phrase it refers to. In English, on the other hand, the position is more flexible.

Attenti! When *also* refers to a whole sentence or phrase, you cannot use **anche**. **Inoltre** is used instead.

Ieri mi sono alzato tardi, sono andato in piscina e poi ho studiato un po'. **Inoltre**, la sera, sono andato al cinema.

*Yesterday I got up late, went swimming and then studied a bit. **Also,** in the evening I went to the cinema.*

✦ Esercizi

11 Give the Italian equivalent of the English, using **anche** each time.

(a) *I went to Rome, Milan, Bergamo, Trento and Turin and then I also went to Bari.*

(b) *Really? You went to Bari as well?*

(c) *Marta is intelligent. – Yes, but Marina is also intelligent/Marina is intelligent too.*

(d) *Marina is sensitive. – Yes, but she's also cheerful.* (**allegra**)

solo: *only*	Mangio **solo** pesce *I only eat fish* Ho mangiato **solo** pesce *or:* Ho **solo** mangiato pesce *I only ate fish* Vieni domani? No, vengo **solo** stasera. *Are you coming tomorrow? No, I'm only coming this evening* Puoi venire domani? No, posso venire **solo** stasera *or:* Posso **solo** venire stasera *Can you come tomorrow? – No, I can only come this evening*	**Solo** comes before the word or phrase it refers to. When used with compound tenses or a verb + infinitive, its position may be flexible, but if a word is especially emphasised, **solo** will precede that word.
	Lo farei, **solo che** sono molto stanco *I would do it, only I'm very tired* Mi piacerebbe comprarlo, **solo che** non me lo posso permettere *I'd like to buy it, only I can't afford it*	When *only* refers to a whole phrase or sentence, it is translated as **solo che**.

✦ **12** Give an Italian equivalent of the English using **solo** each time.

(a) *We've only got one car.*

(b) *Today I'm only studying geography. (and no other subject)*

(c) *We're only free next Monday, because after (that) we're leaving.*

(d) *Yesterday I only read two chapters. (and no more)*

(e) *Did you buy any rolls? No, I only bought bread.*

(f) *They can only come next week, not before.*

✦ **13** The following is part of a review of *Una storia semplice*, a short novel published in 1989, the day after the death of the author, Leonardo Sciascia. Read the text, then answer the questions.

Il telefono squilla inaspettato alla viglia della festa. E la voce, con una calma quasi caricaturale, chiede addirittura del questore.* Chi chiama* è Giorgio Roccella, un diplomatico* che da moltissimo tempo non faceva ritorno nella sua vecchia casa siciliana; e chiama perché proprio nella sua vecchia casa ha trovato qualcosa di molto strano e intende riferirlo alle autorità. Così inizia la complicatissima 'Storia semplice' di Sciascia, dove in pochissime pagine … si condensano tutte le contraddizioni insite* in una società soggetta alla mentalità mafiosa.

Ma quando la mattina dopo il brigadiere si reca a casa del Roccella … trova lo stesso uomo con cui aveva parlato al telefono stecchito*, in una posa che sembra suggerire suicidio ma che non convince per nulla il bravo agente. Subito cerca di far notare tutte le stranezze di quella morte, ma si scontra con una inspiegabile superficialità dei suoi superiore, intenzionati a far chiudere il caso al più presto. …

A poco a poco la storia si dipana* e comincia a presentare situazioni aggrovigliate* non facilmente comprensibili, che finiscono per* mostrare la brutta maschera di cui si vestono troppo spesso le istituzioni* **…** Sciascia voleva 'scandagliare* scrupolosamente le possibilità che forse ancora restano alla giustizia',* ma la conclusione a cui giunge il libro* … conferma la sua poetica* pessimistica.

(Rosario Gambera http://jazzalnero.blogspot.com)

• chiede … del questore *asks for … the police commissioner* • chi chiama *the person who calls* • diplomatico *diplomat* • insite *inherent* • stecchito *stone dead* • si dipana *unfolds* • aggrovigliate *complex, tangled* • finiscono per *end up by* • di cui … istituzioni *with which institutions all too often clothe themselves* • scandagliare *to probe, examine* • giustizia *the law* • a cui giunge il libro *reached/arrived at by the book* • poetica *vision, viewpoint*

(a) In paragraph 1 identify an adjective used as an adverb and give the English equivalent.

(b) In the same paragraph identify two intensifiers. Which word or phrase does each modify? Can you find English equivalents?

(c) In paragraph 2 pick out two adverbs of time and an adverbial phrase.

(d) In paragraph 3 identify as many adverbs and adverbial phrases as you can.

(e) Give the English equivalent of **le possibilità che forse ancora restano alla giustizia**.

(f) Give the Italian equivalent of: (i) *He spoke to the director, no less*; (ii) *He died in that very hotel*; (iii) *Gradually I began to understand*.

5 Comparatives and superlatives

Comparatives and superlatives are particular forms of descriptive adjectives and adverbs. Comparatives (**i comparativi**), take two main forms: inequality or equality, e.g. *Anne is **more/less** talkative **than** Maria; George ran fast**er than** Tom* (inequality); *Peter is **as** tall **as** Carlo; We walked **as** far **as** you did* (equality).

Superlatives (**i superlativi**) describe what is the most or the least. e.g. *The exam was **the most** difficult one ever; He is **the least** talented singer; I arrived the lat**est** of all*. A second superlative, known as an absolute superlative, is expressed in English by *extremely/very*, e.g. *The exam was **extremely** hard; I arrived **very** late*.

◎/+ 5.1 Regular comparatives

(a) Comparative adjectives and adverbs: forms

Descriptive adjectives, most adverbs of manner and a few adverbs of time, place and quantity have comparative forms. These are formed by placing **più** and **meno** in front of them.

più/meno + adjective	Agnese è **più generosa** di sua sorella *Agnese is more generous than her sister* I cani sono **meno intelligenti** dei gatti *Dogs are less intelligent than cats*	**Più/meno** are invariable, but the adjectives change to agree in number and gender with the word they refer to. Note that the adverbs do not change.
più/meno + adverb	Pino corre **più rapidamente** di prima *Pino runs more quickly/faster than before* Pierluigi abita **meno lontano** di te *Pierluigi lives less far (away) than you*	
più/meno + adverbial phrase	Lavorano **con più entusiasmo** del solito They *are working more enthusiastically than usual* Siamo rimasti **meno a lungo** questa volta *We stayed less long this time*	**Più** or **meno** usually go between the preposition and the noun, or sometimes before the whole adverbial phrase.

Attenti! Notice that **meno** can be expressed in English not only as *less* but also as *not as …*

I cani sono meno intelligenti dei gatti.	*Dogs are **not as intelligent** as cats.*
Pierluigi abita meno lontano di te.	*Pierluigi doesn't live **as far** as you.*
Siamo rimasti **meno** a lungo questa volta.	*We didn't stay **as long** this time.*

◎/+ (b) Uses: comparisons of inequality: 'more/less than'

Comparative adjectives and adverbs are both used in comparisons of inequality to describe things in terms of *more or less … than* something else. In Italian *than* is expressed in a variety of ways, most frequently by **di** or **che**.

Expressing 'than': di

di before a noun or adjective	La chiesa di San Clemente è più antica **della Cappella Sistina** *The church of San Clemente is older than the Sistine Chapel* Pino è meno sensibile **di Paolo** *Pino is less sensitive than Paolo* Le azioni parlano più forte **delle parole** *Actions speak louder than words* Giampaolo studia con meno entusiasmo **di suo fratello** *Giampaolo studies less enthusiastically than his brother*	**Di** expresses *than* when there are two terms of comparison, i.e. when comparing a single quality or action between two people or things. Note that **di** is joined to the relevant definite article.
di before a pronoun	Luigi è più giovane **di te/di lei** *Luigi is younger than you/ her* Cammina più rapidamente **di me** *He/She walks faster than me* Questi libri sono meno utili **degli altri** *These books are less useful than the others* La nostra macchina è meno vecchia **della tua** *Our car is not as old as yours* Il tuo appartamento è più moderna **del nostro** *Your flat is more modern than ours*	**Di** precedes different pronouns, e.g. personal (disjunctive), indefinite, possessive.
di quello + **di** + noun	La nostra macchina è più vecchia **di quella di Giorgio** *Our car is older than Giorgio's* Il tuo appartamento è meno moderno **di quello di Ivo/ di quello della zia/di quello dei miei** *Your flat is more modern that Ivo's/than my aunt's/than my parents'*	Before a possessive noun (which is preceded by **di**), **di** is followed by **quello**, which agrees with the noun possessed. Note that **i miei** is used as a noun meaning *parents*.
di quello + adjective	La popolazione italiana è più alta **di quella svizzera** *Italy's population is higher than Switzerland's (population)* I treni inglesi sono meno puntuali **di quelli italiani** *English trains are less punctual than Italian ones/trains*	The demonstrative pronoun **quello** is used after **di**, to avoid repeating the same noun. **Quello** agrees with the noun.
di before numbers and quantifiers	Ho speso più **di cento euro** *I've spent more than 100 euros* Mi danno meno **del tre per cento** di interesse *I get less than 3% interest* Ne ho comprati/e più **di una dozzina** *I bought more than a dozen (of them)*	For more on quantifiers and comparisons, see p. 81.
di with set expressions	La lezione è stata meno interessante **del previsto/del solito** *The lesson was less interesting than expected/ than usual* Ha bevuto più **del necessario** *He drank more than (was) necessary*	The main ones are: **del previsto, del solito, del normale, del necessario**.
➕ di before most adverbs and expressions of time	Sono più felici **di prima/una volta** *They are happier than before* Scrive meno spesso **dell'anno scorso** *He writes less often than last year* Sembri meno depresso **di/che ieri** *You seem less depressed than yesterday* **But:** Sono più stanco **che mai** *I am more tired than ever*	Exceptions which take **che** are **mai** and, optionally, **ieri**, as well as time expressions beginning with a preposition, e.g. **in passato**.

Expressing 'than': *che*

Che is used when there is one term of comparison, i.e. when directly comparing two qualities, activities or entities to a single person, action or thing. The comparison is often between two words of the same grammatical category.

✚ **che +** nouns, adjectives, and adverbs	Mi piacciono più i gatti **che (non) i cani** *I like cats more than (I like) dogs* Sono scarpe più eleganti **che comode** *The shoes are more elegant than comfortable* Grazie, ne ho più **che abbastanza** *Thanks, I have more than enough*	**Non** may optionally be used after **che**, especially when this avoids the repetition of a verb.
✚ **che +** prepositions and infinitives	Fa più freddo qui **che (non) da voi** *It is colder here than (it is) where you are* Emila pensa più a sé **che agli altri** *Emilia thinks more about herself than others* È più riposante andare in montagna **che (non) al mare** *It is more restful to go to the mountains than (to go) to the sea*	

Di normally precedes **altro**, but note the expression **più <u>che</u> altro**.

> **Più che altro** è una gran bugiarda   *More than anything she is a great big liar.*

⚠ **Attenti! Di** and **che** can both go before a noun. Look at the different way they are used and notice that the meaning can change. Compare:

> Io ti vedo **più** spesso **di** Giovanni   *I see you more often than (I see) Giovanni*
> Io ti vedo **più** spesso **che** Giovanni   *I see you more often than Giovanni does (sees you)*

In example 1, a single subject and action (*I see more often*) is related to two terms of comparison (*you/Giovanni*). In example 2, two subjects (*I/Giovanni*) are related to one term of comparison (*see you more often*).

◎/✚ Esercizi

1 Complete the sentences using the correct comparative adjective or adverb and the right word for *than*. Remember to link **di** to the definite article where necessary.

(a) La luce è (*faster than*) il suono.

(b) Ada è (*less studious than*) sua sorella.

(c) Mi alzo (*later than*) i miei genitori.

(d) Carla è (*taller than*) loro.

(e) Mangiano la frutta (*less often than*) te.

(f) La casa di Nita è (*bigger than*) la mia.

(g) La tua macchina è (*older than*) di Giorgio.

(h) Le tasse italiane sono (*lower than*) svedesi.

✚ **2** Now complete these sentences, using **di** or **che** to express *than*.

(a) È più facile capire (*than to speak*) una lingua.

(b) Erano più spaventati (*than angry*).

(c) I suoi capelli sono più corti (*than mine*).

(d) Piera si è vestita (*more quickly than*) prima.

(e) Sandra ha meno (*than ten years old*).

(f) È stato accoltellato più (*than thirty times*).

(g) La strada è più percorribile (*than last year*).

(h) Mara è più sicura di sé (*than in the past*).

✚ **3** Complete the following sentences using **di** or **che** as appropriate.

(a) Le scarpe nere sono (*more elegant than*) quelle rosse.

(b) Le scarpe nere sono (*more elegant than*) comode.

(c) Enzo beve (*more wine than*) acqua.

(d) Enzo beve (*more wine than*) Pino.

(e) Mi sento (*more depressed than*) prima.

(f) Mi sento (*more depressed than*) mai.

✚ Expressing 'than': *di quello che/di quanto* + **verb**

When a finite verb follows *than* there are two main constructions.

di + quel(lo) + finite verb	È più tardi **di quello che pensi** *It's later than you think* La città era meno brutta **di quel che mi aspettavo** *The town was less ugly than I expected* Il teatro è più lontano **di quanto pare** *The theatre is further than it seems/looks* La casa è più grande **di quanto immagini** *The house is larger than you imagine.*	✚ **di quanto** tends to be preferred when size or amount is in focus. Note that comparisons of inequality before finite verbs more often take the subjunctive.
di quanto + finite verb		

✚ Esercizio

4 Spot the finite verbs. Look at the sentences below and decide which three comparisons are made with finite verbs. Then give the Italian equivalent of the English.

(a) *Driving in Naples is more dangerous than driving in London.*

(b) *Driving in Naples is more dangerous than you think.*

(c) *Looking after the children is more stressful than it seems.* (**occuparsi dei bambini**)

(d) *Looking after the children is more stressful than going to work.*

(e) *Eating in company is more fun than eating alone.*

(f) *Eating in company is more expensive than you imagine.*

◎/✚ (c) Uses: comparisons of equality: 'as ... as', 'as much/as many as'

Comparisons of equality inìvolve likening one thing or action to another to express sameness. In Italian the phrases most commonly used are: **così ... come; tanto ... quanto/come; altrettanto ... che.**

Così ... come: 'as ... as'

Così (*as/so*) ... **come** (*like*) are used to express similarity and never change their form. In similes **così** is totally omitted.

Adjective + **come** + noun	Giovanna è magra **come** un chiodo *Giovanna is as thin as a rake (lit. nail)* Il mare oggi è liscio **come** l'olio *Today the sea is as flat as a millpond (lit. as smooth as oil)*

Così come is commonly used to emphasise sameness before verb clauses or when a verb is understood/implicit.

✚ **Così come:** *(just) as/like*	Le cose sono andate **così come** avevo previsto *Things turned out just as I had predicted* È proprio **così come** ti ho detto *It's just as/like I told you* Tu mi piace **così come** sei *I like you (just) as you are* Si sentiva coccolato **così come** a casa *He felt pampered just like (he was) at home* Negli olii, **così come** nei disegni, l'artista ritrae sé stesso *In his oils, just as in his drawings, the artist depicts himself*

In many comparisons with adjectives and adverbs **così** tends to be omitted, especially when the context makes the meaning obvious.

(**così**) + adjective + **come**	Lui è (**così**) felice **come** te *He is as happy as you* L'albergo era (**così**) lussuoso **come** speravo *The hotel was as luxurious as I was hoping* La macchina di mio figlio è (**così**) grande **come** la mia *My son's car is as big as mine** Maurizio è (**così**) generoso **come** mio fratello *Maurizio is as generous as my brother**	After **come,** personal pronouns are disjunctive (**me, te,** etc.). *If size, quantity or degree rather than similarity are stressed, **tanto ... quanto** is more often used (see tables below).
(**così**) + adverb + **come**	Luisa guida (**così**) veloce **come** Luigi/te *Luisa drives as fast as Luigi/as you* Non viene (**così**) spesso **come** una volta *He doesn't come as often as he once did/as he used to*	

✚ *Tanto ... quanto:* 'as much/many as', 'as ... as'

This expression focuses on degree, extent or amount rather than on similarity. **Tanto** and **quanto** are used as adverbs or adjectives. As adjectives they must agree in number and gender with the noun they refer to.

In direct comparisons between words of the same grammatical category, both **tanto** and **quanto** are expressed.

Agreements made when **tanto ... quanto** are adjectives (i.e. when **tanto** precedes a noun)	Ho provato **tanta** rabbia **quanta** paura *I felt as much rage as fear* Ho comprato **tante** pere **quante** mele *I bought as many pears as apples* Sprecano **tanta** energia **quanta** ne consumano *They waste as much energy as they consume* Ho mangiato **tanti** cioccolatini **quanti** ne hai mangiati tu *I ate as many chocolates as you did*	**Tanto** and **quanto** are used here to express direct comparison between two nouns, verbs and verbal clauses. Note that **ne** may replace the noun following **quanto**, but an agreement must still be made. See p. 115–16 for **ne.** **Tanto ... come** is an alternative, usually before personal pronouns.
tanto ... come	***An alternative to the above would be:*** Ho mangiato **tanti** cioccolatini **quanti** te *I ate as many chocolates as you.* However, this sounds clumsy, so **come** may replace **quanto**: Ho mangiato **tanti** cioccolatini **come** te	
No agreements with **tanto ... quanto** as adverbs (i.e. with **tanto** before adjectives, other adverbs, verbs and prepositions)	Carla è **tanto** simpatica **quanto** brava *Carla is as nice as (she is) clever* Ida scrive **tanto** male **quanto** parla *Ida writes as badly as she speaks* Quel disgraziato beve **tanto quanto** mangia *That idiot drinks as much as he eats* Mi piace **tanto** partecipare **quanto** vincere *I like taking part as much as winning* Lidia lavora **tanto** per sé **quanto/che** per gli altri *Lidia works as much for herself as for others*	**Tanto** and **quanto** are used here to express direct comparisons between two adjectives, adverbs, verbs, infinitives and propositions. **Quanto** is sometimes replaced by **che.**

When a comparison focuses on a single adjective or verb, **tanto** is usually omitted.

(tanto) ... quanto: omission of tanto	La macchina di mio figlio è (tanto) grande quanto la mia *My son's car is as big as mine* Maurizio è (tanto) generoso quanto mio fratello *Maurizio is as generous as my brother* Ida guadagna (tanto) quanto te *Ida earns as much as you/you do*	After quanto, personal pronouns are disjunctive (me, te, etc.).

✦ *Altrettanto che:* '(just) as'

Altrettanto che is usually preferred to **tanto ... quanto** for emphasis or when two actions are compared.

altrettanto che: (*just*) *as* No agreements	È altrettanto duro lavorare che studiare *It is just as difficult to work as it is to study* Trovare un idraulico è altrettanto difficile che trovare un buon medico *Finding a plumber is (just) as hard as finding a good doctor* È altrettanto impossibile parlare al manager che (parlare) al direttore *It's (just) as impossible to speak to the manager as (it is) to the director*	Altrettanto is commonly used with che before infinitives, or when an infinitive is implied (as in the third example here). For more on altrettanto, see p. 93.

◎/✦ Esercizi

5 Give the Italian equivalent of these common English similes, matching up the adjectives and nouns given below:

fresco • sordo • sano • rosso ... una campana • un peperone • un pesce • una rosa

(a) *She came back from the race* (**gara**) *as fresh as a daisy.*

(b) *My grandmother is as deaf as a post*

(c) *My grandfather is as fit as a fiddle.*

(d) *You're as red as a beetroot!*

✦ **6** Choose between **così ... come** or **come** to complete the sentences with an Italian verson of the English.

(a) La casa è rimasta (*just as*) era cento anni prima.

(b) Dovrei risparmiare di più, (*just like*) mia cugina.

(c) Non è più (*as amusing as*) prima.

(d) Barbara non è poi (*as stupid as*) pensi.

✦ **7** Set the the record straight and contradict these speakers, using comparisons of equality. There may be more than one possibility.

(a) Lisa è più generosa di Elena. – Ma, no, Elena è senz'altro (*as generous as Lisa*).

(b) Mirella è più ingenua che stupida. – Ti sbagli, Mirella è (*as stupid as she is naïve*).

(c) Tu guadagni meno di me. – Non è vero. Io guadagno (*as much as you do*).

(d) Quei ragazzi dormono più di quanto studiano.– Ma che dici? Studiano (*as much as they sleep*).

✚ 8 Complete the statements and answers. First, use the adjectives given with appropriate comparisons of equality; then, for a bit of revision, contradict each statement by completing the comparisons of inequality.

(a) Secondo te viaggiare in motocicletta è (*just as dangerous as*) viaggiare in bicicletta? – No, in realtà viaggiare in motocicletta è (*less dangerous than travelling by bike*). (**pericoloso**)

(b) Sono convinto che prendere l'autobus è (*just as convenient as*) prendere la metropolitana (comodo). – Non credo. Prendere l'autobus è (*much more convenient than taking the tube*). (**comodo**)

◎/✚ 5.2 Irregular comparatives

Some adjectives and adverbs have irregular comparative forms.

(a) Comparative forms of *buono, cattivo, grande, piccolo*

These four adjectives have both irregular and regular comparative forms.

Adjective	Irrregular comparative	Regular comparatives
buono *good*	**migliore** *better*	più buono *better* meno buono *less good*
cattivo *bad*	**peggiore** *worse*	più cattivo *worse* meno cattivo *less bad*
grande *big*	**maggiore** *bigger/larger, major*	più grande *bigger/larger* meno grande *less big*
piccolo *small*	**minore** *smaller, lesser/minor*	più piccolo *smaller* meno piccolo *less small*

◎/✚ (b) Uses: *piu buon* or *migliore; piu cattivo or peggiore*

The meanings of the regular and irregular comparatives of **buono** and **cattivo** are rarely truly identical, although they may in some cases be interchangeable. The following gives a general guide to their use, but a dictionary will help for specific cases.

Interchangeable forms

La tua minestra è **più buona** di quella che abbiamo mangiato ieri *Your soup is better/nicer/tastier than the one we ate yesterday* Questa minestra è decisamente **migliore** di quella che abbiamo mangiato ieri *This soup is distinctly better (superior to) than the one we ate yesterday* È stato un film **più buono/migliore** di quello che mi aspettavo *It was a better (more enjoyable) film than I expected/It's a better (superior/better made) film than I expected*	The regular and irregular forms are sometimes interchangable, mainly with reference to food. **Più buono** focuses on taste, while **migliore** tends to be less personal and subjective and denote better quality/superiority. Similar distinctions apply to **più cattivo** and **peggiore**. See also table on p. 82.

Più buono, più cattivo only

In the following cases **più buono/più cattivo** have a restricted meaning and cannot be replaced by **migliore** or **peggiore**.

Gianna è una persona **più buona** di Emilia *Gianna is a more decent/better/kinder person than Emilia* Quel ragazzo/cane è diventato **più cattivo** *That boy/dog has become naughtier/more vicious* L'odore dei pini/delle fogne è **più buono/più cattivo** che mai *The smell of the pines is better/nicer than ever/The smell of the sewers is worse/more horrible than ever*	**Più buono** and **più cattivo** are used to describe moral characteristics – personality and human/animal nature. They are also used to describe taste and smell, or subjective feelings relating to ability and performance (see e.g. in table above: **un film più buono ...** *a more enjoyable/better film*).

Migliore/peggiore only

In these cases **migliore/peggiore** are almost always used in preference to **piu buono/cattivo**.

La Rolls Royce è **migliore** della Fiat *A Rolls Royce is better than a Fiat* Ha trovato una soluzione **migliore** della mia *He/She has found a better solution than mine* Le sue condizioni di salute sono **peggiori** del previsto *His/Her state of health is worse than expected* **But compare below:**	**Migliore** and **peggiore** are more commonly used to express *better* and *worse* when making objective evaluations or describing physical or intellectual qualities. Note, however, that they may sometimes be replaced by their adverbial forms, **meglio** and **peggio** (see below.)
Le sue condizioni di salute sono **peggio** del previsto *His/Her state of health is worse than expected* Questa stoffa mi pare **meglio** dell'altra *This material seems better than the other one to me* Lui mi sembra **peggio** di un politico corrotto *To me he seems worse than a corrupt politician* Roma è **meglio** di Napoli *Rome is better than Naples*	✚ In colloquial Italian, the adverbs **meglio** and **peggio** are often preferred to the adjectives **migliore** and **peggiore** when used with **essere, sembrare** and **parere**. See also p. 82.

◎/✚ (c) Uses: più grande or maggiore; più piccolo or minore

Maggiore and **minore** tend to be more used in formal contexts than the regular comparative forms of **grande** and **piccolo**, but not always.

La città è diventata **più grande** *The city has got bigger* La casa di Carlo è **più piccola** della mia *Carlo's house is smaller than mine*	**Più grande/più piccolo** almost always describe concrete objects, unlike **maggiore** and **minore.**
Enrico ha una sorella **maggiore/più grande** *Enrico has an older/bigger sister* Ho parlato con il fratello **minore/più piccolo** *I spoke to the younger/smaller brother*	**Maggiore** and **minore** are interchangeable with reference to age.
È stata una spesa **maggiore/più grande** del previsto *It was a greater/bigger expense than expected* La regione ha alloggiato una percentuale **minore/più piccola** di immigrati *The region has accommodated a smaller percentage of immigrants*	With abstract nouns, the regular and irregular forms may all be used to express size or number, but **maggiore** and **minore** are more formal.
Sono zone di **maggior** interesse *They are areas of major/particular interest* È piuttosto un poeta **minore** *He is more of a minor poet* È un concerto per pianoforte in Do **maggiore** *It's a piano concerto in C major*	✚ **Maggiore/minore** *major/minor* Often express degree of importance. Note the final **-e** is dropped before a noun.

◎/✚ Esercizi

1 Using each of the comparatives below only once, decide where to place them to complete the sentences:

più buone • migliore • più cattivo • peggiore

  (a) Compro sempre il formaggio all'alimentari: la qualità è — che nei supermercati.

  (b) Quelle polpette hanno un sapore meraviglioso, sono molto — di quelle che faccio io.

  (c) La crisi si è rivelata — del previsto.

  (d) Il professore è sempre stato molto severo, ma adesso è diventato — che mai.

✚ **2** Choosing appropriate comparatives complete the following sentences. There is sometimes more than one possibilty.

  (a) Ho due fratelli: il (*older/bigger*) si chiama Andrea e il (*younger/smaller*) si chiama Bruno.

  (b) Se vuoi riuscire, devi fare uno sforzo (*greater/bigger*).

  (c) È una sonata è in chiave (*minor*).

  (d) Ha ascoltato con (*greater/more*) interesse di prima.

  (e) Sono sondaggi di (*minor/lesser*) importanza.

◎/✚ (d) Comparatives of *molto* and *poco*: form and use

Molto and *poco* are both adjectives and adverbs which have almost identical irregular comparative forms

Adjective	Adverb	Comparative adjective	Comparative adverb
molto *much/lots/many*	molto *very/a lot*	**più** *more*	**(di) più** *more*
poco *little/not much/not many/few*	poco *little/not much*	**meno** *less/fewer*	**(di) meno** *less*

Più and *meno* as adjectives and adverbs

Carlo ha molti soldi: purtroppo ha **più** soldi che buon senso *Carlo has lots of money: unfortunately he has more money than sense* Mangio poca pasta: mangio **meno** pasta che riso *I eat little pasta: I eat less pasta than rice*	**Più and meno as adjectives** Note that the comparative adjectives **più** and **meno** are invariable, unlike **molto** and **poco**.
Mi piace molto Roma ma Bologna mi piace **di più** *I like Rome a lot but I like Bologna more* Lavoro il doppio di mio fratello ma guadagno **(di) meno** *I work twice as much as my brother but earn less* Abbiamo sempre risparmiato poco e adesso **meno** che mai *We have always saved little/never saved much and now, less than ever*	**Più and meno as adverbs** **Di** in front of **più** and **meno** is more common, but not always necessary, at the end of a sentence. To refresh your memory on the use of **di/che** to express *than*, see pp. 73–4.

✚ Further adverbial uses: *più* and *meno* with quantifiers

Quest'anno abbiamo <u>molti allievi</u> **in più** *This year we have many more pupils* Ho ricevuto <u>duecento euro</u> **in meno** *I received two hundred euros less* Quest'anno pagano <u>il 0,5 per cento di interesse</u> **in più** *This year they are paying 0.5 per cent interest more/an extra 0.5 per cent* 'Per <u>qualche dollaro</u> **in più**' è il titolo di un vecchio film westerm *'For a Few Dollars More' is the title of an old Western*	**In** is used before **più** or **meno** directly after numbers and quantifiers + a noun. Note that **altro** can be used before numbers to express *more*. See 4.4, p. 69.

✚ *Più* and *meno* in adverbial phrases and with phrasal verbs

Più and **meno** are used as adjectives and adverbs in the following cases. Note that their English equivalent is adverbial.

Studiano con molto entusiasmo, con **più** entusiasmo dell'anno scorso *They are studying very enthusiastically, more enthusiastically than last year* Ho molta fame, ho **più** fame che sete *I'm very hungry, I am more hungry than thirsty* Si è fatto molto male, **più** male di Lidia *He hurt himself a lot, more than Lidia* Devi stare **più** attento/a questa volta *You must be more careful this time*	**Più** and **meno** are used before nouns or adjectives in adverbial phrases (e.g. **con entusiasmo**) or with verbs composed of infinitive + noun/adjective (e.g. **aver fame, farsi male, stare attento**).

◎/✚ Esercizi

──

3 **More and less.** Provide the Italian equivalent of the English.

    (a) La domenica dormo (*more*) che durante la settimana.

    (b) Devi cercare di mangiare (*less*).

    (c) Bisogna consumare (*more*) proteine e (*less/fewer*) grassi.

    (d) Fa troppo caldo per mangiare; ho (*more*) sete che fame.

    (e) Ha superato l'esame con (*less*) facilità dell'anno precedente.

✚ 4 Complete the sentences by providing the correct Italian equivalent of the English.

    (a) Mi hanno dato (*three hundred extra/more euros*).

    (b) L'anno prossimo ci saranno (*four thousand fewer jobs*). (**posti di lavoro**)

    (c) Il 58% delle italiane vuole perdere (*a few more kilos*).

    (d) Purtroppo ci sono (*so many more cars*) sulle nostre strade rispetto a vent'anni fa.

✚ 5 Using the verbs and adverbs below, plus **più** or **meno**, give the Italian equivalent of the English.

    (a) parlare con pazienza   *She spoke less patiently than before.*

    (b) ascoltare con attenzione   *This time they listened more attentively.*

    (c) avere molta fretta   *I am in much less of a hurry today.*

    (d) avere molta voglia di   *I am much more keen to help him now.*

(e) Comparatives of *bene* and *male*: form and use

Bene and *male*: forms

Bene and **male** are adverbs with irregular comparative forms, plus a regular form with **meno** only. Like all adverbs, they are invariable.

Adverb	Comparative adverbs	Examples
bene *well*	**meglio** *better* **meno bene** *less well*	Conosco bene Parigi, ma conosco **meglio** Roma *I know Paris well, but I know Rome better* Abbiamo mangiato **meno bene** del previsto *We ate less well than expected*
male *bad(ly)*	**peggio** *worse* **meno male** *less badly*	Gianni suona male il violino ma suona ancora **peggio** il pianoforte *Gianni plays the violin badly but plays the piano even worse.* Il lavoro è stato fatto **meno male** del previsto *The job was less badly done than expected*

Attenti!

- Note that like **bene** and **male**, **meglio** and **peggio** precede direct objects. See also 4.2, p. 57.
- As a comparative **meno bene** is used more often than **meno male**, but note the common expression **meno male**:

  Meno male che hai finito!   *Thank goodness/Just as well* (lit. *less bad) you have finished!*

- The phrases **più bene** and **più male** exist, but not as comparatives meaning *better* and *worse*. With the verbs **voler bene a** *to love* and **fare male a** *to hurt*, the comparatives **più bene** and **più male** both mean *more.*

  Io ti voglio **più bene** che mai   *I love you more than ever* (lit. *I want more good for you*)

  Mi fa **più male** adesso   *It is hurting me more now* (lit. *It makes me more harm*)

From the examples above, you can see that the comparative adjective **più** is combined respectively with the nouns **bene** (*good*) and **male** (*harm*) to mean *more.*

✚ Special use of *meglio* and *peggio*: to be better/worse at (doing) something

Io gioco bene a tennis, ma lui è **meglio** di me *I play tennis well but he is better* (plays better) *than me* A calcio lui è **peggio** di me *He is worse than I am* at (playing) *football*	**Essere meglio/peggio** is generally used rather than the adjectives **migliore** and **peggiore,** because a verb is understood.
Io gioco bene a tennis, ma lui è **più bravo** di me A calcio lui è **meno bravo** di me	Often, **essere più/meno bravo**, *to be better/worse at*, is used instead.

◎/✚ Esercizi

6 Complete the following sentences using **meglio, migliore, peggio** and **peggiore**.

     (a) Parla italiano (*better*) di me.

     (b) Oggi mi sento male, (*worse*) di ieri.

     (c) Non mi piace il mio lavoro, sto cercando un posto (*better*).

     (d) Non ho mai comprato una macchina (*worse*).

✚ 7 Choose which of the alternatives given is the most appropriate. In several cases either is possible, but in one case there is an incorrect possibility.

(a) Ogni volta che rifaccio il compito mi sembra **peggio/peggiore** di prima.

(b) La situazione politica qua è brutta ma da voi mi pare **meglio/migliore**.

(c) Oggi il tempo è stato **peggio/peggiore** del previsto.

(d) Sono bravo a scacchi, ma lui è **meglio/migliore** di me.

(e) Conosco bene Bologna ma conosco **meglio/migliore** Padova.

✚ 8 Find one or more Italian equivalents for the following.

(a) *He is better at football than me.*

(b) *They are better at tennis but worse at rugby.*

(c) *Your team is worse than mine.*

✚ 9 Give the English equivalent of these pairs of sentences. Refer to **Attenti!** p. 74 if you need help.

(a) Tu mi ami meno di Giorgio.

(b) Tu mi ami meno che Giorgio.

(c) Tu mi capisci meglio di Maria.

(d) Tu mi capisci meglio che Maria.

✚ 10 Transform the sentences below into comparative statements. Use the English as a guide.

(a) Ti voglio bene.   (*I love you*)   *I love you more than before.*

(b) Mi fa molto male   (*It hurts me a lot*)   *It hurts me more than ever.*

(c) Sto molto bene.   (*I am very well*)   *I am much better now.*

(d) Stanno molto male.   (*They are very unwell*)   *They are much worse than yesterday.*

◎/✚ 5.3 Emphatic comparatives

Emphatic comparatives are used with both regular and irregular adjectives and adverbs.

(a) Comparatives with *sempre* and *ancora*: 'more and more', 'even more', etc.

Divento **sempre** più pigro *I am getting/lazier and lazier/more and more lazy/increasingly lazy* Marco torna a casa **sempre** più tardi la sera *Marco is coming home later and later/increasingly late in the evening*	***More and more …/less and less …*** In Italian *more and more …/less and less …* is expressed by **sempre** placed before the regular comparative adjective or adverb/adverbial phrase.
Legge con **sempre** meno attenzione *He/She is reading less and less attentively* Si comportano in modo **sempre** più strano *They are behaving more and more strangely* Lo usano **sempre** meno di frequente *They use it less and less frequently* Ho sempre meno voglia di andarci *I feel less and less like going*	✚ With adverbial phrases, e.g. **con attenzione**, **in modo strano**, or with phrasal verbs, e.g. **avere voglia di**, the position of **sempre** is variable.
Ha **sempre** meno amici *She/He has fewer and fewer friends* L'idea mi piace **sempre** di più *I like the idea more and more/I increasingly like the idea* Vivono in condizioni **sempre** peggiori *They are living in worse and worse/increasingly bad conditions* Gli affari vanno **sempre** meglio *Business is going better and better/is going increasingly well*	✚ **Sempre** is placed directly in front of irregular comparatives: **(di) più, (di) meno, maggiore, minore migliore, peggiore, meglio, peggio**.

Angelo è **ancora** <u>più antipatico</u> di Luigi *Angelo is even more unpleasant than Luigi* Sono arrivati **ancora** <u>più tardi</u> del solito *They arrived even later than usual* Lo devi rileggere <u>con</u> **ancora** <u>più attenzione</u> *You must read it again even more carefully* Mi sono fatto **ancora** <u>più male</u> *I have hurt myself even more*	*Even more/even less* **...** **Ancora** precedes regular comparative adjectives, adverbs and adverbial phrases. It is placed identically to **sempre** in adverbial phrases and with phrasal verbs (see p. 83).
Per le piccole imprese le prospettive sono **ancora peggiori** *For small businesses the prospects are even worse* La riunione è andata **ancora meglio** del normale *The meeting went even better than normal* Ieri sono stato chiuso fuori e, **ancora peggio**, ho perso il portafoglio *Yesterday I was locked out and, what's worse, I lost my wallet*	✚ **Ancora** directly precedes the irregular comparatives **migliore**, **peggiore**, **meglio**, **peggio**. Note the idiomatic use of **ancora peggio**.

✚ (b) 'The more ... the more'; 'the less ... the less'

These comparisons are similarly expressed in Italian and English, but in Italian there is no definite article with the comparatives.

più ... più/ meno	**Più** bevono **più** antipatico diventano *The more they drink, the more unpleasant they become* **Più** mi critichi **meno** ti do retta *The more you criticise me, the less attention I pay (you)*
meno ... più/ meno	**Meno** mangi **più** peso perdi *The less you eat, the more weight you lose* **Meno** ci vediamo **meno** litighiamo *The less we see each other, the less we argue*
più ... meglio/ peggio	**Più** passa il tempo **meglio** sto *The more time passes, the better I feel* **Più** ci penso, **peggio** è *The more I think about it, the worse it gets*
meno ... meglio/peggio	**Meno** ci sentiamo **meglio** è *The less we are in contact, the better it is* **Meno** lavoro, **peggio** sto *The less I work, the worse I feel*

Tanto or **quanto** may precede **più**, especially with adjectives or adverbs.

tanto/quanto più ... quanto/ tanto più	La verità è **tanto più** difficile da sentire **quanto più** a lungo la si è taciuta *Truth is (all the) harder to hear the longer it has been suppressed* (kept quiet) **Tanto più** numerose le leggi, **quanto più** è corrotto uno stato *The more numerous the laws the more corrupt a state is* **Quanto più** già si sa, **tanto più** bisogna ancora imparare *The more you know already the more you have still to learn*

Note the expression **tanto più vicino quanto più lontano** *so near and yet so far.*

◎/✚ Esercizi

1 Rewrite these statements twice to make them more emphatic, using the English as a guide.

(a)	È difficile trovare un lavoro.	*increasingly hard/harder and harder*	*even harder*
(b)	È poco probabile.	*less and less likely*	*even less likely*
(c)	Beve spesso.	*more and more often*	*even more often*

(d) Ascoltava con attenzione.   *more and more attentively*   *even more attentively*

(e) Fa freddo.   *less and less cold*   *even less cold*

✚ 2 Now do the same with the following, taking care to use an appropriate comparative form of the irregular adjectives and adverbs given. In a few instances you may find there are two possibilities.

(a) Ci sono pochi posti di lavoro.   *fewer and fewer*   *even fewer*

(b) I risultati sono buoni.   *better and better*   *even better*

(c) Ho fatto un grande sforzo.   *increasingly big*   *even greater*

(d) L'idea mi piace poco.   *less and less*   *even less*

(e) Abbiamo speso molto.   *more and more*   *even more*

✚ 3 Give the Italian equivalent of the following.

(a) *The more he reads, the less he understands.*

(b) *The more I eat, the more depressed I become.* **(deprimersi)**

(c) *The less we see each other, the better it is.*

(d) *The harder I try, the worse it gets.* **(sforzarsi)**

◎ 5.4 Regular relative superlatives

Relative superlative forms of adjectives and adverbs correspond in English to *the most … the least*. They are termed 'relative' superlatives because they are used with reference to the highest or lowest degree of something amongst a group. It is important to note they are usually identical in form to regular comparatives (p. 72), apart from the use of the definite article.

(a) Adjectives and adverbs: forms and use

Superlative adjectives are formed by placing **più** or **meno** in front, plus the relevant definite article.

il/la/i/le più/ meno + adjective	È **il** monumento **più** antico *It is the oldest/most ancient monument* È **la** torre **più** alta *It is the tallest tower* Sono **i** manoscritti **più** preziosi *They are the most precious manuscripts* Sono **le** chiese **meno** conosciute *They are the least-known churches*	**Più/meno** are invariable, but the adjectives and articles change to agree with the noun they refer to. The article is used only once.

Note that superlatives can be used as pronouns:

Audrey Hepburn è stata decretata **la più bella** di sempre.
Audrey Hepburn has been voted the most beautiful (woman) ever.

Superlative adverbs are usually preceded by **più** or **meno**, exactly like the comparative form. No article is used, except with **possibile**.

più/meno + adverb	Pino corre **più/meno rapidamente** di tutti *Pino runs more quickly/quicker, faster than before* È l'amica che vedo **più/meno** spesso (di tutte) *She's the friend I see most/least often (of all my girl friends)*	The adverb is often followed by **di tutti.** If there is a clear reference to a feminine noun, **tutte** may be used instead.
✚ **il** + **più/ meno +** adverb + **possibile**	È andato a vivere **il più lontano possibile** dai suoceri *He went to live as far as possible from his in-laws* Domani mi alzerò **il più tardi possibile** *Tomorrow I'll get up as late as possible*	With a superlative adverb the definite article **il** is used only with **possibile** or another qualifier such as **immaginabile/ concepibile**.

Although relative superlative adverbs are usually the same as the comparative adverbs, the context makes the meaning clear.

Per favore, parli **più forte** *Please speak more loudly/louder*	**Comparative**
Ha parlato **più forte** di tutti *He/She spoke the loudest of all* Ha parlato **il più forte** possibile *He/She spoke as loudly as possible*	**Relative superlatives**

 Attenti! Note that in relative superlative constructions with **possible**, the English equivalent is often *as … as possible*.
Do not confuse this with comparisons of equality. Compare:

Mangia il più possibile. *He eats as much as possible/the most possible.*
Mangia tanto quanto beve. *He eats as much as he drinks.* (comparative)

(b) 'The most/least of/in'

In English, relative superlatives are often followed by *in* or *of*, which in Italian is usually expressed by **di**, linked where necessary to the definite article.

One of the most/least of/in	La regina d'Inghilterra è **una delle** donne **più** ricche del mondo *The queen of England is one of the richest women in the world* La Gioconda è **fra i** dipinti **più** famosi di tutti i tempi *The Mona Lisa is one of the most famous paintings of all time* È stato votato **fra gli** undici uomini **meno** 'sexy' del mondo *He has been voted one of the twelve least sexy men in the world*	This is expressed by **uno/a di** + definite article + **più/meno** or, very often, by **fra** + **i/le/gli** (lit. *amongst the*) + **più/meno**.
Some of the most/least of/in	**Fra le** squadre di calcio **più** famose d'Italia ci sono la Juventus, il Milan e il Lazio *Some of the/Amongst the most famous football teams in Italy are Juventus, Milan and Lazio* Il gruppo è proprietario di **alcuni fra i** nomi **più** noti nel settore dell'abbigliamento *The group owns some of best-known names in the clothing sector*	This is expressed by **fra** + **i/gli/le** + **più/meno** or else by **alcuni fra** + **i/gli** and **alcune fra** + **le** + **più/meno**.

◎/✚ Esercizi

1 *The most/least.* Match up the phrases carefully to make the best sense possible.

(a) La stanza meno rumorosa
(b) Le notizie più brutte …
(c) Il ministro più corrotto
(d) L'uomo più odioso

(i) della giornata
(ii) di sempre
(iii) della casa
(iv) del governo

2 *One of the most, some of the most.* Rewrite the sentences below without changing the meaning.

(a) Verdi, Puccini e Rossini sono alcuni dei compositori italiani più rinomati.
e.g. *Verdi, Puccini e Rossini sono fra i compositori italiani più rinomati.*
(b) Gli Stati Uniti è uno dei paesi più ricchi del mondo.
(c) Stromboli, Lipari e Capri sono fra le isole più affascinanti d'Italia.
(d) Il parmigiano è fra i formaggi italiani più conosciuti all'estero.

✦ 3 Construct four Italian sentences using the prompts below.

    (a) Qual è — cellulare —?   *the smallest available*

    (b) Giulia parlava —.   *as loud as she could* (*the loudest possible*)

    (c) È stato — servizio —.   *the slowest imaginable*

    (d) La sua valutazione era —.   *as objective as possible* (*the most objective possible*)

◎/✦ 5.5 Irregular relative superlatives

These are identical in form to irregular comparatives (pp. 85–6), apart from the use of the definite article.

◎ (a) Relative superlatives of *buono, cattivo, grande, picccolo*: forms and use

Like their comparative forms, these four adjectives have both a regular and an irregular relative superlative.

buono *good*	**il migliore** *the best*	**il** più buono/**il** meno buono *the best, the most/least good*
cattivo *bad*	**il peggiore** *the worst*	**il** più cattivo/**il** meno cattivo *the worst/least bad*
grande *big*	**il maggiore** *the biggest*	**il** più grande/**il** meno grande *the biggest/least big*
piccolo *small*	**il minore** *the smallest*	**il** più piccolo/**il** meno piccolo *the smallest/least small*

For the use of the regular or irregular form (**il più buono** or **il migliore**, etc.), see Chapter 5, Comparatives and Superlatives.

✦ Uses: 'the best/worst ... in/of'

Like regular relative superlatives, these adjectives are often followed by *in* or *of*, which in Italian is usually expressed by **di**, linked where necessary to the definite article.

The best/worst/ biggest/smallest of/in	Sono **gli** studenti **peggiori** della classe *or:* Sono **i peggiori** studenti della classe *They are the worst students in the class* Gemma è **la** figlia **maggiore/più grande** dei Bruni *Gemma is the eldest of the Brunis* La Finlandia ha **la minore** percentuale di carcerati di ogni altro paese *Finland has the smallest percentage of prisoners of all other countries* È **la migliore** lavatrice di tutte *It is the best washing machine of all* ***But:*** È **la migliore** macchina fotografica <u>sul</u> mercato *It is the best camera on the market*	Remember that the definite article is used only **once**: either before the noun or before the superlative adjective. You never say 'la figlia la maggiore'. See p. 85. Occasionally the adjective is followed by **su** or **in**. ✦
One of the best/ worst, etc.	È **uno degli** scrittori **migliori** di tutti i tempi *He is one of the best writers of all time*	See also p. 86.
Some of the best/worst, etc.	Sono stati **fra i** giorni **peggiori** della mia vita *They were some of the worst days of my life*	See also p. 86.

(b) Relative superlatives of *molto* and *poco*: forms and use

The adjectives and adverbs **molto** and **poco** have no special relative superlative forms.

Adjective	Adverb	Adjective: relative superlative forms	Adverb: relative superlative form
molto *much/lots/many*	molto *very/a lot*	**più (di tutti)/il maggior numero di** *most*	**(di) più** *most*
poco *little/not much/ not many/few*	poco *little/not much*	**meno (di tutti)/il minor numero di** *least/fewest*	**(di) meno** *least*

✚ The adjective *the most/the least* is expressed in two ways, either by using the comparative form + **di tutti** or **possibile**, or by using the phrases **il maggior/il minor numero di** (lit. *the greatest number of/the smallest number of*).

È la scuola con **più** allievi **di tutti** *It is the school with the most pupils (of all)* Cerca di fare **meno** rumore **possibile** *Try to make as little noise as possible*	⚠ **Adjectival use** With the adjectives **più**/**meno**, no article is used with **possibile**. (Unlike adverbs + **possibile**, see below.)
È la scuola con **il maggior numero** di allievi *It is the school with the most pupils* Questa è la traduzione con **il minor numero di** errori *This is the translation with the least/fewest mistakes*	**il maggior/il minor numero di** + plural noun. The final **–e** of **maggiore**/**minore** is dropped.
Mi piacciono Los Angeles e San Francisco, ma New York è la città che mi piace **di più** *I like LA and San Francisco but the city I like (the) most is NY* Avrà speso **più**/**meno** di tutti *He will have spent the most/the least of all*	**Adverbial use** No article is used, except with **possibile** or another qualifier such as **immaginabile.** See also p. 85.
Avrà speso **il più possibile** *He will have spent as much as possible* Devi fare **il meno possibile** *You must do as little as possible.*	

The relative superlative adverb is the same as the comparative adverb, but the context usually makes it clear which form is intended.

(c) Relative superlatives of *bene* and *male*: forms and use

The relative superlatives of **bene** and **male** are identical in Italian to the comparative (p. 82).

Adverb	Relative superlative	Examples
bene *well*	**meglio** *best*	Michela e Sandra nuotano bene, ma Barbara nuota **meglio** di tutte *Michela and Sandra swim well but Barbara swims the best of all*
male *bad(ly)*	**peggio** *worst*	Si è comportato **peggio** di tutti *He behaved the worst of all* ***But:*** ⚠ Si è comportato **il peggio possibile** *He behaved as badly as/the worst possible*

Attenti! It's time to take stock of comparatives and superlatives to see where Italian and English differ. English makes a distinction between comparative and superlative forms, but not between adjectives and adverbs. In Italian the reverse is true: there are separate forms for adjectives and adverbs, but not for comparatives and superlatives.

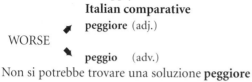

BETTER — **migliore** (adj.) / **meglio** (adv.) *Italian comparative*

BEST — **(il) migliore** (adj.) / **(il) meglio** (adv.) *Italian superlative*

Quella soluzione è senz'altro **migliore**

That solution is undoubtedly <u>better</u> (comparative adjective)

La partita è andata **meglio** del previsto

The match went <u>better</u> than expected (comparative adverb)

È **la** soluzione **migliore**

It's the <u>best</u> solution (superlative adjective)

Ha giocato **meglio** di tutti

He played the <u>best</u> of all (superlative adverb)

The same distinctions apply to *worse* and *worst*:

WORSE — **peggiore** (adj.) / **peggio** (adv.) *Italian comparative*

WORST — **(il) peggiore** (adj.) / **(il) peggio** (adv.) *Italian superlative*

Non si potrebbe trovare una soluzione **peggiore**

You couldn't find a <u>worse</u> solution (comparative adjective)

La giornata andata **peggio** del previsto

The day went <u>worse</u> than exepected (comparative adverb)

È stato **il** consiglio **peggiore** di tutti

It was the <u>worst</u> advice of all (superlative adjective)

Hanno suonato **peggio** di tutti

They played <u>worst</u> of all (superlative adverb)

 **Esercizi**

1 Opinions opinions. Below are some of the questions bloggers have posted on the web about football and food. Complete them, using the relative superlative forms of **buono, cattivo, più** and **meno**.

    (a) Chi è il giocatore (*best of all time*)?

    (b) Chi è (*the worst*) allenatore (*in the world*)?

    (c) Qual è la squadra con (*the most*) punti fatti?

    (d) Quali sono i cibi con (*the least/fewest*) calorie?

    (e) Qual'è (*the best/nicest dish*) che sa cucinare tua madre o tuo padre? (**il piatto**)

2 Now give the Italian equivalent of the English. In the last sentence there is more than one possibility.

    (a) *It was the greatest expense of the year.*

    (b) *She lives in one of the biggest houses in the neighbourhood.*

    (c) *They are some of the worst cars ever.*

    (d) *Angelo and Leo are some of the best players in the team.*

3 Complete the sentences chosing an appropriate superlative form of **molto** and **poco** for the English phases given.

    (a) Cercate di consumare (*the least energy possible/as little energy as possible*).

    (b) Dovete veramente consumare (*the least possible/as little as possible*).

    (c) Devi semplificare il documento (*as much as possible*) per renderlo più chiaro.

    (d) Adele ha fatto (*the most mistakes*). Normalmente ne fa (*the least of all*).

◎/+ 5.6 Absolute superlatives

Absolute superlatives are so called because there is no second term of comparison.

◎ (a) Adjectives: regular forms and uses

Like all adjectives, absolute superlatives agree in number and gender with the nouns they refer to.

Adjective	Absolute superlative	Explanations
scuro *dark* utile *useful* molto *much/many* lungo *long* poco *little/few* simpatico *nice*	scurissimo *very/extremely dark* utilissimo *very/extremely useful* moltissimo *very much/many* lunghissimo *very/extremely long* pochissimo *very little/few* simpaticissimo *very/extremely nice*	-**issimo** is added to the end of the adjective, minus its final vowel. If the adjective ends in -**co** or -**go**, an *h* precedes -**issimo** to keep the hard sound unless the normal plural ends in -**gi** or -**ci**. (Note that **molto** and **poco** have regular absolute superlative forms.)
	molto scuro *very/extremely old* molto utile *very/extremely useful* molto poco *very little* ***But not:* molto molto**	**Molto** + a normal adjective can substitute absolute superlatives except in the case of the adjective **molto**. You cannot say **molto molto**.

Use	Explanations
È un padre **molto egoista** *He is a very selfish father* Sono cresciuto in un ambiente **molto cosmopolita** *I grew up in a very cosmopolitan environment*	Adjectives in -**a** do not have -**issimo** suffixes. **Molto** is used instead.
È una persona straordinaria *He/She is an extraordinary person* È un artista eccellente *He/she is an excellent artist* Ho un terribile raffreddore *I have a terrible cold* **But:** Ho un bruttissimo raffreddore *I have a very bad cold*	Adjectives which already express a superlative concept are not used with -**issimo** or **molto**. Others include: **eccezionale**, **incredibile**, **meraviglioso**, **stupendo**.

(b) Adverbs: forms and use

Like all adverbs, absolute superlatives are invariable.

Adverb	Absolute superlative	Explanations
lontano *far* tardi *late* rapidamente *quickly*	lontanissimo *very/extremely far* tardissimo *very/extremely late* rapid**issima**mente *very/extremely quickly*	-**issimo** is added to the adverb minus its final vowel. When an adverb ends in -**mente**, -**issima** goes before the -**mente** ending and the final vowel is dropped.
bene *well* male *badly* poco *little/not much* molto *much/a lot*	benissimo *very/extremely well* malissimo *very/extremely badly* pochissimo *very/extremely little* moltissimo *very/extremely much*	Absolute superlatives of irregular adverbs are all regular.

Most absolute superlative adverbs except **moltissimo** can be substituted by **molto** + the normal adverb.

Hanno capito **benissimo/molto bene** *They have understood extremely very/perfectly well*   L'esame è andato **malissimo/molto male** *The exam went extremely/very badly*   ***But:***   Ho mangiato **moltissimo** ieri *I ate a great deal yesterday* (not **molto molto**)

(c) Adjectives: irregular forms and use

Buono, **cattivo**, **grande** and **piccolo** have irregular as well as regular absolute superlatives.

buono *good*	buonissimo/**ottimo** *very good extremely good/excellent*
cattivo *bad*	cattivissimo/**pessimo** *very bad/extremely bad/terrible*
grande *big*	grandissimo/**massimo** *very big/extremely big/maximum*
piccolo *small*	piccolissimo/**minimo** *very small/extremely small/minimum*

Use	Explanations
La pasta è **buonissima/ottima** *The pasta is extremely good/excellent* È una **buonissima**/un'**ottima** scelta *It is a very good/excellent choice* È di **cattivissimo/pessimo** umore *He is in an extremely bad/terrible mood* Abbiamo fatto un **pessimo** viaggio *We had a terrible/dreadful journey* Ha fatto **il massimo** sforzo *He made the utmost/maximum effort* È **il** nostro **massimo** poeta *He is our greatest poet* Non ho **la minima** idea *I don't have the slightest idea*	The irregular forms are rarely exactly synonymous with the regular forms, though **buonissimo** and **ottimo** are often interchangeable, as are **cattivissimo/pessimo**. **Massimo** and **minimo** are used with the definite, rather than the indefinite article. **Massimo** has a wide range of equivalents: *largest, greatest, highest, maximum*, etc.

✚ (d) Informal absolute superlatives

In both informal written and spoken Italian it is common for some adjectives and adverbs to be repeated to intensify or emphasise the meaning.

Devi stare **buono buono** *You must be a really good boy.* Fammi un caffè **caldo caldo** *Make me a really/a piping hot coffee* È diventata **rossa rossa** *She went really red/flushed bright scarlet* La principessa viveva in un paese **lontano lontano** *The princess lived in a country far, far away* È stato un pareggio **stretto stretto** *It was a really tight equaliser* Un borghese **piccolo piccolo** *A Very Little Man/A Real Little Bourgeois* (1977 film)	Repetition is typical of the spoken language and fairly colloquial written language, e.g. in fairy stories, songs or in film titles.
Piano piano sono riusciti a liberarlo *Very slowly/gradually they managed to free him* **Quasi quasi** finivo sotto il treno *I very nearly ended up under the train*	**Piano piano** is sometimes written as **pian piano**.
Piano, piano! *Steady!/Take it easy!* Ho fame, **quasi quasi** esco a mangiare una pizza *I'm hungry, I might just go out and have a pizza* Il mio cane zoppicava e stava **mogio mogio** *My dog was limping and looking very sorry for himself/extremely dejected*	In some cases the repeated adjectives or adverbs form expressions of their own.

Other informal absolute superlatives are formed using prefixes or idiomatic phrases.

arci	**arci**contento *extremely happy/over the moon* **stra**grande *vast/ginormous*
stra	**stra**ricco *extremely/mega rich*
super	**super**intelligente *extremely intelligent/ultra-brainy*
ultra	**ultra**rapido *extremely fast*

- Common idioms also function as informal superlatives.

bagnato fradicio *soaking wet*   pieno zeppo *stuffed full, chock-a-block*
ricco sfondato *mega-rich*   stanco morto *dead tired*

◎/✚ Esercizi

1 Form the absolute superlatives of the following adjectives and adverbs. Which are the two odd ones out?

biondo • felice • terribile • largo • antico • comico • ottimista • vicino • rapidamente • bene • tardi • presto

2 Complete the descriptions below by giving the Italian equivalent of the English.

(a) Chiara è la ragazza più allegra della classe. *She is an extremely happy girl.*

(b) Gemma è la studentessa meno simpatica della classe. *She is a very selfish person.*

(c) Riccardo è l'artista più dotato della classe. *He is a very good/excellent artist.*

(d) Pietro è il linguista meno bravo della classe. *He is a terrible linguist.*

(e) Adele è la ragazza che aiuta di più. *She is a really exceptional person.*

✚ **3** Find suitable absolute superlative alternatives for the words in italics. You need to use irregular forms.

(a) I muratori hanno fatto un *bruttissimo* lavoro.

(b) Abbiamo *moltissimo* rispetto per i tuoi amici.

(c) Basta *il più piccolo* pretesto per farlo arrabbiare.

(d) È fortunato perché gode di *buonissima* salute.

✚ **4** Use the relative superlative and an appropriate form of the absolute superlative to answer these questions in Italian.

(a) Sono tornati molto tardi? – *Yes, they came back extremely late, later than everyone.*

(b) Ha lavorato veramente veloce? – *Yes, he worked extremely fast, the fastest of all.*

(c) Ti ha scritto regolarmente? – *Yes, she wrote very regularly, the most regularly of all.*

✚ **5** Now answer these questions by giving the Italian equivalent of the English. As in 4 above, you will need to use both absolute and relative superlatives.

(a) Hanno lavorato bene? (*Yes, they worked extremely well, better than anyone/the best of all.*)

(b) È vero che ti ha aiutato poco? (*Yes, he helped very little, he helped least of all.*)

(c) Insegna davvero così male? (*Yes, he teaches extremely badly, he teaches worst of all the other teachers.*)

(d) Ti piace veramente molto? (*Yes, I like it very much, I like it most of all.*)

✚ **6** The island of Lipari is part of the Aeolian archipelago off the north coast of Sicily. Read this extract taken from a guide to the islands and answer the questions.

Lipari, l'antica Meligunis, è l'isola maggiore dell'Archipelago, nota un giorno quale* emporio dell'ossidiana* e rinomata oggi come il massimo emporio della pomice.* Quest'isola è centro di escursioni indimenticabili per il fascino dei suoi paesaggi. Il centro più importante è Lipari.

La cittadina in parte si estende lungo le due pittoresche insenature* di Marina Lunga e Marina Corta e in parte è appollaiata* attorno al suo Castello, l'antica necropolis. La necropoli classica è una delle più ricche della Sicilia in cui ci hanno recuperato i corredi* di oltre 1300 tombe. Le più antiche risalgono al VI sec. A.C.*

Lipari è l'isola più complessa delle Eolie dal punto di vista geologico e vulcanologico, con fumarole, solfatare e sorgenti termali*. Le più importanti fumarole sono quelle di Bagnosecco; sorgenti termali sono state notate presso Bagnicello ma le più importanti sono quelle di S Calogero. Le acque di S. Calogero sono state utilizzate per fini terapeutici da epoca immemorabile, rivelandosi* sempre di somma efficacia.*

- nota un giorno quale *once famous as* • ossidiana *obsidian – hard volcanic glass*
- pomice *pumice stone* • insenature *inlets* • appollaiata *perched* • recuperato i corredi *recovered the contents* • risalgono al VI sec. A.C. *date from the VI century BC* • fumarole, solfatare e sorgenti termali *smoke holes, volcanic areas of sulphurous gases and hot springs* • rivelandosi *showing itself to be* • di somma efficacia *supremely effective*.

(a) Pick out the relative superlative adjectives and one irregular one.

(b) Identify one irregular absolute superlative adjective.

(c) Reorder the phrase **le più importanti fumarole**.

(d) Replace the following with another equivalent phrase in Italian.

   l'isola maggiore • il massimo emporio • di somma efficacia.

(e) Express the following in Italian: *Lipari is one of the most fascinating islands in Sicily.*

+ 5.7 Further comparatives and superlatives

(a) More comparatives

Altrettanto is very often used in implicit comparisons of equality, i.e. when the second term of comparison is not expressed. It can be an adverb, an adjective or a pronoun.

just as: **altrettanto** as an adverb	Elisa è pigra – Sì, ma Francesca è **altrettanto** pigra *Elisa is lazy – Yes, but Francesca is equally/ just as lazy* Mario ha giocato bene ma Dino ha giocato **altrettanto** bene *Mario played well but Dino played just as/equally well too* Mi sono iscritto a una palestra e Sabrina ha fatto **altrettanto** *I've joined a gym and Sabrina has done the same/likewise/and so has Sabrina*	When **altrettanto** *just as, equally, likewise* is an adverb, it modifies adjectives or other adverbs and verbs. It is invariable.
altrettanto as an adjective and pronoun	Oggi sono arrivati **altrettanti** ospiti *Today just as many guests arrived* Ho raccolto due chili di ciliegie e Carlo ne ha raccolte **altrettante** *I picked two kilos of cherries and Carlo picked as many (as I did)*	When **altrettanto** is an adjective or a pronoun, it agrees with the noun or pronoun it refers to.

Another way to express similarity is to use the adjective **stesso**.

lo stesso di/ **che** *the same as*	Ho fatto **lo stesso** errore **di** ieri *I made the same mistake as yesterday* Ho comprato **la stessa** gonna **di** Mara *I bought the same skirt as Mara* In Italia abbiamo **gli stessi** problemi **che** nel resto del mondo *We have the same problems as in the rest of the world*	**Stesso** agrees with the noun it qualifies. **Che** must be used instead of **di** in front of prepositions.

Differences are expressed in various ways.

a differenza di, in modo diverso, diversamente da *unlike*	**A differenza di** suo padre è molto modesto *Unlike his father he is very modest* Scrivono **in modo** del tutto **diverso** *They write quite unlike each other* **Diversamente da** come riportato, l'incidente non è stato grave *Unlike what was reported, the accident was not serious*	These three constructions all literally mean *differently.*

Piuttosto che and **rispetto a** are frequently used in comparisons.

piuttosto che *rather than, instead of*	Ho deciso di andare a Parigi in treno **piuttosto che** in aereo *I've decided to go to Paris by train instead of by plane* **Piuttosto che** prendere l'ultimo treno perché non dormi da noi? *Rather than catch the last train, why don't you sleep at our place?*	Used to express preferences between two options or to make suggestions. See also **anziché** and **invece di**, 16.3, p. 216.
rispetto a *compared to, than*	Mi hanno pagato duecento euro in meno **rispetto al** mese scorso *I was paid 200 euros less than last month* L'energia solare richiede molto spazio in meno **rispetto a** tutte le altre fonti rinnovabili *Solar energy requires a lot less space than all other renewable sources* Preferisco i cani, perché **rispetto ai** gatti sono pù fedeli *I prefer dogs, because compared to cats they are more faithful*	Used when comparing amounts, but also widely used to express other comparisons.

✚ Esercizi

1 *Just the same*. Complete the replies by giving the Italian equivalent of the English.

    (a) Mio fratello è altissimo. – Certo, (*but you are just as tall*).

    (b) Mio padre guadagna tantissimo. – Lo so, (*but mine earns just as much*).

    (c) Ho raccolto un chilo di funghi. – Bravo, (*but I've picked just as many*).

    (d) Ho prenotato per domani. - Bene, (*I've done exactly the same/likewise*).

2 These people are not interested in change. Give the Italian equivalent of the English.

    (a) *Michele is wearing the same shirt as yesterday.*

    (b) *Giovanna votes for the same party as her parents.*

    (c) *Paolo has the same hairdresser as his brother.*

3 Complete the sentences using each of the given phrases once.

    a differenza di • rispetto a • la stessa che

    (a) Le vendite delle auto sono calate dell'otto per cento — gennaio.

    (b) Qui la temperatura media in marzo è più o meno — in gennaio.

    (c) — di suo fratello non va mai in vacanza in gennaio.

4 Say what the options are, choosing the first one each time and then completing the sentences.

    (a) Preferirei —.   andare a comprare una pizza/andare al ristorante

    (b) Ho intenzione di —.   andare in campeggio/dormire in albergo

    (c) Ho deciso di —.   partire con il treno/prendere la macchina

(b) Comparatives before finite verbs: expressing 'than'

When a comparative of inequality (not equality) is used before a finite verb, there are various ways of expressing *than*.

Lui spende più **di quanto** <u>dovrebbe</u> *He spends more than he should* Il cinema era **meno** lontano **di quanto** ci <u>aveva detto/avesse detto</u> Mario/lo zio *The cinema was less far than Mario/our uncle had told us*	**di quanto** is most commonly used to express *than*. It may precede the indicative – often the conditional – but the subjunctive is also used.
È più pesante **di quanto (non)** <u>pensi</u> *It's heavier than you think/one thinks* Le cose sono molto **più** complicate **di quanto (non)** <u>pensassi</u>/**di quanto** <u>possa sembrare</u> *Things are much more complicated than I thought/than it may seem* Mauro è **meno** astuto **che (non)** <u>sembri</u> *Mauro is less astute than he seems*	**di quanto (non)** or **che (non)** are usually followed by a subjunctive. **Non** is optional as it has no negative meaning.
Lucio è più intelligente **di quel che** <u>sembra</u> *Lucio is more intelligent than he seems/looks* Sandro è **più** simpatico **di quello che** <u>pensavo</u> *Sandro is nicer than I thought* La città è **meno** grande **di come** me la <u>ricordo</u> *The city is less big than/not as big as I remember (it)*	**di quel(lo) che** and **di come** may be followed by an indicative tense. **Di come** especially is used where focus is on likeness.
I miei figli hanno cento e più giochi **di quando** eravamo pioccoli *My children have hundreds more toys than when we were little* Frank Sinatra vende più ora **di quando** era vivo *Frank Sinatra sells more now than when he was alive*	*Than when* is expressed by **di quando** followed by an indicative verb.

(c) Superlatives before finite verbs: expressing 'that'

A superlative before a finite verb takes **che** + a subjunctive. For the subjunctive tense sequence, see, pp. 306–8.

È l'uomo **più simpatico che ci sia** *He's the nicest man (that) there is/ever*	The present subjunctive is used.
È **la** città **più bella che io abbia mai** visto *It is the most beautiful city (that) I have ever seen*	The perfect subjunctive is used.
Era **la** cosa **peggiore che potesse capitare** *It was the worst thing that could happen*	The imperfect subjunctive is used.
Era **la** città **più bella che io avessi mai visto** *It was the most beautiful city (that) I had ever seen*	The pluperfect subjunctive is used.

◎/✛ Esercizi

5 Complete the following sentences, giving the Italian for the English phrases beginning with *than*.

- (a) Tu mangi meno (*than you should*).
- (b) Era più lontano (*than we thought*).
- (c) Sono più anziani (*than they look/seem*).
- (d) Mara è più giovanile (*than I remember her*).
- (e) È più rilassato (*than when he arrived*).

6 Match up the phrases in each column to form complete sentences.

    (a) È il film migliore   **(i)** che io abbia mai letto.

    (b) È la persona più superficiale   **(ii)** che ci siano.

    (c) Sono i vicini più gentili   **(iii)** che io abbia mai visto.

    (d) È il libro peggiore   **(iv)** che conosca.

✚ **7** Read these extracts taken from a magazine article about friendship online. Then,

    (a) identify two irregular comparative adjectives; and, then

    (b) underline as many complete comparative structures as you can.

I social network facilitano le amicizie, ma è anche vero che sulla Rete* i conflitti dilagano* più rapidamente e sono più violenti che dal vivo*: si può arrivare agli insulti peggiori, o a pubblicare foto imbarazzanti della propria ex. Dietro al monitor, infatti, ci si sente più protetti, e anche se si ha un un pubblico più numeroso si dicono cose che mai si direbbero dal vivo. Ma le emozioni restano forti: scoprire che l'amico del cuore non ti ha inserito nella lista dei 'migliori amici' provoca una cocente delusione.*

Su Facebook … si diventa amici degli amici ma anche di gente che non si sa nemmeno chi sia*, perché sono 'amicizie' poco più impegnative di un clic ogni tanto*.

Ma quanto può essere profondo un legame fra gli iscritti al gruppo di Facebook? Certamente meno rispetto ad altri, secondo un esperto di social network. Ma chi investe in questi legami ha più possibilità di ottenere informazioni utili e potenziali nuovi contatti rispetto a chi si chiude nei legami familiari. Anche se, in realtà, Facebook serve più a rafforzare relazioni* iniziate off line che a fare nuove conoscenze.*

('Amici in rete', *Focus* 199, maggio 2009)

• Rete *(inter)net* • dilagano *spread* • dal vivo *face to face, in the flesh* • cocente delusione *bitter disappointment* • non si sa … chi sia *you don't even know who they are* • poco più impegnative … *friendships demanding little more involvement than occasionally clicking online* • relazioni *relationships* • conoscenze *acquaintances*.

---

6 Suffixes

A suffix (**un suffisso**) is a letter or group of letters added to the end of a word. It may change the meaning of the source word or merely modify it, e.g. *friend*, *friend**ship***, *friend**less***; *green*, *green**ish***. In Italian, suffixes are a part of everyday conversation as well as mainly informal writing. They are more common and creatively used than in English to express different emotions and points of view. As a result there are rarely exact equivalents between the two languages.

◎/✚ 6.1 Noun and adjectival suffixes

In Italian, four main groups of suffixes are used with nouns or adjectives: **-ino/-etto, -uccio, -one** and **-accio**. The suffixes are usually added to the source word, minus the final vowel.

Not all nouns and adjectives can be used with suffixes and not all suffixes are used with a given word. (For example, **poverino, poveretto** and **poveraccio** are common, but **poveruccio** or **poverone** are not.)

The use of suffixes often depends on a native speaker's personal preference or origin, but the following are basic guidelines.

◎/✚ (a) *I diminutivi* – diminutives

-ino/a **-etto/a**	un bacino, un bacetto (bacio) *little kiss* un omino, un ometto (uomo) *tiny little/ wee man* un piedino *(piede) tootsie/footsie* un/a poverino/a, un/a poveretto/a (povero) *unfortunate/poor thing* una manina (mano) *tiny hand* un maschietto (maschio) *a baby (newborn) boy* un mesetto (mese) *a month or so* un vizietto (vizio) *slight bad habit, peccadillo* fare l'occhietto/l'occhiolino (occhio) *to wink* (lit. *to make a small eye*)	**-ino/-etto** convey smallness but also sympathy and may suggest something attractive. These suffixes are often used for baby talk, as euphemisms (e.g. **fare il bisognino** *to spend a penny*), or they can be a way of joking and avoiding offence. Note that **omino** is the diminutive of **uomo**, but the initial **-u** is omitted.
	bruttino/a (brutto) *not very good-looking* noiosetto/a (noioso) *a bit boring* piccolino/a, piccoletto/a (piccolo) *teeny-weeny, titchy, tiny* strettino/a (stretto) *narrow and pretty*	
	una borsetta; una borsettina (borsa) *handbag; tiny handbag* un libretto; un librettino (libro) *small book* (e.g. *cheque book, pamphlet*); *titchy, tiny book*	Sometimes a word can combine two suffixes, e.g. **-etto** and **-ino**.

✤ Other diminutive suffixes include:
-ello/a (cattivello *a bit naughty,* stupidello *a bit stupid,* un venticello *nice breeze*)
-ellino/a (un borsellino *tiny bag/purse,* un fiorellino *little flower*)
-icello/a (grandicello *quite big, grown up,* un ponticello *small bridge, footbridge*)
-olino/a (un gocciolino *a little drop,* magrolino *extremely thin, skinny*)
-otto and **-ottello** (bassotto *rather short/shortish,* grassottello *on the plump side*).

Note that **-otto** has various connotations and can also be used as a 'vezzeggiativo', an augmentative and a peggiorative (see examples below).

✤ (b) *I vezzeggiativi* – terms of endearment

There is no exact English equivalent.

| **-uccio/a** | un animaluccio (animale) *a sweet little animal*
un avvocatuccio (avvocato) *a useless/inept lawyer*
una boccuccia (bocca) *a sweet little mouth*
una cosuccia (cosa) *a trifle, an insignificant thing*
una femminuccia (femmina) *a baby (newborn) girl*
un lavoruccio (lavoro) *a petty little job* | **-uccio** can convey terms of endearment often used in children's stories. Words with this suffix express good will and affection – which is sometimes patronising. Consequently they can also have connotations of mediocrity or insignificance. |
| | calduccio (caldo) *nice and warm* (often a noun)
deboluccio/a (debole) *a bit on the weak/dim side* | |

Other 'vezzeggiativi' endings include:
-uzzo/a (un principuzzo *little prince*)
-acchiotto/a (un orsacchiotto *bear cub/teddy,* un lupacchiotto *wolf cub*)
-olo/a (un/una figliolo/a *dear boy/girl*)
-otto (un tigrotto *tiger cub,* un cucciolotto *a little puppy*).

◎/✤ (c) *Gli accrescitivi* – augmentatives

Augmentatives are mostly, but not always, nouns, even when derived from adjectives. Note that when derived from adjectives they can be masculine and feminine if they refer to people, but otherwise they are usually masculine even when the source noun is feminine.

| **-one/a** | un donnone (una donna) *a big, fat, strong woman*
un febbrone (una febbre) *a high temperature*
un grassone una grassona (grasso) *hugely fat man/woman*
un librone (un libro) *a large/important/difficult/overlong book*
un omone (un uomo) *a massive man*
un pancione (una pancia) *a hugh paunch/stomach*
un riccone/una riccona (ricco) *an immensely rich man/woman* | The **-one** ending intensifies the meaning of the source word rather than simply expressing largeness. It can express humorous exaggeration or admiration or it can have a derogatory meaning. |

✚ Other augmentative suffixes include:

-accione/a (un/una spendaccione/a *spendthrift*)

-acchione/a (un/una furbacchione/a *a crafty, sneaky devil*)

-occio (belloccio *handsome in an obvious way*, grassoccio/a *pretty fat, plump, chubby*)

-otto (un giovanotto *a strong young man, a bachelor*, un ragazzotto *a strapping young lad*).

◎/✚ (d) *I peggiorativi* – pejoratives

-accio/a	un libraccio (libro) *a horrible/awful/immoral book* un/una grassaccio/a (grasso) *a disgustingly fat person* un omaccio (uomo) *a horrible man* un/una poveraccio/a (povero) *an unfortunate wretch* un tempaccio (tempo) *terrible weather* fare la linguaccia (la lingua) *to stick out your tongue*	These are widely used to convey unpleasantness and have a pejorative meaning.

✚ Other peggiorative suffixes include:

-astro/a (dolciastro *sickly, cloying*, un poetastro *bad poet*).

Colour is often described with the suffixes **-astro/a**, **-ognolo/a** or **-iccio/a**, usually in slightly pejorative terms: verdognolo, verdiccio (*greenish*), giallastro, giallognolo, gialliccio (*yellowish*), etc.

-azzo/a (un amorazzo *a sordid affair*, un codazzo *a tail of hangers-on*)

-otto/a – this can be a noun or an adjective (un/una sempliciotto/a *a simpleton, dimwit; simple-minded*).

◎/✚ Esercizi

1 Complete the sentences below by substituting the words in italics for a single word, including a suffix each time.

(a) Mio padre è alto e (*abbastanza grasso*) ed è nato in un (*piccolo paese*) di montagna.

(b) Ho conosciuto Daniele (*circa un mese*) fa. È (*una persona molto simpatica*) molto allegro.

(c) Mia figlia va male in francese. È veramente (*piuttosto debole*).

(d) Mirella si veste malissimo con quel (*brutto cappello*) sformato e quelle (*brutte scarpe*) sporche.

(e) Carlo è noioso. Fa sempre dei (*lunghi discorsi*) pieni di (*parole complicate*) incomprensibili.

✚ **2** Choose the appropriate word, according to the definitions given. If in doubt, use a dictionary.

(a) **Difetto:** difettuccio, difettaccio.

Which word do you use if you're tolerant about someone's faults?

(b) **Problema:** problemino, problemaccio, problemone.

If you want to make light of the problem, which word do you use?

(c) **Lavoro:** lavoretto, lavoraccio, lavoruccio, lavorone.

If you have had a terrible time, how would you describe the work?

(d) **Stupido:** stupidello, stupidino, stupidone.

If you don't want to cause offence, which word/s do you use?

(e) **Figura:** Che figuraccia ha fatto! Ha fatto un figurone. Sembra un figurino.

Which phrase would you use to say someone really made a marvellous impression? What do the others mean?

◎/✚ (e) Independent but related meanings

Many nouns and adjectives with suffixes have acquired an independent but related meaning. Here are a few.

Suffix	Derived word	Source word
-ino/a	una banchina *platform, quay*	una banca *bench*
	un finestrino *car/train window*	una finestra *window*
	un girino *tadpole*	un giro *walk, tour*
	un padrino *godfather*	un padre *a father*
	carino *sweet*	caro *dear*
	bellino *pretty*	bello *beautiful*
-ello/a, -etto/a	una bancarella *stall*	una banca *bench*
	una finestrella *computer window*	una finestra *window*
	un fioretto *fencing foil, buttonhole flower*	un fiore *flower*
	una manetta *handle, lever*	una mano *hand*
	il rossetto *lipstick*	rosso *red*
-olo/a, -olino/a	un tovagliolo/tovagliolino *napkin*	una tovaglia *tablecoth*
-uccio/a	una cannuccia *straw*	una canna *reed*
-uzzo/a	una viuzza *alley*	una via *road, street*
-one/a	un bancone *(bar/shop) counter*	un banco *desk*
	un cannone *canon*	una canna *reed*
	un copione *script*	una copia *copy*
	una lumacone *slug*	una lumaca *snail*
	un padrone *boss, master*	un padre *father*
	un pallone *football*	una palla *ball*
	un portone *main/front door*	una porta *door*
-accio/a	un'erbaccia *weed*	erba *grass*
	una parolaccia *swearword*	una parola *word*
-astro/a	un figliastro *stepchild/son*	un figlio *child, son*

✚ Esercizi

3 The English equivalents of the words in the middle column are all mixed up. Match them up, taking the word of origin into consideration and using a bit of guesswork and imagination. If all else fails, use a dictionary.

Source word			Derived word		English equivalent
barba	*(beard)*	A	barbone	1	*briefcase/folder*
bagno	*(bath)*	B	bagnino	2	*test tube*
busta	*(envelope)*	C	bustina	3	*bribe*
busta	*(envelope)*	D	bustarella	4	*(a) tramp (b) poodle*
carta	*(paper)*	E	cartella	5	*crisp*
padre	*(father)*	F	padrone	6	*lifeguard*
padre	*(father)*	G	padrino	7	*audition*
patata	*(potato)*	H	patatina	8	*saucer*
prova	*(test, experiment)*	I	provino	9	*godfather*
prova	*(test, experiment)*	J	provetta	10	*felt tip*
piatto	*(plate)*	K	piattino	11	*small packet, e.g. of sugar*
penna	*(pen)*	L	pennarello	12	*paintbrush*
penna	*(pen)*	M	pennello	13	*owner*

4 Odd ones out: answer the questions and then, using a dictionary if needed, find the English for the other nouns.

    (a) Which two of these are people?

        cappellano • cappellino • capellone • cappelluccio

    (b) Which one of these can you draw with?

        pastella • pastello • pasticcio • pastina

    (c) Which two of the following can you read?

        cartaccia • cartello • cartina • cartone

    (d) Which two of these are used for selling?

        bancarella • banchina • banchetto • bancone

 Attenti! Watch out for false suffixes. Many Italian nouns have endings that are identical to suffix endings such as **-ino, -ello** or **-one,** but which bear no relation to the apparent source word. Always check meanings in a dictionary. Here are a few.

lampo *flash*	lampone *raspberry*	mulo *mule*	mulino *mill*
matto *mad*	mattino *morning*	rapa *turnip*	rapina *armed robbery*
matto *mad*	mattone *brick*	tacco *heel*	tacchino *turkey*
monte *mountain*	montone *ram, mutton*	vite *vine*	vitello *calf, veal*

◎ Esercizio

5 True or false? Say if each statement below is true (T) or false (F). If false, give the meaning of the word.

    (a) Un mattone è una persona molto matta.   **(d)** Il mulino è un piccolo mulo.

    (b) Un postino è un piccolo posto.   **(e)** Un bagnino è un piccolo bagno.

    (c) Un posticino è un bel posto che ti piace.   **(f)** Un rubinetto è un piccolo rubino (*ruby*).

◎ 6.2 Adverbial suffixes

Adverbial suffixes are invariable. They are mainly used with **poco, tardi, male** and **bene.** With the exception of **benino** and **benone,** the choice of suffix depends largely on the personal preference of the speaker, as they are so close in meaning.

bene	benino *quite well* benone *pretty/extremely well*
male	malino, maluccio *not too well*
tardi	tardino tardetto tarduccio *lateish*
poco	pochetto pochettino pochino *a little/tiny bit*

Note that **un fannullone/una fannullona** *a good for nothing,* incorporates the augmentative of **nulla** and the verb **fa** from the phrase **fa nulla** *he/she does nothing.*

◎ Esercizio

1 Rewrite the Italian in italics, using an adverbial suffix.

    (a) Non c'è posto qui. – Ti puoi spostare (*solo un po'*)?

    (b) È andato bene ieri? – Sì, è andato (*abbastanza bene*), credo.

    (c) Aspettiamo mezz'ora, è ancora (*un po' presto*) per partire.

    (d) Come stai adesso? – (*Non molto bene*), purtroppo.

✚ 6.3 Verb suffixes

Some verbal suffixes convey the idea of an incomplete, desultory or intermittent action. They may also suggest a repeated but aimless action and have a pejorative meaning. There are no rules for identifying which suffix conveys which meaning. Check in a dictionary if necessary.

-acchiare **-icchiare** **-ucchiare**	ridacchiare *to snigger* (ridere) scribacchiare *to scribble, write rubbish* (scrivere) dormicchiare *doze fitfully* (dormire) mordicchiare *to nibble* (mordere) leggiucchiare *to flick through, read aimlessly* (leggere) mangiucchiare *to nibble, snack on* (mangiare)
-erellare	canterellare *to hum, sing softly* (cantare) giocherellare *to pass time playing, to fiddle/toy with sth.* (giocare) salterellare *to jump/skip up and down* (saltare) trotterellare *to toddle, trot along* (trottare)
-ettare	fischiettare *to whistle quietly* (fischiare) picchiettare *to tap, drum* (e.g. fingers on table), *to patter* (e.g. rain, hail), *to spatter/splatter* (picchiare)
-igginare	piovvigginare *to drizzle, to 'spit'* (piovere)
-onzolare	gironzolare *to stroll/wander/dawdle about, to lurk* (girare)
-ottare	parlottare *to talk softly, murmur* (often conspiratorial) (parlare)

Eserczi

✚ **1** Read part of this blog written by an anxious pet owner wanting advice about his puppy, then answer the questions.

Buonasera a tutti. – Dopo i primi dubbi arrivano le prime ansie. Ieri sera il mio cagnolino (3 mesi), al risveglio del sonno* ha iniziato a guaire* e non appoggiava per nulla la gamba posteriore destra per terra. Inizialmente ho pensato che gli si fosse addormentata* ma stamattina il piccolo zoppicava* ancora ed era mogio mogio*.

L'ho portato dal veterinario che dopo una radiografia ha escluso qualsiasi rottura* dicendo che potrebbe essersi slogato la caviglia* (cioè la parte che a noi uomini corrisponde alla caviglia). Però, oltre a questo non mi ha detto di fare nulla di particolare.

Ora il cagnolino resta mogio mogio anche perché non appena prova* a giocherellare si vede che prova dolore alla zampetta.

C'è qualcuno a cui è capitato qualcosa del genere*? Si riprenderà presto e tornerà ad essere* il giocherellone che corre in giro per casa mordicchiando a destra e a sinistra?

Grazie per qualsiasi consiglio.

> • al risveglio del sonno *when he woke up* • guaire *to whine* • gli si fosse addormentata *it (his leg) had gone to sleep* • zoppicava *was limping* • mogio mogio *extremely subdued* • ha escluso qualsiasi rottura *he ruled out any break* • potrebbe essersi slogato la caviglia *he could have sprained his leg* • non appena prova *as soon as he tries* • cui è capitato qualcosa del genere *to whom something similar has happened* • tornerà ad essere *will he go back to being*

(a) Identify the three nouns and two verbs with suffixes and find an English version for each.

(b) The puppy owner loves his little dog. How might he describe its nose (**naso**) and eyes (**occhi**)? Use the English as a guide and fill in the gaps below.

Ha un — adorabile e degli — dolcissimi.   *He has an adorable little nose and big soft eyes.*

7 Personal pronouns

A pronoun is a word which stands in place of nouns or noun phrases. Personal pronouns (**i pronomi personali**) are used to substitute the names of people or things. The main categories are: subject, object (direct and indirect), disjunctive, and reflexive. In English personal pronouns include *I, me, you, he, him, she, her, it, we, us, they, them*. There are fewer separate forms than in Italian.

◎/+ 7.1 Subject pronouns

Subject pronouns refer to the subject of a sentence.

(a) Main subject pronouns: forms

Person	Singular		Plural	
1st	**io**	*I*	**noi**	*we*
2nd	**tu** **lei**	*you* (informal) *you* (formal)	**voi** **Loro**	*you* (formal and informal) *you* (very formal)
3rd	**lui, lei**	*he, she*	**loro**	*they*

Different forms for 'you'

- **tu** is the singular familiar *you* used to address a child, a family member, a friend – or an animal.
- **lei** is the singular formal *you*. It is sometimes spelt with a capital *L* to distinguish it from **lei** meaning *she*.
- **voi** is the familiar plural *you* (i.e. the plural of **tu**). It is now also nearly always used for the formal plaral *you*, to speak to people you would address individually as **Lei**.
- **loro** is the formal plural *you* (i.e. the plural of **lei**), sometimes spelt with a capital *L* to distinguish it from **loro**, *they*. However, **loro** is more formal than its singular counterpart, **Lei,** and is not commonly used as the plural formal *you* in spoken Italian. **Voi** is used instead.

Expressing 'it'

- In informal Italian no pronoun is necessary: the context makes the meaning clear:
  Chi è? *Who is it?*
  Non è necessario *It is not necessary*.
  Il gattino è giovane, ha solo due mesi. *The kitten is young, it is only two months old.*
- In more formal contexts the pronouns **esso** and **essa** are used. See p. 105.

(b) Main subject pronouns: uses

In Italian subject pronouns are less frequently used than in English. In most cases there is no need for them, as the form of the verb makes the subject clear:

Quando pago, guardo bene il conto *When I pay, I look at the bill carefully.*

Subject pronouns are used, however, in the following cases.

To stress the subject	Pago **io** questa volta *I'll pay this time.* È un bel vestito, l'hai fatto **tu**? *It's a lovely dress. Did you make it?*	To stress the subject, the pronoun usually follows the verb.
To contrast subjects	**Lui** lavora tanto ma **lei** non fa mai niente *He works so much but she never does anything* L'hai fatto **tu**? – Io no, l'ha fatto **lui** *Did you do it? – I didn't, he did*	The pronoun often follows the verb.
To clarify the subject	Credi che **io/lui/lei** abbia dimenticato? *Do you think I have forgotten?/he/she has forgotten?* Vuoi fare **tu** la spesa o preferisci che la faccia **io/lui/lei**? *Do you want to shop or would you rather I/he/she did?*	If the form of the verb does not make the subject obvious (as in the identical singular forms of some subjunctives), the subject pronoun is needed.
With **anche, neanche, nemmeno, neppure**	Vieni anche **tu**? – Certo che vengo anch'**io** *Are you coming too? – Of course I'm coming too* Non viene neanche **lui** *He's not coming either*	These emphatic words require a subject pronoun after them.

 Attenti! Italian subject pronoun, English disjunctive

In the following cases the English equivalent of the Italian subject pronoun is usually a disjunctive pronoun.

No verb	Chi l'ha fatto? – **Io**. *Who did it? – Me (I did)* Chi ha fame? – **Noi**. *Who is hungry? – Us (We are)* Come sta? – Bene, e **Lei**? *How are you? – Fine and (what about) you?* Non ho voglia di studiare. – Neanch'**io** *I don't feel like studying. – Me neither/Neither do I* Il colloquio sulla diversità culturale ha come tema 'Non **loro** e **noi** ma **tu** e **io**' *The theme of the conference on cultural diversity is 'Not them and us but you and me'*	When there is no verb to indicate the subject, a personal pronoun is essential in Italian. In English, however, disjunctive ('stressed') pronouns are often preferred, e.g. *me* instead of *I*, *us* instead of *we*, and *them* instead of *they*.
Me and …	**Io** e mio fratello arriviamo fra un'ora *Me and my brother/My brother and I are arriving in an hour* **Tu, io,** e Marinella dobbiamo partire subito *You, me and Marinella have to leave at once/You, Mariella and I have to leave at once*	The Italian subject pronoun is always used with a noun phrase or other pronoun. In English, disjunctive pronouns are mostly preferred to the subject pronoun.
It's me/you/ him/her/us/ them	Chi è? – Sono **io** *Who is it? – It is me* (lit. *I*) Sono stati **loro** a chiamare la polizia? – No, siamo stati **noi**. *Was it them who called the police? – No, it was us*	In Italian, subject pronouns are used after the verb for emphasis, but in English, disjunctive (stressed) pronouns are used.

Extra emphasis can be given to the subject by placingi **stesso/a/i/e** after the subject pronoun.

I myself, etc. ✛	È vero, l'hai detto **tu stesso/a** *It's true, you said so yourself* Non so se i Bianchi hanno prenotato, **loro stessi** non si ricordano *I don't know if the Bianchis have booked, they can't remember themselves*	**Stesso/a** follows the relevant subject pronoun. It agrees with the subject and can go before or after the verb.

◎/✛ Esercizi

1 **Tu**, **Lei** or **voi**? Which **you** is appropriate? Choose the correct pronoun to complete each sentence.

    (a) Come sta, signore? – Bene, e —?   **(c)** Noi stiamo bene, e — due, come state?

    (b) Come stai, Aldo? – Non c'è male, e — ?

2 Stress, contrast and contradict. Give the Italian equivalent of the English using appropriate pronouns.

    (a) Javier e Fiona di dove sono? – (*He*) è spagnolo e (*she*) è scozzese.

    (b) Venite anche (*you*)? – No, (*we*) non veniamo, viene solo Marco.

    (c) Che bella lampada! L'hai comprata (*you*), Mariella? – Sì, l'ho comprata (*I*).

    (d) È un bel giardino, lo cura (*you*), signora o suo marito? – Lo curiamo (*us*) due.

✛   **(e)** Sei stato (*you*) a chiamare ieri? – No, (*not me*), forse sono stati (*them*).

3 Clarify matters. Give the Italian equivalent of the English.

    (a) Mina e Elena, siete voi? – *No, it's us, Marta and Ida.*

    (b) Sei tu, Dario? – *No, it's me, Giuseppe.*

    (c) Chi è che vuole una caramella? – *Not me/I don't.*

    (d) Noi andiamo al cinema, *what about you two*?

    (e) Chi è che viene domani? – *Me and my sister.*

    (f) Chi è che fa quel rumore? Sei tu? – *No, it's them, the neighbours.*

✛ (c) Additional subject pronouns: forms and uses

These pronouns are almost exclusively used in written Italian. It is important to be able to recognise them.

Masculine: **egli** *he* **esso** *it* **essi** *they*	Lo scrittore Alberto Moravia morì a ottantadue anni, a Roma. **Egli** fu, per oltre sessant'anni, testimone e interprete del nostro secolo *The writer Alberto Moravia died at 82, in Rome. For over sixty years he witnessed and interpreted (the events of) our century*	**Egli** is very formal and only refers to people. **Esso** refers to animals or things and rarely to people. **Essi** refers to people, animals or things.
Feminine: **ella** *she* **essa** *it* **esse** *they*	La Costituzione Americana fu approvata nel 1787. **Essa** fu il risultato di un lungo processo politico. *The American Constitution was approved in 1787. It was the result of a long political process*	**Ella** is very formal and rare. **Essa** and **esse** refer to people, animals or things.

The impersonal *si*

Si is used as a subject with the 3rd person singular forms of the verb.

Si *One, you,* *we, they,* *people*	In Italia non **si** beve il cappuccino dopo mangiato *In Italy you don't drink cappuccino after a meal* Qui **si** parla italiano *Italian is spoken here/We speak Italian here*	**Si** expresses an impersonal subject which has various English equivalents, including a passive one.

For more on **si**, see p. 127, Indefinites, p. 166 and Chapter 25, pp. 325 and 327–8.

◎ 7.2 Reflexive and reciprocal pronouns

Reflexive pronouns are used with certain verbs mainly to indicate an action that a person does to himself/herself, e.g. **lavarsi** *to wash oneself*. However, they are also used with some verbs which do not express a reflexive action, e.g. **pentirsi** *to be sorry, to regret*.

The three reciprocal pronouns are plural only, because they denote reciprocal actions, i.e. actions people do to each other. They are used with verbs that may not normally be reflexive, e.g. **salutarsi** *to greet each other, to say hello*.

(a) Reflexive and reciprocal pronouns: forms

Person	Singular		Plural	
1st	**mi**	*myself*	**ci**	*ourselves; each other* (reciprocal)
2nd	**ti** **si**	*yourself* (informal) *yourself* (formal)	**vi**	*yourselves* (formal and informal); *each other* (reciprocal)
3rd	**si**	*himself/herself/itself/oneself*	**si**	*themselves; each other* (reciprocal)

(b) Reflexive pronouns: uses

These cannot be omitted in Italian. They mostly precede the verb, except the infinitive, but see also pp. 119–21.

To indicate a reflexive action	**Mi** diverto a scuola *I enjoy myself at school* Maurizio **si** è fatto male *Maurizio hurt himself* Non **ti** vergogni? *Aren't you ashamed (of yourself)?*	A reflexive action 'reflects' back on the subject and is something you do to yourself.
To express non-reflexive meaning	**Vi** comportate male *You are behaving badly* **Si** laureano a giugno *They are graduating in June* **Ci** siamo pentiti sul serio *We were really sorry*	Some verbs have no obvious reflexive meaning in English but reflexive pronouns are essential.
To express possession	**Ti** lavi i capelli? *Are you washing your hair?* **Mi** sono rotto la gamba *I broke my leg* **Si** è messo il cappotto *He put on his coat*	Reflexive pronouns may be used in place of possessives, usually with reference to the body and clothes.

Reflexive pronouns are used in addition to subject pronouns for clarification, contrast and emphasis.

Clarification and contrast	**Io mi** chiamo Angela ma **lei si** chiama Anita *I'm called Angela but she is called Anita* **Noi ci** siamo fermati al semaforo ma loro no *We stopped at the lights but they didn't*	The subject pronoun is essential in front of the reflexive pronoun.
Emphatic use: *I myself, you yourself*, etc. ✚	So che le cose vanno male per loro, ma **mi trovo io stesso/a** in difficoltà *I know that things are going badly for them, but I am in trouble myself* Ada ci dice di alzarci presto, ma **lei stessa si** alza tardi! *Ada tells us to get up early, but she gets up late herself!*	Emphasis is made by using **io/ tu/lui/lei stesso/a, noi/voi/ loro stessi/e** in addition to the reflexive pronouns.

For the agreement of reflexive pronouns and past participles, see p. 132.
For more on reflexives, see Chapter 25, pp. 313–5.

◎/✚ Esercizi

1 Complete the sentences using the appropriate pronoun and verb forms.

(a) Di solito (io − truccarsi) poco.

(b) (Voi − lamentarsi) troppo, ragazzi!

(c) Non (noi − laccarsi) mai le unghie.

(d) (Lui − non ricordarsi) dell'indirizzo.

(e) Perché non (tu − togliersi) la giacca?

(f) (Loro − trattenersi) a Roma per due giorni.

2 Use the correct reflexive verbs below to complete the sentences with the appropriate pronoun and verb forms.

(a) Mio nonno *(falls asleep)* sempre dopo pranzo. (addormentarsi)

(b) I miei figli *(wash themselves and comb their hair)* sempre in fretta. (lavarsi, pettinarsi)

(c) Normalmente io e mia moglie *(wake up)* alle sette e *(we get up)* subito. (svegliarsi, alzarsi)

✚ **3** Complete the sentences by giving the Italian equivalent of the following.

(a) *(I get up early)* ma lui di solito rimane a letto.

(b) *(She washes her hair)* ogni mattina, ma io no.

(c) *(No, he is graduating)* a giugno, ma *(I am graduating)* l'anno prossimo.

(c) Reciprocal pronouns: uses

These are always plural and are identical in form to the plural reflexives, **ci, vi** and **si**. (See table on p. 106.)

Reciprocal use	**Vi** vedete spesso? *Do you see each other often?* **Ci** sentiamo *We'll be in touch (with each other)* **S'**incontrano spesso *They often meet (each other)*	**Ci, vi** and **si** can be used reciprocally to express what people do to each other. **Si** may elide to **s'** in front of **i**.

◎/✚ Esercizi

4 Talk about what people do to each other, using the verbs given.

(a) In Italia quando le persone (*incontrarsi*), (*salutarsi*) e (*darsi*) la mano.

(b) Noi (*vedersi*) raramente ma (*sentirsi*) spesso.

(c) Oggi la gente (*scriversi*) poco. Preferisce (*scambiarsi*) delle e-mail.

✚ **5** Give the English equivalent of the following and say whether the pronoun is used to denote a reflexive or a reciprocal action.

(a) Non siamo in ufficio, ci troviamo di fronte al bar.

(b) A domani, allora; ci troviamo di fronte al bar.

(c) Ciao, ci sentiamo domani.

(d) Sì, ci sentiamo bene tutti e due.

(e) Come si chiamano i suoi nipotini?

(f) Mariella e Paola si chiamano spesso.

◎/✚ 7.3 Direct and indirect object pronouns

These pronouns refer to the object of a sentence. Direct object pronouns (DO) replace direct noun or noun phrase objects. Indirect object pronouns (IDO) replace indirect noun or noun phrase objects. To understand which object pronoun to use, it is necessary to be able to identify the nouns they replace.

(a) Identifying direct and indirect objects

This can seem problematic because in English direct and indirect objects often look identical.

Direct object	I saw **Mario** I saw **him** I helped **Maria** I helped **her** I hate **ice cream** I hate **it**	A DO is a person, animal or thing directly affected by, or involved in, the action of the verb. It can sometimes be identified by asking, *Who?* or *What?*
Indirect object	I sent **Mario** a message I sent **him** a message I bought **Maria** a book I bought **her** a book	An IDO is a person, animal, institution and occasionally a thing less directly involved in the action of the verb than a DO. It may sometimes be identified by asking, *To whom/ what? For whom/what?*
	I told **Mario** (to come) I told **him** I asked **Maria** (a question) I asked **her**	IDO s are mostly used with verbs which also take a DO, whether this is explicitly expressed or not. Of the two objects the IDO is the one which is more distant from the action of the verb. Typical double object verbs are *to give/ say sth. to sb., to buy/make sth. for sb.*

In Italian it is simple to distinguish between direct and indirect <u>noun</u> objects because the indirect object is nearly always preceded by the prepositions **a** or **per**.

Ho dato un libro <u>a Mario</u> *I gave Mario a book* **or** *I gave a book to Mario*

Ho comprato dei fiori <u>per Maria</u> *I bought Maria some flowers* **or** *I bought some flowers for Maria*

However, Italian direct and indirect <u>pronoun</u> objects have forms of their own, which must be learned. See next section.

◎ Esercizio

1 Look at the following sentences. First identify the direct objects (DO) and then the indirect objects (IDO). The number of objects in all is shown in brackets.

(a) *He bought some roses and gave them to his wife. (3)*

(b) *He bought her some roses. (2)*

(c) *Did you ask Francesca to leave? (1)*

(d) *Did you ask her? (1)*

(b) Direct and indirect object pronouns: forms

In Italian many direct and indirect object pronouns are identical. You can see which ones differ in the table below.

Person	Singular		Plural	
	Direct object	**Indirect object**	**Direct object**	**Indirect object**
1st	**mi** *me*	**mi** *(to) me*	**ci** *us*	**ci** *(to) us*
2nd	**ti** *you* (informal) **La/la** *you* (formal)	**ti** *(to) you* **Le/le** *(to) you* (formal)	**vi** *you* (informal and formal)	**vi** *(to) you* (informal and formal)
3rd	**lo** *him/it* **la** *her/it*	**gli** *(to) him/it* **le** *(to) her/it*	**li** *them* (m./m. & f.) **le** *them* (f.)	**gli** *(to) them* (m. & f.) **loro** *(to) them* (m. & f.)

Different forms for 'you' and 'them'

- **la** *you* (DO) and **le** *(to) you* (IDO) are the formal singular forms of address for a man as well as a woman. They are sometimes spelt with a capital letter to distinguish them from the other meanings, *her/to her.*
- **vi** is preferred for both the formal and the informal plural *you*. **Loro** is rarely used as the formal plural *you*.
- **gli** is often used to mean *to them* as well as *to him,* in which case it refers to both men and women. It is used much more than **loro** to mean *to them*, especially in speech.
- **loro** is formal or literary and follows the verb: **Diede loro un libro** *He gave (to) them a book.*

 Attenti! Both **la** and **le** each have three meanings:

- Feminine singular and plural DO pronuns, *it* and *them*.

la	Vedi la casa? Sì **la** vedo	le	Vedi le case? Sì **le** vedo
it	*[...] Yes, I can see it*	*them*	*[...] Yes, I can see them*

- Feminine singular IDO pronouns, *her* and *(to/for) her*.

la	Inviterai Maria? Sì, **la** inviterò	le	Hai scritto a Maria? Sì **le** ho scritto
her	*[...] Yes, I'll invite her*	*to her*	*[...] Yes, I wrote to **her***

- Feminine singular IDO pronouns used for *you* and *to you* in formal address.

la	Scusi, Signora, **la/La** disturbo?	le	Signora Bellini, **le/Le** presento mio marito
you	*Excuse me Signora, am I interrupting?*	*to you*	*Signora Bellini, let me introduce my husband*

(c) Direct object pronouns: uses

Note that the pronouns often precede the verb, unlike English. See the section on position, pp. 119–21.

Replacing DO nouns or noun phrases	La macchina è sporca, **la** devo lavare *The car is dirty, I must wash it* Gli amici di Gianni sono simpatici, **li** inviterò *Gianni's friends are nice, I'll invite them*	The pronouns must agree with the nouns or noun phrases they replace.
lo to replace a whole phrase or sentence	Hai detto che il film era divertente, in realtà non **lo** è *You said the film was amusing, but it isn't really* Quando partono? – Chi **lo** sa? *When are they leaving? – Who knows (it)?* È innamorata di Mario, **l**'ho sempre detto *She's in love with Mario, I've always said so (it)*	The DO pronoun **lo/l'** is used to replace a whole phrase or sentence when these refer to intangible things, e.g. ideas or opinions. It is rarely expressed in English. See also p. 125.
li to refer to m. and f. nouns	Comprerò il pane e il burro. **Li** comprerò *I'll buy the bread and the butter. I'll buy them* **And:** Comprerò il vino e la carne. **Li** comprerò *I'll buy the wine and the meat. I'll buy them*	**Li** *them* is used to refer to masculine nouns only, as well as to masculine and feminine together.
l' before a vowel or **h-**	**L'**ammiri molto? *Do you admire him/her a lot?* **L'**ho/**L'**abbiamo fatto subito *I/We did it at once* **But:** Era triste, vero? Sì, **lo** era *He was sad wasn't he? Yes, he was* **But:** **Li/Le** hai visti/e? *Did you see them?*	**Lo** and **la** can change to **l'** before a vowel or **h-** but this is optional. They are not shortened in front of **è/ero/eri era**, etc. The plural DO pronouns **li** and **le** are never shortened.

The following uses of DO pronouns are also common and important.

Colloquial use: in addition to a DO noun	Franco **l'**ho già visto, ma Enrico no *I've already seen Franco, but not Enrico* (lit. *Franco, I've already seen him*) I pantaloni, quanto **li** hai pagati? *How much did you pay for the trousers?* (lit. *The trousers, how much did you pay for them?*)	The use of both the pronoun and the noun it replaces is common and colloquial. There is no exact English equivalent. See also Chapter 27, pp. 343–4.
lo, **la**, **li** and **le** with **avere**	Hai la piantina? – Sì, **ce l'**ho *Have you got the map? – Yes, I've got it* Avete i passaporti? – Sì, **ce li** abbiamo *Have you got the passports?– Yes, we've got them*	In front of **avere**, **lo**, **la**, **li**, **and le** are preceded by **ce**. This is for pronunciation, as it is hard to say **lo ho**, **la hai**, etc.

Note that the past participles of verbs with the auxiliary **avere** agree with the preceding DO pronouns **lo**, **la**, **li**, **le**. For further details, see also p. 130.

◎ Esercizi

2 Replace the underlined nouns and phrases with the correct pronoun.

(a) I pantaloni bianchi sono bellissimi, perché non … compri?

(b) Quella macchina costa poco, ho intenzione di comprar ….

(c) Conosce mio figlio? – No, non … conosco.

(d) Conoscete le mie cugine? – Certo, … conosciamo da molto tempo.

3 Insert the pronoun corresponding to the English one given.

(a) Angelo, … posso aiutare? (*you*)

(b) Arriveder …, signore, … richiamerò più tardi. (*you* – formal)

(c) Ragazzi, … ringrazio per la bella serata. (*you* – plural)

(d) … accompagno io, Signora Rossi. (*you* – formal)

4 Replace the underlined phrases with one or two pronouns.

(a) Sai dov'è andato? – No, non … so.

(b) Il suo matrimonio andrà male, … ho detto tante volte.

(c) Tu dici che sono tutti disonesti? – Certo, è ovvio che … sono!

(d) Hai la chiave? – Sì … ho.

(e) I clienti hanno i documenti? – Sì, … hanno.

◎/✚ (d) Direct object verbs

The key to fully understanding the use of direct object pronouns lies in understanding the structure of the verbs they are used with.

Verbs with no preposition	Chiamerai **il tassì/Mario**? – Sì, **lo** chiamerò stasera *Will you call the taxi/ Mario? – Yes, I'll call it/him tonight* Vedrai **la mostra/l'amica di Paolo**? – Sì, **la** vedrò *Will you see the exhibition/ Paolo's friend? – Yes, I'll see it/her*	Verbs typically used with direct objects are those without prepositions, e.g. **chiamare qlco./qlcu.** *to call sth/sb.* or **vedere qlco./qlcu.** *to see sth/sb.*

 Attenti! Do not let the English mislead you: some common English verbs take a preposition where the Italian equivalent requires none. The following verbs, therefore, require direct objects in Italian.

English preposition, Italian no preposition	Ascolti spesso la radio? **La** ascolti spesso? *Do you often listen to the radio? Do you often listen to it?* Ho chiesto il conto. **L'**ho chiesto *I have asked for the bill. I have asked for it*	**ascoltare qlcu./qlco.** is *to listen to sb./sth.;* **chiedere qlco.** is *to ask for sth.;* Other similar verbs include **aspettare qlcu./qlco.** *to wait for sb./ sth.;* **guardare qlco./qlcu.** *to look at sb./sth.;* **pagare qlco./qlcu.** *to pay for sth./to pay sb.* (see below).
✚ **pagare**	Hai pagato i biglietti? **Li** hai pagati? *Did you pay for the tickets? Did you pay for them?* Hai visto Dino? – **Lo** hai pagato? *Did you see Dino? Did you pay him? **But:*** **Gli** ho pagato un milione *I paid him a million.* **Le** ho pagato il caffè *I paid for her coffee*	**Pagare** (see above) takes a DO whether it means *to pay for sth.* or *to pay sb..* However, when it has two objects – a person and a thing – an IDO is used for the person and a DO for the sum or thing paid for. See also Chapter 25, p. 323.

✦ Esercizio

5 Give the Italian equivalent of the English.

    (a) Ascolti spesso la radio? – *Yes, I often listen to it.*

    (b) Hai chiesto il conto? – *Yes, I've asked for it.*

    (c) Da quanto tempo aspetti il treno? – *I have been waiting for it for an hour.*

    (d) Quelle scarpe, quanto le hai pagate? – *I paid 150 euros for them.*

(e) Indirect object pronouns: uses

IDO pronouns mostly follow the same rules of position as DO pronouns. See pp. 119–21.

Replacing IDO nouns or noun phrases	Ha prestato una penna a Stefano. **Gli** ha prestato una penna *He lent Stefano a pen. He lent him a pen* Devi rispondere alle gemelle. **Gli** devi rispondere/Devi rispondere **loro** *You must answer the twins. You must answer them* A mia cugina Mirella piace la Francia. **Le** piace la Francia *My cousin Mirella likes France. She likes France*	IDO pronouns replace nouns or noun phrases which function as the indirect object. These are often introduced by **a**. See also p. 113, Indirect Object verbs. Note that to express *to them*, **gli** is more commonly used than **loro**.
Spelling	**Le** ho spiegato la situazione *I explained the situation to her* **Gli** impediranno di venire *They will prevent him from coming*	Unlike some DO pronouns, IDO pronouns are never shortened in front of **h-** or vowels.
Colloquial use: in addition to an IDO noun	**A Giovanni** non **gli** ho detto niente *I haven't told Giovanni a thing* **A Susi** non **le** piace la carne *Susie doesn't like meat*	The use of both the IDO pronoun and the noun it refers to is a common colloquial emphatic use with no exact English equivalent. See also Chapter 27, p. 344.
Instead of the English possessive	**Ti** ho stirato **la** camicia *I've ironed your shirt (for you)* **Le** hanno aggiustato **i** freni *They fixed her brakes (for her)* **Mi** ha rotto **il** vaso *He broke my vase* **Le** hanno distrutto **il** giardino *They destroyed her garden*	The IDO is used often used in conjunction with the definite article. See also Possessives, p. 139.

Other verbs of the type **rompere** and **distruggere** above include:
bruciare *to burn someone's ...*   macchiare *to stain someone's ...*   rovinare *to ruin someone's ...*
rubare *to steal someone's ...*   strappare *to tear/snatch someone's ...* sporcare *to dirty someone's ...*
togliere *to remove someone's ...*

◎ Esercizi

6 Replace the underlined nouns and phrases with the correct pronoun.

    (a) Ho prestato 50 euro <u>a Riccardo</u>. Ieri — ho prestato 50 euro.

    (b) Devi restituire i soldi <u>a Rina</u>. — devi restituire i soldi domani.

    (c) Anna deve 100 euro <u>a suo fratello</u>. Purtroppo — deve 100 euro.

    (d) Lucio dovrà pagare 2,000 euro <u>alla moglie</u>. È vero, – dovrà pagare 2,000 euro.

7 Insert the correct word for *you*.

(a) Signore, — piace il nuovo modello?

(b) Signora, — posso dare una mano?

(c) Ragazzi, — devo chiedere aiuto.

(d) Carlo, — presento mio marito.

(e) Signori, — posso offrire da bere?

8 Helping hand. Complete the sentences using the correct pronoun. Use the English as a guide.

(a) — puoi aggiustare i freni? *Can you fix my brakes (for me)?*

(b) — potresti riparare la bicicletta? *Could you mend her bicycle (for her)?*

(c) — può cambiare 1,000 euro? *Can you change 1,000 euros for us?*

9 Disaster. Complete the sentences using the Italian equivalent of the English pronoun given.

(a) Mio nipote — ha rotto l'orologio. (*my*)

(b) Giulio è rimasto male, la cameriera — ha macchiato la camicia. (*his*)

(c) Maria — ha bruciato la caffetieria. (*their*)

10 Give the Italian equivalent of the English.

(a) *I asked him to buy the bread.*

(b) *Pino, did you tell them (the boys) to come at ten o'clock?*

(c) *Dario, you must answer them (the girls) immediately.*

(f) Indirect object verbs

The key to fully understanding the use of indirect object pronouns lies in understanding the structure of the verbs they are used with. With few exceptions (e.g. **telefonare a**) indirect objects are used with double object verbs, i.e. verbs which can have both a person and a thing as objects, e.g. **dire qlco. a qlcu.** *to say sth. to sb.*, **comprare qlco. per qlcu.** *to buy sth. for sb.* These verbs divide into three main groups, with the following functions.

Expressing *to*, or *to whom* the action is done	Darai il libro **a Gina**? – Sì, **le** darò il libro *Yes, I'll give her the book* Scriverai una lettera **a Pino**? – Sì, **gli** scriverò una lettera *Yes, I'll write him a letter*	Many verbs take **a** before a person, and this is the indirect object. e.g. **dare qlco. a qlcu.** *to give (sth.) to sb.* **scrivere qlco. a qlcu.** *to write sth. to sb.* **rubare qlco. a qlcu.** *to steal sth. from sb.*
Expressing *for whom* an action is done	**Mi** lavi questa maglia? *Will you wash this jumper for me?* **Gli** scaldi il caffe? *Will you heat up the coffee for him?*	The people for whom the actions are done are the indirect objects: **lavare/ scaldare qlco. per qlcu.** *to wash/heat (sth.) for sb.*, **scegliere qlco. per qlcu.** *to choose (sth.) for sb.*
Indirectly expressing the idea of *to*	**Le** piacciono i film di Fellini *She likes Fellini's films* (lit. *Fellini's films are very pleasing to her*) **Gli** servono altri libri? *Does he need any more books?* (lit. *Are other books of use to him?*)	Verbs used impersonally. These all require IDO pronouns to express what in English are subject pronouns (*I, you, he, she, etc.*). For full explanations, see 25.5 and 25.6, pp. 319–24.

Attenti! Person as direct object or indirect object?

The Italian verb structure does not always match the English, so it is not always easy to decide whether the person is the indirect object or not. As you come across new verbs, it is a good idea to make your own list of short phrases to memorise, using clearly differentiated object pronouns such as **lo** (DO) and **gli** (IDO) to make the different use stick in your mind, e.g. **Lo** chiamo *I call him*, but **Gli** telefono, *I phone him*. You'll then remember it's **chiamare qlcu.** (person as direct obect) but **telefonare a qlcu.** (person as indirect object).

✦ Person as direct object

| Aiuterai Dino a fare i compiti? **Lo** aiuterai? *Will you help Dino to do the homework? Will you help him?* Convincerò Matteo a pagare. **Lo** convincerò a pagare *I will persuade Matteo to pay. I will persuade him to pay* | These verbs have no preposition before the person, which is therefore a direct object: **aiutare qlcu. a** *to help sb. to,* **convincere qlcu. a** *to persuade sb. to.* A similar verb is **costringere qlcu. a** *to force, make sb. do sth.* See also 26.5, p. 338. |

✦ Person as indirect object

| Chiederai **a Dino** di venire? **Gli** chiederai di venire? *Will you ask Dino to come? Will you ask him to come?* Hanno consigliato **a Matteo** di rimandare il viaggio. **Gli** hanno consigliato di rimandare il viaggio *They have advised Matteo to postpone the journey. They have advised him to postpone the journey* | These verbs require **a** before the person, which is therefore an indirect object: **chiedere qlco. a qlcu.** *to ask sb. sth.,* **consigliare qlco. a qlcu.** *to advise sb. (to do) sth.* Similar verbs include: **dire, domandare, far sapere, indicare, ordinare, permettere, proibire, promettere.** See also 7.3, p. 112 and 26.5, p. 338 for a full list. |

◎/✦ Esercizi

11 From their infinitives, can you identify which of the verbs below are direct object verbs and which are double object verbs requiring both direct and indirect objects? If necessary, check the meanings in the dictionary.

| ascoltare qlcu. aspettare qlcu. comprare qlco. a/per qlcu. disturbare qlcu. guardare qlcu. | impedire qlco. a qlcu. incorraggiare qlcu. a invitare qlcu. a leggere qlco. a qlcu. mandare qlco. a qlcu. | offrire qlco. a qlcu. portare qlco. a qlcu. pregare qlcu. di prestare qlco. a qlcu. ringraziare qlcu. | scusare qlcu. sentire qlcu. spiegare qlco. a qlcu. telefonare a qlcu. vietare qlco. a qlcu. |

12 Now substitute the underlined words, choosing the correct DO or IDO pronoun each time.

(a) Porterò <u>mia nonna</u> al mare. (la/le)
(b) Porterò dei fiori <u>a mia nonna</u>. (la/le)
(c) Manderò <u>il pacco</u> a Carlo. (lo/gli)
(d) Manderò un fax <u>a Silvio</u>. (lo/gli)
(e) Leggerò <u>l'articolo</u> a Dina e a Lucia. (lo/gli/loro)
(f) Leggerò il riassunto <u>a Dina e a Lucia</u>. (li/gli/loro)

13 Insert the correct word for *you*, choosing between direct and indirect object pronouns.

(a) − ringrazio tanto, signore.
(b) Signore, − mando la conferma domani.
(c) Signora Rodolfi, − disturbo?
(d) Signora, − dispiace se torno più tardi?
(e) − dispiace aspettare, signori?
(f) Signore, − prego di tornare domani.

✦ 14 Give the Italian equivalent of the English using the verbs listed to help decide whether to use a direct or an indirect object pronoun.

(a) *I advised her to leave early* consigliare a qlcu. di *to advise sb. to*
(b) *We must persuade her to help.* convincere qlcu. a *to persuade sb. to*
(c) *You can't force him to come.* costringere qlcu. a *to make/force sb. do sth.*
(d) *I have allowed him to go to the party.* permettere a qlcu. di *to allow sb. to*

✚ **15** *Him*, *her* and *them*. Use the appropriate DO or IDO object pronoun to complete the sentences.

    (a) Non ti preoccupare, — dirò di pagare. (*him*)

    (b) Non c'è problema, — convincerò a pagare. (*him*)

    (c) — dovresti incoraggiare a studiare di più. (*her*)

    (d) — dovresti consigliare di studiare di più. (*her*)

    (e) Ieri — ho invitati a cena. (*them*)

    (f) Ieri — ho offerto la cena. (*them*)

◎/✚ **7.4 Ne**

Ne is an important object pronoun which often has no exact equivalent in English.

(a) The main uses of *ne*

Ne is an invariable pronoun whose principal meanings are *of it/of them*, although in English this is often not expressed.

It replaces nouns or noun phrases relating to quantity and follows the same rules of position as object pronouns (pp. 119–21).

To refer to specific quantity: *of it, of them*	Vorrei 2 etti/4 fette di prosciutto. **Ne** vorrei due etti/4 fette *I would like 200 gr./4 slices of ham. I would like 200 gr./4 slices (of it)* Vorrei mezzo chilo di pere. **Ne** vorrei mezzo chilo *I would like half a kilo of pears. I would like half a kilo (of them)* Quanti figli ha? – **Ne** ho due, un maschi e una femmina *How many children do you have? I have two (of them), a boy and a girl* Quanto/a **ne** vuole? *How much (of it) do you want?* Quanti/e **ne** vuole? *How many (of them) do you want?*	**Ne** replaces numbers and singular or plural nouns which refer to specific quantities. In English this is rarely expressed, but in Italian it is essential. **Ne** must be used with **quanto/a/i/e?**
To refer to unspecific quantity: *some/any, a few, a lot (of)*, etc.	I fagiolini sono buoni, **ne** vuoi? *The beans are good, do you want some/any? (of them)* Hai preso un po' di salame? – Sì, **ne** ho preso un po' *Did you have sone salami? Yes, I've had a little/some (of it)* Il pesce era buono, **ne** ho mangiato troppo *The fish was good. I ate too much (of it)* Quanto **ne** hai preso? – **Ne** ho preso la metà *How much (of it) did you have? – I had half (of it)* **But:** **Lo/Li** prendo tutto/i *I'll take all of it/them*	**Ne** also replaces partitives and nouns relating to unspecific quantities. It cannot be omitted. It must be used, for example, with quantifiers, e.g. **un po' di, poco, molto, tanto, troppo, alcuni, abbastanza, la metà, parecchio**. Note that **ne** is not used with **tutto**.
Agreements	Mangi molta carne? – No, non **ne** mangio **molta** *No, I don't eat much (of it)* Hai molti amici? – Sì, **ne** ho **moltissimi**! *Yes, I have a great many (of them)*	An adjective used with **ne** must agree with the noun **ne** refers to. For the agreement of **ne** with past participles, see p. 131.

◎ Esercizi

1 Shorten the questions and answers below, by substituting **ne** twice each time.

(a) Quante cipolle prende? – Prendo mezzo chilo di cipolle.

(b) Quanto tonno vuole? – Prendo quattro scatole di tonno.

(c) Quanti meloni vuole? – Prendo due meloni.

2 You too. Give the Italian equivalent of the English replies. Begin each one with: **Anch'io ...**.

(a) Consumo pochissimi grassi. – *I eat very little too.*

(b) Consumo tanta frutta e verdura. – *I eat a great deal too.*

(c) Compro molto cibo biologico. *I buy a lot too.*

3 Insert **ne** where necessary in the sentences below.

(a) La minestra è buona, vuoi un po'?

(b) La pasta è fresca, quanta vuole?

(c) Il vino è buono, vuole?

(d) Le salsicce sono eccezionali, volete?

✦ (b) Further uses of *ne*

Ne is used to substitute nouns or prepositional phrases mostly preceded by **di**. In this context it translates variously as (*about//of/without*) ... *it/him/her/them.*

To replace nouns and phrases taking **di**	Abbiamo parlato **di Mario/Gina**. **Ne** abbiamo parlato [...] *We talked about him/her* Hai voglia **di andare al cinema**? **Ne** hai voglia? [...] *Do you feel like it?* Siamo orgogliosi **del loro successo**. **Ne** siamo molto orgogliosi *We are proud of their success. We are very proud (of it)* Amo **il cioccolato**, non **ne** posso fare a meno *I love chocolate, I can't do without it* Tu, cosa **ne** sai? *What do you know about it/them?*	When nouns or phrases are used with many verbs taking **di**, they can be substituted by **ne**. Note that past participle agreements are not made with the noun **ne** refers to. Other verbs taking **di** include: **aver bisogno di** *to need*, **essere contento di** *to be pleased with*, **essere sicuro di** *sure about/of*, **pensare di** *to think about* (opinion).
To replace nouns and phrases taking **da:** passive	Siamo rimasti disgustati **dal loro comportamento**. **Ne** siamo rimasti disgustati *We were disgusted by their behaviour. We were disgusted by it* Ho letto **il libro** e **ne** sono stato conquistato *I read the book and was bowled over by it*	With **da**, **ne** is used only in passive constructions, e.g. **essere distrutto da** *to be destroyed by*, **essere sconvolto da** *to be troubled/upset by.*
To replace phrases of direction taking **da**	Sono tornato **da Roma**. **Ne** sono tornato ieri *I came back from Rome. I came back (from there) yesterday* Ho aperto la cesta e **ne** sono usciti due cuccioli *I opened the basket and out (of there) came two puppies* Sto per uscire di casa; **ne** sto per uscire *I'm about to leave home; I'm about to leave*	**Ne** replaces phrases of direction and movement beginning with **da**, e.g. **tornare da**, **uscire da.** Note that **ne** is also used with the idiomatic verb phrase **uscire di casa**.

For reflexive verbs with **ne**, e.g. **dimenticarsi di** *to forget*, **importarsi di** *to bother about*, see p. 126.

✛ Esercizio

4 Provide the Italian equivalent of the English.

   (a) Hai bisogno di aiuto? – *No thanks, I don't need any.* (avere bisogno di)

   (b) Credi che si dimetterà? – *I am sure of it.* (essere sicuro di)

   (c) Abbiamo parlato dei loro problemi – *We talked about them too.* (parlare di)

   (d) Dimmi quello che è successo. – *But I don't know anything about it.* (sapere di)

   (e) Cosa pensi di quello che ha detto? – *I don't know, what do you think of it?* (pensare di)

   (f) Il mio gattino è adorabile. *I can't do without it.* (fare a meno di)

   (g) Hai sentito la notizia? – *Yes and I was upset by it.* (essere sconvolto da)

   (h) È uscito di casa? *Yes, he's coming out (of there) right now.* (uscire di casa)

◎/✛ 7.5 *Ci*

Ci is extremely common in Italian. It is used as the object pronoun *us* and (*to*) *us*, as well as the reflexive pronoun *ourselves*. (See p. 106 and 109.) In addition, it is also widely used to mean *there* and sometimes *it* or *them*. In this context, **vi** sometimes replaces **ci** in fairly formal writing.

(a) Main uses of *ci*

In Italian it is essential to use **ci** to refer to a place or activity already mentioned.

Location: replacing phrases of place	Vai **a** Milano/**al** mare/**alla** festa/**da** Mario/**in** Francia? – Sì, **ci** vado *Are you going to Milan/to the seaside/to the party/to Mario's/to France? – Yes, I'm going (there)* Se cerchi **dietro** il divano **ci** troverai le scarpe. *If you look behind the sofa you'll find the/your shoes (there)* Sei passato **per** Montorio? Sì, **ci** sono passato la settimana scorsa *Did you go/pass through Montorio? Yes, I passed through (there) last week*	The phrases usually begin with **a** but may begin with **da** or **in** where this means *to*. They may occasionally begin with other prepositions. The closest equivalent is *there*, but this is not always expressed in English.
Replacing verb phrases beginning with **a**	Sei andato **a ballare/a vedere Giulia**? – Sì, **ci** sono andato/a *Did you go dancing/to see Giulia? – Yes, I went (there)*	These phrases usually refer to actions and activities. Note that this is not often expressed in English.
As part of the verb **esserci**	**Ci** sono molti bambini *There are so many children* **C'**è tanto rumore *There is so much noise* **C'**è Tina? No, non **c'**è *No, she's not in* Non **vi** sono rimedi per l'alta disoccupazione *There are no remedies for high unemployment* **Vi** è poco da aggiungere a quello che è stato detto *There is little to add to what has been said*	Before **è, ci** shortens to **c'. C'è/Ci sono** are also used to talk about people being in. Note that in formal contexts, especially in written Italian, **vi** usually replaces **ci**.

◎ Esercizi

1 Insert the appropriate pronouns in the answers to replace the words underlined in the questions.

    (a) Sei stato <u>a Roma</u>? – Sì, sono stato tante volte.

    (b) Andate <u>in centro</u>? – Sì, andiamo fra poco.

    (c) Se andato <u>dal farmacista</u>? – Sì, sono passato stamattina.

    (d) Sei andato <u>a trovare Liliana</u>? – Sì, sono andato ieri.

    (e) Quand'è che vai <u>a far la spesa</u>? – Vado adesso.

2 Using **c'è** or **ci sono** in these sentences, give Italian equivalent of the following.

    (a) *In my flat there are six rooms but there is only one bathroom.* (**un bagno solo**)

    (b) *What is there to eat? – There is spaghetti alle vongole and there is salad.*

    (c) *Is Piero there/in? – No, he's not here/in.*

    (d) *Are Andrea and Massimo in? – No, they're not here/in.*

✦ (b) Further uses of *ci*

Ci can mean *it* or *them* when it replaces noun or verb phrases beginning with **a**.

Replacing noun and verb phrases beginning with **a** ⚠	Sei riuscito **a finire**? – Sì, **ci** sono riuscito […] *Yes I managed to (do it)* Penso **alle vacanze**. **Ci** penso […] *I'm thinking about them* **But:** Hai risposto **a Eva**? – Sì, **le** ho risposto *Did you answer Eva? – Yes I answered her* Penso **a Luciana** ogni giorno. Penso **a lei/La** penso ogni giorno […] *I think of her every day*	Note that **ci** only replaces phrases beginning with **a** when they refer to an action or thing. **But beware:** If the verb + **a** refers to a person, an IDO pronoun is usual. Note, however, that **pensare a** requires a disjunctive or a DO pronoun.
With **metterci** and **volerci**	Quanto **ci** metti per arrivare? *How long do you take to arrive?* **Ci** metto/mettiamo un'ora *I/We take an hour* **Ci** vuole un'ora *It takes an hour* **Ci** vogliono due ore *It takes two hours* **Ci** vuole un'altra forchetta *Another fork is needed* Che cosa **ci** posso fare? *What can I do about it?*	**Ci** is an integral part of these verbs but is not expressed in English. Note that **ci** can be used colloquially with **fare**. See Chapter 25, p. 324 for **volerci**.
ci sento, **ci vedo**	Non **ci** sento più da un orecchio *I can't hear (a thing) in one ear* **Ci** vedi? – No, non **ci** vedo niente *Can you see (anything)? – No, I can't see a thing* Non **ci** vedo niente di scandaloso *I don't see anything scandalous in/about it*	Commonly used with **sentire** and **vedere**, **ci** can mean *a thing*, *anything*, but there is no exact English equivalent.

◎/✦ Esercizi

3 Complete the sentences in Italian using **metterci** and **volerci**.

    (a) (*I take an hour*) per arrivare all'università.

    (b) (*It takes an hour*) per arrivare in centro.

    (c) Quanto (*do they take*) per andare a Genova?

    (d) (*It takes*) tre quarti d'ora se prendi la macchina.

✚ 4 Give the Italian equivalent of the English. There are two cases in which you cannot use **ci**.

    (a) Sei abituato al freddo? – *Yes, I'm used to it.*

    (b) Siete riusciti a farlo? – *Yes, we managed to.*

    (c) Hai risposto a tuo zio? – *Yes, I've answered him.*

    (d) Avete pensato a quello che volete fare? – *No, we haven't thought about it.*

    (e) Pensi spesso ai tuoi fratelli? – *Yes, I often think about them.*

✚ 5 **Ci** can be tricky because of its various meanings and functions. Give the English equivalent of the following sentences and identify the function of **ci** each time. You will need to remember it can also be a DO or IDO pronoun and a reflexive or reciprocal pronoun.

    (a) **Ci** sono pochi treni a quest'ora.

    (b) **Ci** siamo incontrati per caso.

    (c) **Ci** siamo divertiti tantissimo.

    (d) Io penso spesso all'incidente; **ci** pensi anche tu?

    (e) So che ti piace il cinema; **ci** vai spesso?

    (f) Giancarlo **ci** ha chiesto di aiutare domani.

    (g) Il nostro inquilino non **ci** saluta mai.

◎/✚ 7.6 Object pronoun position

The following rules apply to reflexive, DO and IDO pronouns, **ne**, **ci** and combined pronouns (see pp. 106–9 and pp. 123–7).

◎/✚ (a) Invariable positions

Broadly speaking pronouns precede the verb, but there are important exceptions.

Before the verb	**Mi** diverto molto *I enjoy myself a lot* **Lo** comprerò domani *I'll buy it tomorrow* **Gli** ho dato un libro *I gave him a book* **Ne** prendo due *I'll take two* **Ci** vado spesso *I often go*	Apart from **loro**, all relexives and object pronouns normally precede finite verbs, i.e. verb forms which indicate subject and tense and can be conjugated.
loro: after the verb	Ha comunicato **loro** le sue intenzioni *He has communicated his intentions to them* Vuole dare (**a**) **loro** il tempo di pensarci *He wants to give them time to think about it*	**Loro** must follow the verb in all cases and is never attached to it. It is sometimes preceded by **a**.
After infinitives	Ho voglia di divertir**mi** *I feel like enjoying myself* Sto cercando di asciugar**lo** *I am trying to dry it* Sarebbe meglio dir**gli** tutto *It would be best to tell him/them everything* È difficile parlar**ne** *It is hard to talk about it.* Non ho tempo di pensar**ci** *I haven't got time to think about it*	Apart from **loro**, the pronouns are attached to the end of infinitives, whose final **-e** is dropped.

Imperatives: before and after the verb	**Si** accomodi **But**: Accomoda**ti**/ accomoda**tevi** *Do make yourself/selves comfortable* **Li** compri domani **But:** Compra**li**/ comprate**li** domani *Buy them tomorrow* Compriamo**li** domani *Let's buy them tomorrow*	The pronouns come before formal **lei** imperatives but are attached to the end of **tu**, **voi** and **noi** imperatives.
Ecco	Ecco**mi** qui *Here I am* Ecco**li** qua *Here they are* Ecco**ne** un altro *Here's another one* Ecco**ci** di nuovo *Here we are again*	Pronouns are always attached to **ecco** to form one word.
After gerunds ✚	È uscito dal bagno, asciugando**si** in fretta *He came out of the bathroom drying himself in a hurry* **But:** Cosa fai? – Mi sto asciugando *What are you doing? – I'm drying myself*	When gerunds are used alone (i.e. not as part of a finite verb), the pronouns are attached to the end, apart from **loro.**
After participles ✚	Tornata**ci** dopo tanti anni, Lidia è rimasta delusa *Having gone back there after so many years, Lidia was disappointed* **But**: Lidia **ci** è tornata dopo tanti anni *Lidia went back there after so many years*	When past participles are used alone (i.e. not as part of a finite verb), the pronouns are attached to the participle.

◎/✚ Esercizi

1 Rewrite the sentences below, changing verb forms where necessary and placing the pronouns appropriately. Begin with the phrase given. e.g. (a) Preferisco veder-.

(a) Ti vedo più tardi. (Preferisco)

(b) Mi diverto al mare. (Ho intenzione di)

(c) Ci vediamo giovedì. (Non so se)

(d) Ci vediamo giovedì. (È importante)

(e) Edda ci va domani. (So che)

(f) Ci va domani. (È meglio)

(g) Ne compriamo altri. (Perché no?)

(h) Ne compro altri (Ho deciso di)

✚ **2** Substitute the nouns underlined with pronouns and place them correctly in each sentence.

(a) Angelica è uscita, lasciando aperta la finestra.

(b) Luigi ha scritto pregando mia sorella di rispondere.

(c) È caduto, lasciando cadere i bicchieri.

(d) Sto leggendo un racconto a mio figlio.

◎/✚ (b) Variable positions

In the following two cases the different pronoun position is optional and does not normally affect the meaning.

With negative **tu** imperatives	Non **ti** preoccupare/Non preoccupar**ti** *Don't worry* Non **lo** toccare/Non toccar**lo** *Don't touch it*	The pronoun precedes the verb or is joined to the end. The position depends on individual preference.
Optional position with modal verbs ✚	**Le** devo dire di venire?/Devo dir**le** di venire? *Must I tell her to come?* **Lo** sai spiegare o no?/Sai spiegar**lo** o no? *Can you explain it or not?*	The pronoun goes before **potere**, **volere**, **dovere** and **sapere** or is attached to the dependent infinitive.

◎/✛ Esercizi

3 In the commands below, substitute the nouns underlined with pronouns and place them correctly in each sentence.

    (a) Gianna, manda la lettera.

    (b) Signora, spedisca subito questo pacco.

    (c) Ragazzi, parlate di questo oggi.

    (d) Signore, parli a nostro figlio domani.

✛ 4 It makes little difference. Rewrite the sentences to mean the same thing, but changing the pronoun order.

    (a) Mi sai dire se la cena è pronta?

    (b) Mi voglio lavare le mani.

    (c) Lo devo finire stasera.

    (d) Non li posso aiutare.

    (e) Non lo toccare!

    (f) Non ti preoccupare.

✛ 5 It makes a difference! The position of pronouns can alter what you say. Match up the English and Italian meanings below.

    (a) Andiamoci domani.

    (b) Ci andiamo domani.

    (c) Lo facciamo adesso.

    (d) Facciamolo adesso.

    (i) *Let's do it now.*

    (ii) *Let's go tomorrow.*

    (iii) *We're going tomorrow.*

    (iv) *We're doing it now.*

◎/✛ 7.7 Disjunctive pronouns

These are pronouns sometimes known as stressed pronouns, as they are often used used for emphasis or after prepositions.

(a) Main disjunctive pronouns: forms and uses

Person	Singular		Plural	
1st	**me**	*me*	**noi**	*us*
2nd	**te** **Lei**	*you* (informal) *you* (formal)	**voi** **Loro**	*you* (formal and informal) *you* (very formal)
3rd	**lui** **lei**	*him* *her*	**loro**	*them*

Disjunctive pronouns have many forms in common with subject pronouns (only **me** and **te** differ), but they are actually forms of object pronouns. Their position in a sentence usually corresponds to the English.

After prepositions	Lavora per **te/Lei/voi**? *Does he work for you?* Secondo **me** è troppo difficile *In my view (according to me) it's too hard* Tocca a **te** decidere *It's up to you to decide* Mi diverto molto con **te** *I enjoy myself a lot with you*	Disjunctive pronouns follow prepositions like **secondo** or **per**. This is their main use. Note that **tocca a** ... + **me**, **noi**, **te**, **voi,** etc without a dependent verb means *It's my/our/your turn.*
For emphasis: after the verb	Vogliono vedere **lui** *It's him they want to see* (Lo vogliono vedere: *not emphatic*) Cercavo proprio **te** *It's you I was looking for* (Ti cercavo: *not emphatic*) Devo scrivere a **loro**? *Is it them I have to write to?* (Gli devo scrivere? *not emphatic*)	When the object is emphasised disjunctive pronouns are used instead of DO or IDO pronouns. They always follow the verb but not necessarily a preposition.

| For contrast: after the verb | Vuole **me** o **te**? *Does he want me or you?* (**not**: Mi vuole o ti vuole?) Parlerò **a te**, non **a lui** *I'll speak to you, not to him* (**not**: ti parlerò, non gli parlerò) A **lui** piace il teatro ma a **lei** no *He likes the theatre but she doesn't* (**not**: Gli piace il teatro ma non le piace) | When two direct or indirect objects are contrasted they have to be replaced by disjunctive pronouns (preceded by **a** if the object is indirect). |
| With two or more objects: *me and ...* | Ha visto **me** e Franco *He saw me and Franco* Ho dato un gelato a **lui** e a Gino *I gave an ice cream to him and to Gino* | Disjunctive pronouns replace DO or IDO pronouns and follow the verb. |

Disjunctives are also used in exclamations and comparisons. With **stesso** they are used for particular emphasis.

Exclamations	Beato **te**! *Lucky you!* Povero **me**! *Poor me!*	After adjectives in exclamations.
Comparisons	È più ricco di **me** *He is richer than me* Sono ricco come/quanto **loro** *I am as rich as them*	After the prepositions **di**, **come** and **quanto**.
Emphatic forms ✚	Fallo per **te stesso** *Do it for yourself* Quando la vedo, vedo **me stesso** *When I see her, I see myself* Angela parla sempre di **se stessa** *Angela always talks about herself* Bisogna saper controllare **se stessi** *One needs to be able to control oneself*	For added emphasis, **stesso/a/i/e** is often used with disjunctive pronouns. When used with **sé** (see below), the accent is usually dropped.

◎ Esercizi

1 Complete the sentences using disjunctive pronouns.
- **(a)** C'è una lettera per (*me*) e una fattura per (*you*), dottore.
- **(b)** Esci con (*them*) stasera o solo con (*her*)?
- **(c)** Vuoi venire da (*me/my place*) o devi andare da (*him/his place*)?
- **(d)** Secondo (*us*) è pericoloso farlo, e secondo (*you – plural*)?

2 Link the two sentences using the word **o** for (a) and (b) and the phrase **e anche** for (c) and (d).
- **(a)** Mi porti al cinema? Lo porti al cinema? (*Are you taking me or him to the cinema?*)
- **(b)** Le vuoi telefonare? Gli vuoi telefonare? (*Do you want to ring her or him?*)
- **(c)** Li chiamerò. Chiamerò Gina. (*I'll call them and also Gina.*)
- **(d)** Ti manderò una cartolina. Manderò una cartolina ai miei. (*I'll send a postcard to you and to my parents.*)

For **me stesso**, etc., see Exercise 4 below.

✦ (b) Additional disjunctive pronouns: *sé*

Sé is a disjunctive pronoun sometimes used after a preposition instead of **lui, lei** and the plural, **loro**.

Angelo parla sempre di **sé** *Angelo always talks about* himself ***But:*** Angelo parla sempre di lui *Angelo always talks about him* Lo hanno fatto solo per **sé** *They only did it for themselves* ***But:*** Lo hanno fatto per loro *They did it for them* (*others*) ***Note:*** Bisogna imparare a fare da **sé** *One has to learn to do things oneself* È brutto sentire parlare male di **sé** *It's not nice to hear people speak ill of you/oneself*	**Sé** is used when the action refers back to the subject. **Lui, lei** and **loro** are used when the action refers to someone else. Note that when used with an infinitive, **sé** means *you, one (self)*.
La cosa in **sé** non è grave *In itself/As such it's not a serious matter* Le sue intenzioni di per **sé** sono molto buone. *In themselves his intentions are very good*	**Sé** is also used as a disjunctive pronoun referring to things, expressed in English by *itself, themselves* or *as such*.

✦ Esercizi

3 Pick the appropriate pronoun to substitute the English: **sé, lui, lei** or **loro**.

    (a) Eduardo è proprio noioso, parla sempre di (*himself*).

    (b) Angela è veramente innamorata, parla sempre di (*him*).

    (c) Sono piuttosto antipatici, parlano sempre male di (*her*).

    (d) Ida è abbastanza egoista, pensa solo a (*herself*).

    (e) I miei figli vogliono sempre fare tutto da (*themeselves*).

    (f) Amalia vizia i figli, fa proprio tutto per (*them*).

4 Read the sentences below. Decide whether the pronouns in bold are subject pronouns (S) or disjunctive (D) and give their English equivalent.

    (a) L'attrice farà girare un film su **se stessa**.

    (b) È la sua vera storia raccontata da **lei stessa**.

    (c) 'Conosci **te stesso**' è un motto greco.

    (d) È inutile biasimare gli altri: **tu stesso sei** il problema.

    (e) Sono disposto ad andare **io stesso** a prenderti.

    (f) Il blog s'intitola, 'Lettere a **me stesso**'.

    (g) Il ministro parla a vanvera; lo ha detto **lui stesso**.

    (h) Poveretto, dopo la morte della moglie è diventato l'ombra di **se stesso**

◎/✦ 7.8 Direct object pronouns and *ne* combined with indirect object or reflexive pronouns

Direct object pronouns or **ne** are often used in the same sentence with indirect object or reflexive pronouns.

When these pronouns are used together, the IDO and reflexive pronouns change their spelling, except for **loro**.

(a) Forms and position

In the table below, the IDO and reflexive pronouns are listed together: they differ only in the 3rd person, which is highlighted.

IDO and reflexive pronouns	DO pronouns				
	lo	**la**	**li**	**le**	**ne**
mi	me lo	me la	me li	me le	me ne
ti	te lo	te la	te li	te le	te ne
gli	glielo	gliela	glieli	gliele	gliene
le	glielo	gliela	glieli	gliele	gliene
si	se lo	se la	se li	se le	se ne
ci	ce lo	ce la	ce li	ce le	ce ne
vi	ve lo	ve la	ve li	ve le	ve ne
loro	lo … loro	la … loro	li … loro	le … loro	ne … loro
si	se lo	se la	se li	se le	se ne

 Attenti! Unlike English, the Italian pronouns usually come before the verb and the IDO and reflexive pronouns precede the DO pronouns and **ne**. With the exception of **loro** the order of pronouns is as follows:

IDO	+	DO	+	Verb	Reflexive	+	DO	+	Verb
Me		lo		dà	Me		lo		lava
		ne					ne		
To me		*it/some*		*he gives*	*I*		*it/some*		*wash*

Loro *to them* never combines with other pronouns and must follow the verb. When it is used with another pronoun it is often preceded by **a**: **Mando la lettera ai miei** – **La mando (a) loro.**

In speech **gli** usually replace **loro.** (See below.)

✚ (b) Indirect object pronoun combinations

These are used in the following cases.

To replace two objects, direct and indirect	Preparo le tagliatelle per te. **Te le** preparo […] *I'm preparing them for you* Porterò la frutta a Carlo. **Gliela** porterò […] *I'll bring it to him* Porterò un po' di frutta a mia sorella. **Gliene** porterò un po' […] *I'll bring her some/a little*	Combinations of two pronouns are typical with double object verbs.
👁 Italian and English differ	Mi puoi dire chi è? **Me lo** puoi dire? *Can you tell me who he is? Can you tell me? (it)* Puoi chiedere a Lucio di venire? **Glielo** puoi chiedere? *Can you ask Lucio to come? Can you ask him? (it)* Mi permetti di uscire? No, non **te lo** permetto *Will you let me go out? No, I won't let you (do it)* Mi prometti di alzarti presto? – Sì, **te lo** prometto *Do you promise (me) you'll get up early? – Yes, I promise (you it)* Hai capito quello che devi fare? – No, **me lo** spieghi? *Have you understood what you must do? – No, can you explain? (it to me)*	Two object pronouns are always needed with double object verbs like **dire, chiedere, consigliare, permettere, promettere, ricordare, spiegare, far sapere qlco. a qlcu.,** but the English equivalents require only the DO pronoun or even no pronoun at all. See also 7.3(f), p. 113.

| Colloquial use: an extra pronoun | Ma glie**li** ho dati **i soldi**! *But I've given him/her/them the money!*
Allora, glie**li** facciamo, **gli auguri**? *So, shall we say happy birthday to him/her?*
Glielo dico **a Matteo**? *Should I tell Matteo?*
Ma chi **glie**lo spiegherà **a Roberta**? *But who will explain it to Roberta?* | In colloquial speech both DO and IDO pronouns may be used as well as the noun they refer to, though there is no need. There is no English equivalent. (See pp. 110, 112 and 343–4.) |

 Attenti! *glie-* has **four meanings**

When the IDO pronouns **gli** (*to him, to them*) or **le** (*to her, to you*) are used with a DO pronoun or **ne,** they have identical spelling changes and both become **glie-.** Glie- can therefore refer to four different persons: *him, them, her* and the formal *you*. The context usually makes it clear which meaning is expressed.

gli + lo = glielo	Gli do l'indirizzo? *Shall I give him/them the address?*	**Glie**lo do? *Shall I give it to him/to them/ to her/to you?*
le + lo = glielo	Le do l'indirizzo? *Shall I give her/you the address?*	
gli + ne = gliene	Gli do un bicchiere? *Shall I give him/them a glass?*	**Glie**ne do uno? *Shall I give him/them/ her/you one?*
le + ne = gliene	Le do un bicchiere? *Shall I give her/you a glass?*	

◎/✚ Esercizi

1 Rewrite the following sentences, replacing the noun underlined by a pronoun.

- **(a)** Ti manderò <u>il pacco</u> stasera.
- **(b)** Alberto vi spiegherà <u>la situazione</u> domani.
- **(c)** Mi compri due etti <u>di prosciutto</u>?
- **(d)** Fra poco ci spediranno <u>i bliglietti</u>.
- **(e)** Le porterò <u>le riviste</u> lunedì, signora.
- **(f)** Gli daresti un altro po' <u>di vino</u>?

2 Repeat the questions and requests below in shortened form, substituting pronouns for the underlined nouns and phrases.

- **(a)** Mi presti <u>i tuoi appunti</u>? — presti stasera?   (*Will you lend them to me this evening?*)
- **(b)** Ti posso spedire <u>le informazioni</u>? — spedisco adesso?
- **(c)** Signore, Le posso dare <u>il mio numero di casa</u>? — posso dare adesso?
- **(d)** Vi mandiamo <u>la chiave</u>, allora? — mandiamo domani?
- **(e)** Ti troverò <u>della rucola</u> al mercato. — troverò di sicuro.
- **(f)** Le parlo spesso <u>dei miei figli</u>. — parlo spesso.

✚ **3** Allow me! Tell these people you'll do it for them. Use both a DO and an IDO pronoun.

- **(a)** Devo stirare queste camicie. — stiro io, se vuoi. (tu) (*I'll iron them for you if you want.*)
- **(b)** Devo imbucare questa lettera — imbuco io, se vuole (Lei)
- **(c)** Dobbiamo aprire questo pacco. — apro io, se volete. (voi)

✚ **4** Complete the sentences below, using **ne** and another pronoun each time. The English is there to help you.

- **(a)** Queste pere sono mature, signora, — scelgo qualcuna? (*Shall I choose some for you?*)
- **(b)** Sono tre etti di formaggio, signore, — tolgo un po'? (*Shall I take some off for you?*)
- **(c)** I panini, sono freschi, ragazzi, — incarto un paio? (*Shall I wrap a couple for you?*)

✦ **5** Ask who told you each time, using the appropriate pronouns for *you* and not forgetting **lo.**

    (a) Sai che si è sposato Antonio? – Davvero? – *Who told you?*

    (b) Domani sono chiuso, signore, c'è sciopero. – Davvero? *Who told you?*

    (c) Siamo stati bocciati tutti. – Davvero? *Who told you?*

✦ **6** *I promise!* Convince these people of your good intentions. Complete the answers below using appropriate pronouns.

    (a) Mi farai sapere quando arrivi? Sì, — farò sapere senz'altro, — prometto!

    (b) Scusi, mi sa dire quando sarà pronto il lavoro? — dirò domani, signora, — prometto.

    (c) Facci sapere com'è andato, mi raccomando! Certo, — racconterò di sicuro, — prometto!

✦ **7** Give the Italian equivalent of the English.

    (a) *If you (pl.) can't come, will you tell us?*

    (b) *Anna, when you leave, will you let me know?*

    (c) *Ivo, if you want to come can you tell him?*

    (d) *I'll help you Mina, I promise!*

✦ (c) Reflexive pronoun combinations

Reflexive pronouns may be combined with another personal pronoun in the following cases.

To replace a direct noun object	**Mi** lavo le mani **Me le** lavo *I wash my hands. I wash them* Ha vinto Marco. **Se lo** merita *Marco won. He deserves it* **Si** compra sempre *La Repubblica* **Se la** compra sempre *He always buys himself* La Repubblica. *He always buys it for himself* **Si** compra sempre un giornale. **Se ne** compra sempre uno *He always buys himself one*	When a reflexive verb has a direct object this can be replaced by a DO pronoun if it is specific, or by **ne** if the object is unspecific (e.g. preceded by an indefinite article, **un/una**, etc.)
With reflexive verbs taking **di**	**Si** accorge dell'errore? **Se ne** accorge? *Does he see/notice the mistake? Does he notice (it)?* **Vi** rendete conto dell'ora? **Ve ne** rendete conto? *Do you realise the time? Are you aware (of it)?*	**Ne** replaces phrases beginning with **di** and combines with the reflexive pronoun. See p. 116.

Some reflexive pronoun combinations are part of common verbs.

Reflexive verbs with **la: cavarsela sentirsela prendersela**	**Ce la** siamo cavata! *We managed it!* **Te la** senti di venire? – No, non **me la** sento *Do you feel like coming? – No, I don't feel like it* Perché **se la** prende? *Why does he/she take offence?*	Some colloquial reflexive verbs have the pronoun **la** as part of the meaning. The reflexive pronouns change to agree with the subject but **la** stays the same.
Reflexive verbs with **ne**	**Te ne** vai? – Sì, **me ne** devo andare *Are you going? – Yes, I've got to go* **Se ne** frega *He/She doesn't care a damn*	Other colloquial reflexive verbs, e.g. **andarsene**, **fregarsene**, are formed as above with **ne**.

For past participle agreements, see p. 132.

+ Esercizi

8 Using the verbs given below, give the equivalent of the English.

lavarsi • togliersi • comprarsi • occuparsi di • permettersi

(a) I miei capelli sono proprio sporchi! – *Why don't you wash it?* (them)

(b) Mi tiene troppo caldo questo cappotto! – *Why don't you take it off, signora?*

(c) Sono belle quelle fragole! – *Shall we buy ourselves some, then?*

(d) Che freddo che fa! Chiudiamo la finestra? – *Fine, I'll deal with it.* (**occuparsi di**)

(e) Perché non fate un viaggio in Messico? – *We can't afford it.* (**permettersi**)

9 Give the Italian equivalent of the English, using the following verbs.

andarsene • fregarsene • sentirsela • prendersela • cavarsela

(a) *It's late, I'm going.*

(b) *But he couldn't care less!*

(c) *Do you feel like coming to the cinema?* (tu)

(d) *Why do you take offence?* (tu)

(e) *I got by in the exam.* (all'esame)

+ 7.9 Other pronoun combinations

(a) The impersonal *si* with other pronouns

The impersonal and passive **si** (*one, you, we, they, people*) is combined with other pronouns as follows. There are no spelling changes except with **ne**.

With direct and indirect object pronouns	In Italia **si** mangia **il panettone** a Natale. **Lo si** mangia a Natale *You eat it/It is eaten at Christmas* **Si** dice **a me** che è malato. **Mi si** dice che è malato *They tell me/I am told he is ill*	**Si** follows direct and indirect pronouns and does not change its spelling.
With **ne**	**Si** parla tanto **del nuovo film. Se ne** parla tanto *People talk a lot about it*	**Si** precedes **ne** and becomes **se**.

One of the most common combinations is **ci si**. With the impersonal **si** it expresses two different constructions.

Impersonal **si** + **ci** *there*: **ci si**	**Si** mangia male **da Gino. Ci si** mangia male *You eat badly* (there) **Si** riesce **a soddisfare i clienti**? **Ci si** riesce? *Do you/they manage?* (it)	**Si** follows **ci** and becomes **ci si**.
Impersonal **si** or **uno** + the reflexive **si:** **ci si** or **uno si**	**Ci si** diverte al mare/**Uno si** diverte al mare *You have/One has fun at the seaside* **Ci si** stufa/**Uno si** stufa a sentire le stesse domande *You get/One gets bored hearing the same questions* È una persona di cui non **ci si** può fidare *He/She's someone (whom) you can't trust*	With reflexive verbs, **si** is replaced by **uno** or **ci**, as you cannot have the impersonal and reflexive **si** together, making **si si.** Note that **fidare** is reflexive: **fidarsi di**. If phrases such as **al mare** or **al freddo** are also included, these cannot be replaced by yet another **ci** and are simply omitted.
	But note: **Ci si** diverte tanto **al mare. Ci si** diverte tanto *You enjoy yourself a lot* (there) **Ci si** abitua **al freddo. Ci si** abitua *You get used to it*	

For **ci si** as **ci**, *there* + reflexive **si**, see p. 129.

✦ Esercizi

1 Wrong end of the stick. Correct these misconceptions about Italy by completing the sentences using **si** and another appropriate pronoun.

    (a) In Italia, di solito, il Campari si beve come digestivo. – Ma no, … beve come aperitivo!

    (b) In Italia, di solito, la grappa si beve come aperitivo – Ma no, … beve come digestivo!

    (c) In Italia, di solito, il sale si vende solo in tabaccheria. – Ma no, adesso … vende dappertutto!

2 *How do I look?* Rewrite the following sentences replacing the underlined possessives with an IDO pronoun and combining it with **si**. Refer to 8.4, p. 139 if necessary.

    (a) La tua calza si è bucata.   **(c)** La sua giacca si è strappata. *(her)*

    (b) La sua cravatta si è sporcata. *(his)*   **(d)** Il mio bottone si è staccato.

3 Complete the second sentences replacing the underlined phrase with a pronoun and combining it with **si**.

    (a) Su questo materasso si dorme bene. — dorme benissimo!

    (b) In Italia si sta bene. — sta benissimo!

    (c) In questo compito non si capisce niente. Non — capisce assolutamente niente!

    (d) Si riuscirà a fare un bel lavoro. — riuscirà di sicuro.

4 Rewrite the sentences, replacing **uno** with **si**.

    (a) Durante le vacanze uno si alza tardi.   **(c)** D'estate uno si diverte in montagna.

    (b) Uno si veste bene per andare a messa.   **(d)** Uno si abitua al cibo inglese.

✦ (b) *Ci* with other pronouns

Ci precedes some pronouns and follows others. In front of another pronoun it becomes **ce**.

Before **ne**: **ce ne**	Quanta pasta **c'è?** – **Ce n'è** mezzo chilo *How much pasta is there? – There is half a kilo* **Ci** sono molti negozi qui? – Sì, **ce ne** sono tanti *Are there are lots of shops here? – Yes, there are loads of them*	**C'è**, **ci sono** *there is, there are* (from the verb **esserci**) are most commonly combined with **ne**. Note that before another -e, **ce** becomes **c'**.
	Quanto latte **ci** vuole? – **Ce ne** vuole un litro *How much milk does one/you need? – You need a litre* Quante ore **ci** metteremo? – **Ce ne** metteremo due *How many hours will we take? – We'll take two*	**Ci** also combines with **ne** when used as part of **volerci** *to be needed/to take* and of **metterci** *to put in, to take*.

The following combinations are very common, although in the case of the first two, **ci** has no specific English meaning and in the third case may be omitted.

With **avere** before **lo, la, li, le**	Dov'è la piantina, **ce l'**hai tu? *Where is the map, have you got it?* Li hai i biglietti? – Sì, **ce li** ho *Do you have the tickets? – Yes, I've got them*	When **lo, la, li, le** are used with **avere**, **ci** is placed in front purely for ease of pronounciation. See also p. 110.

With **la** as part of **farcela**, **avercela**	**Ce la** fai a portare la valigia? – Sì, **ce la** faccio *Can you manage to carry the case? – Yes, I can manage* Perché **ce l'**hai con me? *Why have you got it in for me/Are you cross with me?*	These common verbs are always used with the invariable pronoun combination **ce la** (**ci + la**).
With DO pronouns and **ci** *there*	Domani Davide va dal dentista, (**ce**) lo porti tu? *Tomorrow Davide is going to the dentist, will you take him (there)?*	When used to replace an expression of place, **ci** is often omitted.

In some cases **ci** *there* comes after another pronoun and there is no spelling change.

After **mi**, **ti, vi**	Quando mi porti al cinema? – **Ti ci** porto domani *When will you take me to the cinema? – I'm taking you (there) tomorrow* Ti siedi spesso sotto l'albero? – Sì, **mi ci** siedo spesso *Do you often sit under the tree? – Yes, I often sit there*	**Ci** comes after the direct object and reflexive **mi, ti, vi** but before the reflexive **si**. (See box below.) In speech, **ci** is sometimes omitted.
Before the reflexive **si**: **ci si**:	Aldo si trova bene a Roma? – Sì, **ci si** trova bene *Does Aldo like it in Rome? – Yes, he likes it (there)*	For more on **ci si**, see p. 127.
With **volerci** after IDO pronouns	Quanto **ti ci** vuole per arrivare? *How long does it take you to arrive?* **Gli ci** è voluto molto tempo *It has taken him a long time*	As part of the verb **volerci**, **ci** combines with indirect object pronouns. (See Chapter 25, p. 324.)

Note that **ci** (*there*) does not combine with the reflexive **ci** or **ci** meaning *us*. It is normally substituted with **là** or omitted:

Ci troviamo bene a Roma. Ci troviamo bene (là). *We like it in Rome. We like it there.*
Aldo ci porta al cinema. Ci porta (là). *Aldo takes us to the cinema. He takes us (there).*

✚ Esercizi

5 You're making preparations for ten guests, but it's not going well. Give the Italian equivalent of the English.

(a) Quanti bicchieri ci sono? (*There are five.*)
(b) C'è della birra in casa? (*No, there isn't any.*)
(c) Abbiamo abbastanza formaggio, vero? (*No, there is very little.*)
(d) Ci sono poche candele. (*It's true, there are very few.*)
   The situation brightens up just a little …
(e) Ho trovato altre candele. (*Good, how many are there?*)

6 Give the Italian equivalent of the following.

(a) *It's too late, I won't make it tonight.*
(b) *It's too difficult, he can't manage it.*
(c) *Dino, why are you cross with me?*
(d) *Does it take you long to get to school?* (tu)

7 **Ci si**: a puzzle. Read the sentences below, give their English equivalent and say which of the three constructions is being used each time: (1) impersonal **si** + reflexive **si**; (2) impersonal **si** + **ci** *there*; (3) **ci** *there* + reflexive **si**.

    (a) In Inghilterra, negli ultimi due anni di liceo, **ci si** specializza in tre o quattro materie.

    (b) Flavia è felicissima a Napoli; **ci si** trova veramente bene.

    (c) È un negozio geniale, **ci si** spende poco.

7.10 Agreement of the past participle with object pronouns

(a) Agreements with direct object pronouns

When used with compound tenses of verbs whose auxiliary is **avere**, direct object pronouns, but not indirect ones, require agreements to be made with the past participles. This is not the case with noun direct objects.

| Agreement with direct object pronouns | Ho preparato **la cena**. **L'**ho preparat**a** [...] *I have prepared it*
 Gli ho preparato **la cena**. **Gliel'**ho preparat**a** [...] *I have prepared it for him*
 Avete restituito **i soldi**? **Li** avete restituit**i**? [...] *Have you given it back?*
 Ti hanno restituito **i soldi**? Te **li** hanno restituit**i**? [...] *Have they given it back to you?* | Agreement of past participles is always made with **lo**, **la**, **li**, **le**, used alone or combined with other pronouns, e.g. indirect obect pronouns. With other DO pronouns – **mi**, **ti**, **ci**, **vi** – agreement is optional and fairly unusual. There is no participle agreement with DO nouns. |

Esercizi

1 *Not yet!* Answer the questions by substituting a pronoun for the noun underlined, and providing the participle with the correct agreement.

    (a) Hanno scelto i libri? – No, non ... hanno ancora ....

    (b) Avete innaffiato le piante? – No, non ... abbiamo ancora.

    (c) Ha mandato la lettera? – No, non ... ha ancora ....

    (d) Hanno prenotato i biglietti? – No, non ... hanno ancora ....

2 *Don't you remember?* Say it's been done already and complete the replies, using the correct pronouns and participle agreements.

    (a) Mi presti i tuoi appunti? – Ma te ... ho prestat... l'altro giorno!

    (b) Ci mandi le fatture domani? – Ma ve ... abbiamo mandat... la settimana scorsa!

    (c) Mi puoi comprare gli stuzzicadenti? – Ma te ... ho comprat... stamattina!

    (d) Ci puoi portare la carta igienica? – Ma ve ... abbiamo portat... ieri!

3 *What have you done!* Express disbelief at this succession of disasters. Complete the sentences below, replacing the underlined words with a pronoun and also making the participle agreements.

    (a) Sai che ho rotto i piatti nuovi di Giulia? – Come! ... hai rott... tutti?

    (b) Sai che ho rovinato la lavatrice di Antonio? – Come! ... hai rovinat... completamente?

    (c) Sai che ho sfasciato la macchina di Rina e Roberto? – Come! ... hai sfasciat... del tutto?

    (d) Sai che ho distrutto il computer di Fabio? – Come! ... hai distrut... totalmente?

◎/✚ (b) Agreements with *ne*

When **ne** is used as a direct object, agreements are usually made with the past participle of verbs taking **avere**.

Agreement with **ne** referring to quantity	Ho venduto **cento libri**. **Ne** ho venduti cento *I've sold a hundred books. I've sold a hundred* **Quanti morti** ci sono stati? – Ce **ne** sono stati almeno venti *How many deaths were there? – There were at least twenty* Aveva mangiato **tante/molte caramelle**. **Ne** aveva mangiate tante/molte *She had eaten loads of/many sweets. She had eaten loads/many (of them)* Hai comprato **dei fiori**? – Sì, **ne** ho comprati tanti *Did you buy any flowers? – Yes, I bought lots*	The past participle usually agrees in number and gender with what **ne** stands for. Note that, with the partitive **dei/delle**, agreement must be made.
✚ Optional agreement	Ha preparato un **po' di minestra**. Te **ne** ha preparata/o un po' *She has prepared some for you* Hai trovato **qualche guida**? – Sì, **ne** ho trovata/o qualcuna *Did you find any guidebooks? – Yes, I found a few*	However, if **ne** refers to quantities which are rather vague, agreement is preferred but optional. Note that with **qualcuno/a**, agreements, when made, are always singular.
✚ Two possible agreements	Ho comprato **tre chili di patate**. **Ne** ho comprati/e tre chili *I've bought three kilos of potatoes. I've bought three kilos* Ho preso **due etti di Gorgonzola**. **Ne** ho presi due etti *I got two hundred grammes of Gorgonzola. I got two hundred grammes*	When **ne** refers to a specific amount of something (a kilo, slice, tin, bottle, etc.), agreement is mostly, but not always, with that specific quantity, rather than with the actual item/s.
✚ No agreement with **di** introducing a phrase	Mi ha parlato **di Giulia**. **Me ne** ha parlato *He spoke to me about Giulia. He spoke to me about her* Si sarà occupato **dei conti**. **Se ne** sarà occupato *He will have taken care of the accounts. He will have taken care of them*	There are no past participle agreements when **ne** replaces a phrase used with a verb taking **di**, e.g. **parlare di**, **occuparsi di**.

✚ Esercizi

4 How much? Making correct participle agreements, say how much you have bought or ordered. There are two answers each time.

- **(a)** Quante pizze hai ordinato? Ne ho ordinat- —.   (molte • quattro)
- **(b)** Quanti fagiolini hai comprato? Ne ho comprat- —.   (tanti • due chili)
- **(c)** Quanto vino hai ordinato? Ne ho ordinat- —.   (parecchio • tre bottiglie)
- **(d)** Quanta marmellata hai comprato? Ne ho comprat- —.   (poca • un barattolo)

5 *Some*, *a few*, *a little*, *a couple*. Supply the correct past participle and agreement/s with **ne**.

    (a) Antonietta ha raccolto dei fiori e me ne ha (dare) alcuni.

    (b) Pierluigi ha comprato delle albicocche e me ne ha (regalare) alcune.

    (c) Mio cognato ha scattato delle bellissime foto e me ne ha (dare) qualcuna.

    (d) Il mio vicino ha trovato dei bicchieri antichi e me ne ha (offrire) qualcuno.

    (e) Giorgio ha riparato le sedie e io ne ho (portare) un paio a casa.

    (f) Simone ha della grappa meravigliosa in casa e ne abbiamo (bere) un po'.

✤ (c) Agreements with reflexive verb past participles

Reflexive verbs take **essere** as their auxiliary, which means past participle agreement is normally with the subject, not the object. In some cases, however, agreement is made with pronoun direct objects.

| Agreement with reflexive past participles | Antonio si è slogato **la caviglia**. **Se l'è** slogat**a** *Antonio has sprained his ankle. He has sprained it*
Bambini, vi siete lavati **le mani**? – No, non **ce le** siamo lavat**e** *Children, have you washed your hands? – No, we haven't washed them*
Maria si è rotta **il braccio**. **Se l'è** rott**o** *Maria has broken her arm. She has broken it*
Mi sono fatto/a tagliare **i capelli**. **Me li** sono fatt**i** tagliare *I got my hair cut. I got it cut* | The past participles of reflexive verbs usually agree with the subject. However, when there is a pronoun direct object, the participle agreement is usually made with the direct object. It is also possible to find agreements with noun direct objects – e.g. **Antonio si è slogata la caviglia.** |

For the agreement of the past participle and the subject, see pp. 254–55.

✤ Esercizi

6 *Poor things*! Express sympathy at these accidents. Finish the sentences by completing all the participle agreements.

    (a) Mio figlio si è slogato la caviglia – Poveretto, se l'è slogat- sciando?

    (b) Mia figlia si è storta il piede – Poveretta, se l'è stort- correndo?

    (c) La mia fidanzata si è bruciata le mani – Poveretta, se le è bruciat- cucinando?

    (d) Il mio fidanzato si è rotto la spalla. Poveretto, se l'è rott- cadendo?

7 Read this extract taken from a recent novel by the writer and lawyer Simonetta Agnello Hornby, then answer the questions. It's Rachele's twentieth birthday and her father wants her to marry.

Compiva vent'anni. Fecero una festicciola* in casa. La sera il padre le disse:

"È ora che prendi marito. Questo giovane medico mi piace, e suo padre è pronto a farsi avanti*."

"Non voglio maritarmi*. Mai."

"Non ti capisco. Vuoi rimanere zitella*?"

"Ho detto che non voglio maritarmi!"

"E se te lo ordina tuo padre?"

"Sul mio corpo e sulla mia anima comando io sola, papà."

"Attenta, te ne pentirai*. Pensaci."

Pochi giorni dopo il padre la chiamò nel suo studio. Non era solo: c'era anche Gaspare*. [...]

"Hai pensato a quello che ti ho detto?" Devo dare una risposta. Lo vuoi?"

"No."

"Ascolta tuo fratello, almeno."

Gaspare stringeva forte le dita attorno allo scaffale.

"Rachele, è un bravo ragazzo, siamo amici. Sarebbe un ottimo cognato per me. ... Ti darebbe una bella famiglia, figli

sani ...

"Vuoi che lo sposi?"

"È un matrimonio adeguato a te. Devi decidere tu."

(Simonetta Agnello Hornby, *Boccamurata*, Feltrinelli, 2007)

> • una festicciola *a little party* • farsi avanti *to come forward* • maritarsi *to get married*
> • zitella *spinster* • pentirsi (di) *to regret* • Gaspare is her brother, with whom she shares a terrible secret

(a) On lines 8 and 17 pick out the two phrases in which subject pronouns are used, then give their English equivalent.

(b) Identify the four direct and four indirect object pronouns used singly, then identify the reflexive pronouns.

(c) Give the English equivalent of: **se te lo ordina tuo padre'**; **te ne pentirai. Pensaci.**

8 Possessives

Possessives (**i possessivi**) are adjectives or pronouns indicating belonging and ownership, e.g. *my, mine, your, yours*.

◎ 8.1 Possessive adjectives and pronouns

(a) Forms

In Italian, possessive adjectives and pronouns have the same forms.

English adjectives and pronouns	Singular Masculine	Feminine	Plural Masculine	Feminine
my, mine	il mio	la mia	i miei	le mie
your, yours (fam.)	il tuo	la tua	i tuoi	le tue
his, her, hers, its	il suo	la sua	i suoi	le sue
your, yours (formal)	il Suo	la Sua	i Suoi	le Sue
our, ours	il nostro	la nostra	i nostri	le nostre
your, yours (pl. fam. and formal)	il vostro	la vostra	i vostri	le vostre
their, theirs *your, yours* (very formal pl.)	il loro	la loro	i loro	le loro

vostro/a/i/e is now normally used for the formal plural: **loro** is rarely used to express *your, yours*.

(b) Possessive adjectives: main uses

Italian possessive adjectives agree in number and gender with the noun they modify, not with the possessor.

È **la tua** camera, Dino? *Is this your room, Dino?* È **il tuo** appartamento, Dino? *Is this your flat, Dino?* Sono **i tuoi** stivali, Anna? *Are these your boots, Anna?* Sono **le tue** scarpe, Anna? *Are these your shoes, Anna?*	Possessive adjectives are mostly used with the definite article and precede the noun they modify. Note that the adjectives agree with the items possessed, not the owner.
Silvia ha trovato **il suo** libro/**la sua** penna *Silvia has found <u>her</u> book/her pen* Sandro ha trovato **il suo** libro/**la sua** penna *Sandro has found <u>his</u> book/his pen* Signor/Signora Fante, ha trovato **il suo/il Suo** portafoglio/**la sua/la Sua** agenda? *Signor/Signora Fante did you find your wallet/diary?*	**Il suo, la sua** both express *his, her* and the formal *your*. They refer to singular objects owned (masculine or feminine) and one owner (male or female). The formal *your* may be written with a capital letter.

Monica ha perso **i suoi** quaderni/**le sue** chiavi *Monica has lost her exercise books/her keys* Roberto ha perso **i suoi/i Suoi** quaderni/**le sue/la Sue** chiavi *Roberto has lost his exercise books/his keys* Signor/Signora Fante, ha perso **i suoi** appunti/**le sue** chiavi? *Signor/Signora Fante, have you lost your notes/your keys?*	**I suoi, le sue** also mean *his, her* and the formal *your*, but they refer to plural objects owned and one owner (male or female). They never mean *their*.
Signori/Ragazzi, mi fate vedere **la vostra** nuova casa? *Will you show me your new house?* **I vostri** quadri sono magnifici *Your pictures are marvellous*	**Vostro** is commonly used for both the familiar and formal plural *your*: **il/la/vostro/a** refer to single objects owned, while **i/le vostri/e** refer to plural objects owned.
Silvia e Sandro hanno trovato **il loro** libro/**i loro** libri *Silvia and Sandro have found their book/their books*	**Il/la/i/le loro** *their* can indicate one or more objects owned, but always more than one owner. They are invariable, apart from the definite article.

◎ Esercizi

1 *Your ...* You're handing people their possessions as they leave the party. Use the appropriate possessive adjective and definite article with the nouns given.

    (a) Claudio, ecco — giacca.
    (b) Letizia, ecco — ombrello.
    (c) Signor Nardi, ecco — cappotto.
    (d) Signori, ecco — impermeabili.
    (e) Ragazzi, ecco — giacche a vento.
    (f) Paolo e Claudia, ecco — zaino.

2 *His, her, their ...* Rewrite the sentences below substituting the appropriate form of **suo** or **loro** for the phrase underlined.

    (a) Non ho mai visto la casa del signor Pirelli. *(his)*
    (b) La casa di Mariella è molto piccola. *(her)*
    (c) Ti piace la nuova casa di Emilia e Patrizio? *(their)*
    (d) L'appartamento di Gianni ha un balcone enorme. *(his)*
    (e) L'appartamento di Gigliola si trova al secondo piano. *(her)*
    (f) L'appartamento dei signori Mancini è in via Manin. *(their)*
    (g) Non mi piacciono le amiche di Sandra. *(her)*
    (h) Siamo usciti con le amiche di Flavia e Fulvio. *(their)*
    (i) I figli del signor Vezzani frequentano l'università. *(his)*
    (j) I figli dei vicini vivono tutti all'estero. *(their)*

3 Find the Italian equivalent of the English phrases given.

    (a) Conosce (*my children*)?
    (b) Questi sono (*our grandchildren*).
    (c) Queste sono (*my nieces*).
    (d) Ti faccio conoscere (*our daughters*).

(c) Possessive adjectives: omission of the article

The definite article is not always used with possessives referring to the family and it may be omitted in some idiomatic phrases.

mia sorella *my sister* **tuo** nonno *your grandfather* **But:** **la mia** sorella **preferita** *my favourite sister* **la mia** sorel**lina** *my little sister* **il tuo bis**nonno *your great-grandfather*	No article is used with singular family members – including **marito** and **moglie** – unless there is an adjective or a suffix/prefix.
le mie sorelle *my sisters* **i tuoi** cugini *your cousins*	The article is always used with plural family members.

la loro sorella *their sister* le loro sorelle *their sisters* il loro nonno *their grandfather* i loro nonni *their grandparents*	Loro always requires an article.
Posso parlare con il tuo babbo? *Can I speak to your Daddy?* Sono uscita con (la) mia mamma *I went out with my mum*	Papà *Daddy* and mamma *Mummy* may optionally be used with the article. Babbo usually requires the article.

Idiomatic expressions

The article is often omitted and the possessive adjective may come after the noun. Here are a few common ones.

Vieni a casa mia/nostra *Come to my/our house* È colpa mia/sua *It is my/his/her fault* Non è compito mio/nostro *It is not my/our job* Sono affari miei/tuoi *It is my/your business*	Sono a tua/vostra disposizione *I am/They are at your/our disposal* Fa tutto a modo suo *He/She does everything his/her way*

◎ Esercizio

4 Introduce family and friends using the appropriate form of the possessive.

    (a) Questo è (*my*) marito e questa è (*our*) figlia, Laura.

    (b) Questo è (*my*) figlio, Claudio e questa è (*his*) fidanzata, Emilia.

    (c) Questa è Alessandra, (*our*) figlia più grande, e questo è (*her*) fidanzato, Alessio.

    (d) Ti presento (*my*) mamma e (*my*) fratellino, Roberto.

    (e) Questa è (*my*) moglie e queste sono (*our*) figlie, Simonetta e Chiara.

(d) Possessive pronouns: main uses

Possessive pronouns agree in number and gender with the nouns they refer to.

Hai trovato i tuoi guanti? – No, ma ho trovato i tuoi *Did you find your gloves? – No, but I found <u>yours</u>*	Possessive pronouns are mostly used with the definite article.
Mia madre lavora nelle relazioni pubbliche, e la tua? *My mother works in public relations, what about <u>yours</u>?*	The article is also used when the pronoun refers to a single family member.
È suo questo portafoglio? – Sì, è mio, ti piace? *Is this your wallet/this wallet yours? – Yes, it's mine, do you like it?* **But:** Questo è il mio portafoglio e questo invece è il tuo *This is my wallet and this one is yours/this is the one that's yours*	No article is used with essere + a possessive, when it means *to belong to* except for emphasis or clarification.
I miei sono in vacanza *My parents are on holiday* Salutami i tuoi *Say hello to your parents/family* I suoi abitano all'estero *His/Her parents live abroad* I suoi di dove sono, signora? *Where are your parents/ is your family from, Signora?*	I miei, i tuoi, i suoi are often used to refer to one's parents or close family.

◎ Esercizi

5 Complete the sentences using appropriate Italian possessive pronouns.

    (a) Tu prendi la tua macchina e io prendo (*mine*).

    (b) Io ho invitato le mie amiche e lei ha invitato (*hers*).

    (c) A me piace il mio professore, a te piace (*yours*)?

    (d) Tu porti tuo padre e io porto (*mine*).

    (e) Io chiederò il permesso ai miei genitori e tu chiedi il permesso a (*yours/your parents*).

6 Substitute the English phrases with the appropriate form of the possessive pronoun, paying attention to the use of the article.

    (a) Enrico, è (*yours*) questo libro? – No, non è (*mine*). (*Mine*) è qui.

    (b) Che bella sciarpa! e (*yours*), signora? – No, non è (*mine*). (*Mine*) è quella nera.

    (c) Ho trovato delle chiavi. Sono (*his*)? – No, non sono (*his*), sono (*mine*).

◎ 8.2 Expressing possession with 's/s' endings

The *'s/s'* endings to English nouns are usually expressed in Italian by **di** or **quello di** before the noun. They are equivalent to both possessive adjectives and pronouns.

L'amica **di** Flavio *Flavio's friend* Le chiavi **di** mio fratello *My brother's keys* La moglie **del** signor Arlacchi *Signor Arlacchi's wife* Il cane **dei** vicini *The neighbours' dog*	**Di** (*of*) expresses the equivalent of the English *'s/s'* ending. If the noun takes a definite article, **di** combines with it.
Sono **di** mio fratello *They are my brother's* È **dei** vicini *It is the neighbours'*	**Essere di** expresses the equivalent of the English *to be somebody's …*
Pino ha mangiato il suo panino e **quello di** sua sorella *Pino ate his roll and his sister's* (lit. *that of his sister*) Ho perso la mia chiave e anche **quella dei** vicini *I've lost my key and the neighbours' as well*	**Quello di:** To avoid repeating a noun. the appropriate form of **quello** is used before **di**.
Vai **da** Fiorella? *Are you going to Fiorella's?* Sono andato **dal** dentista *I went to the dentist's*	**Da** is used for the *'s/s'* ending when this refers to someone's place.

◎ Esercizio

1 Give the Italian for the following.

    (a) *Leonardo's mother is ill.*

    (b) *Signor Palladino's wife is on holiday.*

    (c) *The neighbours' cat is black.*

    (d) *I have found Elisabetta's shoes and Antonio's too.*

    (e) *I have lost Marta's letter and her sister's too.*

    (f) *I'll see you at Giovanni's.*

◎/✚ 8.3 Possessives with other determiners and with *proprio*

◎/✚ (a) Possessive + determiner

Possessives are commonly used with other determiners (articles, possessives, demonstratives, etc. See p. 359).

È **un mio** amico/**una mia** collega *He is a friend/She is a colleague of mine* *Or:* È un amico **mio**/una collega **mia**	**Indefinite article + possessive:** With common nouns such as **amico,** the possessive position is flexible. If placed after the noun it is more emphatic.

Sono ... (**dei**) nostri parenti/parenti nostri ... *relatives of ours* (**dei**) vostri amici/(**degli**) amici vostri ... *friends of yours* (**delle**) sue amiche/amiche sue ... *(girl) friends of his/hers*	**Partitive article + possessive:** The partitive article is often omitted and the possessive position is flexible.
Quel tuo cugino non mi piace *I don't like that cousin of yours* **Quegli** amici **tuoi**/**Quei tuoi** amici non mi piacciono *I don't like those friends of yours* **Questa tua** ossessione è assurda *This obsession of yours is absurd*	**Demonstrative + possessive:** The demonstrative precedes the possessive and agrees with it.
È arrivato con **tre miei** amici/**tre** amici **miei** *He arrived with three friends of mine* Verrà probabilmente con **qualche suo** amico/**qualche** amico **suo** *He'll probably arrive with some friend(s) of his* Mi ha invitato a cena con **alcuni suoi** parenti/**alcuni** parenti **suoi** *He invited me to dinner with a few relations of his*	✚ **A number or an indefinite + possessive:** The position of the possessives is flexible.

◎/✚ Esercizi

1 Explain who the following friends, colleagues, and acquaintances (**conoscenti**) are, using a possessive with the appropriate form of the indefinite or partitive article where required.

    (a) Pietro è (*a friend of mine*).

    (b) Stefania è (*a colleague of his*).

    (c) Alberto è (*an acquaintance of theirs*).

    (d) Sono andato al cinema con (*friends of ours*), Pietro, Tommaso e Elisabetta.

    (e) Sono andato a un convegno con (*colleagues of mine*), Sergio e Nadia.

✚ 2 Now use an indefinite, a number or a demonstrative with the possessive adjective.

    (a) È arrivato con (*three friends of his*).

    (b) Siamo usciti con (*a few clients of ours*).

    (c) Ho litigato con (*those friends of yours*).

✚ (b) *Proprio* as a possessive

Proprio is often used as a focus adverb with various meanings (pp. 63–4), but is also used to emphasise possession.

È importante occuparsi dei **propri** figli *It is important to look after one's (own) children* Bisogna stabilire un buon rapporto con il **proprio** capo *One has to establish a good relationship with one's boss.* Ciascuno ha il **proprio** computer *They each have their own computer* (**Or:** *Everyone/Each person has his own computer*)	**Proprio** is mostly used with impersonal expressions to mean *one's (own)*. With indefinites such as **ciascuno/ognuno** *each/everyone*, it can also mean *his*, *her* or *their own*.
L'ho visto con i miei (**propri**) occhi *I saw it with my (very) own eyes* Trascuri i tuoi (**propri**) interessi *You are neglecting your own interests* Abbiamo portato i nostri (**propri**) bicchieri *We've brought our (very) own glasses*	However, to say *my own*, *our own* or *your own*, **proprio** cannot be used without **mio**, **tuo**, **nostro** or **vostro**, and is frequently dropped.

✦ Esercizio

3 Complete the sentences by substituting the English with an appropriate Italian possessive.

    (a) È importante trovare soddisfazione nel (*one's*) lavoro.

    (b) È necessario esaminare (*one's*) coscienza.

    (c) Ognuno ha diritto alla (*one's own*) opinione.

    (d) Ho pagato con (*my own*) soldi.

✦ 8.4 Omission of the possessive in Italian

Possessives are used far less frequently in Italian than in English, especially where it is clear from the context who or what is possessed. They are often expressed by the following:

The definite article	È uscita con **il** marito *She went out with her husband* Avevano **i** vestiti strappati e **le** scarpe bagnate *Their clothes were torn and their shoes were wet* Ho perso **l'**ombrello/**l'**agenda/**gli** occhiali/**la** patente *I've lost my umbrella/diary/glasses/driving licence* Ha **gli** occhi azzurri e **i** capelli biondi *Her/his eyes are blue and his/her hair is fair*	The definite article is often enough to signify possession on its own. This is usually the case with family, clothes, personal possessions and parts of the body. See also 2.3, pp. 24–5.
Reflexive pronouns	Metti**ti la** giacca/**le** scarpe, Dina *Put your jacket/shoes on, Dina* **Si** è slogato **il** polso/**la** spalla *He sprained his wrist/shoulder* Prepara**ti i** bagagli *Pack your suitcases (luggage)*	Reflexive pronouns make it clear who the possessor is and eliminate the need for a possessive adjective. See also 7.2, p. 106.
Indirect object pronouns	**Gli/le** fa male **il** ginocchio/**la** schiena *His/her knee back/hurts* **Mi** ha stirato **la** camicia *She ironed my shirt* **Ci** ha rubato **l'**orologio *He stole our clock*	Indirect object pronouns may also indicate who the possessor is. See also 7.3, p. 112.
IDO pronouns + reflexive si	**Mi** si è rotto **il** televisore *My TV has got broken* **Ti** si è bloccato **il** computer? *Has your computer crashed?* **Le** si è staccato **un** bottone *One of her buttons has come off*	In these constructions the IDO pronouns also denote the possessor. See also 7.9, p. 127, Ex. 2 and p. 128.

 Attenti! Plural subject, singular possession

English and Italian differ when talking about clothing or parts of the body with reference to several people. In English, if several people are referred to, each of whom possess only one of the items in question, then this item is nevertheless automatically made plural, e.g. *They shook their heads.* To an Italian, this would mean each person had more than one head! More logically, therefore, a singular noun is used in Italian if each person referred to possesses only one of the items mentioned.

    Perché non vi togliete **il** cappotto? *Why don't you take off your coats?*

    Abbiamo perso **la** patente *We've lost our driving licences*

    Ci ha stretto **la** mano *He shook our hands*

    Hanno perso **la** testa *They lost their heads* (fig.)

✚ Esercizi

1 Give the Italian equivalent of the English possessives and nouns below.

    (a) Piove, devi prendere (*your umbrella*).

    (b) Angelo arriverà domani con (*his wife*).

    (c) Fa freddo, perché non ti metti (*your jumper*)?

    (d) Mi fa male (*my foot*).

    (e) Si sono tolti (*their hats*).

9 Demonstratives

Demonstratives (**i dimostrativi**) are adjectives or pronouns which refer to something in terms of whether it is near to or far from the speaker. English demonstratives are *this, these, that* and *those*.

9.1 Demonstrative adjectives and pronouns

(a) *Questo* and *quello*: forms

The adjective and pronoun **questo** *this* has four endings. The singular adjectives, but not the pronouns, may be shortened to **quest'** in front of a vowel.

	Adjectives		Pronouns
Masculine singular	**questo** muro *this wall*	**quest'**edificio *this building*	**questo** *this one*
Masculine plural	**questi** muri *these walls*	**questi** edifici *these buildings*	**questi** *these ones*
Feminine singular	**questa** fabbrica *this factory*	**quest'**aula *this classroom*	**questa** *this one*
Feminine plural	**queste** fabbriche *these houses*	**queste** aule *these classrooms*	**queste** *these ones*

The adjective **quello** *that* has seven forms, whereas the pronoun has only four. Like the definite article, the form of the adjective depends on the gender and initial letter of the word which immediately follows.

	Adjectives			Pronouns
Masculine singular	**quel** muro *that wall*	**quello** specchio *that mirror*	**quell'**edificio *that building*	**quello** *that one*
Masculine plural	**quei** muri *those walls*	**quegli** specchi *those mirrors*	**quegli** edifici *those buildings*	**quelli** *those ones*
Feminine singular	**quella** fabbrica *that factory*	**quell'**aula *that classroom*		**quella** *that one*
Feminine plural	**quelle** fabbriche *those factories*	**quelle** aule *those classrooms*		**quelle** *those ones*

Spelling changes of *quello*

When **quello** precedes another adjective or number, its form may change.

Before other adjectives	**quella** giacca **quell'**edificio **quel** parco **quei** giornali	**quell'**orribile giacca **quel** grande edificio **quello** strano edificio **quell'**immenso parco **quegli** stupidi giornali	The form of the adjective **quello** changes if it precedes another adjective whose initial letter requires a different form.

Before numbers and *altro*	Dammi **quei due** piatti. Dammi **quei due** *Give me those two plates. Give me those two* Dammi **quegli altri** libri. Dammi **quegli altri** *Give me those other books. Give me those other ones*	In front of numbers and the pronoun **altro,** it is always necessary to use the adjectival forms of **quello** even when it is used as a pronoun.

◎ Esercizi

1 You've borrowed many of the contents of your flat. Point out what they are, beginning, 'Ho preso in prestito questo/questa ...', etc.

lampada • sedie • divano • cuscini • armadio • scaffale • specchi

2 You're at the market. Point out the things you want to see, beginning, 'Mi fa vedere quel/quella ...', etc.

borsetta • cravatte • maglione • pantaloni • specchio • anello • orecchini

3 Complete the sentences below using the appropriate form of **quello** twice each time.

    (a) Ho scelto — gonna. Ho scelto — altra gonna.

    (b) Ho scelto — impermeabile. Ho scelto — altro impermeabile.

    (c) Hai visto — programma? Hai visto — strano programma?

    (d) Hai visto — documentario? Hai visto — interessante documentario cinese?

    (e) Non mi piacciono — colori. Non mi piacciono — altri colori.

    (f) Non mi piacciono — edifici. Non mi piacciono — grandi edifici moderni.

(b) Uses of *questo* and *quello*

Questo and **quello** are used for pointing things out or for contrasting them.

Questa è mia figlia e **queste** sono le sue amiche *This is my daughter and these are her friends* **Quei** gigli mi piacciono ma non mi piacciono **quelle** dalie *I like those lilies but I don't like those dahlias*	**Questo** *this* and **quello** *that* always agree with the noun they refer to, whether they are pronouns or adjectives.
Quale penna vuoi? **Quella rossa**? *Which pen do you want? The red one?* Gli stivali di cuoio sono belli, ma preferisco **quelli di camoscio** *The leather boots are nice but I prefer the suede ones* Quale giornale preferisci? – **Quello che leggi tu** *Which newspaper do you prefer? – The one you read*	**Quello** is used before adjectives, adjectival phrases and relatives to mean *them ... one(s)*.
Questo è il bagno ... e **questa qua** è la tua camera *This is the bathroom ... and this is your room right here* Queste quanto costano? E **queste qua**? E **quelle lì,** invece? *How much are these? And these ones (right) here? And what about those ones (over there)?*	**Qui** and **qua** (*here*) and **lì** and **là** (*there*) are often added to **questo** and **quello** for contrast or emphasis: **questo qui/qua** or **quello lì/là.**

A note on a special use of **questo** and **quello:**

Questi and **quegli** are used in the masculine singular only to mean *the latter* (**questi**) and *the former* (**quegli**).

Their form is invariable and their use is confined to formal written texts. However, it is important to be able to recognise their meaning. See the text in Exercise 10, Chapter 25, p. 131 for an example.

◎ Esercizi

4 Which animals are being pointed out at the zoo? Complete the sentences using **quello**.

    (a) Guarda quella tigre! Quale? (*That one*) lì.

    (b) Guarda quel leone! Quale? (*That one*) lì.

    (c) Hai visto quegli ippopotami? Quali? (*Those ones. Those three.*)

    (d) Hai visto quei pappagalli? Quali? (*Those ones. The green ones.*)

    (e) Hai visto quell'elefante? Quale? (*That one?*) No, (*that other smaller one*).

5 Give the Italian equivalent of the following.

    (a) *This is the kitchen and this is bathroom right here.*

    (b) *This is my room here and that's yours there.*

    (c) *How much does this one* (una pasta) *cost? And what about that one?*

    (d) *How much do these cost?* (cartoline) *And what about those ones?*

◎/✚ 9.2 Other ways of expressing 'this' and 'that'

✚ (a) Using *ciò*

Ciò is an invariable demonstrative pronoun used more in writing than in speech.

ciò *that/this*	**Ciò** non m'interessa *That/this doesn't interest me* Ha detto **ciò?** *Did he say that?*	**Ciò** refers to a whole situation or idea. It means *that*, or occasionally *this*.

◎/✚ (b) 'This' and 'that': ideas, actions and situations

When *this* and *that* refer to ideas, actions or situations in English, they no longer correspond exactly to **questo** and **quello** in Italian. Nor do they correspond exactly to the pronoun **ciò**. The use of **questo**, **quello** or **ciò**, referring to ideas and situations, depends essentially on the context and on stylistic considerations. Below are some general observations and guidelines.

questo *that/ this*	**Questo** non m'interessa *That doesn't interest me* **Questo** non mi sembra giusto *That doesn't seem fair to me*	**Questo** (rather than **quello**) usually means *that* when denoting an idea, an event or a situation. It can more formally be substituted by **ciò**.
✚ questo *that's, what a … !*	Dobbiamo firmare tre volte. È assurdo **questo**! *We have to sign three times. That's absurd!* Si è dimesso. – Non è possibile! *He's resigned. – That's impossible/not possible!* Ho perso le mie chiavi. **Che** seccatura! *I've lost my keys. That's/What a nuisance!* Ci sposiamo. – **Che** bello! *We're getting married. – That's/How wonderful!*	**Questo** may follow the verb for emphasis or be omitted altogether. Note that the emphatic English *that* may be conveyed by an Italian exclamatory **che!**

✦ (c) 'This is where', 'that is where'

In Italian **questo** and **quello** are not normally used to express *this* or *that* with *where*.

È qui che compro la verdura ed **è lì che** prendo il pesce *This is where I buy vegetables and that's where I get the fish* **È qui che** dobbiamo scendere? *Is this where we have to get off?* **Era qui che** giocavi da bambino? *Was this where you used to play as a child?* **Qui** lavoro io e **lì** lavora mio marito *This is where I work and that's where my husband works*	In Italian you say, **È qui/qua che** … or **È lì/là che** … This literally means *It is here that …, It is there that …* **Qui, qua, lì** or **là** may also express *This is where …/That is where …*

✦ Esercizi

1 Using **ciò** and **questo**, give your reactions to the following, and find an Italian equivalent of the English. There may be more than one possibility.

  (a) Riccardo è molto depresso. – *That doesn't interest me.*

  (b) Sabrina non è ancora arrivata. – *That doesn't mean she won't come.*

  (c) Silvia guadagna meno di Umberto. – *That doesn't seem fair.*

  (d) Sono divorziati. – *That isn't true.*

2 Saying *that's*. Comment on these situations, using an appropriate Italian equivalent for the English responses below.

  (a) Marco si è rotto la gamba. – *That's a pity, he can't go skiing.* (**andare a sciare**)

  (b) I nuovi clienti non hanno pagato. – *That's embarrassing, what shall we do?*

  (c) Costerà mezzo milione. – *That's absurd!*

  (d) Ho perso le chiavi di casa. – *That's a nuisance! Have you got a spare key?* (**una chiave di riserva**)

  (e) Ti posso dare un passaggio? – *Thank you, that's very kind.*

3 You're being shown round by your host. Ask him some questions, giving the Italian equivalent of the English.

  (a) Questo è il liceo Leopardi. – *Is this where you went to school?*

  (b) Quello lì è il mercato coperto. – *Is that where you shop?*

  (c) Questa qua è la piazza principale. – *Is this where the museum is?*

  (d) Quella lì è una pasticceria rinomata. – *Is that where your daughter works?*

◎/✦ (d) *Ecco*

Ecco is sometimes termed a demonstrative adverb because it can be used to present and point things out. When used alone, its meanings include *behold!, there/here is* and *there/here are*. It can also be used with other words to demonstrate, present, explain or deduce facts.

Ecco il tuo posto. *There is your seat.* Ecco i risultati. *Here are the results.*

ecco perché	**Ecco perché** sono in ritardo *That's why I'm late* **Ecco perché** non funziona *That's why it doesn't work* **È per questo che** sei in ritardo? *Is that why you're late?* **È per questo che** non funziona *This/That is why it doesn't work*	**Ecco perché** is used to say *That's why …, This is why …* It is not used in questions. **Per questo** can be an alternative, especially in questions.

ecco come	**Ecco come** si fa ... *This is how you do it ...* **Ecco come** l'ho saputo ... *That is how I found (it) out ...* È **così** che si fa? *Is this/that how you do it?*	**Ecco come** is used to say *This is how ...*, *That is how ...* **Così** can be used for questions, unlike **ecco come**.
ecco quello che	**Ecco quello che** penso io ... *This is what I think ...* Per cancellare un file, **ecco quello che** bisogna fare ... *To delete a file, this is what you have to do ...* Ah **ecco quello che** bisogna fare *Ah, so that's what you have to do*	**Ecco quello che** is used to say *This is what ...*, *So that's what ...*

For **ecco** and personal pronouns, see p. 120.

✛ Esercizi

4 Using **ecco perché** and **ecco come** where possible, give an Italian equivalent of the English. There may be more than one possibility.

    (a) Il treno si è fermato a Prato. – *That's why I am late.*

    (b) Manca la benzina. – *That's why the car won't start!*

    (c) Non lo sai usare? – *Look, this is how it works ...*

    (d) Come lo sai che Tilda si separa dal marito? – *My brother is a friend of her husband's, that's how I know (it).*

5 Find Italian equivalents to the following, choosing between **ecco quello che** and **quello che**.

    (a) *To access the Internet, this is what you must do ...* (avere accesso a)

    (b) *This is what he told me ...*

    (c) *Yes, that's/it's what I intend to do.* (aver intenzione di)

    (d) *That's not what I mean.*

10 Interrogatives

Interrogatives (**gli interrogativi**) are adjectives, pronouns and adverbs used to ask questions. Question words are *why? where? when? how? who? whose? what? which? how much? how many? how long?*

◎ 10.1 Asking questions

In Italian, as in English, asking a question does not always require a specific interrogative word. In contrast to English, however, in Italian there is no need for a special word order: affirmative and interrogative sentences can be identical in structure, apart from the speaker's rising tone of voice, which indicates that it is a question.

(a) Interrogative and affirmative sentences: word order

In Italian, the order of the subject and the verb is more flexible than in English, as the subject may come after the verb. In English, on the other hand, there is a set word order for interrogative sentences.

Affirmative	Interrogative
Puoi venire domani *You can come tomorrow*	Puoi venire domani? *Can you come tomorrow?*
Lo farà per noi *He/She will do it for us*	Lo farà per noi? *Will he/she do it for us?*
Ti sei alzato tardi *You got up late*	Ti sei alzato tardi? *Did you get up late?*

In Italian, when there is an expressed subject, it may come after the verb. See p. 342.

Mamma è malata/È malata mamma *Mum is ill*	Mamma è malata?/È malata Mamma? *Is Mum ill?*
Bruno e Marco possono venire/Possono venire Bruno e Marco *Bruno and Marco can come*	Bruno e Marco possono venire?/Possono venire Bruno e Marco? *Can Bruno and Marco come?*

(b) Types of questions

Questions can be **direct or indirect**. It is important to be able to recognise them.

Direct questions	Bruno può venire?/Può venire Bruno? *Can Bruno come?*	A direct question represents what the speaker actually said.
Indirect questions	Ho chiesto se Bruno può venire/può venire Bruno *I've asked if Bruno can come* Vorrei sapere se Bruno può venire/può venire Bruno *I'd like to know if Bruno can come* Non so se Bruno può venire/può venire Bruno *I don't know whether Bruno can come* Mi chiedo se Bruno potrà venire/potrà venire Bruno *I wonder whether Bruno will be able to come*	An indirect question reports what was said or introduces a question indirectly. Indirect questions can also include various question words such as **cosa? come? quando? dove? chi**? e.g. **Mi chiedo quando Bruno potrà venire**. See p. 310 for indirect questions with the subjunctive.

Some direct questions are **tag questions,** asked not for information, but for confirmation. They end with tags such *isn't she? won't they? can't you? don't you think? isn't that so? right?*

Tag questions	Si chiama Anna, **vero/non è vero**? *She is called Anna, isn't she?/Her name is Anna, isn't it?/right?* Non puoi venire, **vero**? *You can't come, can you?*	**(Non è) vero**? or **vero?** are added to a positive statement and **vero?** to a negative one.
	Silvia ha ragione, **non ti pare**? *Silvia's right, don't you think?* Perderanno le elezioni, **non è così**? *They will lose the elections, isn't that so/won't they?*	**Non ti sembra/pare?** and **non è così?** are both common tags.

◎ Esercizi

1 Make the following statements into questions and provide English equivalents.

- **(a)** Partono stasera.
- **(b)** Cambiamo discorso.
- **(c)** Non vengono con noi.
- **(d)** È arrivata la posta.

2 Convert the indirect questions below into direct questions.

- **(a)** Vorrei sapere quando viene l'avvocato.
- **(b)** Non so se la signorina è polacca.
- **(c)** Non ho capito cosa vuole la dottoressa.

3 You're just checking on the facts. Give the Italian equivalent(s) of the English.

- **(a)** *The post has arrived, hasn't it?*
- **(b)** *Your name is Carla, isn't it?*
- **(c)** *She's a fascinating woman, don't you think?*
- **(d)** *They're leaving on Monday, aren't they?*
- **(e)** *You haven't paid, have you?* (tu)
- **(f)** *The truth is, they don't want to come, do they?*

◎/+ 10.2 Question words

(a) The main interrogative adverbs: 'when?' 'where?' 'why?' 'how?'

Quando? dove? perché? and **come?** are all invariable and are used in both direct and indirect questions.

quando? *when?*	**Quando** arrivate? *When are you arriving?* Da **quando** lo sai? *Since when have you known (it)?* Da **quando** non ci sentiamo? *When did we last hear from each other?* Per **quando** lo vuole? *When do you want it by?* (lit. *for when*) Non so **quando** arrivano *I don't know when they are arriving*	Prepositions precede **quando.**
dove? *where?*	**Dove** hai comprato il pane? *Where did you buy the bread?* Lei di **dov'è**? *Where are you from?* Non mi ha detto **dove** abita *She hasn't told me where she lives*	In front of **è, dove?** becomes **dov'è?** Prepositions precede **dove?**

quand'è che? *when?* dove'è che? *where?* da quand'è che? *since when?*	**Quand'è che** arriva? *When (exactly) is he arriving? When is he (actually) arriving?/When is it he's arriving?* **Quand'è che** ci possiamo vedere? *When (exactly) can we see each other?* **Dov'è che** l'hai visto? *Where exactly did you see him?/Where is it you saw him?* **Da quand'è che** sei qui? *Since when have you been here?* **Da quand'è che non** ci vediamo? *When did we last see each other?*	**Quand'è che?** and **dov'è che?** (lit. *when/where is it that?*) are used to pin things down. Note that **da quand'è che** (**non**) is used with the present tense. See also **da quant'è** (**non**), p. 153 and p. 242.

 Attenti! The position of **dove?** and **quando?** can trip you up. It is important to note that the expressed subject never precedes the verb as it does in English; i.e. you cannot say, 'Quando i tuoi arrivano?'

Subject position with **quando** and **dove**: Italian and English differ	**Quando** arrivano <u>i tuoi</u>? *When are your parents arriving?* **Per quando** lo vuole, <u>la signora</u>? *When does the lady want it for/by?* **Dove** abita <u>sua figlia</u>? *Where does your daughter live?* **Dove** ha trovato il cadavere, <u>la ragazza</u>? *Where did the girl find the body?* *Or:* I tuoi, **quando** arrivano? La signora, **per quando** lo vuole? Sua figlia, **dove** abita? La ragazza, **dove** ha trovato il cadavere?	With **quando** and **dove**, the expressed subject mostly follows the verb or precedes the question word: if the verb has a direct object, the latter is usually the preferred option in order to avoid two juxtaposed nouns (as in *il cadavere, la ragazza*).

However, with **quand'è che/dove'è che?** the subject may directly precede the verb, as in English, especially when a compound tense is used, although they can go before the question word or after the verb + object as above:

Quand'è che <u>il portiere</u> ha chiamato la polizia? *When was it the porter called the police?*

Perché? *why?* can also be expressed by **per quale ragione/motivo?** It is usually, but not always, followed by the verb.

perché? *why?*	**Perché** vuoi uscire? *Why do you want to go out?* Non ho capito **perché** non esci *I don't understand why you're not going out* **Perché** non vuoi uscire? *Why don't you want to go out?* *But:* **Perché non** vieni con noi? *Why aren't you coming with us?/Why don't you come with us?*	Note that in direct questions **perché non ...?** is also used for suggestions, as in English. **Perché non** can also preface a suggestion: the context makes the meaning clear.
	Non vuoi venire? **Perché no**? *Don't you want to come? Why not?*	*Why not?* is expressed by **perché no?**
Subject position	Ma **perché** <u>i tuoi cugini</u> non vogliono venire? Ma **perché** non vogliono venire, <u>i tuoi cugini</u>? Ma <u>i tuoi cugini</u>, **perché** non vogliono venire? *But why don't your cousins want to come?*	The expressed subject may, as in English, directly precede the verb: alternatively it follows the verb or precedes **perché? per quale motivo/ragione**?

Come? *how?* (and occasionally *what?*) is used in a number of different ways, some of which correspond to the English.

come? how?	**Come** sta? *How are you?/How is she/he?* Mi ha chiesto **come** funziona *He asked me how it works*	The use of **come** here corresponds to the English.
	Come mai sei qui? *How come/Why are you here?* Vorrei sapere **come mai** non è venuta *I'd like to know why (on earth) she didn't come*	**Come mai?** is used to find out why. It is more emphatic than **perché?**
	Come si fa per raggiungere l'autostrada? *How do you get to the motorway?* **Come** devo fare? *What do I do?/How do I do it?* **Come fai** per arrivare al lavoro? *How do you get to work?* **Come fanno** per/ad alzarsi in tempo? *How do they (manage to) get up on time?* Il mio computer ha un guasto. **Come faccio** adesso? *My computer's broken. What do I do now?*	**Come?** + **fare** is used to enquire how people do things, how they manage and what must be done.
	Com'è la sua città? *What's your town like?* **Come sono** i suoi colleghi? *What are your colleagues like?*	**Com'è?** and **come sono?** are used to ask what things are like.
	Come, scusi? *Pardon?/Sorry, what did you say?* Abbiamo vinto un milione. – **Come?** Sul serio? *We have won a million. – What? Honestly?*	**Come?** on its own or with **scusi/a?** is a way of saying you don't understand or of expressing disbelief. Followed by **no,** it is used for emphatic agreement.
	Mi presti la penna? – **Come no!** *Will you lend me the pen? – But of course!*	

For **quanto?** *how much/how long?*, see pp. 152–3.

◎/✚ Esercizi

1 Dove? and **quando?** Here are the answers: you ask the appropriate question each time.

    (a) La signora lo vuole per sabato.   La signora, ——?

    (b) Siamo tutti di Pavia   Voi, ——?

    (c) Mi trovo in Italia da due mesi.   Miriam, ——?

2 Now a few questions to pin things down. Give the Italian equivalent of the English, using the present tense for all verbs.

    (a) Dimmi un po', – *when (exactly) do you* (**tu**) *have to leave*?

    (b) Spiegami un po' – *where* (exactly) *are we meeting this evening*?

    (c) Dimmi un po', – *since when have you* (**tu**) *been waiting*?

3 Using **quando, dove** or **perchè,** give the Italian equivalent(s) of the English: take account of possible different subject positions.

    (a) *When are you leaving?* (voi)   **(d)** *Where are the children going?*

    (b) *When is the train leaving?*   **(e)** *Why are you laughing?* (tu)

    (c) *Where are you going?* (voi)   **(f)** *Why are the girls laughing?*

4 Complete the sentences, giving the Italian equivalent of the English and taking account of subject positions.

    (a) Dimmi (*where the cinema is*). (trovarsi)

    (b) Mi sai dire (*when Maria is coming back*)?

    (c) Mi dispiace, non so (*when the bank opens*).

5 Give the Italian equivalent of the English. You will need to use the same question word in all but one case.

    (a) How come you're late? (*voi*)   **(d)** I don't want to go out. – Why not?

    (b) How do I get into the town centre?   **(e)** Can I have a glass of water? – But of course!

    (c) What's your new job like? (*tu*)   **(f)** I don't knows how this works: what do I do?

✚ **6** Give the Italian equivalent of the English.

    (a) When are Pino and Mariella arriving?   **(c)** Where does Susanna live?

    (b) When exactly does the plane leave?   **(d)** Where exactly does your father work?

(b) The main interrogative pronouns: 'who?' 'whose?' 'what?'

chi? who?	**Chi** viene domani? *Who is coming tomorrow?* Mi ha chiesto **chi** viene *He has asked me who is coming*	**Chi?** refers to people only.
	A chi appartiene? *Who does it belong to?* (lit. *to whom … ?*) **Di chi** stai parlando? *Who are you talking about?* (*about whom … ?*) **A chi** piace il manzo? *Who likes beef?* (lit. *to whom is beef pleasing?*) Dimmi **per chi** lavori *Tell me who you work for*	If **chi** is used with a verb requiring a preposition, this precedes **chi.** Typical verbs include **appartenere a, parlare di, piacere a.**
di chi? whose?	**Di chi** è? *Who does it belong to?/Whose is it?* **Di chi** è questa giacca? *Whose jacket is this?* **Di chi** è quel cappotto? *Whose coat is that?* Non mi ricordo **di chi** è questo portafoglio *I don't remember whose wallet this is*	**Di** is used before **chi** to mean *whose?* (lit. *of whom?*).
	Di chi è quel film?/libro? *Who is that book/film by?*	**Di chi?** can also mean *who by?*
che cosa? what?	**Che cosa** è successo? *What has happened?* **Che** ne so? *How should I know?* (lit. *What do I know about it?*) **Che** vuoi? *What do you want?* **Cosa** facciamo? *What shall we do?* **Che** ne dici se andiamo al cinema? *How about going to the cinema?* (lit. *What do you say to going to the cinema?*)	**Che?** is frequently followed by **cosa** but can be used on its own. **Cosa?** is often used informally on its own.
	A che (cosa) serve? *What is it used for?* **Per (che) cosa** lo vuole? *What do you want it for?*	**Che cosa? che?** and **cosa?** can be preceded by prepositions.

For **chi** as a relative pronoun meaning *those/anyone who*, see p. 184.

◎ Esercizi

7 Give the Italian equivalent of the English. Use **voi** for *you*.

(a)	*Who is that man?*	(e)	*Whose umbrella is this?*
(b)	*Who is that book by?*	(f)	*What have you done?*
(c)	*Who likes ice cream?*	(g)	*What do you need?* (aver bisogno di)
(d)	*Who are you talking about?*	(h)	*What are you talking about?*

8 *Not a clue*: complete the replies below, in Italian, using appropriate interrogative words, plus any prepositions necessary.

(a)	*What does he want?*	–	Non so —
(b)	*What is it for?*	–	Non so — (servire a)
(c)	*What is it made of?*	–	Non so —
(d)	*Who does it belong to?*	–	Non mi ricordo — (appartenere a)
(e)	*Who is it for?*	–	Non ho capito —
(f)	*Who is the book by?*	–	Non ho idea —
(g)	*Whose shoes are these?*	–	Non so proprio —

(c) Interrogative adjectives and pronouns: 'what?', 'which?'

The following are all used as adjectives and pronouns.

che? *what?*	**Che** ora è? *What's the time?* **Che** lavoro fa? *What job do you do?* **Che** scuola fai? *What school do you go to?* **Che** tipo è? *What sort of a person is he/she?*	**Che?** is an invariable adjective It can also be a pronoun. (See table (b) on p. 150.)
	Di che colore è? *What colour is it?* **In che** anno è nato Dante? *What year was Dante born in?* **Di che** anno sei? *What year were you born in?* (i.e. *How old are you?*) Dimmi **da che** parte andate *Tell me which (what) way you're going*	**Che?** can be preceded by prepositions. Note that in English it may sometimes be expressed as *which?*
quale/i? *which (one/s?)*	Dammi il bicchiere. – **Quale**? *Give me the glass – Which one?* **Quale** vuoi, la mela o la pera? *Which (one) do you want, the apple or the pear?* Non so **quali** prendere, le rose o i garofani *I don't know which (ones) to have, the roses or the carnations*	The plural form of **quale** is **quali**. When **quale/i** are pronouns, the meaning is *which one/s?*
	Qual è l'indirizzo?/la capitale d'Italia? *What's the address/the capital of Italy?* (lit. *Which is …?*) **Quali** sono i vostri progetti? *What are your plans?*	Note that when the pronoun **quale** is used with the verb **essere**, it corresponds to the English *what?* **Quale** shortens to **qual** before **è**.
	Quale pasta vuoi, la brioche o la ciambella? *Which cake do you want, the brioche or the doughnut?* **Quali** riviste hai scelto? *Which magazines did you choose?*	The adjective **quale/i** (but not the pronoun) may be replaced by the adjective **che**. (See next table.)

⚠ **Attenti**! As interrogative adjectives, **che** and **quale** are very similar and may occasionally be interchangeable.

che? or quale? which? or what?	Che pasta vuoi? Una brioche o una ciambella? *What (kind of) cake do you want, a brioche or a doughnut?* Da **che/quale** binario parte il treno per Londra? *What/which platform does the London train leave from?* Scusi, da **quale** binario? *Sorry, from which platform?*	Broadly speaking, **che** is used in a general sense to mean *what?* and **quale** (*which?*) is more specific. When clarification and precise information are required, **quale?** is used.

◎/✚ Esercizi

9 Give the Italian equivalent of the following, choosing between **che**? or **quale**? Use the **Lei** form where relevant.

    (a) *What's the time?*

    (b) *What job do you do?*

    (c) *What's your phone number?*

    (d) *What's your favourite sport?*

    (e) *What's your teacher like?(two possibilities, one with come)*

✚ 10 In which of the sentences below could **che**? substitute **quale/i**?

    (a) Qual è la strada migliore?

    (b) Dammi una matita. – Quale vuoi?

    (c) Quali giornali compri?

✚ 11 Guess what the mystery object is. To do so, match up the questions and answers below.

    (a) A che cosa serve questo oggetto?   (i) È rosso.

    (b) Di che cosa è fatto?   (ii) Dipende, ma questo qua è abbastanza grande.

    (c) Che dimensioni ha?   (iii) È rotondo.

    (d) Di che colore è?   (iv) È fatto di gomma o di plastica.

    (e) Che forma ha?   (v) Serve per giocare.

◎/✚ (d) Quanto

Quanto? *how much? to what extent?* is mainly used to talk about quantity or size and occasionally time and place. It can be a pronoun, an adjective and also an adverb.

Pronoun: quanto/a? quanti/e? how much? how many?	Ho preso un po' di benzina – **Quanta**? *I got some petrol – How much?* Ecco le tazze, **quante** ne vuoi? *Here are the cups, how many do you want?* **Quanti** ne abbiamo oggi? *What's the date today?* In **quanti** siete? *How many of you are there?*	As a pronoun, **quanto** agrees with the noun it refers to. It is preceded by prepositions. Note these two expressions.
Adjective	**Quanta** pizza prendi? *How much pizza are you having?* Non so **quante** persone verranno *I don't know how many people will come*	As an adjective, **quanto** also agrees with the noun it refers to.

As an adverb modifying a verb or an adjective, **quanto** is invariable. The position of expressed subjects is flexible, as with **quando?** and **dove?**

Adverb **quanto?**	**Quanto** costano? *How much do they cost?* **Quanto** costano i fagiolini?/I fagiolini **quanto** costano?	Note that as with **quando?** and **dove?** the subject cannot follow the question word as it does in English. It must either precede the question word or follow the verb or adjective. **Quanto** becomes **quant'** before **è**. **Quanto?** *how long?* can also be expressed by **quanto tempo?** Note that **da quanto?** is used with the present tense, not the English perfect. See also table below. For use of tenses with **da,** see pp. 242 and 261.
Size: *how big/ tall/high?*	**Quant'è** grande? *How big is it?* **Quant'è** grande lo studio?/Lo studio **quant'è** grande? *How big is the study?* **Quant'è** alto/a? *How tall is it?* **Quant'è** alta la stanza?/La stanza **quant'è** alta? *How tall is the room?*	
Duration: *how long?*	**Quanto** dura? *How long does it last?* **Quanto** dura il viaggio/Il viaggio **quanto** dura? *How long does the journey last?* **Da quanto** abiti qui? *How long have you lived here for?* **Da quanto** abita qui Giuseppe?/Giuseppe **da quanto** abita qui? *How long has Giuseppe lived here?* **Da quanto non** ci sentiamo? *How long is it since we were in touch/heard from each other?*	
Future: *how soon?*	**Fra quanto** ci possiamo vedere? *How soon can we see each other?*	
Distance: *how far?*	**Quant'è** lontano? *How far is it?* **Quanto** lontano abitano i tuoi?/I tuoi **quanto** lontano abitano? *How far (away) do your parents live?*	

Subjects used with **da quant'è che?** *how long for?* and **da quant'è che (non)?** *how long since?* can follow the question word, as with **perché? quand'è che?** and **dov'è che?** (see p. 148).

Da quant'è che (non) Subject position +	**Da quant'è che** abiti qui? *How long have you been living here for?* **Da quant'è che** <u>tua figlia</u> è malata? *How long has your daughter been ill for?* **Da quant'è che non** ci vediamo? *How long is it since we've seen each other/last met?* **Da quant'è che** <u>i suoi figli</u> **non** si vedono? *How long has it been since your children have seen each other/last met?*	The expressed subject position may correspond to the English: alternatively the subject can either follow the verb or precede **da quant'è che (non)?**

For **quanto** in exclamations, see p. 159.

⊚/✚ Esercizi

12 Give the Italian equivalent of the following.

    (a) *How much spaghetti do you want?* (tu)

    (b) *How much sauce do you want?*

    (c) *How many of you are there?*

    (d) *I don't know how many eggs are left (remain).*

✚ **13** Ask the following in Italian, using **quanto.**

    (a) *How far (away) is your house?*

    (b) *How long do you take to get there?* (**impiegare**)

    (c) *How big is your kitchen?*

    (d) *How wide is it?* (**largo/a**)

    (e) *How soon can we see each other?*

◎/✚ 10.3 Special uses of *perché? che?* and *chi?*

These interrogatives are used in a number of very common colloquial constructions used to ask questions to which no answer is necessarily expected.

◎ (a) Questions with *perché?*

Perché? is used before the infinitive to ask general questions usually relating to indefinite subjects.

Perché? + infinitive: Why should? What's the point of?	**Perché andare in giro** per il mondo se in Italia abbiamo le spiagge più belle? *Why go round the world if we have the best beaches in Italy?/Why should you go round the world ...?* **Perché andare a votare** quando i politici non fanno niente? *Why vote/Why should you vote when politicians do nothing?* **Perché preoccuparsi** se la decisione è presa? *Why worry/What's the point of worrying if the decision has been taken?*	This construction is used as form of conjecture, usually relating to the future. See also Chapter 23, p. 287.
	Ma **perché scrivergli** se non risponde mai? *But why write to him if he never answers?/Why bother to write/ What's the point of writing ... ?*	It can be used in a more definite context, although the subject is not explicit.
	Perché lasciarlo lì se era già morto? *Why leave him/ did they leave him there if he was already dead?*	And it can also be used with reference to the past.

 Attenti! When **perché** is not interrogative (i.e. = *because*), the meaning differs:

Perché fare un testamento per l'UNICEF.   *Reasons to give/for giving money to UNICEF.*

◎/✚ (b) Questions with *che?* and *chi?*

A che serve? What for? What's the point (of)?	Ho chiamato la polizia. – **A che serve**? *I've called the police. – What for?/What's the point?* **A che serve** andare in giro per il mondo? *What's the point of going round the world?*	When followed by the infinitive this is used like **perché** above, but expresses futility more categorically.
The following common expressions are very colloquial and emphatic.		
✚ Che + verb + a fare? What/Why on earth?	Ma **che** gli scrivi **a fare**? Non risponde mai! *What on earth are you writing to him for? He never answers!* Ma **che** ci vai **a fare** in Germania? *What on earth are you going to Germany for?* **Che/Cosa** ci stai **a fare** qui? *What on earth are you doing here?*	This expresses disapproval: the action is pointless, unwelcome or unexpected. Note that in English the gerund (*-ing* form) is used, but not in Italian. See pp. 288 and 290 for further explanations. For the use of **ci**, see Chapter 27, p. 344.
✚ Chi me lo fa fare? What/ Whatever for? How do you do it?	Odio fare il pendolare. **Chi me lo fa fare**? *I hate commuting. Why on earth do I do it?/ Why am I doing this?* Che lavoraccio! **Chi ce lo fa fare**? *What a horrible job! What are we doing it for?/Why on earth are we doing it?* Barbara lavora giorno e notte, **chi glielo fa fare**? *Barbara works night and day, what on earth/whatever for?/How does she do it?*	This much-used expression is used in the context of stressful activities: it can be used with all persons of the verb. The basic structure is: **fare fare qlco a qlcu**. For further explanations, see Chapter 25, pp. 315–16.

✦ Esercizi

1 Complete the sentences by substituting the correct Italian verb in place of the English.

    (a) Perché (*pay*) più del necessario?

    (b) Ma perché (*help him*)? Non è mica un bambino!

    (c) Ma perché (*get angry*)? Non c'è più niente da fare.

    (d) Che lo (*are you calling*) a fare? Non è mai in casa.

    (e) Che ci (*are you going*) a fare a Londra?

    (f) Che ci (*are you doing*) qui?

2 Give the English equivalent of sentences (d)–(f) above.

3 Complete these sentences by inserting the correct pronouns, then give the English equivalent.

    (a) Lavoro ogni weekend. – Ma Giulia, chi ... fa fare?

    (b) Prendiamo la metropolitana tutti i giorni. – Ma chi ... fa fare?

10.4 Distinguishing interrogatives from relatives

Attenti! In English, unlike Italian, interrogative pronouns have some forms in common with relative pronouns. Here is a summary of the differences.

Interrogative		Relative	
who?	➡ **chi?**	*who*	➡ **che**
(*with*, *to*) *whom?*, etc.	➡ **con/a chi?** ecc.	(*with*, *to*) *whom*, etc.	➡ **con/a cui** ecc.
which?	**quale?/che?**	*which*	➡ **che**
(*with*, *to*) *which?*, etc.	➡ **con/a quale/che?** ecc.	(*with*, *to*) *which*, etc.	➡ **con/a cui** ecc.
what?	➡ **che cosa?**	*what*	➡ **ciò che/quello che**
whose?	➡ **di chi?**	*whose*	➡ **il/la/i/le cui**

Interrogatives are used in direct and indirect questions. Note that relative pronouns can be used in questions, but they are not the question word.

who? whom?	**Chi** è venuto? *Who came?* **Con chi** esci? *Who are you going out with? (With whom?)*	Direct questions
	Voglio sapere **chi** è venuto/**con chi** esci *I want to know who came/who you go out with*	Indirect question
who, whom	Il ragazzo **che** è venuto è mio fratello *The boy **who** came is my brother* La ragazza **con cui** esco è sarda *The girl I go out with is Sardinian (with whom ...)*	Relative pronouns
	Il ragazzo **che** è venuto è tuo fratello? *Is the boy who came your brother?*	Relative pronoun in a question
which?	**Quale** macchina ti piace? *Which car do you like?* **Da quale** stazione parti? *Which station do you leave from?*	Direct questions
	Non so **quale** macchina mi piace *I don't know which car I like*	Indirect question

which	La macchina **che** mi piace è la Ferrari *The car (which) I like is the Ferrari* La stazione **da cui** parto è Waterloo *The station I leave from is Waterloo*	Relative pronouns
what?	**Che cosa** hai comprato? *What have you bought?* Mi ha chiesto **che cosa** avevo comprato *He asked what I had bought*	Direct question Indirect question
what	Ti faccio vedere **ciò che/quello che** ho comprato *I'll show you what I bought*	Relative pronouns
whose?	**Di chi** è la Lancia grigia? *Whose is the grey Lancia?* Devo scoprire **di chi** è la Lancia grigia *I have to find out whose is the grey Lancia*	Direct question Indirect question
whose	Mio cugino, **la cui** Lancia è stata rubata, si comprerà una Seicento *My cousin, whose Lancia was stolen, is going to buy himself a Seicento*	Relative pronoun

Esercizio

✚ **1** Complete the following sentences by selecting the correct pronoun: interrogative or relative.

   (a) Dimmi — vuoi. (**che cosa/quello che/ciò che**) *Tell me what you want.*

   (b) Fa' — ti dico. (**che cosa/quello che/ciò che**) *Do what I tell you.*

   (c) Voglio sapere — viene. (**chi/che**) *I want to know who is coming.*

   (d) Gli ospiti — vengono sono italiani. (**chi/che**) *The guests who are coming are Italian.*

   (e) Non mi hai detto con — giochi a tennis. (**con chi/con cui**) *You haven't told me who you play tennis with.*

   (f) La ragazza — esce è simpaticissima. (**con chi/con cui**) *The girl you go out with is extremely nice.*

   (g) Mi dai una penna — funziona? (**quale/che**) *Can you give me a pen which works?*

   (h) Non so — penna funziona. (**quale/che**) *I don't know which pen works.*

11 Exclamations

Exclamations (**gli esclamativi**) express strong emotions such as horror, disgust, delight and admiration. As such, they are particularly a feature of the spoken language. They consist of one or several words and do not need the usual structure of a full sentence to make sense, e.g. ***How wonderful!*** ***What*** *nonsense!*

⊚ 11.1 Exclamations with *che! come! quanto!*

In Italian exclamations are mainly expressed by interrogatives. The most commonly used are **che**, **come**, **quanto** and, more rarely, **quale**.

(a) *Che!*

Che is used in a variety of combinations with nouns, adjectives and pronouns which do not always coincide exactly with the English. The English equivalent of **che!** is *how ... !* or *what ... !* and sometime *so ... !* and *such ... !*

Che before nouns	**Che** delusione *What a disappointment!/How disappointing! It's so disappointing!* **Che** pasticcio! *What a mess/mix-up! What a nuisance!* **Che** disastro/guiao! *What a disaster!/How awful/terrible!* **Che** peccato! *What a shame!/It's such a shame!* **Che** meraviglia! *How wonderful!/It's so wonderful!* **Che** rabbia!/**Che** seccatura! *How annoying! What a nuisance!* **Che** caldo! *How hot it is!/It's so hot!*	Note that the English equivalent to the Italian noun is sometimes an adjective.
	Che piacere sentirti! *How nice to hear from you!* **Che** peccato non poterci andare *What a shame we can't go*	
Che before adjectives	**Che** bello! *Great!/How nice!* **Che** strano! *How odd!* **Che** buffo! *How funny/amusing!*	**Che!** + masculine singular adjectives expresses a general comment.
	Che bella! *How lovely/beautiful she is!* (Com'è bella!) **Che** bravi/e! *How clever (they are)!/Well done!* (Come sono bravi/e!)	**Che!** + an adjective agreeing with the noun it modifies is used for specific people or things. A more formal alternative is **come!** + **essere**. See p. 158.

 Attenti! Not all adjectives can be used on their own with **che!** Emphatic ones like **assurdo**, **favoloso**, **meraviglioso**, **squisito**, **stupendo** are used with a noun: you cannot say 'che favoloso/ meraviglioso', but you can say 'che giacca favolosa', 'che panorama stupendo', etc.

Che before nouns and adjectives	**Che** faccia tosta! *What a cheek!* **Che** bei bambini! *What lovely children!* **Che** vino squisito! *What a delicious wine!* **Che** film assurdo! *What an absurd/ridiculous film!* **Che** scarpe favolose! *What fabulous shoes!*	Note that **bello** can be used alone with **che**: che belli!
Che + noun or adjective + **quello** or **questo**	**Che** meraviglia **quella** casa! *What a wonderful house!/How lovely that house is! It's such a lovely house!* **Che** simpaticone **quel** ragazzo! *What a lovely guy that boy is!/He's such a lovely guy that boy!* **Che** carina **questa** borsa! *What a nice/pretty bag (that is)! It's such a nice/pretty bag!/How nice/ pretty this bag is!*	In colloquial Italian an exclamation with **che** + noun or adjective is reinforced by adding **quello** or **questo** followed by the subject. See also the less colloquial **com'è! come sono**!, below.
Che ... che + verb	**Che** faccia tosta **che** ha! *What a cheek he's got!* **Che** stupido **che** sei! *How stupid you are!* **Che** male **che** giocano! *How badly they play!*	**Che**! comes before a noun, adjective or adverb followed by the relative pronoun **che** (*that*), and a finite verb.

Quale! is a rarely used literary form of **che! Quale coraggio!** *How brave!*

◎ **Esercizi**

1 How do you react? Chose the most appropriate exclamation(s) to fit the situation.
- **(a)** *Your friends say they can't come:* **che delusione! che peccato! che noia!**
- **(b)** *You've missed your flight:* **che guaio! che disastro! che sorpresa!**
- **(c)** *Your friend has gone to the wrong meeting place:* **che pasticcio! che rabbia! che meraviglia!**

2 How nice! You are full of praise for everything. Emphasise your admiration, using **che!** with the adjectives and nouns given. Don't forget to make the adjectives agree with the nouns.
- **(a)** quel giardino (bello)
- **(b)** quella casa (meraviglia)
- **(c)** quei ragazzi (simpatico)
- **(d)** quella ragazza (amore)
- **(e)** questi orecchini (carino)
- **(f)** questa maglietta (bellino)

3 Can you comment on these actions? Give the equivalent of the English.
- **(a)** *You've got locked out: How stupid I am!*
- **(b)** *You're not enjoying the concert: How badly they play!*
- **(c)** *Your partner has lost his diary: How careless you are!*

(b) *Come!*

The English equivalents of **come!** are *how!*, *so!* and *such!*

Come before complete sentences	**Come** mi dispiace! *How sorry I am!/I'm so sorry!* **Come** cantano bene! *How well they sing! They sing so well!* **Come** fa freddo qui dentro! *How cold it is in here!/ It's so cold in here!*	**Come!** is used before a complete clause or sentence and is less colloquial than **che!**
Com'è/come sono + adjective + **quello/questo**	**Com'è** simpatica quella gente! *How nice those people are!/What nice people they are!/They are such nice people!* **Com'è** pesante questa valigia! *How heavy this suitcase is!/What a heavy suitcase this is!/This suitcase is so heavy!/It's such a heavy suitcase!* **Come sono** distratti quei ragazzi! *How careless those boys are!/Those boys are so careless!/ They're such careless boys!*	**Com'è!** and **come sono!** are used before adjectives followed by a demonstrative. In colloquial Italian this is often replaced by **che**, e.g. **Che simpatica quella gente!** (see table above).

(c) *Quanto!*

The English equivalent of **quanto!** is *what! how!* and occasionally *such!* or *so (much)!*

Quanto before nouns	**Quanta** gente! *What a lot of people! Such a lot of people!* **Quante** bugie raccontano! *What a lot of lies they tell!/They tell such a lot of lies!*	**Quanto!** *what a lot!* usually emphasises amount. As an adjective it agrees with the nouns it refers to.
Quanto before verbs	**Quanto** hai speso! *What a lot you've spent!/You spent such a lot!* **Quanto** sei cambiata! *How you've changed!/You've changed so much!* **Quanto** mi piace! *How (much) I love it!/I love it so much!*	There is no agreement when **quanto!** is used as an adverb modifying verbs.
Quanto before **essere**	**Quant'**è piccola questa stanza! *How small this room is!/This room is so small!* **Quant'**è bella tua figlia! *How beautiful your daughter is! Your daughter is so beautiful!* **Quant'**è stato difficile l'esame! *How hard the exam was! The exam was so hard!*	**Quanto!** + **essere** is sometimes used like **come!** + **essere** especially when quantity or degree are in focus. It is invariable but changes to **quant'** before **è**.

◎ **Esercizi**

4 Rewrite the statements below to make them into exclamations, using **che** or **quanto** as appropriate. Use the English as a guide.

    (a) C'è molto rumore qui dentro.   *What a lot of noise in here!*

    (b) È un rumore tremendo.   *What a terrible noise!*

    (c) È gente antipatica.   *What horrible people!*

    (d) C'è molta gente in giro.   *What a lot of people around!*

5 Use **quanto** or **come** to complete the following. Sometimes either is possible.

    (a) — dorme quel ragazzo!   (c) — sono lenti!

    (b) — soldi hai speso!   (d) — mi dispiace!

6 What do you say? Select one or more of the exclamations below to match the situation given.

    (a) You've been invited   (i) Che bella!   (ii) Che bello!   (iii) Com'è bello!
         to a concert.

    (b) *That's odd, your friend hasn't* (i) Com'è strano! (ii) Quant'è strano! (iii) Che strano!
         turned up.

    (c) *The ice cream is delicious.*   (i) Che squisito!   (ii) Che buono!   (iii) Che gelato squisito!

    (d) *That boy's so clever!*   (i) Com'è bravo!   (ii) Quant'è bravo!   (iii) Che bravo!

(d) *Chi!*

Chi! is used in only a few exclamations. These are, however, extremely common.

Ma **chi** si vede!/Ma guarda **chi** c'è! *Look who's here!*
Ma **chi** si crede di essere! *Who does he//she think he/she is!*
A **chi** lo dici! *You're telling me!*

+ 11.2 Other exclamations

Not all exclamations (or interjections, as they are also called) are expressed using interrogatives. In Italian, as in English, the spoken language is rich in a wide range of expressions conveying all manner of spontaneous emotions. Many of these are personal or regional and often subject to the whims of fashion. The ones listed here are some of the most common and enduring: learners should beware of using any but the most innocuous, e.g. the ubiquitous 'mamma mia!', but it is nevertheless important to be able to grasp the nuances of the emotions conveyed. Note that each individual exclamation may be used in different contexts to express different emotions.

Astonishment/ surprise, disbelief	Accipicchia!	*Good gracious!/Goodness gracious me!/ Would you believe it!* (slightly precious form of **Accidenti!**)
	Accidenti!	*Goodness me!/Goodness! Good God! Good grief!*
	Caspita!	*Goodness!/Crikey!/You don't say!*
	Mamma mia!	*Good heavens!/Goodness me!/Good God!*
	Santo cielo!	*Heavens above!*
	Non me lo dire!	*You don't say! No! Never!/Well I never!*
	Ma dai! Ma va!	*Come on!*

Ha preso 110 e lode. **Accidenti!/Caspita!** *He got full marks with distinction. Goodness!* **Ma dai,** non è mica possible che abbia vinto! *Come on, he can't possibly have won!*

Admiration and approval	Accipicchia!	*My goodness!/Well, well!/Wow!*
	Bello/a!, Bellissimo/a!	*Lovely!* (this agrees with the noun)
	Fantastico/a! Stupendo/a!	*Fantastic! Great!/Stunning!* (this agrees with the noun)
	Mica male!	*Not bad!*
	Però!	*Well, well! I say!*
	Caspita!	*I'll say so!*
	Bene!/benissimo!/bravo/i!	*Good!/Well done!/Good for you!*
Encouragement and persuasion	Avanti!	*Come on!*
	Forza!	*Get a move on!/Play up!/Come on!*
	Coraggio!	*Cheer up!/Chin up!/Take heart!*
	Su!	*Come on!/Cheer up!*
	Dai!	*Go on!*

È buono? **Caspita!** *Is it nice? I'll say so!* **Avanti!** Non fare il timido *Come on, don't be shy* **Forza** Roma! *Come on Rome!* (football team) **Coraggio!** Fra poco finiscono gli esami *Cheer up, the exams will soon be over* **Dai,** non essere cattivo, fallo per noi *Go on, don't be mean, do it for us!*

Disagreement, disapproval and refusal	Macché!	*Certainly not!*
	Nemmeno per idea/per sogno!	*Absolutely not!/Not on your life!*
	Ma che dici!	*Nonsense! Rubbish!*
	Ma che mi racconti!	*What nonsense!/Rubbish!*
	Ma scherzi!	*You must be joking/kidding!/Of course not!*
	Per carità!	*God forbid!/Not on your life!/Good heavens no!*

Franco è il più bravo di tutti. – **Ma che dici**! È proprio scemo! *Franco is the best of all. – Nonsense! He's really thick!*

Ci vai alla festa di Lucia? – **Per carità!** Sono sempre noiose! *Are you going to Lucia's party! Not on your life! They're always boring!*

Irritation, annoyance and anger	Accidenti! Accidentaccio! Caspita! Santa pazienza!/Santa pace! (Ma) insomma! Santo cielo!/Santo dio!/Dio buono! Accidenti e te/lui/lei ecc. Cacchio!/Cavolo! Mannaggia! Va' a quel paese! Ignorante! Scemo! Stronzo!	*Bother!/Damn!/Blast it!* *Damnation!/Bother and blast!* *Damn (it all)!/Blow!/Look here!* *Good grief!/For crying out loud!* *What now!/Look here/For goodness sake!* *For heaven's sake!/For Christ's sake!* *Damn you!/him!/her!* etc *Bloody hell!* (familiar) *Blast!* (familiar) *Go to hell!* (familiar) *Idiot!* *Idiot!/Fool!* (familiar) *Bastard!/Arsehole!* (vulgar)

Accidenti! Ho dimenticato la benzina! *Bother!/Damn! I forgot to get petrol!*

Caspita! È più di un'ora che aspetto! *Damn it all/Look here, I've been waiting for over an hour!*

Insomma, cosa vuoi? Lasciami in pace! *For heaven's sake, what do you want? Leave me alone!*

Santo cielo, non potresti smettere di suonare per un po'! *For goodness sake, couldn't you stop playing for a bit?*

Concern, trepidation, alarm, dismay and disappointment Commiseration	per carità! mamma mia! o dio!/dio mio! madonna! ma guarda! (che) peccato! ahimé! povero te!/poveretto!	*Please!/For goodness sake!/Whatever you do, please …!* *Good heavens!/Oh God!/Good God!* *Good God!/My God!/Oh God!/Oh dear!* *Good God!/Heavens!* *Oh dear!/That's a shame!* *What a shame!* *Alas!/Alack!* (can be humorous) *(You) poor thing!*

Per carità non dirlo a nessuno! *For goodness sake (whatever you do), don't tell anyone!*

Madonna! Che vento stasera! *Good God! What a terrible wind tonight!*

✦ Esercizio

1 Complete the sentences below, using appropriate interjections. There may be several possibilities each time.

(a) (*Bother!*) ho dimenticato di chiudere la porta a chiave!

(b) Corrado ha dato del tu al preside! – (*You don't say!*) E che cosa gli è successo?

(c) Come sto? – (*Wow! Fantastic!*), sembri una diva con quel vestito!

(d) Abbiamo finito tutti quanti i compiti. – (*Well done!*)

(e) Alberto è stato ricoverato in ospedale. – (*Oh dear!*), che cos'ha?

(f) Non vengo prima delle sei stasera – (*For goodness sake!/Damn it!*), me lo potevi dire prima!

(g) Vieni con noi domani? – (*You must be joking!/Of course not!*), domani c'è l'esame! – (*My goodness/Oh dear*), avevo dimenticato!

(h) Vuoi un'altra fetta di torta? – (*Heaven forbid!/Good heavens no!*), sto a dieta!

12 Indefinites

Indefinites (**gli indefiniti**) refer to unspecific people, things, places and amounts. They are words like *someone, anyone, something, anything, somewhere, anywhere, every, all*. They can be pronouns or adjectives and sometimes both.

◎/✚ 12.1 Indefinite pronouns

(a) *Qualcosa* and *qualcuno*

Qualcosa *something* is normally masculine and invariable. It is always used with a singular verb.

qualcosa *something* *anything*	C'è **qualcosa** che non va *There is something wrong* C'è **qualcosa** che non va? *Is there anything wrong?* Mi piacerebbe vincere **qualche cosa** *I would like to win something*	Note that **qualcosa** also expresses the English interrogative *anything*. **Qualche cosa** is a slightly less common alternative to **qualcosa**, also masculine and invariable.
	Mi sa dire **qualcosa di** più? *Can you tell me anything more?* Bisogna trovare **qualche cosa di** veramente speciale *You need to find something really special*	**Di** follows **qualcosa/qualche cosa** in front of adjectives or adverb + adjective. See also p. 42.

Qualcuno *someone/somebody* is always used with a singular verb, although it often refers to plural persons.

qualcuno *someone,* *anyone,* *some people*	Fa' venire **qualcuno** *Get someone to come* C'è **qualcuno** in casa? *Is anyone at home?* **Qualcuno** ha mai letto 'A Ciascuno il suo'? *Has anyone ever read 'Each to his own'?*	Note that **qualcuno** also expresses the English interrogative *anyone/ anybody*. **Qualcuno** *some people* can also be expressed by **chi**: C'è chi dice che troppa vitamina C fa male. (See 13.5, p. 184.)
	Qualcuno dice che troppa vitamina C fa male *Some people say that too much vitamin C is harmful*	

Qualcuno/a may be used to refer to identified people or objects rather than to people in general. In this case, agreement is made with the gender of the noun referred to.

qualcuno/a *some, a few* *(of)*	Hai incontrato qualche amico/a a Milano? – Sì, **qualcuno/a** *Did you meet any friends in Milan? – Yes, a few/the odd one* Ho visto i quadri. **Qualcuno** era veramente eccezionale *I've seen the pictures. Some were really outstanding* Le pesche sono buone, te ne do **qualcuna**? *The peaches are good, shall I give you a few?*	**qualcuno/a** is the pronoun equivalent of the adjective **qualche** (p. 168). It is always singular even if it refers to plural nouns.

| ✚ qualcuno/a di + noi/voi/ loro *some/any of us/you/them* | Qualcuno di voi ha una penna? *Have any/some of you got a pen?/Has anyone got a pen?* Qualcuna di noi ragazze ti accompagnerà *Some/one (or other) of us girls will go with you* Mi è piaciuta solo qualcuna delle foto *I only liked some/a few of the photos/the odd photo* | Qualcuno/a di + noi, voi, loro, or qualcuno/a + a noun or a number, is always used with a singular verb to refer to things as well as people. The verb is always singular in Italian. |

When **qualcuno** is used to refer to plural persons or things, **alcuni/e** + a plural verb can be used but it is less colloquial. However, it is used instead of **qualcuno** in the phrase *some … others*:

Alcuni sono grandi, e altri sono piccoli.   *Some are big and others are small.* (See page 171.)

◎/✚ (b) *Niente, nulla* and *nessuno*

Niente and **nulla** are masculine and invariable. They both mean *nothing/not … anything*.

| niente/nulla *nothing/not … anything* | Non ho detto **niente/nulla** *I said nothing* Non hai visto **niente/nulla**? *Didn't you see anything?* | **Niente** has wider uses than **nulla**; see, e.g., 2.6 p. 32 and 14.1, p. 187. |
| | Cos'hai comprato? – **Niente di** straordinario *What have you bought? – Nothing out of the ordinary* Non è accaduto **nulla di** particolare *Nothing much happened* | **Di** follows **niente/nulla** in front of adjectives or adverb + adjective. See also 3.1, p. 42. |

The pronoun **nessuno** *no one/nobody* is always singular, even when referring to more than one person or object, but its gender may change to agree with the noun referred to.

nessuno *no one, not anyone*	**Nessuno** è venuto *No one came* Non c'è **nessuno** qui *There's no one here* Non c'è **nessuno** qui? *Isn't there anyone here?*	**Nessuno** is invariable when referring to an indeterminate person or group of people.
nessuno/a *none/not one, not any*	Hai ricevuto qualche regalo/cartolina? – No, **nessuno/nessuna** *Have you received any presents/postcards? – No, none*	When **nessuno/a** refers to objects, it agrees with their gender.
✚ nessuno/a di *none (of), neither, not either*	Ha tre figli. **Nessuno di** loro vuol fare il medico […] *None of them want to become doctors* **Nessuna delle** mie sorelle è sposata *None of my sisters are married* (or, if there are two, *Neither of my sisters*) Ho due cappotti. Non mi piace **nessuno dei** due […] *I don't like either of them*	**Nessuno/a di + noi, voi, loro,** or **nessuno/a** + a noun or a number is always used with a singular verb to refer to things as well as people. See also **né l'uno né l'altro**, p. 167.

For **nessuno** as an adjective, see p. 169.

 Attenti! In a question, you may hear **nessuno** or **niente** colloquially used to mean *anyone* or *anything*:

C'è nessuno in casa? *Is there anyone at home?*
C'è niente per me? *Is there anything for me?*

✦ (c) *Qualcuno, qualcosa, nessuno, niente + altro*

Altro follows these indefinites to mean *else*.

qualcun altro nessun altro *someone/no one else*	C'è **qualcun altro** *There's someone else* Non c'è **nessun altro** *There's no one else*	**Qualcuno** and **nessuno** drop their final vowel. **Qualcosa** and **niente** also drop their final vowel and require an apostrophe. Note that **altro** may be used on its own as short for **qualcos'altro** or **nient'altro**.
qualcos'altro nient'altro/non ... altro *something else,* *nothing else,* *anything else*	Ho visto **qualcos'altro** *I saw something else* Non c'è **nient'altro/Non** c'è **altro** *There's nothing else* Vuole **altro**? *Do you want anything else?* Non mi serve **altro** *I don't need anything else*	

For *everyone/everything else*, see 12.3, p.172. For *somewhere/anywhere/nowhere/everywhere …
else*, see 12.5, pp. 174–5.

◎/✦ Esercizi

1 Complete the sentences by inserting the Italian equivalent of *something, anything, someone, anyone, nothing, no one.*

(a) C'è — che non capisco.

(b) C'è — alla porta.

(c) Non c'è — nel cassetto.

(d) Non c'è — in giro. *(around)*

(e) C'è — in casa?

(f) Posso fare — ?

2 Give the Italian equivalent of the English using appropriate indefinite pronouns.

(a) *Do you want anything/something? (Lei)*

(b) *I don't know anyone called Carlo.*

(c) *There's someone on the phone.*

(d) *I don't need anything.*

(e) *Is there anyone/someone at the door?*

(f) *Has anyone seen my glasses?*

3 Answer the following questions using indefinite pronouns.

(a) Avete scattato delle belle foto? – *Yes, some/a few/the odd one.*

(b) Hai ricevuto qualche bel regalo? – *Yes, some/a few/the odd one.*

(c) Avete dei progetti interessanti per quest'estate? – *No, none.*

(d) Mi serve un foglio di carta. – Ce n'è *(some/a few)* sulla scrivania.

(e) Hai per caso qualche busta? – Sì, ce n'è *(some/a few)* nel cassetto.

✦ **4** Give the Italian equivalent of the English and complete the following sentences using indefinite pronouns.

(a) *(None of)* miei cugini ha la patente. *(can drive)*

(b) *(A few of)* mie amiche arriva domani.

(c) Ti potrà accompagnare *(some of us)*.

(d) Può venire *(any of you)*?

(e) *(None of us)* ti può aiutare.

(f) *(A few of them)* parla inglese.

✦ **5** Express the following in Italian, using the correct forms of **nessuno** or **qualcuno**.

(a) *None of my friends wants to be a doctor.* (**fare il medico**)

(b) *I don't like any of my aunts.*

(c) *Are any of your children married? (use the plural 'you')*

(d) *My parents have interesting jobs but neither of them went to university.* (**fare l'università**)

(e) *My brother took two photos but I don't like either of them.*

(f) *There's no more room in the car; some of you must walk.* (**andare a piedi**)

✚ 6 Give the Italian equivalent of the following. Use **Lei** for *you*.

(a) *Can you ask someone else?* (**chiederlo a**) (e) *I have nothing else to say.*

(b) *Are you having anything else?* (**prendere**) (f) *Haven't you got anything else?*

(c) *No one else can do it.* (**saper fare**) (g) *Didn't you see anyone else?*

(d) *Have you got anything else to do?*

◎/✚ (d) *Ognuno* and *ciascuno*

Ognuno and **ciascuno** are always singular but their gender changes to agree with the noun referred to. They are frequently synonymous.

ognuno *everyone*	**Ognuno** ha il diritto di essere protetto dalla legge *Everyone has the right to be protected by the law*	**Ognuno** refers to individual members of a collective whole. See also **tutti** (p. 170), which is more specific and familiar.
ognuno/a *every one, all of* ✚	C'erano 18 stanze e in **ognuna** c'era un orologio *There were 18 rooms and in every one/all of them there was a clock* Ho provato tre vestiti, **ognuno** più bello dell'altro *I tried on three dresses, every/each one more beautiful than the next*	**Ognuno/a** also refers to individual people and things. Note that adjectives modifying **ognuno** are also singular (e.g. **bello**).
ognuno/a di *all, every one (of)* ✚	**Ognuno di voi** deve dare una mano *All/Every one of you must give a hand* **Ognuna delle** quattro fabbriche ha fatto fallimento *All four factories went bankrupt*	**Ognuno/a di** + **noi**, **voi**, **loro** or + **ognuno di** + a noun or a number is used with a singular verb.

Although **ognuno** and **ciascuno** are often used interchangeably, **ciascuno** is preferred in distributive or partitive constructions.

ciascuno *each one, each person* ✚	**Ciascuno** cercava di salvare gli altri *Each one/Everyone tried to save the others* Erano tempi in cui **ciascuno** sognava di emigrare *They were times when everyone/ each person dreamt of emigrating*	**Ciascuno** is occasionally used instead of **ognuno** when individuals are highlighted more than a group.
ciascuno/a *each* ✚	Le rose costano 6 euro **ciascuna** *The roses each cost 6 euros lire/cost 6 euros each* Ai ragazzi ho dato una penna **ciascuno** *I gave the boys a pen each/I gave each of the boys a pen*	**Ognuno** would not be used in clearly partitive constructions.
ciascuno/a di *each of* ✚	**Ciascuno/a di** voi avrà 250 euros *Each (one) of you will have 250 euros* Ho fatto un regalo a **ciascuna delle** mie amiche *I gave each of my girlfriends a present* Ha offerto un libro a **ciascuno dei** tre ragazzi *He gave each of the three boys a book*	**Ciascuno di** + **noi**, **voi**, **loro** and also **ciascuno di** + a noun or number is used with a singular verb. This emphasises each individual rather than a collective whole.

See p. 168 for **ciascuno** as an adjective.

✚ Esercizi

7 Complete the sentences using the appropriate form of the pronoun **ognuno.**

(a) — ha diritto alla pensione.

(b) In — delle stanze c'erano dei fiori.

(c) — dei cinque figli è sposato.

(d) — di voi deve pagare domani.

(e) Devi compilare la domanda in — delle sue parti.

8 Complete the sentences using the correct form of the pronoun **ciascuno.**

(a) Le cartoline costano un euro 20 centesimi —.

(b) I panini costano tre euro —.

(c) Il generale ha dato una medaglia a — destino.

(d) Alle mie figlie ho dato

(e) I miei figli hanno un computer —.

(f) — di noi è libero di scegliere il proprio dei soldati.

9 Give the Italian equivalent of the English.

(a) *Everyone needs affection.*

(b) *Every one of his daughters married a rich man.*

(c) *In all four restaurants the waiters are unpleasant.*

(d) *All of you must make an effort.*

(e) *Each of you deserves a prize.* (meritare)

(f) *The lilies are expensive. They cost 10 euros each.*

◎/✚ (e) *Uno/a* and *l'uno/a*

Uno/a can refer to people or objects. It is usually singular but the gender changes to agree with the noun referred to.

uno *one/you* ✚	**Uno** potrebbe pensare che non sia vero *One might think it isn't true* **Or:** Si potrebbe pensare che non sia vero	**uno** can be used as the indefinite impersonal *you*, but the impersonal **si** is more common. (See p. 325.) However, with reflexive verbs, **uno** may replace the impersonal **si** to avoid **si** (impersonal) + **si** (reflexive).
uno instead of the impersonal **si** ✚	**Uno** si trova benissimo dagli zii *You have/One has an extremely good time at my uncle and aunts'*	
uno/a *someone*	C'è **uno** qui che ti cerca *There's someone/ some man (or other) here looking for you* È venuta **una** che voleva parlarti *Some woman (or other) turned up wanting to speak to you*	**uno/a** can be used a bit like **qualcuno** but changes gender. It is slightly more indefinite in meaning.
uno/a *one*	Se vuoi una penna, ne ho **una** in tasca *If you want a pen, I've got one in my pocket*	When **uno** means *one* (in number), its gender agrees with the noun it refers to.
l'uno/a *each*	Le cartoline costano un euro 20 centesimi **l'una** *The postcards cost one euro 20 cents each* I piatti? Li ho pagati 60 euro **l'uno** *I paid 60 euros each for them*	**l'uno/a** agrees in gender with the noun it refers to. See also **ciascuno/a**, p. 168.

✚ The following constructions may require a plural verb. Both **uno** and **altro** remain singular but vary in gender.

(o) l'uno o l'altro *one or (the) other, either* ✚	**L'una o l'altra** delle ragazze si faranno vive/si farà viva *One or other of the girls will turn up* Quale giornale compro? – Puoi comprare **l'uno o l'altro**, per me è lo stesso *Which paper shall I buy? – You can buy either one/one or the other, it's all the same to me* Compro tutt'e due i vestiti? – No, sono cari, prendi **o l'uno o l'altro** *Shall I buy both dresses? No, they're expensive, take one or the other*	When **l'uno/a o l'altro/a** are the subject of the sentence, the verbs can be singular or plural. **o l'uno o l'altro** is used more specifically to express a choice between two: *one or the other, but not both.*
l'uno e l'altro *both, either* ✚	Non so quale maglione prendere, mi piacciono **l'uno e l'altro** *I don't know which jumper to have, I like both of them* Sono belle sedie, vanno bene **l'una e l'altra** *They are lovely chairs, either/both will do*	**l'uno/a e l'altro/a** The verb is usually plural. This is also commonly expressed by **tutt'e due** (p. 173).
né l'uno né l'altro *not either, neither* ✚	Questi orologi non mi piacciono, non voglio **né l'uno né l'altro** *I don't like these watches, I don't want either (of them)* Non funziona/funzionano **né l'una né l'altra** macchina *Neither car works*	**Né l'uno/a né l'altro/a** The verb can be singular or plural. See also **nessuno/a di**, p. 163.

✚ Esercizio

10 Complete the answers below by giving the Italian equivalent of the English. In two of the sentences there are two possible versions.

    (a) I bicchieri quanto li hai pagati? – Li ho pagati 65 euro (*each*).

    (b) Quale espressione si usa di più? – Vanno bene (*either one/both*).

    (c) Possono venire Silvio e Luciano? – Mi dispiace, puoi far venire (*one or the other*).

    (d) Mi presti una di quelle calcolatrici? – Mi dispiace, non funziona (*neither of them*).

✚ (f) *Chiunque*

| *anyone (at all)* | **Chiunque** lo sa fare *Anyone can do it*
Lo sa fare chiunque *Anyone can do it*
Non sono cose che puoi dire a **chiunque**! *They aren't things you can say to (just) anyone* | **Chiunque** is invariable and refers only to people. There is more emphasis when it follows the verb. |
| *whoever, no matter who, whichever* | Non voglio vederlo, **chiunque** sia *I don't want to see him, no matter who/whoever he is*
Chiunque di voi verrà/venga, sarà il benvenuto *Whichever of you comes will be welcome* | **Chiunque** is often followed by a verb in the subjunctive. |

Note that the relative pronoun **chi** can express *whoever, anyone who*, but it is slightly more specific than **chiunque**, e.g. Chi ha freddo può aprire la finestra *Anyone who is/Whoever is/Those who are cold can open the window*. See also p. 184.

✦ Esercizio

11 Give the English equivalent of the following.

(a) Non è niente: l'avrebbe fatto chiunque.

(b) È semplice: lo sa fare chiunque.

(c) Chiunque chiami, digli che sono fuori.

(d) Chiunque di voi dovrà essere pronto ad aiutare.

◎/✦ 12.2 Indefinite adjectives

(a) *Ogni, ciascuno* and *qualche*

Ogni, **qualche** and **ciascuno** all precede the noun they modify. **Ogni** and **qualche** are invariable and widely used in speech. **Ciascuno,** which is less common, is always singular but its gender varies.

ogni *every, all* ◎	**Ogni** cittadino deve votare *Every citizen must vote/All citizens must vote* Mi ha sconsigliato **ogni** genere di antidepressivo *He advised me against all types of antidepressants*	**Ogni** is used in a general sense, denoting people or objects as part of a group. It is always used with a singular noun and verb.
✦ **ciascuno/a** *each*	**Ciascun** ragazzo/allievo deve fare uno sforzo *Each boy/pupil must make an effort* **Ciascuno** studente riceverà un diploma *Each student will receive a certificate* C'è una guida diversa per **ciascuna** esigenza *There is a different guide for each/every requirement* **Ciascun**'agenda è diversa, con la copertina dipinta a mano *Each diary is different, with a hand-painted cover*	**Ciascuno** emphasises individuality, 'one by one'. It has four singular adjectival forms based on the indefinite article. **Ogni** may often replace it, just as *every* and *each* are sometimes interchangeable in English. Nevertheless, **ciascuno** is used to stress each individual part.

Ogni is more common than **ciascuno**, to which it is roughly equivalent, but not in the following cases.

✦ ogni or **ciascuno** ⚠	C'è un posto **ogni** dieci candidati *There's a job for every tenth candidate* C'è un treno **ogni** due ore *There's a train every two hours* I prezzi aumentano **ogni** anno *Prices go up every/each year*	**Ogni**, but not **ciascuno**, is used with numbers or to say how often something happens. See also **tutto** + article, which is a little more specific and familiar, p. 170.
	I bambini devono prendere una pallina con **ciascuna** mano *The children have to take a ball in each hand*	**Ogni** cannot refer to two people or things.

For **ciascuno** as a pronoun, see p. 165.

Qualche is a very common adjective.

qualche *some, any, a few*	Ho **qualche** dubbio *I have some/a few doubts* Ho bisogno di perdere **qualche** chilo *I need to lose the odd kilo/a kilo or two* C'è **qualche** posto libero? *Are there any seats free?/Is there a seat free?* L'ho incontrato in **qualche** bar *I met him in some bar or other*	**Qualche** has a range of meanings. It is always used with a singular noun and verb, although its meaning is mostly plural, except when it signifies *some or other*. See also **alcuni**, p. 171 and 2.6, p. 32.

For **ogni** and **qualche** with **altro**, see p. 172.

⊚/✚ Esercizi

1 Complete these sentences using **ogni** or **qualche.**

(a) Mi saluta — volta che mi vede.

(b) — volta mi saluta, ma non sempre.

(c) Vado in Italian — anno.

(d) Ci vediamo fra — anno.

(e) — studente deve munirsi di una tessera.

(f) C'è — studente che non ha la tessera?

✚ **2** Complete the sentences by using **ciascuno** or **ogni,** as appropriate.

(a) (*Each*) concorrente ha ricevuto un premio.

(b) In (*every/all of the*) camera c'è un minibar.

(c) (*Every/All*) studente deve superare una prova.

(d) Vado al mare (*every*) estate.

(e) Hanno fatto le stesse domande a (*each*) allieva.

(f) (*All/Every*) artista è sensibile.

(g) (*Each*) artista vede le cose in modo diverso.

(h) (*Each/Every*) volta che mi vede mi dà dei soldi.

⊚/✚ (b) *Nessuno* and *alcuno*

The adjectives **nessuno/a** and **alcuno/a** are formed like **ciascuno.**

nessuno/a *no, not any*	**nessun** ragazzo **nessun** allievo **nessuno** studente **nessuna** ragazza **nessun'**allieva Non vedo **nessuna** difficoltà *I can see no difficulty*	**Nessuno** has only singular forms but changes gender to agree with the noun modified.
alcuno/a no, whatsoever ✚	Non c'è **alcuna** prova *There is no proof whatsoever/absolutely no proof* Non c'era **alcun** dubbio *There was no doubt whatsoever/absolutely no doubt*	**Alcuno/a** is a more emphatic form of **nessuno**. But note that the plural form, **alcuni/e**, does not have a negative meaning. See pp. 32–3.

For **nessuno** as a pronoun, see p. 163. See also Articles, p. 33, Negatives, p. 187.

⊚/✚ Esercizi

3 Supply the correct form of the adjective **nessuno** to complete the sentences.

(a) Non c'è — problema.

(b) Non abbiamo — alternativa.

(c) Non hai fatto — sforzo!

(d) Non ho — voglia di farlo.

✚ **4** Make sentences (a) and (b) above more emphatic using **alcuno/a**.

✚ (c) *Qualsiasi* and *qualunque*

Qualsiasi and **qualunque** are virtually synonymous and have two main uses.

qualsiasi, qualunque *any* (*whatsoever*)	Per me **qualsiasi** giorno va bene *Any day is fine for me* Posso venire in **qualsiasi** momento *I can come at any time* Mi dà un cognac? – Di quale marca? – Una **qualsiasi** [...] *What make? – Any one will do/Any old one* È una segretaria **qualsiasi** *She's a very average secretary*	Note that, when placed after the noun/pronoun, the meaning can be pejorative. See also p. 175 for **in qualsiasi momento.**

	Per lei farei **qualsiasi/qualunque cosa** *I would do anything for her*	**Qualsiasi/qualunque cosa** are used to say *anything (whatsoever, at all).*
whatever, whichever	Avrai successo, **qualsiasi** corso tu scelga *You'll be successful whatever/whichever course you choose* **Qualsiasi** cosa tu possa dire, non ti crederò *Whatever you say I won't believe you*	**Qualsiasi** and **qualunque** are often followed by a verb in the subjunctive. See p. 308.

✦ Esercizi

5 Answer the questions in Italian taking care to give the correct equivalent of *any*.

    (a) A che ora ti chiamo? – *At any time.*   **(c)** Che vino beviamo? – *Any one you want.*

    (b) Che colore preferisci? – *Any colour is fine.* **(d)** Un whiskey? Che marca vuoi? – *Any will do.*

6 Give the English equivalent of the following.

    (a) Accetterò la tua decisione, qualunque sia.   **(b)** Per lui Elisabetta farebbe qualsiasi cosa.

◎/✦ 12.3 Indefinite adjectives and pronouns

The following indefinites agree in number and gender with the noun they refer to, and all adjectives precede the noun.

(a) *Tutto, tanto, molto, parecchio, troppo, poco*

tutto *everything* **tutti** *everyone*	Ho sistemato **tutto** *I've arranged everything* Lo sanno **tutti** *Everyone knows it*	These pronouns are used in a general sense to mean *everything* and *everyone.*
tutto/a/i/e *all*	Sono venuti/e **tutti/tutte** *They all came/ Everyone came* La mangi **tutta?** (la pizza) *Will you eat it all/all of it?*	When the pronoun **tutto** refers to specific people or things, it agrees with the noun it refers to.
tutto + article *all, the whole, every*	Ho lavorato **tutta la** giornata *I've worked all/the whole day* **Tutti i** bambini vanno a scuola *All children go to school* Lavoro **tutti i** giorni *I work every day*	As an adjective **tutto** is followed by a noun with the definite article.
tutto/a quanto/a *absolutely everything, the entire/whole lot*	Ho fatto **tutto quanto** possibile *I've done absolutely everything possible* Il dolce era squisito, l'ho mangiato **tutto quanto** *The pudding was delicious, I ate the (whole) lot* Ho girato **tutta quanta** l'isola *I've been round the entire island*	**Tutto/a quanto/a** can be a pronoun or an adjective. Both **tutto** and **quanto** agree with the noun they refer to. When followed by a noun, the definite article is always used.
tutti/e quanti/e *absolutely all/ every single one*	Andiamo **tutti quanti** a Parigi *All/Every (single) one of us is going to Paris* Vengono **tutte quante le** ragazze? *Are absolutely all the girls coming?* **Tutti quanti i** biglietti sono stati prenotati *Absolutely all the tickets/Every single ticket has been booked*	Note that **tutti/e quanti/e** is followed by plural nouns.

For **tutt'e due tutt'e tre**, *both,* all three, etc., see 12.4, p. 173.

Like **tutto** these indefinites are adjectives and pronouns. In the table below, examples with adjectives are listed first.

| molto, poco, parecchio, tanto, troppo | C'è **tanta/troppa/poca** disoccupazione *There is so much/too much/little unemployment* **Molti/parecchi/pochi** miei amici sono disoccupati *Many/Lots/Few of my friends are unemployed* | These are all similarly used as both adjectives and pronouns and agree with the noun they refer to. |

◎/✚ (b) *Alcuni, certi, vari* and *diversi*

In the following two tables examples with adjectives are given first.

alcuni/e some, a few	Oggi ho pranzato con **alcune** amiche *Today I had lunch with a few/some girlfriends* Gli operai hanno protestato. **Alcuni** hanno fatto sciopero [...] *Some/a few went on strike* **But:** Hai pranzato con qualche amica? *Did you have lunch with some girlfriends?* Qualcuno (di loro) ha fatto sciopero? *Did some (of them) go on strike?*	**Alcuni/e** is most common in the plural. Note that in questions it is usually replaced by **qualche** (adjective) or **qualcuno** (pronoun). See p. 32. For the singular form **alcuno**, see p. 33.
certi/e certain, some, a few un certo/una certa a certain ✚	Ho avuto **certe** difficoltà *I've had certain/some difficulties* Ha telefonato **un certo** signor Barilla *A (certain) Mr Barilla phoned*	**Certi/e** is close in meaning to **alcuni**. In the singular it is used with an indefinite article. See also 3.3, p. 46.
vari/e, diversi/e, various, several, quite a few, a number of ✚	Ci sono **varie** soluzioni *There are various/quite a few solutions* Ce ne sono **varie/diverse** *There are quite a few* Abito qui da **diversi** anni *I've lived here for several years* **But:** È malato da **diverso** tempo *He has been ill for quite a while*	**Diversi/e** and **vari/e** are usually only used with plural nouns and are close in meaning. See also 3.3, p. 46 for different meaning and position.

◎/✚ (c) *Altro* and *altrettanto*

| (un) altro/a another altri/e other | C'è **un'altra** possibilità *There is another possibility* Ce n'è **un'altra** *There is another one* Ce ne sono **altre**? *Are there any others?* **But:** C'è **altro**? *Is there anything else?* Non mi serve **altro** *I don't need anything else* | In the singular **altro** is used with an indefinite article except when it is short for **qualcos'altro** or **nient'altro** (p. 164). (See also p. 172.) |
| altrettanto/a/i/e just as much, just as many ✚ | Lui ha **altrettanta** paura *He is just as frightened* Questo mese ti mando 850 euro e il mese prossimo te ne mando **altrettanti** *This month I'm sending you 850 euros and I'll send you the same next month* | **Altrettanto** is used for comparing like. As an adjective and pronoun it agrees with the noun it refers to. See also 5.7, p. 93. |

For **altro** meaning *more* before quantifiers, see 4.4, p. 69.

+ (d) Indefinites used with *poco* and *altro*

Ogni, **qualche** and most of the indefinites in tables (a) and (b) above can be used with **altro** and a few with **poco**.

Indefinites + **poco/a** **pochi/e**	Ho comprato **troppo** poca carne *I've bought too little meat* Ci sono **molto** pochi clienti *There are very few clients* Ce ne sono **molto** pochi *There are very few of them*	Indefinites before the adjective and pronoun **poco** are adverbs, so these remain invariable and agreement is only necessary with **poco**. See also 4.2, pp. 56–7. ⚠
Indefinites + **altro/a/i/e** *many/some/few, etc. … other*	Ci sono **troppe** altre/**molte** altre/**alcune** altre/**poche** altre possibilità *There are too many other/many other/a few other/ few other possibilities* Ce ne sono **troppe** altre *There are too many others*	Indefinites before the adjective and pronoun **altro** are classed as adjectives, so agreements are necessary with both **altro** and the other indefinites. See also 4.2, pp. 56–7. ⚠
ogni/qualche + **altro/a** *some/ every/all, etc. … other*	Ci deve essere **qualche altra** possibilità *There must be some other possibility/ies* Hanno scartato **ogni altra** possibilità *They have rejected every other possibility/all other possibilities* Scrivi su **ogni altra** riga *Write on every other line*	**Ogni** and **qualche** are singular invariable adjectives (p. 168), so agreement is made only with **altro**.

Gli altri *the others* and **il resto** *the rest* are used with **tutti** and **tutto** respectively to express *everyone else* and *everything else*.

tutti gli altri *everyone else* tutto il resto *everything else*	**Tutti gli altri** sono a casa *Everyone else is at home* Mi ha lasciato **tutto il resto** *He left me everything else*	**Gli altri** comes after after **tutti**, and this literally means *all the others*. **Il resto** follows **tutto**, which lit. means *all the rest*.

- For *someone/something else, anyone/anything else, no one/nothing else*, see 12.1, p. 164.

◎/+ Esercizi

1 Substitute the English with appropriate forms of **tutto**.

(a) Abbiamo organizzato (*everything*).

(b) Vengono (*everyone*)?

(c) Siamo (*all*) qui.

(d) Hanno dimenticato (*all the*) libri.

(e) Sono stato a letto (*the whole/all*) giornata.

(f) Lavoro (*every*) sere.

(g) Vengono (*absolutely everyone*) da noi.

(h) La minestra ti fa bene. La devi mangiare (*the whole lot*).

(i) (*The entire*) commissione sarà rieletta.

(j) (*Every single*) studenti sono stati bocciati.

+ 2 Odd ones out: identify the inappropriate sentences.

(a) Which sentence cannot be used to say what you paid? Is it grammatical?

(i) Ha pagato molto.

(ii) Ha pagato parecchio.

(iii) Ha pagato diverso.

(iv) Ha pagato poco.

(b) Cecilia says she has got a lot of work. What's the phrase she wouldn't use? Does it mean anything?

(i) Ho tanto da fare.

(ii) Ho altro da fare.

(iii) Ho parecchio da fare.

(iv) Ho molto da fare.

(c) Angelo has made quite a few mistakes. Which three phrases wouldn't he use? What do they mean?

   (i) Ho fatto vari errori.   (iv) Ho fatto alcuni errori.

   (ii) Ho fatto diversi errori.   (v) Ho fatto altri errori.

   (iii) Ho fatto errori diversi.   (vi) Ho fatto altrettanti errori.

✚ 3 Which one of these phrases is grammatically inaccurate?

   (a) Ci sono molte altre possibilità.   (c) Hai mangiato molta poca verdura.

   (b) Ho troppe altre cose da fare.   (d) Ci sono troppo pochi insegnanti.

✚ 4 Give the Italian equivalent of the following.

   (a) *There must be some other solution.*   (c) *Everyone else has gone home.*

   (b) *Every other seat is taken.* (occupato)   (d) *You can take everything else.* (tu)

◎/✚ 12.4 Indefinites and quantity

(a) 'Both'/'either', 'all three/four/five', etc., 'most'

If a noun accompanies any of these constructions it is always preceded by a definite article.

tutti/e e due ✚ **entrambi/e** ✚ **ambedue** *both/either*	Sono venuti **tutt'e due/entrambi** *They both came* Sono partite **tutt'e due/entrambe le** ragazze *Both girls have left* Vanno bene **tutt'e due/entrambi i** colori *Both colours are fine/either colour is fine* Ci sono case su **entrambi/ambedue i** lati *There are houses on both sides/either side*	**Tutti e due** (m.) and **tutte e due** (f.) are often replaced by **tutt'e due**, and are more widely used than the plural adjective and pronoun **entrambi/e**. The pronoun and adjective **ambedue** is invariable and less widely used.
tutti/e e tre/ quattro … *all three, four, etc.*	Sono venuti **tutti e quattro** *All four (of them) came* **Tutti e tre gli** imputati erano in aula *All three (of the) accused were in court* Sono stati condannati **tutti e sette i** dirigenti *All seven directors have been found guilty*	With numbers above two, **tutti/e** is not shortened before **e**. Note that *of* is not expressed in Italian, but a definite article is always used before a following noun. See also **ognuno dei/delle tre, quattro, cinque**, etc., 12.1, p. 165.
✚ **la maggior parte di** *the majority/most (of)*	**La maggior parte della** mia famiglia abita all'estero *Most of my family lives abroad* **La maggior parte dei** miei amici sono stranieri *Most of my friends are foreign* **La maggior parte di** noi non siamo d'accordo *Most of us don't agree*	**la maggior parte di** can be followed by plural or singular verbs. After plural nouns the verb is usually in the plural. After pronouns the verb matches the pronoun (e.g.. **noi … siamo**). For **la maggioranza**, see p. 12.
✚ **(la) gran parte di** *a sizeable/ considerable number/ proportion, a great deal (of), most of/the bulk of*	**Gran parte** degli abitanti è rimasta senza casa *A large number of the inhabitants have been left homeless* **La gran parte** dei rifiuti tossici viene dal Nord *Most of the toxic waste comes from the North* **La gran parte** degli italiani tifano per il Barcellona *Most Italians support Barcelona*	**(la) gran parte di** is less specific in meaning than **la maggior parte.** A singular verb after a plural noun is more common.

For **tutto/a/i/e quanto/a/i/e** *the entire, absolutely all,* see 12.3, p. 170.

◎/✚ Esercizi

1 Find the Italian equivalent of the English to complete the sentences.

(a) (*All three*) case danno sul mare.

(c) (*All four of*) mie sorelle sono insegnanti.

(b) (*All five*) appartamenti sono lussuosi.

(d) (*All six*) giudici sono corrotti.

✚ **2** Give the Italian equivalent of the English to complete the sentences.

(a) (*Most/The majority of my relatives*) abitano in Germania.

(b) (*Most of them/the majority*) sono dottori.

(c) (*A good deal of the penisula*) sarà coperta di nuvole.

(d) Ha perso (*most of/the bulk of his fortune*).

✚ **3** Complete the sentences giving the Italian equivalent of the English and using **entrambi/e** or **tutt'e due.**

(a) Quali delle due giacche mi sta meglio? – Puoi mettere l'una o l'altra, (*they both suit you*.)

(b) A chi chiedo aiuto? A Carlo o a Riccardo? – Puoi chiedere all'uno o all'altro, (*they are both experts.*)

(c) Quale colore ti sembra più adatto? Il bianco o il nero? (*Either is fine, they are both lovely.*)

◎/✚ 12.5 Indefinites expressing place and time

(a) 'Somewhere', 'nowhere', 'anywhere', etc.

All the following expressions are invariable.

da qualche parte *somewhere, anywhere*	Ho lasciato i miei occhiali **da qualche parte** *I've left my glasses somewhere* Li hai visti **da qualche parte**? *Have you seen them anywhere?*	Note that in questions, **da qualche parte** means *anywhere*.
da nessuna parte *nowhere, not anywhere*	Non li vedo **da nessuna parte** *I can't see them anywhere* Non li trovi **da nessuna parte**? *Can't you find them anywhere?*	In questions, **da nessuna parte** means *not anywhere*.
dappertutto *everywhere*	Li ho cercati **dappertutto** *I've looked everywhere for them* Le donne spuntano **da tutte le parti**! *Women are popping up all over the place/everywhere!*	An alternative is **da tutte le parti** *all over the place*.
✚ **dovunque** *anywhere*	Li puoi comprare un po' **dovunque/ dappertutto** *You can buy them more or less anywhere* Si trovano **dovunque/in qualsiasi posto** *You can find them anywhere*	**dovunque** may be replaced by **dappertutto** or by **in qualunque/qualsiasi posto.**
✚ **dovunque** *wherever, everywhere, anywhere*	**Dovunque** siano, li troverai *Wherever they are, you'll find them* **Dovunque** io vada, lo porto con me *I take it with me wherever/everywhere I go* Possiamo andare **dovunque** tu voglia *We can go wherever you like* **Or:** Possiamo andare **dove** vuoi tu *We can go wherever you like/anywhere you want*	When **dovunque** means *wherever*, it is used with the subjunctive and is fairly elevated in style. In speech, **dove** avoids the use of **dovunque** + subjunctive.

✚ (b) 'Somewhere else', 'nowhere else', 'anywhere else', etc.

To express *else*, **altra** is placed after **qualche or nessun'** to agree with (**la**) **parte**.

da qualche altra parte/ altrove *somewhere else*	Saranno **da qualche altra parte/ altrove** *They will/must be somewhere else* Si vendono **altrove/da qualche altra parte/in qualche altro** posto? *Are they sold anywhere else?*	Other meanings are *elsewhere, anywhere else.* **Altrove** is more formal. An informal alternative is **in qualche altro posto**.
da nessun'altra parte *nowhere else*	Non si vede **da nessun'altra parte** *It is nowhere else to be seen/You can't see it anywhere else/elsewhere* Non si trovano **da nessun'altra parte** *You can't find them elsewhere/ anywhere else*	Other meanings are: *not ... anywhere else, not ... elsewhere.*
da tutte le altre parti *everywhere else*	Ho cercato **da tutte le altre parti** *I've looked everywhere else* Si usa l'euro **da tutte le altre parti/** in ogni altro paese/in tutti gli altri paesi *They use the euro everywhere else/in all other countries*	Alternatives include **in ogni altro posto/luogo.** It is also common to use a noun and say: *in all other countries/shops,* etc.

✚ (c) A note on indefinites and time

in ogni momento/ in qualsiasi momento *at any time, at all times*	In Tibet una rivolta è possible **in ogni momento** *In Tibet a revolt is possible at any time* Chi possiede un telefonino è rintracciabile **in ogni momento** *People who own mobile phones can be traced at all times/at any time* Si può spegnere il computer **in qualsiasi momento** *The computer can be turned off at any time (whatsoever)/whenever you want*	**In qualsiasi momento** is slightly more formal and indefinite.
ogni volta *whenever, any/every time*	**Ogni volta che** mi vede mi fa un sacco di complimenti *Whenever he sees me he pays me a load of compliments* Posso partire **quando** vuoi *I can leave whenever you want* **Quando** sei di passaggio vieni a trovarmi *Any time you're passing, drop in*	*Whenever* in Italian is usually expressed by **ogni volta che, tutte le volte che,** or simply by **quando**.

✚ Esercizi

1 Give the English equivalent of the following.

(a) Ho lasciato la mia agenda da qualche parte. (d) Non si vende da nessun'altra parte?

(b) Andiamo da qualche altra parte. (e) Queste scarpe si trovano dappertutto.

(c) Non vado da nessuna parte. (f) Hanno cercato da tutte le altre parti.

2 Now give the Italian equivalent of the English. (Use *tu* for 'you' where relevant.)

(a) *Have you seen him anywhere?* (d) *I don't want to go anywhere.*

(b) *I have met you somewhere.* (conoscere) (e) *I don't want to go anywhere else.*

(c) *Shall we go somewhere else?* (f) *I've looked everywhere/all over the place.*

3 Give the English version of these Italian phrases taken from advertisements.

(a) Con il nuovo software puoi trovare un tassì in ogni momento.

(b) Devi essere pronto a partire in ogni momento.

(c) Si può mangiare in qualsiasi momento della giornata se si ha un'alimentazione sana.

4 Now give the Italian version of the English.

(a) *I eat whenever I want to, at any time of the day.*

(b) *Whenever you feel like it, come and see me.* (tu)

(c) *I need to be in touch at all times/at a moment's notice.*

13 Relative pronouns

Relative pronouns (**i relativi**) link main clauses with subordinate clauses, introducing additional information about a preceding subject or object (the antecedent), e.g. *The girl* **who** *has arrived is my sister*; *The book* **that** *I bought was expensive*. In English, the main relative pronouns are *who, whom, whose, which* and *that*. *When, where* and *why* can also be relative pronouns

◎/✛ 13.1 Main relative pronouns

In Italian relative pronouns can never be omitted, unlike English.

(a) *Che* and *il quale*

che who, whom, which, that	È un giovane **che** studia molto *He's a young man who studies a lot* È la ragazza **che** ho incontrato *She's the girl (whom) I met* Ho visto un film **che** mi è piaciuto *I've seen a film (that/which) I liked*	**Che** is invariable and can be the subject as well as the object of the relative clause. It is important to note that **che** refers to people as well as things. When used with prepositions, **che** becomes **cui**. See pp. 178–80.

Il quale, etc., can be used like **che**, but usually when it is the subject, not the object of the relative clause.

il quale who (whom), which, that	Alla festa c'era anche il mio ragazzo, **il quale** si è sentito male *My boyfriend, who was also at the party, was taken ill* In Italia ci sono tante leggi in vigore **le quali** non servono più *In Italy there are so many laws in existence which no longer serve a purpose*	**Il quale** agrees with the noun it refers to and has four forms: **il/la quale** and **i/le quali**. For this reason it is used for clarity in long sentences to make clear the antecedent (i.e. the noun it refers to). See also below, 'Avoiding ambiguity'.
	Ho incontrato qualcuno **che** conosci *I've met someone (whom) you know* (not **il quale**) Ho incontrato qualcuno **con il quale** hai fatto l'università *I've met someone you went to university with (with whom you went)*	Unless used with a preposition, **il quale** etc. is unlikely to be used to refer to the direct object. Compare the examples here. (See p. 179 for prepositions + **che/il quale**.)
Avoiding ambiguity	La sorella di Marco **che** parte domani … *(Is the sister or Marco leaving?)* **La sorella** di Marco, **la quale** parte *(the sister is leaving)* La sorella di **Marco**, **il quale** parte *(Marco is leaving)*	Sometimes **il quale**, etc. is preferable to **che** in order to avoid ambiguity; **che** is invariable, so cannot make clear the antecedent.

◎/✚ **(b)** *Il che, ciò/quello che, quanto*

These relative pronouns refer to an entire action or concept rather than to a single noun.

il che *which*	È stato bocciato, **il che** non mi sorprende *He failed the exam, which doesn't surprise me*	**Il che** refers to the whole preceding clause.
quello che, ciò che *what*	**Quello che** mi sorprende è la sua arroganza *What surprises me is his/her arrogance* Fa' **quello che** vuoi *Do what you want* La prego di ricordare **ciò che** è stato detto? *Would you please remember what has been said?*	**Quello che, ciò che** both literally mean *that which*. **Ciò che** tends to be used in more formal contexts. For **tutto/i quello/i che** and **tutto ciò che**, see p. 184.
✚ quanto *what, (all) that*	Apprezzo molto **quanto/quello che** hai fatto *I appreciate a lot what/all (that) you have done* Le ha dato **quanto/ciò che** poteva *He has given her what/all (that) he could*	**Quanto** (lit. *how much*) is even more formal than **ciò che**. It tends to be used when the idea of quantity is implicit.

◎/✚ **Esercizi**

1 Link the information about the people and things below into a single sentence using a relative pronoun.

    (a) Marta è un'amica. Marta mi è molto simpatica.

    (b) Eduardo è un lontano cugino. Edoardo lavora a Parigi.

    (c) I signori Colucci sono i vicini. I signori Colucci litigano tanto.

    (d) La Rinascente è un grande magazzino. La Rinascente si trova nelle maggiori città italiane.

    (e) 'Roma città aperta' è un film di Rossellini. Non ho mai visto 'Roma città aperta'.

2 Give the Italian equivalent of the following, taking care to use relative pronouns.

    (a) *The flat I rented is on the first floor.* (affittare)

    (b) *The man you met is the landlady's husband who is leaving today.* (la padrona)

    (c) *They have raised the rent, which isn't fair.* (l'affitto)

✚ **3** Identify the three sentences below in which both **che** and **il quale**, etc. can be used. (Remember that **il quale** is not used as a direct object.) Then, for the remaining two, supply the appropriate pronoun.

    (a) A Parigi abbiamo trovato un ristorante italiano — ci è molto piaciuto.

    (b) La borsa — ho comprato è viola.

    (c) È la stazione — è stata bombardata nel 1944.

    (d) In macchina hanno portato anche il cane, — è stato buono buono.

✚ **4** Identify the four relative pronouns *what* below (the others are exclamations and interrogatives). Then give the Italian equivalent of the English relative sentences, using the **tu** form of address.

    (a) *What you're doing is absurd.*   **(e)** *What a horrible colour!*

    (b) *You can do what you want.*   **(f)** *What can I do?*

    (c) *I will do what I can.*   **(g)** *I don't know what to do.*

    (d) *What I don't like is the colour.*

✚ **5** In which one of the sentences above could **quanto** be used as well as **quello che** or **ciò che**?

◎/✚ **13.2 Relative pronouns with prepositions**

When prepositions are used with the relative pronouns **che** and **il quale**, etc., **che** changes form and **il quale** undergoes minor modifications.

⊚/✦ (a) *A cui, etc., al/alla quale, etc.*

Che *who, whom, which* becomes **cui** when used with prepositions, which always precede it.

a + che = **a cui** *to whom/to which* per + che = **per cui** *for whom/for which*	È l'uomo **a cui** ho scritto *He is the man I wrote to/the man to whom I wrote* La ditta **per cui** lavoro è in centro *The firm I work for/The firm for which I work is in the centre of town*	**Cui** is invariable. In Italian it never comes at the end of the sentence. Not all prepositions can be used with **cui**. See below.

Prepositions precede **il quale**, etc.; **quale** itself does not change its form except to agree with its antecedent, but a number of prepositions are joined to the definite article. Here are some examples.

a + il quale = **al quale** a + i quali = **ai quali** a + la quale = **alla quale** a + le quali = **alle quali** *to whom/to which*	È l'uomo **al quale** ho scritto *He's the man I wrote to* Sono gli uomini **ai quali** ho scritto *They are the men I wrote to* È la donna **alla quale** ho scritto *She's the woman I wrote to* Sono le donne **alle quali** ho scritto *They are the women I wrote to*	**Il quale** must agree with the noun it refers to. The definite article is joined to **a**, **da**, **di**, **in**, **su**, and occasionally to **con**, but not to other prepositions such as **per**. See below.

✦ Other prepositions such as **per** remain separate from **il quale** etc.

per + il quale, etc. for *whom/which* **per cui** also common	Gli australiani **per i quali** lavoro sono veramente in gamba *The Australians I work for/for whom I work are really decent* La ditta **per la quale/per cui** lavoro è in centro *The firm I work for/for which I work is in the centre of town*	Instead of **per i quali/la quale**, etc., it is possible to use **per cui**.

The following prepositions are generally used with **il quale**, etc., rather than with **cui**.

Other prepositions: **contro, dentro, senza, secondo** + **il quale**, etc	Questo è l'albero **contro il quale** si è schiantata la macchina *This is the tree the car crashed against/ against which the car crashed* È una legge **secondo la quale** è vietato fumare nei luoghi pubblici *It is a law according to which it is forbidden to smoke in public places*	Instead of these prepositions + **il quale**, etc., it is possible but less common to use **cui**. For a list of other prepositions, see 15.3, pp. 205–6.
Compound prepositions, e.g. **davanti a, in fondo a, a causa di, lontano da**	C'era un lunghissimo corridoio **in fondo al quale** si trovava una porta chiusa *There was a very long corridor at the end of which was a closed door* Vive rinchiuso in un suo mondo a parte, **fuori del quale** non riesce a vivere *He lives cooped up in a separate world of his own, outside which he cannot exist* (<u>not</u> fuori di cui)	Compound prepositions are more often used with **il quale**: **a, di** or **da** is combined with the definite article. Note that **fuori** (**di**) and **invece** (**di**) are never used with **cui**.

Attenti! Watch out for **hidden prepositions**.

Note that a preposition may be required where in English there is none, e.g. **aver bisogno di**, *to need*, **rispondere a** *to answer*.

Italian and English differ	I libri **di cui/dei quali** ho bisogno sono troppo cari *The books I need are too expensive* (i.e. *of which I have need*) Sono domande **a cui/alle quali** non posso rispondere *They are questions I can't answer* (i.e. *to which I cannot reply*)

For clarification you need to use a preposition + **il quale**, etc., not a preposition + **cui: il quale** avoids ambiguity better than a preposition + **cui** because the definite article pinpoints the noun referred to.

Preposition + **il quale** for clarification	*I saw my brother's girlfriend, to whom I gave the books* Ho visto la ragazza di mio fratello **a cui** ho dato i libri *(Who got the books?)* Ho visto **la ragazza** di mio fratello **alla quale** ho dato i libri *(the girl)* Ho visto la ragazza di **mio fratello al quale** ho dato i libri *(the brother)*

✦ **(b) Relatives with numbers and quantifiers: 'some', 'one', 'two', 'ten ... of whom/which'**

The preposition **di** is used with either **il quale** or **cui** to express quantity.

one of whom/which some of whom/which	Abbiamo tre computer, **uno dei quali/di cui uno** non funziona *We have three computers one of which doesn't work* Hanno tre figli, **due dei quali/di cui due** sono architetti *They have three sons two of whom are architects* Mia nonna ha vari anelli, **alcuni dei quali/di cui alcuni** sono di valore *My grandmother has quite a few rings, some of which are valuable*	**Del quale** and sometimes **di cui** are used with numbers and quantifiers (e.g. **alcuni, molti, ognuno**). **Del quale** usually follows the number or quantity, but **di cui** tends to precede it.

◎/✦ Esercizi

1 How do you relate to these people? Link the two sentences into one by replacing the underlined phrases with suitable relative pronouns. Provide an alternative one each time.

   (a) Il professor Binni è un insegnante. Ho molto rispetto <u>per il Professor Binni</u>.

   (b) Carlotta è la nipote. Ho regalato una bicicletta <u>a Carlotta</u>.

   (c) Aldo e Stefano sono colleghi. Lavoro <u>con Aldo e Stefano</u> da due anni.

   (d) Fiorella è la mia assistente. <u>Senza Fiorella</u> non potrei lavorare.

   (e) Il signor Feroni è il nostro capo. <u>Secondo lui</u>, siamo tutti pigri.

✦ **2** You are describing these places from the photos. Link the two sentences into one by replacing the underlined phrases with suitable relative pronouns.

   (a) Questo è il Duomo. <u>Accanto al Duomo</u> si trova il Battistero.

   (b) Qui c'è una bella piazza. <u>In centro alla piazza</u> c'è un monumento ai caduti della Grande Guerra.

   (c) Queste sono le due fontane. <u>Dietro alle due fontane</u> si vede il museo.

   (d) Qui ci sono i giardini pubblici. <u>Di fronte ai giardini pubblici</u> si trova la stazione.

✚ **3** Complete these sentences with appropriate relatives.

    (a) Ho due stampanti, — una non è mia.

    (b) Qui ci sono tre calcolatrici, due — sono rotte.

    (c) Mi ha dato delle cartelle, alcune — sono sparite.

    (d) Abbiamo cenato con degli amici — uno è deputato.

    (e) Hanno sette figlie ognuna — è bellissima.

◎ (c) Relatives expressing time, space and manner

In Italian, the relatives expressing time, space and manner/reason tend to differ from the English: for example, *when* is rarely **quando** in relative constructions, and *why* is not usually **perché**.

Time and place: in cui *when and where*	Il 1986 è **l'anno in cui** è nato mio fratello *1986 is the year (when) my brother was born* È **la casa in cui**/**dove** sono nato/a *It's the house where (in which) I was born*	**In cui** (lit. *in which*) can mean *when* and also *where,* and is used after words like **giorno**, **data**, **momento** and **periodo. Dove** is also used as a relative to say *where.*
Manner: in cui *how*	Non mi piace **il modo in cui** ti parla *I don't like the way (in which) he talks to you*	**In cui** is also used after **modo** or **maniera** to mean *the way (in which).*
Reasons: per cui *why*	Non è **la ragione per cui** è venuto *It's not the reason (why) he came* Hai capito **il motivo per cui** l'ha fatto? *Do you understand the reason (why) he did it?*	**Per cui** can mean *why* (lit. *for which?*). It is used with both **la ragione** or **il motivo** *reason.*

Il quale, etc. can replace **in/per cui** in the examples above.
  È l'anno **nel quale** ... È la casa **nella quale** ...
  Non è la ragione **per la quale** ...

◎ Esercizio

4 Family matters. Give the Italian equivalent of the English.

    (a) *1905 is the year my grandfather was born.*

    (b) *The reason(s) he emigrated are not clear.*

    (c) *The house in London he lived in was bombed during the war.* (**è stata bombardata**)

◎/✚ 13.3 Relatives with special verbs

(a) Relatives with *piacere, servire, mancare,* etc.

⚠ **Attenti!** When using relative pronouns with verbs such as **piacere (a)**, **servire (a)** and **mancare (a),** it is essential to distinguish between the grammatical subject and object, because these differ in Italian and English. Compare:

a cui: Italian indirect object ➡ English subject	*che*: Italian subject ➡ English direct object
Sono gli amici **a cui piace** tanto Roma *They are the friends who like Rome so much* (lit. *to whom Rome is so pleasing*) Il signore **a cui serve** un'altra forchetta è al tavolo due *The man who needs another fork is at table two*	È la ragazza **che** mi piace di più *She's the girl (whom) I like most* (lit. *She's the girl who is most pleasing to me*) È un libro **che** non mi serve *It's a book (that) I don't need* (lit. *It is a book which is not necessary to me*)

When the relative refers to the Italian grammatical subject, **che** is used in preference to **il quale**. Both **a cui** and **al quale**, etc. are used with reference to the Italian indirect object.	
Gli amici **ai quali/a cui** piace ... Il signore **al quale/a cui** serve ...	**Il quale** not used.

✦ (b) Relatives with some passive and impersonal constructions

In passive and impersonal constructions, the English subject is the Italian direct or indirect object, so again take care: with verbs requiring **a** before a person, the English subject *who* is the Italian indirect object *to whom*. See also Chapter 25, pp. 319–20.

Impersonal and passive: *a cui* **Italian indirect object ➡ English subject**	Active: *che* **Italian and English subjects coincide**
Gli operai **a cui** hanno rifiutato un aumento sono in sciopero *The workers who were refused a rise are on strike* (lit. *The workers to whom they refused a rise*) *Or:* Gli operai **a cui** è stato rifiutato un aumento .... (lit. *The workers to whom a rise was refused*) La signora **a cui** hanno mandato la fattura non ha pagato *The woman who was sent the invoice has not paid* (lit. *The woman to whom they sent the invoice* ...) *Or:* La signora **a cui** è stata mandata la fattura ... (lit. *to whom the invoice was sent*)	Gli operai **che** hanno rifiutato di lavorare *The workers who refused to work* ... La signora **che** ha mandato la fattura *The woman who sent the invoice* ...
Gli operai **ai quali** hanno rifiutato ... La signora **alla quale** hanno mandato la fattura ...	

✦ Esercizio

1 Che or **cui**? Decide which of the sentences in each pair requires **che** and which **a cui**.

(a) È l'unico studente — piace l'insegnante   *He's the only student who likes the teacher.*
È l'unico insegnante — mi piace.   *He's the only teacher I like.*

(b) I profughi — hanno concesso l'asilo sono bosniaci.   *The refugees who were given asylum are Bosnian.*
I profughi — hanno richiesto l'asilo sono bosniaci.   *The refugees who asked for asylum are Bosnian.*

(c) La signora — mi ha offerto il posto è molto gentile.   *The woman who offered me the job is very nice.*
La signora — hanno offerto il lavoro lo ha rifiutato.   *The woman who was offered the job turned it down.*

✦ 13.4 'Whose'

In Italian, how to say *whose* depends on whether it refers to the subject or the object of a sentence.

(a) 'Whose': subject of the relative sentence

There are two main forms used as the subject of a sentence.

il cui **la cui** **i cui** **le cui**	Il pittore Tintoretto, **il cui** vero nome era Jacopo Comin, è nato a Venezia Verdi, **la cui** prima moglie morì nel 1840, si risposò nel 1859	**Cui** is preceded by the appropriate definite article denoting who or what is possessed. It is placed before the noun.
di + il/la quale, **i/le quali**	È un film **del quale** non ricordo il titolo È una canzone **della quale** non conosco le parole	**Di + quale** is used with the definite article of the noun denoting the possessor and is placed after the noun.

Either of the forms above are commonly used to express *whose*. Where there is ambiguity, the use of **del quale, della quale,** etc. is usually clearer than **il, la cui,** etc.

<table>
<tr><td>Il mio amico, la cui casa è in vendita è simpaticissimo.</td><td>My friend, whose house is for sale, is extremely nice.</td></tr>
<tr><td>Il mio amico, la casa del quale è in vendita, è simpaticissimo.</td><td></td></tr>
</table>

When a verb requiring a preposition is involved (e.g. **contare su, fidarsi di**), the use of **cui** is more common than **quale.** As a rule the preposition combines with the article in front of **cui.**

È una persona **sul cui** giudizio puoi contare.	*He is a person whose judgement you can rely on.*
È un uomo **del cui** parere mi fido sempre.	*He is a man whose opinion I always trust.*

(b) 'Whose': object of the relative sentence

di cui + **verb +** **definite** **article**	Ho parlato con una signora **di cui** mi sfugge sempre **il** nome *I spoke to a woman whose name always escapes me* Ho un account **di cui** non ricordo il password *I've got an account whose password I can't remember*	When *whose* + noun are the object of the verb in the relative clause, **di cui** is placed before the verb, followed by the definite article + noun.

 Attenti! When *whose* is interrogative it is **di chi?**, e.g. Di chi sono questi guanti? *Whose gloves are these?/Whose are those gloves?* See Interrogatives, p. 150.

✚ Esercizio

1 Form a single sentence from each pair below by replacing the underlined phrases using a construction with **cui.**

(a) Ho appena incontrato una signora.   La sua figlia conosce Anna.   *(a woman whose daughter …)*

(b) Mia cugina si sente molto sola.   Le sue figlie abitano a Parigi.   *(my cousin whose daughters …)*

(c) Il camion ha provocato l'incidente.   I suoi freni non funzionavano.   *(the lorry whose brakes …)*

(d) È un romanzo di fantascienza.   Non mi ricordo l'autore.   *(the novel whose author …)*

(e) Abita in un paesino.   Mi dimentico il nome del paesino.   *(a village whose name …)*

◎/✚ 13.5 Other relative pronouns

✚ quello/a/ quelli/e che *the one(s) which,* *whichever*	Ho comprato la rivista, **quella che** compritu *I've bought the magazine, the one (which)* *you buy* Quale prendo? – **Quello che** vuoi *Which one can I take? – Whichever/The one* *you want*	Apart from meaning *what* (p. 178), **quello che** is used to refer to specific things or people and must agree with the noun it modifies.
quelli che *those* *who/those of you* *who*	**Quelli che** si trovano in difficoltà mi possono consultare *Those who are having problems can ask me*	**Quelli che** can also refer to people in general. It is close in meaning to **chi**, but a bit more specific (see below).
✚ coloro che *those who*	È un nuovo registratore digitale su disco per **coloro che** desiderano ascoltare un suono stereo digitale *It is a new digital CD recorder for those who* *wish to hear a digital stereo sound*	**Coloro che** is mainly used in written Italian and is less used than **quelli che** and **chi.** Its singular forms, **colui** (*he who*) and **colei** (*she who*), are quite rare.
tutto quello/ciò che ✚ tutto quanto *everything (that),* *all that,* *whatever*	Fa tutto **quello/ciò che** vuole *He does everything (that) he wants/* *whatever he wants* Milano è la vera capitale di **tutto quanto** è nuovo *Milan is the true capital of all that is new*	**Tutto quello che** and **tutto ciò che** are similarly used. **Tutto quello che** is a bit less formal. The literal meaning is *all that which.* **Tutto quanto** is the most formal.
tutti quelli che *everyone/all those* *who*	**Tutti quelli che** si trovano in difficoltà mi possono consultare dopo *All those who/Everyone who is having* *problems can consult me afterwards*	**Tutti quelli che** is used when referring to a general group of people. **Tutte** **quelle che** is possible if the group is female.
tutti/e quelli/e che *all those which*	Le mele sono cadute e ho raccolto **tutte** **quelle che** non erano marce *The apples have fallen and I gathered all* *those which weren't rotten*	This is used to refer to things and must agree with the noun it refers to.
✚ chi *people who/those* *who/anyone who/* *whoever/he who*	C'è **chi** non sa né leggere né scrivere *There are people who can neither read nor* *write* **Chi** si trova in difficoltà mi può consultare *Whoever is having/Those who are having* *problems can consult me* Guarda **chi** c'è! *Look who's here!* (lit. *look at he who is here*)	**Chi** is always used with a singular verb, although it may have a plural meaning. It refers to unspecified people only and is commonly used in spoken as well as written Italian.
✚ chi ... chi *some (people) ...* *others*	**Chi** leggeva, **chi** dormiva *Some (people) were reading, others were* *sleeping*	**Chi ... chi** is more common in written Italian than spoken Italian. It refers to people only.

⊕/✚ Esercizi

1 Give the Italian equivalent of the English. Use **tu** for *you*.

    (a) Quale piatto prendo? – *The one you prefer.*

    (b) Quali riviste compro? – *The ones you want.*

    (c) Non mi piace quella ragazza. – Quale? – *The one who studies medicine.* (**fare medicina**)

    (d) Mi presti qualche libro? – *Of course, take whichever/the ones you want.*

    (e) *Those of you who arrive late will have to come back tomorrow.*

2 Use each of the relative pronouns below twice to complete the sentences.

tutto quello che • tutti quelli che

    (a) Grazie per — hai fatto.

    (b) Puoi fare — vuoi.

    (c) — hanno studiato quest'anno saranno sicuramente promossi.

    (d) Questi libri non mi servono più, puoi prendere — vuoi.

✚ **3** These questions refer back to Exercise 2.

    (a) In which of the above sentences, could **tutto ciò che** be used?

    (b) In which of the sentences could the relative pronoun be translated as *whatever*?

✚ **4** Identify the sentences below in which **chi** is used as a relative pronoun and provide an English equivalent.

    (a) Mi dispiace, ma chi non ha la tessera non può mangiare alla mensa.

    (b) Devo sapere entro domani chi vuole iscriversi al corso.

    (c) La scadenza per chi vuole iscriversi al corso è il 3 settembre.

    (d) È un posto ideale per chi desidera riposarsi.

    (e) L'albergo Miramare pensa a chi desidera il relax totale.

    (f) C'è chi preferisce i cani e chi invece preferisce i gatti.

✚ **5** In which sentence(s) above can **quelli che** not be used instead of **chi**?

6 Times are hard. The readers of a woman's magazine have been asked to blog and say what they won't give up under any circumstances:

In questo momento di crisi economica abbiamo chiesto alle nostre blogger: 'A che cosa di non strettamente necessario non siete comunque disposte a rinunciare?' Ecco i risultati del sondaggio.

Assolutamente non voglio rinunciare a:

• un weekend con lui (53%)

• il viaggio di Natale (14%)

• un paio di stivali nuovi (20%)

• una borsa nuova (14%)

Whether you are male or female, think about what you can't give up or do without. Give as many answers as you can, including at least one which begins:

One thing I will never give up is … (use **rinunciare a**) and another beginning:

One thing I can't do without is … (use **fare a meno di**)

14 Negatives

Negatives (**le negazioni**) are used to contradict the meaning, or part of the meaning, of a sentence. They include various parts of speech such as adverbs or indefinites. Typical negative words are *no*, *not* and *nothing*. In Italian, negatives are made with single words but more often with two.

◎ 14.1 Single negatives

(a) The main negatives: use before verbs

In Italian the main single negatives are **no** *no* and **non** *not*. Their use does not always correspond to the English.

no *no*	Vieni domani? – **No** *Are you coming tomorrow? – No*	**No** is used like *no* in English to contradict a whole question.
non *not*	Vieni domani? – (No) **non** vengo *Are you coming tomorrow? – (No), I'm not coming* Hai finito? – No, **non** ho finito *Have you finished? – No, I haven't finished*	**Non** is used within a sentence and placed immediately before the word it negates – usually a verb. If there is an auxiliary, **non** precedes it, unlike in English.
	Non lo trovo *I can't (cannot) find it* **Non** mi piace *I don't like it*	**Non** goes before object pronouns.

With verbs of thinking, believing, hoping and opinion, e.g. **pensare**, **credere**, **parere**, **sembrare**, the expression **di no** may be used when the negation comes at the end of the sentence.

di no *not* *not ... so*	Viene anche Matteo? – Spero/Credo **di no** *Is Matteo coming too? – I hope/think not* (i.e. *I don't think so*) Matteo ha finito gli esami? – Mi pare **di no**/ Credo **di no** *I think not **Or note also:*** Non mi pare/Non credo *I don't think so* Non sembra *It doesn't seem so*	**Di no** corresponds to *not* at the end of a sentence or to *not .... so*, e.g. *I think not/I don't think so.* Note that **non** is also used, but not with **sperare**, as you cannot say *I don't hope so.*
o no, o meno *or not*	Non so se viene **o no**/**o meno** *I don't know if he's coming or not* Fammi sapere se puoi aiutare **o no**/**o meno** *Let me know if you can help or not **But:*** Vieni **o no**? *Are you coming or not?*	In Italian, the literal equivalent of *or not* is *or no* and *or less*. In direct questions **o meno** is not normally used.

(b) Negatives before nouns, adjectives, etc.

Non and other negatives such as **niente** may be used in constructions before nouns, adjectives, prepositions, etc.

non *not*	Ma io viaggio in seconda classe, **non** in prima *But I travel second class, not first class* Lo fa per me, **non** per te *He is doing it for me, not you* Giuliano mi sembra triste, **non** arrabbiato *Giuliano seems sad to me, not angry.*	**Non** may precede adverbial phrases, prepositions or adjectives, for example. It is usually used for emphasis in contradictions.

nessuno *no, not one*	**Nessun** cliente si è presentato *No clients/Not one/a single client turned up*	**Nessuno** is used for emphasis. See also Chapter 2 and Chapter 12.
niente *no*	**Niente** caffè, grazie *No coffee, thanks* **Niente** zucchero per me *No sugar for me*	**Niente**, but not **nessuno**, is commonly used to decline an offer. Note that as a question **niente** may be used in the affirmative to make an offer. See also 12.1, p. 163.
	Niente caffè? *Any coffee? (No coffee?)* **Niente** zucchero per lei? *Any sugar for you? (No sugar for you?)*	

◎ Esercizio

1 Give Italian equivalents of the English replies.

    (a) Ti chiami Edda? – *No, my name isn't Edda, it's Emma.*

    (b) Pioverà domani? – *I don't think so. – I hope not!*

    (c) Perché lo chiami? – *Because I'd like to know if he's paid or not.*

    (d) Prendi l'aereo? – *No, I like to travel by train, not by plane.*

    (e) Prendiamo un bicchierino insieme? – *No, I'm sorry, no wine today.*

◎ **14.2 Negatives used without *non***

It is possible to make a sentence negative without **non,** using other negatives instead.

senza + infinitive	Sono andati via **senza** salutarci *They went away without saying goodbye* È partito **senza** dire niente *He left without saying anything* Hanno risolto la questione **senza** nessuna difficoltà *They have resolved the problem without any difficulty*	**Senza** is often used before infinitives or other negatives such as **niente** and **nessuno**. Note that in English the negative element is often *any, anything,* etc.
nessuno niente neanche nemmeno neppure mica	**Nessuno** è venuto (Non è venuto nessuno) *No one came* **Neanche** loro lo sanno (Non lo sanno neanche loro) *They don't know either* **Mica** è venuto, sai (Non è mica venuto, sai) *He didn't actually come, you know*	The negative word goes before the verb and is usually more emphatic than with **non**. (See double negatives, p. 188.)
ancora no assolutamente (no) nient'affatto mai/mai più mica per niente/ nulla	Sei pronto? – **Ancora no** … *Not yet* Gli darai i soldi? **Assolutamente (no)!/** **Nient'affatto** … *Certainly not!/Definitely not!/No way!* Torneresti in quell'albergo? – **Mai più!** … *Never again/Never ever!* Ti piace? – **Mica** male! … *Not bad!* Ti dispiace? – **Per niente** … *Not at all/Not in the least/slightest*	The negative word(s) may often be used without a verb. **Assolutamente** may be followed by **no**.

Note that in questions, **niente** and **nessuno** may be used colloquially with an affirmative meaning:

    Hai bisogno di **niente**?   *Do you need anything?*

◎ Esercizio

1 The right word for the right situation. Choose the appropriate response from the ones given. There is the odd case where either will do.

    (a) Ti piace l'appartamento? – Mica male/Meno male!

    (b) Hai studiato il testo? – Niente/Nient'affatto!

    (c) Che cosa ti ha detto? – Niente/Per niente.

    (d) Quand'è che si sposano? – Mai più/Mai!

    (e) Ti piacerebbe tornarci? – Mai/Mai più!

    (f) È stato interessante? – Assolutamente (no)/Per niente!

    (g) Hai capito? – Per niente/Nient'affatto!

    (h) Hai intenzione di pagare la multa? – Assolutamente no/Mai!

◎/✛ 14.3 Double negatives

(a) Forms

In Italian many negatives involve two words because **non** is used with other negative words. They are as follows.

non … nessuno [pronoun] *no one, nobody*	**non … ancora** *not yet, still*
non … nessun/o/a [adj.] *no, not any, none*	**non … più** *no longer, not any more, not again*
non … niente/nulla *nothing, not anything*	**non … mai** *never, not ever*
non … né … né *not (either) … nor*	**non … mai più** *never/not ever again*

non … neanche		**non … affatto**	*not at all*
non … nemmeno	*not even/not either*	**non … per niente**	*not in the least/slightest*
non … neppure		**per nulla**	
non … mica	*just, really, actually not*	**non … assolutamente** *in no way*	

Many of these are almost synonymous and their use may depend on style or individual preference.

◎/✛ (b) The position of double negatives

The position may vary depending on the tense, the emphasis or the personal style of the speaker. The following examples provide guidelines.

Non inviterò **nessuno** *I won't invite anyone* **Non** prendo **niente** *I'm not having anything* **Non** voglio invitare **né** Maria **né** Anna *I don't want to invite either Maria or Anna*	In most cases, **non** goes before the verb and the negative word immediately follows.
Non legge **mai** il giornale *He never reads the paper* **Non** ha **mai** letto un giornale *He has never read a paper* **Non** deve **più** uscire *He must not go out again*	The negatives **ancora**, **più**, **mai**, **mai più** and **mica** directly follow a simple tense verb but usually come before a past participle or infinitive. See also Adverbs, p. 60.

✚ The position of these negatives depends in part on emphasis or personal style.

Non mi convince **per nulla** *You don't convince me at all/in the least* **Non** mi è piaciuto **per niente/affatto/Non** mi è **per niente/affatto** piaciuto *I didn't like it at all* **Non** mi hai **assolutamente** convinto *You haven't convinced me in any way/at all* **Non** può **assolutamente** capire *He just can't understand*	**Per nulla/per niente** etc. follow simple tense verbs, but with compound verbs their position is flexible: they may go before or after past participles and infinitives. **Per niente** tends to follow the verb, while **assolutamente** is more likely to come before a past participle or infinitive. **Affatto** is very variable.

◎/✚ Esercizi

1 Give the Italian equivalent of the English, paying attention to the position of the negatives.

- **(a)** *I haven't seen anyone.*
- **(b)** *He has never seen Mont Blanc.*
- **(c)** *He hasn't left yet.*
- **(d)** *I don't want to eat anything.*
- **(e)** *She never wants to help.*
- **(f)** *I don't want to come any more.*

✚ **2** Use the negative words below to produce the Italian equivalent of the English given. There may be more than one possibility, but make sure that you use each phrase at least once.

non ... affatto • non ... assolutamente • non ... per niente

- **(a)** *I don't like it at all.*
- **(b)** *I don't know him at all.*
- **(c)** *He isn't in the least unpleasant.*
- **(d)** *You simply mustn't leave.*

✚ (c) Different positions and meanings of double negatives

The position of **non neanche, non nemmeno** and **non neppure** affects the meaning.

not even **non ... neanche** **non ... nemmeno** **non ... neppure**	**Non** lo so **neanche** *I don't even know* **Non** mi piace **nemmeno** *I don't even like it* **Non** puoi **neanche** telefonare? *Can't you even/at least phone?* Tom **non** ha **neppure** chiamato *Tom didn't even call*	When **neanche, nemmeno, neppure** mean *not even,* they have the same position as **ancora, più, mai, mai più** (see p. 188).
not either **non ... neanche** **non ... nemmeno** **non ... neppure**	**Non** lo so **neanch'io** *I don't know either* **Non** piace **nemmeno a me** *I don't like it either* **Non** hai chiamato me e **neppure Tom** *You didn't call me or Tom either* **Non** sa scrivere e **neanche leggere** *He can't write or read either* **Non** puoi telefonare **nemmeno tu?** *Can't you phone either?*	When **neanche, nemmeno** and **neppure** mean *not either*, they are placed immediately before the item they emphasise. If this is the subject, it is placed at the end.

✚ Esercizio

3 What's the difference? Give the English equivalent of the sentences below.

- **(a)** (i) Giacomo non ha nemmeno chiamato.
- **(b)** (i) Non ci sono andato neppure io.
- **(c)** (i) Non mi piace neanche.
- (ii) Non ha chiamato nemmeno Giacomo.
- (ii) Non ci sono neppure andato.
- (ii) Non piace neanche a me.

◎/✚ 14.4 Further uses of negatives

(a) *non ... mica*

Mica is colloquial and widely used in speech to reinforce **non.**

| **non ... mica**
just, really,
actually, not | **Non** è **mica** vero *It's just not/isn't actually true*
Non è **mica** colpa mia *It's certainly not my fault*
Non mi piace **mica** *I don't really/just don't like it*
Non vuole **mica** venire *He just doesn't want to come*
Non verranno **mica**
They won't actually come/There's no way they'll come
Non ti sei **mica** offeso?
You're not offended, are you/by any chance? | **Mica** has the same
position as **ancora,**
più, mai, mai più
(p. 188).
In questions, **mica** can
have the meaning of *by*
any chance? |

◎/✚ Esercizi

1 Surely not? You're hoping your worst fears won't be realised. Put the following into Italian.

    (a) *You haven't forgotten to post the letter by any chance?*

    (b) *You didn't actually invite the neighbours, did you?*

    (c) *Surely you haven't left the oven on, have you?* (**lasciare acceso il forno**)

✚ **2** Rewrite the underlined phrases using **(non) ... mica or assolutamente no** to make the negative expressions more emphatic. Use the English as a guide to the emphatic version.

    (a) <u>Non gli ho detto che parto</u>, ma secondo me lo sa.   *I haven't actually told him I'm leaving, but I guess he knows.*

    (b) <u>Non ho intenzione di pagare</u>; il lavoro è fatto male.   *I'm certainly not going to pay; they've done a bad job.*

    (c) Ti scuserai, allora? – <u>No! Non è stata colpa mia</u>.   *Will you apologise, then? – No! It definitely wasn't my fault.*

    (d) La situazione è penosa; <u>lui non capisce</u> che è pieno di debiti.   *It's a painful situation; he just can't see (doesn't understand) that he's up to his eyes in debt.*

    (e) Credi che potrebbe aiutare qualche prestito da parte tua? – Ma no! <u>Non posso e non voglio aiutare</u>.   *Do you think the odd loan from you might help? Absolutely not! I simply can't and don't want to help.*

✚ (b) *Non ... nessuno/niente/nulla* with other negatives

Non nessuno and **non niente/nulla** can be used with **ancora, mai, mai più, mica** and **più.**

| With simple
tenses | **Non** legge **mai niente** *He never reads anything*
Non vede **più nessuno** *He doesn't see anyone any more*
Non aiuterà **mai più nessuno** *He will never help anyone ever again*
Non darò **niente** a **nessuno** *I won't give anyone anything* | **Nessuno** and **niente**
generally come after the
second negative word.
Note that if they are both
used, **nessuno** comes
last. |
| With
compound
tenses
and verb +
infinitive | **Non** ho **ancora** fatto **niente** *I haven't done anything yet*
Non ho **mica** visto **nessuno** *I didn't actually see anyone*
Non vuole **più** aiutare **nessuno** *He doesn't want to help anyone again* | **ancora, mica, mai**
and **più** usually go
before participles and
dependent infinitives, but
nessuno and **niente**
always follow. |

✦ Esercizio

3 Find the Italian equivalent of the English, using two negative words in addition to **non** each time.

(a) *He never explains anything.*

(b) *He won't offend anyone again/any more.*

(c) *There is nothing left.*

(d) *I haven't found anything yet.*

(e) *I didn't actually find anything.*

(f) *I won't say anything to anyone.*

✦ (c) Negatives with the subjunctive

Using negatives sometimes involves the use of a subjunctive verb.

non dico che, etc.	**Non dico che** sia una buona *soluzione* *I'm not saying it's a good solution* **Non è detto che** possa venire *He won't necessarily be able to come* **Non è che** sia difficile, ma non mi va di farlo *It's not that it's difficult, but I don't feel like doing it*	Subjunctives are often needed when the reality of what is said is denied. Other expressions include **non è vero/possibile che** and **non perchè** (*not because*). See pp. 300–1.
nessuno che, niente che	**Non** c'era **nessuno che** lo potesse aiutare *There was no one who could help him*	These require a subjunctive, especially in written Italian. See p. 310.
non sapere/non capire ... se/come	**Non so come** abbiano fatto *I don't know how they did it* **Non si capisce se** sia vero o meno *It's not clear whether it's true or not* (lit. *One doesn't understand whether*)	These are indirect questions. There is an increasing tendency to use the indicative. See p. 310.

For exercises on the subjunctive, see pp. 301–2.

15 Prepositions

Prepositions (**le preposizioni**) are words like *at, in, to, by,* which are used to express a wide variety of relationships, the most common of which is location in time and place: *in an hour, at two o'clock, by midnight*; *in the drawer, at the station*. Other relationships include possession, purpose, cause and manner. Prepositions can be one word, sometimes two and occasionally a whole phrase.

This chapter deals with prepositions used with nouns, pronouns or adjectives. For verbs and prepositions, see Chapter 26.

◎ 15.1 The use of prepositions: general observations

- Prepositions often acquire different meanings in different contexts and have a large number of uses that can vary, especially in everyday Italian. Use depends on a number of things, including the region someone is from and the differing degrees of formality or informality being used. The examples in this unit present the most common norms.
- Prepositions can be simple (one word) or complex (two or more words), e.g. **per** *for*, **con** *with*; **in fondo a** *at the end/bottom of*; **dall'altra parte di** *on the other side of*.
- Prepositions are invariable, although some modify their form when combined with the definite article.
- Unlike in English, prepositions almost always precede nouns and noun phrases, including interrogative and relative phrase, e.g. Non sa per che cosa lo vuole *He doesn't know what he wants it for.*
- It is necessary to repeat prepositions where they refer to several people or things individually. In English this is not always essential. Compare:

Lo troverai nel cassetto o nell'armadio,	*You'll find it in the drawer or the cupboard,*
o forse nella mia borsetta.	*or possibly (in) my handbag.*
Quest'anno siamo stati in Sicilia,	*This year we've been to Sicily,*
a Malta e nelle Seychelles.	*Malta and the Seychelles.*

If, on the other hand, the nouns are considered as a unit, repetition is not necessary.

Ho scelto un libro per Giovanni e Barbara.	*I chose a book for Giovanni and Barbara (for both of them together).*

◎ 15.2 The main simple prepositions

The following are the eight most commonly used prepositions. All except **per** and **fra/tra** can form one word with the definite article. They are otherwise invariable.

a *to, at, in*	**con** *with*	**da** *from, by, at, to*
di *of*	**fra/tra** *between*	**in** *in, into, at, to*
per *for*	**su** *on, onto*	

For other simple prepositions, such as **lungo** *along*, see pp. 205–6.

(a) The uses of *a*

To denote the recipient of an action

A function unique to **a** is to indicate the recipient of an action, direct or indirect. The English equivalents often differ from the Italian.

Who or what is affected: *to, for, from* The preposition is often not expressed in English	Dico **ai** figli di comportarsi bene *I tell my children to behave (say to)* Darò il libro **a** Anna *I'll give the book to Anna* Il riposo fa bene **a** tutti *Rest is good for everyone*
	Al vecchietto gli è stato rubato il portafoglio *The old man's wallet was stolen (from him)* **A** Carlo gli ho fatto un caffè *I made Carlo a coffee* (for Carlo) For further explanations, see pp. 329–30 and Chapter 27, p. 344.

To express place

A is commonly used to express different aspects of place, focused on location: *where.*

Destination: motion to a place: *to*	Vado **a** Roma *I'm going to Rome* (see also **in**, p. 197) Telefono **a** Parigi/**a** Giorgio *I'm phoning (to) Paris/Giorgio*
Location: where: *at, on*	Mi fermo **al** semaforo *I stop at the traffic lights* La casa si trova **all'**angolo/**a** sinistra *The house is on the corner/on the left* Abito **al** primo piano *I live on the first floor*
Direction and distance: *no English equivalent*	È un paesino **a** nord est di Roma *It's a village (to the) northeast of Rome* Abito **a** cento chilometri da Roma *I live 100 km (away) from Rome*
Position on the body: *in, on, round*	È ferito **al** braccio *He is wounded in the arm* **Al** collo aveva una catenina d'oro *She had a gold chain round her neck* ***But:*** Ha un cappello strano **in** testa *He's got a strange hat on his head*
Non-literal expressions of place: *on, in*	L'ho sentito **alla** radio *I heard it on the radio* Chi c'è **al** telefono? *Who's on the phone?* Sono **a** pagina 17 *I'm on page 17* Mi siedo **al sole/all'**ombra *I sit in the sun/shade* ***But:*** **sotto** la pioggia *in the rain*

To express time

A is mostly used to express *when* and *how often.*

The time, time of day, festivals, months: *at, in*	**a** che ora? *at what time?* **a** mezzogiorno/**alle** due *at midday/at two o'clock* **all'**alba/**al** tramonto *at dawn/sunset* **al** weekend *at the weekend* **a** Natale/**a** Pasqua *at Christmas/Easter* **a** marzo/maggio *in March/ May* (also **in** marzo, **in** maggio, etc., see p. 194)
Future time and duration: *until, to*	**a** domani/**a** presto/**a** lunedì *Until tomorrow/See you tomorrow/soon/ on Monday* Rimandano la riunione **a** martedì *They are postponing the meeting until Tuesday* Sarà aperto da lunedì **a** venerdì *It will be open from Monday until/ to Friday*
How often: *per/a*	Mi lavo i denti due volte **al** giorno *I clean* (lit. *wash*) *my teeth twice a day*
a + noun can replace English phrases beginning with *when*	Lo farà **al** suo ritorno *He'll do it when he returns/on his return* **Alla** partenza piansero tutti *When they left/On their departure everyone cried*

For description

A is frequently used as part of adjectival or adverbial phrases which describe what something is like or how it is done.

Distinguishing features – design, construction and food: no equivalent	un vestito **a** fiori *a flowered dress* carta **a** righe *lined paper* una casa **a** tre piani *a three-storey house* pattini **a** rotelle *roller skates* gelato **al** limone *lemon ice cream* una bistecca **ai** ferri *grilled steak*
Manner and means: how things are done or what with: *on, by, in*	**a** cavallo *on horseback* **a** piedi *on foot* **a** memoria *by heart* fatto/scritto **a** mano *made/written by hand/handmade/handwritten* scritto **a** matita *written in pencil* ***But:* in** corsivo *in italics* **in** grassetto *in bold* **in/a** stampatello *in capitals*

For **a** with other prepositions, see p. 206.

◎ Esercizio

1 Give the Italian equivalent of the English.

    (a) *I live on the top floor.* (**ultimo**)

    (b) *The restaurant is on the corner, on the right.*

    (c) *The bookshop is 200 metres from my house.*

    (d) *I live in a town southwest of London.* (**sud ovest**)

    (e) *There is an interesting film on television.*

    (f) *Your mother's on the phone.*

    (g) *See you in December, at Christmas.*

    (h) *What time are you coming, Ida?*

For more on **a** see also Exercise 2, p. 195, Exercises 1 and 2, pp. 197–8 and Exercise 4, p. 200.

(b) The uses of *in*

To express place

In expresses location and motion to a place.

Where: *in, on*	Abito **in** Italia *I live in Italy* (see p. 197) L'ho messo **nella** busta *I put it in (to) the envelope* Ci vediamo **nel** parco *See you/We'll see each other in the park* Leggo **in** treno/autobus/metropolitana *I read on the train/bus/tube*
Destination and motion to a place: *to, into* ⚠ Note the use of **in** with **entrare** and **salire**	Vado/telefono **in** Italia *I'm going to Italy/I'm phoning (to) Italy* (see also **a**, p. 193) Sono salito **in** macchina *I got into the car* È entrata **nel** negozio *She went into/entered the shop*

To express time

In expressions of time, **in** has fairly restricted uses which need to be distinguished from that of some other prepositions, e.g. **a**, **di** and **fra**.

Months, seasons, years and centuries: *in*	Sono nato **in** ottobre/**in** autunno/**nel** 1980/**nel** ventesimo secolo *I was born in October/in autumn/in 1980/in the twentieth century* See also **di** for seasons (p. 199) and **a** for months (p. 193)
Time taken: *in* ⚠ **In** does *not* express future time	È un libro che si legge **in** un paio d'ore *It's a book you read in a couple of hours* ***But:*** Il lavoro sarà pronto **fra** un paio d'ore *The work will be ready in a couple of hours* (see p. 205)

Other uses

In is used as part of adjectival or adverbial phrases which describe how something is done. It is also used in some expressions of quantity.

Means: transport, colours, materials	Vado **in** macchina/metropolitana *I go by car/tube* Parto **in** treno/aereo *I'm going by train/plane I'm taking the train/a plane* Ci sono molte donne **in** nero *There are many women in black* I pavimenti sono **in** marmo *The floors are (made of) marble* (See also **con** for transport (p. 203) and **di** for colour/material (p. 198).)
Quantity: numbers and averages: *of, for, on*	**In** quanti siete? *How many of you are there?* Siamo **in** cinque/in pochi *There are five of us/few/not many of us* Sono venuti **in** quattro/venti *Four/Twenty of them came* Si gioca **in** tre *Three of you play/It's a game for three* **In** media ne consumano due litri al giorno *On average they consume two litres a day*

◎ Esercizi

2 Give the Italian equivalent of the English using **in** with an appropriate verb.

(a) *I must go to France.*
(b) *I must ring Italy.*
(c) *I'm going by plane.*
(d) *Let's go into/enter the shop.*
(e) *Do you live in England?*
(f) *It's in the drawer.* (**il cassetto**)
(g) *I sleep on the train.*

3 Answer the questions, giving the Italian equivalent of the English using **in** or **a**.

(a) A chi devi telefonare? – *I have to phone my cousin* (f.) *in Italy, in Rome.*
(b) È difficile imparare a guidare? – *No, you can learn in (a) few months.*
(c) In quanti siete? – *There are six of us.*
(d) Quand'è che è nato Piero? – *He was born in April at 5, at dawn.*

(c) The uses of *da*

To express place

An important use of **da** is to express where something comes from, in addition to motion from, through and to a place.

Origins: *where from*	C'è una lettera per te **dalla** Francia *There's a letter for you from France* La parola deriva **dal** latino *The word comes from the Latin* **Da** dove viene questo vino? *Where does this wine come from?* *But:* **Di** dove sei? *Where are you from?* (See **di**, p. 199.)
Distance: *from*	Quanto dista **da** Milano? *How far is it from Milan?*
Motion away: *from, out of* ⚠ Note the use of **da** with **partire** and **uscire**	Il treno parte **dal** binario 2 *The train leaves from platform 2* Sono partiti **da** Imola/**da** qui alle due *They left Imola/here at two* È uscito **dalla** stazione *He came out of the station*
Motion from: *out of, off, from*	Lo ha tolto **dalla** borsa *He took it out of/from the bag* Lo ha tolto **dal** muro *He took it off/from the wall* Guardare **dalla** finestra *To look out of the window*

Motion through: *through, by*	Siamo passati **da** Ginevra *We passed through Geneva* È entrato/passato **dalla** finestra *He came/went in by the window* Devi uscire **dalla** porta di dietro *You have to go out/leave by the back door* (See also **per**, p. 201 and **di**, p. 199.)
Motion to: *to*	Vado **dal** medico/**da** Ugo *I'm going to the doctor's/Ugo's* (See also **a** and **in**, p. 197.)

For actions

Da expresses the agent of an action and a variety of other related uses.

Agent: who or what by: *by*	E' amato **da** tutti *He is loved by everyone* La città è stata distrutta **dal** terremoto *The town was destroyed by the earthquake* E' un libro scritto **da** Pasolini *It's a book written by Pasolini* **But:** un libro/un film di Pasolini *a book/a film by Pasolini.* (See also **di**, p. 198.)
The cause of an action: *with, from, for*	Tremavo **dal** freddo *I was shivering from/with cold* Saltava **dalla** gioia *He was jumping for joy*
Things to be done: *to* **da** + infinitive verb	Ho due capitoli **da** leggere *I've got two chapters to read* Vuoi qualcosa **da** mangiare? *Do you want something to eat?* È una cosa **da** tenere in mente *It's something to bear in mind* **Note:** Ho **da** fare *I've got a lot to do* Non c'è niente **da** fare *It's no good/hopeless*
How things are done	Ci vado **da** solo *I'm going alone* Voglio fare **da** me *I want to do it (by) myself* E' uno spettacolo **dal** vivo *It's a live show*

To express time

Da is mostly used to express duration in time.

How long: *for, since, ago*	Sono qui **da** un'ora/domenica *I have been here for an hour/since Sunday* Studiavo medicina **da** anni *I had been studying medicine for years* È partito **da** due ore *He has been gone for two hours*
How long: *from … to*	Lavora **dalla** mattina **alla** sera *She works from morning till night* **D'**ora in poi starò attento *From now on I'll be careful*
A period in the past: *when, as*	**Da** bambino/**Da** giovane ho vissuto a Roma *As a child/When I was a child/When I was young I lived in Rome*

For description

Da expresses the purpose and value of things, as well as physical characteristics.

Purpose – what an object is used for: no English equivalent	un ferro **da** stiro *an iron* un campo **da** tennis *a tennis court* una sala **da** pranzo *a dining room* un bicchiere **da** vino *a wine glass* una tazzina **da** caffè *a coffee cup* un cavallo **da** corsa *a racehorse* **But:** un bicchiere di vino, una tazzina di caffè *a glass of wine, a cup of coffee* un cavallo **di** razza *a thoroughbred* (see p. 198.)
Characteristic of: *like, as,* or, also, *'s*	Mi tratta **da** imbecille *He treats me like an idiot* Devo fare **da** guida *I've got to act as the guide* È morto **da** eroe *He died like/as a hero/He died a hero's death* Ha una faccia **da** straniero *He has the look of a foreigner/a foreigner's face* Fa una vita **da** cane *He leads a dog's life*

Physical characteristics: *with*	una ragazza **dagli** occhi azzurri *a girl with blue eyes/a blue-eyed girl* la giraffa è un animale **dal** collo lungo *the giraffe is an animal with a long neck* (**Con** can substitute **da**, see p. 202.)
Physical disabilities: *in*	cieco **da** un occhio *blind in one eye* sordo **da** un orecchio *deaf in one ear* zoppo **da** una gamba *lame in one leg*
The value of something: *worth*	un francobollo **da** 41 centesimi *a 41 cent stamp* (*a stamp worth …*) un biglietto **da** 100 euro *a 100 euro note* (*a note worth …*) ***But:*** una multa **di** 500 euro *a 500 euro fine* (i.e. *it amounts to*)

 Esercizi

4 Give the English equivalent of the following.

(a) Sono partito da Londra ieri.

(b) Sono uscito dall'ufficio alle sette.

(c) L'aereo parte dall'uscita numero 34.

(d) Siamo entrati dalla finestra.

(e) Non guardare dalla finestra.

(f) Da studente mi piaceva viaggiare.

(g) Sono qui da sabato.

(h) Vuoi qualcosa da bere?

5 Da or di? Complete these sentences using the correct Italian equivalent of *by*.

(a) Il Kosovo è stato distrutto (*by*) la guerra.

(b) Il film è girato (*by*) Franco Zeffirelli.

(c) È un libro (*by*) Leonardo Sciascia.

(d) È un libro scritto (*by*) Umberto Eco.

For more on **da**, see also Exercises 1 and 2, pp. 197–8; Exercises 3 and 4, pp. 199–200; Exercise 5, p. 200.

⚠ Attenti! *In, a,* or *da*?

When talking about about being in a place or going to a place, take care not to confuse the uses of **in**, **a**, **da**: *in, at, to*. In Italian their use depends largely on the category of place, but in many cases these must be learned.

in: *in/at, to*	**Sono in …/Vado in …** **in** Europa/**in** Italia/**in** Piemonte/**in** Sicilia/ **in** farmacia/**in** città/**in** ufficio/**in** banca/**in** montagna	With: continents, countries, regions, some islands, shops ending in **-ia**, familiar places.
a: *in/at/to*	**Sono a/Vado a** … **a** Roma/**a** Capri/**alla** Standa/**allo** stadio/ **all'**università/**a** scuola/**a** casa	With: towns, some islands, shops (unless they end in **-ia**), many public places, and the word *home*.
da: *in/at, to*	**Sono da …/Vado da…** **da** Gianni/**dalla** zia/**dagli** amici/**dai** Bianchi/ **dal** medico/**dal** farmacista/**da** 'Carlino'/loro	With: places connected with people, such as family, friends, professional people, shopkeepers and shops or restaurants named after people.

For more on the use of prepositions and the article with geographical place names, see Articles, pp. 27–8.

 Esercizi

6 *Where are you going?* Choose **a**, **da** or **in** – with the definite article if necessary – to say you're going to the following places. Begin: **Vado …**

(a) Italia

(b) Sicilia

(c) Toscana

(d) Capri

(e) Bari

(f) il supermercato

(g) la Rinascente

(h) farmacia

(i) piscina

(j) Franco

(k) il parrucchiere

(l) il medico

(m) lo zoo

(n) il mare

(o) casa

(p) campagna

7 *Where are you meeting?* Choose between **a, da** and **in**. Begin: **Ci vediamo …**

(a) casa mia	**(d)** la fermata dell'autobus	**(g)** il bar	**(j)** il ristorante
(b) biblioteca	**(e)** trattoria	**(h)** banca	**(k)** 'Gigino'
(c) Franca	**(f)** mia sorella	**(i)** fruttivendolo	**(l)** centro

(d) The uses of *di*

Di is one of the most frequently used prepositions. Its main function is specification and description: it provides extra information about a noun to define it more precisely.

To specify possession and origin

Di is used to specify various aspects of ownership.

Possession and relationships: *'s*	la casa **di** Anna *Anna's house* la divisa **della** scuola *the school('s) uniform* la figlia **del** padrone *the boss's daughter*
Origin: *of*	È figlio **di** immigrati *He is the son of immigrants* È nata nel 1900 **di** genitori scozzesi *She was born in 1900, of Scottish parents*
Authorship: *by*	È un'opera **di** Verdi *It's an opera by Verdi* Sono dipinti **di** Botticelli *They are paintings by Botticelli* Regia/musica **di** … *Production/music by …*

To specify quantities

Di is used with specific amounts and also has an important partitive function.

Quantities and measurement: no English equivalent, but **di** is essential	un aumento **di** duemila euro *a 2,000-euro rise* un pacco **di** quattro chili *a four-kilo package* La superficie è **di** 350 metri quadrati *The surface area is 350 square metres* Il percorso più lungo è **di** 8 km *The longest route is 8 km*
Partitive use: *some, of*	Ho **dei** libri interessanti *I have some interesting books* (see pp. 30–31.) Molti **di** loro sono vecchissimi *Many of them are very old* La metà **di** loro sono in tedesco *Half of them are in German*

For reference, comparison and description

Di is used to specify topics or make comparisons. It is also used as part of adjectival or adverbial phrases which describe what something is like or for and how it is done.

Specifying subject/ topic: *about, of*	Parliamo **della** situazione in Italia *Let's talk about the situation in Italy* **Di** che cosa si tratta? *What's it about?*
With comparatives and superlatives: *than, in, of*	È più alto **di** me *He is taller than me* La donna più simpatica **del** mondo *The nicest woman in the world* La più simpatica **di** tutte *The nicest of all*
How it is done: no English equivalent for **di**	È arrivato **di** corsa *He came in a rush* L'ho fatto **di** nascosto *I did it secretly* Si è alzato **di** scatto *He got up all of a sudden*
Specification of type: no English equivalent	la partita **di** calcio *the football match* un libro **di** geografia *a geography book* un'uscita **di** sicurezza *an emergency exit*
What it is like: colours, materials and substances: no English equivalent	È vestita **di** nero *She is wearing black* Ho una camicetta **di** seta *I have a silk blouse* È una torta **di** cioccolato *It's a chocolate cake* **Di** che colore è? *(of) What colour is it?* **Di** che cosa è fatto? *What's it made of?* (See also **in**, p. 195.)

To express time and place

Di is used mostly to refer to habitual time as well as to geographical origin and motion from. It is also part of adjectival phrases of time.

To express the usual time or season: *in, at, on*	Veniva **di** sera/**di** notte/**di** domenica/**d'**estate/**d'**inverno *He used to come in the evening/at night/in the summer/winter* ***Note also:*** Veniva **la** sera Studiava **la** domenica (see Articles, p. 21) Veniva **in** estate/**in** inverno/**in** autunno/**in** primavera (see **in**, p. 194)
To specify, age, time, seasons: no exact English equivalent	un ragazzo **di** dodici anni *a twelve-year-old boy* il treno/il volo **delle** 17.00 *the five o'clock train/flight* le sette **di** mattina/**di** sera *seven in the morning/in the evening* una notte **d'**estate *a summer night*
Origin: with the names of towns or areas, not countries or regions: *from*	**Di** dove sei? *Where are you from?* Sono **di** Roma/Sono **del** Sud *I'm from Rome/from the South* ***But:*** Siamo toscani/italiani *We are Tuscan, from Tuscany/Italian, from Italy*
Distance and motion: *from, through*	Abito a due passi **di** qui *I live a stone's throw from here* Si entra/passa **di** qui/qua *You enter through here/this way* Esco **di** qui/**di** casa alle sette *I leave here/home at seven* (See also **per**, p. 201 and **da** (note below).)
from … to	***Note also:*** **di** porta **in** porta *from door to door*

 Attenti! Both **di** and **da** can be used to express motion from (see **da**, p. 195).

Di is more usual than **da** before **qui/li, qua/là** or familiar places such as **casa** or **scuola**:

Bisogna passare di qui.   *You have to come this way/through her.*
Esce di casa alle sette.   *He leaves home at seven.*

Da is more usual with **partire, lontano** and emphatic statements: in these instances it is used with **qui**:

È partito da qui ieri sera.   *He left here last night.*
Non è lontano da qui.   *It's not far from here.*
Da qui non esci!   *You're not leaving here/getting out of here!*

©/✦ Esercizi

8 Give the English equivalent of:

(a) una cintura di sicurezza

(b) la casa di Mauro

(c) un dipinto di Leonardo

(d) un aumento di 2,000 euro

(e) una bottiglia di due litri

(f) una giornata d'inverno

9 Give the Italian for the following.

(a *a language teacher*

(b) *the prime minister's wife*

(c) *a novel by Manzoni*

(d) *a ten-year-old girl*

(e) *the eight o'clock flight*

(f) *a five-hour journey*

(g) *eight in the evening*

10 Insert the correct preposition – **di** or **da**.

(a) Vuoi una tazza — caffè o preferisci un tè?

(b) Mi ha regalato sei tazzine — caffè.

(c) Ho bisogno di due francobolli — un euro.

(d) Ha pagato una multa — 400 euro.

(e) Gina è — Pisa, è pisana.

(f) Gina è arrivata — Pisa.

11 Complete the words for clothing and personal effects below using **di**, **a** or **da**. Bear in mind that **a** usually denotes design or how something is made, **da** generally indicates what something is for, while **di** tells you what something consists of.

(a) un anello — oro (*a gold ring*)

(b) un abito — sera (*an evening dress*)

(c) una gonna — fiori (*a flowery skirt*)

(d) un cappello — paglia (*a straw hat*)

(e) occhiali — sole (*sunglasses*)

(f) una camicia — quadretti (*a checked shirt*)

+ 12 **Di** or **da**? Choose the appropriate preposition each time.

(a) Dobbiamo entrare (dalla/della) porta principale?

(b) Si può entrare (da/di) qui?

(c) A che ora uscirai (dalla/della) riunione?

(d) A che ora esci (di/da) casa la mattina?

(e) Uscite tutti (di/da) qui!

(f) Partite (da/di) qui o (da/di) casa?

(e) The uses of *per*

The main meaning of **per** in English is often stated to be *for*. However, **per** also has a number of other important meanings, such as *to, along, around* and *through*.

To express purpose, intention and cause

Purpose – who and what for: *for* **Note also:** *on*	Lavora **per** me *He works for me* Vorrei delle pasticche **per** la gola *I'd like some pastilles for my throat* L'ho fatto **per** scherzo *I did it as a joke (for a laugh)* È un libro **per** bambini *This is a book for children (a children's book)* **Note also**: È andato **per** affari *He went on business* Ha speso gran parte dei suoi soldi **per** donne, alcol e automobili *He spent most of his money on women, drink and cars*
Inclination: *for*	Ha una passione **per** la musica *He has a passion for music*
Intention: *to, in order to*	Sono venuti **per** aiutare *They have come to help* È uscita **per** fare la spesa *She has gone out to do the shopping* (see also **a,** Chapter 26, p. 334)
Cause: *because of/on account of, out of* **Per** indicates why something happens	È **per** questo che non ti piace? *Is that why/Is it because of that you don't like it?* Il traffico è bloccato **per** la nebbia *The traffic is held up because of the fog* Ha sofferto molto **per** il freddo *He suffered a lot on account of the cold* L'ha fatto **per** ripicco/**per** curiosità *He did it out of spite/curiosity*

 Attenti! Take care when expressing *the reason for/why*.

Note that in the following expressions **di**, not **per**, is used:

Non ho capito il motivo/la ragione **del** loro successo.

I don't understand the reason for their success.

But *the reason (why)* is il motivo/la ragione **per cui**:

Non ho capito il motivo/la ragione **per cui** sono venuti.

I don't understand the reason why they have come. (See also Relatives, p. 181)

For destination, distances and motion through or around a place

Per is used to express movement towards, along and around a place. It occasionally refers to location.

Destination, distance, motion along: *for, along*	Prendo il treno **per** Bolzano *I'm taking the train for/to Bolzano* Camminava **per** strada *He was walking along the street** Sono ritornato **per** un'altra strada *I came back by another route/a different way/along another road* Ho guidato **per** 500 chilometri *I drove for 500 kilometres*
Motion through and around: *around, through, by, about on, throughout* **Per + tutto/a** means *thoughout/all over*	È entrato **per** la porta principale *He came in through the main entrance* È uscito **per** la porta di servizio *He left by the tradesman's entrance* (see also **da**, p. 196) Il treno passa **per** Milano *The train goes through Milan* Girava **per** la casa *She was wandering through/about/around the house* Ho viaggiato **per** tutta l'Europa *I've travelled all over Europe*
Location	Mi sono seduto **per** terra *I sat down on the ground* Ha delle idee strane **per** la testa *He has some odd ideas in his head*

* When *along* means *beside*, **lungo** is used: camminavo lungo il fiume *I was walking along/by the river*. See also p. 205.

In time expressions

Per expresses the time for which something lasts.

Duration: how long *for*	Ha piovuto **per** un'ora/una settimana *It rained for an hour/a week* Ci ho pensato **per** almeno un anno *I thought about it for at least a year*
Specific point in time: *for, by*	Ho un appuntamento **per** domani *I have an appointment for tomorrow* **Per** quando lo vuole? *When do you want it for/by?* – **Per** sabato/**per** le cinque *For/By Saturday/five o'clock* (see also **entro**, p. 205)

Other uses

How or by what means: *by*	L'ho mandato **per** posta/**per** via aerea *I sent it by post/by air* È meglio comunicare **per** email *It's best to communicate by email* Mi ha preso **per** il braccio *He took me by the arm* ***Note also:*** **per** iscritto *in writing* **per**/in ordine alfabetico *in alphabetical order*
With numbers: there are various English equivalents	il venti **per** cento *twenty per cent* Due **per** cinque fa dieci *Two by/times five equals ten* Devi dividere **per** dieci *You must divide by ten* Sono entrati due **per** due *They came in two by two* Li ho mangiati poco/uno **per** volta *I ate a few/one at a time*

◎/✛ Esercizi

13 Give the Italian equivalent of the phrases in English.

    (a) Che lavoro fa? – *I work for an airline company.* (**una compagnia aerea**)

    (b) Lei è qui in vacanza? – *No, I'm here on business.*

    (c) Lei per che cosa è qui? – *I'm here to learn Italian. It's for my job.*

    (d) Quanto si trattiene a Milano? – *I'm staying for a month.* (**mi trattengo**)

    (e) È libero domani? – *I'm sorry, I have lots of appointments for tomorrow.*

14 Match up the phrases to complete the sentences and give the English equivalent.

    (a) La macchina non è partita stamattina   **(i)** per la lontananza del fidanzato.

    (b) Non è venuto alla festa   **(ii)** per il freddo.

    (c) Mia figlia soffre molto   **(iii)** per timidezza.

15 Complete the sentences by giving the Italian equivalent of the English.

    (a) I tifosi giravano (*through/about*) la città.

    (b) Erano seduti (*on the ground*).

    (c) L'ho incontrato (*in the street*).

✛ **16** Complete the sentences using **in**, **da** or **per**.

    (a) Sono saliti tutt'e due — macchina.

    (b) Siamo scesi — treno in fretta.

    (c) Siamo passati — lui verso le otto.

    (d) Passiamo — Milano fra un mese.

    (e) Sono ritornato — un'altra strada.

✛ **17** **Revision**. Give the Italian equivalent of the English. Distinguish between the uses of **da**, **di** and **per**.

    (a) *Mirella is forty but she has the voice of a young girl.* (**una ragazzina**)

    (b) *I have seen the children's room.*

    (c) *This is a children's game.*

    (d) *They treat her like an adult.*

    (e) *The reason for the delay is not clear.*

    (f) *The reason he came is not clear.*

(f) The uses of *con*

In modern Italian, **con** does not usually combine with the definite article, though the forms **col** (**con** + **il**) and **coi** (**con** + **i**) are used in speech. Its main meaning is *with*.

Company: who and what with: *with, together with*	Vengo **con** mio fratello *I'm coming with my brother* Esco **con** il cane *I'm going out with the dog* (Note that **insieme a** can also be used like **con**, see p. 207)
What accompanies what: *with, and*	Prendo il pollo **con** insalata mista *I'm having chicken with mixed salad* Il pesce **con** le patate fritte è un piatto tradizionale inglese *Fish and chips is a traditional English dish*
Distinguishing features: *with*	È una ragazza **con** i capelli biondi *She is a girl with fair hair* Ho comprato delle scarpe **con** i tacchi alti *I bought some high-heeled shoes* (See also **da**, p. 197)

Relationships: *with, to*	È cortese/gentile **con** tutti *He is polite/nice to/with everyone*
Means: transport: *by* Instrument: *with*	È partito **con** il treno *He went by train/took the train* Andiamo **con** la macchina? *Shall we go by car?* (See also **in**, p.195) L'ha colpito **con** un martello *He hit it with a hammer* Lui disegna **con** la matita *He draws with a pencil*
How – manner: *with, to*	Parla **con** convinzione *He speaks with conviction* Ascolta **con** attenzione *He listens attentively* **Con** mia sorpresa/mio stupore sono stati promossi *To my surprise/amazement they passed (the exam)*
Cause and effect: *with, in view of/ because of, despite*	**Con** il tempo che fa, preferisco rimanere a casa *In view of the weather I prefer to stay at home* **Con** tutti i problemi che ha, è sempre allegra! *Despite all her problems she is always cheerful*
Time: *as (at the same time as), with*	Arrivammo **col** tramonto del sole *We arrived as the sun set* È arrivato **con la** bella stagione *He arrived with the fine weather*

◎ Esercizi

18 Link up the pairs, using **con**.

    (a) una coca cola   **(i)** servizi

    (b) un appartamento   **(ii)** la panna

    (c) un gelato   **(iii)** la cannuccia

19 Consequences. Match up the phrases to say what the consequences are.

    (a) Con questi voti   **(i)** non ho voglia di uscire.

    (b) Con questo maltempo   **(ii)** non ti potrai mai laureare.

    (c) Con questo mal di gola   **(iii)** dovresti smettere di fumare.

20 Substitute the prepositions **in** and **da** with **con,** making any necessary changes.

    (a) Andiamo in macchina.   **(c)** È un uomo alto dai baffi lunghi.

    (b) Sono partito in treno.   **(d)** È una signora elegante dai capelli biondi tinti.

(g) The uses of *su*

The principal uses of **su** relate to place, but it has other common uses as well.

To express place

Position: *on*	Era seduta **sulla** sedia rossa *She was sitting on the red chair* **Note also:** L'ho letto **sul** giornale *I read it in the newspaper* L'ho visto **su** Canale 2/internet *I saw it on Channel 2/the internet*
Location: *over, above* **Sopra** can sometimes be used instead of **su**	Hanno costruito un ponte **sul** fiume *They have built a bridge over the river* È a mille metri **sul** mare *It's a thousand metres above the sea* Stiamo volando sopra le/**sulle** Alpi *We're flying over the Alps*
Motion onto and up: *onto, up*	Andiamo **sul** balcone *Let's go onto the balcony* La finestra dà **sul** cortile *The window looks onto/overlooks the courtyard* È salito **sulla** collina *He climbed up the hill* Siamo andati **sull'**Etna *We've been up Etna* Ho fatto un viaggio **sul** Nilo *I travelled up the Nile*

Other uses

Topic/subject: *on, about, concerning*	E' un libro **sulla** Cina *It's a book on/about/concerning China* Ho letto molto **sul** problema *I've read a lot about the problem* ***Note:*** Si raccontano molte cose **su di** lei *People say a lot of things about her* (After **su**, **di** is needed before a personal pronoun. See p. 206.)
Cause and manner: no single English equivalent	È stato un furto **su** commissione *It was a theft carried out to order* Il vestito è stato fatto **su** misura *The dress was made to measure* Stanno studiando **sul** serio *They are studying in earnest/seriously*
Approximation: *about, around*	Costa **sui** trecento euro *It costs about/around three hundred euros* È un uomo **sui** trent'anni *He is a man of about thirty* Verrò **sul** tardi *I'll come/fairly late* **Note**: **su** is used with the definite article here. ***Note also***: **su** per giù *roughly, approximately*
Quantity: *out of*	Ha preso nove **su** dieci *He got nine out of ten* Venti allievi **su** trenta *Twenty out of thirty pupils* Aperto 24 ore **su** 24 *Open 24 hours*

◎ Esercizio

21 Give the English equivalent of the following.

(a) Ho lasciato i documenti sulla scrivania.

(b) Il gatto è salito sul tetto.

(c) *'Il ponte sul fiume Kwai'* è un film piuttosto vecchio.

(d) È un film sulla guerra in Giappone.

(e) Siamo stati sul Monte Bianco.

(f) Il viaggio costa sui due milioni.

(g) Ho letto la notizia sul giornale.

(h) Ho lasciato l'ombrello sull'autobus.

(h) The uses of *fra* and *tra*

Tra and **fra** are interchangeable. Their basic meaning is *between* and *among*. They express relationships of space and time as well as relationships between people and things.

To express place and time

Note that in Italian, *between* and *among* are the same: there is no distinction, unlike in English.

Place: *between, among*	La casa si trova **fra** due strade *The house is between two roads* Gli ulivi crescono **tra** i fiori *The olive trees grow among the flowers* La luce filtra **fra** i rami *The light filters through (between) the branches* ***Note also:*** Me lo trovo sempre **fra** i piedi *He's always under* (lit. *between*) *my feet*
Place, figurative: *between, among, amidst*	Vive **tra** la speranza e la disperazione *He lives/is torn between hope and despair* Mi trovo **tra** due fuochi *I am caught between the devil and the deep blue sea/in the crossfire* **Fra** tutti questi problemi non so che fare *Amongst/Amidst all these problems I don't know what to do*

Place ahead: *in, ahead*	**Fra** qualche chilometro c'è una stazione di servizio *There's a petrol station in a few kilometres/a few kilometres ahead* **Fra** duecento metri comincia l'autostrada *The motorway starts in two hundred metres/two hundred metres ahead*
Time: *between*	Arrivo **fra** le due e le tre *I'm arriving between two and three*
Future time: *in*	Parto **fra** un'ora *I'm leaving in an hour* Sarò a casa **fra** un mese *I'll be home in a month*

With reference to people, institutions, etc.

Interaction: *between, among, amongst, amidst*	Mio figlio ha scelto **fra** tre università *My son chose between three universities* È scoppiata la guerra **tra** gli stati balcanici *War broke out between the Balkan states* **Tra** loro c'è molta stima *There's a lot of respect between them* Siamo **fra** amici *We're among friends* C'è un medico **fra** voi? *Is there a doctor amongst you?* **Note also: Fra** me (e me) pensavo che ... *I was thinking to myself that ...*
Partitive: *(out) of, amongst/some of*	**Fra** i suoi amici preferisco Enzo *Out of his friends, I prefer Enzo* Sono **fra** gli uomini più ricchi d'Italia *They are amongs/some of the richest men in Italy* (see also 5.4, p. 86.) **Fra di** loro si capiscono molto bene *They understand each other well* (After **fra**, **di** may be used before a personal pronoun. See p. 206.)

◎ Esercizio

22 Give the English equivalent of the following.

(a) Arrivo fra le cinque e le sei.
(b) Arrivo fra una settimana.
(c) Mario è seduto fra la cugina e il nonno.
(d) Fra i miei cugini preferisco Luciano.
(e) L'incrocio si trova fra due chilometri.
(f) La nuova casa si trova fra Genova e Livorno.
(g) Si vede la casa fra gli alberi.
(h) Fra di loro c'è un'intesa speciale.

◎/✚ 15.3 Other prepositions

(a) Simple prepositions

Apart from the eight simple prepositions dealt with on pp. 192–205, the other ones commonly used are:

attraverso *across, through*
contro (**di**) *against*
dentro (**a/di**) *inside*
dietro (**a/di**) *behind, round*
dopo (**di**) *after*
durante *during*
eccetto/meno/salvo/tranne *except, apart from*
entro *by, within (a certain time)*
fuori (**di/da**) *outside*

lungo *along, by*
nonostante/malgrado *despite*
oltre (**a**) *beyond, over, besides*
presso (**di**) *at (sb.'s place), with, near*
secondo *according to*
senza (**di**) *without*
sopra (**a/di**) *above, over*
sotto (**di**) *under, below, beneath*
verso (**di**) *towards, at about*

✚ Simple prepositions used with other prepositions: *a* and *di*

Some of the prepositions on p. 205 and **su** (p. 204) are followed by **a** or **di**, depending on the word that follows.

Before a noun	Before a personal pronoun	Explanations
contro il muro *against the wall* dentro la (alla) scatola *inside the box* dietro il (al) negozio *behind the shop* dopo la partita *after the match* senza soldi *without money* sopra la (alla) porta *above the door* sotto la neve *under the snow* sul divano *on the sofa* verso il fiume *towards the river*	contro di me *against me* dentro di sé *within himself* dietro a/di te *behind you* dopo (di) te *after you* senza (di) te *without you* sopra a/di noi *above us* sotto di lui *below/beneath him* su di lui *about/on him* verso di lei *towards her*	**A** is occasionally used before a noun or pronoun. **Di** is often used before pronouns. Note the expression **dietro** l'angolo *round the corner.*

If, however, the personal pronoun is modified or linked to another word, **di** is not used:

> Si raccontano tante schiocchezze   *People are talking so much rubbish*
> su lui e il fratello.   *about him and his brother.*

Note that **fra/tra** optionally require **di** before personal pronouns. (See p. 205.)

✚ Using *fuori* with *di* and *da*

Fuori *outside, out of* can be used both with and without prepositions, depending on the meaning. To indicate location, **fuori** may be used without a preposition in a few common expressions. Otherwise it takes **di**. Note that **di** is used before **qui** or personal pronouns. With **da**, **fuori** is used to express motion from.

fuori or **fuori di** to express location: *outside*	Abita **fuori** città *He lives outside/out of town* In questo momento è **fuori** casa/**fuori** città/**fuori** Roma *At the moment he's not at home/not in town/out of Rome* **Note also:** Non mangiare **fuori** pasto *Don't eat between ('outside') meals*
	È sconosciuto **fuori** d'Italia *He's unknown outside Italy* **Fuori di** qui! *Get out of here!* È **fuori di** sé *He is beside himself ('outside' himself)*
fuori + da: to express motion from: *out of*	L'ha tirato **fuori dal** cassetto *He took it out of the drawer* È uscito **fuori dalla** stazione *He came out of the station*

✚ Esercizi

1 Read the sentences below and add the preposition **di** where necessary.

    (a) Ci vediamo dopo cena.   **(e)** Mauro è fuori città oggi.

    (b) Marina andrà in vacanza dopo me.   **(f)** Non è mai stato fuori Italia.

    (c) Abita verso il centro.   **(g)** Non riesco a lavorare senza un po' di musica.

    (d) Non ho nessun obbligo verso lui.   **(h)** Senza te non riesco a lavorare.

2 Add **di** where necessary, and also indicate where **a** is possible.

    (a) Il portafoglio è dentro la borsa.   **(d)** Le chiavi sono dietro te.

    (b) Dentro me sono molto arrabbiato.   **(e)** Oltre te non conosco nessuno.

    (c) Le scarpe sono dietro la porta.   **(f)** Oltre i libri, ci hato dato delle videocassette.

(b) Complex prepositions and prepositional phrases

These consist of two or more words. Some of the most common relate to place.

a destra/sinistra di *on the right/left of*
accanto a *beside, next to*
dall'altra parte di *on the other side of*
da parte di *by*
davanti a *in front of, outside*
a fianco di *next to, alongside*
fino a *as far as, until*
di fronte a *opposite*
giù per/su per *down/up (along)*
in cima a *at the top of*

in fondo a *at the end/bottom of*
in mezzo a *in the middle of, amongst*
insieme a/con *(together) with*
intorno a *around*
lontano da *far from*
nel centro/mezzo di *in the centre of*
vicino a *near (to)*
a causa di *because of*
prima di *before*

Examples

The use of most of the prepositions listed above is fairly straightforward, but note the varying English equivalents in the following:

davanti a	Il burro è **davanti a** te *The butter is in front of you*
	Ci vediamo **davanti al** cinema *We'll see each other outside the cinema*
in fondo a	La toilette è **in fondo al** corridoio *The toilet is at the end of the corridor*
	La nave è **in fondo al** mare *The ship is at the bottom of the sea*
	La citazione è **in fondo alla** pagina *The quote is at the bottom of the page*
in mezzo a	Non mi piace stare **in mezzo a** tanta gente
	I don't like being amongst so many people
nel centro di	La fontana è **nel centro della** piazza
	The fountain is in the middle/centre of the square
prima di	Saremo lì **prima di** mezzogiorno *We'll be there before midday*
	Ci sono altri candidati **prima di** te
	There are other candidates before/in front of you

Using *da parte di*

Da parte di is used to clarify by whom an action is, will be or was carried out. It is generally used when this action is represented by a noun or infinitive. The English equivalents vary.

of	Non è giusto **da parte del** Ministero rifiutare le loro rivendicazioni *It is not fair of*
's	*the Ministry to reject their demands/The Ministry's rejection of their demands is*
by	*unfair/The rejection of their demands by the Ministry is unfair*
on the part	Le manifestazioni contro la guerra **da parte dei** londinesi sono state inutili
of	*Londoners' demonstrations against the war were useless/The demonstrations by*
	Londoners against the war were useless

Attenti! English and Italian differ: a look at the position of prepositions

In English, unlike in Italian, a preposition frequently ends a sentence, sometimes followed by *it*, e.g. *I don't want the soup, there's a fly in it/I don't want the soup with the fly in.*

In Italian the equivalent construction is quite different. The pronoun *it* is never expressed, and the preposition comes before the noun it governs, preceded by **con** (*with*), or occasionally **senza** (*without/with no*).

Ho mangiato un lampone **con dentro** una formica! *I've eaten a raspberry with an ant inside (it)!*

È una bella casa **con dietro** un enorme giardino. *It's a lovely house with a hugh garden behind (it).*

Complex prepositions drop **a**:

È un giardino stupendo **con in mezzo** un tempietto.   *It's a stunning garden with a small temple in the middle.*

Often the Italian ignores the preposition and pronoun altogether, or uses an adjective instead:

Porta un vestito macchiato.   *She's wearing a dress with a stain on (it)/a stained dress.*

Ha mandato la lettera senza il francobollo.   *He sent the letter with no stamp on (it).*

◎/✚ Esercizi

3 Using each of the prepositions below once, you tell your friend you're parked in the following places:

di fronte al … • **accanto alla …** • **davanti a …** • **nel …**
• **in fondo alla …** • **dall'altra parte della …**

  (a) *in the courtyard*   **(d)** *on the other side of the street*

  (b) *next to his car*   **(e)** *at the end of the street*

  (c) *opposite the cinema*   **(f)** *outside his house*

✚ **4** Supply the appropriate prepositional phrase to complete the sentences.

  (a) L'omicidio del boss mafioso — di sconosciuti è rimasto un mistero.

    *The murder of the mafia boss **by** persons unknown has remained a mystery.*

  (b) La creazione di spazi verdi — Comune è stato applaudito.

    *The **local council's** creation of green spaces has been praised.*

  (c) L'imbarcazione in Sicilia — alleati è avvenuto nel luglio del 1943.

    *The **Allied** landing in Sicily took place in July 1943.*

  (d) La decisione di vendere — azionisti è stato condannato.

    *The **shareholders'** decision to sell has been condemned.*

✚ **5** Give an Italian equivalent for each of the following:

  (a) Ha mangiato un gelato (*with a cherry on top*).

  (b) Ho frequentato una scuola (*with a pub next to it*).

  (c) Lavoro in un ufficio (*with a hugh tree outside*).

  (d) Abbiamo comprato una casa (*with a park opposite*).

  (e) La piazza è bellissima, (*with two fountains in the middle*).

  (f) L'ambasciata sembra una fortezza (*with an electric fence round it*). (**recinto elettrico**)

✚ 15.4 Adjectives used with prepositions

Many common adjectives are followed by one or more prepositions. Their use often differs from the English.

(a) Adjectives followed by one preposition

Adjectives taking *a*

abituato a *accustomed/used to*	disposto a *prepared/willing to*
addetto a *in charge of/responsible for (something)*	indifferente a *indifferent to*
attento a *careful of, beware of*	interessato a *interested in*
costretto a *forced to*	nocivo a *harmful to*
deciso/risoluto a *determined to*	uguale a *like, the same as*

Adjectives taking *di*

ansioso di *anxious/keen to*	innamorato di *in love with*
capace di *capable of*	macchiato di *stained with*
consapevole/conscio di *aware/conscious of*	pieno di *full of*
contento di *pleased to, satisfied with*	responsabile di *responsible for, in charge of*
convinto di *convinced of/about*	sicuro di *sure of/about*
farcito/imbottito di *stuffed with*	soddisfatto di *satisfied with*
felice/lieto di *happy/pleased to*	stanco/stufo di *tired of/sick of, fed up with*
fornito di *equipped/supplied with*	vestito di *dressed in/wearing*

Adjectives taking *con*

antipatico con *unpleasant to*	simpatico con *pleasant to*
buono con *kind to*	sposato con *married to*
gentile con *nice to*	

Adjectives taking *da*

diverso da *different from/to*	lontano da *far from*
indipendente da *independent of*	

+ Esercizi

1 Describe these people by completing the sentences using **a** or **di**.

    (a) Pina è molto interessata — imparare il greco.

    (b) Alberta è proprio decisa — cambiare casa.

    (c) Ida è ansiosa — partire ma Delia non sembra disposta — muoversi.

    (d) Diego è molto soddisfatto — suo lavoro, è responsabile — tutto il reparto.

2 Give the Italian equivalent of the English.

    (a) *I am fed up with my job.*   **(c)** *He is nice to me.*

    (b) *I am pleased with the results.*   **(d)** *She is married to an engineer.*

+ (b) Adjectives with different dependent prepositions

bravo **a**, bravo **in** *good at*	È bravo **a** scuola *He's good at school* È bravo **a** tennis/**a** scacchi *He's good at tennis/chess* È brava **in** matematica/**in** geografia *She's good at maths/geography*	**Bravo a** with the word *school* and games you play; **bravo in** followed by subjects of study.
circondato **di**, circondato **da** *surrounded by*	Sono circondati **dal** nemico *They are surrounded by the enemy* È circondato **di** affetto/**di** mistero *He/It is surrounded by affection/by mystery*	Literal meaning. Figurative meaning.
coperto **di** *covered in/with* coperto **con** *covered with* coperto **da** *covered by*	coperto **di** sangue/polvere/neve/cioccolato *covered in blood/dust/snow/chocolate* coperto **con** (pellicola di) aluminio *covered with/wrapped in foil* un corpo coperto **dalla** neve *a body covered by the snow*	**Coperto di** is more common.

costituito **da/di** *comprising/consisting of*	L'appartamento è costituito **da/di** una sola stanza *The flat consists of a single room*	There is no difference.
dipinto **di**/dipinta **in** *painted (in)*	La stanza è dipinta **di** verde *The room is painted green* Ho dipinto la porta **in** nero *I painted the door in black*	Little difference. **In** stresses the colour more.
generoso **con**, generoso **verso**	È molto generoso **con** tutti/**con** te *He is very generous to everyone/to you* Si è dimostrato generoso **verso** gli avversari *He proved to be generous towards his adversaries*	**Con** for material generosity; **verso** for moral generosity.
libero **di** *free (to)* libero **da** *free of*	Sei libero **di** fare quello che vuoi *You are free to do what you want* È libero **da** ogni preoccupazione *He is free of all worries*	**Di** before a verb; **da** before noun.
pronto **a/per** *ready/ willing to/for*	Siamo pronti **a** decollare *We're ready to take off* Sono pronto **a** tutto *I am ready for anything* Siamo pronti **per** il decollo *We are ready for takeoff*	**Pronto a** before a verb and **tutto**; **pronto per** before a noun.

+ Esercizio

3 Complete the sentences using the correct prepositions.

(a) Angelo è bravo — palavolo.

(b) Pietro è bravo — scuola, soprattutto — italiano.

(c) L'appartamento è costituito — tre piccole stanze.

(d) Il divano è coperto — una stoffa indiana.

(e) Il vecchio pianoforte è coperto — polvere.

(f) Simona era tutta pronta — uscire.

+ 15.5 Nouns and prepositions

Here are just a few nouns that are commonly used with prepositions.

l'amore **per** *a love of* un'antipatia **per** *a dislike of/aversion to* l'assuefazione **a** *an addiction to* la capacità **di** *the ability to* la causa **di** *the cause of* un desiderio **di** *a desire for* un esperto **di** *an expert on*	(un) esperto **in** *(an) expert in/at* l'odio **contro/verso** *(a) hatred of* una passione **per** *a passion for* una predisposizione **a** *an aptitude for* il responsabile **di** *the person in charge of* una sensibilità **per** *a talent, sensitivity for* una simpatia **per** *a liking for*

A note on **esperto di/in**: **esperto in** is more common as an adjective.

È un esperto di cibi transgenici/ di Dante/del Medio Oriente.	*He is an expert on genetically modified food/Dante/the Middle East.*
È esperto nell'uso dei colori/nelle previsioni del tempo.	*He is expert in the use of colour/ in forecasting the weather.*

✚ Esercizi

1 Give the Italian equivalent of the English.

(a) *The cause of the accident is not clear.*

(b) *My sister is an expert on Medieval Italy.*

(c) *His love of animals is well known.*

(d) *Her aversion to cats was extraordinary.*

✚ **2** Look at the following newspaper report about a cyclist in Milan fined for jumping the lights at two in the morning. Some of the prepositions have been deleted. Reconstruct the text by inserting the appropriate prepositions given below.

> a (× 2) • con • da • dalla • del • di • in (× 2) • nella • per • sulla

Passa col rosso alle due di notte, è il primo ciclista multato[1] in città

Due di notte, un'occhiata in giro e via libera. La fidanzata lo aspetta (1) casa, Francesco pedala (2) viale Tibaldi e passa (3) il semaforo rosso. Due vigili in moto lo inseguono e lo fermano: 200 euro di verbale*, sei punti (4) meno (5) patente. È nel deserto d'agosto che il primo ciclista milanese cade (6) rete* del nuovo pacchetto sicurezza (7) governo*, che per le due ruote* inasprisce le sanzioni* e, come (8) gli automobilisti, decurta* punti (9) patente. La vittima non l'ha presa bene: «Ho provato (10) giustificarmi – racconta Francesco Collepardo, 35 anni – in giro non c'era davvero nessuno, mancavano due giorni a Ferragosto*. Niente (11) fare. Capisco il principio, ma un minimo (12) fattore umano deve esserci sempre».

(La Repubblica Milano, 25 agosto 2009: http:/milano.repubblica.it/dettaglio)

> multato *fined* • il verbale *fine, ticket* • la rete *net* • pacchetto … governo *government safety package* • le due ruote *bicycles* (lit. *two wheels*) • inasprisce le sanzioni *makes stricter penalties* • decurta *to dock, take off* • mancavano … a Ferragosto *it was two days before the feast of the Assumption* (an important August holiday when people tend to leave town)

16 Connectives

Connectives (**i connettivi**) are those all-important words or phrases such as *and, or, but, since, instead of, even if* that link sentences or different parts of a sentence and which crucially affect the meaning. They are vital linguistic building blocks which make it possible to develop more fluent, precise and complex language. Their many uses include: adding or clarifying information; giving alternatives or reasons; expressing contrast, conditions or exceptions and defining temporal relationships. They can have coordinating or subordinating functions.

Coordination

*You can have butter **and** jam. You can have butter **or** jam* (simple sentence: see p. 212) *I opened the window **and** shut the door. I opened the window **but** shut the door* (compound sentence: see p. 353)	The simplest connectives have a coordinating function. They connect or coordinate two similar items of equal importance within simple or compound sentences.

Subordination

Subordinating connectives tend to express a more precise meaning than coordinating ones.

She called her brother (main clause) ***because*** *he was ill* (subordinate clause) *She called her brother* (main clause) ***although*** *he was ill* (subordinate clause: see p. 360)	Many connectives have a subordinating function when used in complex sentences (p. 358) to introduce a dependent or subordinate clause.

A sentence can of course contain both coordinating and subordinating connectives: e.g. *She picked up the phone **and*** (coordinating) *called her brother, **although*** (subordinating) *it was late.*

Traditionally connectives are classified as conjunctions (e.g. *and, but, although, since*), but they also include different grammatical categories such as adverbs, prepositions and pronouns. All these categories are included but not discussed here; attention is focused entirely on the various communicative functions of connectives in speech and writing.

◎/✦ 16.1 Adding information

◎/✦ (a) *Le copulative*

These connectives are known in English as copulative because they couple together two items.

e	Caterina **e** Michela sanno nuotare *Caterina **and** Michela can swim* Studi con Anna **e** Giulio? *Do you study with Anna **and** Giulio?* Aveva piovuto **ed erano** bagnati fradici *It had rained **and** they were soaking wet*	Used in affirmative statements and questions. **Ed** is used before words beginning with **e-**.
e non (non) … né	Non studio inglese **e non** voglio farlo *I'm **not** studying English **and** I do **not** want to* **Non** studio inglese, **né** voglio farlo *I'm **not** studying English, **nor** do I want to*	These are both used in negative statements and questions. **Non … né** is more emphatic.

anche ⚠️ **pure**	Va bene, prendo **anche** quello *Fine, I'll **also** take that one/I'll take that one **too/as well*** Vado a Roma e vado **anche** a Bari *I'm going to Rome and I'm **also** going to Bari/I'm going to Bari **as well*** Spero che verranno **pure** loro *I hope they will come **too*** Mi ha aiutato molto, è **pure** riuscito a sbloccare il lavandino *He helped me a lot, he **even/and** he **also** managed to unblock the sink*	⚠️**Anche** goes before the word it qualifies and rarely translates *also* at the beginning of a sentence. See also Adverbs, pp. 63 and 69. **Pure** can be used like **anche**.
inoltre/ **in più,** **per di più**	Vado a Roma. **Inoltre/In più** vado a Bari *I'm going to Rome. **Also/In addition** I'm going to Bari* Non ha pagato l'affitto **e per di più** mi ha insultato *She didn't pay the rent and **what's more/on top of that**, she insulted me*	These, and not **anche**, express *also* at the beginning of a sentence. **Per di più** is emphatic.
oltre a **a parte**	**Oltre a** Roma ho visto Napoli ***Besides/As well as/In addition to** Rome I saw Naples* **Oltre a** vedere il Colosseo ho visitato il Vatican ***As well as/Apart from** seeing the Colosseum, I visited the Vatican* **A parte** noi due, c'erano Marina e Ugo ***Apart from/Besides** us two, Marina and Ugo were there*	**Oltre a** and **a parte** precede nouns and pronouns. **Oltre a** may be followed by an infinitive. Both can also mean *except*. See p. 221.
fra l'altro	No, non vengo, non m'interessa. Poi, **fra l'altro** i biglietti sono cari *No, I'm not coming, it doesn't interest me. **And (then) anyway/furthermore/what's more**, the tickets are expensive*	Very common. **Fra l'altro** can also mean *incidentally*.
✚ **come** **pure**	Gli insegnanti fanno sciopero, **come pure** gli studenti *The teachers are on strike **and so are** the students/**as well as/just like** the students* Lucio si è offeso, **come pure** mio marito *Lucio took offence, **and so did/just like** my husband*	Lit. *like also*. It is a common and useful way of avoiding the clumsy repetition of a verb.

✚ (b) *Le correlative*

These connectives, known in English as correlatives, link more than one item and add emphasis.

sia … sia **sia … che**	Possono venire **sia** Caterina **che** Michela ***Both** Caterina **and** Michela can come* Vado in piscina **sia** d'inverno **sia/che** d'estate *I go swimming in **both** summer and winter/in summer and winter **alike*** Non importa chi cucina oggi: può farlo **sia** l'una **che** l'altra *It doesn't matter who cooks today, **either of** them can do it*	This generally means *both … and*, or occasionally *either… or*. Unlike o … o (p. 216), it never expresses opposing, excluding alternatives.
né … né	Non sono amico **né** di Anna **né** di Giulio ***Neither** Anna **nor** Giulio are my friends* **Né** mia sorella **né** suo marito bevono/beve vino/Non bevono **né** mia sorella **né** suo marito ***Neither** my sister **nor** her husband drink wine*	If the verb has two preceding subjects, it can be singular or plural; when the subjects follow, the verb is plural.

non solo ... ma (anche)	**Non solo** ha perso l'orologio, **ma** ha (**anche**) dimenticato la riunione ***Not only*** *did he lose his watch **but** he (**also**) forgot the meeting* **Non solo** il padre **ma anche** i figli hanno il diritto di scegliere ***Not only*** *the father, **but** the sons **too** have the right to choose*	When **ma anche** is followed by a different subject from the first one, the latter determines the person of the verb.
non solo	Si è rotto il braccio. **Non solo**: il poveretto si è anche spaccato un dente *He's broken his arm **and that's not all/what's more**: the poor thing has also broken a tooth*	This refers to a whole clause or sentence.
✚ tanto meno	Non si può condannarli, **tanto meno** punirli *You can't condemn them, **let alone** punish them*	Links verbs and avoids repetition.

◎/✚ Esercizi

1 Complete the text below by using the connectives given.

e anche • e • inoltre • in più • oltre a

Durante le vacanze sono andato in giro con mio fratello. Abbiamo visitato tutta la Campania, (1 *and also*) la Sicilia. (2 *Also/In addition*) siamo stati nelle isole Eolie al largo della Sicilia. In Campania abbiamo visto Napoli, Salerno, Amalfi (3 *and*) Ravello. In Sicilia siamo stati un po' dappertutto. (4 *As well as*) visitare le città principali di Messina, Palermo, Catania, Siracusa e Trapani, siamo stati nel centro, a Enna e (5 *in addition*) abbiamo visitato Erice e il tempio di Segesta.

✚ **2** Give the English equivalent of the following sentences.

(a) Sia Emilio che Elisabetta sono stati promossi.

(b) Emilio è stato promosso, come pure Elisabetta.

(c) Né Giorgio né Giovanna sono stati promossi.

(d) Dopo la festa Giorgio è tornato ubriaco. Non solo: è stato fermato dalla polizia.

◎/✚ 16.2 Clarifying information

◎/✚ (a) *Le dichiarative*

These connectives, known in English as declaratives, are commonly used to define, correct, explain or confirm.

per esempio, ad esempio	Ti posso vedere presto, **per esempio** alle otto *I can see you early, **for example** at eight*	**Ad esempio** is slightly more formal.
cioè	Torno più tardi, **cioè** all'una *I'll be back later, **that is** at one.* Sono proprio stufo – **Cioè?** – **Cioè** non ci voglio andare! *I'm really fed up. – **What does that mean?** – **It means** I don't want to go*	Widely used to express and request more specific information.
✚ ossia	È un esperto di micologia, **ossia** dello studio dei funghi *He is an expert in micology, **that is to say**, in the study of mushrooms*	Very like **cioè**, but typical of formal written Italian.

voglio dire	**Voglio dire** che è disonesto *I mean he is dishonest*	Informal.
✚ **in altre parole**, **in altri termini**, **vale a dire (che)**	Il capo mi ha detto di non metter piede nella ditta, **in altre parole** mi ha licenziato *My boss has told me not to set foot inside the firm, **in other words** he has sacked me* È una lettera anonima, **vale a dire** non firmata *It's an anonymous letter, **that is to say** it is not signed*	**In altre parole/termini** can be used in the same way. **Vale a dire** is typical of written Italian.
o meglio, **piuttosto**, **più che**	Gli telefonerò – **o meglio/piuttosto** gli manderò una mail *I'll phone him – **(or) rather**, I'll send him an email* **Piu che** un conoscente, è un amico *He's a friend **rather than** an acquaintance (more of a friend than …)*	These can be used as a way to specify or to correct oneself.
✚ **si tratta di**	**Si tratta di** un incendio doloso, non di un semplice incidente ***It is** arson, not just an accident* **Si tratta dei** problemi di una coppia separata ***It's about** the problems of a separated couple.* **Di** che cosa **si tratta**? *What is it/this about?*	Used to specify what something is about. It literally means *it is a question of*, but often translates as *this/it is*.
✚ **anzi**	Ti chiedo, **anzi,** ti prego di aspettare *I'm asking you, **in fact** I'm begging you to wait* Sei veramente gentile, **anzi**, sei proprio un angelo! *You're so kind, **in fact** you're an absolute angel!*	Used emphatically to specify. **Anzi** more commonly contradicts. See p. 218.

⚠ **Attenti!** You need to differentiate between the following:

ecco	**Ecco!** Avevo ragione io, Mauro non ha pagato! ***You see!/There!** I was right, Mauro hasn't paid.* Non m'interessa, **ecco!** *I'm not interested, **so there!**/I'm **just not** interested*	Commonly used to reinforce a point.
✚ **infatti** **già**	Pietro viene stasera. – **Infatti**, me l'ha già detto *Pietro is coming tonight. – **That's right/Indeed/ I know,** he's already told me* Pietro viene stasera. – **Già!** Avevo dimenticato *Pietro's coming tonight. – **Of course/That's right.** I had forgotten*	**Infatti** does not often mean *in fact*. Like **già** it expresses agreement: it is used to confirm what has just been said, while **già** acknowledges you have remembered something.
✚ **infatti** **in effetti**	Hai perso il treno, allora? – **Infatti.** *So did you miss the train then? – **Indeed/That's right/Yes I did*** È un ragazzo timido – **Infatti**, l'ho sempre notato *He is a shy boy – **That's right**, I've always noticed it* È un'allieva timida – Sì, **in effetti** non parla mai in classe *She is a shy pupil – Yes, **the fact/the truth is** she never talks in class*	These are virtually synonymous, but **in effetti** introduces extra detail beyond simple confirmation. It has the additional meaning of *the truth is*. Compare **in realtà** *in fact*, p. 218.

◎/✚ Esercizi

1 Make things clear. Substitute the English connectives with an appropriate Italian one, choosing from the list below.

cioè • già • ecco • infatti • o meglio

    (a) Ho telefonato a Marta, (*that is*) a mia cognata.

    (b) Ho invitato la suocera, (*or rather*) l'ha invitata mia moglie!

    (c) Domani è festa. – (*Of course/That's right!*), avevo dimenticato.

    (d) Alberto è bugiardo. – (*Indeed!/That's right!*) È tanto che lo so.

    (e) Alberto è stato arrestato per frode. – (*There! You see!*) lo sapevo che è un tipo disonesto.

✚ **2** Now do the same with these connectives:

infatti • in effetti • anzi

    (a) È meglio partire più tardi. – Sì, (*that's right/indeed*), così evitiamo il traffico.

    (b) Sandra mi sembra piuttosto depressa. – Sì, (*that's right/in fact*) non esce più.

    (c) È un bellissimo film, (*in fact*) è un capolavoro!

◎/✚ 16.3 Expressing alternatives

◎/✚ (a) *Le avversative* (1)

These are known as adversative or disjunctive connectors, and express choice or alternatives.

o oppure **o ... o/** **oppure**	Vuoi una birra **o** un caffé? *Would you like a beer **or** a coffee?* Possiamo andare da Mirella **oppure** rimanere qui *We can go to Mirella's **or else** we can stay here/We can **either** go to Mirella's **or** we can stay here* **O** lo faccio io **o/oppure** lo fai tu ***Either** I do it **or (else)** you do* Verrà/verranno **o** mio figlio **o/oppure** mia sorella ***Either** my son or my sister will come*	These all express opposing alternatives. When a verb has two subjects it may be singular or plural especially when the subjects follow. See also Indefinites, **o l'uno o l'altro**, p. 167.
altrimenti	Devo andarmene, **altrimenti** sarò in ritardo *I must leave, **otherwise** I'll be late*	**Altrimenti** is used only before a verb.
invece di ✚ **piuttosto**	**Invece di** scrivergli perché non gli mandi un sms? ***Instead of** writing to him why don't you text him?* **Invece di** Sandro, perché non sposi **piuttosto** Andrea? ***Rather than** Sandro, why don't you marry Andrea **instead**?*	**Invece di** precedes infinitives, nouns or pronouns. See also p. 217. **Piuttosto** often comes after the verb.
✚ **piuttosto che (di)** ✚ **anziché**	**Piuttosto che** fare tardi, prenderò un taxi ***Rather than** be late, I'll take a taxi* Secondo me è timido **piuttosto che** freddo *I think he is shy **rather than** cold* Preferisco parlare con te **anziché** con il professore *I prefer to speak to you **instead of** the teacher*	**Che** is more commonly used than **di** with **piuttosto. Anziché** is similar but expresses a more definite alternative.

◎/✚ Esercizi

1 Complete the sentences in Italian, substituting the English.

    (a) Cosa prendete?   *we have beer or wine.*

    (b) Facciamo quello che vuoi tu,   *we can either stay here or (else) go to the cinema.*

    (c) Dobbiamo rispondere subito,   *otherwise we'll lose the contract.*

    (d) È meglio parlargli direttamente   *instead of sending an email.*

✚ **2** Give the Italian equivalent of the following.

    (a) *Rather than eat sweets, why don't you eat fruit?*

    (b) *I want to work with her rather than with him.*

    (c) *I prefer to go alone rather than wait.*

    (d) *Don't drink coffee, have a lemon tea instead.*

◎/✚ 16.4 Comparing, contrasting and contradicting

◎/✚ (a) *Le avversative* (2)

These adversative connectives introduce contrasting or opposing ideas.

ma **però**	Noi usciamo, **ma** Lucio non viene *We're going out **but** Lucio's not coming* Non posso parlare adesso; ti chiamo domani, **però** *I can't talk now, **but/however** I'll call you tomorrow*	**Però** can be used like **ma** but can also end a sentence.
comunque	È vero che si sta bene qui, **comunque** sabato devo partire *It's true that it's nice here, **however/but anyway** on Saturday I have to leave*	Very common. Precedes the verb. After the verb it means *come what may/anyway* (p. 222).
invece, mentre	Io studio a Bari, Tommaso **invece** studia a Milano *I'm studying in Bari, Tommaso **however/on the other hand**, is studying in Milan* Io studio a Bari **mentre** Tommaso studia a Milano *I'm studying in Bari **while/whereas** Tommaso is studying in Milan* Mio fratello ha scelto medicina, **mentre** io **invece** ho scelto architettura *My brother has chosen medicine, **whereas I (on the other hand)** have chosen architecture*	Very common. Both are used to compare and contrast. **Mentre** often reinforces **invece**. For **invece (di)**, see p. 216.
viceversa **al contrario**	Avevano promesso di finire il lavoro oggi, **viceversa** non hanno neppure incominciato *They promised to finish the work today, **but instead/ whereas** they haven't even started* Gli avevo chiesto di non dirle niente, e lui, **al contrario**, le ha riferito tutto *I had asked him not to tell her anything, **but instead/on the contrary**, he told her everything*	These both introduce opposing actions. **Viceversa** is quite informal. It can also correspond to the English *vice versa*.
solo che	Sarei venuto ieri, **solo che** i figli sono malati *I would have come yesterday, **only/but** the children are ill*	This is quite informal and very common.
eppure ✚ **tuttavia**	Tu dici che è pigro, **eppure** ha ottimi risultati *You say he is lazy, **and yet/nevertheless** he has excellent results* Era stanco morto, **tuttavia** ha giocato a tennis *He was dead tired, **nevertheless/all the same** he played tennis*	Similar in meaning. **Eppure** is more informal.

✦ d'altra parte, del resto	Non mi piace viaggiare in aereo. **D'altra parte** è rapidissimo *I don't like going by plane. **On the other hand** it is very quick* Antonio si è comportato male, anche Stefania, **del resto** *Antonio behaved badly, **but then/on the other hand** so did Stefania*	These are all used to evaluate and weigh things up. **Del resto c**an be used like **d'altra parte** but also has other meanings.
✦ da un lato ... dall'altro, da una parte ... dall'altra	**Da un lato** ha ragione, **dall'altro** no ***On the one hand** he's right, **on the other** he isn't* **Da una parte** è un po' bugiardo, **dall'altra**, però, è un tipo proprio simpatico ***On the one hand** he's a bit of a liar, **on the other**, however, he's a really nice guy*	**Da un lato ... dall'altro** and **da una parte ... dall'altra** are identical in meaning.

◎/✦ (b) *Le oppositive o sostitutive*

 These are used to contradict and to say that something else is true. **Attenti!** Do not confuse **invece** and **in realtà:**

invece ✦ in realtà	Katia ha promesso di venire, **invece** è andata al cinema *Katia promised to come **but** she has gone to the cinema **instead*** Sembra un ragazzo timido. **In realtà** è piuttosto aggressivo *He seems a shy boy. **In actual fact/In reality** he is quite aggressive/He's **actually** quite aggressive*	Very common. See also p. 217. **In realtà** is used to contradict or correct a previous statement. Do not confuse with **infatti** (p. 215).
anzi	Non è per niente stupido. **Anzi!** *He's not stupid at all. **On the contrary/Far from it!*** Disturbo? – **Anzi**, mi fa piacere *Am I interrupting you? – **Not at all**, you're welcome*	Very common. Mostly used to contradict, but also to reinforce/clarify (see also p. 215).
✦ bensì	La crisi non è dovuta a fattori economici, **bensì** a problemi politici *The crisis is **in fact not** due to economic factors **but** to political problems (instead)*	An emphatic form of **ma**. It is only used after negatives.

◎/✦ Esercizi

1 Contrast and compare. Complete the sentences by substituting the English with suitable Italian connectives.

- **(a)** Io studio legge (*but*) mia sorella studia architettura.
- **(b)** Io studio legge (*whereas*) mia sorella studia architettura.
- **(c)** Io studio medicina, (*however*) non mi piace molto!
- **(d)** Io sono nato a Torino, Leonardo (*on the other hand/however*) è nato a Palermo.
- ✦ **(e)** Sta male, (*nevertheless*) ha intenzione di dare l'esame.
- ✦ **(f)** Non mi piace viaggiare in aereo, (*on the other hand*) è molto comodo.

✦ **2** Complete the sentences by including the connectives given.

anzi • invece • in realtà • viceversa

- **(a)** Avevo intenzione di studiare, ma — ho cenato da amici.
- **(b)** Non è una persona antipatica, — è gentilissima.
- **(c)** Leopoldo mi ha portato a cena ma — non avevo fame.
- **(d)** Maurizio ha detto che arrivava di sicuro, ma — non si è fatto vivo.

⊙/+ 16.5 Expressing reasons, purpose, cause and effect

⊙/+ (a) Le *causative*

The following connectives are known as causal in English, as they explain reasons or cause.

⚠ **Attenti!** In Italian, *because* and especially *because of* is expressed in a variety of ways. Look carefully at the following tables.

perché	Preferisco non venire **perché** piove tanto *I'd rather not come **because** it's raining so much* **But:** **Siccome/Visto che** piove tanto, preferisco non venire **Because** *it's raining so much I'd rather not come*	Does not begin a sentence. Instead, use **dato che, dal momento che, poiché, siccome, visto che** (see below).
per questo **per**	È **per questo** che sono in ritardo *It's **because of this/that** I'm late/**That's why** I'm late* Non siamo venuti **per** il freddo *We didn't come **because of** the cold*	See also Prepositions, p. 200.
a causa di + noun **+ (per/è)** **colpa mia/** **tua**, etc., **per causa** **mia/tua**, etc.	Sono in ritardo **a causa dell'**incidente/**a causa di** Giulio *I am late **because of** the accident/Giulio* Sono in ritardo **per colpa tua** *I am late **because of** you* È **colpa sua** se sono in ritardo *It's **because of** him/her that I am late/It's **his/her fault** that I am late* Hanno traslocato **per causa mia** *They moved **because of/on account of** me* È scoppiata una rissa **per causa sua** *A brawl broke out **because of him/on his account***	**A causa di** is followed by a noun, not a pronoun. To say *because of me/you* etc., **per colpa mia/tua** etc., or **è colpa mia**, etc. are used. **Per causa mia**, etc. can also be used.
+ grazie a **è merito** **tuo, suo**, etc.	La festa è andata bene **grazie al** bel tempo/**a** Roberto/**a** loro *The party went well **thanks to/because of** the weather/Roberto/them* **È merito tuo** se la festa è andata bene *It's **thanks to/because of** you the party went well*	**Grazie a** or **È merito tuo/suo**, etc. are used when the cause is positive.

Unlike **perché**, the following connectives may begin a sentence. Note, however, that with the exception of **siccome**, they may also be placed elsewhere.

siccome **dato** **che/dal** **momento** **che,** **visto** **che,** **+ poiché** **+ giacché**	**Siccome** è ricco, può viaggiare molto **Because/Since** *he is rich, he can travel a lot* **Dato che/Dal momento che** siamo senza soldi, è assurdo pensare a cambiare casa **Since/As** *we have no money, it's absurd to think about moving* **Visto che** sei qui, mi puoi aiutare/Mi puoi aiutare **visto che** sei qui **Since/Seeing that/As** *you are here, you can help me* **Poiché** si era fatto tardi, rimasero fino al giorno seguente/Rimasero fino al al giorno seguente, **poiché** sia era fatto tardi **Since/As** *it had got late, they stayed until the following day* **Giacché** non ci sono obbiezioni, possiamo cominciare **Since/As** *there are no objections we can begin*	**Siccome** must begin the sentence. **Dal momento che** also means *as soon as*. **Giacché** and, to a lesser extent, **poiché** are more formal and used in writing.
+ Gerund	**Avendo perso** il treno, sono rimasto da loro **As/Since** *I had missed the train I stayed at their place*	See also Gerunds, p. 294.

◎/✛ Esercizi

1 Complete the following sentences using a suitable Italian equivalent of the English. More than one version may be possible.

    (a) (*Since/Seeing that*) sei qui, mi puoi aiutare.

    (b) (*Because/Since*) la banca è chiusa, sono rimasto senza soldi.

    (c) (*Since/As I had*) perso la chiave, sono rimasto chiuso fuori.

2 Give the Italian equivalent of the following.

    (a) *Because it's your birthday we can eat out.*

    (b) *We can't leave because of the strike.*

    (c) *Is that why he's angry?*

✛   **(d)** *It's because of you that I passed the exam.* (**sono stato promosso**)

✛   **(e)** *I'm late because of you.*

◎/✛ (b) *Le finali*

These are connectives of intention and purpose.

per + infinitive	Sono venuti **per** festeggiare l'Anno Nuovo *They have come **to** celebrate the New Year*	This is the simplest way of expressing intention.
perché, ✛ **affinché**	Te lo dico ora **perché/affinché** lo sappia prima degli altri *I'm telling you now **so that** you know before the others*	These take the subjunctive. **Affinché** is typical of very formal Italian.
✛ **al fine di**	**Al fine di** meglio comprendere la situazione che stiamo vivendo, io propongo un'analisi più approfondita ***In order to** better understand the situation we are experiencing, I propose/suggest we analyse it more deeply*	**Al fine di** is typical of a formal register.
✛ **pur di** + present infinitive	Sono disposti a ridursi lo stipendio **pur di** non perdere il lavoro *They are willing to drop their salaries **just as long as** they don't lose their jobs/**to make sure** they don't lose their jobs* Ecco che il governo si inventa una qualunque cosa **pur di** distrarre gli italiani dalla crisi *And so here we have the government coming up with all manner of things **to make sure they/just to** distract Italians from the crisis*	**Pur di** + the infinitive is a common way of expressing what is specifically done to achieve a goal in difficult circumstances.
✛ **in modo da** + infinitive, **in/di modo che**	Bisogna organizzarci **in modo da** evitare lavoro inutile *We have to organise ourselves **so that** we avoid unnecessary work* Farò **in modo che** loro possano andare a casa presto *I'll **see to it that** they can go home early* Gli hanno fatto bere mezza bottiglia di whiskey **in modo che** si ubriacasse *They made him drink half a bottle of whisky **so that** he got/would get drunk*	These focus on future intentions with respect to outcome (see next section). **In/di modo che** mostly takes the subjunctive (p. 309).

◎/✚ (c) *Le conclusive e consecutive*

These express conclusions and consequences, focusing on outcome and on what happens next.

| allora,
così,
quindi,
sicché,
perciò,
dunque,
✚ pertanto | Era senza soldi **e allora** ho dovuto prestargli venti euro *He had no money **and so/so then** I had to lend him 20 euros*
Ero senza macchina, **allora/così/quindi** sono venuto a piedi *I didn't have the car **so/therefore** I walked*
Il telefono era rotto, **sicché/perciò** non ho potuto chiamare *The phone was broken **and so/therefore** I couldn't call*
Penso **dunque** sono *I think **therefore** I am* | These can all be used in very similar ways. **Perciò** is a little more formal. **Pertanto** is very formal and used in writing.
For **dunque**, see also p. 227. |
| per cui

di
conseguenza
tanto
✚ tanto che | È caduto per strada, **per cui** è arrivato tardi *He fell in the street, **so that** he arrived late*
Si è addormentato. **Di conseguenza** non ha sentito il telefono *He fell asleep. **As a result** he didn't hear the phone*
E' inutile arrabbiarsi, **tanto** è troppo tardi *There's no point getting cross **because anyway** it's too late*
Cinzia lo trova proprio antipatico, **tanto che** non gli parla mai *Cinzia really dislikes him, **to the extent that/so the result is** she never talks to him* | These put more emphasis on the outcome than the above connectives. |

◎/✚ Esercizi

3 Consequences. Match up the sentences and give the English equivalents.

(a) La macchina è guasta …   (i) in modo da poter risparmiare di più.

(b) Si è rotto la gamba …   (ii) quindi la devo portare dal meccanico.

(c) Sono diminuiti i profitti …   (iii) per cui non ha potuto andare a sciare.

(d) Ho organizzato le cose …   (iv) di conseguenza hanno chiuso una fabbrica.

✚ **4** What for? Complete the sentences using appropriate connectives.

(a) È arrivato — controllare la situazione.

(b) A mia nonna le abbiamo comprato un letto nuovo — stesse più comoda.

(c) Bisognerebbe confrontare i due testi — di determinare con precisione le loro origini.

(d) Farebbe qualsiasi cosa — non perdere la moglie

◎/✚ 16.6 Making exceptions, concessions and conditions

◎/✚ (a) *Le eccettuative*

These connectives express exceptions.

| a parte,

oltre (a),

salvo,
tranne,
meno (che)

✚ all'infuori di/ad eccezione di | Ho letto tutto, **a parte** la conclusione *I've read everything **apart from/except** the conclusion*
Oltre Paolo, non è venuto nessuno
***Apart from/Except for** Paolo, no one came*
Sono partiti tutti, **meno/salvo/tranne** lui
*They have all left **except** him*
Ha pensato a tutto, **meno che** alla moglie
*He thought of everyone **except for** his wife*
All'infuori di sua sorella, parlavano tutti tedesco
***Apart from** his sister they all spoke German* | *Apart from/except (for)* can be expressed by any of these. **Che** usually follows **meno** before a preposition. More formal alternatives are **all'infuori di/ad eccezione di.** |

eccetto, fuorché	Mi puoi chiedere tutto quello che vuoi, **eccetto/ fuorché** andare in aereo *You can ask me to do whatever you want, **apart from/save/except** going by plane*	Mostly used with infinitive verbs.
+ a prescindere da	**A prescindere dal** fatto che non abbiamo soldi, non ho voglia di andare all'estero ***Apart from the fact/Leaving aside the fact that** we have no money, I don't feel like going abroad*	**Lasciando da parte** could be more informally used instead.

◎ Esercizio

1 Using appropriate connectives complete the following sentences. There may be more than one possibility.

(a) Io mangio di tutto (*except*) il baccalà. (*salt cod*)

(b) Non ha obiettato nessuno, (*except*) tuo fratello.

(c) (*Apart from*) mia madre, nessuno parla inglese.

(d) Chiedimi tutto, (*apart from*) invitare quella gente!

◎/+ (b) *Le concessive*

These connectives express concession – *although*, *despite*, etc. Many take the subjunctive.

in ogni caso ad ogni modo lo stesso, **+** comunque	Non ho voglia di vederlo e **in ogni caso** parto stasera *I don't feel like seeing him and **in any case/anyway** I'm leaving this evening* Non vinceranno, secondo me. **Ad ogni modo,** vedremo cosa succede *In my view they won't win. **Anyway/Anyhow/At any rate** we'll see what happens* Io vengo **lo stesso/comunque** *I'm coming **all the same/anyway**/I'm **still** coming* Fai come vuoi, io parto **comunque** *Do what you want, I'm leaving **anyway/come what may***	These are all very common. No subjunctive is used. For **comunque**, see also Le avversative p. 217; Le condizionali, p. 224.
anche se	**Anche se** è mio cugino, mi è antipatico ***Even though/Although** he is my cousin, I don't like him*	This is only used with the subjunctive when expressing a hypothesis. See Subjunctives, p. 309.
+ benché, sebbene	**Benché/Sebbene** sia difficile, ci riuscirai ***Although** it is hard, you will manage*	Used with the subjunctive. See p. 309.
+ pur + gerund	**Pur sapendo** che era troppo tardi, gli ho telefonato ***Although** I knew/**Despite** knowing it was too late, I phoned him* **Pur** non **avendo capito** molto, gli è piaciuto il film ***Although** he had not/**Despite** not having understood much, he liked the film*	Used if the subject of both verbs is the same. See Gerunds, p. 294.

+ **malgrado, nonostante**	È arrivato in tempo **malgrado/nonostante** la neve *He arrived on time **despite** the snow* Uscirono, **malgrado/nonostante** facesse freddo *They went out **although/despite the fact** it was cold*	Used with a noun. For subjunctive verb, see also Subjunctives, p. 309.
+ ammesso che	Quali sono, **ammesso che** ce ne siano, gli effetti dei film violenti sulla società? *What, **if any**, are the effects of violent films on society?/ **If you accept** they exist, what effects do violent films have on society?*	Used with the subjunctive, it often expresses scepticism or lack of conviction. See Subjunctives, p. 309.

◎/✚ Esercizi

2 Complete the sentences by substituting the English with an appropriate Italian connective.

(a) Io voglio andarci (*even though*) è lontano.

(b) Mi sono divertito (*despite*) la pioggia.

(c) So che c'è sciopero ma io parto (*all the same*).

(d) La partita è cominciata male per loro, ma (*anyhow*) sono riusciti a vincere.

✚ **3** Find an appropriate Italian connective to substitute the English.

(a) (*Although*) sia lontano, vale la pena di andarci.

(b) (*Even if you accept that*) esista il riscaldamento globale, cosa ci possiamo fare?

(c) (*Despite the fact*) fosse malato, sua figlia non andava mai a trovarlo.

(d) (*Although he was/Despite being*) molto malato, ha voluto andare in ufficio.

◎/✚ (c) *Le condizionali*

These connectives express hypotheses and conditions. Most of them are used in complex sentences and can take the subjunctive.

se **+**	**Se** vuoi, ti posso aiutare *If you want, I can help you* **Se** costa poco lo comprerò *If it's cheap I'll buy it* **Se** fossi in te, non lo farei *If I were you I wouldn't do it*	For **se** + future, see p. 249. For **se** + subjunctive, see p. 305.
in caso di	Chiamatemi **in caso di** emergenza *Call me **in the event of** an emergency/if there is an emergency*	
magari	Possiamo **magari** andare al cinema *We can **maybe/perhaps** go to the cinema*	For use with the subjunctive, see p. 305.
semmai, caso mai	Ti chiamerò domani, **semmai/casomai** *I **might possibly/I'll maybe** call you tomorrow/I'll call you tomorrow **if need be*** Non credo di aver dimenticato niente. **Caso mai** te lo faccio sapere subito *I don't think I've forgotten anything. **If so/if I have**, I'll let you know at once*	These are widely used. Their meanings are similar, though not identical.
+ semmai, caso mai + subjunctive	**Semmai** dovesse rispondere domani, fammelo sapere *If he answers/should answer tomorrow, let me know* Le do il mio numero **caso mai** mancasse qualcosa *I'm giving you my number **in case** anything should be missing/**in the** (unlikely) **event that** something is missing*	Both **semmai** and **caso mai** may be used with the past subjunctive. See p. 309.

nel caso che	**Nel caso che** dovesse dimenticare la chiave, ce n'è un'altra nel vaso *In case/if he forgets/**Should** he forget his key, there's another one in the vase*	**Qualora** and, to a lesser extent, **nel caso che** are more
qualora ✚	**Qualora** avesse bisogno le consiglierò ***Should** you need it, I will advise you*	formal than **semmai** and **caso mai**.
anche se ✚	**Anche se** fosse vero, non ci crederei ***Even if** it were true I wouldn't believe it* **Anche se** l'avesse saputo, non avrebbe cambiato idea ***Even if** he had known he wouldn't have changed his mind*	With the subjunctive (p. 309), **anche se** is used for hypotheses. With no subjunctive, it = *even though* (p. 222).
per quanto/ comunque ✚	**Per quanto** lo so le cose stanno come *prima* ***As far as** I know things are the same as before* **Per quanto** difficile sia, ci riuscirai ***However** hard it may be, you will manage* Non ti scoraggiare **comunque** vadano le cose *Don't get discouraged **however** things go*	Both sometimes used with the subjunctive. For **comunque** without the subjunctive, see pp. 217 and 222.
ammettendo che ✚	Anche **ammettendo che** le votazioni fossero manipolate, resta il fatto che il presidente rimarrà al potere *Even **supposing** that the vote was rigged, the fact remains that the President will stay in power/Even **assuming** the vote may have been rigged ...*	This has a variety of meanings including *suppose/what if?* Used with different subjunctive tenses (see p. 309).

✚ Esercizio

4 Complete the sentences using appropriate Italian connectives.

    (a) (*As far as*) lo so, è sposato da due anni.

    (b) Quest'anno andiamo in ferie (*however*) vadano gli affari.

    (c) Non so se saranno d'accordo, (*in that case/possibly*) li chiamo domani.

    (d) (*Suppose/What if*) trovassi un appartamento, lo compreresti?

    (e) (*If/Should*) tu non potessi venire, fammelo sapere subito.

✚ The following conjunctions express more specific, restricted conditions.

a meno che	Lo pulisco io, **a meno che** tu non abbia voglia di farlo *I'll clean it, **unless** you feel like doing it*	Used with subjunctive (see p. 309).
a condizione di/a patto di	Accetto di viaggiare con la tua macchina, **a patto di/a condizione di** poter contribuire alle spese di viaggio *I'll accept travelling in your car **on condition that/as long as** I can contribute to the travel expenses*	**di** + infinitive is used when the subject of both clauses is the same.
a condizione che/a patto che	Ti darò i soldi **a condizione che/a patto che** tu me li restituisca *I'll give you the money **on condition that/providing that** you return it*	**che** + subjunctive is used when each clause has a different subject (see p. 300).
purché	Non m'importa quello che fa, **purché** sia felice *I don't mind what he does **as long as/provided that** he's happy*	Used with subjunctive (see p. 309).

+ Esercizio

5 Give the English equivalent of the Italian.

(a) Mi va bene qualsiasi orario purché io lo sappia prima.

(b) Ci troviamo in biblioteca a meno che non sia chiusa.

(c) Ti accompagno a condizione di essere tornato prima delle dieci.

(d) Gli perdono solo a patto che chieda scusa a mia sorella.

◎/+ 16.7 Time sequence

Le temporali

These important connectives signal when something happens in relation to something else.

| all'inizio, prima, poi, dopo, in seguito, alla fine | **All'inizio** ho rifiutato. **Poi, dopo** un po' ho cambiato idea, e **alla fine** ho accettato *At first I refused. Then, after a while I changed my mind and in the end I accepted* **Prima** ero impiegato alle poste, **poi, in seguito**, ho lavorato per il Comune *First I was employed in the post office, then subsequently I worked for the Council* | These basic connectors are used in simple or compound sentences to indicate a sequence of actions or events. |

The following are used to locate points in time.

allora, a quell'epoca, a quel tempo/in quei giorni	**Allora/A quell'epoca** erano poveri *Then/In those days they were poor* Ero a Roma quando è morto mio padre. **In quei giorni** ho sofferto molto *I was in Rome when my father died. I suffered a lot at that time*	Distant past. Distant past in relation to a specific time span/event.
negli ultimi giorni/tempi	**Negli ultimi tempi** ha smesso di salutarmi *Recently/Of late he has stopped saying hello*	Recent past.
nei giorni scorsi	**Nei giorno scorsi** il tempo è peggiorato *The weather has got worse in the last few days*	Very recent past.
in questi giorni	**In questi giorni** mi occupo io dei suoi bambini *I'm looking after her children at the moment/at present/these days* (present) **In questi giorni** ho passato molte ore al computer *In/Over the last few days I've spent many hours at the computer* (recent past) **In questi giorni** avrò molto da fare *In the next few days I'll have a lot to do* (future)	This can be used with reference to the present, to the recent past and also to the future.
nei prossimi giorni	Ho intenzione di vederli **nei prossimi giorni** *I intend to see them in the next few days*	Future.

✚ The following time connectives are used in complex sentences to introduce subordinate clauses.

prima di + infinitive **prima che +** subjunctive **prima che me ne/te ne/se ne dimentichi**	Li chiamerò **prima di** partire *I'll call them **before** I leave* Ha rifatto il letto **prima di** uscire *She made the bed before she left* Li chiamerò **prima che** partano *I'll call them **before** they leave* Ha rifatto il letto **prima che** arrivassero *She made the bed **before** they arrived* **Note also:** **Prima che** me ne dimentichi/**Prima di** dimenticarmene, ti do le chiavi di casa ***Before** I forget, I'll give you the house keys*	**prima di** is used when the subject of both clauses is the same. **prima che** is used when each clause has a different subject. See also Subjunctive p. 301. **prima che** is often used with the subjunctive of **dimenticarsi** even when the subjects are the same.
appena	**Appena** arrivi, chiamami *Call me **as soon as** you arrive* **(Non) appena** avrai una risposta, fammelo sapere ***As soon as** you get a reply, let me know*	See pp. 249, 250–1 and 271 for use with the future, future perfect and past anterior.
dopo che **dopo +** past infinitive **dopo +** noun	Riceverà i risultati **dopo che** sarai partito *He will receive the results **after** you (will) have left/leave* Riceverà i risultati **dopo che** sarà partito *He will receive the results **after** he (will) have left/he leaves* L'ho saputo solo **dopo esser arrivato** (**dopo che** ero arrivato) *I found out only **after arriving**/I had arrived* Ti chiamerò **dopo averlo visto** (**dopo che** l'avrò visto) *I'll call you **after having seen him**/after I (will) have seen him* Riceverà i risultati **dopo** la tua partenza *He will receive the results **after** your departure* L'ho saputo **dopo** il mio arrivo *I found out **after** my arrival*	**dopo che** can be used whether the subjects of the clauses are different or the same. **dopo +** past infinitive is used when the subject of both clauses is the same. See also pp. 251 and 267. **dopo +** a noun substituting the verb is a very common alternative. See p. 271.
fino a + time expression	Dobbiamo aspettare **fino a** domani/**fino alla** settimana prossima *We must wait **until** tomorrow/next week*	This indicates time *until*.
finché + verb	Puoi rimanere **finché** vuoi *You can stay **as long as** you like* **Finché** fa caldo, sono felice ***As long as** it's hot, I'm happy* **Finché** c'è vita c'è speranza ***While** there's life there's hope*	This is followed by the indicative.
finché/fino a quando (non) **che +** subjunctive	Abbiamo aspettato/Non abbiamo cenato **finché/fino a quando** (**non**) sono tornati *We waited/We did not eat supper **until** they returned* Aspettiamo/Resta con me **finché/fino a quando** saranno tornati *or* non siano tornati *Let's wait/Stay with me **until** they have returned/return* Aspettiamo **che** siano tornati *Let's wait **until** they have returned* Abbiamo aspettato **che** tornassero *We waited **for** them **to** return*	If the action is not certain to take place, the subjunctive is preferred. The use of **non** is stylistic and has no negative meaning. (See also p. 301.) **Che** is often used after **aspettare** instead of **finché**.

◎/✦ Esercizi

1 Pick out all the connectives in brackets which make sense within each sentence, then name the odd one out each time.

(a) Da studente ho vissuto a Firenze. (**A quell'epoca/A quel tempo/In questi giorni**) avevo pochissimi soldi.

(b) Spero di vederti (**nei giorni scorsi/nei prossimi giorni/in questi giorni**).

(c) (**Negli ultimi tempi/Nei prossimi giorni/In questi giorni**) ho avuto tanto da fare.

(d) (**In questi giorni/In quel momento**) non faccio niente di bello.

✦ **2** Match up the two parts of the sentences by finding the equivalent of the English phrase.

(a) Chiamami (*before you leave*)

(b) Fammelo sapere (*before they leave*)

(c) Chiamalo (*as soon as you arrive*)

(d) Mi metterò in contatto (*after I have seen him*)

(e) Fammi sapere qualcosa (*after she leaves/has left*)

(i) appena arrivi.

(ii) prima di partire.

(iii) dopo averlo visto/dopo che l'avrò visto.

(iv) prima che partano.

(v) dopo che sarà partita/dopo la sua partenza.

✦ **3** Complete the sentences by using the appropriate Italian phrases.

(a) Rimango qui (*until*) sabato.

(b) Puoi stare da noi (*as long as*) vuoi.

(c) Starò qui (*until*) siano tornati.

(d) Abbiamo aspettato (*until*) non sono tornati.

◎/✦ 16.8 Initiating, concluding and generalising

Clarity and fluency of speech and writing is enhanced by the ability to use connectives to initiate, conclude, summarise and generalise.

(a) Initiating

prima di tutto, per cominciare	**Prima di tutto/Per cominciare**, vorrei ringraziare tutti *First of all/To begin with*, I'd like to thank everyone	These open out a topic. **Per cominciare** is quite formal.
allora	**Allora**, cominciamo **Right (then)**, let's begin	Informal.
anzitutto, innanzitutto	**Anzitutto/Innanzitutto** è necessario chiamare la banca *First and foremost* it is necessary to call the bank **Anzitutto/Innanzitutto** quello che ha detto non è vero, e in ogni caso non ti riguarda *In the first place/First of all/Firstly* what he said is not true, and in any case it doesn't concern you (*It's none of your business*)	These can be used like the above, but are often used to respond to questions and prioritise things.

✦ These connectives can be used to round off a topic and initiate another one.

dunque, allora, ora	**Dunque,** come dicevo, ci sono tre problemi *So/Right, as I was saying, there are three problems* **Allora/Ora**, a questo punto è essenziale valutare i rischi *So/Now, at this point, it is essential to evaluate the risks*	These tend to begin a sentence and can all be used colloquially.
a proposito	Ho visto Maria ieri. **A proposito,** hai deciso cosa facciamo domani? *By the way/Incidentally, have you decided what we're doing tomorrow?*	Switching topics. Used to initiate a totally new topic.

◎/✚ (b) Concluding and summing up

These are all used for drawing things to a close.

infine, per terminare, in conclusione	**Infine/Per terminare/In conclusione**, vorrei ringraziare il dottor Bianchi ***Finally/To end with/To conclude,*** *I'd like to thank Doctor Bianchi*	Quite formal.
in poche parole, a dirla breve	**In poche parole** non abbiamo tempo da perdere ***In short****, there is no time to lose* **A dirla breve,** le cose vanno malissimo ***In short*** *things are going very badly*	These are both used to summarise.
tutto sommato, dopotutto	**Tutto sommato**, è la soluzione migliore ***All things considered/All in all*** *it's the best solution* Sono favorevole alla proposta; **dopotutto** non abbiamo niente da perdere *I suppport the proposal;* ***after all/when all's said and done*** *we have nothing to lose*	These can be used both to summarise and to assess.
insomma	**Insomma**, dobbiamo prendere una decisione ***Basically/In a nutshell/The fact is****, we have to make a decision* Alla festa c'erano tanti amici; è stata una bella serata **insomma** *There were lots of friends at the party;* ***all in all*** *it was a lovely evening* **Insomma,** che vuoi? ***Look here/For heaven's sake****, what do you want?*	Informal. Used more for summing up than assessing. Colloquially, **insomma** can convey exasperation.
✚ in fin dei conti, in ultima analisi	**In fin dei conti/In ultima analisi**, non c'è altro da fare ***At the end of the day/When it comes down to it/Ultimately/In the final analysis*** *nothing else can be done*	As with **tutto sommato**, etc., these are all used when making a final assessment.

◎/✚ (c) Generalising

in generale	Si può dire **in generale** che la nuova politica ha avuto successo ***Generally speaking*** *it can be said that the new policy has been popular*	Used to express a global view, avoiding details.
in genere/in generale	**In genere/In generale** i negozi aprono alle otto ***As a rule*** *shops open at eight*	Used to express norms and habit.
in fondo in sostanza	**In fondo** non mi piace guidare ***Basically*** *I don't like driving/I don't* ***actually*** *like driving* **In sostanza** ci sono due possibilità *There are* ***essentially*** *two possibilities*	Both used in a similar way. **In fondo** is more colloquial.

+ per lo più, in linea di massima	I nostri clienti sono **per lo più** italiani *Our clients **by and large** are Italian/Our clients are **mostly** Italian* **In linea di massima** sono d'accordo *I agree **on the whole*** Diversi studi hanno evidenziato che **in linea di massima** i lavori sono fattibile *Various studies have shown that the works are **broadly speaking** feasible*	Sometimes used to avoid specifying numbers, often conciliatory/diplomatic.
+ nel complesso	**Nel complesso** sono molto soddisfatto dei risultati ***On the whole/All in all/All things considered**, I am very pleased with the results*	This can be used like **in generale**.

+ Esercizi

1 Complete these sentences using an appropriate connective.

    (a) (*So/Right*), dove eravamo rimasti?

    (b) Siamo tornati sul Web. Scusate il ritardo! (*First*), ecco alcune spiegazioni: si sono rotti due dischi sulla catena del server e anche il disco USB che ospita il backup.

    (c) È difficile definire l'identità iraniana: (*broadly speaking*) è un misto di elementi persiani, islamici e occidentali, con tutti i paradossi che questo comporta.

    (d) Le elezioni libanesi hanno dimostrato che (*when it comes down to it*) la politica interna non è stata proprio 'interna'.

    (e) Appartengono a famiglie (*on the whole*) forse più ricche delle nostre.

2 The following is a magazine article on how to save water and avoid high bills. Read the text and identify the Italian connectives that correspond to the English ones given below.

actually/on the other hand • also • as far as … is concerned • as long as/until • basically • but also • however • on the one hand … on the other • since • as much as (even) • this is • too/as well/also

Tra i tanti rincari* di questi giorni, ce n'è uno che rischia di passare inosservato. E che **invece** (1) merita una doppia attenzione: quello* dell'acqua. **Da una parte** (2a) la spesa per l'acqua comincia a incidere sensibilmente sul* bilancio delle famiglie, **dall'altra** (2b) il suo consumo è **anche** (3) un problema sociale. L'aumento della popolazione e l'utilizzo industriale, assieme al mutamento del clima, rischiano di rendere la situazione sempre più difficile. **Insomma** (4), risparmiare sull'acqua fa bene al portafoglio **ma anche** (5) alla salute del pianeta. Tagliare i consumi si può, basta un'attenzione quotidiana.

In bagno, meglio lavarsi nella vasca* o nelle doccia? **Per quanto riguarda** (6) il consumo, fare la doccia permette di consumare in media un terzo dell'acqua necessaria a riempire la vasca. Significa più o meno un risparmio di cento litri di acqua ogni mattina. …Attenti* **però** (7) a non metterci troppo tempo*, **visto che** (8) dal getto della doccia possono uscire **anche** (9) venti litri al minuto. **Anche** (10) il water* è un grande consumatore d'acqua. I sistemi più spreconi* sono quelli a maniglia*, in cui l'acqua scorre **fino a che** (11) si tiene aperta. In cucina una buona idea è applicare un frangigetto*. **Si tratta di** (12) un piccolo dispositivo* che immette aria nel flusso e aumenta il volume del getto d'acqua: in un anno può far risparmiare migliaia di litri.

(Adapted from 'Sei consigli contro l'acqua troppo … salata',
Di Tutto, 31 ottobre 2008)

> • rincari *price rises* • 'quello' refers to 'rincaro' • incidere sensibilmente sul *to affect considerably* • vasca *bath tub* • Attenti *Take care* • non metterci troppo tempo *not to take too long about it* • water *the toilet* • sprecoli *wasteful* • a maniglia *with a handle* • un frangigetto *diffuser spray* • dispositivo *appliance/device*

3 Complete the article below from a gardening magazine on the classification of old roses, substituting the English connectives with Italian ones chosen from the list below.

cioè • comunque • infatti • ma • mentre • nonostante si tratti di • non solo • perciò

Rose antiche

Molte di queste rose **not only** (1) sono tuttora* disponibili sul mercato, **but** (2) stanno riacquistando popolarità. È assai difficile sapere con esattezza quale ragruppamento inserire in questa categoria **despite the fact that it is** (3) un argomento* discusso presso* le varie società internazionali della rosa. Alcuni specialisti, **in fact** (4) pensano che debbano far parte di tale* gruppo le vecchie rose europee e da giardino, quelle, **that is to say** (5) in coltura prima dell'avvento delle rose cinesi e delle Tea*. ... Altri sostengono che le rose della Cina e le Tea sono tra le più antiche rose da giardino e che, **therefore** (6), vanno, di diritto, inserite* in questo gruppo ...

However (7), **whereas** (8) ora è possibile stabilire quali rose porre in questa categoria, risulta arbitraria* la data al di là della quale le rose sarebbero da considerare* antiche.

(*Gardenia*, novembre 1991)

> • tuttora *still* • argomento *subject* • presso *amongst* • tale *that* (formal) • le Tea *tea roses* • vanno ... inserite *must ... be included* • risulta arbitraria *is arbitrary* • sarebbero da considerare *should be considered*

17 Numerals and units of measurement

There are two types of numerals (**i numerali**): cardinal numbers which are used for counting (*one, two, three*, etc.) and **ordinal numbers**, used to order items in a series (*first, second, third,* etc.).

◎ 17.1 Cardinal numbers

(a) Numbers 0–100

0	zero	**10**	dieci	**20**	venti	**30**	trenta
1	uno	**11**	undici	**21**	ventuno	**31**	trentuno
2	due	**12**	dodici	**22**	ventidue	**32**	trentadue, *etc.*
3	tre	**13**	tredici	**23**	ventitré	**40**	quaranta
4	quattro	**14**	quattordici	**24**	ventiquattro	**50**	cinquanta
5	cinque	**15**	quindici	**25**	venticinque	**60**	sessanta
6	sei	**16**	sedici	**26**	ventisei	**70**	settanta
7	sette	**17**	diciassette	**27**	ventisette	**80**	ottanta
8	otto	**18**	diciotto	**28**	ventotto	**90**	novanta
9	nove	**19**	diciannove	**29**	ventinove	**100**	cento

Spelling

Quanti piatti ti servono? – **Uno/Un** piatto va bene *How many plates do you want? – One/ One plate is fine* Quante tazze ci sono? – **Una** sola/C'è **una** tazza sola *How many cups are there? – Only one/ There is only one cup*	All cardinal numbers are invariable except for **uno**. This becomes **un** when used before a masculine noun and **una** with a feminine noun.
Quanti studenti hanno firmato? – **Ventotto/ Ventotto** studenti; **Cinquantuno/ Cinquantun(o)** ragazzi *How many students have signed? – Twenty-eight/Twenty-eight students; Fifty-one/Fifty-one students*	When **uno** and **otto** are part of numbers above 20 the final vowel of **venti, trenta**, etc. is omitted. The final **-o** of **uno** (but not **otto**) may be omitted when the number is used with a noun.
Ha **diciott'**anni/**vent'**anni/**cinquant'**anni Siamo aperti **ventiquattr'**ore su 24	Other numerals may lose their final vowel before another noun beginning with a vowel.
Mi ha dato **sessantatré** sterline *He gave me sixty-three pounds*	When **tre** is part of another number, it is written with an accent.

(b) Numbers from 100

100	cento	**200**	duecento	**1.001**	milleuno
101	centouno	**201**	duecentouno	**1.008**	milleotto
102	centodue	**300**	trecento	**1.211**	milleduecentoundici
108	centootto	**400**	quattrocento	**2.000**	duemila
111	centoundici	**500**	cinquecento	**2.001**	duemilauno
120	centoventi	**600**	seicento	**2.008**	duemilaotto
121	centoventuno	**700**	settecento	**2.011**	duemilaundici
128	centoventotto	**800**	ottocento	**2.100**	duemilacento
128	centotrenta	**900**	novecento	**2.200**	duemiladuecento
140	centoquaranta	**1.000**	mille	**3.000**	tremila
150	centocinquanta	**1.001**	milleuno	**100.000**	centomila
160	centosessanta	**1.008**	milleotto	**1.000.000**	un milione
170	centosettanta	**1.011**	milleundici	**2.000.000**	due milioni
180	centottanta/centoottanta	**1.100**	millecento	**1.000.000.000**	un miliardo
190	centonovanta	**1.200**	milleduecento	**2.000.000.000**	due miliardi

Spelling and punctuation

quattrocentootto *four hundred and eight* **ottocentottanta** *eight hundred and eighty*	Note that **otto** and **undici** are not elided after **cento**, **duecento, trecento**, etc. but **ottanta** sometimes is.
novemilaottocentoventi *nine thousand eight hundred and twenty* **But:** **un milione (e) quattrocentomiladuecentodieci** *one million four hundred thousand two hundred and ten*	The numbers are spelt as one word except with numbers above **un milione**.
Cento/Duecento euro *A hundred/Two hundred euros* **Mille**/Due**mila** euro *A thousand/Two thousand euros* Un **milione**/Due **milioni** di euro *A million/Two million euros* Un **miliardo**/Due **miliardi** di euro **But:** Un milione (e) duecento euro Due miliardi (e) cinquecentomila euro	**Cento** is invariable, but **mille**, **milione** and **miliardo** change. **Cento** and **mille** are used without an indefinite article, unlike English. However, **milione** and **miliardo** are preceded by the article **un** and followed by **di** unless additional numbers are used. **Un miliardo** is a thousand million – an American billion.
Sono stati uccisi 2.800 prigionieri *2,800 prisoners were killed*	In Italian, full stops are used where in English commas are required. The reverse is true with regard to decimal points (see Percentages, p. 233).

◎ Esercizio

1 Give the Italian equivalent of these phrases.

(a) *one kilo*

(b) *one slice*

(c) *seventeen books*

(d) *nineteen pages*

(e) *thirty one students*

(f) *forty eight hours*

(g) *three chapters*

(h) *twenty three girls*

(i) *a hundred pounds*

(j) *two hundred pounds*

(k) *a thousand euros*

(l) *ten thousand euros*

(m) *a million pesetas*

(n) *five million dollars*

(o) *three million five hundred thousand euros*

(c) Uses of cardinal numbers

 Attenti! Their use does not always correspond to the English.

Percentages ⚠	Solo **il** 35,5 (trentacinque virgola cinque) per cento **della** popolazione ha votato *Only 35.5 (thirty-five point five) per cent of the population has voted* **Il** 53 per cento **degli** intervistati ha/(hanno) paura del futuro *53 per cent of those interviewed are afraid of the future*	Cardinal numbers are used with the definite article **il/l'** and the preposition **di**. The decimal point is a comma (**virgola**) in Italian. If there is a clear reference to a plural subject, a plural verb may sometimes be used.
Price and speed ⚠	Costa 30 euro **al/il** chilo *It cost 30 euros per kilo* Viaggiava a 200 chilometri **l'ora/all'**ora *It was going at 200 km per hour*	Cardinal numbers are used with the definite article, which is sometimes combined with **a**.
Years ⚠	**Il** duemiladodici sarà un anno bisestile *Two thousand and twelve will be a leap year* Sono nato **nel** millenovecentosessantotto *I was born in nineteen sixty-eight*	The year is written as one word and the definite article is required, sometimes combined with **in**.
Dates	È il 29 (ventinove) ottobre, l'8 (otto) settembre, l'11(undici) marzo *It's the twenty-ninth of October, the eighth of September, the eleventh of March* Arrivo il primo (1) o il due (2) maggio *I'm arriving on May the first or second*	With the exception of the first of the month, cardinal numbers are used, with the definite article **il** – or **l'** before **otto** and **undici**. The first is **il primo** (see Ordinal numbers, pp. 234–5).
Phone numbers ⚠	Il mio numero è ventuno trentotto zero due *My number is 21 38 05* Il mio fax è quarantacinque sessantasette ottantuno nove *My fax is 45 67 81 9* Il prefisso è zero due zero sette *The prefix is zero two zero seven* Per un emergenza chiamate **il** centotredici *Call 113 for an emergency*	The main phone number is given in pairs of digits. The prefix or extension tends to be given digit by digit. If the number is three digits, it is normally said as one number. Note that numbers tend to be masculine except when telling the time (see below).
Telling the time ⚠	È **l'**una *It's one o'clock* Sono **le** cinque *It's five o'clock* La riunione inizia **alle** venti *The meeting begins at eight pm*	Cardinal numbers are used with the feminine definite article (which refers to the feminine noun **ora/e** *hour/s*). The 24-hour clock is very common.
Plural verbs ⚠	Duecento euro non bastano/non sono sufficienti *Two hundred euros is not enough* Diecimila euro sono tanti *Ten thousand euros is a lot (of money)*	Unlike English, verbs used with numerals above **uno** must be plural.

◎ Esercizi

2 Insert the correct figure in words each time.

    (a) *(Ten per cent of)* automobilisti non sono assicurati.

    (b) *(Fifty-one per cent of)* popolazione ha votato.

    (c) L'olio costa *(25 euro per)* litro.

    (d) *(2002)* è stato un anno brutto per gli agricoltori.

(e) Per chiamare fuori bisogna fare (9).

(f) Il mio numero di telefono è (02 39 24 81) interno (750).

3 Give these times in Italian, also giving the 24-hour clock version where relevant.

(a) *ten o'clock (a.m.)*

(b) *one o'clock (p.m.)*

(c) *eight o'clock (p.m.)*

(d) *11 o'clock (p.m.)*

◎ 17.2 Ordinal numbers

(a) Forms and uses

primo	1st	**sesto**	6th	**undicesimo**	11th	**sedicesimo**	16th
secondo	2nd	**settimo**	7th	**dodicesimo**	12th	**diciassettesimo**	17th
terzo	3rd	**ottavo**	8th	**tredicesimo**	13th	**diciottesimo**	18th
quarto	4th	**nono**	9th	**quattordicesimo**	14th	**diciannovesimo**	19th
quinto	5th	**decimo**	10th	**quindicesimo**	15th	**ventesimo**	20th

I miei hanno festeggiato il **cinquantesimo** anniversario del loro matrimonio *My parents have celebrated their fiftieth wedding anniversary*	Ordinal numbers above **decimo** are formed by adding **-esimo** to a number, minus its final vowel (except if the number ends in **tré** or **sei**: **quarantatreesimo** *forty-third* **ventiseiesimo** *twenty-sixth,* etc.
I, II, III, ... XXV 1°, 2°, 3°, ... 25° *1st, 2nd, 3rd, ... 25th*	Ordinal numbers can be abbreviated in two ways: with Roman numerals or with the symbol °.
Prendi la **terza** (strada) a sinistra *Take the third (road) on the left* Sono sempre **i primi** ad arrivare *They are always the first to arrive*	Ordinal numbers can be used as adjectives or pronouns, and agree in number and gender with the noun they refer to.
il **Terzo** Mondo *the Third World* il **diciottesimo** secolo *the eighteenth century* **But:** Umberto Secondo (II) *Umberto the Second* Paolo Sesto (VI) *Paul the Sixth*	The numbers go before the noun unless used with the names of monarchs and popes.
Il **primo** secolo a.C (avanti Cristo) *The first century* BC Il **quinto** secolo d.C (dopo Cristo) *The fifth century* AD	As in English, ordinal numbers can be used for centuries, but from the thirteenth century onwards, cardinal numbers are also used in Italian. See below.

(b) Special uses: centuries

 Attenti! In Italian there are two ways of expressing centuries. In English, only ordinal numbers are used, but Italian uses both ordinal and cardinal numbers. The latter are used especially with reference to art and literature.

The thirteenth century	Il tredicesimo secolo	Il Duecento
The fourteenth century	Il quattordicesimo secolo	Il Trecento
The fifteenth century	Il quindicesimo secolo	Il Quattrocento
The sixteenth century	Il sedicesimo secolo	Il Cinquecento
The seventeenth century	Il diciassettesimo secolo	Il Seicento
The eighteenth century	Il diciottesimo secolo	Il Settecento
The nineteenth century	Il diciannovesimo secolo	L'Ottocento
The twentieth century	Il ventesimo secolo	Il Novecento
The twenty-first century	Il ventunesimo secolo	Il Duemila

Il Duecento, **il Trecento**, etc. are shortened forms of *twelve hundreds* (1200), *thirteen hundreds* (1300), etc. They are always spelt with a capital letter:

Macchiavelli è nato nel 1498: è nato nel Quattrocento/nel quindicesimo secolo.

Macchiavelli was born in 1498: he was born in the fifteenth century.

◎ Esercizi

1 Give the Italian for the following.

- **(a)** *the first of October*
- **(b)** *The Second World War*
- **(c)** *the Third World*
- **(d)** *the tenth time*
- **(e)** *the twentieth anniversary*
- **(f)** *Elizabeth II*
- **(g)** *the eighth century* AD

2 Express these centuries in a different way.

- **(a)** il ventesimo secolo
- **(b)** il quattordicesimo secolo
- **(c)** il Quattrocento
- **(d)** l'Ottocento

◎/✚ 17.3 Other numbers

◎ (a) Fractions

Fractions	un terzo, un quarto, un quinto *a third, a quarter, a fifth* due terzi, tre quarti, due quinti *two-thirds, three-quarters, two-fifths*	Fractions are mostly expressed by using cardinal and ordinal numbers. The denominator (**terzo**, **quarto**, etc.) is plural if the numerator is plural. See also below.
mezzo as an adjective	mezzo secolo/chilo *half **a** century/half **a** kilo* mezza bottiglia/porzione *half **a** bottle/half **a** portion*	(**un**) **mezzo** is *(one/a) half*. If used as an adjective, it agrees with the noun to which it refers and precedes it. Unlike English, no article is used.
mezzo as a noun	Ho mangiato una porzione e **mezzo**/e **mezza** *I ate one and **a** half portions/a portion and **a** half* Ho preso tre chili e **mezzo** di patate *I got three and **a** half kilos of potatoes* Sono le due e **mezzo/mezza** *It is half past two*	It comes after the noun it refers to and is usually invariable, although in speech, agreement is often used. When used to tell the time it can also agree with **ora** in speech.
Three-quarters is **but (i) tre quarti sono**	**Sono** rimasti **tre quarti** della sua fortuna *Three-quarters of his fortune was left* (**l**) **due terzi** del territorio **sono** dedicati all'agricoltura *Two-thirds of the territory is given over to agriculture*	With plural fractions, note that plural verbs are required and that sometimes the definite article is used as a stylistic choice.

✚ (b) Half and multiples

(la) metà	La metà di otto è quattro *Half (of) eight is four* (**La**) **metà** degli studenti **deve/devono** passare le vacanze a casa *Half (of) the students have to spend their holidays at home* Più **della metà** dei soldati **sono** stati uccisi *More than half the soldiers were killed* Ho speso (**la**) metà del mio stipendio *I've spent half (of) my salary*	The noun for *half* is (**la**) **metà.** If **metà** refers to plural subjects, a plural verb is sometimes used.

	Lo vendono a **metà** prezzo *It's (being sold) half price* Sono a **metà** strada *I'm halfway* Arrivo a **metà** giugno *I'm arriving in mid-June*	When used as an adjective there is never an article with **metà**. **Metà** also means *mid-*.
Multiples	Ha pagato **il doppio/triplo del** prezzo normale *He paid twice/double/three times the normal price*	Multiples are preceded by **il/l'**, and **di** combines with the definite article.

✦ (c) Collective numbers and approximation

una decina	*about ten/10 or so*	un paio	*a pair*
una dozzina	*about twelve/12 or so; a dozen*	un centinaio	*about a hundred/100 or so*
una quindicina	*about fifteen/15 or so*	un migliaio	*about a thousand/1,000*
una ventina	*about twenty/20 or so*		*or so*
una trentina *etc.*	*about thirty/30 or so, etc.*		

Collective numbers can be singular or plural: in the singular they express approximation.

Singular collective numbers	C'è **una dozzina di** uova *There are a dozen/about 12 eggs* C'era/C'erano solo **una decina di** ospiti *There were only about ten guests* Alla festa è venuto/sono venute **un centinaio di** persone *About a hundred people came to the party*	Numbers ending in **-ina** and **-aio** are preceded by the indefinite article and followed by **di**. When these singular numbers refer to plural subjects, a plural verb is often, but not always, preferred.
Plural collective numbers	Ha scritto **decine di** lettere *He wrote scores of letters* Sono venute **centinaia** di ospiti *Hundreds of guests came*	There is a slight shift in meaning when collective numbers are plural. **Centinaio** and **migliaio** have plural feminine forms in **-a**. See Nouns, p. 12.

For expressions involving the Italian equivalents of *most*, *both* and *all*, see Indefinites, pp. 167, 173 and 170.

◎/✦ Esercizi

1 Complete these sentences in Italian by substituting the English.

  (a) Io risparmio (*a quarter*) del mio stipendio.

  (b) Gianni spende (*a third*) della sua paga per l'affitto.

  (c) Mio padre ha investito (*three-quarters*) del suo capitale.

  (d) (*Two-thirds*) degli impiegati sono stati licenziati.

✦ **2** Complete these sentences in Italian choosing between **mezzo/a** and **metà**.

  (a) Hanno bevuto (*half a*) bottiglia.

  (b) Hanno bevuto una bottiglia (*and a half*).

  (c) Hanno bevuto (*half of the*) vino.

  (d) Ho letto solo (*half*) pagina.

  (e) Ho letto (*half (of) the*) libro.

  (f) L'ho comprato a (*half*) prezzo.

✦ **3** Give the Italian for the following.

  (a) *There were about a hundred guests.*

  (b) *There were about twenty students.*

  (c) *There are about a thousand demonstrators.*

  (d) *There are thousands of demonstrators.* (**manifestanti**)

18 The present indicative tense

The present indicative tense (**l'indicativo presente**) is called 'indicative' because it expresses or indicates facts, usually, but not always, in relation to what is happening now, what is universally the case or what usually happens. It is, however, a very versatile tense: depending on the context, it can also relate to actions in the future or past.

18.1 The present indicative tense: regular forms

Regular verbs present an unchanging pattern of forms which can be deduced from the infinitive. There are three categories, known as **conjugations:** the first ends in **-are,** the second in **-ere** and the third in **-ire**. Note that the third conjugation ending in **-ire** has two regular patterns.

	-are portare *to wear, to bring*	**-ere** vendere *to sell*	**-ire** dormire *to sleep*	**-ire** preferire *to prefer*
io	port**o**	vend**o**	dorm**o**	prefer**isco**
tu	port**i**	vend**i**	dorm**i**	prefer**isci**
lui/lei/Lei	port**a**	vend**e**	dorm**e**	prefer**isce**
noi	port**iamo**	vend**iamo**	dorm**iamo**	prefer**iamo**
voi	port**ate**	vend**ete**	dorm**ite**	prefer**ite**
loro	port**ano**	vend**ono**	dorm**ono**	prefer**iscono**

The present tense of reflexive verbs is exactly like other present tense verbs, but is always used with the reflexive pronouns. (See Personal pronouns, p. 107.)

	-are lavarsi *to wash (oneself)*	**-ere** mettersi *to put on*	**-ire** divertirsi *to enjoy oneself*	**-ire** stupirsi *to be amazed*
io	mi lav**o**	mi mett**o**	mi divert**o**	mi stup**isco**
tu	ti lav**i**	ti mett**i**	ti divert**i**	ti stup**isci**
lui/lei/Lei	si lav**a**	si mett**e**	si divert**e**	si stup**isce**
noi	ci lav**iamo**	ci mett**iamo**	ci divert**iamo**	ci stup**iamo**
voi	vi lav**ate**	vi mett**ete**	vi divert**ite**	vi stup**ite**
loro	si lav**ano**	si mett**ono**	si divert**ono**	si stup**iscono**

 Attenti! The majority of third conjugation **-ire** verbs take the **-isco** pattern, so it is worth learning the relatively small number which do not, as many of them are very common. Verbs like **dormire/divertirsi** are:

aprire *to open*, avvertire *to warn, notify*, bollire *to boil*, coprire *to cover*, cucire* *to sew*, divertir(si) *to enjoy*, fuggire *to run away*, investire *to invest*, offrire *to offer*, partire *to leave*, pentir(si) *to regret*, riempire* *to fill*, scoprire *to discover*, seguire *to follow*, sentire *to feel, to hear*, servire *to serve*, soffrire *to suffer*, vestirsi *to dress*

* See table below.

Verbs which take either ending are:

applaudire *to applaud*, assorbire *to absorb*, inghiottire *to swallow*, mentire *to lie*, nutrire *to nourish*, starnutire *to sneeze*, tossire *to cough*

Spelling changes

Regular verbs ending in **-ciare, -giare, -sciare, -gliare, -care** or **-gare** require minor spelling changes.

cominciare mangiare lasciare sbagliare	(tu) cominci (tu) mangi (tu) lasci (tu) sbagli	(noi) cominciamo (noi) mangiamo (noi) lasciamo (noi) sbagliamo	The **-i** of the stem is dropped before the **tu** and **noi** endings (which begin with **-i**) to avoid forms like cominci**i**, cominci**iamo**.
giocare pagare	(tu) giochi (tu) paghi	(noi) giochiamo (noi) paghiamo	An **-h** is added before the **tu** and **noi** endings (which begin with **-i**) in order to keep the hard sound. See Spelling, p. 347.

The two **-ire** verbs, marked * in the list on pp. 237–8, also require minor spelling changes.

riempire	(io) riempio (lui/lei) riempie (loro) riempiono	An **-i** is inserted before the vowels **-o** and **-e** in the **io/lui/lei** and **loro** forms
cucire	(io) cucio (loro) cuciono	An **-i** is inserted before the **-o** in the **io** and **loro** forms to keep the soft sound.

◎ Esercizi

1 Choose which of the forms of the verbs given in each sentence below is correct.

abitare • leggere • scrivere • studiare • dormire

(a) Dove (abitono/abitano) i tuoi?

(b) Che cosa (leggono/leggano) i vostri figli?

(c) Che cosa (scrivete/scrivate) in classe?

(d) Dove (studiete/studiate) a Roma?

(e) Giacomo (dorma/dorme) fuori stasera?

(f) Elena (mangia/mangie) fuori domani?

2 The verbs used in the sentences below are all **-ire** verbs, but which pattern do they follow? Give the infinitive of each verb and say whether it takes the **-isco** pattern or the **-o** pattern.

(a) Offrono loro da bere.

(b) Preferite il gelato?

(c) Partiamo domani.

(d) Soffrono molto il freddo.

(e) Seguiamo un corso di francese.

(f) Quand'è che finite il lavoro?

(g) Capite quando parlo?

(h) Ci vestiamo sempre in fretta.

3 Spell it right. Give the correct present tense form of the verbs in brackets.

(a) Tu (mangiare) troppo.

(b) Tu (pagare) troppo di affitto.

(c) Perché non (cominciare – noi) subito?

(d) (Giocare – noi) spesso a bridge.

4 Complete the sentences using the appropriate present tense form of the reflexive verbs given.

(a) Rita e Anna (annoiarsi) a casa nostra.

(b) Renato e Luca (perdersi) sempre a Londra!

(c) Giovanna e Paola (divertirsi) da me.

(d) Aldo (stupirsi) della loro stupidità!

◎/+ 18.2 The present tense: irregular forms

Irregular present tense forms are important, as other verb forms are based on them (e.g. the imperative and the present subjunctive). The main present tense irregularities can be grouped into the following categories:

(a) Very common irregular verbs: **avere**, **essere**, **dare** and **stare**;
(b) Other common patterns of irregularity, e.g. vowel changes;
(c) Contracted infinitive verbs, e.g. **bere**, **dire**, **fare**, **trarre**, **porre**, **condurre**;
(d) The modal verbs: **dovere**, **potere**, **volere**, **sapere**.

◎ (a) Common irregular present tenses

Infinitive	Present tense	Similar verbs
avere *to have*	ho hai ha abbiamo avete hanno	
essere *to be*	sono sei è siamo siete sono	
andare *to go*	vado vai va andiamo andate vanno	
uscire *to go out*	esco esci esce usciamo uscite escono	riuscire *to manage, succeed*
dare *to give*	do dai dà diamo date danno	ridare *to give back*
stare *to be, to stay*	sto stai sta stiamo state stanno	sottostare *to underlie*

◎/+ (b) Other common patterns of irregularity

These fall into four main categories. For the full present tenses, see Appendix B, pp. 355–6.

Verbs with **-g** in 1st person sing. (**io**) and 3rd person pl. (**loro**)	**rimanere** *to stay* (rimango/rimangono) **salire** *to go up* (salgo/salgono) **scegliere** *to choose* (scelgo/scelgono) **togliere** *to remove* (tolgo/tolgono) **valere** *to be worth* (valgo/valgono)
Verbs with **-g** in the **io** and **loro** forms and a vowel change in the **tu**, **lui/lei** forms	**tenere** *to hold* tengo/tengono/tieni/tiene **venire** *to come* vengo/vengono/vieni/viene **See also: contenere** *to contain*, **trattenersi** *to stay*, **intervenire** *to intervene*
Verbs with vowel changes in the stem except for the **noi** and **voi** forms or just the **io** and **loro** forms **+**	**sedere** *to sit* siedo, siedi, siede, sediamo, sedete, siedono **morire** *to die* muoio muori muormoriamo, morite, muoiono **udire** *to hear* odo, odi, ode udiamo, udite, odono **apparire** *to appear* appaio, appari, appare, appariamo, apparite, appaiono **parere** *to seem* paio, pari, pare, pariamo, parete, paiono
Verbs with minor spelling changes **+**	**piacere** *to please* piaccio, piaci, piace, piacciamo, piacete, piacciono (an extra **-c** in the **io, noi** and **loro** forms)

(c) Contracted infinitives

A few verbs have infinitives known as 'contracted' because they are nearly all shortened versions of longer Latin verbs from which they are derived. To form many of the tenses of these verbs, it is necessary to learn their expanded stem.

Infinitive and stem	Present tense	Similar verbs
bere *to drink* ➡ **bev-**	bevo bevi beve beviamo bevete bevono	
dire *to tell, to say* ➡ **dic-**	dico dici dice diciamo dite dicono	contraddire *to contradict* disdire *to cancel*
fare *to do, to make* ➡ **fac-**	faccio fai fa facciamo fate fanno	rifare *to redo* stupefare *to amaze*
condurre *to lead* ➡ **conduc-**	conduco conduci conduce conduciamo conducete conducono	tradurre *to translate* produrre *to produce*
porre *to place* ➡ **pon-**	pongo poni pone poniamo ponete pongono	proporre *to propos* supporre *to suppose*
trarre *to draw, to pull* ➡ **tra-**	traggo trai trae traiamo traete traggono	attrarre *to attract* distrarre *to distract, entertain*

(d) Modal verbs

Modal verbs are nearly always used before another infinitive verb to modify its meaning by indicating the attitude of the writer/speaker to the action.

dovere *to have to*	devo/debbo devi deve dobbiamo dovete devono/debbono
potere *to be able to*	posso puoi può possiamo potete possono
sapere *to know how to*	so sai sa sappiamo sapete sanno
volere *to want to*	voglio vuoi vuole vogliamo volete vogliono

The English equivalents of these verbs often vary according to the tense in which they are used. See pp. 264 and 276.

Sapere can be used both as a normal verb without a dependent infinitive (see p. 319) and as a modal verb:

Sanno scrivere. *They know how to write.*
Mi sa dire quando arrivano? *Can you tell me when they are arriving?*

◎/✚ Esercizi

1 Insert the correct forms of the present tense in both the question and the answer.

   (a) Giulio, … tempo di prendere un caffè? – Mi dispiace, non … tempo. (**avere**)

   (b) Sandra, dove … di casa? – … in via Carducci, numero 12. (**stare**)

   (c) Lucia, che … domani? – Domani … una lunga passeggiata in campagna. (**fare**)

   (d) Lino, … l'esame oggi? – No, lo … domani. (**dare**)

   (e) Antonella, dove … stasera? – Stasera … da Alessandro. (**andare**)

2 Rewrite the sentences below changing the form of the verb according to the person indicated. Give the infinitive of each verb.

(a) Esco spesso la sera. (*io* ➡ *noi*)

(b) Vado raramente all'estero. (*io* ➡ *noi*)

(c) Cosa propone? (*lui/lei* ➡ *loro*)

(d) Ma cosa mi dici? (*tu* ➡ *voi*)

(e) Traduciamo un articolo. (*noi* ➡ *io*)

(f) Dov'è? (*lui/lei* ➡ *loro*)

(g) Siamo in anticipo. (*noi* ➡ *io*)

3 Insert the correct present tense form of these modal verbs.

(a) Scusa, (volere – io) partire adesso, non (potere – io) aspettare.

(b) (Potere – tu) venire subito o (dovere – tu) chiedere permesso?

(c) Non (sapere – noi) ancora se (dovere – noi) lavorare domani.

(d) Se non (volere – voi) aspettare, (potere – voi) mangiare adesso.

✦ **4** Using Appendix B if necessary, complete the sentences with the correct form of the verb given.

(a) Se tu — a casa, ci — anch'io. (**rimanere**)

(b) Se lui — a Milano — anche loro. (**rimanere**)

(c) Tu — sempre i vini migliori, mentre io — quelli peggiori! (**scegliere**)

(d) Io — con mia sorella, tu con chi — ? (**venire**)

(e) Io — qui per dieci giorni, ma loro — per almeno un mese. (**trattenersi**)

(f) Io — qua, voi dove —? (**sedersi**)

 ## 18.3 Uses of the present tense

◎ **(a) Main uses of the present indicative (1)**

Habitual actions or states	Cosa fai la domenica? *What do you do on Sundays?* Vado spesso in Italia *I often go to Italy* Mi piace leggere *I like reading*	This refers to things that happen regularly. The use is the same as in English.
General truths	Il latte fa bene *Milk is good for you* Londra è la capitale della Gran Bretagna *London is the capital of Great Britain*	This use is the same as in English.
What is going on now ⚠	Cosa fai? *What are you doing?* Leggo il giornale *I'm reading the paper* Pranziamo insieme *We are having lunch together*	In Italian the present tense also expresses the English *-ing* form. See pp. 243–4 and top of table p. 242.

⚠ **Attenti!** *Do, does* and *can.* Note the following differences from Italian.

Il pesce lo mangio, ma la carne no.   *I do eat fish but I don't eat meat.*

Suoni la chitarra?   *Do you play the guitar?*

With verbs of perception (e.g. *to see, to hear*), there is no Italian equivalent of *can* unless permission or ability are involved.

Lo vedi? – Sì, lo vedo benissimo   *Can you see him? – Yes, I can see him really well.*

But: Posso venire? *Can I come?* (permission)

Posso/Riesco a vedere la torre solo   *I can see the tower only if I go onto the*
se mi metto sul balcone.   *balcony.* (ability)

✦ Esercizio

1 Give the Italian equivalent of the following, using each of the verbs below at least once.

alzarsi • bere • dire • essere • fare • fare colazione • pranzare • riuscire a • sentire

    (a) *I get up early and have breakfast at seven.*

    (b) *Great Britain is an island and Italy is a peninsula.* (**isola, penisola**)

    (c) *Do you drink coffee in the morning?* (**voi**)

    (d) *Are they still having lunch?* (still, **ancora**)

    (e) *What job do you do?* (**tu**)

    (f) *What is he saying? I can't hear him.*

    (g) *I can't open the window.*

◎/✦ (b) Main uses of the present indicative (2): expressing future and past

The Italian present tense is very often used to express actions referring to the immediate future and can it also refer to the past. These are important and common uses.

Immediate or definite future	Cosa **fate** domani? – Andiamo a Pisa *What are you doing tomorrow? – We're going to Pisa* Ti **richiamo** fra poco *I'll call you back soon*	The present is used to express definite future plans or intentions.
To be about to: **stare per**	**Sta per** piovere *It's about to rain* Non mi posso trattenere, **sto per** andare dal medico *I can't stop, I'm about to go to the doctor's*	The future – what is about to happen – is expressed by the present tense of **stare** followed by **per** and the infinitive**.**
How long for and since: **da**	**Da** quanto tempo **sei** qui? – **Sono** qui **da** un mese *How long have you been here? – I have been here for a month* **Da** quanto non ci **vediamo**? – *How long is it since we last met/saw each other?* **Aspettate da** molto tempo? – **Aspettiamo dalle** due *Have you been waiting long? – We have been waiting since two*	**da** + present tense is used when the verb refers to an action which originates in the past and continues uninterrupted into the present. This corresponds to the English perfect tense + *for/since*. For **da quanto** (**non**), see also Chapter 10, p. 153.
✦ **da** + **essere** + **che**	**Da** quant'**è che** sei qui? *How long have you been here?* **È da** molto **che** sei qui? *Have you been here long?* È un'ora **che** aspetto *I have been waiting for an hour*	***essere*** + ***che*** + present tense is more colloquial. Note that **da** is not used when the meaning is *for*.
✦ **Historic present**	**Squilla** il telefono. **Rispondo** e **sento** una voce strana *The phone rings. I answer and hear this strange voice …* Giuseppe Verdi **nasce** nel 1901, a Busseto *Verdi was born in 1901, in Busseto*	This is often used in speech to make a story more dramatic. In writing it is much used in historic narrative/biography.

  Attenti! Expressing *since* and *for*. The present is not used in the following two instances: Completed past actions are expressed by **da** + the perfect (**passato prossimo**) tense:

    Dal 1945 ci **sono state** varie   *Since 1945 there have been several*
    guerre in Europa.   *wars in Europe.*

Da quando ci **siamo incontrati** gli ho scritto due volte.

I have written to him twice since we met.

The present is not used with **per** *for,* because it expresses actions that are over and done with:

Ho portato gli occhiali per due anni.

I wore glasses for two years (and no longer do).

◎/✚ Esercizi

2 Give the Italian equivalent of the following, using each of the verbs once.

andare • chiamare • partire • sentirsi • stare per

(a) *When are you* (**voi**) *leaving for Paris?*

(d) *We'll be in touch soon.*

(b) *Tomorrow I'm going to the cinema.*

(e) *We are about to leave.*

(c) *I'll call you* (**tu**) *next week.*

3 How long for? Answer the following questions in Italian.

(a) Da quanto tempo impari l'italiano? – *I have been learning Italian for two years.*

(b) Da quand'è che vi conoscete? – *We have known each other for three months.*

(c) Da quant'è che non ci sentiamo? – *We haven't spoken since last year.*

(d) È da molto che sei in Italia? – *I have been in Italy since September.*

(e) Lo aspetti da molto tempo? – *I have been waiting for him since Saturday.*

✚ **4** Choose the appropriate tense in the sentences below and provide the English equivalent.

(a) Porto/Ho portato gli occhiali da due anni.

(b) Porto/Ho portato gli occhiali per due anni.

(c) Dal 2008 cambio/ho cambiato casa quattro volte.

(d) Dal 2008 abito/ho abitato nello stesso posto.

(e) Da quando ci conosciamo scrive/ha scritto ogni settimana a sua madre.

(f) Da quandi ci conosciamo scrive/ha scritto cinque libri.

◎/✚ 18.4 The present continuous

The English present continuous focuses on an activity in the process of taking place at the time of speaking. In Italian this can be expressed with the normal present tense or with the present tense of the verb **stare**, followed by the gerund of the verb required. The gerund only has two endings, **-ando** and **-endo**.

◎ (a) Regular and irregular forms of the present continuous

Regular forms have **-ando** endings for **-are** verbs and **-endo** endings for both **-ere** and **-ire** verbs. Irregular verbs with 'contracted' infinitives expand their stem and form the gerund with an **-endo** ending only.

Regular forms			Irregular forms		
Infinitive	***stare* + gerund**		**Infinitive**	***stare* + gerund**	
parlare	sto		bere	sto	**bev**endo
leggere	stai	parl**ando**	dire	stai	**dic**endo
finire	sta	legg**endo**	fare	sta	**fac**endo
partire	stiamo	fin**endo**	trarre	stiamo	**tra**endo
	state	part**endo**	proporre	state	**propon**endo
	stanno		produrre	stanno	**produc**endo

◎/✚ (b) Uses of the present continuous

The Italian present continuous has a far more restricted use than the English present continuous, and can nearly always be replaced by the normal present indicative.

Non può venire al telefono, **sta preparando** un rapporto *He can't come to the telephone, he's preparing a report* In questo momento Nina **sta chiacchierando** con il cugino *Right now Nina is chatting to her cousin* (or **chiacchiera**)	**Stare** + gerund is used when emphasising an action developing and taking place right now.
Si stanno divertendo *They are enjoying themselves*	Personal pronouns normally precede **stare**.
Oggi Nina **porta** una minigonna (***not:*** sta portando) *Today Nina is wearing a mini skirt* Oggi Nina **va a trovare** il cugino (***not:*** sta andando) *Today Nina is going to visit her cousin*	✚ **Stare** + gerund is only used to express actions in progress, not a state of affairs. It cannot be used to express future actions expressed in English by the *-ing* form.

Stare + gerund can also be used with the future and the imperfect; see pp. 247 and 265.

◎/✚ Esercizi

1 Answer the questions using an appropriate present tense form of the verbs given.
- **(a)** Volete venire a cena con noi? – No, mi dispiace, in questo momento (studiare).
- **(b)** Posso parlarti un attimo? – No, mi dispiace, (leggere) un rapporto.
- **(c)** Vieni al cinema con me? – Adesso non posso, (fare) i compiti.
- **(d)** I bambini, cosa (fare)? – (divertirsi) in giardino.

✚ **2** In which of the following sentences is it impossible to use **stare** + gerund?
- **(a)** *What are you doing this evening?*
- **(b)** *What are you doing in Rome?*
- **(c)** *Who are you talking to?*
- **(d)** *Where are you going tomorrow?*

19 The future tense

The future indicative tenses are used to express what will happen after the time of speaking. There are two forms: the simple future (**il futuro semplice**), which corresponds to the English *will*: e.g. **Will** *you leave?* The future perfect (**il futuro anteriore**) corresponds to *will have*: e.g. **Will** *you* **have** *left?*

◎/✛ 19.1 The simple future

(a) Regular forms

There are only two regular future tense forms: **-are** and **-ere** verbs follow an identical pattern, as do both types of **-ire** verbs.

-are and -ere		-ire	
port**are**	prend**ere**	fin**ire**	dorm**ire**
port**erò**	prend**erò**	fin**irò**	dorm**irò**
port**erai**	prend**erai**	fin**irai**	dorm**ira**
port**erà**	prend**erà**	fin**irà**	dorm**irà**
port**eremo**	prend**eremo**	fin**iremo**	dorm**iremo**
port**erete**	prend**erete**	fin**irete**	dorm**irete**
port**eranno**	prend**eranno**	fin**iranno**	dorm**iranno**

Spelling changes

-ciare	comin**cerò** comin**cerai** comin**cerà**, etc.	The **-i** of the stem is omitted in front of **-e**, as it is not needed to keep the soft sound of the infinitive.
-giare -sciare	man**gerò** man**gerai** man**gerà**, etc. las**cerò** las**cerai** las**cerà**, etc.	
-care -gare	gio**cherò** gio**cherai** gio**cherà**, etc. pa**gherò** pa**gherai** pa**gherà**, etc.	An **-h** is added to verb stems ending in **-c** and **-g** in order to keep the hard sound of the infinitive.
sedere *to sit* **possedere** *to own*	**siede**rò **siede**rai **siede**rà, etc. **possiede**rò **possiede**rai **possiede**rà, etc.	These verbs have an **-i** in the complete future conjugation, including **noi** and **voi** forms. There is also a less commonly used regular future (**sederò**, etc.).

◎ Esercizi

1 Choose the correct form of the verbs given.

   (a) Fra poco (scriverò/scivirò) quella lettera. (**scrivere**)

   (b) Domani Enrico (dormerà/dormirà) da me. (**dormire**)

   (c) (Tornaranno/Torneranno/Tornerano) domani con i loro amici. (**tornare**)

2 Provide the correct future form of the verbs given.

   (a) Se vuoi (io – giocare) con te stasera.

   (b) Se volete vi (noi – spiegare) il gioco.

   (c) Quand'è che (loro – cominciare) a studiare?

   (d) Quand'è che (tu – festeggiare) il tuo successo?

(b) Irregular forms

In the future tense there are two patterns of irregularity, with endings in **-ro** and in **-rrò**. These are added directly to the stem (which in some cases is irregularly formed), without the **-e** or **-i** of the regular future endings. The stem is the part of the verb minus the **-are**, **-ere**, **-ire** infinitive endings.

Verbs with *-rò* endings

Note the stem formations. In **1** below, **essere** has an irregular stem (**sa-**); in **2**, the verb stems are regular (**and-**, **av-**, etc.); in **3**, the verbs retain the vowel of the infinitive before the **-rò** ending.

1 essere	sarò	sarai	sarà	saremo	sarete	saranno
2 andare	andrò	andrai	andrà	andremo	andrete	andranno
avere	avrò	avrai	avrà	avremo	avrete	avranno
cadere	cadrò	cadrai	cadrà	cadremo	cadrete	cadranno
dovere	dovrò	dovrai	dovrà	dovremo	dovrete	dovranno
potere	potrò	potrai	potrà	potremo	potrete	potranno
sapere	saprò	saprai	saprà	sapremo	saprete	sapranno
vedere	vedrò	vedrai	vedrà	vedremo	vedrete	vedranno
vivere	vivrò	vivrai	vivrà	vivremo	vivrete	vivranno
3 dare	darò	darai	darà	daremo	darete	daranno
dire	dirò	dirai	dirà	diremo	direte	diranno
fare	farò	farai	farà	faremo	farete	faranno
stare	starò	starai	starà	staremo	starete	staranno

Udire *to hear* can have a regular or irregular future (**udirò** or **udrò**, etc.). The latter is more common.

Verbs with *-rrò* endings

Other verbs, including all those with **-arre**, **-orre**, and **-urre** infinitives, also omit the vowel of the regular future endings but double the **-r**. Note the stem formations. In **1** below, the stem is formed by dropping the **-ere/ire** infinitive endings, along with the consonant (usually **-l** or **-n**) that precedes them; in **2** below, the verbs retain the vowel of their infinitive in the stem.

1 parere	parrò	parrai	parrà	parremo	parrete	parranno
rimanere	rimarrò	rimarrai	rimarrà	rimarremo	rimarrete	rimarranno
tenere	terrò	terrai	terrà	terremo	terrete	terranno
valere	varrò	varrai	varrà	varremo	varrete	varranno
venire	verrò	verrai	verrà	verremo	verrete	verranno
volere	vorrò	vorrai	vorrà	vorremo	vorrete	vorranno
2 bere	berrò	berrai	berrà	berremo	berrete	berranno
trarre	trarrò	trarrai	trarrà	trarremo	trarrete	trarranno
porre	porrò	porrai	porrà	porremo	porrete	porranno
ridurre	ridurrò	ridurrai	ridurrà	ridurremo	ridurrete	ridurranno

- All **-arre**, **-orre** and **-urre** verbs are similarly formed.

◎ Esercizi

3 Complete the sentences using the correct future tense form of the verb given.

    (a) Fra poco (io – andare) a casa e (fare) il bucato.

    (b) Domani (tu – dovere) stare a casa o (potere) uscire?

(c) I nostri figli (rimanere) a Rimini e ci (vedere) dopo le vacanze.

(d) La settimana prossima (io – avere) moltissimo da fare, ma (io – essere) disponibile venerdì.

(e) Martedì vi (noi – dire) se (noi – venire) o no.

(f) (Tu – tradurre) l'articolo o lo (dare) a qualcun altro?

 19.2 Uses of the future

(a) Main uses of the future tense (1)

In Italian, particularly in informal conversation, the present tense is often preferred to the future. Nevertheless, the future is likely to be used for the following.

Definite future events/facts	Oggi c'è la partita, non **sarà** mica facile parcheggiare *The match is on today, it won't be at all easy to park* Mi dispiace, **arriverò/sarò** in ritardo *I'm sorry, I will arrive/be late/I am going to arrive/be late* ***But:*** Oggi **vado** alla partite *Today I'm going to the match*	The future is used to say what will happen next, but the present is often preferred for definite future plans/intentions (see p. 242). Note that the Italian future expresses both the English simple future (*I will*) and the '*be going to*' + infinitive form which has no Italian equivalent.
Firm beliefs and predictions	Sono convinto che lui **avrà** successo *I am convinced he will be successful/that he is going to be successful* **Verrà** senz'altro *He will definitely come*	
On-the-spot decisions	Luisa non c'è – La **chiamerò** più tardi, allora *Luisa's not in – I'll call her later then* Oggi c'è sciopero – **Rimarrò** a casa allora *There's a strike today – I'll stay at home then*	The present tense is actually also used, especially in informal conversation.

Note that the continuous form of the future (**stare** + gerund) is commonly used for the following:

Events taking place in the near future	Domani a quest'ora **staremo mangiando** la pizza/**staremo prendendo** l'aperitivo di fronte al lago *Tomorrow at this time we will be eating a pizza/having an aperitif in front of the lake*	The future continuous is mainly used to express actions or events likely to be taking place soon. Its other use is for speculation (see table below).

⚠ **Attenti!** The following are amongst the most common uses of the future in everyday Italian.

Speculation and probability	Quanti anni **avrà**? *How old could/(will) he be/I wonder how old he is?* **Avrà** settant'anni *He must be/will be/is probably seventy* Dove **saranno**? *Where can/could they be?* **Saranno** in centro *They must be/I expect they are in town*	Note that the conjectural use of the future does not strictly refer to the future and that there are a range of English equivalents. See also the future perfect, p. 250.
	Cosa **staranno facendo**? *What can/could they be doing?* Dove **staranno andando** a quest'ora? *Where can/could they be going at this hour?*	The continuous form of the future (**stare** + gerund) is mainly used as a hypothetical future.

Concession	**Avranno** ragione, ma sono proprio antipatici *They may be right, but they are really unpleasant* **Sarà** un collega ma non mi fido di lui *He may be a colleague but I don't trust him*	Like the above, this does not actually refer to the future. It is widely used to express scepticism. See also future perfect, p. 250.
Orders	**Farai** come ti ho detto *You'll do as I say* **Ti scuserai** con lui *You will apologise to him*	Like English, the future can be used as a command.

◎/✦ Esercizi

1 Say what is bound to happen next, using the correct future tense forms of the verbs given.

    (a) Guarda che nuvoloni! – (Piovere) di sicuro.

    (b) Marco non ha studiato. – (Essere) sicuramente bocciato.

    (c) Abbiamo perso il treno. Purtroppo (arrivare) in ritardo.

2 Getting better all the time? When it comes to politics you know better. Make your predictions.

    (a) Le tasse (aumentare) e gli stipendi (restare) fermi.

    (b) Gli automobilisti (affollare) le strade e (inquinare) l'ambiente.

    (c) Per gli anziani la vita (diventare) più dura. (Lavorare) di più e alla fine (ottenere) una pensione più piccola di prima.

3 You make some decisions on the spur of the moment. Give an Italian equivalent of the English.

    (a) Lo sai che Marina è all'ospedale? – *I'll go and see her, then.* (**andare a trovare**)

    (b) Hanno chiuso l'autostrada. – *We'll take the statale (road), then.* (**prendere la statale**)

    (c) È il compleanno di Giacomo. – *I'll send him a card, then.* (**mandare una cartolina di auguri**)

4 Say what you're planning to do. Give the Italian equivalent of the English. Take care to use the appropriate tense.

    (a) *Tomorrow I'm going/going to go to Turin.*

    (b) *We're taking/going to take the train at five o'clock.*

    (c) *I'm sending/going to send my mother some flowers.*

5 You're looking at photos of relatives you haven't seen for ages. Give the Italian equivalent of the English using a future tense each time.

    (a) *He must be at least sixty.* (**almeno**)   **(c)** *I expect he's married.*

    (b) *I wonder what job she does?*   **(d)** *She may be rich, but she's really stupid!*

✦ 6 Complete the horoscopes below by putting the verbs in brackets into the future tense.

    Cancro La Luna vi (**1 spingere**) a valutare un piccolo problema in modo poco obiettivo; ma con il passare delle ore (**2 cambiare – voi**) il vostro punto di vista. Problemi in vista in campo amoroso: (**3 tendere – voi**) a chiedere molto ma a dare poco. (**4 Toccare**), quindi, a voi* prevenire momenti di tensione cercando* di essere più affettuosi e concilianti con il partner.

    Bilancia L'umore (**5 vedere**) diversi alti e bassi. Nella seconda parte della giornata (**6 essere**) raggiante*; nella mattina, invece, un'ombra di malinconia (**7 spegnere**) il vostro entusiasmo. In ambito affettivo*, non rinunciate al dialogo con il partner. Simpatie improvise vi (**8 riempire**) di emozioni: per qualcuno* il cuore (**9 potere**) battere per una persona conosciuta di recente.

    Sagittario Sbagliare è umano, l'importante è riconoscere gli errori compiuti* e fare il possibile per rimediare*. Un po' di sana autocritica vi (**10 aiutare**) a capire il motivo di un recente fallimento. Secondo le stelle, nel sociale* (**11 avere – voi**) mille opportunità; (**12 dovere – voi**) però usare tutto il vostro fascino e tutta la vostra abilità, se (**13 volere – voi**) ottenere un risultato.

> Tocca … a voi *it's up to you* • cercando *by trying* • raggiante *radiant* (*your mood*) •
> In ambito affettivo *on the emotional plane* • per qualcuno *for some* • compiuti *made* •
> rimediare *make up for it* • nel sociale *socially speaking*

(b) Main uses of the future tense (2): time clauses and conditions

Time conjunctions and **se** are used at the beginning of subordinate clauses: in Italian they are usually followed by the future, unlike English.

After connectives of time	Appena lo **saprò** te lo dirò *As soon as I know, I will tell you* Quando **sarò** grande farò il medico *When I grow up I will be a doctor* Fino a quando **rimarrà** qui, non andremo d'accordo! *As long as he stays here, we will not get on!* **Note:** Appena lo **sai**, me lo **dici**? *As soon as you know, will you tell me?*	In standard Italian the future is preferred after **appena, dopo che, fino a quando/finché** and **quando** when there is a future in the main clause. Colloquially the present tense is common. See also Connectives p. 226.
The future after **se**	Se **avrò/ho** tempo, **passerò** a prenderti *If I have time I'll come by and pick you up* Se **bombardano** la città, **uccideranno** molta gente *If they bomb the city they will kill lots of people* **Note:** Se **rimani** qui, **fai** tardi *If you stay here, you'll be late*	When the main clause verb is a future, the future or the present is used in the subordinate **se** clause. The future makes the action less definite. Note that the present tense in *both* clauses is colloquial and expresses certainty.

✦ Esercizi

7 Here are some definite promises and predictions you have made. Express them in Italian using **tu**.
- (a) *If you give me a hand, I'll buy you an ice cream.*
- (b) *If you lend me the car, I'll pay for the petrol.*
- (c) *If you don't hurry up, we'll be late.* (**sbrigarsi**, **fare tardi**)

8 What will happen if? Give the Italian equivalent of the English.
- (a) Se non aumentano gli stipendi quest'anno … *teachers will go on strike.* (**fare sciopero**)
- (b) Se i rifornimenti non arrivano presto … *people will starve.* (**morire di fame**)
- (c) Se non riusciranno a salvare le foreste equatoriali … *the Earth's climate will change.*

9 Using **finché (non)/fino a quando, appena** and **quando**, give an Italian equivalent of the following.
- (a) *I'll stay as long as he stays.*
- (b) *I'll stay here until he arrives.*
- (c) *I'll phone you as soon as he writes.*
- (d) *When they pay me I'll buy you a dress.*

✦ 19.3 The future perfect

(a) The future perfect: verb forms

The future perfect (**il futuro anteriore**) is made up of the future of the auxiliary **avere** or **essere** plus the past participle of the verb. (See p. 253 for which auxiliary to use.)

pagare	tornare
avrò pagato	sarò tornato/a
avrai pagato	sarai tornato/a
avrà pagato	sarà tornato/a
avremo pagato	saremo tornati/e
avrete pagato	sarete tornati/e
avranno pagato	saranno tornati/e

(b) Uses of the future perfect (1)

What will have happened	Domani a quest'ora **avrò dato** l'esame *By this time tomorrow I will have sat the exam* Le due non ci conviene, **saremo** già **partiti** *Two o'clock is no good for us, we will already have left*	As in English, the future perfect is used in Italian to say what will have taken place by a certain time.
Speculation and supposition ⚠	Dove **saranno andati/e**? *Where can/could they have gone?* **Saranno** già **partiti** *They must have/will have already left* Ti **sarà costato** un occhio dalla testa *It must have/I bet it cost you an arm and a leg*	These are is some of the most common uses of the future perfect, although they do not strictly refer to the future. See also the simple future, p. 247.
Concession ⚠	**Avrà cambiato** idea, ma mi sembra strano *He may have changed his mind but I think it's odd*	

✚ Esercizi

1 Complete the sentences in Italian to say what will have happened.

  (a) Fra una settimana … *you will have forgotten him.*

  (b) Quando leggerà questa lettera … *I will already have left.*

  (c) A quest'ora domani … *Giovanni will have returned/will be back.*

2 A friend hasn't turned up. What could have happened? Give the Italian equivalent of the following.

  (a) *Could he have gone the wrong way?* (**sbagliare strada**)

  (b) *He must have had an accident.*

  (c) *He may be a good driver but the weather is bad.* (**un bravo guidatore**)

✚ (c) Uses of the future perfect (2): time clauses and conditions

In standard Italian, the future perfect is used with conditions and time expressions to express an action that will take place in the future before another one.

After conjunctions of time	Non appena **avrò finito**, ti verrò a trovare *As soon as I (will) have finished I will come and see you* Quando **sarò arrivato**, ti chiamerò *When I (will) arrive I'll call you* Passerò a trovarvi una volta che/quando **avrò cenato** *I'll call round and visit you once I (will) have had supper*	A simple future in the main clause (e.g. **ti verrò** …) is used with the future perfect after **(non) appena**, **dopo che**, **fino a quando/finché (non)**, **quando**, **una volta che**. In colloquial Italian the future perfect is often avoided. (See alternatives in (d), p. 251).

se + future perfect conditions	Se **avremo finito**, ti chiameremo alle quattro *If we have finished, we'll call you at four*	A simple future in the main clause (e.g. **ti chiameremo**) is used with the future perfect in a **se** clause. For colloquial alternatives, see below.
With imperatives	Appena **avrai pagato**, fammelo sapere *Let me know when you (will) have paid*	An imperative in the main clause may be used with the future perfect, but colloquially the perfect is used. See below.

(d) Alternatives to the future perfect

In colloquial Italian, the future perfect is often replaced by other tenses.

Simple future or present	Non appena **finirò/finisco** ti verrò/vengo a trovare *As soon as I finish ...* Se **finiremo/finiamo** in tempo ti chiamerò alle quattro *If we finish on time I'll call you at four*	After **se, (non) appena** and **fino a quando/finché (non)**, the future or the present are common in speech.
Passato prossimo	Se **abbiamo finito**, cercherò di chiamarti *If we've finished, I'll try and call you* Non appena **ho finito** ti passo a prendere *As soon as I've finished, I'll come by and pick you up* Appena **hai pagato** fammelo sapere *As soon as you've paid, let me know*	The **passato prossimo** may be used after **se, (non) appena, quando, dopo che, una volta che** and when there is an imperative in the main clause. The present tense may replace the future in the main clause.
dopo + past infinitive	Potrò/Posso venire a trovarvi dopo **aver visto** mia figlia *I can come and see you after I have seen my daughter*	Note that if the subjects in both clauses are the same, **dopo** can be followed by a past infinitive. See pp. 226 and 267.

✛ Esercizi

3 Give the Italian equivalent of the English.

  (a) Potrò passare a prenderti alle sette ... *if I have finished my homework.*
  (b) Ti restituirò il libro ... *when I have read it.*
  (c) Ti inviterò da me ... *once I have sorted out the flat.* (**sistemare**)
  (d) Ti verrò a trovare ... *after I have done the shopping.*

4 Now make the statements above more of a definite promise, using **appena**. Note the change in tense.

  (a) Passo a prenderti ...
  (b) Ti restituisco il libro ...
  (c) Ti invito da me ...
  (d) Ti vengo a trovare ...

5 Give a colloquial Italian equivalent of the following.

  (a) *Come and see me when you've finished.*
  (b) *Send him the book once he has paid.*
  (c) *When he divorces he will remarry at once.*

20 The past indicative tenses

Past tenses express states, actions or events related to the past. There are four main Italian indicative past tenses: the perfect (**il passato prossimo**), the imperfect (**l'imperfetto**), the pluperfect (**il trapassato prossimo**) and the simple past (**il passato remoto**).

◎/+ 20.1 The *passato prossimo*

The perfect tense in Italian is called **il passato prossimo** ('near past') and expresses completed past actions which are sometimes related to the present. It can correspond to two forms of the English past tense, e.g. **ho mangiato** can be both *I have eaten* and *I ate*.

(a) Regular forms of the *passato prossimo*

The **passato prossimo** is composed of the present tense of an auxiliary verb – **avere** or **essere** – plus the past participle of the verb required. The regular past participles end in: **-ato** (**-are** verbs), **-uto** (**-ere** verbs) and **-ito** (**-ire** verbs).

Auxiliary: *avere*	cant**are** *to sing*	ricev**ere** *to receive*	fin**ire** *to finish*	Auxiliary: *essere*	and**are** *to go*	cad**ere** *to fall*	usc**ire** *to go out*
ho				sono	andato/a	caduto/a	uscito/a
hai				sei	andato/a	caduto/a	uscito/a
ha	cantato	ricevuto	finito	è	andato/a	caduto/a	uscito/a
abbiamo				siamo	andati/e	caduti/e	usciti/e
avete				siete	endati/e	caduti/e	usciti/e
hanno				sono	andati/e	caduti/e	usciti/e

- The past participles of verbs taking **essere** change to agree with the subject.
- The verb **avere** itself takes the auxiliary **avere** and has a regular past participle: **ho avuto**, etc.
- **Essere** takes the auxiliary **essere** and has an irregular past participle: **sono stato**, etc. (see p. 253).

Reflexive verbs

The **passato prossimo** of regular reflexive verbs all take the auxiliary **essere** preceded by the reflexive pronouns. The partciples are regularly fomed with **-ato**, **-uto** and **-ito** endings and agree with the subject.

Auxiliary: *essere*	alz**arsi** *to get up*	sed**ersi** *to sit down*	divert**irsi** *to enjoy onself*
mi sono	alzato/a	seduto/a	divertito/a
ti sei	alzato/a	seduto/a	divertito/a
si è	alzato/a	seduto/a	divertito/a
ci siamo	alzati/e	seduti/e	divertiti/e
vi siete	alzati/e	seduti/e	divertiti/e
si sono	alzati/e	seduti/e	divertiti/e

Attenti! Which auxiliary – **avere** or **essere**?

In order to use not only the **passato prossimo** but also all other compound tenses (future perfect, pluperfect, past conditional and **trapassato remoto**), you need to understand which of the two auxiliary verbs to use:

There is no foolproof formula for chosing the auxiliary, but the following are useful guidelines:

- The choice of auxiliary often depends on whether a verb is transitive or intransitive. A transitive verb is a verb which can be used with a direct object, e.g. **comprare** *to buy* or **vendere** *to sell*. An intransitive verb cannot be used with a direct object. e.g. **andare** *to go* or **partire** *to leave*.
- Transitive verbs usually take **avere**.
- Reflexive verbs generally take **essere,** whether they are transitive or intransitive. (There is a list of verbs taking **essere** on p. 349 of Appendix B.)
- Intransitive verbs are more complicated: many, such as **riuscire** *to succeed*, always take **essere**. However, a considerable number take **avere**, e.g. **camminare** *to walk*, **dormire** *to sleep*, **parlare** *to talk* or **viaggiare** *to travel*.
- Some verbs can take either **avere** or **essere**, depending on the context or function of the verb. For more details on auxiliaries, see Auxiliaries (2), p. 256.

(b) Irregular forms of the *passato prossimo*

Irregularities in the **passato prossimo** concern the form of the past participle. Many common -**ere** verbs have an irregular past participle, as do all contracted infinitive verbs. Only a few -**are** and -**ire** verbs are irregular. Below are some common patterns of irregular past participles, together with an example of each. There is a more comprehensive list in Table 1 of Appendix B on pp. 350–2. Most of the following past participles should be learned.

-asto -esto -isto -osto	rimanere chiedere vedere rispondere	**rimasto** **chiesto** **visto** **risposto**	-anto -ento -into -unto	piangere spegnere vincere giungere	**pianto** **spento** **vinto** **giunto**
-arso -erso -orso	apparire perdere correre	**apparso** **perso** **corso**	-elto -olto	scegliere togliere	**scelto** **tolto**
-atto -etto -itto -otto -utto	fare dire scrivere rompere distruggere	**fatto** **detto** **scritto** **rotto** **distrutto**	-erto -orto	aprire morire	**aperto** **morto**
-aso -eso -iso -oso -uso	persuadere prendere decidere esplodere chiudere	**persuaso** **preso** **deciso** **esploso** **chiuso**	-ato -ito -uto	essere stare esistere bere venire vivere	**stato** **stato** **esistito** **bevuto** **venuto** **vissuto**
-esso -osso -usso	mettere muovere discutere	**messo** **mosso** **discusso**	-iuto	piacere conoscere	**piaciuto** **conosciuto**

◎ Esercizi

1 Complete the questions below using the correct past participle of the verbs given.

- (a) Hai — una pizza? (**ordinare**)
- (b) Avete — la lettera? (**ricevere**)
- (c) Hai — il problema? (**capire**)
- (d) Siete — in centro? (**andare**)
- (e) È — per strada? (**cadere**)
- (f) Sei — ieri? (**partire**)

2 Complete the sentences choosing the correct auxiliary and form of the past participle.

- (a) (*I have made*) un errore madornale. (**fare**)
- (b) (*He answered*) subito. (**rispondere**)
- (c) Luca, (*have you opened*) la finestra? (**aprire**)
- (d) Ieri sera (*I stayed*) da Ornella. (**stare**)
- (e) Oggi (*I stayed*) a casa. (**rimanere**)
- (f) L'anno scorso (*they came*) da noi. (**venire**)

3 Complete the sentences using the correct auxiliary and past participle of the verbs given.

- (a) Mi — alle sette. (**alzarsi**)
- (b) Mi — male in autobus. (**sentirsi**)
- (c) Mi — accanto a Rita. (**sedersi**)
- (d) Mi — il cappotto. (**mettersi**)
- (e) Mi — le scarpe in casa. (**togliersi**)

(c) Uses of the *passato prossimo* (1)

As mentioned on p. 252, the **passato prossimo** is equivalent to two English tenses, e.g. *he has taken/he took*. These depend on the context.

Expressing completed actions in the past	Stamattina **ha preso** il treno per Napoli *This morning he took the train for Naples* Ieri mi **ha telefonato** due volte *Yesterday he phoned me twice* Che bella città, Cagliari! Ci **sono andato** trent'anni fa *What a beautiful city Cagliari is! I went there thirty years ago*	Despite its name, the **passato prossimo** is used to refer not only to recent actions but also to events in the distant past, especially if these are still vivid in the speaker's mind.
Expressing an ongoing situation or action	Non **ho** mai **preso** sonniferi *I have never taken sleeping tablets* Oggi Mirella mi ha già **telefonato** dieci volte *Mirella has already phoned me ten times today* **Siamo** sempre **andati** in Sicilia per Pasqua *We have always gone to Sicily for Easter*	The **passato prossimo** is often used with words such as **sempre**, **già** or **mai** to express an action that is, or may well be, repeated. Note that in this case the English equivalent is *have/has …*

◎ Esercizio

4 Give the English equivalent of the following.

- (a) Conosco bene la Sardegna. Ci sono stato molte volte. Mi è sempre piaciuta.
- (b) L'anno scorso sono stato in Sardegna. Mi è piaciuta moltissimo.
- (c) Hai preso l'aereo o hai viaggiato in treno? – Ho preso la macchina, è più comodo.
- (d) Giulia, ho preso la macchina. Te la riporto stasera.

◎/✛ (d) Uses of the *passato prossimo* (2): past participle agreements

Agreements with the subject: verbs taking **essere**	**Ada** dov'è andat**a**? *Where has Ada gone?/Where did she go?* **Le ragazze** si sono divertit**e** *The girls enjoyed themselves* **Modena** mi è molto piaciut**a** *I liked Modena a lot*	When **essere** is used, the past participle agrees with the subject. Note that, with **piacere**, it agrees with the object/person liked – e.g. Modena – as this is actually the grammatical subject. See also p. 319.

Agreements with direct object pronouns: verbs taking **avere**	Ieri ho vist**o** Ada (noun direct object, no agreement). **L**'ho vist**a** (direct object pronoun object) *I saw Ada yesterday. I saw her* Ho parlato con Ada. Le ho parlato (**le** is an indirect object pronoun, no agreement)	When **avere** is used, the past participle agrees with the preceding pronoun direct objects **lo**, **la**, **li** and **le***, but not with *noun* direct objects or pronoun *indirect* objects. It never agrees with the subject.
✚ Agreements with direct object pronouns: reflexive verbs	**Ada** si è lavat**a** le mani. Aldo si è lavat**o** le mani *Ada/Aldo has washed her/his hands* (agreement with the subject of a reflexive verb). Se **le** è lavat**e** *She/He has washed them* (agreement with pronoun direct object of reflexive verb).	Reflexive verb past participles agree with the subject (see first row). However, when there is a direct object pronoun (**lo**, **la**, **li** and **le**), agreement is made with that object rather than with the subject. See also p. 132.

* Past participle agreement with the direct object pronouns **mi**, **ti**, **ci** and **vi** is optional and less common.

◎/✚ Esercizi

5 Your day. You're Giorgio's wife. Say what you did yesterday, using the verbs given and making any necessary participle agreements.

Ieri io e mio marito Giorgio (**1 alzarsi**) presto e (**2 andare**) tutti e due a lavorare. Io (**3 arrivare**) in ufficio alle otto e mezzo e (**4 lavorare**) tutta la giornata. Io (**5 annoiarsi**) da morire! (**6 Tornare**) a casa verso le sei e dopo cena io e Giorgio (**7 fare**) una lunga passeggiata. (**8 Camminare**) per un'ora, dopodiché (**9 tornare**) a casa e (**10 vedere**) un bel film che ci (**11 piacere**) molto. Devo dire che noi (**12 dormire**) bene!

✚ **6** Complete the sentences making participle agreements where necessary.

  (a) Hanno scritt– la lettera? L'hanno scritt–?
  (b) Avete lett– i giornali? Li avete lett–?
  (c) Hai parlat– con Franca? Non, non le ho parlat–.
  (d) Angelo, ti sei mess– la giacca? No, non me la sono mess–, fa troppo caldo.

◎/✚ (e) Uses of the *passato prossimo* (3): tense sequence

The **passato prossimo** in a main clause can be used with various different tenses in subordinate clauses, depending on whether reference is being made to the future, to the present situation, to the immediate past or to a more distant past. Notice that the sequence differs, depending on whether the **passato prossimo** is linked to the present or very recent past (as in 1 below), or to the more distant past (as in 2).

Main clause	Subordinate clause		Time referred to
1 **Mi ha detto che** ➡	↗ parte/partirà ➡ sta male *He has told me (that)* ↖ ha perso il portafoglio	↗ *he is leaving/will leave* ➡ *he is unwell* ↖ *he lost/has lost his wallet*	Future: **domani** Ongoing: **oggi** Past: **ieri**
2 **Mi ha detto che** ➡	↗ ✚ partiva/sarebbe partito ➡ stava male *He told me (that)* ↖ aveva perso il portafoglio	↗ *was leaving/would leave* ➡ *he was unwell* ↖ *he had lost his wallet*	Future: **l'indomani** Ongoing: **quel giorno** Past: **il giorno dopo**

- In **1** above, after the **passato prossimo** in the main clause, the present or future are used to refer to the future; the present tense is used to refer to the ongoing situation/concurrent events, while the **passato prossimo** refers to past events/situations.
- In **2** above, after the **passato prossimo** in the main clause, the imperfect or past conditional refer to the 'future in the past' (see p. 278); the imperfect to the ongoing situation/concurrent events (see p. 226); while the pluperfect expresses past events/situations (see p. 259).

◎/✚ Esercizi

7 Choose an appropriate tense to complete the sentences, using the English as a guide.

   (a) Ha appena detto che — (avere) intenzione di dare le dimissioni. (… *he intends to* …)

   (b) Ha appena detto che — (dare) le dimissioni. (… *he has handed in his notice*)

   (c) Mi ha detto ieri che — (avere) intenzione di dimettersi. (… *he intended/was intending to* …)

   (d) Mi ha detto ieri che — (dare) le dimissioni. (… *he had handed in his notice*)

✚ **8** Give the Italian equivalent of the following.

   (a) *He has (just) told me that he booked yesterday.*

   (b) *He told me (yesterday) that he hadn't booked.*

   (c) *He told me that he was intending to book the following week.*

◎/✚ (f) More on the use of auxiliaries

Check that you have read the guidelines on the use of auxiliaries on p. 253. Here are some further uses.

Verbs used impersonally: **essere**	Gli spaghetti non mi **sono piaciuti** *I didn't like the spaghetti* (lit. *the spaghetti were not pleasing to me*) Gli **è capitata** una cosa strana *Something odd happened to him*	All verbs used impersonally take **essere**. The past participle agrees with the Italian grammatical subject. (In English this is the object, i.e. who or what is liked.) See pp. 319–20.
✚ Modal verbs: **avere** preferred	Fausto non **è potuto partire** ieri (**partire** takes **essere**) *Fausto was not able to leave yesterday* Fausto **ha potuto studiare** in pace (**studiare** takes **avere**) *Fausto was able to study in peace* ***But most usual:*** Fausto non **ha potuto partire** ieri	Strictly speaking modal verbs (see p. 240) take the auxiliary normally required by the following infinitive. Increasingly, however, the tendency is to use **avere** even when the following verb takes **essere**.
✚ After **essere** and some key verbs: **avere** essential	Non **ho** potuto **essere** presente *I didn't manage to be there* **Ha** voluto **restare** neutrale *He was determined to stay neutral*	When **essere**, **diventare**, **risultare**, **sembrare** and **restare** are used after a modal verb, the auxiliary is always **avere**.
✚ Modal + reflexive verbs: **avere** or **essere**	Ho dovuto alzarmi *or* Mi sono dovuto/a alzare *I had to get up* Hanno voluto riposarsi *or* Si sono voluti riposare *They wanted to rest*	Both constructions are used in speech. Note that with **avere** the reflexive pronoun comes first and there are no past participle agreements.

✚ Either **essere** or **avere**. Other verbs, especially those which can be used both transitively and intransitively, may take either **avere** or **essere**. Some of the most common are: **aumentare**,

cominciare, diminuire, finire, salire, scendere, cambiare, migliorare, peggiorare, toccare.
There is a more complete list in Appendix B on p. 350.

Transitive use: **avere**	**Ho salito** le scale *I climbed the stairs* Non **ha toccato** niente *He didn't touch anything* **Ha cominciato** a gridare *He began to shout* **Hai finito** di criticarlo? *Have you stopped criticising him?*	The verb takes **avere** when it is transitive and there is a direct object. When the verb is followed by **a** or **di** + infinitive, it is considered transitive.
Intransitive use: **essere**	**Sono salito** in macchina *I got into the car* Gli **è toccato** pagare per loro *He had to pay for them* Il film **è cominciato** tardi *The film began late* La lezione **è finita** *The lesson has finished*	When the verb has no direct object, it is intransitive and takes **essere**.

✚ In the case of some common verbs like **correre**, **saltare** and **volare** (which can be used transitively and intransitively), the rules are not so clearcut. Their use needs to be learned.

With **avere**	**Ho corso** cinque chilometri/tanto/per due ore *I ran five kilometres/so much/for two hours* **Ha saltato** il muretto/la cena/dalla gioia *He jumped over the wall/skipped supper/jumped for joy* **Abbiamo volato** di notte *We flew at night*	**Avere** is the most common auxiliary with these verbs even when there is no obvious direct object.
With **essere**	**Sono corso** a casa/verso il bosco *I ran (to) home/towards the wood* **È saltato** giù dall'albero *He jumped down from the tree* La vespa **è volata** via *The wasp flew away*	These verbs take **essere** only when they are accompanied by a phrase of direction indicating to or from a place (**a casa**, **via**).

A few verbs can take either auxiliary, irrespective of whether they are transitive or intransitive, without any change in meaning.

vivere	**È vissuto** fino a ottant'anni *He lived until he was eighty* **Ha vissuto** dei brutti momenti *He lived (through) some bad moments* È un tipo che **ha vissuto** molto *He's someone who's lived a lot (i.e. been through a lot)*	**Essere** is possible when **vivere** is intransitive, but **avere** is increasingly common for both transitive and intransitive uses of **vivere**.
Verbs referring to weather	**Ha/È** piovuto per un'ora *It has rained for an hour* Ieri notte **ha/è** nevicato senza sosta *Last night it snowed without stopping*	Either auxiliary is acceptable. In speech, **avere** is more common than **essere**.
Other verbs	L'aereo **ha/è** decollato con un'ora di ritardo *The plane took off an hour late* La messa **è durata/ha durato** tre ore *The Mass lasted three hours* Il telefono **ha/è** squillato a mezzanotte *The phone rang at midnight*	The most common are: **atterrare** *to land*, **decollare** *to take off*, **durare** *to last*, **squillare** *to ring*.

◎/✚ Esercizi

9 Rewrite the sentences below using the **passato prossimo**. Use the correct auxiliary and agreements each time.

(a) Quella chiave mi serve per aprire il portone.

(b) Quei soldi non mi bastano per stasera.

(c) In quella casa mi succedono delle cose strane.

(d) Mi piace quella coppia allegra.

✚ **10** There's more than one way of saying the same thing. Which two verbs below can have a different form?

(a) Non sono potuto partire.

(b) Non ho voluto vederlo.

(c) Hai dovuto cambiare treno?

(d) Sei dovuto tornare a casa?

✚ **11** Rewrite the sentences below, making sure the meaning is the same.

(a) Ci siamo dovuti fermare.

(b) Elena si è dovuta riposare.

(c) Ho potuto sposarmi presto.

(d) Marta non ha voluto fidanzarsi.

✚ **12** Choose the correct auxiliary to complete the sentences and make any necessary participle agreements.

(a) Ho/Sono cambiato casa il mese scorso.

(b) La casa ha/è molto cambiato.

(c) La nuova legge non ha/è migliorato niente.

(d) La situazione non ha/è migliorato da ieri.

(e) L'ape ha/è volato via.

(f) Ho/Sono volato in prima classe.

(g) Ho/Sono corso fino all'angolo.

(h) Ho/Sono corso per molto tempo.

◎/✚ 20.2 The imperfect

The imperfect tense (**l'imperfetto**) is a past tense which expresses unfinished states or actions. It corresponds to four forms of the English past tenses: e.g. studiavo = *I used to study, I would study, I was studying, I studied.*

(a) Regular forms of the imperfect

The majority of verbs have regular imperfect forms. The endings are stressed on the last but one syllable, except in the **loro** form. You need to get used to this.

-are	andare	-ere	avere	-ire	uscire
	andavo		avevo		uscivo
	andavi		avevi		uscivi
	andava		aveva		usciva
	andavamo		avevamo		uscivamo
	andavate		avevate		uscivate
	andavano		avevano		uscivano

(b) Irregular forms of the imperfect

There are few irregularities. These relate to **essere** and to verbs with contracted infinitives. The verbs with contracted infinitives usually expand their stem and use the regular **-ere** endings. (See also the present tense, p. 240.) The stress pattern is the same as for regular imperfects.

essere	ero eri era eravamo eravate erano
-arre verbs (**trarre**)	traevo traevi traeva traevamo traevate traevano
-orre verbs (**opporre**)	opponevo opponevi opponeva opponevamo opponevate opponevano

-urre verbs (**produrre**)	produc**evo** produc**evi** produc**eva** produc**evamo** produc**evate** produc**evano**
bere	bev**evo** bev**evi** bev**eva** bev**evamo** bev**evate** bev**e**v**ano**
dire	dic**evo** dic**evi** dic**eva** dic**evamo** dic**evate** dic**e**v**ano**
fare	fac**evo** fac**evi** fac**eva** fac**evamo** fac**evate** fac**e**v**ano**

Dare and **stare** form the imperfect with regular **-are** endings: **davo, stavo,** etc.

◎/✚ (c) Uses of the imperfect (1)

The imperfect is used to describe past events which have no specific beginning or end.

A past state of affairs	**Era** tardi e **faceva** freddo *It was late and it was cold* **Eravamo** felici di vederli *We were happy to see them*	This can be physical, temporal, mental or emotional.
A habitual or repeated action in the past	**Pioveva** sempre in montagna *It always used to rain/It would always rain/It always rained in the mountains* **Andava** a messa tutte le domeniche *She used to go/would go/went to Mass every Sunday*	This is often expressed in English as *used to* or *would*.
Ongoing actions	**Pioveva** e la gente **correva** a casa *It was raining and people were running home* Lisa **piangeva** mentre sua sorella **urlava** *Lisa cried/was crying while her sister screamed/was screaming*	See also p. 265 for the imperfect continuous.

⚠ **Attenti!** Expressing 'could'

✚ • When *could* expresses permission and ability, it corresponds to the imperfect of three different verbs: **potere** *to be able to*, **sapere** *to know (how to)* and **riuscire** *to succeed/manage*:

Poteva uscire solo la domenica.	*She could only go out (was only allowed out) on Sundays.* (permission)
Non **riuscivo** ad aprire la porta	*I couldn't (manage to) open the door.* (ability)
Sapeva cucinare ma non **sapeva** usare un PC.	*She could cook but she couldn't use (didn't know how to use) a PC.* (ability)

• However, with verbs of perception (e.g. *to see, to hear*) there is no Italian equivalent of *could* unless ability or permission are explictly involved. Compare:

Lo **sentivo** benissimo.	*I could hear him clearly.*
But: Lo **potevo sentire** soltanto quando aprivo la porta.	*I could only hear him when I opened the door.*
Vedevo tutta la città dal mio balcone.	*I could see the whole city from my balcony.*
But: **Riuscivo a vedere** la città soltanto se mi mettevo in punta dei piedi.	*I could only see the town if I stood on tiptoe.*

• *Could* may also be expressed by the imperfect of **potere** when referring to events which might have, but didn't, take place:

| Perché non sei venuto? **Potevi** chiamare, almeno. | *Why didn't you come? You could at least have called.* (See p. 262) |

• It is important to note that *could* also expresses the conditional (p. 276) as well as future tense constructions used for speculation (p. 247).

⊚/✚ Esercizi

1 Things aren't what they used to be. Recall the good old days by completing the sentences.

    (a) Adesso la città è piena di macchine. Trent'anni fa … *there were very few cars.*

    (b) Al giorno d'oggi la gente ha paura di uscire di notte. Vent'anni fa … *no one was afraid.*

    (c) Al giorno d'oggi tutti i giovani bevono tanto. Anni fa … *they drank/used to drink very little.*

    (d) Adesso nessuno va più a Messa. Ai miei tempi … *everyone went/used to go to Mass.*

2 There has been a break-in next door. Answer the questions, giving the Italian equivalent of the English.

    (a) Non ha sentito niente quando hanno rotto il vetro della finestra? – *No, I was listening to the radio.*

    (b) Sono passati per il giardino? – *I don't know, I was preparing supper in the kitchen.*

    (c) Non ha visto nessuno fuori? – *It was dark, but yes, there was someone. He was wearing a ski jacket* (una giacca a vento) *and a woollen hat. I saw him as he was getting into a white van.* (un furgoncino)

3 Read this extract taken from a short story by Primo Levi, the writer and chemist. The child Maria is watching a house painter at work.

    (a) Complete the description by providing the correct form of the verbs given.

    In cucina c'era un uomo molto alto, vestito in un modo che Maria non aveva mai visto prima. (**1 Avere**) in testa una barchetta fatta con un giornale, (**2 fumare**) la pipa e (**3 dipingere**) l'armadio di bianco.

    (**4 Essere**) incomprensibile come tutto quel bianco potesse stare in una scatoletta così piccola, e Maria (**5 morire**) dal desiderio di andare a guardarci dentro. L'uomo ogni tanto (**6 posare**) la pipa sull'armadio stesso, e (**7 fischiare**); poi (**8 smettere**) di fischiare e (**9 cominciare**) a cantare; ogni tanto (**10 fare**) due passi indietro e (**11 chiudere**) un occhio … Faceva insomma tante cose strane e nuove che era interessantissimo starlo a guardare* …

    (Primo Levi, 'Titanio', in *Il sistema periodico*, 1975)

> era interessantissimo starlo a guardare *it was very interesting being there watching him*

    (b) Give the English equivalent of the following two phrases: (i) **che Maria non aveva mai visto prima**; (ii) **era interessantissimo starlo a guardare**. Refer to pp. 266 and Chapter 23, p. 290 respectively if you need help.

✚ **4** Give the Italian equivalent of the following, using the imperfect. There may be several possibilities.

    (a) *I couldn't open the window.*

    (b) *It was dark: I could hear them but I couldn't see them.*

    (c) *I could only hear them if they shouted.*

    (d) *I couldn't dance but I could sing.*

✚ (d) Uses of the imperfect (2): *da* + imperfect to express the pluperfect

⚠ **Attenti! Da** used with the Italian imperfect is equivalent to an English pluperfect.

How long for and since: **da**	Nel 1988 **insegnava** già **da** cinque anni *In 1988 she had already been teaching for five years* (and still was teaching) **Abitavamo** a Genova **dal** 1990 *We had been living/had lived in Genoa since 1990* (and still were living) Lo **consocevo da quando** avevamo fatto il militare insieme *I had known him since we had done military service together* (and still knew him)	**Da/da quando** + the imperfect express the English pluperfect tense when referring to a past action or state which has not been completed or interrupted, i.e. which is ongoing. **Da quant'era che** or **da quanto tempo** *how long?* are often used in questions. **Essere che** + imperfect is a more colloquial equivalent.
	Voleva sapere **da quant'era che ci trovavamo** a Roma *He wanted to know how long we had been in Rome* (and still were)	
	Era un settimana **che ci trovavamo** a Roma *We had been in Rome for a week*	

Note, however, that **da** and especially **da quando** are also used with the pluperfect, as in English, when expressing *completed* past actions, as opposed to ongoing past actions:

Dalla fine dell'anno precedente **aveva scritto** due libri.	*Since the end of the previous year* *he had written two books.*
Da quando aveva perso la moglie non era più uscito di casa.	*Since he had lost his wife he had no* *longer left the house.*
Da quando si era laureata non gli aveva più rivolto la parola.	*Since she had graduated she had no* *longer spoken a single word to him.*

✚ Esercizi

5 Give the Italian equivalent of the English, taking care to use the correct tense.

   (a) *I hadn't seen her since December.*
   (b) *I had known her since I was three.*
   (c) *He had been waiting for an hour.*
   (d) *Since 1980 she had had three husbands.*

6 Ancient history. You're quizzing your grandfather about his life. Complete the conversation in Italian, choosing between the imperfect and pluperfect tenses.

   (a) **Question:** Quando è scoppiata la guerra … *how long had you been teaching in Milan?*
       Answer: *I had been teaching for two years, since I had got married.*

   (b) **Question:** Eravate fidanzati da molto tempo?
       Answer: *Yes, we had been engaged for six years.*

   (c) **Question:** E poi la guerra ti ha separato dalla nonna. Per quanto tempo?
       Answer: Per tanto tempo. Quando sono tornato dalla guerra *we hadn't seen each other for three years and I had never seen my daughter!*

7 The following comes from an account of political exile in a remote part of the South in Fascist Italy. The author was a doctor and painter, Carlo Levi.

   (a) Read the text and identify the pluperfect tenses.

   Ero da poco nella cucina della vedova* e le chiedevo le prime notizie del paese, quando si batté alla porta, e alcuni contadini chiesero timidamente di entrare. Erano sette o otto, vestiti di nero, con i cappelli neri in capo, gli occhi neri pieni di una particolare gravità. – Tu sei il dottore che è arrivato ora? – mi chiesero. – Vieni, che* c'è uno che sta male. Avevano saputo subito in Municipio* del mio arrivo, e avevano sentito che io ero dottore. Dissi che ero dottore, ma da molti anni non esercitavo; – che certamente esisteva un medico nel paese, che chiamassero quello*; e che perciò non sarei venuto. Mi risposero che in paese non c'erano medici, che il loro compagno stava morendo. – Possibile che non ci sia un medico? – Non ce ne sono. – Ero molto imbarazzato: non sapevo davvero se sarei stato in grado, dopo tanti anni, che non mi ero occupato di medicina, di essere di qualche utilità. Ma come resistere alle loro preghiere?

(Carlo Levi, *Cristo si è fermato a Eboli*, 1945)

> • **vedova** *widow* • **che** *because* • **in Municipio** *the town hall* • **che chiamassero quello** *they should call him*.

(b) Identify the two phrases with imperfect tenses whose English equivalent is a pluperfect.

(c) Finally, refer to Chapter 21, p. 278 if necessary and give the English equivalent of:
(i) **non sarei venuto** and (ii) **non sapevo … se sarei stato in grado … di essere di qualche utilità**.

◎/✚ (e) Further uses of the imperfect

There are cases when the imperfect does not, strictly speaking, refer only to the indeterminate past.

To be about to: **stare per**	**Stavo per** uscire quando mi hai chiamato *I was about to go out when you called me*	When used in the imperfect, **stare per** expresses what was about to happen.
✚ Referring to the future 'in the past'	Tu mi hai detto che non **veniva** più *You told me he wasn't coming/wouldn't come any more* Ci aveva spiegato che **pagava** più tardi *He had explained that he was paying/would pay later*	In Italian, as in English, the imperfect can refer to the future in a past tense narrative. This is common in informal Italian, especially if the event referred to is definite. Otherwise a past conditional is often required. See p. 278.
✚ Hypothetical events	Hai già scritto? – Sì – Bene, altrimenti lo **facevo** io. *… Good, otherwise I was going to do it/I would have done it myself* Non vengono più? – Me lo **potevi** dire almeno! *… You could/might at least have told me!*	In informal spoken Italian the imperfect is generally used to refer to events which might have, but didn't happen. See past conditional, p. 277 for equivalent more formal written forms.
	Facciamo che **eravamo** grandi e tu **eri** una principessa *Let's pretend we're grown up and you're a princess*	The imperfect is used in children's imaginary games, whereas in English the present is used.
✚ Impossible conditions with **se**	Se mi **chiamavi** ti **venivo** a prendere *If you had called me I would have come and picked you up*	The imperfect can be used very informally in both clauses. See p. 305 for more formal written constructions.
✚ Immediacy of narrative	Quarant'anni fa **moriva** lo statunitense Herbert Kalmus che, nel primo decennio del XX secolo, aveva inventato il 'tecnicolor' *The American Herbert Kalmus, who (had) invented 'technicolor' in the 1910s, died forty years ago*	The use of the imperfect instead of the **passato prossimo** or **passato remoto** (p. 267) is a particularly common feature in journalism. The effect is to make the events more immediate or dramatic. It is important to recognise rather than use the imperfect in this way.

◎/✛ **Esercizi**

8 You were not prepared for what was going to happen. Complete the sentences by substituting the English.

    (a) Non sapevo che … *they were coming so soon.*

    (b) Mio figlio non mi aveva detto che … *he was sleeping out.*

    (c) Mio marito non mi aveva avvertito che … *he was bringing twenty guests to dinner.*

    (d) Nessuno mi aveva detto che … *they were about to sell the house.*

✛ **9** How might you have protested about the above situations? Supply the correct form of the verb using the English as a guide.

    (a) Loro me lo (potere) dire, almeno! *They could/might have …*

    (b) Me lo (dovere) dire, almeno! *He should have …*

    (c) Mi (potere) avvertire almeno! *You could/might have …*

✛ **10** You would have helped your friend out if you had known. Supply the correct form of the verbs given.

    (a) Ho dovuto prendere un tassì. – Ma se lo (sapere) ti (venire) a prendere.

    (b) Ho perso la mia carta di credito. – Ma se me lo (dire) ti (prestare) dei soldi.

    (c) Giovanni non ha capito quello che bisogna fare. – Ma bastava chiamarmi e glielo (spiegare) subito!

See also conditions with **se** and the subjunctive, pp. 305–6.

◎/✛ **20.3 The imperfect and the *passato prossimo***

Deciding whether a verb should be in the imperfect or **passato prossimo** is not always straightforward. This is partly because in English the same form of the verb can often be used for both imperfect and perfect tenses, e.g., depending on the context, *I watched* can express the imperfect **guardavo** and the *passato prossimo* **ho guardato**.

(a) Imperfect or *passato prossimo*: the main contrasts

Ongoing v. completed action	Mentre Lina **guardava** la TV Gino **preparava** la cena *While Lina watched TV Gino prepared/was preparing supper* Mentre Lina **guardava** la TV Gino **ha preparato** la cena *While Lina was watching TV Gino prepared the supper*	**Guardava … preparava** expresses an ongoing past action taking place simultaneously with the watching of TV. **Guardava … ho preparato** is used to signify the fact that the action was completed while Lina watched TV.
Description v. completed action	Da bambino **non mi piaceva** il mio insegnante di storia *As a child I didn't like/didn't use to like my history teacher* Quando ho incontrato Michele per la prima volta **non mi è piaciuto** *When I first met Michele I didn't like him (didn't take a liking to him)*	**Non mi piaceva** is used to describe a state of affairs relating to an unspecified length of time, whereas **non mi è piaciuto** expresses an event that happened at a given time.

 Attenti! Take care to distinguish between the Italian equivalents of *was* and *were*:
    era or **è stato; erano** or **sono stati**?

As shown in (a) above, the **passato prossimo** expresses completed actions or events (E), while the imperfect describes ongoing states or situations (D). Compare:

    Era una bella serata d'estate.   *It was a beautiful summer's evening.* (D)

    Grazie, **è stata** una bella serata.   *Thank you, it was/has been a lovely evening.* (E)

Occasionally either tense is possible – with only a slight shift in meaning.

Erano difficili gli esami?   *Were the exams hard?* (D)
Sono stati difficili gli esami?   *Were the exams hard? i.e. Have the exams been hard (to do)?* (E)

✛ (b) Imperfect or *passato prossimo*: modal verbs and *conoscere*

There is usually a shift of meaning when these verbs are used in the imperfect as opposed to **the passato prossimo.** It is particularly interesting to note that in the imperfect, **dovere**, **potere** and **volere** often express actions *which have not yet taken place* – rather than ongoing actions in progress. However, when used in the **passato prossimo** these verbs are used normally to express completed actions. **Sapere** and **conoscere** *to know* have different shifts in meaning.

Verb	Imperfect	*Passato prossimo*
dovere	A che ora **dovevi** partire? *At what time were you supposed to/meant to leave?* **Dovevo** far la spesa *I was supposed to/I used to have to do the shopping*	A che ora **hai dovuto** partire? *At what time did you have to leave? (and did)* **Ho dovuto** fare la spesa *I had to/have had to do the shopping*
potere	Ho chiamato per dire che non **potevo** venire presto venerdì *I called to say I couldn't come early on Friday*	Non **ho potuto** venire presto venerdì *I couldn't come early on Friday (was not able to and didn't)*
volere	**Voleva** offrirci da bere *He wanted to offer us a drink* (it was his intention) **Non voleva** studiare *She didn't want to study* (but did she?)	**Ha voluto** offrirci da bere *He insisted on buying us a drink (and did)* **Non ha voluto** studiare *She refused/ has refused to study (and didn't)*
sapere	**Sapevo** che era in ospedale *I knew he was in hospital* **Non sapevano** rispondere alle domande *They didn't know how to answer the questions*	**Ho saputo** che era in ospedale *I found out/learned he was in hospital* **Non ho saputo** rispondere alle domande *I wasn't able to answer/proved incapable of answering the questions*
conoscere	A Londra **conoscevo** molti italiani *In London I knew/used to know/was acquainted with many Italians*	A Londra **ho conosciuto** molti italiani *In London I met/got to know many Italians*

For more on modal verbs see special verb constructions, p. 319.

✛ Esercizi

1 Express the following in Italian, choosing the correct tenses.

    (a) *On Tuesday while Anna listened to the radio Pietro made supper.*

    (b) *On Wednesday Anna cleaned the house while Pietro prepared a lecture.* (**una lezione**)

    (c) *Yesterday we went to a party. It was a wonderful evening.*

    (d) *Yesterday we went for a walk because it was a lovely evening.*

    (e) *Last year I went to Corsica. I liked it a lot.*

    (f) *When I lived in London I liked visiting the museums.*

2 Complete the sentences, choosing the correct Italian form of the verb.

    (a) *(I was supposed to)* partire alle tre ma il treno è in ritardo.

    (b) *(I had to)* partire subito, mia figlia si è sentita male.

(c) Purtroppo (*I couldn't see*) il professore perché era malato

(d) Mi hanno detto che (*I couldn't see*) il medico prima di lunedì.

(e) (*I found out*) dalla segretaria che il mio capo era in vacanza.

(f) (*I knew*) che il mio capo era in vacanza.

◎ 20.4 The imperfect continuous

This English tense focuses on an activity in the process of taking place in the past at the time of speaking. In Italian, this is expressed by the imperfect tense of the verb **stare**, followed by the gerund of the verb required.

(a) Regular forms of the imperfect continuous

Infinitive	stare + gerund	
pensare **leggere** **finire** **partire**	stavo stavi stava stavamo stavate stavano	parl**ando** legg**endo** fin**endo** part**endo**

(b) Irregular forms of the imperfect continuous

Irregular forms have an irregular gerund used with stare as with regular forms. The irregularities concern verbs with contracted infinitives and verbs in **-arre**, **-orre** and **-urre**, which all end in **-endo**.

Infinitive	stare + gerund	
bere **dire** **fare** **trarre** **proporre** **produrre**	stavo stavi stava stavamo stavate stavano	**beve**ndo **dice**ndo **face**ndo **trae**ndo **propon**endo **produc**endo

(c) Uses of the imperfect continuous

In Italian, this verb form has a more restricted use than the past continuous in English.

An action in progress	**Stavo ascoltando** la radio quando ho sentito l'esplosione *I was listening to the radio when I heard the explosion* **Or:** **Ascoltavo** la radio quando ho sentito l'esplosione	**Stavo** + gerund emphasises an action in the process of taking place in the past – often when something else intervenes. It can usually be replaced by the Italian simple imperfect with no significant change of meaning.
Not a state of affairs	Che cosa **portava**? *What was she wearing?* Non so che cosa **faceva** a Roma *I don't know what she was doing in Rome* **Era seduta** in giardino *She was sitting in the garden*	**Stavo** + gerund is not used to express a state of affairs in the past, i.e. it must emphasise an action in progress. It cannot therefore be used with such verbs as **essere, stare, rimanere, sedere, volere**.

Esercizio

1 Look at Exercise 2 on p. 260 about the break-in. Which of the actions could be expressed using the imperfect continuous? Provide these alternative forms.

◎/✚ 20.5 The pluperfect

The pluperfect (**il trapassato prossimo**) is a tense which expresses actions that have taken place before another in the past. It is often recognisable in English by the characteristic *had* before a past participle: *I went to meet them, but they **had** already **left***.

(a) Forms of the pluperfect

The pluperfect is composed of the imperfect tense of the auxiliary verb (**avere** or **essere**), plus the past participle of the verb required. The past participle of verbs with the auxiliary **essere** must agree with the subject in number and gender.

Verbs with *avere*		Verbs with *essere*			
avevo avevi aveva	compr**ato** ricev**uto** dorm**ito**	ero eri era	and**ato/a**	cad**uto/a**	part**ito/a**
avevamo avevate avevano		eravamo eravate erano	and**ati/e**	cad**uti/e**	part**iti/e**

- Irregular pluperfects use the regular imperfect auxiliary and simply have irregular past participles, e.g. **avevo fatto** un errore *I had made a mistake*; **ero rimasto** a casa *I had stayed at home*.
- The pluperfect uses auxiliaries in the same way as the **passato prossimo**. See pp. 253 and 256.

◎/✚ (b) Uses of the pluperfect

The pluperfect is used to express an action or situation occurring before another one in the past.

Expressing an action preceding another in the past	Quando siamo usciti **aveva smesso** di piovere *When we came out it had stopped raining* Una volta che **aveva finito** di studiare andava a trovare gli amici *Once he had finished studying he used to go and see his friends* **Era** sempre **stato** un marito modello finché un giorno sparì *He had always been a model husband until one day he disappeared*	The pluperfect is used with the other past tenses – the **passato prossimo**, the imperfect and the simple past (**passato remoto**). These express the past action nearest in time, while the pluperfect expresses what took place before then.
✚ English and Italian differ	Mi ha dato il numero che **avevo chiesto** *He gave me the number I (had) asked for* Mi ha chiesto dov'**ero nato/a** *He asked me where I was (had been) born*	Note that in English the pluperfect is not always rigorously used, but in Italian an action preceding another in the past must be pluperfect.

✚ Simultaneous events: no pluperfect except in reported speech	Quando mi ha visto mi ha dato un bacio *On seeing me/When he saw me, he gave me a kiss* **But:** Ha detto che quando mi aveva visto mi aveva dato un bacio *He said that on seeing me/when he saw me he gave/had given me a kiss*	However, when expressing past actions that are more or less simultaneous, the pluperfect is not generally used except in reported speech.

◎/✚ Esercizio

1 Complete the sentences using the pluperfect form of the verb given in all but one case. Can you spot it?

  (a) Ieri Patrizio mi ha portato i libri che io gli (chiedere) l'altro giorno.

  (b) Mio fratello (laurearsi) in medicina ma non ha mai voluto fare il medico.

  (c) Quando Marcello (bere) era meglio non ascoltarlo.

✚ **(d)** Il funzionario voleva sapere dove (nascere) io e mio fratello.

✚ **(e)** Non mi ha dato il numero che (chiedere).

✚ **(f)** Quando (uscire), ho visto Enzo che saliva le scale.

✚ **(g)** Mi ha spiegato che quando (uscire) aveva visto Enzo che saliva le scale.

✚ (c) Alternatives to the pluperfect

In Italian the pluperfect is often avoided by using more succinct constructions.

Avoiding the pluperfect: infinitives and participles	**Dopo aver sentito** la notizia si è messa a piangere *After she had heard/After having heard the news, she began to cry* **Pensavo di/Mi sembrava di aver visto** Clara *I thought I had seen Clara* **Una volta/Appena finito** di studiare uscivo con gli amici *Once I had/As soon as I (had) finished studying, I used to go out with my friends*	If the subjects are the same in both clauses **dopo** can be used with a past infinitive and **appena** or **una volta** can be used with a past participle. The past participle can also be used alone. See also pp. 226 and 296.

✚ Esercizio

2 Give the Italian equivalent of the English, avoiding the pluperfect where possible.

  (a) *As soon as I (had) left the house I was taken ill.* (**sentirsi male**)

  (b) *After I had finished the exams I found myself a job.*

  (c) *I had already left when they arrived.*

  (d) *Once my wife had left hospital, I was able to go back to work.* (**uscive da**)

◎/✚ 20.6 The simple past: *il passato remoto*

The simple past or past historic (**il passato remoto**) is used to express completed past actions, e.g. **ci andai** *I went*. It is used in formal written Italian, but is also common in speech, for example in the south of Italy and in some parts of Tuscany. In northern Italy, however, it is usually replaced by the **passato prossimo** in speech.

(a) Regular forms of the *passato remoto*

-are comprare *to buy*	-ere vendere *to sell*	-ire domire *to sleep*
comprai	vendei	dormii
comprasti	vendesti/vendetti	dormisti
comprò	vendè/vendette	dormì
comprammo	vendemmo	dormimmo
compraste	vendeste	dormiste
comprarono	venderono/vendettero	dormirono

The alternative -**etti**, -**ette**, -**ettero** endings of -**ere** verbs are widely used, especially in speech.

✚ (b) Irregular forms of the *passato remoto*

A large number of verbs are irregular in the **passato remoto**, but most of them follow a consistent pattern.

There are only three verbs whose entire **passato remoto** has no clear link to the stem, but they also follow a basic pattern: i.e. the 1st person singular (**io**) is similar in form to the 3rd persons singular and plural (**lui/lei** and **loro**).

Passato remoto of common irregular verbs: completely irregular conjugations

essere	**fui**	fosti	**fu**	fummo	foste	**furono**
dare	**diedi/detti**	desti	**diede/dette**	demmo	deste	**diedero/dettero**
stare	**stetti**	stesti	**stette**	stemmo	steste	**stettero**

For all other irregular **passato remoto** verbs, it is possible to conjugate the whole tense simply by learning the **io** form. You can see in the table below that:

● the 1st person singular is similar in form to the 3rd persons singular and plural.
● the remaining **tu**, **noi** and **voi** forms follow the pattern of the regular -**ere** verb endings based on the stem.

Passato remoto of other common irregular verbs

avere	**ebbi**	avesti	**ebbe**	avemmo	aveste	**ebbero**
conoscere	**conobbi**	conoscesti	**conobbe**	conoscemmo	conosceste	**conobbero**
chiudere	**chiusi**	chiudesti	**chiuse**	chiudemmo	chiudeste	**chiusero**
mettere	**misi**	mettesti	**mise**	mettemmo	metteste	**misero**
prendere	**presi**	prendesti	**prese**	prendemmo	prendeste	**presero**
rimanere	**rimasi**	rimanesti	**rimase**	rimanemmo	rimaneste	**rimasero**
rispondere	**risposi**	rispondesti	**rispose**	rispondemmo	rispondesti	**risposero**
scegliere	**scelsi**	scegliesti	**scelse**	scegliemmo	sceglieste	**scelsero**
togliere	**tolsi**	togliesti	**tolse**	togliemmo	toglieste	**tolsero**
vincere	**vinsi**	vincesti	**vinse**	vincemmo	vinceste	**vinsero**
nascere	**nacqui**	nascesti	**nacque**	nascemmo	nasceste	**nacquero**
vedere	**vidi**	vedesti	**vide**	vedemmo	vedeste	**videro**

Passato remoto of contracted infinitive verbs

The stem of these verbs is an expanded version of the infinitive (see p. 240). The verbs all have the same consistent **passato remoto** pattern: the 1st person singular and the

3rd persons singular and plural are similar, while the **tu**, **noi** and **voi** forms are based on the expanded stem (i.e. **bev, dic, fac, tra, pon, conduc**).

bere	bevvi	bevesti	bevve	bevemmo	beveste	bevvero
dire	dissi	dicesti	disse	dicemmo	diceste	dissero
fare	feci	facesti	fece	facemmo	faceste	fecero
trarre	trassi	traesti	trasse	traemmo	traeste	trassero
porre	posi	ponesti	pose	ponemmo	poneste	posero
condurre	condussi	conducesti	condusse	conducemmo	conduceste	condussero

Note that **bere**, **dire**, **trarre** and **condurre** (above) all have double consonants in the 1st and 3rd persons. Similar verbs include: cadere (**caddi**), discutere (**discussi**), leggere (**lessi**), muovere (**mossi**), rompere (**ruppi**), scrivere (**scrissi**), sapere (**seppi**), tenere (**tenni**), venire (**venni**), vivere (**vissi**), volere (**volli**).

Most other irregular **passato remoto** verbs are in Appendix B, pp. 353–6.

◎/✚ Esercizi

1 Complete the sentences chosing the correct **passato remoto** form of the verb given.

    (a) Dopo il loro matrimonio (comprare) una casa al mare.

    (b) Dopo l'omicidio del figlio, la famiglia (ricevere) una lettera ononima.

    (c) Finiti gli esami, Agnese (dormire) per ventiquattr'ore.

    (d) (Sedersi – loro) vicino alla finestra.

✚ **2** Look at the list above of 11 irregular **passato remoto** verbs (**cadere,** etc.).

    (a) Give the whole **passato remoto** conjugation of **leggere** and **scrivere**.

    (b) Choose the correct form of the verbs given to complete the sentences below.

        (i) (Vennero/Venero) troppo tardi per vederlo. (**loro**)

        (ii) (Vennisti/Venisti) troppo tardi per vederlo (**tu**)

        (iii) Il nonno (visse/vissi) a lungo in Etiopia. (**lui**)

        (iv) Per sei mesi, allora, voi soldati (viveste/vivesti) sotto tenda? (**voi**)

◎/✚ (c) Uses of the *passato remoto*

The **passato remoto** is essentially a written tense, although in some parts of Italy it is used in speech. (See comments p. 267.) Beginners should avoid its use in speech in favour of the **passato prossimo** as the main past tense of everyday spoken Italian. However, it is important to recognise and understand the forms, as they are widely used in modern written Italian.

Literary and academic past tense	I monaci **uscirono** in fila e la chiesa **rimase** deserta *The monks filed out and the church was left deserted*	The **passato remoto** expresses events which are over and done with. It is the characteristic narrative tense of formal written Italian.
No link to the present	Lo hai visto di recente? <u>not</u> Lo vedesti di recente? *Have you seen him recently?*	Unlike the **passato prossimo** it does not express actions linked to the present.
Sequence of tenses	Mi **disse** che sarebbe venuto l'indomani *He said he would come the following day* Mi **spiegò** che la fidanzata era svedese *He explained that his fiancée was Swedish* **Seppi** che aveva vissuto a lungo *all'estero* *I found out he had lived abroad for a long time*	See table 2, p. 255 for a similar sequence of tenses. For the use of the **passato remoto** in dependent time clauses with **quando**, **appena**, see p. 271.

✦ Combining the *passato remoto* and *passato prossimo*

As already mentioned, the **passato remoto** can be used in spoken and written Italian – sometimes actually in conjunction with the **passato prossimo**. The former expresses events that are distant – or 'history' in the mind of the speaker/writer – irrespective of the actual amount of time which has elapsed. The **passato prossimo** is used for events that stick in the mind, however distant in time, to which the speaker still feels connected. Here is an example taken from a letter written by a couple to a magazine, in which the **passato prossimo** at the beginning and the end (in bold italics) is used to express the enduring intensity of their love.

Ci siamo innamorati ma poi **scoppiò** la guerra mondiale. La vita ci **portò** su strade diverse, **ci sposammo** con altre persone. Ora, rimasti vedovi tutt'e due, ***abbiamo scoperto*** che quell'antico sentimento non era mai finito.	*We fell in love, but the world war broke out. Life drew us along different paths, we married other people. Now that we are both widowed, we have discovered that our old feelings for each other had never died.*

✦ Esercizi

3 The following has been adapted from a story about a rabbit.

Fu allora che vide un coniglio in una gabbia. Era un coniglio bianco, di pelo lungo e piumoso … Fuori della gabbia, sul tavolo, c'erano dei resti d'erba e una carota. Marcovaldo pensò a come doveva essere infelice, chiuso là allo stretto*, vedendo quella carota e non potendola mangiare. E gli aprì lo sportello della gabbia. Il coniglio non uscì … Marcovaldo prese la carota, gliel'avvicinò, poi, lentamente la ritrasse per invitarlo a uscire. Il coniglio lo seguì …

(Italo Calvino, 'Il coniglio velenoso', in *Marcovaldo*, Einaudi, 1963)

> chiuso là allo stretto *cooped up in there*

    (a) Identify the nine **passato remoto** verbs. Give their infinitive, **io** and **tu** forms.

    (b) Substitute the **passato prossimo** for the **passato remoto** and rewrite the story in the 1st person as though you were telling it about yourself. Begin: **È stato allora che** …

4 This extract is adapted from a short story by Cesare Pavese. The narrator, Nino, his young son, along with Pietro, with whom Nino is infatuated, return from a village party. Reconstruct the text, inserting the correct **passato remoto** form of the verbs, but with one exception: there is a **passato prossimo** verb. Can you spot where it should go?

Fu quella notte che (**vedere – io**) Pietro ballare e Nino prendersi gli scapaccioni* perché lo rincorreva* … Verso la fine della festa Nino cascava dal sonno e Pietro lo (**prendere**) in spalla* e ce ne (**venire – noi**) via. Eravamo taciturni, come sempre succede dopo ogni festa e disordine; il fresco di settembre ci teneva svegli … Ai piedi della collina Pietro se lo (**togliere**) di spalla*, lo (**posare**) a terra e lo (**costringere**) a camminare. Nino (**aprire**) appena gli occhi, (**abbandonare**) una mano a ciascuno di noi e (**venire**) avanti a testa bassa. …

Quella notte del ritorno l'ho nel cuore come l'ultima dell'infanzia di Nino. I canti, la stanchezza, l'eccitazione sotto la luna me ne (**fare**) qualcosa d'irreale e di triste …

E l'indomani Nino, come se lo sapesse, (**restare**) nell'orto a leggicchiare e (**venire**) a pranzo contento e ancora asssonato*.

(Cesare Pavese, 'L'Eremita', in *Racconti*, Einaudi, 1953)

> • prendersi gli scappacioni *getting his ears boxed* • rincorreva *he was following him around* • in spalla *on his shoulders* • se lo … dispalla *took him off his shoulders* • assonato *sleepy*

✦ **20.7 The past anterior**

The **trapassato remoto** (known in English as the past anterior) is in essence an alternative pluperfect. It is used mainly in conjunction with the **passato remoto** to express past actions and events preceding the **passato remoto**. Its use is fairly limited, as it is used almost exclusively in written, formal or literary Italian, unlike the normal pluperfect (**trapassato prossimo**).

(a) Forms of the *trapassato remoto*

The **trapassato remoto** is formed with the **passato remoto** of **avere** or **essere** plus the past participle of the verb.

With **avere**	**ebbi** portato **ebbi** ricevuto **ebbi** finito *I had brought I had received I had finished*
With **essere**	**fui** arrivato **fui** caduto **fui** uscito *I had arrived I had fallen I had gone out*

The *trapassato remoto* of **avere** is **ebbi avuto**, but **essere** has no **trapassato remoto** form: you cannot say 'fui stato', etc. Similarly, there is no **trapassato remoto** form for passive verbs.

(b) Uses of the *trapassato remoto*

The **trapassato remoto** is used for action or events completed immediately before the action of the main verb. However, its use is fairly restricted, and in some circumstances it may be replaced by the **passato remoto** or participles and nouns.

Andò a casa appena/quando **ebbe mangiato** *He went home as soon as/when he had eaten* Dopo che **furono partiti** Gemma si mise a piangere *After they had left, Gemma began to cry*	Conventional use: Used in a dependent clause, after **appena**, **quando**, **dopo che** when there is a simple past (**passato remoto**) in the main clause.
Arrivarono due jeep con gli americani. Appena ci **videro**, **si fermarono** *Two jeeps with Americans arrived. On seeing us/As soon as they saw us, they stopped* Quando **partì** a fare il militare le **diede** un anello *On leaving/When he left to do military service he gave her a ring*	Use of **passato remoto**: When **appena** or **quando** links two verbs whose action is more or less simultaneous, the **passato remoto** is generally used instead of the **trapassato remoto**.
Quando **fu al corrente** dell'incidente corse subito in ospedale *When he heard about/was informed of the accident, he immediately rushed to the hospital* Quando **furono riempite** tutte le scatole, i ragazzi si misero a fumare *When all the boxes had been filled, the boys began to smoke.*	**Passato remoto** with essere and passives: The **trapassato remoto** is not used with **essere** or passives: instead the **passato remoto** tends to be used, rather than the pluperfect (e.g. **furono riempite** rather than **erano state riempite**).

The **trapassato remoto** tends to be further avoided with the use of nouns or participles.

Dopo mangiato andò a casa *After he had eaten he went home* **Appena tornati** i ragazzi, cominciarono a bisticciare *As soon as the boys (had) got home, they began to quarrel* **Dopo la loro partenza** Gemma si mise a piangere *After they had left, Gemma began to cry*	A past participle or a noun often replace the **trapassato remoto**. See also pp. 226, 267 and 296.

✦ Esercizi

1 Supply the correct form of the verb in brackets. The **trapassato remoto** is used only once.

(a) Quando (finire) di parlare, scoppiò a ridere.

(b) Quando (finire) di parlare, è scoppiato a ridere.

(c) Quando (sentire) squillare il campanello, Luciano si nascose subito.

(d) Quando (sentire) squillare il camapanello, Luciano si è nascosto subito.

2 The following is taken from a novel by Primo Levi, *Se non ora, quando?* It describes the journey of survivors of Nazi persecution as they travel across Europe from Russia to Italy in the years 1943–45. In this extract, two of the protagonists, Mendel and Leonid, have just met.

(a) Read the text, then identify the two pluperfect verbs.

(b) Next, give the English equivalents of: (i) **quando fu soddisfatto** and (ii) **quando tutte e dieci furono tagliate**.

(c) The main narrative tense is the **passato remoto**, but nevertheless, in (b) (i) and (ii) the **passato remoto (fu soddisfatto, furono tagliate)** is used after **quando** to express actions preceding the main actions: explain in both cases, (i) and (ii), why the **trapassato remoto** is not used?

(d) Finally, can you explain why the verbs **sputava**, **affilava**, **controllava** are not in the **passato remoto**?

Fumarono per qualche minuto in silenzio. Mendel aveva cavato di tasca un coltellino, aveva raccolto da terra un ciottolo*, ci sputava sopra a intervalli, e ci affilava contro la lama*; ogni tanto ne controllava il filo* provandolo sull'unghia del pollice*. Quando fu soddisfatto, incominciò a tagliarsi le altre unghie, manovrando il coltellino come se fosse una sega*. Quando tutte e dieci furono tagliate, Leonid gli offerse un'altra sigaretta: Mendel rifiutò. No, grazie. Io veramente non dovrei fumare, ma quando trovo tabacco fumo.

(Primo Levi, *Se non ora, quando?* Einaudi, 1982)

> • ciottolo *pebble* • ci affilava … contro *sharpened the blade against it* • ne controllava il filo *he would check its edge* • provandolo sull'unghia del pollice *testing it on his thumb nail* • sega *saw*

3 Revision. This comes from the novel *Alténopis* by Fabrizia Ramondino. The extract recounts what happened when the news that World War II was over reached the narrator's village.

(a) Read the text and underline or note down the past tenses in the following order: (i) passato remoto (main narrative tense); (ii) passato prossimo; (iii) imperfect; (iv) pluperfect. Consider the relationship of the other past tenses to the **passato remoto**, then answer the questions below.

Una sera il carrettiere* arrivò ballando fino alla tabaccheria, agitando dei giornali come un tamburello. "È finita la guerra! – gridava. È finita la guerra!" Era vero, la guerra era finita. … Lo aveva saputo quella mattina ad Alténopis* …

Tutto il villaggio si radunò* nella piazza e di finestra in finestra, di porta in porta, correva la voce: "È finita la guerra!"

Tutti cominciarono ad abbracciarsi, le donne piangevano; fu chiamato don Candido, ad aprire la chiesa. … Nostra madre l'aveva saputo due ore prima alla radio, ma non aveva detto niente, perché non riteneva fosse una gran notizia, o perché, incredula e diffidente*, pensava fosse una notizia falsa; non credeva alla radio e ai giornali, ma solo ai libri.

(Fabrizia Ramondino, *Alténopis*, Einaudi, 1988)

> • carrettiere *carter* • Alténopis *name given to Naples in WWII by the Germans* • si radunò *gathered* • diffidente *suspicious*

(b) Give English equivalents for: (i) **È finita la guerra**; (ii) **la guerra era finita**; (iii) **l' aveva saputo.**

(c) Finally, identify the two imperfect subjunctives. Why is the indicative not used? (Refer to Chapter 24, p. 300 if necessary.)

21 The conditional

The conditional form of the verb (**il condizionale**) generally expresses hypothetical or imaginary events and situations, as well as events dependent on a condition. This form often corresponds to *would* and *would have*: **Would** *you* **go** *tomorrow?* **Would** *you* **have left** *so early?*

⦿/+ 21.1 Regular and irregular forms of the conditional

(a) Regular forms of the conditional

The conditional form has similarities with the future. Like the future, there are two regular forms: **-are** and **-ere** verbs, which follow an identical pattern, as do both types of **-ire** verb endings.

-are and -ere				-ire	
-are	portare	**-ere**	prendere	finire	dormire
	porterei		prenderei	finirei	dormirei
	porteresti		prenderesti	finiresti	dormiresti
	porterebbe		prenderebbe	finirebbe	dormirebbe
	porteremmo		prenderemmo	finiremmo	dormiremmo
	portereste		prendereste	finireste	dormireste
	porterebbero		prenderebbero	finirebbero	dormirebbero

- As with the future tense, verbs with **-care** and **-gare** endings require the addition of an **-h** to keep the hard sound of the infinitive: e.g. **cercare** – cercherei, **pagare** – pagherei.
- Verbs in **-ciare**, **-giare** and **-sciare** drop the **-i** of the stem, as it is not needed to maintain the soft sound of the infinitive, e.g. **cominciare** – comincerei, **mangiare** – mangerei, **lasciare** lascerei.
- Note that, as with the future, **sedere** *to sit* has an **-i** in the conditional: **siederei, siederesti, siederebbe**, etc.

(b) Irregular forms of the conditional

These also have similarities with the future and form their verb stem in the same way. There are two patterns of irregularity, with endings in **-rei** and **-rrei**. These are added directly to the stem (which in some cases is irregularly formed), without the **-e** or **-i** of the regular conditional endings.

Verbs with -rei endings

Note the stem formations. In **1** below, **essere** has an irregular stem (**sa-**); in **2**, the verb stems are regular (**and-**, **av-**, etc.); in **3**, the verbs retain the vowel of the infinitive as part of the stem.

1 essere	sarei saresti sarebbe saremmo sareste sarebbero
2 andare avere potere	andrei andresti andrebbe andremmo andreste andrebbero avrei avresti avrebbe avremmo avreste avrebbero potrei potresti potrebbe potremmo potreste potrebbero
3 dare fare	darei daresti darebbe daremmo dareste darebbero farei faresti farebbe faremmo fareste farebbero

Similar verbs include: **cadere, dovere, sapere, vedere, vivere, dire, stare**. See Appendix B, pp. 353–6.

Verbs with -rrei endings

Other verbs, including all those with -**arre**, -**orre** and -**urre** infinitives, also omit the vowel of the regular conditional endings but double the -**r**. Note the stem formations. In **1** below, the stem is formed by dropping the -**ere**/-**ire** infinitive endings, along with the consonant (usually -**l**- or -**n**-) that precedes them; in **2** below, the verbs retain the vowel of their infinitive in the stem.

1 parere	parrei	parresti	parrebbe	parremmo	parreste	parrebbero
rimanere	rimarrei	rimarresti	rimarrebbe	rimarremmo	rimarreste	rimarrebbero
tenere	terrei	terresti	terrebbe	terremmo	terreste	terrebbero
venire	verrei	verresti	verrebbe	verremmo	verreste	verrebbero
valere	varrei	varresti	varrebbe	varremmo	varreste	varrebbero
volere	vorrei	vorresti	vorrebbe	vorremmo	vorreste	vorrebbero
2 bere	berrei	berresti	berrebbe	berremmo	berreste	berrebbero
trarre	trarrei	trarresti	trarrebbe	trarremmo	trarreste	trarrebbero
porre	porrei	porresti	porrebbe	porremmo	porreste	porrebbero
ridurre	ridurrei	ridurresti	ridurrebbe	ridurremmo	ridurreste	ridurrebbero

◎ Esercizi

1 Select the correct form of the conditional.

    (a) Mariella, tu lo (lavaresti/laveresti) veramente con acqua calda?

    (b) Ma voi due (cerchereste/cercereste) davvero un altro lavoro?

    (c) Lo (prenderemo/prenderemmo), ma è troppo caro.

2 Complete the sentences using the correct conditional forms.

    (a) (Venire – io) volentieri ma ho un appuntamento.   **(d)** (Potere – voi) aiutare?

    (b) (Volere – loro) partire, ma c'è sciopero.   **(e)** Mi (fare – tu) un favore?

    (c) (Rimanere – tu) fino a domani?   **(f)** Non (andare – io) mai con loro.

◎/✚ (c) Main uses of the conditional

Polite requests and diplomacy	Mi **faresti** un favore? *Would you do me a favour?* **Avrei** bisogno di almeno un chilo *I need/I'll be needing at least a kilo* Ti sembra ubriaco? – Non **saprei** *Does he seem drunk to you? – I wouldn't know*	The use of the conditional, rather than the present, makes things less blunt and direct. The English equivalent is not always *would*.
Hypothetical or uncertain events	Al mio posto che cosa **faresti?** *What would you do in my place?* **Uscirei** volentieri, ma non mi sento bene *I would love to go out, but I don't feel well*	The conditional is used to express actions which often depend on an obstacle or unspoken condition.
✚ Conditions with **se**	Ti **accompagnerei** se avessi più tempo *I would go with you if I had more time* **Sarei** già a casa se non avessi perso il treno *I would already be at home if I hadn't missed the train*	The conditional is used with past subjunctives. With **piacere** and **volere** an indicative verb may follow **se**.
	Mi piacerebbe venire se Ida è d'accordo *I would like to come if Ida agrees*	

Attenti! *Would* can be used to express tenses other than the conditional.

- It is important to distinguish the conditional *would* from the imperfect habitual *would*:

  Mi daresti una mano?   *Would you give me a hand?* (conditional)

  Mi dava spesso una mano.   *He would often give me a hand.* (imperfect)

- *Would not* can also express the **passato prossimo** or imperfect of the verb **volere**:

  Gli hanno chiesto di venire,   *They asked him to come, but he wouldn't.*

  ma non ha voluto farlo.   *(i.e. didn't)*

◎/✛ Esercizi

3 Be polite and ask diplomatically. Rewrite the commands and statements below using the conditional.

    (a) Umberto, dammi un bicchiere di vino.   **(c)** Signora, ho bisogno di una crema più leggera.

    (b) Anna e Cristina, fatemi un favore.   **(d)** Signore, me lo prepari per stasera.

4 What would you be willing to do if there were no obstacles? Use the correct form of the verbs given.

    (a) Ti (dare un passaggio), ma devo andare a prendere mia figlia.

    (b) (Tradurre) l'articolo ma non ho tempo.

    (c) Il vino lo (bere) volentieri, ma prendo antibiotici.

5 What would you do in someone else's shoes? Give the Italian equivalent of the English.

    (a) Al tuo posto … *I would not reply.* (**rispondere**)

    (b) Al suo posto, signore … *I would propose another solution.* (**proporre**)

    (c) Al mio posto … *he would get angry.* (**arrabbiarsi**)

✛ **6** The following is taken from a magazine article entitled **E se non ci fosse la luna?** *What if there were no moon?*

    (a) Complete the article by inserting the conditional verbs given below.

avremmo • farebbero • mancherebbe • potrebbe • potremmo • sarebbe • sarebbero

Se mancasse il nostro satellite* **(1)** un clima instabile. E giornate molto brevi.

In assenza della Luna il giorno **(2)** più breve: **(3)** durare solo 6 ore. Infatti le maree* prodotte dalla Luna dissipano energia e di conseguenza la Luna si allontana dalla terra rallentandone la rotazione … Oggi la lunghezza della giornata aumenta di 2,3 millisecondi al secolo, e la distanza Terra-Luna cresce di 3,8 cm all'anno.

Se non ci fosse la luna, **(4)** un pezzo di cultura e della nostra stessa identità:non ci **(5)** i lunari*, le poesie di Leopardi*, i licantropi*, i luna park*, i romanzi di fantascienza come quelli di Jules Verne (*Dalla Terra alla Luna*) e HG Wells (*I primi uomini sulla Luna*), *I* piani di colonizzazione lunare della Nasa, il disco *The dark side of the moon* dei Pink Floyd … Non **(6)** 'volere la luna' né avere la 'luna storta'*. E come **(7)** gli sposini senza la loro 'luna di miele'?

(*Focus*, maggio 2009)

> • satellite *satellite*, i.e. *the moon* • maree *tides* • i lunari *almanacks* • Leopardi *19th-century poet famous for a poem about the moon* • i licantropi *werewolves* • i luna park *funfairs* • avere la 'luna storta' *to be in a bad mood/in a huff*

    (b) Find English equivalents for: **volere la luna** and **luna di miele**.

✦ (d) Special uses of the conditional

In the conditional, modal verbs, **piacere** and **essere** have a range of meanings and functions.

dovere *should,* *ought to,* *supposed* *to,* *must*	**Dovresti** chiedere uno sconto *You should/ought to ask for a discount* **Dovremmo** studiare domani *We should/ought to/are supposed to study* *tomorrow* **Dovrebbero** essere arrivati *They should/must have arrived*	There are three main uses: giving advice; expressing obligation – what you are meant or supposed to do; expressing probability.
potere *could,* *may,* *might*	**Potreste** darci una mano? *Could you give us a hand?* **Potremmo** andare da Paolo oppure **potremmo** stare qui *We could go to Paolo's or we could stay here* La strada è buona, **potrebbe** essere a Roma ormai *It's a good road, he could be in Rome by now* Con questa nebbia **potrebbe** arrivare in ritardo *With this fog, he could/may/might arrive late*	There are three main uses: expressing polite requests – *could*; expressing a definite possibility; expressing a hypothesis or vague possibility – what could or is likely to be the case: *could/* *might/may.*
sapere *could,* *would*	Mi **saprebbe** dire a che ora tornano? *Could you tell me what time they are coming back?* Non so se **saprebbe** rispondere *I don't know if he could/would be able to answer*	Polite requests (see also **potere**). Expressing ability.
volere *would like*	**Vorrei** delle informazioni *I would like some information* **Vorrebbe** venire martedì *He would like to come on Tuesday* Non **vorresti** venire con noi? *Wouldn't you like to (i.e. don't you want to) come* *with us?*	Expressing wishes. The conditional literally means *would want/be wanting* but is expressed as *would like.*
piacere *would like*	Mi **piacerebbe** vederlo *I would like to see him* Ti **piacerebbe** venire con noi? *Would you like to come with us?*	Expresses what would give you pleasure. *Would like* is also the conditional of **volere** (see above).
essere	Ma questo, cosa **sarebbe**, scusa? *So what's this meant to be, may I ask?* E lui, chi **sarebbe**? *And who's he supposed to be/who might he be?*	Can be used to express irritation or scepticism.

 Attenti! *Could* is expressed in Italian by more than one verb and more than one tense.

- Both the conditional and imperfect of **potere** can be expressed as *could* in English:

  Mi potresti aiutare?   *Could you help me?* (conditional)
  Non poteva sempre aiutare.   *He couldn't always help.* (imperfect)

- Both the conditional and imperfect of **sapere** may be expressed as *could* when this refers to ability:

  Mi sapresti spiegare questo? *Could you* (are you able to) *explain this to me?* (conditional)
  Sapeva leggere a tre anni.   *He could read at three.* (imperfect)

For full explanations, see pp. 259 and 264.

✚ Esercizio

7 Give the English equivalent of the Italian.

(a) Dovresti andare dal medico.

(b) Dovrei partire alle tre ma non ho fatto il biglietto.

(c) Dovrebbero già essere a casa ormai.

(d) Potresti venire alle due?

(e) Hai detto che potevi venire alle due.

(f) Potrebbe essere dalla zia oppure dalla nonna.

(g) Mi sapresti dire se sono tornati?

(h) Non sapeva dirmi niente.

(i) Giulia vorrebbe rimanere a Pisa.

(j) Le piacerebbe rimanere a Pisa.

8 In which sentences above are the verbs not conditional?

✚ 21.2 The past conditional

(a) Forms of the past conditional

The past conditional (**il condizionale passato**) generally corresponds to the English *would have*, and is made up of the conditional of the auxiliary **avere** or **essere** plus the past participle of the verb.

pagare	tornare
avrei pagato	**sarei** tornato/a
avresti pagato	**saresti** tornato/a
avrebbe pagato	**sarebbe** tornato/a
avremmo pagato	**saremmo** tornati/e
avreste pagato	**sareste** tornati/e
avrebbero pagato	**sarebbero** tornati/e

✚ Esercizio

1 Supply the correct auxiliary verb to complete the past conditional.

(a) (io) — venuto/a prima.

(b) (io) — telefonato ieri.

(c) (loro) — partiti/e più tardi.

(d) Mi — arrabbiato/a.

(e) Si — seccato/a.

(f) Ci — divertiti/e.

(b) Uses of the past conditional

Hypothetical and impossible events

The past conditional very often refers to what might have but did not happen.

| Hypothetical events | Hai scritto la lettera? – Sì. – Bene, altrimenti **l'avrei scritta** io. …
Good, otherwise I would have written it myself
Al tuo posto **sarei venuto** prima *In your place/shoes I would have come earlier*
Me lo **avresti potuto** dire! *You could/might have told me!* ***Or:*** Me lo potevi dire! | The past conditional is used to refer to events which might have, but did not, take place. It can also express wishes that could not have been realised. In colloquial Italian, the imperfect may substitute the past conditional. See p. 262. |
| I would have liked … | Mi **sarebbe piaciuto** venire, ma avevo un appuntamento *I would have liked (i.e. enjoyed) to have come but I had an engagement*
Avrei voluto avvertirlo, ma era già partito *I would have liked to have warned him, but he had already left* | Note that the past conditional of **piacere** and **volere** are identically expressed in English, but in Italian the former is used to express pleasure and the latter to express intention. |

Unrealised conditions	Ti **avrei accompagnato** se avessi avuto più tempo *I would have gone with you if I had had more time* Se avesse i soldi **sarebbe partito** ieri *If he had the money he would have left yesterday*	The past conditional is used with the pluperfect subjunctive (and sometime the imperfect subjunctive) to express events which have not taken place. See also p. 305.

Events which could take place

When used in reported or indirect speech, the past conditional can also express events and situations which could actually take place: in essence it is used as a 'future in the past' to report what is expressed as a future in direct speech.

⚠ Italian and English differ. The past conditional for the 'future in the past'	Sono sicuro che verrà ➡ Ero sicuro che **sarebbe venuto** *I am sure he will come* ➡ *I was sure he would come* Chiamerò presto ➡ Mi ha/Mi aveva detto che **avrebbe chiamato** presto *I will call soon* ➡ *He told me/He had told me he would call soon* ***Or:*** Ero sicuro che **veniva** *I was sure he was coming/would come* Mi aveva detto che **chiamava** presto *He had told me he would call soon*	The past conditional expresses the future with respect to a main clause past tense (imperfect, perfect and pluperfect). In English this is a simple conditional. The imperfect is a common colloquial alternative. (See p. 262.)
	Ogni volta che sentirò la musica, penserò a te ➡ Disse che ogni volta che avesse sentito la musica, **avrebbe pensato** a lui *Every time I hear the music I will think of you* ➡ *He said that every time he heard the music he would think of him*	When there are two futures in direct speech, the future in the subordinate clause becomes a pluperfect subjunctive in reported or indirect speech. See also p. 305.

Unconfirmed facts: a special use

 Attenti! English and Italian differ.

A quanto dicono, la ragazzina **sarebbe** la figlia illegittima dell'attore *The girl is apparently the actor's illegitimate daughter* Secondo le rivelazioni del settimanale britannico, il ministro **avrebbe intrecciato** una torrida storia d'amore con la trentunenne modella. *According to the revelations of the British weekly, the minister had become involved in a steamy affair with the 31-year-old model*	The conditional and the past conditional are both used to report unconfirmed facts where in English present or past tenses are used. This is typical of news items.

✚ Esercizi

2 Say how you would have reacted in the following circumstances.

    (a) Non hanno fatto la fila, sono passati davanti a noi. Voi cosa avreste fatto? – *We would have protested*.

    (b) Sono arrivati con tre ore di ritardo. Tu come avresti reagito? – *I would have been angry.*

    (c) Mi hanno fatto pagare troppo. Tu cosa avresti fatto? – *I would have complained.*
    (lamentarsi)

3 *I would like … I would have liked.* Answer in Italian, using the appropriate conditional form of the verb used in the question: **piacere** or **volere**.

    (a) Ti sarebbe piaciuto andare? – *Yes, I would have liked to go (have gone). I would like to go tomorrow.*

    (b) Avresti voluto parlargli? – *Yes, I would have liked to speak to him. I would like to speak to him soon.*

    (c) Gli sarebbe piaciuto venire? – *Yes, he would have liked to come. He would like to come next week.*

    (d) Avresti voluto finire il lavoro? – *Yes, I would have liked to finish the job. I would like to finish it soon.*

4 Give the Italian equivalents of the English. There are two alternatives each time.

    (a) *I was convinced she would phone/she was going to phone.*

    (b) *They knew she would leave/she was going to leave.*

    (c) *He told me he would arrive at four/he was arriving at four.*

5 Give the English equivalent of the Italian.

    (a) Il ministro non sarebbe disposto a dare le dimissioni.

    (b) L'aereo sarebbe caduto dieci minuti dopo il decollo.

    (c) Il rapinatore avrebbe sparato due volte.

See also Exercise 6, p. 306 for the conditional used with the subjunctive.

22 The imperative

Imperatives (**gli imperativi**) are verb forms used for giving orders or making suggestions, e.g. *Wait! Don't come. Let's have a coffee.*

22.1 The formation of the imperative

(a) Regular forms of the imperative

In Italian, unlike English, there are separate imperative forms depending on who is being addressed.

- **Tu** imperatives are used to address one person in a familiar way.
- **Lei** imperatives are the most common way of addressing one person formally.
- **Voi** imperatives are used to address several people, both those addressed individually as **tu** and those addressed formally as **Lei**. (In some parts of Italy **voi** may be used to address one person formally.)
- **Loro** imperatives are rarely used with several people individually addressed as **Lei**: **voi** is generally preferred.
- The **noi** form of the verb is used to make suggestions (*let's … let's not/don't let's …*).

	-are aspettare *to wait*	**-ere** prendere *to take*	**-ire** finire *to finish*	**-ire** sentire *to hear*
tu	**aspetta** **non aspettare**	prendi **non prendere**	finisci **non finire**	senti **non sentire**
Lei	aspetti non aspetti	prenda non prenda	finisca non finisca	senta non senta
voi	aspettate non aspettate	prendete non prendete	finite non finite	sentite non sentite
noi	aspettiamo non aspettiamo	prendiamo non prendiamo	finiamo non finiamo	sentiamo non sentiamo
Loro	aspettino	prendino	finiscano	dormano

Attenti! Regular verbs have no separate imperative form:

- **Tu**, **noi** and **voi** imperatives are identical to their present tense forms. It is important to note, however, that **tu** imperatives of **-are** verbs are identical to their present tense 3rd person singular form.
- **Lei** and **loro** imperatives are identical to their present subjunctive forms (pp. 298–9).
- Negative imperatives: it is important to note that the **tu** forms are composed of the verb infinitive, preceded by **non**. For all other forms, **non** precedes the normal imperative.
- Regular reflexive imperatives are formed as in the table above, but with reflexive pronouns (see table p. 282).

(b) Irregular forms of the imperative

Verbs with an irregular present tense

If a verb has an irregular present tense, its imperative forms are also irregular and identical. See also the lists of irregular present tenses on pp. 239–40 Here are a few examples.

Infinitive	tu: identical to present tense	voi: identical to present tense	Lei: identical to present subjunctive	noi: identical to present tense
bere	bevi (non bere)	(non) bevete	(non) beva	(non) beviamo
salire	sali (non salire)	(non) salite	(non) salga	(non) saliamo
uscire	esci (non uscire)	(non) uscite	(non) esca	(non) usciamo
venire	vieni (non venire)	(non) venite	(non) venga	(non) veniamo
sedersi	siediti (non sederti*)	(non) sedetevi	(non) si sieda	(non) sediamoci

* Or **non ti sedere**; see Imperatives with object and reflexive pronouns, pp. 282–3.

✚ The eight main irregular imperatives

These verbs are entirely or partly irregular. The list below is complete. Irregularities are marked in bold.

Infinitive	tu	voi	Lei
avere	**abbi**	**abbiate**	**abbia**
essere	**sii**	**siate**	**sia**
sapere	**sappi**	**sappiate**	sappia
stare	**sta'* /stai**	state	**stia**
andare	**va'* /vai**	andate	vada
dare	**da'* /dai**	date	dia
dire	**di'***	dite	dica
fare	**fa'* /fai**	fate	faccia

⚠ **Attenti! Pronoun use:** when the five forms asterisked above are followed by a pronoun, the initial letter of that pronoun is doubled, except in the case of **gli**:

Fammi vedere.   *Let me see.*   Falle vedere.   *Let her see.*

But:

Fagli vedere.   *Let him see.*

For more on pronoun position with imperatives, see below.

 Esercizi

1 Give the **tu**, **Lei** and **voi** imperative forms of the phrases below.

    (a) parlare più piano

    (b) scendere subito

    (c) finire il lavoro

    (d) partire subito

2 Give the negative **tu** and **voi** imperatives of the phrases (a)–(d) above.

3 What are the **tu** and **Lei** imperatives of the following phrases?

    (a) scegliere una canzone

    (b) rimanere un po' di più

    (c) tenere la destra

    (d) venire dentro

    (e) tradurre il brano

✛ 4 Rewrite the sentences below by substituting the **tu** imperative for the **Lei** form. Then provide **voi** imperatives for sentences (a)–(c).

      (a) Abbia pazienza, è inutile arrabbiarsi.

      (b) Stia tranquillo, finiremo in tempo.

      (c) Faccia quello che vuole, per me è lo stesso.

      (d) Dica a mio marito che farò tardi stasera.

      (e) Dia l'assegno a mio cugino.

✛ (c) Pronouns and imperatives

Reflexive imperatives

These are formed exactly like other imperatives. Note that the negative **tu** imperative is formed with **non** + infinitive, and that in this case there are two possible reflexive pronoun positions: either before or after the infinitive (see Imperatives with object and reflexive pronouns below). It is also important to note where the spoken stress falls.

	accomodarsi *to come in, sit down*	**mettersi** *to put on/to put oneself*	**servirsi** *to help oneself*
tu	accomodati non accomodarti/ti accomodare	mettiti non metterti/non ti mettere	serviti non servirti/non ti servire
voi	(non) accomodatevi	(non) mettetevi	(non) servitevi
Lei	(non) si accomodi	(non) si metta	(non) si serva
noi	(non) accomodiamoci	(non) mettiamoci	(non) serviamoci
loro	(non) si accomodino	(non) si mettano	(non) si servano

 Attenti! Pay attention to the stress patterns:
Irrespective of whether the infinitive is stressed on the final vowel (e.g. **accomodarsi**) or on the previous vowel (e.g. **mettersi**), the stress pattern is the same for all imperatives except the **tu** negative form:

- In **tu, lei** and **loro** imperatives the spoken stress is on the vowel of the stem.
- In **noi** and **voi** imperatives the stress falls on the penultimate vowel of the verb ending.
- In the **tu** negative form the stress falls where it normally does in the infinitive. For -**are** and -**ire** verbs, this is on the infinitive vowel ending. For -**ere** verbs, the stress is usually in the stem (**mettere, perdere, ricevere**), but some common verbs have the stress on the infinitive vowel ending (e.g. **avere, rimanere, sedere, tenere**).

Imperatives with object and reflexive pronouns

Pronouns are usually attached to the end of the **tu, voi** and **noi** imperative forms but always come before the **Lei** and **Loro** forms.

tu	voi	noi	Lei	Loro
Prendi**lo** *Take it* Sbriga**ti** *Hurry up*	Prendete**lo** *Take it* Sbrigate**vi** *Hurry up*	Prendiamo**lo** *Let's take it* Sbrighiamo**ci** *Let's hurry up*	**Lo** prenda *Take it* **Si** sbrighi *Hurry up*	**Lo** prendano *Take it* **Si** sbrighino *Hurry up*

With negative **tu** imperatives, pronoun position is usually flexible and does not significantly alter the meaning: it can be attached to the verb or precede it.

Non prender**lo**/Non **lo** prendere.   *Don't take it.*

 Attenti! With the **noi** form, take care to distinguish a suggestion from a statement. The key is the pronoun position. Pronouns are joined to the end of **noi** imperatives but otherwise precede finite verbs. Compare:

Andiamoci subito.   *Let's go (there) right away.* (**noi** imperative)
Ci andiamo subito.   *We are going (there) right away.* (**noi** present tense)
Divertiamoci.   *Let's enjoy ourselves/have fun.* (**noi** imperative)
Ci divertiamo.   *We enjoy ourselves/have fun.* (**noi** present tense)

✛ Esercizi

5 Give the Italian equivalent of the following, using **tu** and **Lei** imperatives.

(a) *Do it at once.* (**fare**)   (b) *Tell her to come.* (**dire a**)   (c) *Go (there).* (**andare**)

6 Give the negative **tu** and **Lei** imperatives of (a) and (c) above.

7 Give the English equivalent of the following using **tu** imperatives and then **voi** imperatives. Notice where the spoken stress falls.

(a) *Wake up!*   (d) *Ask him to come.* (**chiedere a**)
(b) *Finish it.*   (e) *Put on your coat.* (**mettersi**)
(c) *Sit down.* (**sedersi**)   (f) *Have fun!* (**divertirsi**)

8 Which of the sentences below are suggestions?

(a) mettiamolo qui   (d) andateci domani
(b) lo mettiamo qui   (e) ci andiamo domani
(c) non metterlo qui   (f) andiamoci domani

◎/✛ 22.2 Uses of the imperative

(a) Main uses

To give orders	**Esci** di qui! **Uscite** di qui! *Get out (of here)!*
To give instructions	**Prenda** la prima strada a sinistra *Take the first road on the left* **Fate soffriggere** la cipolla *Fry the onion*
To make suggestions or invitations	**Facciamo** una pausa *Let's take a break* **Non prendiamo** un tassì *Don't let's take a taxi*
To make requests	**Abbi** pazienza! *Bear with me!*
To advise and persuade	**Non fumare tanto** *Don't smoke so much* **Stammi bene** *Take care* **Siate** prudenti ragazzi *Be careful everyone* Per ricevere la tua calcolatrice, **spedisci** subito il buono! *To receive your calculator, send off the coupon immediately!*

- In advertisements the **tu** form is very common, although **voi** and (very occasionally) **Lei** forms are also used.
- For general instructions, see also p. 285.

◎ Esercizi

1 Give the Italian equivalent of the following. Use the **Lei** imperative unless specified.

    (a) *Do sit down.* (also **voi** form)

    (b) *Pass me the salt.*

    (c) *Give me a bit of bread, please.*

    (d) *Make us a coffee, please.*

    (e) *Bring us the bill, please.*

2 These are some of the instructions you gave when you took your nieces and nephews on an outing. What would you have said if you had only taken one of them?

    (a) Guardate bene prima di attraversare la strada.

    (b) State attenti!

    (c) Non toccate niente

    (d) Non sedetevi lì!

    (e) Uscite di qui.

    (f) Sbrigatevi!

3 Match up the questions and answers. Which answers are **noi** imperatives?

    (a) Aspettiamo Giulio?

    (b) Cosa fate?

    (c) Perché non andiamo al cinema?

    (d) Andate al cinema?

    (i) Aspettiamo Giulio.

    (ii) Sì, ci andiamo fra poco.

    (iii) Sì, aspettiamolo allora.

    (iv) Ottima idea, andiamoci.

◎/✚ (b) Special uses of imperative forms

The imperatives of **dare**, **sentire**, **dire** and **fare** have common colloquial uses.

dare	Non te lo dico. – Ma **dai**, non è mica un segreto! *I'm not telling you. – Go on, it's not actually a secret*	Lit. *give*. Used for persuasion or encouragement.
sentire	**Senti,** è inutile aspettare *Look, it's useless to wait*	Lit. *hear,* like the English *look* or *hey*. The **lei** form is used to attract attention in a shop or restaurant.
	Senta! Ci porti il pane per piacere *Excuse me! Bring us the bread, please*	
dire	Carlo, ti voglio parlare. – **Dimmi** *Carlo. I need to speak to you. – Go ahead*	Lit. *tell me*. The **tu** form is a common way of encouraging someone to speak. while the **lei** form is used in shops to offer help.
	Mi dica, signora *Can I help you, Madam?*	
non dire	**Non me lo dire**! *You don't say!* **But:** **Non dirmelo** *Don't tell me*	With **dire** the position of the pronouns alters the meaning. But see also p. 283.
fare	**Fammi pensare** *Let me think/see* **Fatti sentire** *Get in touch*	These expressions are commonly used.

✚ Note also the imperative uses of **sapere** and **volere**.

sapere	Se le scriverai presto, **sappi** che la farai felice *I'd like you to know/You should know that if you write to her soon, you'll make her happy* **Sappiate** che con me non si scherza! *You'd better know that you can't mess around with me!*	The **tu** and **voi** imperative forms are commonly used to emphasise what you want someone to know.
volere	**Voglia** gradire i miei migliori saluti *Please accept my very best wishes/Yours faithfully*	The **lei imperative** form is often used to end formal letters.

◎/✚ (c) Other imperatives

The infinitive as imperative

The infinitive is not only used as the negative **tu** imperative form. It is very often used in all kinds of impersonal instructions such as public notices and announcements.

spingere *push* **rallentare** *slow down* **lavare ad acqua fredda** *wash in cold water* **allacciare le cinture** *fasten (your) seatbelts* **non sporgersi** dal finestrino *do not lean out of the window*	The infinitive is used when there is an indeterminate readership.

Other impersonal imperatives

In advertisements, in newspapers and on TV and radio, both the **tu** and the **voi** forms are widely used to address an unknown readership.

Intestino pigro? **Risveglialo** con gusto! **Scopri** un biscotto buonissimo, ricco di fibre prebiotiche *Sluggish digestion? Wake it up/Kick-start it with something nice! Discover a delicious biscuit rich in prebiotic fibres*	**Tu** is particularly prevalent in advertisements.
Tagliate le banane a fettine e **grigliatele** leggermente *Cut the bananas into slices and lightly grill them* Per evitare il mal d'auto **evitate** percorsi accidentati o strade con molte curve *To avoid car sickness, avoid bumpy or winding roads*	**Voi** is often used to give instructions and advice, e.g. in recipes. However, the infinitive is also used (see Exercise 7, p. 286), with a more impersonal effect.

✚ In general public announcements, **essere pregato/i** + an infinitive is used in preference to an imperative.

Il signor Cardelli **è pregato di** presentarsi immediatamente alla porta d'imbarco numero 12 *Would Mr Cardelli please go immediately to gate number 12?* **Siete pregati di** rimanere seduti *We ask you/You are asked to remain seated*	This is a common way of making polite public announcements.

✚ Questions as imperatives

The imperative is quite often avoided in order not to sound too abrupt or authoritarian. It is substituted by a variety of polite requests, for example, a question in the present tense; **potere/volere** + infinitive or **ti/le/vi dispiace** + infinitive.

	Imperative *Bring me some water*	Alternative (i) *Can/Could you/Would you bring me some water?*	Alternative (ii) *Do you mind bringing me some water?*
tu	Portami un po' d'aqua	Mi porti un po' d'aqua? Puoi/Vuoi portarmi un po' d'aqua?	Ti dispiace portarmi un po' d'aqua?
lei	Mi porti un po' d'aqua	Mi porta un po' d'aqua? Può/Vuol(e) portarmi un po' d'aqua?	Le dispiace portarmi un po' d'aqua?
voi	Portatemi un po' d'aqua	Mi portate un po' d'aqua? Potete/Volete portarmi un po' d'aqua?	Vi dispiace portarmi un po' d'aqua?

To be extra polite, the conditional may also be used instead of the present:

Mi porteresti un po' d'aqua?/Potresti portarmi un po' d'aqua?

Would you/Could you bring me some water?

Le dispiacebbe portarmi un po' d'aqua?

Would you mind bringing me some water?

◎/✛ Esercizi

4 What do you say? Pick the appropriate expression.

  (a) *You try to attract the shop assistant's attention:* Senti!/Senta!

  (b) *You can't believe your ears:* Non dirmelo!/Non me lo dire!

  (c) *You want your friend to pay attention:* Senti/Ascolti.

5 Ask for what you want in Italian, using the **Lei** form.

  (a) (i) *Can/Could you bring me the bill?*   (ii) *Bring me the bill.*

  (b) (i) *Make me a coffee.*   (ii) *Can you make me a coffee?*

6 Look at the general instructions in the infinitive on p. 285 (**spingere**, **rallentare**, etc.) and give their **tu** form.

7 Here are some instructions from a magazine on looking after a Christmas tree before bringing it into the house. Rewrite it as if you were telling an acquaintance (**Lei**) what to do.

Evitare le piante a radice nuda che perdono presto gli aghi. **Scegliere** piuttosto un albero in un vaso. **Mettere** la pianta all'aperto e **a̲nnaffiare** abbondantemente quando la temperatura è sopra lo zero. Nei giorni successivi **tenere** il terriccio (*compost*) umido. Prima di portarla in casa **spruzzare** i rami.

✛ **8** This is taken from a leaflet on child health on holiday. Read the information about adder bites, then change the instructions as though you were telling friends, by replacing the infinitives in bold with **voi** imperatives.

Morso di vipera: la vipera è l'unico velenoso* presente in Italia. È diffusa* in tutte le regioni ad eccezione della Sardegna.

Nella sede* del morso, più spesso un arto* inferiore, compare* immediatamente un forte dolore e poco dopo una spiccata* tumefazione … Le misure di pronto soccorso al malcapitato* devono essere volte ad* impedire la diffusione del veleno inoculato:

  – **Distendere** il paziente evitandogli sforzi fisici.

  – **Legare** un laccio emostatico* (o ciò che di simile si dispone), a monte del* morso, avendo cura di rimuoverlo per pochi istanti ogni 10 minuti …

  – **Iniettare** siero antiofidico*: metà nella parte colpita e metà per via intramuscolare alla radice dell'arto interessato*.

  – In alternativa **praticare** una incisione tra i segni lasciati dai denti (della vipera) e **spremere** la ferita fino al sanguinamento*.

  – **Trasportare** il paziente all'ospedale più vicino.

(In vacanza con i bambini)

> • velenoso *poisonous creature* • diffusa *refers to* la vipera • sede *site (of the bite)* • un arto *limb* • compare *appears* • spiccata *pronounced* • malcapitato *victim* • volte a *aimed at* • laccio emostatico *tourniquet* • a monte del *above* • siero antiofidico *antisnake serum* • radice dell'arto interessato *the joint of the limb concerned* • fino al sanguinamento *until it bleeds*

23 Non-finite verb forms

Non-finite verb forms have no specified subject or tense. They are: the infinitive (e.g. *to eat*); the gerund (e.g. *singing*); and participles – past and present (e.g. *established, establishing*). Unlike finite verbs, these forms cannot be conjugated because they do not have separate forms for each person or tense. However, they are widely used in Italian and are extremely versatile parts of speech.

◎/✛ 23.1 The infinitive

There are two infinitive forms: the simple infinitive (**l'infinito presente**) and the past infinitive (**l'infinito passato**).

(a) Forms of the simple infinitive

The simple infinitive (**l'infinito presente**) is the form used in the dictionary to identify a verb: *to see, to go*, etc.

-are/-arsi	-ere/-ersi	-ire/-irsi	Italian infinitives generally end in **-are**, **-ere** or **-re**, but also in **-arre**, **-orre** and **-urre**. Reflexive infinitives mostly end in **-arsi**, **-ersi** and **-irsi**, though some end in **-orsi** and **-ursi**.
parlare lavarsi	perdere iscriversi	dormire stupirsi	
-arre/-arsi	**-orre/-orsi**	**-urre/-ursi**	
trarre sottrarsi	porre opporsi	condurre ridursi	

 Attenti! The reflexive infinitive **si** changes to match the subject of the verb on which the infinitive depends.

Conviene iscriver**si**.	*It is advisable to enrol.*	Vogliamo iscriver**ci**.	*We want to enrol.*
Devi iscriver**ti**, Maria.	*You must enrol, Maria.*	Volete iscriver**vi**.	*You want to enrol.*

◎/✛ (b) Uses of the simple infinitive

The infinitive is used a great deal in Italian. It is important to note that its English equivalents include gerunds (e.g. *shouting*) and finite verbs (*he shouts*) as well as the standard infinitive forms *to shout, to speak*, etc.

After prepositions and prepositional phrases	Sono venuto per **aiutare** *I have come to help* È partito senza **salutarci** *He left without saying goodbye to us* Lavati le mani prima di **mangiare** *Wash your hands before eating/you eat*	Others include: **fuorché, invece di, oltre a, piuttosto che, tranne**. Note that **prima che** takes the subjunctive (see p. 301)
After verbs taking prepositions	Ha cominciato a **gridare** *He began to shout/shouting* Ricordati di **chiamarmi** *Remember to call me*	The final **-e** of the infinitive is dropped when it is followed by a pronoun.

After modal verbs	Devo **uscire** *I have to go out* So **nuotare** *I can swim* Potrei **farlo** domani *I could do it tomorrow*	**Dovere, potere, volere** always require an infinitive verb. For **sapere** see also p. 319.
Two infinitives together	È andato via senza **poter vedere** la figlia *He went away without being able to see his daughter*	If the modal verb itself is in the infinitive, it drops the final **-e** before another infinitive.

In the following cases the infinitive is used only when the subject in both clauses of a sentence is the same. If the subjects differ, a subjunctive verb is used, generally after **che**.

After exclamations with **che**	Che bello **essere** qui! *How nice to be here!* Che strano **vedersi** dopo tanto tempo! *How odd to see each other after so long!* Che peccato **dover partire** *What a pity to have to leave/that we have to leave*	See p. 300 for **che peccato che, che strano che**, etc. + subjunctive.
After impersonal verbs and expressions	È importante **studiare** *It is important to study* Bisogna **partire** *It is necessary to leave* Non vale la pena **andarci** *It is not worth going* Tocca a te **farlo** *It's up to you to do it*	For the subjunctive with **è importante che, bisogna che**, etc. see p. 300.
After verbs of emotion	Preferisco **stare** qui *I prefer to stay here* Le dispiace **ripetere**? *Do you mind repeating?* Non m'interessa **imparare** a guidare *I'm not interested in learning to drive*	Others include: **piacere, odiare, sperare, temere**. For their use with the subjunctive, see p. 300.
✚ After verbs of opinion, belief, knowing and doubt + **di**	Crede di **essere** malato *He believes he is ill* Penso di **venire** *I am thinking of coming/I think I will come* Non credo di **poter venire** *I don't think I can come*	Others include: **dire, dubitare, sembrare, parere, sapere**. For their subjunctive use, see pp. 300–1.

The following uses are also important.

For general advice	Da **vedere** *What to see/Must be seen* Dove **stare/dormire** *Where to stay* Con chi **viaggiare** *Who to travel with* Come **arrivare** *How to get there*	As in English, the infinitive is used for advising an indeterminate readership, usually after **da**, or **dove, chi**, etc.
Indirect speech	Marco sa cosa **fare**/dove **andare**/con chi **parlare**/come **andarci** *Marco knows what to do/where to go/who to talk to/how to get there* Hanno discusso come meglio **proteggere** l'ambiente *They discussed how best to protect the environment*	In indirect speech, as in English, the infinitive follows **cosa, dove, chi, come**, etc. For **perché** + infinitive, see p. 309.
✚ Direct speech: conjecture and possibility	**Che fare?** *What do you do?/What should you do?/What does one do?/What's to be done?* **Cosa dire** se qualcuno si rifiuta di pagare? *What do you/should you/does one say if someone refuses to pay?*	Unlike English, the infinitive is used in an indefinite context after interrogatives: the subject is unspecific.
	Uscire con loro? Ma scherzi! *Go out with them? You must be joking!* **Perdonarlo**? Mai! *Forgive him? Never!*	The infinitive sometimes stands on its own and usually refers to an unwelcome possibility.

✚ As a noun	**Piangere** non serve a niente *Crying is pointless/It's pointless to cry* Non sopportava **l'abbaiare** del cane *He couldn't stand the barking of the dog* Con il/Col **passare** del tempo il dolore si attenua *As time passes the pain lessens*	Italian infinitives can correspond to the English *-ing* form used as a noun. In formal Italian and in some set phrases, the infinitive used as a noun can be preceded by the masculine articles **il/l'/lo**.
As an imperative	**Tirare** (on a door) *Pull* **Non correre!** *Don't run!*	See also pp. 280 and 285 for full explanations.
✚ With verbs of perception	L'ho visto **arrivare** *I saw him arrive*	See also pp. 315–8.

◎/✚ Esercizi

1 Complete the sentences by giving the Italian equivalent of the English.

    (a) Non devi partire … *without paying.*

    (b) Ti vedrò … *before I leave.*

    (c) Non so … *how to thank you* (**tu**)

    (d) Bisogna … *change trains in Milan.*

    (e) Che strano … *to see you here!*

    (f) Mio figlio mi ha detto … *where to go.*

✚ **2** Give the Italian equivalent of the English.

    (a) *I like travelling by train.*

    (b) *I'm thinking of leaving.*

    (c) *I hope to see you soon.*

    (d) *I doubt I can come.*

✚ **3** Complete the sentences.

    (a) Abbiamo discusso (*how to improve*) i risultati.

    (b) Come si fa a (*improve*) i risultati?

    (c) Come (*do you improve*) i risultati?

✚ **4** Give the Italian equivalent of the English.

    (a) *Eat it? You must be joking!*

    (b) *Go for a walk? No, I'm too tired.*

    (c) *My favourite pastime is playing cards.*

    (d) *Having a shower saves water.*

✚ **5** Read this newspaper article about a new letter scanning service in Switzerland.

    (a) Identify the infinitives in the article.

    (b) Which three Italian infinitives are dependent on a preposition?

    (c) Which one depends on an interrogative word?

    (d) What is the grammatical function of the other infinitives?

Il nuovo servizio della Posta Svizzera

Il servizio prevede la scansione* della lettera ancora chiusa e l'invio di una e-mail con l'immagine della busta.

Tocca poi al destinatario* della lettera comunicare alla Posta cosa fare della busta chiusa:

- Aprirla e scansionare il contenuto per consentire all'utente di leggerla online.
- Spedirla, sempre chiusa, a un indirizzo a scelta*.
- Riciclarla.
- Passarla in una macchina tritadocumenti* e distruggerla.
- Archiviare il contenuto.

(*La Repubblica*, 22 giugno 2009)

> • prevede la scansione *provides for the scanning* • tocca poi al destinatario *it is then up to the addressee* • a scelta *of his/her choice* • macchina tritadocumenti *shredder*

✦ (c) Further uses: Italian infinitive – English gerund

 Attenti! In Italian, unlike English, the infinitive is used to express simultaneous actions, whereas in English the gerund (*-ing* form) is used. In the following cases it is important not to use the Italian gerund.

Sta tutta la giornata **ad ascoltare** la musica *He spends* (lit. *stays*) *all day listening to music* **Ho passato** la giornata **a pensare** ai miei problemi *I spent the day thinking about my problems* I bambini **erano occupati a costruire** castelli di sabbia *The children were busy building sandcastles* **Era seduta a guardare** la TV *She was sitting watching TV* **Eccolo a girare** di notte per la città *There he is/was, wandering through the city at night*	To express simultaneous actions, **a** + the infinitive is used after **stare** *to be*, **rimanere** *to stay*, **trovarsi** *to find oneself*, **passare** *to spend* (*time*), **essere occupato** *to be busy*, or after verbs expressing position: **essere seduto/ disteso** *to be sitting/lying*, etc. The construction may also follow **ecco.** See also Verbs and prepositions, p. 335.

✦ Esercizio

6 Complete the sentences by giving the Italian equivalent of the English.

    (a) Sta a letto tutta la giornata … *reading novels.*

    (b) Erano seduti intorno al tavolo … *playing bridge.*

    (c) Hanno passato la giornata … *mending the car.*

    (d) Era distesa sul divano … *eating chocolates.* (**cioccolatini**)

◎/✦ 23.2 The past infinitive

The past infinitive (**l'infinito passato**) corresponds literally to forms such as *to have seen, to have gone,* but the English equivalents are more varied than these standard forms.

(a) Forms of the past infinitive

The past infinitive is made up of the infinitive of **avere** or **essere**, plus the past participle of the verb.

The final **-e** of **avere** (and sometimes **essere**) may be dropped. Reflexive forms have the pronoun **si** attached to **essere**, but, as with the simple infinitive, the reflexive pronoun changes to match the subject on which the infinitive depends.

aver mangiato	**aver** ricevuto	**aver** dormito/finito
essere andato/a/i/e	**essere** venuto/a/i/e	**essere** partito/a/i/e
essersi lavato/a/i/e	**essersi** seduto/a/i/e	**essersi** divertito/a/i/e

✦ Past infinitives of modal verbs

Note that the past infinitive of modal verbs is followed by the simple infinitive. The usual auxiliary is **avere**, whatever auxiliary the following verb normally takes.

È assurdo … **aver**	**dovuto** **potuto** **voluto**	mangiare/venire	*It is absurd to have …*	*had to* *been able* *wanted to*	*to eat/come*

Pronoun position and participle agreements

Position	Mio marito è contento di non aver**lo** comprato *My husband is glad he didn't buy it* (lit. *not to have bought it*)	Object and reflexive pronouns are always attached to the auxiliaries **essere** or **avere**.
Agreement	Credo di **essere partito/a** alle undici *I think I left at eleven* È un peccato **non essere arrivati** prima *It's a shame not to have arrived earlier* È in carcere per **averla uccisa** *He is in jail for having killed her* **But**: È in carcere per **aver ucciso** Maria	The past participles of infinitives taking **essere** agree with the subject of the verb in the main clause. If this is indefinite, the agreement is always masculine plural. The past participle of infinitives taking **avere** only agrees with a preceding direct object pronoun. (See also Past tenses, p. 255.)

◎/✚ Esercizi

1 'I am pleased to have …' Give the past infinitive form of the following simple infinitives. Sono contento di:

    (a) pagare i debiti   **(b)** ricevere il pacco   **(c)** uscire con te   **(d)** divertirsi

✚ **2** Complete the sentences, giving the Italian equivalent of the English.

    (a) È un peccato … *to have had to leave.* (**dover partire**)

    (b) Mi dispiace … *not to have been able to come.* (**non poter venire**)

✚ **3** Complete the following in Italian, making the necessary participle agreements.

    (a) Sono contento di aver comprato i pantaloni. – *I am pleased I bought them.*

    (b) È un sollievo aver venduto la casa. – *It's a relief to have sold it.*

    (c) È un peccato *not to have left together.* (**partire**)

    (d) È un peccato *not to have travelled together.* (**viaggiare**)

✚ (b) Uses of the past infinitive

The past infinitive is used after a variety of tenses to refer to completed actions preceding the time of speaking, whether this is future, present or past. Otherwise, with a few exceptions, its uses coincide with those of the simple infinitive. It is important, for example, to note that, like the simple infinitive, the past infinitive is used only when the subject of the verbs in both clauses is the same. Otherwise the subjunctive is used. (See p. 300.)

After prepositions and prepositional phrases	Andrò a Milano dopo **aver visto** Gianni *I'll go to Milan after I have seen/after seing (after having seen) Gianni* Mi ha chiamato prima di **aver avuto** la risposta *He called me before he (had) got (having got) the reply* Ero partito senza **averlo visto** *I had left without seeing him/having seen him*	You will notice from the first example that the English equivalents of the past infinitive are varied. Note also that **dopo** is only used with a past infinitive. For **dopo che** and **prima che** + the subjunctive, see p. 301.
After verbs taking prepositions	Mi ricordo di **averlo letto** *I remember having read it/I read it* Mi vergogno di **aver imbrogliato** Dino *I'm ashamed that I cheated Dino* Ti ringrazio/Grazie per **avermi chiamato** *Thanks for calling/having called me*	Note that **grazie per** and **ringraziare** are only used with a past infinitive.

| After modal verbs | Devo **aver sbagliato** *I must have made a mistake*
Potrei **averlo dimenticato** *I might/could have
forgotten it* | **Dovere, potere, volere**
always require an infinitive verb.
For **sapere** see also p. 319. |

In the following cases, the past infinitive is used only when the subject in both clauses of the sentence is the same. If the subjects differ, a subjunctive verb is used after **che**.

After exclamations with **che**	Che peccato non **esserci andati**! *What a shame not to have gone/that we didn't go* Che bello **averti visto** *How lovely to have seen you!*	For the subjunctive use, **che peccato che**, etc., see p. 300.
After impersonal verbs	Bisognava **averlo capito** prima *It was necessary to have understood that before/It was necessary for us to have understood that before*	For the subjunctive use, **bisognava che**, etc., see p. 300.
After verbs of emotion	Sono contento/a di **esserci andato/a** *I am pleased I went (to have gone) there* Mi dispiace non **aver potuto aspettare** *I am sorry I couldn't wait/that I couldn't wait*	For the subjunctive use, **sono contento che**, etc., see p. 300.
After verbs of saying, belief, opinion and doubt	Dice di **essere stato** da Mario *He says he has been at Mario's* Eravamo sicuri di **averlo visto** We *were sure we had seen him*	For the subjunctive use, **pensare che** etc., see p. 300.

✦ Esercizi

4 Complete these sentences in Italian.

    (a) Che sollievo di … *to have found the keys.*

    (b) È un peccato … *not to have gone there.*

    (c) Dubito di … *(that) I have understood.*

    (d) Mi dispiace … *(that) I had to leave.*
       (dover partire)

5 Simple or past infinitive? Give the Italian equivalent of the English.

    (a) *I went out without having breakfast.*

    (b) *They left without having paid.*

    (c) *Thank you for helping us.*

    (d) *I'll come and see you after I've talked
    to him.*

6 Give the English equivalent of the following.

    (a) Credo di partire lunedì.

    (b) Credo di essere partito lunedì
    scorso.

    (c) Sono felice di vederlo domani.

    (d) Sono felice di averlo visto ieri.

    (e) Non posso sposarmi prima di finire
    gli studi.

    (f) Non posso sposarmi prima di aver finito
    gli studi.

◎/✦ 23.3 The gerund

The gerund (**il gerundio**) is used to provide additional information about the main verb, e.g.
Mi sono rotto la gamba <u>giocando</u> a calcio *I broke my leg **playing** football.*
There are two forms: simple gerunds (e.g. *playing*) and past gerunds (e.g. *having played*).

(a) The forms of simple and past gerunds

The simple gerund (**il gerundio presente**) is invariable except for the reflexive **si**, which changes to **mi**, **ti** etc. depending on who the gerund refers to. It has two forms only: **-ando** is added to the stem of **-are** verbs, and **-endo** is added to the stem of **-ere** and **-ire** verbs.

-are ➡ ando	-ere ➡ endo	-ire ➡ endo
parlare **parlando**	ricevere **ricevendo**	dormire/finire **dormendo/finendo**
lavarsi **lavandosi**	sedersi **sedendosi**	divertirsi **divertendosi**

The gerunds of irregular verbs all end in **-endo**, e.g. **bere** ➡ **bevendo**, **dire** ➡ **dicendo**, **fare** ➡ **facendo**. See pp. 243 and 265 for the full forms.

The past gerund (**il gerundio passato**) consists of the gerund of **avere** or **essere**, plus the past participle. It is invariable except for past participles, which follow the rules of agreement with the subject or object (see p. 254–5).

-are	-ere	-ire
parlare avendo parlato	**ricevere** avendo ricevuto	**dormire/finire** avendo dormito/finito
andare essendo andato/a/i/e	**venire** essendo venuto/a/i/e	**partire** essendo partito/a/i/e
lavarsi essendosi lavato/a/i/e	**sedersi** essendosi seduto/a/i/e	**divertirsi** essendosi divertito/a/i/e

Pronoun position

Pronouns are normally attached to the end of simple gerunds and to the auxiliary of past gerunds unless they are part of a finite verb, e.g. the present or imperfect continuous.

Portando**lo** a casa.   *Bringing it home.*

Avendo**lo** portato a casa.   *Having brought it home.*

But: **Lo** sto portando a casa.   *I am bringing it home.*

(b) Uses of the simple and past gerund

The simple gerund is more frequently used than the past gerund.

Expressing simultaneous actions: *while/as*	**Svegliandomi** stamattina, mi è venuta in mente la soluzione *As I woke up this morning the solution came to mind* (lit. *waking up this morning …*) L'appetito viene **mangiando** *One's/Your appetite comes while/as you eat* (with eating)	Simple gerunds only. The simple gerund expresses what is going on while another action takes place. Note that the English equivalent is often *as/while*, followed by a finite verb.
Modality: *how*	È entrata, **piangendo** *She came in, crying* Risponde sempre **sorridendo** *He always replies smiling* (with a smile)	Simple gerunds only.
Under what conditions: *by* and *if*	**Leggendo** quel libro imparerai un sacco di cose *You will learn a load of things by reading/if you read that book* Ho imparato l'italiano **ascoltando** una cassetta *I learned Italian by listening to a cassette* **Sbagliando** s'impara *You learn by* (making) *your mistakes*	Simple gerunds only.

Cause: since/ because ✚	**Essendo** tardi ho dovuto partire *Since it was late I had to leave* **Avendo fatto** la spesa è tornata a casa *Since she had/When she had/Having done the shopping she went home*	Simple and past gerunds. Sometimes the gerund is simply used for concision rather than to emphasise cause. This is typical of formal written Italian.
Concession: despite/even though/ although ✚	**Pur essendo** ricco era tirchio *Even though he was rich he was mean* **Pur avendo preso** l'ombrello si è bagnato *Although he took/Despite having taken the umbrella he got wet*	**Pur** (pure) + simple or past gerund. See also p. 222.
In continuous tenses	Stiamo **pranzando** *We are having lunch* Stavano **pranzando** *They were having lunch* Staranno **pranzando** *They will be/must be having lunch*	**Stare** + the simple gerund express the English present, imperfect and future continuous. See pp. 243–4, 265 and 247.

✚/⚠ **Attenti!** Same subject as main verb

It is important to note that the gerund usually has the same subject as the main verb. A gerund cannot be used if it refers to a subject which differs from the main verb subject. **Che** or **mentre** + a finite verb must be used instead.

Passeggiando lungo il fiume ho visto tua figlia **Facendo** la spesa ... ho incontrato Maria **But:** Ho incontrato Maria **che faceva** la spesa Ho incontrato Maria **mentre faceva** la spesa	*As I walked along the river I saw your daughter* *While (I was) doing the shopping I met Maria* *I met Maria (who was) doing the shopping* *I met Maria while she was shopping*

An exception to the above rule is with impersonal expressions.

Essendo buio, mi sono perso	*Since it was dark, I got lost*

◎/✚ **Esercizi**

1 How do you do it? Answer the questions in Italian using the correct form of the gerund.

(a) Che bella casa. Come hai fatto a comprarla? – (Lavorare) come un matto e (risparmiare) la metà dello stipendio.

(b) Studi tanto di notte, come fai a resistere? – (Bere) caffè e (fumare) come un turco!

(c) Gli affari vanno benisssimo, come ha fatto? – (Studiare) il mercato e (offrire) un servizio sempre migliore.

✚ **2** While/As I was ... Express some of the events of your day in Italian, using a simple Italian gerund where appropriate.

(a) *Going into town I met Giuseppe on the bus.*

(b) *As I crossed Piazza della Repubblica I saw the police arresting two men.*

(c) *On my way home/As I was going home, I saw Letizia talking to Adriano.*

✚ **3** Why not? Explain why you didn't do the following things, using the correct form of the past gerund.

(a) Perché non sei uscito con noi? – Beh, (essere) malato mi è sembrato più prudente.

(b) Come mai non hai voluto vedere il film? – Beh, (sentire) le critiche mi è passata la voglia.

(c) Come mai avete rifiutato l'invito? – Beh, (mangiare) così male l'altra volta, abbiamo preferito andare da Laura!

✚ 4 Gerund or infinitive? Express the following in Italian.

(a) *I hate waiting.*

(b) *They were sitting there waiting for me.*

(c) *She ran off screaming.* (**scappare via**)

(d) *Screaming is pointless.*

✚ 5 Read this extract from an essay by the detective writer Andrea Camilleri. Identify the gerunds, then give the English equivalent of each.

Un pomeriggio dell'estate del 1932, avevo 7 anni, pigliai* il coraggio a due mani e, approfittando della dormitina pomeridiana* dei genitori, mi impadronii di una chiave proibitissima, salii una rampa di scale e mi trovai davanti alla porta del 'tetto-morto', il solaio*. Intuivo che doveva essere un luogo pieno di tesori per le mie fantasie, ma l'accesso me ne era severamente negato. In effetti, oltre che inondato di polvere, era alquanto* pericoloso: non essendo pavimentato*, bisognava camminare da una trave* all'altra, evitando le fragili traversine* che si sarebbero potute spezzare* sotto il peso.

(Andrea Camilleri, 'Il mio debito con Simenon', in *Racconti quotidiani*, Oscar Mondadori, 2008)

> • pigliai *I seized* • dormitina pomeridiana *afternoon snooze* • 'tetto-morto', il solaio *'dead (space) roof', attic/loft* • alquanto *rather* • non … pavimentato *there being no flooring* • trave *beam, joist* • traversine *cross-beams* • si sarebbero potute spezzare *which could have given way/snapped*

✚ 6 This is an extract from Umberto Eco's novel *Il nome della rosa*. There has been a murder. The narrator, Adso, and his master, the friar Guglielmo, come out of the church into the cloister and spot one of the monks, Berengario, whose behaviour they find suspicious. Read the text and focus on the phrases in bold.

E mentre doppiavamo* il lato orientale del tempio* scorgemmo Berengario **che usciva** dal portale del transetto* … Guglielmo lo chiamò, quello* si arrestò e lo raggiungemmo …

"Dunque, pare che tu sia stato l'ultimo a vedere Adelmo* vivo", gli disse.

Berengario vacillò come stesse per* cadere in deliquio*:

"Io?" domandò con un filo di voce*. Guglielmo aveva buttato la sua domanda quasi a caso*, probabilmente perché Bencio* gli aveva detto di **aver visto i due* confabulare** nel chiostro dopo vespro*. Ma doveva avere colto nel segno* e Berengario **stava chiaramente pensando** a un altro e veramente ultimo incontro*, perché cominciò a parlare con voce rotta,

"Come potete dire questo, io l'ho visto **prima di andare a riposare** come tutti gli altri."

(Umberto Eco, *Il nome della rosa*, Bompiani, 1980)

> • doppiavamo *walked along* • tempio *church* • portale del transetto *the transept door* • quello *he* (i.e. Berengario) • Adelmo *the murdered man* • come stesse per *as if he were about to* • in deliquio *into a faint* • con un filo di voce *in a whisper* • aveva buttato … a caso *had hit on his question almost by chance* • Bencio (a scholar from Uppsala whom they had already interrogated) • i due (i.e. Adelmo and Berengario) • confabulare *conferring* • vespro *Vespers* • doveva avere colto nel segno *he must have struck home* • ultimo incontro *reference to the Day of Judgment*

(a) Give the English equivalent of the four phrases in bold.

(b) **che usciva**: why can this not be **uscendo**?

(c) **di aver visto**: express this with a finite Italian verb.

(d) **i due confabulare**: express this phrase with a finite verb. (For a grammatical explanation, see Chapter 25, Verbs of perception, p. 318).

(e) **stava … pensando**: is this a finite or non-finite construction? (Refer to Chapter 20, p. 265 if you need help.)

◎/+ 23.4 The past participle

The past participle (**il participio passato**) is the form of the verb which is used with **avere** and **essere** in compound tenses (see p. 359). It is also used in passive constructions (see p. 325–6). On its own the past participle can be used to introduce a concise dependent clause, and it is mostly, though not exclusively, typical of formal written Italian.

(a) Forms of the past participle

Regular forms of the past participle end in **-ato**, **-uto** and **-ito** (see p. 252), but there are many irregularities, especially of **-ere** verbs (see p. 253).

bagnare ➡ bagnato *wet*	temere ➡ temuto *feared*	pulire ➡ pulito *clean*

Pronoun position and participle agreements

| Agreement | Una volta **fatto**, non ci penso più *Once it's done I don't think about it any more/I put it out of my mind* **But**: Una volta **imboccata** la strada, vedrete la casa a sinistra *Once you have turned into the road you'll see the house on the left* Una volta **arrivati** alla stazione, vi consiglio di prendere un tassì *Once you have arrived at the station I advise you to take a taxi* | With verbs taking **avere**, the past participle is invariable unless there is a direct object. In this case the participle agrees with the object. With verbs taking **essere,** past participles agree with the subject of the verb. |
| **+** Pronoun position | Trovato**si** solo, si spaventò *On finding himself alone, he became frightened* | Pronouns are attached to the participle. This is not used in speech. |

◎/+ (b) Uses of the past participle

Apart from being used in compound tenses with either **essere** or **avere** as auxiliaries, the past participle has the following uses.

| As a participle | **Data** la situazione, io rimango qui *Given the situation, I'm staying here* Ecco, **detto fatto**! *Right, no sooner said than done!* | In Italian if the participle qualifies a noun, it agrees with it in number and gender. |
| As an adjective | Mi devi mandare i contratti **firmati** (che sono stati firmati) *You must send me the signed contracts* | Used as adjectives, past participles agree with the noun they modify. They often replace a relative clause. |

The past participle is often used to replace longer clauses. It is used with a variety of tenses, as the participle simply refers to actions preceding the main verb, irrespective of tense.

| Expressing as soon as, once | Una volta **arrivati** al semaforo, dovete girare a destra *Once you've got to/arrived at the traffic light you have to turn right* **Or:** *Having arrived at the traffic lights you have to turn right* | The participle here could also express *having arrived*, but the English equivalent is usually a whole clause with a finite verb. The past participle is often preceded by (**non**) **appena,** or **una volta**, especially in speech. |

✚ Expressing *when … after*	**Finita** la partita, torneremo a casa *When the match ends, we'll go home* **Finita** la partita, siamo tornati a casa *When the match ended, we went home* **Finita** la partita, eravamo tornati a casa *After the match had ended, we had gone home*	The past participle can replace *when/after* + a finite verb in a dependent clause. Note the variety of tenses possible in the main clause. The participle here cannot express *having finished*, as the subjects in the two clauses are different. See below.

✚ When the subjects in both clauses are the same, the past participle is often used instead of the past gerund or past infinitive (*having …* and *after having …*).

> **Finiti** i soldi si mise a cercare un lavoro
> *Or:* **Avendo finito/Dopo aver finito** i soldi si mise a cercare un lavoro
> *Having run out of money/When he had run out of money, he set about looking for a job*

◎/✚ Esercizi

1 Rewrite the following, making each sentence more concise by using a past participle to replace the verbs in italics and changing the word order where necessary.

    (a) Una volta che *aveva fatto* la spesa Luisa è tornata a casa.

    (b) Appena *saranno finite* le lezioni, andremo in centro.

    (c) Una volta che *siete arrivati* in albergo, mi dovete chiamare.

    (d) Appena *hai passato* il ponte e la farmacia, troverai la strada a destra.

2 Look back at the text by Camilleri in Exercise 5 on p. 295 and give the English equivalent of **oltre che inondato di polvere**.

✚ **3** Complete the sentences by giving the Italian equivalent of the English.

    (a) *When the car was mended*, hanno potuto partire.

    (b) *When the boat left*, sono tutti tornati a casa.

    (c) *After she received the bad news*, Marinella si ammalò.

✚ **4** Express the following in Italian.

    (a) *Having resolved the problem, he felt calmer.* (**tranquillo**)

    (b) *Having finished his exams, he went on holiday.*

    (c) *Having just found my glasses I managed to lose my keys!*

(c) A note on the present participle

The present participle (**il participio presente**) is formed by adding -**ante** to the stem of -**are** verbs and -**ente** to the stem of -**ere**, -**ire** and irregular verbs. Like adjectives ending in -**e**, the present participle has a plural in -**i**:

amare ➡ **amante/amanti** *loving*	vincere ➡ **vincente/vincenti** *winning*	partire ➡ **partente/partenti** *leaving*

Nowadays it is mostly used as an adjective or noun, and is recognisable in such familiar words as: **arrogante, sorridente, insegnante, studente**.

The present participle is used increasingly rarely as a verb, and is found mostly in bureaucratic language. It tends to replace a relative clause.

    La circolare ministeriale n. 533 **istituente**   *The ministerial circular **establishing** …*
    il modello 45 …

    Il registro degli atti non **costituenti** reato …   *The register of acts not **constituting** a crime …*

24 The subjunctive

The subjunctive (**il congiuntivo**) is a form of the verb known as a mood. This is used to express a variety of attitudes such as uncertainty, possibility, emotions and desires. In Italian there are four subjunctive tenses, but in English subjunctive forms are rare and usually old-fashioned: *If your father were here, he would be happy. So be it.*

◎/+ 24.1 The present subjunctive

(a) Regular forms

The easiest way to form the present subjunctive is to start from the present tense and change the **io** form.

	parlare: o ➡ i	vendere: o ➡ a	dormire: o ➡ a	finire: o ➡ a
Indicative	parl**o**	vend**o**	dorm**o**	finisc**o**
Subjunctive	parl**i**	vend**a**	dorm**a**	finisc**a**

The full conjugations are as follows: note that -**ere** and -**ire** verbs have identical endings.

io	parl**i**	vend**a**	dorm**a**	finisc**a**
tu	parl**i**	vend**a**	dorm**a**	finisc**a**
lui/lei/Lei	parl**i**	vend**a**	dorm**a**	finisc**a**
noi	parl**iamo**	vend**iamo**	dorm**iamo**	fin**iamo**
voi	parl**iate**	vend**iate**	dorm**iate**	fin**iate**
loro	parl**ino**	vend**ano**	dorm**ano**	finisc**ano**

- The singular forms of the present subjunctive are identical (e.g. io/tu/lui/lei **parli**). This means that if the context does not make the subject clear, then subject pronouns are used.
- All the forms except **noi** and **voi** are based on the **io** 1st person form (e.g. **finisco ➡ finisca/finiscano** but **finiamo, finiate**).
- The **noi** forms are identical to the indicative present, but the **voi** forms all end in -**iate**.
- Spelling. As with future and conditional tenses, verbs with -**care** and -**gare** endings require the addition of an -**h** to keep the hard sound of the infinitive: e.g. **cercare** – cer**chi**, **pagare** – pa**ghi**. Verbs in -**ciare**, -**sciare** and -**giare** drop the -**i** of the stem, as it is not needed to keep the soft sound of the infinitive: e.g. **lasciare** – lasc**i**, **mangiare** – mang**i**.

◎/+ (b) Irregular forms of the present subjunctive

Verbs with an irregular indicative present

Irregularities in the present indicative are reflected in the present subjunctive: if a verb has an irregular indicative present tense, then its present subjunctive is also irregular. As with the regular present subjunctive (see above), all the forms except **noi** and **voi** are based on the 1st person singular (**io**). The following are some of the most common irregularities.

Infinitive	Indicative	Subjunctive					
andare	vado	**vada**	vada	vada	andiamo	andiate	vadano
bere	bevo	**beva**	beva	beva	beviamo	beviate	bevano
dire	dico	**dica**	dica	dica	diciamo	diciate	dicano
dovere	devo/debbo	**debba**	debba	debba	dobbiamo	dobbiate	debbano
fare	faccio	**faccia**	faccia	faccia	facciamo	facciate	facciano
potere	posso	**possa**	possa	possa	possiamo	possiate	possano
rimanere	rimango	**rimanga**	rimanga	rimanga	rimaniamo	rimaniate	rimangano
tenere	tengo	**tenga**	tenga	tenga	teniamo	teniate	tengano
venire	vengo	**venga**	venga	venga	veniamo	veniate	vengano
volere	voglio	**voglia**	voglia	voglia	vogliamo	vogliate	vogliano
uscire	esco	**esca**	esca	esca	usciamo	usciate	escano

Debba is the most common form of the present subjunctive of **dovere**, but **deva** also exists. Although all the subjunctive **voi** forms end in -**iate**, there are a few which are not based on the **voi** indicative forms:

dite ➡ **diciate**, dovete ➡ **dobbiate**, fate ➡ **facciate**, potete ➡ **possiate**, volete ➡ **vogliate**

Very irregular forms

The following five common verbs are the only ones not derived from the present indicative **io** form.

Infinitive	Indicative	Subjunctive					
avere	ho	**abbia**	abbia	abbia	abbiamo	abbiate	abbiano
essere	sono	**sia**	sia	sia	siamo	siate	siano
dare	do	**dia**	dia	dia	diamo	diate	diano
sapere	so	**sappia**	sappia	sappia	sappiamo	sappiate	sappiano
stare	sto	**stia**	stia	stia	stiamo	stiate	stiano

Note that the present continuous **stare** + gerund can be made subjunctive: **sto leggendo** ➡ **stia leggendo**.

◎/✚ **Esercizi**

1 Form the present subjunctive of the verbs given to say what you want others to do.
   (a) Vuoi che io gli (mandare) il pacco?
   (b) Voglio che tu gli (scrivere) qualcosa.
   (c) Voglio che loro (dormire) subito!
   (d) Vuoi che lo (finire) io?
   (e) Vuole che tu lo (pagare) adesso.
   (f) Voglio che loro (cominciare) presto.

2 Ask what others prefer you to do by using the correct subjunctive form of the verb.
   (a) Preferisci che lo (fare) io?
   (b) Preferisce che ci (andare) io?
   (c) Preferisci che glielo (dare) io?
   (d) Preferite che glielo (dire) io?

✚ 3 Have a guess. Can you form the present subjunctive singular form of the verbs below? They have irregular indicative present tenses. If necessary, consult the irregular present tense verb section on pp. 239–40.
   (a) contenere
   (b) intervenire
   (c) riuscire
   (d) produrre
   (e) opporre
   (f) attrarre

◎/✚ (c) The main uses of the present subjunctive

The subjunctive is frequently used in Italian but its use has become increasingly flexible, especially in the spoken language. In many cases it is a question of personal or stylistic choice. The following are guidelines to some of the most common uses.

In independent sentences: *let …* *may …* ✚	**Che** venga quando gli pare *Let him come when he wants* **Viva** l'Italia! *Long live Italy!* (lit. *May Italy live*)	The subjunctive can express a wish – usually heartfelt.
Maybe, perhaps	**Può darsi che** sia vero *It may be true/* *Perhaps it's true* ***But:*** Forse è vero	The subjunctive is always used after **può darsi che** but not with **forse**, which means the same.

The present subjunctive is also used to form some imperatives. (See p. 281.)

In the cases which follow, note:

(i) A subjunctive is used in a dependent clause when its subject differs from the main clause subject. If the subjects are the same, an infinitive is often used instead of a subjunctive (see p. 288).
(ii) The present subjunctive is used when the action in the dependent clause is possible and refers mainly to the present or future.
(iii) The main clause verb is usually in the present or the future tense and occasionally in the **passato prossimo.** See pp. 306–8 for a full explanation of the subjunctive tense sequence.

With verbs expressing emotion and feeling	**Mi auguro che** tornino presto *I hope they will return soon* **Ho paura che** sia troppo tardi *I'm afraid it's too late* **Che peccato che** Barbara sia malata *What a shame that Barbara is ill*	Others include: **sperare, piacere, dispiacere, preferire, temere, non vedere l'ora** (*to look forward to*), **essere contento,** **è incredibile/bello/strano … che.**
Expressing need, possibility, probability and uncertainty	**È facile/difficile che** arrivino lunedì *They are likely/unlikely to arrive on Monday* **Non è detto che** vengano *It's not definite that they are coming/* *They won't necessarily come*	See also: **avere bisogno che, bisogna che, è necessario che, è possibile/probabile che, mi/ti/gli capita che.**
Expressing value judgements	**Non importa che** sia ricco *It doesn't matter that he is rich* **È naturale che** siano arrabbiati *It's natural they should be angry*	Also: **non vale la pena che, conviene che, è … logico/meglio/normale/importante/essenziale … che.**
With verbs of thinking, believing and opinion	**Mi pare che** vadano via domenica *I think they're going away on Sunday* **Avrà l'impressione che** io sia gelosa *He will have the impression I am jealous* **Direi che** sia depresso *I would say he's depressed*	Others include: **credere, pensare, ritenere, supporre, immaginare, sembrare.** ⚠ The subjunctive is not used with **dico che.** See p. 301.

+ Expressing hearsay and doubt	**Si dice che** abbia una casa che vale 100 milioni *It is said she has a house worth 100 million* **Non so che cosa** lui stia leggendo *I don't know what he's reading*	See also: **non so se, non capisco se, dubitare**. See also Negatives, p. 186. ⚠ **No** subjunctive with **dico che**.
+ Denial and negation	**Non dico che** sia antipatica ma si comporta male *I'm not saying she is unpleasant but she behaves badly*	Also: **negare, non è che**. ⚠ **Dico che** does not take the subjunctive.
+ Wishes, requests, orders and permission	**Vuoi che** lo faccia io? *Do you want me to do it?* **Permette che** glielo dica? *Will you let me tell him?*	Other verbs include: **chiedere, insistere, lasciare, pregare, pretendere, esigere, evitare, ordinare, proporre, suggerire**.
+ With some connectives of time	Chiamalo **prima che** vada via *Call him before he goes away* **È ora che** Ivo mi aiuti *It's time Ivo helped me* **But:** Chiamalo prima di andare via *Call him before you leave* È ora di aiutare Ivo *It's time to help Ivo*	Others include: **finché/ fino a quando** (**non**). Note also **aspettare che**. If the subjects are the same in both clauses, **prima, è ora** and **aspettare** are followed by **di** + an infinitive. See also p. 226.

⚠ **Attenti!** No subjunctive
- The future indicative can replace the present subjunctive in affirmative sentences with verbs of opinion, belief and emotion: the use of the subjunctive depends largely on the speaker's degree of conviction.

  Penso che sarà/sia difficile convincerlo.   *I think it will be hard to persuade him.*
  Spero che verranno/vengano.   *I hope they come.*

- Expressions such as **dire che, essere evidente/ ovvio/vero che** do not require subjunctives:
  È chiaro che sta male.   *It's clear he is unwell.*
  Dicono che è brava.   *They say she is clever.*

  However, **si dice che, direi che** and **non dico che** do require the subjunctive, as they express hearsay and negation:

  Si dice che sia brava …   *It is said/They say she is clever …*
  Direi che sia brava …   *I would say she is clever …*
  Non dico che sia brava …   *I'm not saying she is clever …*

 Esercizi

4 You tell others what needs to happen. Express the English in Italian.

(a) Nicola, non hai ancora pagato l'affitto? *It's essential that you pay it soon.*

(b) Silvana e Giorgio non hanno spedito il pacco? *It's important that they send it tomorrow.*

(c) Voi non sapete se venite domani? *But it's necessary for me to know today.*

5 Discuss possibilities using the appropriate form of the verb. The English is given to help.

(a) È difficile che (venire) tutti quanti. (*It's unlikely that they will all come.*)

(b) È possibile che il treno (essere) in ritardo. (*It's possible that the train may be late.*)

(c) Non è detto che loro (tornare) stasera. (*They won't necessarily come back tonight.*)

6 Say how you feel, using the expressions in the order given to begin the sentences. Make the necessary changes to the verb.

mi fa piacere che • mi dispiace che • temo che • che peccato che • ho paura che • non è giusto che

(a) Tu stai meglio.

(b) Lei non ha più tempo.

(c) Loro vogliono lamentarsi di nuovo.

(d) Loro non possono venire.

(e) Lucio è malato.

(f) Lo fanno loro.

7 Express your thoughts and impressions using the correct form of the verb given.

(a) Ho l'impressione che Carlo (bere) troppo.

(b) Mi sembra che Luca (mangiare) tanto.

(c) Non credo che loro (rimanere) stasera.

(d) Non dico che (tradire) la moglie.

✚ **8** Make requests and demands using the correct form of the verb given.

(a) Giovanni, lascia che lo (fare) tuo fratello. *(Giovanni, let your brother do it.)*

(b) Lavinia permetti che io (finire) il mio discorso? *(Lavinia, will you allow me to finish what I'm saying?)*

(c) Voglio che Simone mi (dare) una mano. *(I want Simone to give me a hand.)*

✚ **9** Select the correct form of the verb. Beware – not all of the sentences require a subjunctive verb. In a few cases either is possible.

(a) Sono sicuro che Anna è/sia infelice.

(b) Non dico che lui è/sia antipatico.

(c) Dici che sono/siano tutti corrotti?

(d) Si dice che lui ha/abbia miliardi.

(e) Spero che tu torni/tornerai.

(f) Temo che sia/sarà troppo tardi.

✚ **10** Change the subject. Rewrite the last part of the second sentence using the appropriate verb form.

(a) Mi dispiace non poter venire. – Mi dispiace che Lei …

(b) Non credo di riuscire a farlo in tempo – Non credo che lui …

(c) Prima di andar via voglio parlarti. – Prima che tu …

✚ **11** Identify the sentences which require a subjunctive in Italian and supply the correct form of the verb.

(a) *I prefer to do it.*

(b) *I prefer you to do it.*

(c) *I want to come.*

(d) *I want them to come.*

(e) *It's important to understand.*

(f) *It's important you understand.*

✚ **12** Identify the subjunctives in these questions taken from a magazine quiz:

- Preferisci che le persone ti considerino: creativo, preciso, organizzato?
- Pensi che le persone che ti vogliono bene concentrino la loro attenzione sui tuoi difetti?
- Ritieni che le basse performance delle persone che ti stanno attorno spesso rallentino i tuoi progressi nello studio o nel lavoro?
- Ti capita che* le persone che ti stanno attorno ti dicano che pretendi* troppo da loro?

(Focus, novembre 2008)

> Ti capita che *Does it happen that* • pretendi *expect*

✚ 24.2 The past subjunctives

There are three past subjunctive tenses: the perfect, the imperfect and the pluperfect.

(a) Forms and uses of the perfect subjunctive

This is formed with the present subjunctive of **essere** and **avere** plus the past participle of the relevant verb.

	parlare	partire
io	abbia parlato	sia partito/a
tu	abbia parlato	sia partito/a
lui/lei/Lei	abbia parlato	sia partito/a
noi	abbiamo parlato	siamo partiti/e
voi	abbiate parlato	siate partiti/e
loro	abbiano parlato	siano partiti/e

 Remember that **avere** takes the auxiliary **avere** (**abbia avuto**) and **essere** takes **essere** (**sia stato**). See p. 252.
Irregularities concern the past participles only. To revise their use, see p. 253.

Uses of the perfect subjunctive

The perfect subjunctive shares the same basic uses as the present subjunctive (see pp. 300–1). Its time frame is also the present, but it refers to a completed action preceding the time of speaking. It may be used in conjunction with the following main verb tenses, but always with reference to the present.

Main verb	Examples
Present Future	Immagino che si **siano divertiti** *I expect/imagine that they enjoyed themselves* Penseranno che tu non **abbia avuto** tempo di scrivere *They'll think that you haven't had/didn't have time to write*
Passato prossimo Conditional	Mi è dispiaciuto che tu **non abbia vinto** il premio *I was sorry you did not win the prize* Direi che **abbia sbagliato** *I would say he has made a mistake*

See pp. 306–8 for the complete sequence of tenses with the subjunctive.

✛ Esercizi

1 Complete the sentences by giving the Italian equivalent of the English.

(a) Sarà contento che tu … *you came/have come.*

(b) Ho l'impressione che … *he has not understood.*

(c) Non credo che … *they want to come.*

(d) Direi che … *they have forgotten.*

2 Give the Italian equivalent of the English.

(a) *I imagine it has been difficult.*

(b) *Maybe he has already left.*

(c) *It's odd that they haven't called.*

(d) *Do you think he has had an accident?*

(b) Forms of the imperfect subjunctive

This is formed from the stem of the verb as follows.

	parlare	vendere	finire
io	parlassi	vendessi	finissi
tu	parlassi	vendessi	finissi
lui/lei/Lei	parlasse	vendesse	finisse
noi	parlassimo	vendessimo	finissimo
voi	parlaste	vendeste	finiste
loro	parlassero	vendessero	finissero

The **io** and **tu** forms are identical. If the context does not make the meaning clear, the subject pronouns are used.

The only irregularities are **essere**, **dare**, **stare** and verbs with contracted infinitives. The regular -**ere** endings are used in all these cases except for **essere**.

essere	fossi	fossi	fosse	fossimo	foste	fossero
dare	dessi	dessi	desse	dessimo	deste	dessero
stare	stessi	stessi	stesse	stessimo	steste	stessero
bere	bevessi	bevessi	bevesse	bevessimo	beveste	bevessero
dire	dicessi	dicessi	dicesse	dicessimo	diceste	dicessero
fare	facessi	facessi	facesse	facessimo	faceste	facessero
trarre	traessi	traessi	traesse	traessimo	traeste	traessero
porre	ponessi	ponessi	ponesse	ponessimo	poneste	ponessero
condurre	conducessi	conducessi	conducesse	conducessimo	conduceste	conducessero

Note that the imperfect continuous **stare** + gerund can be made subjunctive: **stare leggendo** ➡ **stessi leggendo**.

(c) Forms of the pluperfect subjunctive

This is formed from the imperfect subjunctive of **avere** or **essere** plus the past participle of the verb.

	parlare	**partire**
io	avessi parlato	fossi partito/a
tu	avessi parlato	fossi partito/a
lui/lei/Lei	avesse parlato	fosse partito/a
noi	avessimo parlato	fossimo partiti/e
voi	aveste parlato	foste partiti/e
loro	avessero parlato	fossero partiti/e

Irregularities concern the past participles only. To revise them, see p. 253. Remember that **avere** takes the auxiliary **avere**, while **essere** takes **essere**: **avessi avuto**; **fossi stato**.

✚ Esercizi

3 Insert the correct imperfect subjunctive form of the verb given.

    (a) Voleva che (io – tornare) il giorno dopo.

    (b) Sperava che (tu – potere) aiutare.

    (c) Era contento che (noi – studiare).

    (d) Non sapevo se (voi – capire) anche l'arabo.

4 Provide the correct imperfect subjunctive form of the verb given.

    (a) Pensavo che Matilda (essere) in Australia!

    (b) Credevo che voi (avere) da fare.

    (c) Era contento che noi (stare) con lui.

    (d) Era ora che Marco ci (dare) una mano.

    (e) Mi dispiaceva che Giulio e Antonio (bere) tanto.

    (f) Volevo che tu lo (tradurre) in fretta.

5 Complete the sentences by giving the Italian equivalent of the English.

    (a) Pensavo che ... *they had returned.*

    (b) Era contento che ... *we had studied.*

    (c) Non sapevo se ... *you* (tu) *had understood.*

    (d) Era strano che ... *he had gone out early.*

(d) Specific uses of imperfect and pluperfect subjunctives

Imperfect and pluperfect subjunctives share the basic uses of the subjunctive (see p. 309). They differ from the present and perfect subjunctive in that they generally (but not always) refer to a past time frame and express finished actions or hypothetical events. Their main specific uses are as follows:

With words expressing hypotheses	Si comporta **come se** fosse un genio *He behaves as though he were/was a genius* **Magari** avessi finito! *If only I had finished!*	See p. 309.
Possible conditions	**Se dovessi passare** per Pisa, mi farò sentire *If I (should) come through Pisa, I'll look you up/get in touch* **Se dovessi vedere** Ida, che cosa le dico? *If I happen to see Ida, what shall I say?*	The use of **se dovessi** in conjunction with a future (or present) rather than a conditional verb (see box below) is common when you want to suggest that the action is by no means definite.
	Se **dovessi** vincere il Totocalcio, non so cosa farei *If I were to win/If I won the lottery I don't know what I would do* Se **avessi** più tempo, ti aiuterei *If I had more time I would help you*	The imperfect subjunctive is used to refer to hypothetical cases, where the action is still possible, usually, but not exclusively, in conjunction with the simple conditional.
Unrealised conditions	Se mi **avessi chiamato,** sarei andata a prenderti *If you had called me I would have gone to collect you* ***But:*** Se non **avessi bevuto** tanto starei meglio! *If I hadn't drunk so much I would feel better!*	The pluperfect subjunctive is used when the condition has not been met, usually, but not exclusively, with the past conditional (see **Se non avessi bevuto … starei meglio**). See also p. 278 and **Attenti!** below.

 Attenti! Pluperfect subjunctive plus past conditional also expresses 'future in the past'

This combination expresses not only unrealised conditions but also hypotheses or possible conditions and promises recounted in the past (the 'future in the past': see p. 278 and Exercise 4, p. 279). This may sometimes seem ambiguous, but the context usually makes the meaning clear. Compare:

1. Ho sempre pensato che se mi **fossero venuti** i dolori a casa, **avrei aspettato** quasi fino all'ultimo momento prima di andare in ospedale.
   I have always thought that if I were to go/went into labour at home I would wait until almost the last minute before going to hospital. (Hypothesis)

2. Penso che se mi **fossero venuti** i dolori a casa, **avrei aspettato** quasi fino all'ultimo momento prima di andare in ospedale.
   I think that if I had gone into labour at home, I would have waited until almost the last moment before going to hospital. (Unrealised condition)

In the first example, the pluperfect subjunctive in the subordinate clause and the past conditional in the main clause are expressing a feasible hypothesis for the future – expressed in the past. The direct speech underpinning the sentence involves two verbs in the future: **Se mi verranno i dolori … aspetterò** …

In the second example it is clear that the events have not taken place.

For the subjunctive sequence of tenses, see chapter 24.3.

✦ Esercizi

6 What would happen if … What would have happened if …? Complete the sentences.

   (a) *If you came/were to come to my place* … potremmo partire insieme.

   (b) *If they had arrived earlier* … non avremmo perso il treno.

   (c) *If I lost/were to lose my job* … sarebbe un disastro.

   (d) *If he had not quarrelled with the boss* … non avrebbe perso il posto.

   (e) *If I earned more* … avrei già pagato i debiti.

   (f) *If I hadn't broken my leg* … ti aiuterei a traslocare.

7 In which two sentences above could the imperfect subjunctive of **dovere** + the infinitive replace the imperfect subjunctive?

8 Rewrite the sentences below, reporting what was actually said. Begin with the phrases given.

   (a) Se cambierai lavoro, non ti parlerò mai più. (Mi ha detto che se io …)

   (b) Daremo un premio a chiunque risolverà/avrà risolto il problema. (Dissero che …)

   (c) Ti compreremo la macchina quando ti sposerai/ti sarai sposato. (Hanno detto che gli …)

✦ 24.3 The subjunctive sequence of tenses

The majority of subjunctives occur in a subordinate clause. The appropriate tense to use depends on its temporal relationship to the main clause, i.e. (i) future/posterior, (ii) contemporaneous or 'ongoing', (iii) past/previous time.

(a) Present/future tense main verbs

Main clause	Subordinate clause	Time referred to
1. Future and present indicative*	✔ **future/present subjunctive/present indicative*** ➡ **present subjunctive** ◤ **imperfect/perfect subjunctive**	Future: **domani/fra poco**, etc. Now: **oggi/in questo momento**, etc. Past: **ieri, di recente**, etc.
Examples Credo che *I believe that*	✔ partirà/parta/parte domani ➡ stia male in questo momento ◤ stesse male ieri sera ◤ abbia perso il portafoglio di recente	*he will leave/will be/is leaving tomorrow* *he is unwell at the moment* *he was feeling unwell last night* *he has lost his wallet recently*

* In colloquial Italian the present indicative may be used instead of the present subjunctive to refer to the future. See p. 301.

⚠ **Attenti**! The subjunctive tense sequence is subject to variation and does not always conform to watertight rules. For example, the **passato prossimo** may have the same subjunctive tense sequence as in the table above, especially when it refers to recent events.

   Mi è dispiaciuto che tu non **abbia vinto** ieri.   *I was sorry that you didn't win yesterday.*

   Ho temuto che questo film ti **possa** dispiacere.   *I have been/was afraid that you might not like this film.* (now or very soon)

Compare with the following example, which is a past time frame (see table below):

Ho temuto che quel film ti potesse dispiacere.	*I was afraid that you may/would not like that film.* (at the time)

✛ (b) Past tense main verbs

Main clause	Subordinate clause	Time referred to
2. All past tenses	✔ **past conditional/imperfect subjunctive/indicative*** ➡ **imperfect subjunctive** ◀ **pluperfect subjunctive**	Future: **l'indomani/il giorno dopo** Now: **quel giorno/in quel momento** Past: **il giorno prima/ precedente**
Examples Credevo/Ho creduto che *I believed that* Avevo creduto che *I had believed that*	✔ sarebbe partito/partisse/(partiva) il giorno dopo* ➡ stesse male quel giorno ◀ avesse perso il portafoglio il giorno prima ✔ sarebbe rimasto/rimanesse/rimaneva di più ➡ fosse malata quel giorno ◀ fossero rimasti al mare	*he would leave/would be/was leaving the next day* *he was feeling unwell that day* *he had lost his wallet the day before* *he would stay/would be/was staying longer* *she was ill that day* *they had stayed at the seaside*

* In colloquial Italian the imperfect indicative may be used instead of the subjunctive or past conditional to refer to the future. See p. 262.

✛ (c) Tense sequence with conditional verbs in the main clause

The sequence of tenses after conditionals depends in part on whether the time frame is past or present.

Main clause	Subordinate clause	Time referred to
3. Present and past conditionals	✔ **imperfect subjunctive** ➡ **imperfect subjunctive** ◀ **pluperfect subjunctive**	Future Now Past
Examples Sarebbe meglio che la **chiamasse** lui *It would be best if he called her/if he were to call her* Mi sarebbe piaciuto che Mara **venisse** con la figlia *I would have liked Mara to come with her daughter* Non avrei mai sospettato che **fosse** straniero *I would never have guessed he was a foreigner* Sarebbe stato meglio se mi **avessero consultato** *It would have been better if they had consulted me*		Future Future Now Past

Sometimes, for greater immediacy, the present conditional may be followed by the present or perfect subjunctive, rather than by the imperfect or pluperfect subjunctive.

Direi che **abbiano** ragione *I would say they are right*	Now
(Direi che **avessero** ragione) *I would say they were right*	Now
Non si direbbe che **sia stata** lei a lasciarlo	Recent past
You wouldn't say/couldn't tell that she is one who has left him	
(Non si direbbe che **fosse stata** lei a lasciarlo)	Past
You couldn't tell it was her who left him	
Sembrerebbe che nessuno **abbia visto** il ladro	Recent past
It would seem that no one has seen the thief	
(Sembrerebbe che nessuno **avesse visto** il ladro	Past
It would seem that no one had seen the thief	

✚ Esercizi

1 Give the English equivalent of these sentences and identify the time relationship between the subjunctive and the main verb: F (future), C (contemporaneous), P (past).

(a) Speriamo che vengano presto.

(b) Speravo che venissero presto.

(c) Sono contento che tu stia qui.

(d) Ero contento che loro stessero insieme.

(e) Crederà che tu non abbia fatto niente.

(f) Sembrava che nessuno avesse visto niente.

(g) Sarebbe assurdo che pagasse lui.

(h) Non si direbbe che avesse studiato.

2 In which two sentences do the subjunctives not refer to future time with respect to the main verb?

(a) Ho insistito che scrivesse subito.

(b) Avevo chiesto che venissero più tardi.

(c) Mi piacerebbe che tu imparassi il francese.

(d) Credo che abbia avuto un incidente.

(e) Credo che fosse qui ieri.

(f) Avrei voluto che pagasse lui.

3 Complete the sentences by providing the Italian equivalent of the English, using a subjunctive verb each time.

(a) Era strano che … *no one was there.*

(b) Era strano che … *no one had replied.*

(c) Mi sarebbe piaciuto che … *them to come.*

(d) Era un peccato che Angela … *had not come.*

4 Make the commands and requests below less abrupt by beginning with the expressions below and making the necessary changes to the verbs.

mi piacerebbe che tu • sarebbe meglio che Lei • mi farebbe piacere se tu • vorrei che voi

(a) Vieni con noi.

(b) Lo dica a loro, non a me.

(c) Fallo subito.

(d) Me lo spiegate?

✚ 24.4 Further uses of the subjunctive

(a) The subjunctive with indefinites and connectives

Most of the following indefinites and connectives can be used with all subjunctive tenses.

Indefinites	Non essere scoraggiato, **comunque** vadano le cose *Don't be discouraged, however things go* Io ti appoggio **qualunque cosa** tu abbia fatto *I support you whatever you've done*	Others include: **chiunque, qualunque/qualsiasi, dovunque.** See pp. 170–4.

Concession and condition	**Benché** avesse voglia di venire, non è stato possibile *Although he felt like coming, it wasn't possible* Anche **ammesso che** ti abbiano provocato, la tua reazione è stata eccessiva *Even allowing for the fact that you may have been provoked, your reaction was extreme*	Others include: **nonostante, sebbene, per quanto, a condizione che, a meno che, a patto che, purché.** See also pp. 222–4.
	Che sia vero o no, non m'interessa *Whether it's true or not doesn't interest me* **Che io sappia**, non è ancora laureato *As far as I know he hasn't got his degree yet*	**che** + subjunctive is often used to express indifference to the facts: it precedes the main clause. **Che io sappia** is a set phrase.
Contradiction, cause, purpose	Te lo dico **perché** tu sappia come regolarti *I'm telling you so that you know what to expect*	Others include: **non perché** (*not because*), **di/in modo che, affinché** (*so that*). See also p. 220.
Exceptions	Devo parlargli **senza che** gli altri lo sappiano *I have to talk to him without the others knowing* **But**: Eravamo vicini senza saperlo *We were neighbours without knowing it*	Others include **eccetto/salvo che/tranne** (*except*). If the subjects are the same in both clauses, the infinitive follows. See also p. 221.
Hypotheses	**Magari fosse** vero! *If only it were true!* **Caso mai dovesse** piovere, ti passo a prendere *If it should rain/If by any chance it should rain, I'll come by and pick you up*	**Caso mai, magari, anche se** *even if*, **come se** *as if*, are used with imperfect and pluperfect subjunctives only.
	Nel caso che tu **debba** contattarmi, ti lascio il mio numero *I'll leave you my number in case you have to contact me* Gli ho lasciato il mio numero **nel caso che** mi **dovesse** contattare *I left him my number in case he should need to contact me* **Ammettendo che sia** vero, cosa farai? *Supposing it's true, what will you do?* **Ammettendo che riuscisse** a sposarlo, la poveretta se ne pentirebbe! *Suppose she did manage to marry him, the poor thing would regret it!*	**Ammettendo che** *supposing,* and **nel caso che,** may be followed by any subjunctive tense. **Anche se** takes the indicative when it means *even though* (see p. 222).

 Attenti! *Il fatto che* and *che* + subjunctive

The subjunctive is normally always used after **il fatto che** *the fact that*:

    Il fatto che tu sia giovane non è una scusa.   *The fact that you are young is no excuse.*

    Il fatto che fosse malato lo ha aiutato un po'.   *The fact he was ill helped him a little.*

But: not if followed by **è**:

    Il fatto è che sono golosi.   *The fact is that they are greedy.*

However, **il fatto di** may be used more impersonally with the infinitive:

Non è una scusa il fatto di essere giovane.   *It's no excuse to be young.*

Che is always followed by the subjunctive, but only when it precedes the main verb.

Che avesse pianto era ovvio.   *It was obvious she had been crying.*

But: Era ovvio che aveva pianto.

✚ Esercizi

1 Rewrite the sentences below replacing **ma** and **se** with the words given and providing the correct form of the verb.

   (a) È stanco, *ma* non ha fatto niente oggi. (benché/sebbene)

   (b) Andremo in piscina *se* non fa freddo. (a condizione che)

   (c) Possiamo stare a casa *se* tu non vuoi uscire. (a meno che)

   (d) Lo farò *ma* nessuno lo saprà. (senza che)

   (e) Ti lascio la chiave *se* ne hai bisogno. (nel caso che)

   (f) Anche *se* è antipatico hai fatto male a parlargli in quel modo. (ammesso che)

2 Complete the sentences by giving the Italian equivalent of the English.

   (a) *The fact that her son did not study* … le pesava molto.

   (b) *As far as I know* … suo figlio non studia.

   (c) Era evidente che … *they were not willing to help.* (essere disposto a)

   (d) *That they were not willing to help…* era evidente.

(b) The subjunctive in relative and interrogative clauses

All subjunctives may be used in relative clauses introduced by superlative, indefinite or negative antecedents (i.e. the word or phrase to which **che** refers).

After a superlative antecedent to a relative clause	È la ragazza **più simpatica che** io **conosca** *She's the nicest girl I know* È la coppia **più generosa che** io **abbia** mai **conosciuto** *They are the most generous couple I have ever met* È **l'unica** soluzione **che abbia** un senso *It's the only solution that makes sense*	A superlative antecedent is a phrase containing an adjective with **più**, **meno** or **solo**, **unico**, **primo**, **ultimo**.
After an indefinite antecedent to a relative clause	Ci sono circostanze che giustificano la prescrizione di antidepressivi ai bambini? – **Nessuna che** mi **venga** in mente … – *None that I can think of* Non conosco **nessuno che** lo abbia fatto *I don't know anyone who has done it* Bisogna trovare **qualcuno che** lo sappia fare *You need to find someone who knows how to do it* **But:** Conosco qualcuno che lo sa fare *I know someone (specific) who knows how to do it*	Common indefinite antecedents are **nessuno, niente, qualcuno, qualcosa, uno**. These must refer to someone or something unspecified that may not exist.
After an interrogative antecedent	**Non so chi** sia *I don't know who he is* **Non capisco come** l'abbiano fatto *I don't understand how they did it* **Voleva sapere dove** fossero andati *He wanted to know where they had gone*	Interrogative antecedents are words like **chi**, **che cosa**, **come**, **dove**, **quando**, **perché**. Also **se** used, e.g., with **non sapere, non capire, chiedersi, domandarsi** and **voler sapere**. In spoken Italian the indicative is often used.

✚ Esercizi

3 Express the following in Italian.

    (a) *It's the most beautiful place there is.*

    (b) *It's the most beautiful place I have ever seen.*

    (c) *He was the only teacher who had ever helped me.*

4 Select the appropriate verb each time. In some cases either is possible.

    (a) Non conosco nessuno che sa/sappia quattro lingue.

    (b) Conosco qualcuno che sa/sappia quattro lingue.

    (c) Hai comprato un abito che ti sta/stia molto bene.

    (d) Devi trovare un abito che ti sta/stia bene.

✚ **5** The following is part of a Tuscan fairy story entitled 'La novella dell'enigma' ('The Tale of the Riddle').

    (a) Identify the subjunctives, then answer the questions that follow.

C'era una volta una povera donna che aveva un figlio disubbidiente e senza voglia di lavoro; ormai faceva la vita del vagabondo girando tra il letto e l'osteria, l'osteria e il letto.

Venne un giorno nella piazza un banditore* a leggere un editto del re per cui* chiunque avesse voluto, sarebbe potuto andare a presentarsi alla principessa a porgli un enigma: se la ragazza avesse saputo dare la soluzione, il pretendente avrebbe subito mozzata* la testa; se invece la donna non fosse riuscita a interpretarlo l'avrebbe sposato.

The young man sets off, determined to win the princess's hand by devising a riddle she cannot answer. Although he succeeds, the princess is unwilling to marry him, but agrees to spend one night with him, surrounded by guards and servants, in a vast bed with a porcupine skin between them. He nevertheless wins her hand by his cunning and wit.

Si erano appena messi tra le lenzuola, a distanza di parecchi metri uno dall'altro, quando il ragazzo disse:

"Serenissima principessa, vi* pare che stiano bene tutte queste guardie alle porte?"

"No" dovette rispondere la principessa.

"Guardie, avete sentito? La principessa non gradisce* la vostra presenza: fuori tutti!"

Le guardie se ne andarono e dopo qualche momento il ragazzo domandò:

"Vi dispiacerebbe, serenissima principessa, se si chiudessero le porte e le finestre, che* viene tanto freddo?"

"No" dovette rispondere anche questa volta la ragazza, che cominciava ad avere simpatia per quel giovanotto che era tanto astuto e simpatico.

"Servi, che aspettate? La principessa vuole che si chiuda tutto!"….

Dopo ancora un poco:

"Vi sembra che per dormire, graziosa principessa, ci sia bisogno ancora di tutti questi servi in camera?"

"No" disse la principessa che si stava divertendo a vedere quanto era scaltro* quel ragazzo. …

Erano appena usciti i servitori che il ragazzo disse:

"E ora vi offendereste, gentile fanciulla*, se io levassi questa pelle d'istrice*?"

"No."

"E vi sembra fatto bene che due giovani come noi debbano passare una notte insieme stando così lontano?"

"No."

"E vi offendereste mia cara se ora vi dessi un bacio?"

('La novella dell'enigma', in *Fiabe toscane*, Arnoldo Mondadori, 1984)

> banditore *town crier* • per cui *which proclaimed/said that* • mozzata *chopped off* • vi *used throughout as the archaic equivalent of* le *(to) you* • non gradisce *does not appreciate* • che *because* • scaltro *crafty* • fanciulla *damsel, young girl* • pelle d'istrice *porcupine skin*

(b) Give the subjunctive tense and infinitives of: **stiano, chiuda, sia, debbano**.

(c) Give the subjunctive tense and infinitive of: **si chiudessero, levassi, dessi**.

(d) In paragraph 2 look at the three main points of the King's edict (see below), bearing in mind they are presented as the town crier's reported speech (**un editto per cui** ...):

(i) chiunque **avesse voluto**, sarebbe potuto andare a presentarsi alla principessa.

(ii) se la ragazza **avesse saputo** dare la soluzione, il pretendente avrebbe subito mozzata* la testa.

(iii) se invece la donna **non fosse riuscita** a interpretarlo l'avrebbe sposato.

Give the English equivalent for each point, then for each one say what you think the town crier's actual words might have been in Italian.

Finally, say whether the pluperfect subjunctives in bold refer to the past or the future. Refer to **Attenti!** on p. 305 if you need help.

25 Special verb constructions

◎/✚ 25.1 Reflexive constructions

Many Italian verbs have a reflexive construction, which means that the subject and object coincide, e.g. **lavarsi** *to wash oneself*, **vestirsi** *to dress oneself*. These verbs are always used with reflexive pronouns (see p. 106) and usually with the auxiliary **essere** in compound tenses. There are variations on the basic reflexive construction, but broadly speaking they can be divided into reflexive and reciprocal verbs (**i verbi riflessivi, i verbi reciproci**).

(a) Uses of reflexive and reciprocal verbs

For the complete present tense reflexive verb forms, see p. 237 and, for the **passato prossimo** in full, see p. 252.

Mi lavo *I wash myself* **Mi lavo** le mani *I wash my hands*	Reflexive verbs are those which express an action that a person does to or for himself/herself directly, or indirectly.
Si chiama Adriana *Her name is Adriana* (lit. *She calls herself Adriana*) **Ci alziamo** alle sette *We get up at seven*	Note that the English equivalents may not include the words *myself, yourself, himself*, etc.
Mi sono preso/a una polmonite *I went and caught pneumonia* Ho preso una polmonite *I caught pneumonia* ✚	Many common non-reflexive verbs followed by an object are made reflexive, especially in spoken Italian, simply for greater emphasis or dramatic effect. Others include **bere/bersi, comprare/comprarsi, fumare/fumarsi, mangiare/mangiarsi.**

Some verbs with reflexive forms express **reciprocal meanings**, i.e. actions that people do to each other.

Vi vedete spesso? *Do you see each other often?* **Ci** siamo abbracciati *We embraced/hugged each other* **Si** sono scritti *They wrote to each other* *But:* La gente **si guardava**, impaurita *People were looking at each other in fright*	In reciprocal constructions, **ci**, **vi** and **si** + plural verb forms are used, except with words like **la gente**, which expresses a plural concept but is singular in form.

Verbs with reciprocal meanings include: **abbracciarsi, aiutarsi, amarsi, baciarsi, chiamarsi, conoscersi** (*to know each other, to become aquainted/to meet*), **guardarsi, insultarsi, odiarsi** (*to hate each other*), **parlarsi, picchiarsi** (*to hit each other*), **rispettarsi, scriversi, sentirsi** (*to be in touch (with each other)*), **stimarsi** (*to respect each other*), **trovarsi** (*to meet up (with each other)*), **vedersi, volersi bene** (*to love each other*).

(b) Verbs which can be either reflexive or non-reflexive

Numerous verbs have both a reflexive and a non-reflexive form, often without a fundamental change in meaning.

Mi **sono** fermato a Milano *I stopped in Milan* (lit. *I stopped myself*) **Ha** fermato il treno *He stopped the train* Si **sono** salutati *They said hello to each other* Li **ho** salutati *I said hello to them*	⚠ Note that the non-reflexive forms are used transitively, with a direct object (e.g. **treno**, **li**), and that their auxiliary is **avere**, not **essere**.

Verbs used in this way include most reciprocal verbs plus the following:
alzarsi/alzare *to get up/to raise, to put up,* **dimenticarsi/dimenticare** *to forget,* **conoscersi/conoscere** *to know oneself/to know,* **divertirsi/divertire** *to enjoy oneself/to amuse somebody,* **laurearsi/laureare** *to graduate/to confer a degree,* **lavarsi/lavare** *to wash,* **mangiarsi/mangiare** *to eat,* **mettersi/mettere** *to put on/to put, to place,* **muoversi/muovere** *to get going/to move something,* **offendersi/offendere** *to take offence/to offend,* **pettinarsi/pettinare,** *to comb/do hair,* **preoccuparsi/preoccupare** *to worry,* **ricordarsi/ricordare** *to remember/to remember, to remind,* **salutarsi/salutare** *to greet,* **salvarsi/salvare** *to save (oneself),* **scusarsi/scusare** *to apologise/to excuse somebody,* **sedersi/sedere** *to sit, be seated/to sit down,* **sentirsi/sentire** *to feel/to hear,* **spogliarsi/spogliare** *to undress, strip,* **stancarsi/stancare** *to get tired/to tire,* **tagliarsi/tagliare** *to cut (oneself),* **togliersi/togliere** *to take off/remove,* **trattenersi/trattenere** *to stay/to hold back, restrain, detain,* **trovarsi/trovare** *to find oneself, to be/to find*
Some verbs have different meanings in their reflexive and non-reflexive forms, e.g. **comportarsi** *to behave,* **comportare** *to involve.*

 Attenti! Some verbs can have a reflexive, reciprocal and non-reflexive use. Note especially:

chiamarsi/chiamare	sentirsi/sentire	trovarsi/trovare	
Come ti chiami? *What's your name?*	Mi sento male *I feel bad/unwell*	Si trova a Pisa *He/She is in Pisa*	Reflexive
Si chiamano tutti i giorni? *Do they call each other every day?*	Ci sentiamo ogni giorno *We are in touch (with each other) every day*	Dove ci troviamo stasera? *Where shall we meet up/each other tonight?*	Reciprocal
Chiamate il medico *Call the doctor*	Sento il telefono *I can hear the phone*	Hai trovato la chiave? *Have you found the key?*	Non-reflexive

Reflexive form, no reflexive meaning

Perché ti arrabbi? *Why are you angry?* Flavio si comporta male *Flavio behaves badly*	A number of Italian verbs with reflexive forms have lost their original reflexive meanings. The majority of these express a feeling, a state or an attitude of mind.

Similar verbs include: **accorgersi** *to notice, to realise,* **addormentarsi** *to fall asleep,* **annoiarsi** *to be/get bored,* lagnarsi *to complain, to moan,* **meravigliarsi** *to be amazed,* **offendersi** *to take offence,* **pentirsi** *to regret,* **rendersi conto** *to realise/be aware,* **ribellarsi** *to rebel,* **stufarsi** *to get fed up,* **stupirsi** *to be amazed/surprised,* **vantarsi** *to boast,* **vergognarsi** *to be ashamed.*

◎/✚ **Esercizi**

1 Give the Italian equivalent of the following: half of them are not reflexive constructions.

(a) *He washed himself.*	**(e)** *We kissed each other.*
(b) *He washed the car.*	**(f)** *They kissed us.*
(c) *I dressed my daughter.*	**(g)** *I felt unwell.*
(d) *I got dressed.*	**(h)** *I felt a pain.* (**un dolore**)

✚ **2** Give the English equivalent of the following and say whether the pronoun is used to denote a reflexive or a reciprocal action.

(a) Non siamo in ufficio, ci troviamo di fronte al bar.

(b) A domani, allora; ci troviamo di fronte al bar.

(c) Ciao, ci sentiamo domani.

(d) Sì, ci sentiamo bene tutti e due.

(e) Come si chiamano i suoi nipotini?

(f) Mariella e Paola si chiamano spesso.

For further practice of reflexive constructions see p. 318, Exercise 3; Chapter 7 Exercises 1–3, p. 107; Chapter 18, Exercise 4, p. 238; Chapter 20, Exercise 3, p. 254.
For reflexive verbs used with parts of the body and clothing, see pp. 24 and 139.
For agreements of the past participle of reflexive verbs, see pp. 132 and 255.

25.2 Causative verbs

Causative verbs are made up of two parts: **fare** or **lasciare** + an infinitive, e.g. **far venire qlcu.** *to get* ('cause') *sb. to come/to make sb. come.* They are used in two ways:

- to express making or letting someone do something, e.g. **far aspettare qlcu.** *to make sb. wait*; **lasciar ascoltare qlcu** *to let/allow sb. to listen.* This category also includes verbs which may refer to things rather than people, e.g. **far durare qlco.** *to make sth. last.*
- to express having something done by someone else, e.g. **far pulire qlco.** *to get/have something cleaned.*

(a) Making or letting somebody do something

Note that in Italian the object position differs from the English.

| Noun and pronoun object position | Puoi far aspettare **i clienti**? *Can you make/let/get the clients to wait?*
 Li puoi far aspettare?/Puoi far**li** aspettare? *Can you get them to wait?*
 Bisogna far durare **l'acqua** *You have to make the water last*
 Bisogna **farla** durare *You have to make it last*
 Ho lasciato passare **il camion** *I let the lorry pass*
 L'ho lasciato passare *I let it pass*
 Ha fatto arrabbiare **Pino** *She made Pino angry*
 Lo ha fatto arrabbiare *She made him angry* | In Italian, unlike English, the noun object comes after the verbs. The object pronouns follow the regular rules of object pronoun position

 If a reflexive verb such as **arrabbiarsi** follows **fare**, reflexive pronouns are omitted. |

Notice that the construction becomes a little more complicated if the agent of the action is named, as well as its direct object.

a before the agent	Perché non fai cantare quella canzone **ai bambini?** *Why don't you get the children to sing that song?* Lascia fare il lavoro **a Edda** *Let Edda do the work*	The noun agent of the action is usually preceded by **a**. The pronoun agent is either an indirect personal pronoun (e.g. **gli**, **le**, **loro**) or, for emphasis, a disjunctive, preceded by **a** (e.g. **a loro**, **a lei**).
Pronoun subjects	Perché non **gli** fai cantare quella canzone? ***Or:*** Perché non fai cantare **loro** quella canzone? (formal) Perché non fai cantare quella canzone **a loro**? *Why don't you get them to sing that song?* Lascia**le** fare il lavoro *Let her do the work* Lascia fare il lavoro **a lei** *Let her do it*	

(b) Getting or having something done

This concerns actions performed for the subject by someone else.

Noun and pronoun object position	Farò riparare la **macchina** *I'll get the car mended* **La** farò riparare *I'll get it mended* Mi faccio tagliare **i capelli** *I get my hair cut* Me **li** faccio tagliare *I get it cut*	As in section (a) above, the noun object comes after the verbs. The object pronouns follow the regular rules of object pronoun position (see pp. 119–20).

Notice that if the agent of the action is named, as well as its direct object, the former is preceded by **da**.

da before the agent	Farò riparare la macchina **da mio cognato** *I'll get my car mended by my brother in law* (i.e. *the car will be mended by him*) Mi faccio tagliare i capelli **dalla suocera** *I get my hair cut by my mother in law* (*My hair is cut by her*)	**Da** is used to express by whom something is done. It is always required when there is an implicit passive meaning and also when the causative verb **fare** is reflexive.
Pronoun subjects	**Gli** farò riparare la macchina *I'll get him to mend the car* **Le** faccio tagliarmi i capelli *I get her to cut my hair*	An indirect object pronoun is used for a pronoun agent.

 Attenti! Direct or indirect object pronouns?

You need to take account of the number of objects. Compare the following:

fare + one object + two objects	Fal**la** studiare di più *Get **her** to/Make **her** study more* Fal**le** studiare **i verbi** *Get **her** to study **the verbs*** Fa**glieli** studiare *Get **her** to study **them***	If the construction has one object, a direct object pronoun is required for the person (e.g. **la**). If there are two objects, an indirect object pronoun is required for the person. If both objects are pronouns, the object of the infinitive verb is direct (e.g. **li**).
lasciare + one object + two objects	**Lo** lasceremo scegliere *We will let **him** choose* **Gli** lascerei fare **quello che vuole** ***Or:* Lo** lascerei fare **quello che vuole** *I would let **him** do **what he wants***	Occasionally **lasciare** can take a direct object pronoun for the person even when the infinitive has another object.

(c) Alternative causative constructions

lasciare che + subjunctive	Lascia che lo **facciano** loro/i ragazzi *Let them/the children do it*	This is often used in place of **lasciare** + infinitive, but only when the dependent infinitive has a different subject from **lasciare**.
rendere	La solitudine lo **ha reso** malato/ lo **ha fatto diventare** malato *Solitude has made him ill*	**Rendere** means *to make, to cause* (something to become) and may substitute **far diventare.**

(d) Italian causative verbs ➡ English non-causative equivalents

Fare/Lasciare + infinitive also correspond to some common English non-causative constructions:

far cadere *to knock over*, **far conoscere** *to introduce sb., to acquaint sb. with*, **far entrare** *to show/let sb. in*, **far notare** *to point out*, **far pagare** *to charge sb.*, **farsi prestare** *to borrow*, **far sapere** *to inform, let sb. know*, **fare vedere** *to show*, **lasciar cadere** *to drop*, **lasciar perdere** *to forget about, ignore*, **lasciar stare** *to leave alone.*

Bisogna **fargli vedere** il conto. *We must show him the bill.*

– Ma **lascia perdere**, non pagherà mai. *– Forget it, he'll never pay.*

✚ Esercizi

1 Give the English equivalent of these sentences.

(a) Fate entrare Luigi.

(b) Perché fai aspettare Luigi?

(c) Perché non fai pagare la multa a Luigi?

(d) I capelli me li faccio tagliare da Luigi.

2 A or **da**? Select the correct form to complete the sentences.

(a) Si fa sempre ingannare (a/da) quell'uomo.

(b) Perché non ti fai prestare il libro (a/da) Ivo?

(c) Come fai a far prendere la medicina al/dal gatto?

3 Say who does what and repeat it in shortened form.

(a) *I got my sister to play the piano. – I got her to play the piano.*

(b) *I made Dino to the shopping. – I made him do the shopping.*

(c) *I let my brother drive the car. – I let him drive the car.*

(d) *I got the mechanic to adjust the brakes. – I got him to adjust the brakes*

4 Express in Italian what you get/got others to do and repeat it in shortened form.

(a) *I get the house cleaned. – I get it cleaned.*

(b) *I make my son get up. – I make him get up.*

(c) *I let my daughter go out. – I always let her go out.*

5 This is the advice you get from your friends about your children. Complete the sentences in Italian.

(a) (*Make him*) studiare di più.   (c) (*Let her*) uscire di più.

(b) (*Make him*) studiare medicina.   (d) (*Let her*) scegliere le materie che preferisce.

✦ 25.3 Verbs of perception

Verbs of perception such as **sentire, vedere, ascoltare** and **guardare** are often used before other infinitives, e.g. **sentir arrivare qlcu.** *to hear sb. arrive*, **veder partire qlcu.**, *to see sb. leave*. These follow slightly different rules from **fare** or **lasciare** + infinitive. Note that the word order may differ from the English.

Noun object position	Sentirai cantare Pavarotti? *Will you hear Pavarotti sing?* Ho visto uscire di casa Elena ***Or:*** Ho visto Elena uscire di casa *I saw Elena leave the house*	The noun direct object of the first verb often follows the infinitive, unlike English. But if the infinitive is modified by a phrase or if it has an object, the order can be similar to the English.
Personal pronoun position	**Lo** hai visto picchiare il cane? *Did you see him hit the dog?* **Li** ho sentiti dire che sei un bugiardo *I heard them say you are a liar*	When both the infinitive and the main verb have a direct object, the person is normally expressed as a DO pronoun.
Alternatives to the infinitive after **sentire, vedere,** etc.	Ho sentito piangere il bambino *I heard the baby cry* **Sentivo** il bambino **che piangeva** *I could hear the baby crying* ***But:* Sentivo che** il bambino piangeva *I could hear that the baby was crying*	**che** + a finite verb replaces the infinitive after **sentire, vedere,** etc. when the emphasis is on an action which is/was taking place. The subject precedes **che**. ***But:*** If **che** precedes the subject (**il bambino**), the meaning is different.

✦ Esercizi

1 Rewrite the following, substituting the noun given for the pronoun.
- **(a)** Dobbiamo ascoltarlo cantare. (Pavarotti)
- **(b)** L'ho guardato giocare. (mio figlio)
- **(c)** L'abbiamo visto passare. (il corteo)
- **(d)** L'ho sentito uscire di casa. (il vicino)

2 There has been a robbery. Express in Italian the questions asked by the inspector.
- **(a)** *Did you hear the dog bark?*
- **(b)** *Did you see the men leave?*
- **(c)** *Did you hear them slam the door?*
- **(d)** *Did you hear the neighbours shouting for help?*

3 The following is taken from a novel by Lara Cardelli entitled *Volevo i pantaloni*. Anna's mother is having hysterics, convinced that her daughter's reputation is irrevocably compromised as a result of her meeting with a boy.

(a) Provide the correct form and **passato prossimo** tense of the reflexive verbs in brackets.

Mia madre era stesa a terra, vicino al tavolo, con le mani aperte che toccavano un piatto rotto*! (**Avvicinarsi – io**) per vedere se era ancora viva e ho visto la sua mano stringere il piatto rotto: era viva e ora cercava di alzarsi. Con un po' di fatica (**alzarsi**), quando è stata in piedi (**girarsi**) dalla mia parte e mi ha visto. Allora ha cominciato a urlare, sempre più forte. Mi urlava improperi* terribili, uno dopo l'altro, e tremende* maledizioni. E io correvo, correvo e scappavo, giravo intorno al tavolo perché certo mia madre non si fermava mentre gridava, anzi, si arrabbiava sempre di più perché non riusciva a colpirmi. Poi ha smesso, è andata nella stanza da letto e (**buttarsi**), a peso morto, sul lettone.

(Lara Cardella, *Volevo i pantaloni*, Arnoldo Mondadori, 1989)

> un piatto rotto *a broken plate* • improperi *abuse, insults* • tremende *awful*

(b) Look at the phrases **mi ha visto** and **mi urlava improperi terribili**. Are the pronouns **mi** reflexive or personal pronouns? Refer to Chapter 7 if you need help. Define them and give the English equivalents of these phrases.

(c) Identify a verb of perception with two objects; give its English equivalent. (See above.)

(d) Give the Italian equivalent of (i) *I saw the man hit the boy* and (ii) *I saw the man hitting the boy*.

◎ 25.4 *Sapere* and *conoscere*

(a) *Sapere*

Sapere can be used as a modal verb and as a normal verb without a dependent infinitive.

Sanno scrivere *They can write/know how to write* **Mi sa** dire quando arrivano? *Can you tell me when they are arriving?* (Mi può dire quando arrrivano?)	As a modal verb, **sapere** expresses knowing how to do something. It also expresses possibility. In the latter case **potere** can be used instead, without any significant change in meaning. See also *can*, p. 241.
So che Gianni è malato *I know Gianni is ill* **So** tre lingue/il tuo indirizzo/numero *I know three languages/your address/number* Lo **sai** a memoria? *Do you know it by heart?*	When **sapere** is used as a normal verb. it implies complete knowledge of something and is used to express knowing a fact, a language or something by heart.

(b) *Sapere* v. *conoscere*

Conosco Gino/Pisa/'la Primavera' di Botticelli? *I know Gino/Pisa/Botticelli's 'Primavera'* **Conosci** bene questa strada? *Do you know this road well?*	**Conoscere** is used to express being or becoming acquainted with someone, something (e.g. a book or picture) or a place, including a road. For **conoscere**, meaning *to meet*, see p. 264.
Ho bisogno di **sapere** la strada che va Ferrara a Cabana *I need directions to get from Ferrara to Cabana*	**Sapere la strada** means *to know the way*, i.e. how to get somewhere.

Sapere, but not **conoscere**, may precede **che** + clause: you never say 'conosco che'.

◎ Esercizio

1 Do you know? Complete the sentences using the relevant forms of **conoscere** and **sapere**.

sai • conoscete • sappiamo • sa • conosci • so

    (a) Io purtroppo — solo l'italiano.

    (b) Mark, tu non — l'Italia?

    (c) Signora, scusi, — quando apre l'ufficio di turismo?

    (d) Ragazzi, — quella poesia? – Certo, la — a memoria!

    (e) Fiorella, lo — il mio indirizzo e il telefono?

◎/✛ 25.5 *Piacere*

(a) The forms and uses of *piacere*

The verb **piacere** *to please* is used when referring to things or actions you like, but it is not directly equivalent to the English verb *to like*. In Italian you literally say that something is pleasing to you. The 3rd persons **piace** and **piacciono** are the key. **Piace** (*it/he/she is pleasing*) is used if you like one thing or like doing something, and **piacciono** (*they are pleasing*) is used to say you like several things. Notice how the grammatical structure differs in English and Italian: the Italian subject is actually the English direct object.

Subject + verb + DO		IDO +	verb	+ subject	
I like	*ice cream*	Mi	piace	il gelato	*(Ice cream is pleasing to me)*
I like	*skiing*	Mi	piace	sciare	*(Skiing is pleasing to me)*
I like	*desserts*	Mi	piacciono	i dolci	*(Desserts are pleasing to me)*

The table on p. 319 shows that in Italian the person who likes something is grammatically an indirect object. The indirect object pronouns **mi**, **ti**, **gli**, **le**, **ci**, **vi**, **loro** therefore normally express the English subject pronouns *I, you, he, she, we, you, they.*

mi ti gli, le Le ci vi (a) loro gli	piace piacciono	*I like* *You like* (informal) *He, she likes* *You like* (formal) *We like* *You like* (plural) *They like* *They like* (colloquial)	Le piace il vino *She likes wine* Le piace cucinare *She likes cooking* Le piacciono le fragole *She likes raspberries*

Attenti!

- Notice that **gli piace/piacciono** means both *he likes* and *they like*. **Gli piace l'Inghilterra** *He likes/They like England.* The context usually makes it clear whether **gli** means *he* or *they.*
- When **loro** is used for *they* (usually in a formal context), it tends to be accompanied by **a**, e.g. **A loro piace l'Inghilterrra.**
- **loro** can be used alone, but only after the verb: **L'Inghilterra piace loro** *They like England.*
- Notice also that **piace**, but never **piacciono,** can be followed by an infinitive verb.
- Finally, notice that with **piacere,** direct object pronouns, e.g. *it, them,* are not expressed in Italian:

È un bel fim, ti piace?	*It's a good film, do you like it?*
Mi piacciono le ostriche, mi piacciono molto.	*I like oysters, I like them a lot.*

  (See also p. 323.)

Piacere with *a*: naming and emphasising the subject

When naming the person/s or things who like something, it is necessary to place the preposition **a** *to* in front (see (i) in the table below). When expressing emphasis or contrast, or with **anche** and **neanche**, disjunctive pronouns preceded by **a** are used instead of indirect object pronouns (see (ii) below).

a Carlo ai cani a mia moglie a tutti a nessuno ad alcuni ad altri alla maggior parte	(i) piace piacciono	*Carlo likes …* *Dogs like* *My wife likes …* *Everyone likes …* *No one likes …* *Some like …* *Others like …* *Most (people) like …*	a me a te a Lei a lui/a lei a noi a voi a loro	(ii) piace piacciono	*I like* *You like* *You like* *(formal)* *He/she/it likes* *We like* *You like* *They like*

In very colloquial Italian, both the disjunctive and the indirect object pronoun may be used after **a**:

A me non **mi** piace per niente!	*I don't like it at all!*
A te non **ti** piace?	*Don't you like it?*

✚ In the following examples, note the use of **a me sì, a lei no**, etc. to express *I do, she/he does*, etc., and *I don't, he/she doesn't*, etc. This avoids repetition of the verb.

Emphatic use/ contrast	**A lei** non piace la carne, ma ma **a me**, sì/**a me** non piace *She doesn't like meat but I do/I do like **it*** **A Federico** piace il pesce ma **a lei** no/**a lei** non piace *Federico likes fish but she doesn't/she doesn't like **it*** I musei sono noiosi; **ai miei amici** non piacciono *Museums are boring; my friends don't like **them*** Carlo è generoso, **a noi** piace molto *Carlo is generous, we like **him** a lot*	Note also that the DO pronouns *it*, *them*, *him*, etc. are not expressed in Italian. This is because in Italian what is liked is not the grammatical direct object of **piacere**. (See pp. 319–20.)
With **anche** and **neanche**	Gli spaghetti piacciono **a lei** e anche **a loro** *She likes spaghetti and so do they* Il vino non piace neanche **a loro** *They don't like wine either*	

◎/✚ Esercizi

1 Piace or **piacciono**? Insert the correct form of **piacere**, using an appropriate pronoun. Note that for *you* there are several alternatives.

(a) (*I like*) il gelato.

(b) Non (*you like*) gli spaghetti?

(c) (*She likes*) cucinare.

(d) (*Do you like*) pranzare all'aperto?

(e) (*Does he like*) l'uva o preferisce le arance?

(f) (*Does she like*) le fragole o preferisce i lamponi?

2 Give two English equivalents for these sentences.

(a) Le piace viaggiare?

(b) Gli piacciono i film giapponesi?

3 Complete the sentences by giving the Italian equivalent of the English.

(a) Franco, ti piace il nuovo corso? – *Yes, I like it very much.*

(b) Signora Marini, le piacciono i fiori? – *Yes, I like them a lot.*

(c) Antonio e Roberto, vi piace andare in palestra? – *Yes, we like it very much.*

4 Supply the missing words and ask who likes what.

(a) Tutti: la musica lirica? (*Does everyone like opera?*)

(b) I tuoi figli: andare a teatro? (*Do your children like going to the theatre?*)

✚ **5** Provide the emphatic form of **piacere** for sentences (a), (b), (c) and (e) in Exercise 1 above.

✚ **6** Complete the sentences using the appropriate form of **piacere** with a pronoun subject.

(a) Ad Elena piace leggere, ma … *he doesn't.*

(b) Ad Enrico non piace la frutta, ma … *she does.*

(c) Ci piace il calcio. – *They like it too.*

(d) Non mi piace suonare il pianoforte. – *I don't like it either.*

✚ **7** You and your partner's likes and dislikes: give the Italian equivalent of the English.

(a) *He likes tomatoes but I don't.*

(b) *She doesn't like coffee but I do.*

(c) *My husband likes playing tennis and so do I.*

(d) *I don't like lentils but my wife does.* (**le lenticchie**)

✛ (b) Further uses of *piacere*

Compound tenses	Gli **è piaciuta** la pizza *He liked the pizza* Ti **sono piaciuti** i fagiolini? *Did you like the beans?*	**Piacere** always takes the auxiliary **essere**, so its past participle agrees with the subject (which in English is the object, i.e. the item liked).
Use with subjunctive	Gli piace **che** tu sia qui *He is pleased you are here* Mi piacerebbe **che** venissero *I would like them to come*	The subjunctive is used after **che** when the subject of **piacere** is different from the subject of the verb that follows. See Subjunctive, p. 300.
Use with the **io** and **tu** forms	Io **piaccio** a Aldo *Aldo likes me* Tu **piaci** a Mirella *Mirella likes you.*	Although **piacere** is mostly used in the 3rd persons of the verb, it is also possible to use it in the first or second persons. Note the double **-c** in the **io** form.

(c) Other ways of expressing 'like'/'dislike'

essere simpatico/ antipatico a	(Tu) mi sei simpatico *I like you* (Voi) gli siete simpatici *He likes you* (Io) le sono antipatico/a *She dislikes me* (Io) sono simpatico/a tutti *Everybody likes me*	The meaning is literally 'to be likeable/not likeable to ... me, you, him, everybody', etc. The subject pronouns **tu**, **voi**, **noi**, etc. are not essential.

✛ Esercizi

8 You've been away as a family. Say who liked what, using the **passato prossimo**.

   (a) Mia moglie: l'albergo di lusso.

   (b) Mia suocera: i negozi.

   (c) I miei figli: la piscina.

   (d) Io e mio suocero: le passeggiate in montagna.

9 Give the Italian equivalent of the English without using **piacere.**

   (a) *He likes Mirella.*

   (b) *She likes Bruno.*

   (c) *They don't like me.*

◎/✛ 25.6 Other verbs used impersonally

Verbs used impersonally are verbs like **piacere** which are nearly always used in the 3rd persons singular and plural.

(a) Main verbs used impersonally

accadere *to happen* avvenire *to happen* bastare *to be enough* bisognare *to be necessary* capitare *to chance, happen to* convenire *to be advisable/best* dispiacere *to be sorry*	importare *to matter/mind* interessare *to interest* occorrere *to be needed* parere *to seem* rincrescere, *to regret* sembrare *to seem* servire *to be of use*	spettare *to be up to something* succedere *to happen* toccare *to have to, be somebody's turn* volerci *to take, to be necessary* mancare *to lack, to be missing/insufficient, to be absent/not there*

◎/✛ (b) Uses of verbs used impersonally

The basic construction is the same as **piacere**: the verb is generally in the 3rd person singular or plural, used with indirect object pronouns. Depending on their meaning, the verbs in (a) above can be followed by nouns, adjectives or infinitives. The following are the uses they have in common with **piacere**.

Singular verb + singular noun Plural verb + plural noun	Mi **serve** una penna *I need a pen* Ci **servono** due bicchieri *We need two glasses* M'**interessa** il cinema *I'm interested in the cinema* Ti **interessano** i film francesi? *Are you interested in French films?*	In Italian you literally say *A pen is of use to me, Two glasses are of use to us, The cinema is of interest to me*, etc.
No DO pronouns	Mi serve *I need **it*** M'interessano *I am interested in **them***	The English direct object pronouns *it, them,* etc. are not expressed in Italian.
mi, **ti**, **gli**, **le** etc. = *I, you, he, she*, etc.	**Le** dispiace *She is sorry* **Ti** conviene partire presto *You should leave early* (*It's best for you to leave early*)	Indirect object pronouns (**gli, le**, etc.) express the English subject pronouns (*he, she*, etc.).
a + noun or other pronoun subject	**A mia figlia** dispiace non poter venire *My daughter is sorry not to be able to come* **A Dino** conviene chiamare prima *Dino should call first* **A molti** mancano i soldi per andare in vacanza *Many people lack the money to go on holiday*	To express noun or other pronoun subjects, e.g. indefinite pronouns, the preposition **a** precedes them.
Emphatic use	Tocca **a te** andare, non a me *You'll have to go, not me/It's your turn to go, not mine* Non spetta **a lui** decidere *It's not up to him to decide*	For emphasis, **a** is used before a disjunctive pronoun instead of **mi**, **ti**, **gli**, **le**, **ci**, **vi** and **loro**.
Compound tenses ✛	Che cosa gli **è successo**? *What's happened to him?* Ti **sono successe** delle cose strane! *Some odd things have happened to you!*	**Essere** is used as the auxiliary in compound tenses. The past participle agrees with the grammatical subject.

The following are specific uses not shared with **piacere**.
When followed by an infinitive, some verbs require **di** in front.

di before infinitive	Le dispiace **farlo**? *Do you mind doing it?* **But:** Capita spesso alle mie figlie **di andarci** *My daughters often go (happen to go) there*	Infinitives mostly directly follow the 3rd person singular of the verb (see also examples above). But **accadere**, **capitare** and **succedere** are preceded by **di**.

With some verbs the English equivalent mirrors the Italian structure.

mi, ti, gli, le = to/for me, you, him, etc.	**Le** bastano due etti? *Are 200 grammes enough for you?* **Mi** pare ridicolo *It seems ridiculous to me*	Note that with **bastare, parere** or **sembrare**, the indirect object pronouns are expressed as *to* or *for me/you*, etc.
No pronouns	**Basta** scrivere presto. *It is enough to write soon* **Sembra** difficile *It seems difficult* **Bisogna** studiare *You have to study*	Some verbs can also be used without the pronouns **mi, ti, gli**, etc.
volerci	**Ci vuole** mezz'ora/**Ci vogliono** trenta minuti *It takes half an hour/30 minutes*	**Volerci** is always used with **ci** only. See also p. 118.

◎/✚ Esercizi

1 Complete the questions using the verbs given, with an appropriate pronoun.

(a) Fabrizio, (bastare) due fette di prosciutto?

(b) Flavia, (servire) altro?

(c) Signor Mancini, (mancare) qualcosa?

(d) Nino e Sandro, (convenire) andare in aereo.

(e) Lidia, se non capisci (bastare) chiedere aiuto.

(f) Signori, (bisognare) stare molto attenti.

✚ **2** Rewrite the sentences putting the verb into the **passato prossimo**.

(a) Mi dispiace partire così presto.

(b) Ci succedono delle cose strane.

(c) Non gli capita mai di arrivare in ritardo.

(d) Gli tocca pagare una multa.

◎/✚ 25.7 Further impersonal constructions

(a) Five impersonal constructions

Indefinite or impersonal constructions are those where the specific agent of the action is either unknown, not expressed or unimportant. In English this type of construction corresponds to such sentences as: *It is advisable to wait*; *One should be more careful*; *You never know*; *They say it will rain*. In Italian there are five main impersonal constructions.

Verbs used impersonally	Domani **pioverà** *Tomorrow it will rain* **Sembra** impossibile *It seems impossible*	There is no identifiable subject.
3rd person plural verb	**Dicono** che è ricco sfondato *They say he is stinking rich* (i.e. *It is said that …*)	The 'they' must refer to unspecified people.
The impersonal **tu**	**Puoi** apprendere l'inglese con comodo, a casa tua *You can learn English at your leisure in your own home*	This refers to a generic 'you'. As in English, this implies that the speaker or writer is including him/ herself.
uno	Perché **uno** dovrebbe andare in pensione a 65 anni? *Why should someone have to/Why should people have to retire at 65?* A quei tempi **uno** si alzava alle cinque di mattina *In those days people/you used to get up at five o'clock in the morning*	As a subject pronoun, **uno** is close to **si** (p. 325), and may be rendered in English by *you/someone* or *people* rather than simply by *one*. **Uno** is used instead of **si** with reflexive verbs to avoid the repetition of the reflexive and impersonal **si** (see Exercise 4, p. 128).

The fifth and most widely used impersonal construction is **si.**

The impersonal **si**	Come **si dice**? *How does one/How do you say it?* **Si sta bene** qui *It is nice here* D'estate **si mangia** spesso all'aperto *In the summer people often eat outdoors*	Most verbs – transitive or intransitive – can be made impersonal by using **si** as the subject with the 3rd person *singular* form of the verb. Its English equivalents vary. For the passive use of **si**, see pp. 327–8.
✚ Use with pronouns	**Lo si** fa ogni tanto *You/People do it now and again* **Ci si** vive bene *You/People live well there* Non **se ne** parla molto *People don't talk much about it*	**Si** comes after direct object pronouns but before **ne**. See also Pronouns, pp. 127–8 for further explanations and exercises.
✚ Use with adjectives	Quando **si è giovani**, non si pensa alla vecchiaia *When you're young you don't think about old age*	Adjectives referring to an impersonal **si** must always be masculine plural, but note that the verb remains singular.
✚ Use in compound tenses	Si **è dormito** bene ieri sera *Everyone/People/We slept well last night* Si **è parlato** spesso di lui negli ultimi tempi *We/People have talked a lot about him recently* Si **è mangiato** la pizza in fretta *One/We ate the pizza in a hurry*	**Si** is always used with **essere**, whether or not the verb normally takes **avere**. In the latter case the past participle does not usually change. However, when there is a direct object (e.g. **pizza**) an agreement may be made (see **si passivante**, p. 327–8).
	Si **è partiti** presto per evitare il traffico *They/We left early so as to avoid the traffic*	If the verb normally takes **essere**, the past participle is always masculine plural, but **essere** remains singular.

For the infinitive used impersonally, see Chapter 23, p. 288.

◎/✚ Esercizi

1 You are computer illiterate and need to know how to reboot, save, highlight and download. Select the appropriate form of the verb.

(a) Come si (riavviare) il computer?
(b) Come si (archiviare) un file?
(c) Come si (evidenziare) il testo?
(d) Come si (scaricare) una cartella?

✚ 2 Insert the **passato prossimo** form of the verb, making past participle agreements if necessary.

(a) La fiera del libro era affollatisssima, purtroppo non si (vedere) molto.
(b) I miei mi dicevano che lo zio era ricco sfondato. Non si (capire) mai come avesse fatto.
(c) Si doveva partire per Parigi, per cui si (andare) prestissimo a votare.

For exercises on **si** used with other pronouns, see p. 128.

✚ 25.8 The passive

Verbs are said to be in the passive when the action is done to the subject, as opposed to the action being performed by the subject, e.g. *The Mafia **shot** the judge* (active); *The judge **was shot** by the Mafia* (passive). The passive form makes the performer of the action less important and the verb becomes more impersonal. This is why the passive is more common in academic or technical and scientific writing than in everyday speech. It is also common in journalism.

(a) Forms and uses of the passive (1)

Only transitive verbs, i.e. verbs which take a direct object, can be made passive. This means that verbs like **essere, andare**, **venire** and **dormire** have no passive forms. (You could not say, for example, *I was slept.*) The main way of forming the passive is by using **essere** in the appropriate tense followed by the past participle.

Simple tenses	Passive form	Compound tenses	Passive form
Present Future Imperfect Past definite	**sono** rispettato **sarò** rispettato **ero** rispettato **fui** rispettato	Passato prossimo Future perfect Pluperfect	**sono stato** rispettato **sarò stato** rispettato **ero stato** rispettato
Present subjunctive Imperfect subjunctive	**sia** rispettato **fossi** rispettato	Perfect subjunctive Pluperfect subjunctive	**sia stato** rispettato **fossi stato** rispettato
Present conditional	**sarei** rispettato	Past conditional	**sarei stato** rispettato
Infinitive	**essere** rispettato	Past infinitive	**essere stato** rispettato

> **Passive modal verbs**:
> **dovere**, **volere** and **potere** are used like **essere**, followed by the passive infinitive, e.g.
> **devo** essere rispettato (present); **dovrò** essere rispettato (future); **dovevo** essere rispettato (imperfect)

Note that there is no passive of the **trapassato remoto** (see p. 271).

Agreements	La casa sarà vendut**a** *The house will be sold* Gli orari sono cambiat**i** *The timetables are changed*	The past participle always agrees with the subject in number and gender.
da for the agent: *by*	È stato ucciso **da** un pazzo/**dal** veleno *He was killed by a madman/by the poison*	To say who or what performs the action, **da** (+ definite article if necessary) is used.

✦ Esercizio

1 Make these sentences passive using the auxiliary **essere**.

(a) Le macchine inquinano la città.
(b) Troveranno il colpevole.
(c) A giugno gli insegnanti correggevano sempre gli esami.
(d) Il pubblico accetterebbe queste tasse nuove?
(e) Non è giusto che il governo critichi gli insegnanti.
(f) Carlo non deve riparare la macchina.

(b) Forms and uses of the passive (2): alternative auxiliaries

The auxiliary **essere** is often replaced by other verbs, most of which can be used in simple passive tenses only.

Using **venire**	Il portone **viene** (è) sempre chiuso a chiave *The door always gets/is always locked* Se non stai attento **verrai** (sarai) licenziato *If you're not careful you'll get/be sacked*	**Venire** is sometimes synonymous with **essere**, but emphasises habit. It tends to stress the action more and is often equivalent to *get* … It is only used in simple tenses.

Using **rimanere**	Il conducente **rimase** (fu) ucciso *The driver got/was killed* Il passante **è rimasto** (è stato) ferito *The passer-by got/was wounded*	Used mainly in the simple past, **passato prossimo** and pluperfect, it replaces **essere** to express a strong impact.
Using **andare**	Durante la guerra i quadri **andarono** (furono) perduti *During the war the pictures went missing/ got lost/were lost* Tutta la casa **andò** (fu) distrutta *The whole house got/was destroyed*	**Andare** is normally used only in the 3rd person. In the simple past it expresses the idea of *get …* with verbs like **perdere** or **smarrire** *to lose*, **distruggere** *to destroy*, **sprecare** *to waste*.
andare for necessity or obligation	**Va** fatto subito (dev'essere fatto) *It must be done at once* **Andrebbe** fatto più tardi (dovrebbe essere fatto) *It should/ought to be done later* **Andrà** fatto domani (dovrà essere fatto) *It will have to be done tomorrow* **Andava** fatto ieri (avrebbe dovuto essere fatto) *It should have been done yesterday*	The present, the conditional, the future and the imperfect of **andare** are much used in this way, and avoid the more complex use of **dover essere** + past participle.

✦ Esercizi

2 Substitute forms of **venire** or **rimanere,** for **essere,** as appropriate.

    (a) Le finestre **sono** pulite ogni mese.

    (b) I ragazzi **erano** spesso puniti.

    (c) La città **è stata** distrutta.

    (d) Noi tutti **siamo stati** stupiti dalle sue parole.

3 The house is falling apart. Say what must be done using **andare** to complete the sentences.

    (a) Il tetto (*must be*) riparato.

    (b) La cucina (*ought to be*) rinnovata.

    (c) I soffitti (*will have to be*) rifatti.

    (d) Le finestre (*should have been*) pulite.

(c) Alternative constructions to express the passive (1): the passive *si*

In English the passive is more frequently used in the spoken language than in Italian, where active verb constructions are often preferred to passive ones.

One of the main alternatives to the passive with **essere** or other auxiliaries, is the passive **si** (**il si passivante**). This is a very common construction used with active transitive verbs only, to express a passive meaning. It is frequently preferred to the passive. Note that the verb and object agree in number. Compare these different constructions:

English passive	**The passive *si***	**The passive** (less used)
Italian is spoken *Many languages are spoken* *Toilet paper is not sold in the chemist's* *Postcards are sold at the station*	**Si parla** italiano **Si parlano** molte lingue La carta igienica non **si vende** in farmacia **Si vendono** cartoline alla stazione	L'italiano **è/viene parlato** Molte lingue **sono/vengono** parlate La carta igienica non **è/viene venduta** in farmacia Le cartoline **sono/vengono vendute**

Attenti! Passive or impersonal **si**?

Strictly speaking, the main grammatical differences are:

- The passive **si** is used with transitive verbs only and can be both singular and plural.
- The impersonal **si** (p. 325) is used with both transitive and intransitive verbs in the singular only.

When the two constructions are used with transitive verbs, the learner may potentially be confused, since the meaning of a passive **si** may sometimes be indistinguishable from that of an impersonal **si**. For example, in the table, where the verbs used are transitive, the sentences may also be translated as impersonal sentences, e.g.

They don't sell toilet paper at the chemist's. They sell postcards at the station.

In modern Italian, the distinction between the passive and impersonal **si** tends to be blurred, especially if there is a plural direct object. On the whole, when a direct object is involved, people tend nowadays to use the **si passivante** for both passive and impersonal meanings. For example, the sentence **Si sentono spesso strani rumori** is used to express not only the passive – *Strange sounds are often heard* – but also the impersonal *One often hears strange noises* (which strictly speaking is **Si sente strani rumori**). In practice, the learner should be able to interpret the meaning from the context without any difficulty.

The passive *si* in compound tenses

Si is always used with **essere** whether or not the verb normally takes **avere**. The past participle agrees in number and gender with the subject.

English passive	The passive *si* with active verb	The passive (less used)
The situation was not understood	Non **si è capita** la situazione	La situazione non **è stata capita**
A lot of money was wasted	**Si sono sprecati** tanti soldi	Tanti soldi **sono stati sprecati**
The pizza was eaten in a hurry	**Si è mangiata** la pizza in fretta	La pizza **è stata mangiata** in fretta

✦ Esercizio

4 Substitute the passive constructions using the passive **si**.

    (a) Domani il pacco *verrà spedito*.

    (b) Di solito il formaggio *viene mangiato* prima del dolce.

    (c) La città bombardata *è stata abbandonata*.

    (d) Il prezzo non *è stato preso in considerazione*.

    (e) La settimana prossima tutte le finestre *dovranno essere pulite*.

5 This extract is taken from the Italian Save the Children website. It concerns child soldiers. Read it and:

    (a) Find as many passive verbs as you can.

    (b) Give the English equivalent of the sentence which begins: **Si ritiene infatti**.

Milioni di bambini sono costretti ad assistere o a prendere parte a* orrendi atti di violenza in conflitti armati dove vengono impiegati come bambini soldato.

Quello del* bambino soldato non è un fenomeno nuovo, ma il fatto di contare su di loro per imbracciare le armi e partecipare ai conflitti ha conosciuto un incremento drammatico negli ultimi anni. La tecnologia moderna ha prodotto armi da peso ridotto* che possono essere utilizzate persino dai bambini più piccoli che sono considerati reclute* più abili e veloci in battaglia. Si ritiene infatti che siano più 'malleabili', più inclini ad ubbidire agli ordini e che abbiano meno rimorsi a compiere gesti efferati.*

È molto difficile fare una stima* precisa del numero di bambini – soldato ma nel 2007 l'Unicef ha stimato che perlomeno 250,000 bambini in tutto il mondo sono rimasti coinvolti in conflitti armati, utilizzati come soldati, messaggeri, spie, portatori, cuoche, e che le bambine sono state obligate a fornire prestazioni sessuali. Al di là dei numeri reali* e malgrado la condanna internazionale, i bambini continuano ad essere arruolati.

(www.savethechildren.it)

> assistere o a prendere parte a *to witness or take part in* • Quello del … refers to **fenomeno** • armi da peso ridotto *light arms* • reclute *recruits* • efferati *ferocious, savage* • fare una stima *to estimate* • Al di là dei numeri reali *irrespective of the true numbers*

---

6 This is taken from a specialist magazine article on the discovery of another complex of catacombs in Rome's via Latina. Identify (i) the impersonal **si** construction, (ii) the **si** passivante and (iii) a passive verb, and give their English equivalents.

La scoperta del nuovo nucleo cimiteriale nell'area della via Latina dimostra ancora un volta che, pur essendo già note e praticabili a Roma una sessantina di catacombe* … tuttavia non si è ancora individuato tutto. In particolare alcuni complessi … non sono stati ancora trovati oppure si è incerti sulla loro identificazione. Restano, ad esempio, alcuni punti oscuri … nella ricostruzione della topografia cimiteriale della vi Aurelia e dell'area compresa tra l'Appia e l'Ardeatina.

(Archeo, agosto 1994)

> pur essendo già note e praticabili …. una sessantina di catacombe *although around 60 catacombs are already known and accessible*

---

7 In chapter 5, p. 96 read the article about friendships on the Web, and identify examples of the impersonal **si** and the **si passivante**.

(d) Alternative constructions to express the passive (2)

The passive with verbs taking people as indirect objects

In Italian, unlike English, an indirect object cannot be the subject of a passive sentence. This means that Italian verbs which take **a** before a person, e.g. **dare a**, **dire a**, **consigliare a**, cannot express the passive in the same way as the English. In Italian you cannot say 'Mia figlia è stata detta di venire' (*My daughter was told to come*), or 'Tommaso è stato consigliato di aspettare' (*Tommaso was advised to wait*). Instead, a 3rd person impersonal construction is used.

	Third person plural (impersonal 'they', see p. 324) + **a** + noun
My aunt was told to come (**dire a**)	**Hanno detto** a mia zia di venire A mia zia (le) **hanno detto** di venire (*colloquial use of the IDO pronoun + the noun*)
Tommaso was advised to wait (**consigliare a**)	**Hanno consigliato** a Tommaso di aspettare A Tommaso (gli) **hanno consigliato** di aspettare (*colloquial use*)

In the following examples, the verbs also take **a** before a person, but in addition are used with a noun direct object. In these cases it is possible to use both the 3rd person construction and a passive construction. In the latter case, the direct object becomes the subject, but never the person: you cannot say 'Carla è stata offerta un bicchiere di vino'.

	Third person plural (impersonal 'they', see p. 324) + **a** + noun
Carla was offered a glass of wine (**offrire a**) *My daughter has had her bag snatched* (**scippare a**)	**Hanno offerto** un bicchiere di vino **a Carla** A Carla (le) hanno offerto un bicchiere di vino (*colloquial*) **Hanno scippato** la borsa **a mia figlia** A mia figlia (le) hanno scippato la borsa (*colloquial*)
	Passive construction:
A glass of wine was offered to Carla *My daughter's bag has been snatched*	A Carla **è stato offerto** un bicchiere di vino/Un bicchiere di vino **è stato offerto** a Carla **E stata scippata** la borsa di mia figlia/La borsa di mia figlia **è stata scippata**

Personal pronouns as indirect objects

When pronouns rather than nouns are the indirect objects, passive structures are possible when there is also a direct object (e.g. *book*, *a rise*), but the 3rd person constructions are far more commonly used. Note that the person is expressed as an indirect object pronoun.

English passive	**Impersonal 3rd person**	**Passive**
He was given the book *We were promised a rise* *He was offered a drink*	Gli **hanno dato** il libro Ci **hanno promesso** un aumento Gli **hanno offerto** da bere	(Il libro gli **è stato dato**) (Ci **è stato promesso** un aumento) (Gli **è stato offerto** da bere)

 Attenti! Verbs like **scippare qlco. a qlcu.** *to snatch something from somebody/to snatch somebody's*, including **rubare, rompere, distruggere** and **incendiare** (see also Chapter 7, pp. 112–5), can technically be used in a passive construction with a person and direct object. However, the tendency is to use the impersonal *they*:

A mia sorella hanno rubato l'anello.   *My sister had her ring stolen.*
Le hanno rubato l'anello.   *Her ring was stolen.*

When there is no person involved, these verbs can be made passive:

L'anello è stato rubato.   *The ring was stolen.*

The passive with verbs taking people as direct objects

There is no restriction on the use of the passive when the person is the direct object, as this can be made the subject of a passive sentence. However, the 3rd person construction is still often preferred.

Ada was invited to the party *We were called at five*	Ada **è stata invitata** alla festa/**Hanno invitato** Ada alla festa **Siamo stati/e chiamati/e** alle cinque/**Ci hanno chiamato** alle cinque
He was persuaded to participate	**È stato convinto** a partecipare/**Lo hanno convinto** a partecipare

✚ Esercizi

8 Using each of the verbs below once, express the following in Italian (there may be more than one possibility). Take care to notice which verbs take a person indirect object (i.e. are preceded by **a**).
chiamare qlcu. • **chiedere qlco. a qlcu.** • **derubare qlcu. di qlco.** • **telefonare a qlcu.**
• **rubare qlco. a qlcu.**

    (a) *Aldo was called yesterday.*

    (b) *Patrizia was telephoned at nine o'clock.*

(c) *Antonio was robbed of his wallet.*

(d) *Gemma's bicycle has been stolen.*

(e) *Mario was asked to move the car.*

9 Express the following in Italian, providing any possible alternative versions. Use the following verbs.

costringere qlcu. a + infinitive • **dare qlco. a qlcu.** • **dire qlco. a qlcu.** • **impedire a qlcu. di** + infinitive **incendiare qlco. a qlcu.**

(a) *I was told to arrive early.*

(b) *They were prevented from voting.*

(c) *He had his shop burned.*

(d) *She was given the wrong timetable.*

(e) *We were forced to pay the fine.*

10 Revision. This comes from an article in a magazine about the Greeks' views on death. Read the passage, then answer the questions relating to the words in bold.

Notoriamente più gaudenti e solari* **degli** egizi, i greci avevano le idée più chiare sulla vita **che** sulla morte. Non a caso, i culti in materia* si chiamavano 'misteri' e **di quelli più importanti non si sa moltissimo**. Ma di una cosa erano sicuri: il corpo **andava seppellito***, altrimenti l'anima **avrebbe vagato** senza pace per 100 anni. Ma anche dopo una degna sepoltura*, la prospettiva non era rosea. **Fatta** la conoscenza del barcaiolo Caronte* e del **cagnaccio** Cerbero, **si finiva** nel regno di Ade*. Questi*, dopo un processo* sommario, giudicava i defunti* e li precipitava nel Tartaro*, se cattivi, oppure li destinava alla felicità dell'Eliseo*; non prima di **avere fatto dimenticare loro tutte le brutture*** del mondo **bevendo** dalle acque del Lete*.

(*Specchio Della Stampa*, 6 febbraio 1999)

> gaudenti e solari *pleasure-loving and sunny* • in materia *on the subject (of death)* • seppellire *to bury* • sepoltura *burial* • barcaiolo Caronte *the boatman Charon* • Ade *Hades* • Questi *the former* (i.e. Charon) • processo *trial* • i defunti *the dead* • Tartaro *Tartarus* (the underworld) • L'Eliseo *the Elysian fields* (equivalent of Heaven) • brutture *horrors* • il Lete *Lethe, the river of oblivion*

(a) Give the English equivalent of: (i) **di quelli più importanti non si sa moltissimo**; (ii) **si finiva nel regno di Ade**; (iii) **il corpo andava seppellito**. (See pp. 325 and 327.)

(b) What part of speech is **fatta**? What is its English equivalent here in the phrase **fatta la conoscenza**? Now find another way of saying the same thing in Italian. (Refer to Chapter 23, pp. 296–7 if necessary.)

(c) (i) Give the English equivalent of **non prima di avere fatto dimenticare loro tutte le brutture del mondo**. Now (ii) express the phrase less formally by using **gli** instead of **loro**. For help, see p. 316 in this chapter.

(d) Define **bevendo** grammatically and give its English equivalent here. (See Chapter 23, p. 293.)

(e) Look at the two comparatives on line 1 to see how **than** is expressed in Italian. If necessary, go to Chapter 5, pp. 73–4, to revise the use of **di** and **che** in comparisons.

(f) Give the English equivalent of **l'anima avrebbe vagato**. (Refer to Chapter 21, p. 278 if necessary.)

(g) What is **un cagnaccio**? Why is Cerberus so called? (Look at Chapter 6, p. 99 if necessary.)

26 Verbs and prepositions

Prepositions such as **a** or **di** are often used with verbs to link them to nouns, pronouns or infinitive verbs, and they can have a significant impact on the meaning. There are some major differences between their use in English and Italian:

1 Some English verbs require a preposition where Italian ones do not – and vice versa.
2 Many Italian verbs take di while others take a – and they may both be translated in English as to.
3 Other Italian verbs take prepositions such as **con, in, per** or **su**, but these do not always correspond exactly to the English.
4 Italian prepositions only precede the infinitive form of the verb, whereas English prepositions can also precede gerunds (the -*ing* form).

This chapter provides reference tables, plus an analysis of the main areas of difference between Italian and English use. The lists given are not exhaustive but include the most common verbs.

◎ 26.1 Italian verbs without prepositions

The following verbs are followed by a preposition in English, but not always in Italian.

(a) No Italian prepositions before nouns or pronouns

English and Italian differ	English verb + preposition: Italian verb with no preposition
ascoltare *to listen to* guardare *to look at*	Ascolta la musica, ascoltalo *Listen **to** the music, listen to it* Bisogna guardare la strada! *You have to look **at** the road*
English and Italian differ	**English verb + preposition: Italian verb with no preposition before a noun or pronoun (but taking *di* before an infinitive: see p. 336)**
aspettare *to wait for* cercare *to look for* sognare *to dream about* chiedere* *to ask for sth.*	Aspetto mia sorella, l'aspetto *I am waiting **for** my sister, I am waiting **for** her* Cerco i miei occhiali, li cerco *I am looking **for** my glasses/**for** them* Ha sognato la guerra *He dreamed **about** the war* Ho chiesto un aumento *I asked **for** a rise*

* **Chiedere** may actually be followed by **di** before a noun or pronoun, but the meaning changes slightly (see p. 335).

 Attenti! Pagare *to pay (for)* is not often used with prepositions, but its use differs from the verbs above.

To pay (for) a thing or to pay a person: no preposition	Ho pagato le bibite e l'albergo Le ho pagate, l'ho pagato Ho pagato il conto, ho pagato Mimi, l'ho pagata	*I've paid for the drinks and the hotel* *I've paid for them, I've paid for it* *I've paid the bill, I've paid Mimi, I've paid her*
To pay for sb.; to pay sb.'s …	Pago sempre per lui Gli pago sempre l'affitto Le pago spesso la cena	*I always pay for him* *I always pay his rent* *I often pay for her dinner*

For **pagare**, see also Pronouns, p. 111.

(b) No Italian prepositions before certain infinitives

In English, many verbs are followed by the preposition *to* before an infinitive, unlike the following categories of Italian verbs.

No Italian preposition after the infinitives of most verbs used impersonally or with *essere* + adjective

(Exceptions: **accadere di**, **capitare di** and **succedere di** *to take place, happen to*; see p. 323.)

see p. 323.

bastare *to be enough to* bisognare *to be necessary to* convenire *to be a good idea to/best (to)* dispiacere *to be sorry to/mind …ing* interessare *to be interested to/in …ing* piacere *to like to/…ing* spettare *to be one's duty/up to s.b to*	essere difficile *to be difficult to* essere facile *to be easy to* essere giusto *to be fair to* essere importante *to be important to* essere meglio *to be better/best to* essere necessario *to be necessary to* essere utile *to be useful to*
Examples: Bisogna uscire *You have **to** go out* Non m'interessa vederlo *I'm not interested **in** seeing him* Gli spetta farlo *It's up to him **to** do it* Non è facile capire *It's not easy **to** understand* **Note**: In some cases there is no preposition in English either: Mi conviene partire *I had better leave*	

No Italian prepositions after modal verbs and verbs of liking/disliking

dovere *to have to* potere *to be able to*	sapere *to know* volere *to want to*
amare *to like, to love to/…ing* desiderare *to wish, to want to* detestare *to detest, hate to/…ing*	preferire *to prefer to* odiare *to hate to/…ing* osare *to dare (to)*
Examples: Devo studiare *I have **to** study* Preferisci pagare adesso? *Do you prefer **to** pay now?* **Note:** in some cases there is no preposition in English either: Ti dispiace chiamare più tardi? *Do you mind calling later?* Detesto aspettare *I hate waiting (to wait)*	

◎/+ 26.2 Verbs taking *a*

The following Italian verbs are all followed by **a**. Some, but not all, of their English equivalents take the preposition *to*.

(a) The main categories of verbs taking *a*

There are three main categories.

Verbs taking *a* before a noun or pronoun only

assistere a *to attend sth.* assomigliare a *to look like sb.* aver diritto a *to be entitled to* disubbidire a *to disobey sb.*	partecipare a *to take part in sth.* sopravvivere a *to survive, outlive sb.* ubbidire a *to obey sb.* voler bene a *to love sb.*
Examples: Ho assistito **alla** cerimonia *I attended the ceremony* Tu assomigli **a** tuo padre *You look like your father* Devi ubbidire **al** professore *You must obey the teacher*	

Verbs taking *a* before nouns, pronouns and infinitives

abituarsi a *to get used to*	giocare a *to play (at)*
dedicarsi a *to devote oneself to*	rassegnarsi a *to resign oneself to*
fare bene a *to be good for, to be right to*	rinunciare a *to give up, refrain from*
fare male a *to be bad for, to be wrong*	tenere/tenerci a *to be keen on/to value*

Examples: Mi abituo **al** freddo/**ad** alzarmi presto *I get used to the cold/to getting up early*
Il fumo fa male **a** tutti/fa male **alla** salute *Smoking is bad for everyone/for your health*
Hai fatto male **a** non ascoltarlo *You were wrong not to listen to him*

For **pensare a** *to think about*, see p. 339.

Verbs taking *a* before infinitives only

affrettarsi a *to hurry/rush to*	impegnarsi a *to undertake to*
aver torto a *to be wrong to*	mettersi a *to start/get down to/set about ...ing*
cominciare a *to begin to/start ...ing*	prepararsi a *to get ready to*
continuare a *to continue to/go on ...ing*	provare a *to try to*
decidersi a *to make up one's mind to*	riuscire a *to manage to*
iniziare a *to start to/to begin ...ing*	scoppiare a *to burst into/out ...*
imparare a *to learn to*	tardare a *to delay ...ing*

Examples: Hai torto **a** criticare il tuo amico *You're wrong to criticise your friend*
Hanno continuato **a** chiacchierare *They continued to chat/carried on chatting*
Sofia è scoppiata **a** piangere/è scoppiata **a** ridere *Sofia burst into tears/burst out laughing*

✚ (b) Special uses of *a* before infinitives

The following Italian verbs all take **a** before an infinitive as above, but depending on the context there are three possible meanings.

Verbs of position, movement and emotion used with *a*

alzarsi a *to get up to/and ...*	rimanere a *to stay/stand and ...*
andare a *to go to/and ...*	sedersi a *to sit and ...*
annoiarsi a *to get bored ...ing*	stare a *to stop, stay to/and ...*
correre a *to run/race to/and ...*	stancarsi a *to tire of ...ing**
divertirsi a *to enjoy ...ing*	stufarsi a *to get fed up ...ing**
fermarsi a *to stop to/and ...*	

* These verbs may also take **di** (see p. 335).

 Attenti! Three possible meanings: with the verbs in (b) above, **a** is used in three ways:

1 To express intention. a may be used as a synonym of **per** to express intention, *(in order)* to.
    Sono venuto **a/per**/fare una telefonata.   *I have come to (in order to) make a phone call.*
    Mi sono alzato **a/per** salutare Gino.   *I got up to (in order to) greet Gino.*

(In these sentences it is not clear whether the action actually took place.)

2 To express consecutive actions, i.e. an action which has taken place soon after the first one. This can be expressed in English as and. If it is not clear whether the action has taken place, the English uses to. The context usually makes it clear.
    Sono andato **a** fare la spesa.   *I went and did/to do the shopping.*
    Sono stato/rimasto **a** chiacchierare con loro. *I stayed and chatted/to chat with them.*
    Ci siamo fermati a guardare il temporale.   *We stopped and watched/to watch the storm.*

3 To express simultaneous actions, i.e. actions taking place at the same time.

Si è divertito a guardare la partita.	*He enjoyed himself/had fun watching the match (while he watched).*
Si stanca a studiare tanto la sera.	*He gets tired studying so much in the evening (while he studies).*
Sta tutta la giornata ad ascoltare la musica.	*He spends all day listening to the music.*

For further examples of verbs used to express simultaneous actions, see Chapter 23, p. 290.

+ Esercizio

1 Refer to the notes above, then mark each sentence below 1, 2 or 3 according to which type you think it is. Then complete the sentences, giving the Italian equivalent of the English. In which sentence could **per** also be used?

    (a) È venuto (*to make/and made*) una telefonata, dopodiché è andato via.

    (b) Sono venuto qui (*to/in order to make*) una telefonata, ma il telefono è guasto.

    (c) Siamo rimasti (*to see/and saw*) la partita.

    (d) Si annoiavano (*hearing*) sempre le stesse canzoni.

◎/+ 26.3 Verbs taking *di*

Very large numbers of Italian verbs are followed by the preposition **di**, literally *of*, in English. However, the English equivalents involve a number of different prepositions, or sometimes none at all.

(a) Verbs taking *di* before nouns, pronouns and infinitives

Di before nouns and pronouns only

caricare di *to load, to burden*	macchiarsi di *to stain oneself with*
coprirsi di *to cover oneself, get covered in*	sporcarsi di *to dirty oneself, get dirtied with*
fare di *to do with*	riempirsi di *to fill oneself up with*
innamorarsi di *to fall in love with sb./sth.*	sapere di *to taste/smell of*
informarsi di *to find out*	ubriacarsi di *to get drunk on*

Examples: Mi sono innamorato **di** Maria/**di** lei *I've fallen in love with Maria/her*
Cosa facciamo **dei** resti? *What shall we do with the leftovers?*
Si sono riempiti **di** caramelle *They stuffed themselves with sweets*
Sa **di** bruciato/di muffa *It tastes/smells burnt/musty*

Di before nouns, pronouns and infinitives

Note that some of these verbs can also take **a** (see /!\ overleaf).

aver bisogno di *to need (to)*	fidarsi di/a *to trust, rely on/dare (to)*
aver paura di/a *to be frightened of*	godere di/a *to enjoy, to enjoy ...ing*
aver vergogna di/a *to be ashamed of/to*	rendersi conto di *to be aware of, to realise that*
aver voglia di *to desire, to feel like ...ing*	ricordar(si) di *to remember (to)*
accorgersi di *to notice, realise (that)*	scusarsi di *to apologise, be sorry for/that*
chiedere di *to ask to, to ask after*	stancarsi di/a *to get tired (of)/...ing*
dimenticar(si) di *to forget (to)*	stufarsi di/a *to be fed up (of)/sick of ...ing*
essere contento di *to be pleased with/to*	vergognarsi di/a *to be ashamed of/of ...ing/that*
essere orgoglioso di *to be proud of/to*	

Examples: Mi sono stancato **del** corso/**di** studiare *I've got tired of the course/of studying*
Mi sono accorto **delle** difficoltà *I have realised the difficulties*
Non ti sei accorto **di** aver perso la borsa? *Didn't you notice (that) you had lost your bag?*

Attenti! *Di* or *a*?

Some of the verbs in the table above may also be followed by **a** – usually expressing a slightly different meaning.

- In some cases the use of **a** or **di** is a matter of personal style or preference:

  Si vergogna **di/a** dirlo.   *He is ashamed to say it.*

  Non mi fido **di/a** lasciarlo solo in casa.   *I don't dare leave him alone in the house.*

- With some verbs, **di** refers to a concrete possibility or specific instance, while **a** is used to refer to an unspecific, repeated or hypothetical action (*when/if*):

  Ho paura **di** vederlo.   *I'm frightened of seeing him/that I will see him.*

  La sera ha paura **a** uscire da sola.   *In the evening she's afraid of going out alone/ when she goes out alone.*

- Some verbs, e.g. **godere, stancarsi, stufarsi**, are mostly used with **di** but use **a** to express simultaneous actions (see p. 335):

  Mi sono stufato **di** studiare.   *I'm fed up of studying.*

  Arturo si stufa **a** sentire sempre gli stessi discorsi.   *Arturo gets fed up of always hearing the same stories (i.e. when he hears …).*

✚ Esercizio

1 Give the Italian equivalent of the English, using the verbs given with either **di** or **a**.

  (a) *I have got fed up with waiting.* (**stufarsi**)

  (b) *I get tired studying in the evening.* (**stancarsi**)

  (c) *Aren't you ashamed to cheat/of cheating people?*

  (d) *I'm ashamed that I cheated Carla.* (**imbrogliare**)

◎/✚ (b) Verbs taking *di* before infinitives only

Verbs taking **di** before an infinitive are very numerous. They can be divided into two broad categories: those in which **di** is nearly always expressed in English as *to*, and those in which **di** is expressed as *that*.

Di as 'to'

With the following verbs, **di** is mostly expressed in English as *to*, or the … *ing* verb form.

aspettare di *to wait to*	preoccuparsi di *to take care/the trouble to*
aver il diritto di *to have the right to*	rifiutare/si di *to refuse to*
aver fretta di *to be in a hurry to*	rischiare di *to risk, be in danger of …ing*
aver intenzione di *to intend to*	scegliere di *to choose to*
aver ragione di/a *to be right to*	sforzarsi di *to strive, endeavour, try hard to*
aver voglia di *to desire/feel like …ing*	smettere di *to cease, stop, give up doing sth.*
cercare di *to try to*	sognare di *to dream of …ing*
finire di *to stop doing sth.*	tentare di *to attempt, try to*

Examples: Abbiamo intenzione **di** chiamarlo *We intend to call him*
Hai finito **di** mangiare? *Have you finished/stopped eating?*
Rischiano **di** perdere tutto *They are in danger of losing everything*

Di as 'that'

With certain verbs, **di** is the equivalent of *that* when used in constructions with a dependent clause in which the subject is the same as in the main clause, e.g. *I think (that) I understand.*

accettare di *to agree to/that* capire di *to understand that* credere di *to believe that* decidere di *to decide to/that* dire (di) *to say (that) you have* dubitare di *to doubt that* fingere/fare finta di *to pretend to/that* negare di *to deny that*	pensare di *to think (that), to plan to* parere di *to seem to/that* promettere di *to promise to, that* ritenere di *to consider (that)* sembrare *to seem/think that* sperare di *to hope to/that* temere di *to be afraid/fear that*

Examples: Dice **di** essere troppo stanco *He says (that) he is too tired*
Ha accettato **di** pagare *He has agreed to pay/that he will pay*
Ha capito **di** aver sbagliato *She/He understood that she/he had made a mistake*
But: where the subjects differ, the verb is followed by **che** + the subjunctive (see p. 300):
Ha capito che Lena aveva sbagliato *She/He understood that Lena had made a mistake*

- For similar verbs, e.g. **accorgersi di**, **vergognarsi di**, see also the table on p. 335.
- For more on **credere**, and **pensare**, see pp. 339–40.

◎/✚ Esercizi

2 Verbs of beginning, stopping, trying and deciding: do you know when to use **di** and when to use **a**? Complete the sentences with the appropriate preposition.

(a) Comincia — piovere.

(b) Si è messo — gridare.

(c) Abbiamo finito — mangiare.

(d) Ha smesso — piovere.

(e) Ho provato — giustificarmi.

(f) Ha cercato — aiutarli.

(g) Ho tentato — persuaderli.

(h) Mi sono sforzato — studiare.

(i) Mi sono decisa — lasciarlo.

(j) Ho deciso — partire.

✚ 3 Give an Italian equivalent of the following, using a preposition with the verb given.

(a) *I think (that) I'll come early.* (**pensare**)

(b) *She hopes (that) she will get the job.*

(c) *I doubt that I can help.*

(d) *I'm afraid (that) I am late.*

◎/✚ 26.4 Verbs used with *con, da, in, per, su*

con	congratularsi con *to congratulate sb.* cominciare/iniziare con *to begin with*	finire/terminare con *to end in* scambiare con *to exchange, swap for*
	Examples: Mi sono congratulato **con** lui *I congratulated him* La partita è terminata **con** un pareggio *The match ended in a draw* Ho scambiato l'anello **con** un braccialetto *I swapped the ring for a bracelet*	
da	dipendere da *to depend on*	travestirsi da to *disguise oneself/dress up as*
	Examples: Dipende **dalla** moglie *He depends on his wife* Si sono travestiti **da** demoni *They dressed up as demons*	
in	cambiar(si) in *to change into/for* relegare in *to relegate/banish to*	trasformar(si) in *to transform/turn oneself into*
	Examples: Per fortuna è cambiato **in** meglio *Luckily he has changed for the better* È stato relegato **in** un museo di provincia *It was relegated to a provincial museum*	
per	finire per *to end up* denunciare per *to accuse of*	preoccuparsi per *to be worried about* scambiare per *to mistake for*
	Examples: Mi ha scambiato **per** mio fratello *He mistook me for my brother* E'stato denunciato **per** genocido *He was accused of genocide*	

su	contare su *to count on* dare su *to overlook/look out onto*	incidere su *to affect* informarsi su *to find out about*
	Example: La finestra dà **sul** cortile *The window looks onto the courtyard*	
in/su/per ⚠	Navigare: navigare **in/per** mare *to sail, sail (on) the sea*; navigare **in/su** Internet *to surf the web;* navigare **su** un fiume/canale/lago *to sail on a river/canal/lake*	

◎/+ 26.5 Further uses of *a* and *di*: requests, commands, promises and refusals, etc.

In Italian, most common double object verbs, especially those expressing commands, requests, prohibition, etc., are used in one of two ways: either with a direct object person plus **a** before a dependent infinitive, or with an indirect object person preceded by **a** and followed by **di** before a dependent infinitive. It is therefore important to know which verbs take a direct object person and which an indirect object person (see the discussion on pp. 111, 113–4). In addition, knowing which pattern these verbs follow is important for the correct use of personal pronouns (Exercise 14, p. 114) and also for the correct use of passive constructions (pp. 329–30).

Verbs taking a direct object person: *a* before the infinitive

aiutare qlcu. a *to help sb. to* convincere qlcu. a *to persuade sb. to* costringere qlcu. a *to force sb. to* forzare qlcu. a *to force/push sb. to* invitare qlcu. a *to invite sb. to* incoraggiare qlcu. a *to encourage sb. to*	obbligare qlcu. a *to oblige sb. to* persuadere qlcu. a *to persuade sb. to* spingere qlcu. a *to push sb. to* **But:** pregare qlcu. **di** *to beg sb. to*
Examples: Puoi convincere Giorgio **a** lavare la macchina? *Can you persuade Giorgio to wash the car?* Ho incoraggiato Costanza **a** fare un po' di sport *I encouraged Costanza to do a bit of sport*	

Verbs taking an indirect object person: *a* before the person, *di* before the infinitive

accadere/capitare/succedere a qlcu. di *to happen (to sb.) that ...* (lit. *to happen to sb. to ...*) chiedere a qlcu. di *to ask sb. to* comandare a qlcu. di *to order sb. to* consentire a qlcu. di *to allow sb. to* consigliare a qlcu. di *to advise sb. to* dire a qlcu. di *to tell sb. to* domandare a qlcu. di *to ask sb. to* impedire a qlcu. di *to prevent sb. from ...ing* offrire a qlcu. di *to offer to do sth.* ordinare a qlcu. di *to order sb. to*	perdonare a qlcu. di *to forgive sb. for ...ing* permettere a qlcu. di *to allow sb. to* proibire a qlcu. di *to prohibit sb. from ...ing* promettere a qlcu. di *to promise sb. that* proporre a qlcu. di *to propose sb. does sth.* ricordare a qlcu. di *to remind sb. to* sconsigliare a qlcu. di *to advise sb. against ...ing* suggerire a qlcu. di *to suggest sb. does sth.* vietare a qlcu. di *to forbid sb. to* **But:** insegnare a qlcu. **a** *to teach sb. to*
Examples: Ho detto **a** Nadia **di** venire fra poco *I told Nadia to come soon* Ho promesso **a** mia figlia **di** accompagnarla *I promised my daughter I would go with her* È mai capitato **ai** tuoi figli di essere chiusi fuori? *Have your children ever been locked out?*	

✚ Esercizi

1 Complete the sentences by inserting the correct prepositions. Refer to the table above if necessary.

(a) Perché non la inviti — venire?

(b) Perché non le chiedi — venire?

(c) Lo devi costringere — pagare

(d) Gli devi ordinare — pagare.

2 Now complete the sentences by substituting the correct Italian pronoun and providing the right preposition.

(a) Ieri (*him*) ho proibito — uscire.

(b) Domani (*him*) convincerò — uscire.

(c) Ieri (*her*) ho chiesto — rimanere.

(d) Domani (*her*) costringerò — rimanere.

3 Give the English equivalent of the following.

(a) *I told Simona to come later.* (**dire**)

(b) *I invited Angelo to come.* (**invitare**)

(c) *I asked Martina to leave.* (**chiedere**)

(d) *I reminded Susi to phone.* (**ricordare**)

(e) *He made Susi phone.* (**costringere**)

(f) *She begged Fabrizio to write.* (**pregare**)

◎/✚ 26.6 Different preposition, different meaning

Some verbs can take more than one preposition or no preposition at all, and this usually affects the meaning.

Parlare di/a; pensare di/a

Preferisco parlare **di** Lucia/**della** situazione politica *I prefer to talk about/discuss Lucia/the political situation*	**Parlare di** is used to refer to a topic of discussion: a person or a thing.
Vorrei parlare **a** Lucia *I would like to talk to Lucia* **Also:** Vorrei parlare **con** Lucia	**parlare a**: this expresses connection with sb.; **con** is also used.
Cosa hai pensato **degli** esami? *What did you think about/of the exams?* Pensi **di** venire? *Are you thinking of/planning to come?* Penso **di** partire presto *I think I'll leave early/I plan to leave early*	**pensare di** means to have an opinion about sb. or sth. Before an infinitive it can also mean *to plan to*.
Pensi **agli** esami? *Are you thinking about the exams?* Ha pensato **a** tutto *She has thought of/seen to everything* Hai pensato **a** prenotare i biglietti? *Have you got around to booking/booked the tickets?* Penso sempre **a** te *I always think of you*	**pensare a**: this expresses connection, not opinion. It also means *to see to*, *to arrange*, *to sort out*, *to get around to*.

✚ *Credere a/in; credere*

Credi **a** Giorgio? *Do you believe Giorgio?* **Gli** credi? *Do you believe him?* Bisogna credere **a** se stessi *You have to believe in yourself* Non credeva **ai** giornali *She didn't believe in newspapers* Credi **alle** streghe/**agli** Ufo)? *Do you believe in witches/in UFOs?* **Ci** credi? *Do you believe in them?*	**credere a** indicates belief or faith in a person or thing, or in the fact that something exists (but not God).

credere **in** Dio/**nello** Spirito Santo/**nella** giustizia/ **nella** sua onestà *to believe in God/in the Holy Ghost/in justice/in his honesty* **Ci** credo (nella giustizia, in Dio) *I believe in it/him*	**credere in** indicates belief in the existence of God or of human qualities.
Crede sempre quello che dice Ivo *He always believes what Ivo says (is true)* **Lo** crede *He believes it*	**credere** without a preposition is used to mean *to think sth. is true.*

◎/✛ Esercizi

1 Complete the sentences using **pensare** with **a** or **di** as appropriate.

(a) Che cosa pensi ... la proposta?   (d) Che cosa pensi ... fare?

(b) Che cosa pensi ... Bruno?   (e) Hai pensato ... Bruno?

(c) Pensi ... domani?   (f) Hai pensato ... prenotare?

✛ 2 Give the Italian equivalent of the following.

(a) *You can believe what you want.*   (d) *Can I talk to you about Gianni?*

(b) *Do you believe Marina? Do you believe her?*   (e) *Can I talk to Gianni?*

(c) *Do you believe in God?*   (f) *He talked to me about his job.*

✛ 3 This passage will help you to revise a large number of points and you will need to read it several times. It is taken from the beginning of a short story entitled 'Un giocattolo per Natale' by the writer Gianni Rodari. The narrator has gone out to search for Christmas presents, scouring the shops for elusive old-fashioned children's toys. The first time you read this, pay particular attention to the use of prepositions. Then answer the questions.

Eccomi dunque a vagare* di negozio in negozio, a sospirare* di vetrina in vetrina, sempre più incerto, sempre più confuso. Ero partito con l'orgoglioso proposito* di comprare ai ragazzi i giocattoli che io stesso avevo desiderato da bambino, senza mai riuscire a farmeli regalare*. Ma quei giocattoli, ora, non esistevano più. O erano relegati negli angolini* e nei sottoscala a coprirsi di polvere. In primo piano e in prima linea* apparivano giocattoli nuovi, per me assolutamente misteriosi. Non capivo che cosa fossero, come potessero funzionare e divertire. Forse, prima di uscire, avrei dovuto frequentare un corso sul giocattolo moderno, più che altro elettronico. Ma una scuola del genere*, dove genitori e nonni potessero rifare i loro studi e informarsi sui gusti dei loro figli e nipoti, cresciuti nell'era atomica, ... questa scuola esisteva o no?

– Venga, – disse una vocetta, – entri, si guardi in giro, non stia lì a mettere radici* sul marciapiede. La voce proveniva da un ometto sbucato* da uno stretto e basso botteghino senza vetrina. Chi sa da quanto tempo mi ero fermato in quel punto*, dopo ore d'inutile vagabondaggio, chi sa da quanto mi studiava lo strano omuncolo* sorridendo dietro i suoi occhialoni, l'unico oggetto grande di una faccia in cui tutto era piccolo: gli occhi, il naso, la bocca, i baffetti, il pizzetto nero sul mento.

– Ma lei vende giocattoli? – domandai sospettoso.

– Forse, – rispose l'ometto*. – Se qualcuno li compra, io li vendo.

(Gianni Rodari, 'Un giocattolo per Natale', in *Il gioco dei quattro cantoni*, 1980)

> vagare *to wander* • sospirare *to sigh* • proposito *intention* • senza ... farmeli regalare *without ever managing to get them given to me* • angolini *nooks and crannies* • In primo piano e in prima linea *In the foreground and at the front* • del genere *like that* • radici *roots* • sbucare *to emerge, pop out* • in quel punto *on that spot* • omuncolo = ometto *tiny man*

(a) Identify the prepositions which go with the following verbs: **comprare**; **riuscire**; **relegare**; **informarsi**.

(b) Give the English equivalents of: (i) **Eccomi ... a vagare ... a sospirare**; (ii) **erano relegati ... a coprirsi di polvere**; (iii) **non stia lì a mettere radici nel marciapiede** (refer to pp. 290 and 335 if necessary).

(c) Give the English equivalent of: (i) **di negozio in negozio**; (ii) **da bambino**; (iii) **sul giocattolo moderno**; (iv) **in quel punto**; (v) **di una faccina**.

(d) Look at the phrase: **senza mai riuscire a farmeli regalare**. Give the Italian equivalent of: (i) *I wanted to get the toys given to me;* (ii) *I wanted to get them given to me.* (See Chapter 25, p. 316.)

(e) Identify the three imperfect subjunctive verbs. Explain their use in terms of their antecedents. (See Chapter 24, p. 310.)

(f) In the context of the story what parts of speech are: **venga, entri, si guardi, non stia**?

(g) Look at the following phrase: **un ometto sbucato da uno stretto e basso botteghino senza vetrina**. How would you translate **sbucato**? (Refer to Chapter 23, p. 296 if you need help.) Consider also the position of the adjectives.

(h) **Da** with the pluperfect or imperfect. Consider these two phrases: (i) **da quanto tempo mi ero fermato** *how long I had stood* ... and (ii) **da quanto mi studiava lo strano omuncolo** *how long the strange little man had been studying me*. Why is **studiare** in the imperfect and **fermarsi** in the pluperfect? (Refer to Chapter 20, p. 259 if you need help.)

(i) Nouns. (i) Apart from **ometto** and **omuncolo**, can you spot six nouns used with suffixes? (ii) On line 5 of the text find an invariable noun.

27 Elements of syntax: Italian word order

Word order is an important aspect of language, and in Italian it is particularly flexible compared to English. As has been shown in previous chapters, changes in the Italian word order often express shifts of meaning and emphasis which are differently conveyed in English (for example, by different tone of voice, inflection and stress). This chapter highlights the most characteristic differences between Italian and English word order, and aims to remind the learner of the main areas of divergence.

◎/+ 27.1 Subject position

The basic components of a sentence in both English and Italian are: subject, verb and object. However, they are not always combined in the same way. The main variations concern the position of the subject and object in relation to the verb.

Expressed subject before the verb

- In Italian, as in English, the expressed noun subject commonly comes before the verb:
  Mia figlia ha perso un dente.   *My daughter has lost a tooth.*
- However, in Italian pronoun subjects are used mostly only for emphasis or clarification. This means the verb may begin the sentence when the subject pronoun is not expressed:
  Ha perso un dente.   *She has lost a tooth.* (See p. 103.)
- In a question, unlike English, the subject may come before or after the verb:
  Sua figlia ha perso un dente?/Ha perso   *Has your daughter lost a tooth?*
  un dente, sua figlia? (See p. 146.)
  As a general rule of thumb, what follows the verb is most in focus, so in the last example of the two above it is the subject following the verb (i.e. **sua figlia**) which is emphasised.

Expressed subject after the verb

This is far more common in Italian than in English:
- As mentioned above, what follows the verb is most in focus.
- This principle also applies to subject pronouns: they follow the verb for emphasis and contrast:
  Pago io questa volta.   *I'm paying this time.* (See p. 104.)
- Irrespective of who or what is in focus, if the subject is long, it may follow the verb:
  Debbono far parte di gruppo   *Old European and garden roses should*
  le vecchie rose europee e da giardino.   *form part of this group.* (See p. 230.)
- The subject tends to follow many common Italian verbs – again irrespective of emphasis.

Verbs which often precede the subject

Bastano venti piatti *Twenty plates are sufficient* **Mancano** due studenti *Two students are missing/absent* **È successo** qualcosa di strano *Something odd has happened*	Some verbs used impersonally (p. 322). (Remember the English subject is sometimes the Italian object; see p. 320.)

Sono passati dieci anni *Ten years have passed* **È arrivata** mia sorella *My sister has arrived* Ieri **ha telefonato** mio cugino *Yesterday my cousin phoned*	Many verbs taking **essere** mostly relating to time, movement and place (but also to communication, with **avere**, e.g. **chiamare**, **telefonare**, **suonare**).
Apparve un uomo incappucciato, vestito di nero *A hooded man appeared, dressed in black (There appeared …)* **Scoppiarono** due bombe nel mercato *Two bombs exploded in the market*	The subject tends to follow the verb when dramatic events/actions are related.
Vennero massacrati duecento bambini *Two hundred children were massacred* **Andò/Fu distrutta** tutta la casa *The whole house was destroyed*	The subject generally follows a passive verb, especially with dramatic events.

- It is possible for the subject to precede the verb for special effect, e.g. **Venti piatti bastano!** – the emphasis is then on the verb.

Questions with *dove* and *quando*

- In questions with **dove** and **quando**, the expressed subject never precedes the verb as it does in English; i.e. you cannot say, 'Quando i tuoi arrivano?' Alternatively the subject may precede the question word.

Quando arrivano <u>i tuoi</u>?	*When are your parents arriving?*
Dove abita <u>sua figlia</u>?	*Where does your daughter live?* **Or:**
<u>I tuoi</u>, **quando** arrivano? <u>Sua figlia</u>, **dove** abita?	

See also the subject position with with **perché? quand'è che? quant'è che?** (pp. 148 and 153).

The subject after prepositional phrases

- The subject may come after prepositions or prepositional phrases. This is also the case in English (e.g. *For my birthday he gave me a car. At exactly 6 o'clock he left the house*), but in Italian the phenomenon is more marked. Prepositions and prepositional phrases may come before the subject for emphasis, or in the cases of long sentences, for clarity.

È rimasta un mistero: **di** lei si sa pochissimo.	*She has remained a mystery: very little is known about her.*
Dal getto della doccia possono uscire almeno 20 litri d'acqua al minuto.	*At least 20 litres of water per minute can flow from the shower head.*
Alla festa della nonna sul lago di Garda hanno assistito tutti i parenti, compresi i nipotini e bisnipotini, ansiosi tutti quanti di darle gli auguri.	*All the relatives attended Grandma's party on Lake Garda, including the grandchildren and great grandchildren, all keen to wish her a happy birthday.*

◎/✛ 27.2 Object position

(a) The recapitulation of objects: noun + pronoun

One of the most striking differences between colloquial Italian and English sentence structure is the repetition of the same object in both noun and pronoun form, usually placed before the subject and verb. In what is known as a 'moving to the left', the object becomes the topic of the sentence and the subject tends to be stressed.

Two objects before subject and verb: stressing the subject

I pantaloni, quanto **li** hai pagati? *How much did you pay for the trousers?* **Quella storia** me **la** contò più volte mia nonna *My grandma told me that story several times* Per ora noi **uno stipendio ce** l'abbiamo *For now we (at least) have a salary*	**Direct noun object + DO pronoun(s)** Note that the word order may occasionally differ depending on the focus: **Quanto <u>li</u> hai pagati, i pantaloni?** (particular stress on the cost). See below. See also 7.3, p. 110.
A Lidia non **le** è piaciuto lo spettacolo *Lidia didn't like the show* **A Ennio**, non **gliene** importa niente *Ennio doesn't care a bit about it*	**Indirect noun object + IDO pronoun(s)** Verbs used impersonally are often used with reiterated objects. See also 7.3, p. 112.
A Tommaso gli hanno consigliato di aspettare *Tommaso was advised to wait* **A Carla le** è stato offerto un altro posto *Carla's been offered another job*	Passive constructions (see p. 330) are also used with reiterated objects.
A mia figlia le ho regalato una collana *I've given my daughter a necklace*	**Indirect noun object + IDO pronoun(s)** Constructions with double object verbs (p. 108).

✚ Prepositional phrases + *ci* or *ne* before subject and verb

   • Prepositions or prepositional phrases preceding the subject (see p. 343) may be repeated in pronoun form by **ci** or **ne**.

Che **ci** stai a fare **a Roma/qui?** *What on earth are you doing in Rome/here?* **In Italia** non **ci** vanno mai *They never go to Italy* **Sulla scrivania ci** ho lasciato la chiave e i soldi *I've left the key and money on the desk* **Con Marta** non **ci** vado d'accordo *I don't get on with Marta* **Contro** il ciottolo **ci** affilava la lama *He was sharpening the blade on/against the stone*	**Ci** is used with verbs and constructions beginning with **a, in, su, con, contro** and the adverb **qui.**
Di lui non **se ne** parla più *No one talks about him any more/He is no longer talked about* **Di scarpe ne** avrà centinaia *She must have hundreds of shoes* **Di benzina ne** è rimasta pochissima *There's very little petrol left*	**Ne** is used mainly with verbs and constructions taking **di**, e.g. **parlare di**, partitives and uncountable nouns.

◎/✚ (b) Other aspects of object position

Moving the object to the right

In very informal speech the object may be moved to the right, leaving the pronoun before the verb: the object at the end is less important, with the focus usually on the verb:

   Lo vuoi o no, questo gelato?   *Do you want this ice cream or not?*

   Quanto li hai pagati, i pantaloni?   *So what did you pay for the trousers, then?*

Direct noun object with causative verbs

- In Italian the noun DO follows the verb. See p. 315.

| Perché fai aspettare **i clienti**? | *Why do you make the clients wait?* |
| Farò riparare **la macchina.** | *I'll get the car repaired.* |

Object position with adverbs of manner and quantity and some adverbs of frequency

- In Italian, these usually follow the verb and precede the direct noun object, unlike English. See 4.2 pp. 57, 60 and Chapter 5.2, p. 82.

| Conosco bene **Arturo** ma conosco meglio **Pino.** | *I know Arturo well but I know Pino better.* |
| Non apprezzano abbastanza **il professore.** | *They don't appreciate the teacher enough.* |

◎ 27.3 The position of adverbs

The position of adverbs has been dealt with at length in Chapter 4. As a general rule of thumb, adverbs follow the verb. However, some adverbs may change position and alter the meaning:

Change in position, shift in meaning

Adverbs which change their meaning depending on position include:

anche	**Anche** Renata parla inglese *Renata too/as well speaks English* Renata parla **anche** inglese *Renata speaks English too/as well* (p. 69)
ancora	Hai **ancora** voglia di uscire? *Do you still want to go out?* Hai voglia di uscire **ancora**? *Do you want to go out again?* (p. 68)
appena	Ha aperto **appena** la finestra *He barely/only just opened the window* Ha **appena** aperto la finestra *He has just opened the window* (p. 58)
molto, tanto	Gli piace **molto** giocare a tennis *He likes playing tennis a lot/He is very fond of playing tennis* Gli piace giocare **molto** a tennis *He likes to play tennis a lot* (p. 58)
neanche	Enrico non ha **neanche** chiamato *Enrico hasn't even called* Non ha chiamato **neanche** Enrico *Enrico hasn't callled either* (p.189)
sempre	Bisogna **sempre** chiudere il cancello *You must always close the gate* Bisogna chiudere **sempre** il cancello *You must close the gate at all times* (pp. 60–1)
spesso	Gli piace **spesso** andare in palestra *He often likes to go to the gym* Gli piace andare **spesso** in palestra *He likes to go to the gym often* (pp. 60–1)
solo	**Solo** Luciano mangia pesce *Only Luciano eats fish* Luciano mangia **solo** pesce *Luciano only eats fish* (p. 70)

◎/+ 27.4 The position of adjectives

In Italian, the flexible position of adjectives within sentence is another feature which sets it apart from English. In English, adjectives generally come before the noun, but in Italian, most adjectives can go in any position with respect to the noun: it all depends on their function. The position of adjectives is dealt with in Chapter 3, pp. 44–50.

The position of single adjectives

- After the noun when they have a specifying or restrictive function:
  lo schermo televisivo
  un ragazzo napoletano

una scatola rettangolare
una storia d'amore *a love story*
una gonna lunga
un diamante prezioso (p. 44.)

- Before the noun when they have a generic descriptive, metaphorical or rhetorical function:
un suggestivo panorama
una lunga fila
un prezioso aiuto *invaluable help*
un terribile incidente (p. 45.)

✚ The position of several adjectives

When more than one adjective is used, adjectival position depends both on the function, as above, and on the descriptive importance of the adjective.

- Adjectives of equal descriptive importance are usually linked by **e** (see p. 47).

Specifying	una camica bianca e nera *a black and white shirt*
Generic	uno stretto e basso corridoio *a low, narrow corridor*

- If adjectives are of different descriptive importance, the one which most closely defines the noun immediately comes after it, directly followed by the other one (usually in reverse order to the English, see p. 48):

Specifying	un vino bianco frizzante *a sparkling white wine*
Generic	un film poliziesco banale *a banal crime film*

- It is common for many generic adjectives to precede the noun and for specifying ones to follow (see also p. 49):

Porta delle **nuove** scarpe **rosse** e **vecchi** pantaloni **neri**
She is wearing new red shoes and old black trousers

- The same adjectives can vary their position, unlike English (see also p. 49):

Specifying	un vino biologico **squisito** *a delicious organic wine* un corso d'inglese **noioso** *a boring English course* scarpe nere **nuove** *new black shoes*
Generic	uno **squisito** vino biologico *a delicious organic wine* un **noioso** corso d'inglese *a boring English course* **nuove** scarpe nere *new black shoes*

Compito

In your own time, reread the texts from the book to try and identify some of the features of sentence structure mentioned in this chapter.

Appendix A Spelling and pronunciation

The alphabet

In Italian there are 21 letters in the alphabet plus five letters, **j**, **k**, **w**, **x**, and **y**, which are only used in foreign words.

j k w x y	il **j**olly *joker* (in cards) il **k**imono *kimono* il **w**eekend lo **x**ilofono *xylophone* lo **y**oga **But w pronounced as v:** il walzer *waltz* Walter *Walter*	These are mostly pronounced as in English, but in a few words of German origin **w** is pronounced like the English **v**.

Spelling

Italian spelling is fairly simple because the relationship between the letters and the sounds is consistent. On the whole there is no variation from one word to another. (Compare this with the English *comb*, *tomb*, *bomb*, etc.) However, some combinations of letters are pronounced and spelt differently from the English. The main ones are given here.

Spelling	Approximate English sound	Examples
ce ci	English **ch**	cento (like *cherry*) Cina (like *cheese*)
che chi	English hard **k**	anche (*monkey*) chilo (*keen*)
ge gi	English **j**	geloso (*jet/generous*) magico (*tragic/jilt*)
ghe ghi	English hard **g**	lunghe (*rogue*) larghi (*gear*)
sce sci	English **sh**	scende (*shed*) scippo (*sheep*)
sche schi	English hard **sk**	pesche (*sceptic/schedule*) boschi (*skip/school*)
gli	no exact English equivalent	figlio, famiglia (the closest equivalent is *million*)
gn	no exact English equivalent	lasagne gnocchi signore (the closest equivalents are *new*, *canyon* or *onion*)
h	not pronounced at the beginning of a word	ho/hobby (*honour*)

Accents

Grave accents	la citt**à** il caff**è** cos**ì** dormir**ò** pi**ù** da *from* d**à** *gives* e *and* **è** *is* si *one, you, him/herself* s**ì** *yes*	Used to indicate that the stress falls on the final vowel. They also distinguish between words with the same spelling but different meanings.

Acute accents	perché *because* benché *although* ne *of it, of them* né *neither*	Much less common. Used to indicate a 'closed' *e* sound (like *Jill*) as opposed to an 'open' *e* (like *bed*). They also distinguish between words with the same spelling but different meanings.
With capitals	**È/E'** un mistero *It's a mystery*	When used, accents are also required on capital letters but may also be written as an apostrophe.

Capital letters

In Italian, capitals are less used than in English. Unless they begin a sentence, the following are not used with capitals:

io *I* Titles Weekdays and months Languages and nationalities Streets, piazzas, etc. In organisation or book/play/film titles the first word only is capitalised, with the exception of newspapers. Formal titles: note that capitals may be used in formal contexts.	Lo faccio io Il signor Perruta l'avvocato Agnelli sabato domenica marzo aprile l'italiano mi piace gli americani un paese europeo Abito in via Daniele Manin/in piazza del Duomo Il signore degli anelli *The Lord of the Rings* Sogno di una notte di mezza estate *A Midsummer Night's Dream* **But**: La Repubblica Il Corriere della Sera Il presidente della reppublica italiana **or** della Republica Italiana Il ministero dell'economia e delle finanze **or** dell'Economia e delle Finanze

Capitals are otherwise used much as in English, but note that the formal personal pronouns (**Lei, La, Le**) and related adjectives for *you* (**Suo, Sua, Suoi, Sue**), may be spelt with a capital letter, although the tendency is increasingly to use lower case.

Appendix B Italian verbs

A verb is a word which typically express a physical or mental action, a state or a process, e.g. *to eat, to think, to be, to regret, to age*. Verb forms change depending on who or what is the subject of the action (**the person**), when this takes place (**the tense**) and what the attitude or perception of the speaker is (the **mood**). In dictionaries – and in this appendix – verbs are listed in the **infinitive** form, e.g. *mangiare to eat*, etc.

The Italian verb

Italian verbs are grouped into three conjugations defined by their infinitive endings: **-are** (1st conjugation), **-ere** (2nd conjugation) and **-ire** (third conjugation). These determine the pattern the verbs follow and the forms they take with the different persons. Not all verbs follow a regular pattern, especially in the **-ere** second conjugation. Some second conjugation verbs have endings such as **-arre -orre** or **-urre** and are known as contracted infinitive verbs. (See p. 240.) Their irregularities must be learned.

In Italian there are three tense types:

Simple	Single-word tense: present, future, conditional, past simple	mangio *I eat* mi sposerò *I will marry* partirei *I would leave* mangiai *I ate* uscii *I went out*
Compound	Auxiliary (**avere** or **essere**) + participle: **passato prossimo**, pluperfect, passives, etc.	ho mangiato *I have eaten* sono uscito *I have gone out* avevo mangiato *I had eaten* ero uscito *I had gone out* è stato mangiato *It has been eaten*
Continuous/ Progressive	Auxiliary (**stare**) + gerund: present/future and past continuous	sto mangiando *I am eating* stavo uscendo *I was going out* starà mangiando *he/she will be/must be eating*

From the above you can see that progressive tenses are always used with **stare** as an auxiliary, but compound tenses use both **essere** *to be* or **avere** *to have*. It is important to know when to use these. This appendix is designed as a reference to help you deal with some of the main difficulties of Italian verbs: their irregular forms and the use of auxiliaries.

A guide to the use of auxiliaries

In Italian, the rules for the use of **avere** and **essere** as auxiliaries are not always clearcut. This is not a comprehensive list, but below are the main verbs taking **essere**; they are less numerous than those which take **avere**.

Verbs taking *essere*

andare *to go*	esistere *to exist*	ritornare *to return*
apparire *to appear*	essere *to be*	riuscire *to manage, to succeed*
arrivare *to arrive*	fuggire *to flee, to escape*	scadere *to run out, to expire*
cadere *to fall*	giungere *to arrive at, to reach*	scappare *to dash, to rush off*
costare *to cost*	intervenire *to intervene*	sparire *to disappear*
crollare *to collapse*	morire *to die*	stare *to stay, to be*
dipendere *to depend*	nascere *to be born*	svenire *to faint*
divenire *to become*	partire *to leave*	tornare *to return*
diventare *to become*	pervenire *to arrive, to come to*	uscire *to go out*
emergere *to emerge*	restare *to stay*	valere *to be worth*
entrare *to enter, to come in*	rimanere *to stay*	venire *to come*

Verbs taking either *essere* or *avere*

Some verbs can take either **essere** or **avere** as an auxiliary depending on whether they are being used transitively or intransitively, i.e. with or without a direct object (see also p. 253).

aumentare *to increase, to go up* bruciare *to burn* cambiare *to change* cessare *to cease* cominciare *to begin* correre* *to run* crescere *to grow* diminuire *to decrease, to reduce*	finire *to finish* guarire *to get well, to cure* iniziare *to begin* invecchiare *to grow old, to age* migliorare *to improve* passare *to pass, to spend time* peggiorare *to deteriorate* salire *to go up, to get in*	saltare* *to jump* scivolare *to slip* servire *to be necessary, to serve* scendere *to go down, to get out of* terminare *to end, put an end to* toccare *to touch, to have to* volare* *to fly* vivere* *to live*

- Verbs marked * may take the auxiliary **avere** even when used intransitively. See pp. 256–7.

Irregular verb tables (1): simple past and past participle

This table lists verbs whose simple past and past participles are nearly all irregular, but whose other forms are regular. Both the **io** and **tu** forms of the simple past are given so that you can conjugate the whole tense.

Infinitive	Simple past	Past participle
accendere *to light, to turn on*	accesi accendesti	acceso
accorgersi *to realise*	accorsi accorgesti	accorto
aprire *to open*	aprii/apersi apristi	aperto
assistere *to attend*	(regular form)	assistito
chiedere *to ask*	chiesi chiedesti	chiesto
chiudere *to close*	chiusi chiudesti	chiuso
conoscere *to know*	conobbi conoscesti	conosciuto
coprire *to cover*	coprii/copersi copristi	coperto
correre *to run*	corsi corresti	corso
crescere *to grow*	crebbi crecesti	cresciuto
decidere *to decide*	decisi decidesti	deciso
deludere *to disappoint*	delusi deludesti	deluso
deprimere *to depress*	depressi deprimesti	depresso
difendere *to defend*	difesi difendesti	difeso
dipingere *to paint*	dipinsi dipingesti	dipinto
dirigere *to direct*	diressi dirigesti	diretto
discutere *to discuss*	discussi discutesti	discusso
distinguere *to distinguish*	distinsi distinguesti	distinto

Infinitive	Simple past	Past participle
distruggere *to destroy*	distrussi distruggesti	distrutto
dividere *to divide*	diviso dividesti	diviso
emergere *to emerge*	emersi emergesti	emerso
escludere *to exclude*	esclusi escludesti	escluso
fingere *to pretend*	finsi fingesti	finto
fondere *to melt*	fusi fondesti	fuso
friggere *to fry*	frissi friggesti	fritto
giungere *to reach*	giunsi giungesti	giunto
includere *to include*	inclusi includesti	incluso
invadere *to invade*	invasi invadesti	invaso
leggere *to read*	lessi leggesti	letto
mettere *to put, to place*	misi mettesti	messo
mordere *to bite*	morsi mordesti	morso
muovere *to move*	mossi muovesti	mosso
nascere *to be born*	nacqui nacesti	nato
nascondere *to hide*	nascosi nascondesti	nascosto
offendere *to offend*	offesi offendesti	offeso
offrire *to offer*	offersi offendesti	offerto
perdere *to lose*	persi perdesti	perso/perduto
persuadere *to persuade*	persuasi persuadesti	persuaso
piangere *to cry*	piansi piangesti	pianto
prendere *to take*	presi prendesti	preso
proteggere *to protect*	protessi proteggesti	protetto
ridere *to laugh*	risi ridesti	riso
risolvere *to solve, to resolve*	risolsi risolvesti	risolto
rispondere *to answer/reply*	risposi rispondesti	risposto
rodere *to gnaw*	rosi rodesti	roso
rompere *to break*	ruppi rompesti	rotto
scendere *to go down*	scesi scendesti	sceso
sconfiggere *to defeat*	sconfissi sconfiggesti	sconfitto
scoprire *to discover*	scoprii/scopersi scopristi	scoperto

Infinitive	Simple past	Past participle
scrivere *to write*	scrissi scrivesti	scritto
scuotere *to shake*	scossi scuotesti	scosso
soffrire *to suffer*	soffrii/soffersi soffristi	sofferto
sommergere *to submerge*	sommersi sommergesti	sommerso
sorgere *to rise*	sorsi sorgesti	sorto
sorridere *to smile*	sorrisi sorridesti	sorriso
spargere *to scatter*	sparsi spargesti	sparso
spendere *to spend*	spesi spendesti	speso
spingere *to push*	spinsi spingesti	spinto
stringere *to squeeze, to tighten*	strinsi stringesti	stretto
succedere *to take place/happen*	successe (*3rd person only*)	successo
tingere *to die*	tinsi tingesti	tinto
uccidere *to kill*	uccisi uccidesti	ucciso
vincere *to win*	vinsi vincesti	vinto
volgere *to turn*	volsi volgesti	volto

Verbs with similar patterns

The following common verbs have the same pattern as the ones (in bold) given in the table above:

assistere: consistere, esistere, insistere, resistere; **deprimere:** esprimere, sopprimere; **fondere:** confondere, diffondere; **giungere:** aggiungere; **leggere:** correggere, eleggere; **mettere:** permettere, promettere, smettere; **piangere:** rimpiangere; **rodere:** corrodere, esplodere; **rompere:** corrompere, interrompere; **scrivere:** descrivere, iscrivere/si; **scuotere:** riscuotere; **stringere:** costringere, restringere; **vincere:** convincere; **volgere:** rivolgere/si, sconvolgere, svolgere

Irregular verb tables (2): very irregular verbs

The following table lists the main Italian verbs with irregularities in most tenses.

- Only irregular forms are given. If a particular form of a verb does not appear in the table, this means it is regular: e.g. **andare** has a regularly formed imperfect, simple past and past participle all based on the infinitive. These are therefore not given.
- Most irregular present tenses are given in full, but only the **io** forms of irregular future, conditional and subjunctive forms are given. Very irregular present and imperfect subjunctives are given in full. For the simple past, the 1st person (irregular) and 2nd person (regular) are given.
- Only one example each is given of **-arre, -orre** and **-urre** verbs. Their compounds have identical irregularities.
- The few imperative irregularities are not included. These can be found on p. 281 and are indicated on the following table with an asterisk (*) next to the infinitive form.

Infinitive	Present	Future and conditional	Imperfect	Subjunctive	Simple past	Past participle
andare* *to go*	vado vai va andiamo andate vanno	andrò, andrei		*Present:* vada		
apparire *to appear*	appaio appari appare appariamo apparite appaiono			*Present:* appaia	apparvi/apparsi apparisti	apparso
avere* *to have*	ho hai ha abbiamo avete hanno	avrò, avrei		*Present:* abbia abbia abbia abbiamo abbiate abbiano	ebbi avesti	
bere *to drink*	bevo bevi beve beviamo bevete bevono	berrò, berrei	bevevo	*Present:* beva *Imperfect:* bevessi	bevvi bevesti	bevuto
cadere *to fall*		cadrò, cadrei			caddi cadesti	
cogliere *to gather*	colgo cogli coglie cogliamo cogliete colgono			*Present:* colga	colsi cogliesti	colto
compiere *to carry out, to complete*	compio compi compie compiamo compite compiono	compirò, compirei	compivo	*Present:* compia *Imperfect:* compissi	compii, compisti	compiuto
condurre *to lead*	conduco conduci conduce conduciamo conducete conducono	condurrò, condurrei	conducevo	*Present:* conduca *Imperfect:* conducessi	condussi conducesti	condotto
cuocere *to cook*	cuocio cuoci cuoce cuociamo cuocete cuociono			*Present:* cuocia	cossi cuocesti	cotto
dare* *to give*	do dai dà diamo date danno	darò, darei	davo	*Present:* dia dia dia diamo diate diano *Imperfect:* dessi dessi desse dessimo deste dessero	diedi/detti desti	dato

Infinitive	Present	Future and conditional	Imperfect	Subjunctive	Simple past	Past participle
dire* to say	dico dici dice diciamo dite dicono	dirò, direi	dicevo	Present: dica Imperfect: dicessi	dissi dicesti	detto
dovere to have to	devo devi deve dobbiamo dovete devono	dovrò, dovrei		Present: debba debba debba dobbiamo dobbiate debbano		
essere* to be	sono sei è siamo siete sono	sarò, sarei	ero	Present: sia sia sia siamo siate siano Imperfect: fossi fossi fosse fossimo foste fossero	fui fosti fu fummo foste furono	stato
fare* to do, to make	faccio fai fa facciamo fate fanno	farò, farei	facevo	Present: faccia Imperfect: facessi	feci facesti	fatto
morire to die	muoio muori muore moriamo morite muoiono			Present: muoia		morto
parere to seem	paio pari pare paiamo/pariamo parete paiono	parrò, parrei		Present: paia	parvi paresti	parso
piacere to like, to please	piaccio piaci piace piacciamo piacete piacciono			Present: piaccia	piacqui piacesti	piaciuto
porre to place	pongo poni pone poniamo ponete pongono	porrò, porrei	ponevo	Present: ponga Imperfect: ponessi	posi ponesti	posto
potere to be able to	posso puoi può possiamo potete possono	potrò, potrei		Present: possa		
rimanere to remain, to stay	rimango rimani rimane rimaniamo rimanete rimangono	rimarrò, rimarrei		Present: rimanga	rimasi rimanesti	rimasto
riuscire to succeed	riesco riesci riesce riusciamo riuscite riescono			Present: riesca		

Infinitive	Present	Future/Conditional	Imperfect	Subjunctive	Passato remoto	Past participle
salire *to go up*	salgo sali sale saliamo salite salgono			*Present:* salga		
sapere* *to know*	so sai sa sappiamo sapete sanno	saprò, saprei		*Present:* sappia sappia sappia sappiamo sappiate sappiano	seppi sapesti	
scegliere *to choose*	scelgo scegli sceglie scegliamo scegliete scelgono			*Present:* scelga	scelsi scegliesti	scelto
sciogliere *to dissolve*	sciolgo sciogli scioglie sciogliamo sciogliete sciolgono			*Present:* sciolga	sciolsi sciogliesti	sciolto
sedersi *to sit*	mi siedo ti siedi si siede ci sediamo vi sedete si siedono	mi siederò, mi siederei		*Present:* mi sieda		
soddisfare *to satisfy*	soddisfo soddisfi soddisfa soddisfiamo soddisfate soddisfano	soddisferò, soddisferei	soddisfacevo	*Present:* soddisfi soddisfi soddisfi soddisfacciamo soddisfacciate soddisfacciano *Imperfect:* soddisfacessi	soddisfeci soddisfacesti	soddisfatto
spegnere *to turn off*	spengo spegni spegne spegniamo spegnete spengono			*Present:* spenga	spensi spegnesti	spento
stare* *to be, to stay*	sto stai sta stiamo state stanno	starò, starei	stavo	*Present:* stia stia stia stiamo stiate stiano *Imperfect:* stessi stessi stesse stessimo steste stessero	stetti stesti stette stemmo steste stettero	stato
tenere *to hold*	tengo tieni tiene teniamo tenete tengono	terrò, terrei		*Present:* tenga	tenni tenesti	
togliere *to remove*	tolgo togli toglie togliamo togliete tolgono			*Present:* tolga	tolsi togliesti	tolto

Infinitive	Present	Future and conditional	Imperfect	Subjunctive	Simple past	Past participle
trarre *to draw, pull*	traggo trai trae traiamo traete traggono	trarrò, trarrei	traevo	*Present:* tragga *Imperfect:* traessi	trassi traesti	tratto
udire *to hear*	odo odi ode udiamo udite odono	udirò/udrò, udirei/udrei		*Present:* oda		
uscire *to go out*	esco esci esce usciamo uscite escono			*Present:* esca		
valere *to be worth*	valgo vali vale valiamo valete valgono	varrò, varrei		*Present:* valga	valsi valesti	valso
vedere *to see*		vedrò, vedrei			vidi vedesti	visto/veduto
venire *to come*	vengo vieni viene veniamo venite vengono	verrò, verrei		*Present:* venga	venni venisti	venuto
vivere *to live*		vivrò, vivrei			vissi vivesti	vissuto
volere *to want*	voglio vuoi vuole vogliamo volete vogliono	vorrò, vorrei		*Present:* voglia	volli volesti	

Similar verb patterns

Like **apparire:** scomparire *to disappear*; **cadere:** accadere *to happen*; **compiere:** adempiere *to fulfil*; **condurre:** dedurre *to deduce*, produrre *to produce*, ridurre *to reduce*, tradurre *to translate*; **dire:** benedire *to bless*, contraddire *to contradict*, disdire *to cancel*; **fare:** disfare *to undo*, rifare *to redo*, stupefare *to amaze*; **piacere:** tacere *to be silent*; **porre:** comporre *to compose*, opporre *to oppose*, proporre *to propose*, supporre *to suppose*; **seder(si):** possedere *to own*; **tenere:** appartenere *to belong*, contenere *to contain*, ottenere *to obtain*, trattener(si), *to stay, remain*; **togliere:** accogliere *to welcome*, cogliere *to pick*, sciogliere *to dissolve, to melt*; **trarre:** attrarre *to attract*, distrarre *to distract, amuse*, estrarre *to extract*; **valere:** prevalere *to prevail*; **venire:** avvenire *to happen*, intervenire *to intervene*; **vivere:** sopravvivere *to survive*.

Glossary

This is a glossary of grammar definitions. You will find the main parts of speech defined at the beginning of each relevant chapter (e.g. Articles, p. 17). This section contains additional terms used in the book. If a term is in small capitals, it is further defined in alphabetical order within this glossary or else at the beginning of the relevant chapter in the book itself.

agreement	Refers to the matching of word endings in NUMBER and GENDER to other words they are linked to, e.g. in Italian the form of a noun affects the form of related adjectives or pronouns.
antecedent	A word or phrase to which a following pronoun (often relative) refers. *I spoke to the boy who had broken his leg:* 'the boy' is the antecedent of the relative pronoun 'who'. *That day I spent all the money, which angered him*: 'I spent all the money' is the antecedent of 'which'. Antecedents are usually relative, interrogative, indefinite/negative or superlative. (See also p. 310.)
auxiliary	Auxiliary or 'helper' verbs are **avere**, **essere** and **stare** used in conjunction with a past participle or gerund to form compound tenses.
clause	Part of a sentence containing a SUBJECT and a VERB. A main clause makes sense on its own. The meaning of a subordinate or dependent clause may be unclear on its own, e.g. *I left the house* (main clause) *without speaking* (subordinate clause). *I saw him* (main clause) *when he arrived* (subordinate clause). See also RELATIVE CLAUSE.
collocation	A combination or juxtaposition of words depending on convention and common usage. Often especially relevant when using intensifying adverbs: e.g. *highly intelligent* but not 'highly happy'; *hilariously funny* rather than 'hilariously comic/humorous'.
complex sentence	A sentence with a main clause and one or more subordinate or dependent clauses, e.g. *When it stopped raining* (subordinate clause) *I left the house* (main clause).
compound sentence	A sentence with more than one main clause linked by a COORDINATING CONJUNCTION such as *and*, e.g. *I left the house and I went to the station.* It can also contain subordinate clauses, e.g. *After he had rung me* (subordinate clause), *I left the house and went to the station* (main/independent clauses).
conjugation	Italian VERBS are grouped into three conjugations defined by different infinitive endings: **-are** (1st conjugation), **-ere** (2nd conjugation) and **-ire** (3rd conjugation). Some 2nd conjugation verbs have endings such as **-arre**, **-orre** or **-urre**. See also The Italian verb, p. 349.
context	Refers to the surrounding text of written language or to the accompanying situation of speech. The context is often crucial in determining the meaning of a word, PHRASE, etc., e.g. *That's nice!* can be response to a genuine compliment or the ironic response to an unpleasant remark.
coordinating conjunction	This is a word linking words or clauses of the same kind and of equal importance, e.g. *Do you want beer or wine? I drank beer but he drank wine.*

countable noun	Also known as count nouns, these refer to people or things that have a singular and plural form and can be counted individually, e.g. *house/houses, boy/boys*.
determiner	A word used with a noun to specify its meaning more closely. Typical determiners are articles (*a, the*), demonstratives (*this, that*), possessives (*my, your*) and indefinites (*all* or *many*).
direct and indirect speech	Direct speech refers to the words actually spoken, e.g. *I can come tomorrow.*
double object verb	A verb which can have two objects: both a person and a thing, e.g. *to give* (sth. to sb.), *to offer* (sth. to sb.)
finite verb	A verb form with a definite SUBJECT and TENSE, e.g. *I sing, they played.*
gender	In Italian all nouns are masculine or feminine, even if referring to things. The gender affects the form of the noun and sometimes its meaning.
impersonal use	Impersonal use refers to instances where the specific agent of the action is either unknown, not expressed or unimportant, e.g. *it is incomprehensible, one can't be too careful, you can't blame him.* See Chapter 25, p. 32.
indicative	This refers to the most common MOOD used in verb tenses. It expresses fact and certainty.
intransitive verbs	These are verbs like *to die, to sleep,* whose action does not affect anyone else directly and which are not used with direct OBJECTS. They cannot be used to form PASSIVE tenses. See also p. 253 and Appendix B, p. 350.
literal meaning	This refers to a word-by-word translation which may not be the natural equivalent to the word or phrase in the original language, e.g. **Mi piace il burro** literally means *Butter is pleasing to me*, but the normal equivalent is *I like butter.*
mood	A category of verb tenses which indicates the attitude or perception of the writer/speaker. In Italian, verb tenses can be INDICATIVE (expressing fact), subjunctive (expressing uncertainty, hopes, desires), conditional (awareness of conditions or limitations) or imperative (expressing commands).
non-finite verb	A verb form with no specified subject or tense which is sometimes equivalent to a noun or adjective. There are four main types: infinitive (*to sing is fun*), gerund (*singing is fun*), past participle (*the song sung was sad*) and present participle (*the singing doll was very popular*). See Chapter 23.
number	The number of a noun or verb refers to whether it is singular or plural.
object	The noun, pronoun or noun phrase considered to be affected by the action of a verb, either directly or indirectly: e.g. *I see John/the tower – Who/what do you see?* (direct objects: *John, the tower, who? what?*); *I speak to John – To whom do you speak?/Who do you speak to?* (indirect objects: *John, who?/ whom?*).
passive	See Chapter 25, p. 325.
person of a verb	This refers to the particular form of the verb which depends on who or what performs the action. There are three singular and three plural persons – 1st persons: *I, we*; 2nd persons: *you, you* (plural); 3rd persons: *he, she, it, they.*

phrase	A group of words lacking a finite verb, e.g. *the enormous house* (noun phrase), *having been working* (verb phrase).
quantifier	A word or PHRASE denoting quantity, e.g. *a lot*, *some*, *many*,
relative clause	A SUBORDINATE CLAUSE which modifies a noun and is introduced by a relative pronoun, e.g. *The man <u>who came yesterday</u> is my brother*, *The book <u>that I read</u> is very long*.
simple sentence	A simple sentence consists of one CLAUSE with only one VERB and SUBJECT, e.g. *I left the house*, *I feel tired*.
stem	Sometimes referred to as 'root', this is the basic part of the verb infinitive from which the different TENSES are usually formed, e.g. **pens-** is the stem of **pensare**, **vend-** the stem of **vendere** and **fin-** the stem of **finire**.
style	Style denotes variation in speech or writing. The style (or register) of someone's language may depend on who is being addressed or what the topic and purpose is. Style can be formal, colloquial, slangy, etc. It can also refer to a person's individual use of speech or writing, or to a way of using language at a particular historical period.
subject	Generally the noun, pronoun or noun phrase which performs the action of a verb, e.g., *<u>Peter</u> plays tennis*, *<u>He</u> is eating*, *<u>The black cat</u> disappeared*.
subordinating conjunction	A word which links a main clause to a subordinate clause, e.g. *He went to work <u>although</u> he was ill*.
syntax	The rules governing sentence formation: how words are arranged in a sentence.
tense	Forms of FINITE VERBS which locate the action in time with relation to past, present and future. For simple, compound and progressive tenses, see p. 349.
transitive verbs	Verbs which can be used with a direct OBJECT. In Italian these are nearly always used with the AUXILIARY **avere** (see Appendix B, p. 350). Unlike INTRANSITIVE VERBS, transitive verbs in Italian can be used with the PASSIVE (see p. 326).
uncountable noun	Also known as mass nouns, and used in the singular, these refer to indivisible masses such as foods, substances or abstract concepts, e.g. *gas*, *snow*, *bread*, *rice*, *housing*, *rudeness*.
verbs	See Appendix B, p. 349.

Key to exercises

1 Nouns

1.1 Regular nouns

1 Ho bisogno di lampade, letti, armadi, tavoli, sedie, poltrone, tendine, specchi, tappeti.
2 Abbiamo bisogno di piatti, coltelli, forchette, cucchiai, bicchieri, tazze, scodelle, tovaglioli.
3 lattughe, asparagi, funghi, peperoni, fichi, albicocche, limoni, pesche, arance, ciliegie
4 greci, medici, idraulici, parroci; cuochi, polacchi, tedeschi, turchi
5 chirurghi and drammaturghi. The others end in **-gi**.
6 abitudine f, appendice f, azione f, immagine f, indagine f, opinione f, origine f, unione f.
  amore m, animale m, atlante m, elefante m, esame m, incidente m, infermiere m, ordine m.
7 **(a)** f. f. **(b)** m. m. **(c)** m. f. **(d)** f. m. **(e)** f. m. **(f)** m. f. m.

1.2 Irregular nouns

1 gli atleti/le atlete, i colleghi/le colleghe, i ginnasti/le ginnaste, i tennisti/le tenniste, i pilota/le pilote, i pediatri/le pediatre, i poeti
2 l'analisi, la crisi, il dilemma, il diploma, la moglie, il problema, il programma, il sistema
3 **Masculine**: il clima/i climi, il/i delta, il pianeta/i pianeti **Feminine**: la cometa/le comete, l'/le eclissi, l'/le oasi
4 **Masculine**: il/i frigo, lo/gli stereo, il/i video **Feminine**: l'/le auto, la/le foto, la/le moto
5 computer m, cursore m, database m, fax m, file m, software m, mouse m, modem m. E-mail is feminine.

1.3 Compound nouns

1 gli accendisigari, gli apribottiglie, gli aspirapolvere, i cavatappi, i portacenere, i portasapone, gli stuzzicadenti, i tagliaerba, i tritacarne, i tritadocumenti, i tritarifiuti
2 **Regular plural**: i portafogli, i sottotitoli **Invariable**: i portachiavi, i portamonete, i/le portavoce, i doposcuola, i dopobarba, i senzatetto

1.4 Defective nouns

1 **(a)** I bagagli sono qui (Il bagaglio è qui).
  (b) Ho bisogno di informazioni.
  (c) Ha troppi soldi.
  (d) I media devono essere indipendenti.
  (e) Non ho spiccioli.
  (f) L'uva è senza semi?
  (g) È nuovo, il tuo pigiami?
  (h) Le notizie sono buone.

1.5 Collective nouns

1 **(a)** era **(b)** C'è **(c)** sono arrivati **(d)** sono stati

1.6 More on gender

1 contralto, mezzosoprano
2 levatrice (*midwife*), regina (*queen*)
3 **(a)** Maria è diventata un architetto molto bravo.
  (b) Mio figlio è diventato una guida molto conosciuta.
  (c) James Bond, l'agente 007, è una spia famosa inventata da Ian Fleming.
  (d) Le vittime più tragiche sono state **or:** sono stati i bambini.
4 **(a)** le orecchie **(b)** uova **(c)** paia **(d)** migliaia **(e)** centinaia
5 l'arancia, il fico, la pesca, la mandorla, l'oliva

6   le braccia, le ciglia, le dita, le ginocchia, le labbra, le mani (*odd one out because it is f. in the singular and its plural ends in* -i)

7   **(a)** la fine   **(c)** la capitale   **(e)** banca   **(g)** nella buca
    (b) il capitale   **(d)** la morale   **(f)** il manico   **(h)** un tavolo

8   **(a)** estensione f, equatore m, abitante m, altitudine f
    (b) il clima, il lago, il confine
    (c) i pianeti m, le varietà, f, gli archipelaghi m, le supercficie f, i delta m
    (d) la Tanzania, le Seychelles

2   Articles

2.1   The indefinite article

1   Ho fatto un frullato di frutta, un arrosto, un'insalata, uno zabaglione, una zuppa inglese, uno spezzatino, un sugo di pomodoro

2   **uno:** studente, scienziato, spettatore, psichiatra, psicologo. **un:** signore, soldato, sacerdote, pediatra, profugo, produttore, poliziotto

3   **un:** amico, appartamento, elicottero, etto, ingresso, ispettore, ombrello, operario, uccello, ufficio
    un': amica, automobile, enciclopedia, estate, inchiesta, isola, offerta, opinione, uscita, uniforme

4   **(a)** una; un'   **(b)** uno; un   **(c)** un; uno   **(d)** un'; una

5   **(a)** Sono medico. *I'm a doctor.*
    (b) È un bravo medico. *He's a good doctor.*
    (c) È uno studente che studia tanto. *He's a student who studies a lot.*
    (d) Sono studente. *I'm a student.*
    (e) È cattolica tua zia? *Is your aunt a Catholic?*
    (f) Mia zia è una cattolica molto tradizionale. *My aunt is a very traditional Catholic.*

2.2   The definite article

1   l'asciugamano, la carta igienica, il dentifricio, il sapone, lo shampoo, la spugna, il rasoio

2   lo gnu, la scimmia, lo scoiattolo, il serpente, lo struzzo, lo yak, la zanzara

3   lo zodiaco, il Capricorno, l'Acquario, i Pesci, l'Ariete, il Toro, i Gemelli, il Cancro, il Leone, la Vergine, la Bilancia, lo Scorpione, il Sagittario

4   Mi fa vedere le espadrille, i mocassini, le pantofole, i sandali, le scarpe da tennis, gli scarponi, gli stivali, gli zoccoli

5   l'antisemitismo, il razzismo, il sessismo, la xenofobia; l'intolleranza *is a general term, the other words are specific forms of intolerance.*

6   **(a)** l'; il   **(b)** il; lo   **(c)** il; l'   **(d)** l'; lo

7   **(a)** I cani sono animali fedeli. *Dogs are faithful animals.*
    (b) I cani che abbiamo visto erano adorabili. *The dogs we saw were adorable.*
    (c) In Italia i bambini vanno a scuola a sei anni. *In Italy children go to school at six.*
    (d) Ieri i bambini erano stanchi. *The children were tired yesterday.*
    (e) La guerra risolve poco. *War doesn't solve much.*
    (f) La guerra nei Balcani è stata una tragedia. *The Balkans war has been a tragedy.*

8   **(a)** Non mi piace il tè, ma adoro il caffè.
    (b) Mi piace tanto il tennis, ma non mi piace il calcio.
    (c) Detesto l'inverno, ma adoro la primavera.
    (d) La vita è bella.
    (e) Il tempo vola.
    (f) Il lavoro è necessario.

9   **(a)** Mi piace l'italiano.
    (b) Parli greco? Non, ma parlo bene **lo** spagnolo.
    (c) Al liceo studio tedesco e inglese.
    (d) Dottor Binni, le presento **il** signor Giusti.

10 (a) venerdì   (c) **la** sera   (e) lunedì 10 giugno
     (b) **il** martedì   (d) **il** 5 febbraio 1993   (f) **il** 27 maggio

11 (a) **La** Gran Bretagna è un'isola.
     (b) **Il** Messico confina con **gli** Stati Uniti.
     (c) Cuba e Haiti non sono paesi ricchi.
     (d) **La** Sardegna e **la** Sicilia sono isole e regioni italiane.

12 (a) and (c) have an article missing:
     (a) Dammi **il** tuo libro.
     (c) Avete visto **il** mio cappotto?

13 (a) Faccio il medico.   (c) Ho bisogno di fare la doccia.
     (b) Maria sta facendo il bagno.   (d) Non ho fatto il biglietto.

14 (a) Roma è una bella città.
     (b) **L'**Aia si trova in Olanda.
     (c) Lipari è un'isola affascinante.
     (d) Mi ha fatto vedere **la** Parigi di Sartre e Camus.
     (e) Oggi Gianni non è andato a scuola.
     (f) Studia **alla** scuola di suo fratello.
     (g) Siamo arrivati **la** primavera dell'anno scorso.
     (h) Siamo arrivati in primavera.

15 (a) L'Olivetti, la Pirelli e la Fiat sono famose società italiane.
     (b) La Juventus è in testa alla serie A.
     (c) Leonardo e Michelangelo erano grandi artisti.
     (d) (Il) Petrarca e (il) Leopardi erano grandi poeti.
     (e) La Morante e la Ginzburg sono note scrittrici italiane.
     (f) Giuseppe Verdi è morto fra gli 86 e gli 87 anni, credo.

2.3 Special uses of the definite and indefinite article

1 (a) Ha i capelli biondi, gli occhi azzurri, la pelle chiara e le orecchie a sventola.
     He has got blond hair, blue eyes, fair skin and ears which stick out.
     (b) Ha il raffreddore e mal di gola ma non ha la tosse.
     He has got a cold and a sore throat, but he hasn't got a cough.
     (c) Purtroppo si è rotto la gamba! *Unfortunately he has broken his leg!*

2 (a) la   (b) il, l'   (c) i, lo   (d) gli

2.4 The prepositional article

1 (a) Vado al mercato, all'aeroporto, allo stadio, alla stazione.
     (b) La carta è nel cassetto. I biscotti sono nell'armadio. La lampada è nello studio. Le matite sono nella scatola.
     (c) Il pane è sul tavolo. La chiave è sull'armadietto. Il dizionario è sullo scaffale. La penna è sulla scrivania.
     (d) Dai giardini si vede la casa. Dagli scalini si vede la fontana. Dalle montagne si vede la pianura.

2 1 della distilleria 2 di Talisker 3 dell'isola 4 sulla riva 5 di Loch 6 dal lunedì 7 al venerdì 8 dalle 9.30 9 alle 16.30 10 della distilleria 11 di Oban 12 nel 1794 13 nel centro 14 della città 15 delle distillerie 16 della Scozia 17 dal lunedì 18 al venerdì 19 Da dicembre 20 a febbraio 21 di apertura 22 a pagamento

3 (a) dei   (b) della   (c) di   (d) nello   (e) nel

4 **Vado ...** a Roma, a Capri, all'isola d'Elba, alle tremiti, a Cipro. **Viviamo ...** a Boston, al Cairo, a Lampedusa, a Malta, nelle Eolie.

5 **Vado ...** in Inghilterra, nei Paesi Bassi, in Asia, in Toscana, in Sicilia. **Lavoriamo ...** in Europa, in Italia, nell'Italia meridionale, in Sardegna, in Emilia Romagna.

6 (a) Passo sempre le ferie in Francia, nella Francia del sud.
     (b) Io lavoro in Gran Bretagna.
     (c) Carlo è nato nel Regno Unito.

7   **(a)** Torino è in Piemonte. È il capoluogo del Piemonte.

     (b) L'Aquila è negli/in Abruzzi. È il capoluogo degli Abruzzi.

     (c) Cagliari è in Sardegna. È il capoluogo della Sardegna

8   **(a)** La capitale della Scozia è Edimburgo.

     (b) La capitale d'Italia è Roma.

     (c) La capitale d'Israele è Gerusalemme.

     (d) La capitale del Canada è Ottawa.

     (e) La capitale di Cuba è l'Avana.

     (f) La capitale delle Filippine è Manila.

9   **(a)** Cipro è situata a sud dellaTurchia.

     (b) Ci sono molti libri e guide sull' isola d'Elba.

     (c) La Sicilia non è lontana dall'Africa.

     (d) Bratislava è in Slovakia, ma non è lontana da Vienna.

     (e) Le Eolie sono al largo della Sicilia.

     (f) Il Canada occupa la parte nord dell'America settentrionale.

10 **(a)** Fiona abita nell'/sull'isola di Skye.

     (b) Donald abita nelle Orcadi.

     (c) Alberto abita a Capri.

     (d) Barbara va all'Isola di Man.

     (e) Alistair va alle Ebridi.

     (f) Sandra va a Cuba.

11 **(a)** Il futuro re di Inghilterra è Carlo, Principe del/di Galles.

     (b) Carlo Alberto di Savoia abdicò nel 1849.

     (c) Nel 1861 Vittorio Emanuele II, re di Sardegna, fu proclamato Re d'Italia.

2.5 The partitive article

1   **(a)** dei   **(b)** degli   **(c)** dell'

2   **(a)** Mi dà del caffè macinato?

     (b) Avete della pasta fresca?

     (c) Devo comprare delle camicie nuove.

     (d) Ho comprato dei pantaloni neri.

     (e) Mi ha prestato degli scarponi da sci.

     (f) Mi serve dello sciroppo per la tosse.

     (g) Ho bisogno di aspirina.

     (h) Non ho fratelli.

     (i) Devo comprare olio, aceto, sale e pepe.

     (j) Volevo mandarini, non arance.

2.6 Partitive expressions and their alternatives

1   **(a)** Mi dà un po' di zucchero?

     (b) Mi porti un po' d'acqua frizzante?

     (c) Mi dà un po' di fagiolini?

     (d) Siamo senza burro.

     (e) Siamo senza soldi.

     (f) Mancano le lenzuola.

2   **(a)** Ho alcune lettere/qualche lettera da scrivere.

     (b) Ho alcuni dubbi/qualche dubbio da chiarire.

     (c) Avete qualche impegno per domani?

     (d) Hai qualche articolo da leggere?

3   **(a)** Non ha alcun valore.

     (b) Non ho nessuna voglia di farlo.

     (c) Non c'è qualche altra possibilità?/Non ci sono altre possibilità?/Non c'è nessun'altra possibilità?

     (d) Non c'è alcun problema/Non c'è problema.

    (e) Non c'è nessun'alternativa/alcun'alternativa.

    (f) Lo ha fatto senza ragione.

4 **(a)** (1) between the ages of 11 and 15 (2) on alcohol (3) 19.5% of minors (4) to minors (5) young people (6) 1.8% of males (7) Italy (8) alcoholic drinks (9) 14.6 in Europe (10) Ireland and Austria

    (b) In Italia circa il 12 per cento dei ragazzi fra/tra gli 11 e i 15 anni consuma bevande alcoliche.

5 **(a)** *No. In this context* **niente** *is not synonymous with* **nessuno**. (See pp. 32, 187.)

    (b) alcuni giorni.

    (c) I medici dicono che non esistono cure per l'influenza ma che è sempre consigliabile il vaccino per i bambini e gli anziani.

3 Descriptive adjectives

3.1 Regular adjectives

1 **(a)** un appartamento spazioso ma scuro/una stanza spaziosa ma scura

    (b) un armadio vecchio ma pulito/una cucina vecchia ma pulita

    (c) uno studente pigro ma simpatico/una studentessa pigra ma simpatica

    (d) un signore ricco ma stupido/una signora ricca ma stupida

    (e) un panorama grigio e brutto/una città grigia e brutta

    (f) un programma lungo e noioso/un'analisi lunga e noiosa

2 **(a)** un fazzoletto bianco/sudicio, fazzoletti bianchi/sudici; una camicia bianca/sudicia, camicie bianche/sudice/sudicie

    (b) un amico turco/greco, amici turchi/greci; un'amica turca/greca, amiche turche/greche.

    (c) un melone fresco/marcio, meloni freschi/marci; una pera fresca/marcia, pere fresche/marce

    (d) un parco pubblico/antico, parchi pubblici/antichi; una piazza pubblica/antica, piazze pubbliche/antiche

    (e) un discorso saggio/necessario, discorsi saggi/necessari; una decisione saggia/necessaria, decisioni sagge/necessarie

    (f) l'autista stanco/ubriaco, gli autisti stanchi/ubriachi; la cantante stanca/ubriaca, le cantanti stanche/ubriache.

3 **(a)** È una collega depressa, lunatica e squilibrata.

    (b) Sua sorella, Cinzia, è aggressiva, sensibile e dolce.

    (c) Il professore è timido, pedante e conformista.

    (d) I miei cugini sono vanitosi, ignoranti ed egoisti.

    (e) Le mie zie sono colte, intelligenti e cosmopolite.

    (f) Gina e Franco sono bravi, simpatici e gentili.

    Sentence (b) expresses disagreement.

4 **(a)** felici e contenti   **(d)** prolungati, stanche morte   **(g)** antisemita, preoccupante

    (b) avvincente   **(e)** arabe, cristiane, ebree

    (c) astronomici, grave   **(f)** umani, xenofoba

5 **(a)** bel   **(b)** bell'   **(c)** bella   **(d)** bei   **(e)** begli

6 **(a)** buon   **(b)** buono   **(c)** buon'/buona   **(d)** buoni   **(e)** buone

7 **(a)** Sant'Andrea, San Giorgio   **(c)** San Pietro, San Zeno   **(e)** le Scale Sante,

    (b) Sant'Agata   **(d)** Santo Spirito   San Giovanni

8 **(a)** un gran peccato   **(c)** grand'armadio   **(e)** piedi grandi

    (b) grand'errore   **(d)** grand' impressione

9 **(a)** Che cosa fai di bello oggi?

    (b) Vorrei bere qualcosa di caldo.

    (c) Non hanno fatto niente di male/sbagliato.

    (d) Non danno nulla di bello al cinema stasera

    (e) Che cosa c'è di straordinario in tutto questo?

    (f) Quello che c'è di strano è la sua indifferenza.

3.2 Irregular adjectives

1 Ho visto:
- **(a)** una lampada liberty.
- **(b)** tappeti multicolori.
- **(c)** delle riviste gay.
- **(d)** dei pappagalli verde smeraldo.
- **(e)** dei pantaloni grigioverdi.
- **(f)** un parasole viola.
- **(g)** dei vestitini sexy.
- **(h)** un boa con piume rosa.

2 **(a)** antidroga **(c)** antiaerei **(e)** angloamericane **(g)** antigienica
(b) antinucleari **(d)** russo-afgano **(f)** antipersona

3.3 The position of single adjectives

1 **(a)** dei soldati americani
- **(b)** un gruppo di suore sorridenti
- **(c)** dei bambini annoiati
- **(d)** dei giovani ubriachi
- **(e)** un monaco buddista con la veste gialla
- **(f)** una signora indiana con il sari di seta
- **(g)** una donna strana con un cappello triangolare
- **(h)** un gatto piccolino in una gabbia molto grande

2 **(a)** D, S **(b)** S, D **(c)** D, S **(d)** S, D **(e)** D, S **(f)** D, S

3 **(a)** Due buste grandi e tre buste piccole, per piacere.
- **(b)** Un caffè lungo in una tazza grande/grande tazza, per piacere.
- **(c)** Prendo il solito caffè, per piacere, e un tè freddo.

4 **(a)** È una cara amica. Ho comprato una giacca cara.
- **(b)** Ci sono diverse soluzioni. Ci sono soluzioni diverse.
- **(c)** Ho parlato con lo stesso direttore. Ho parlato con il/al direttore stesso.
- **(d)** La ammiro, è una donna unica. È l'unica donna per me.

5 **(a)** È un ristorante semplice. **(c)** Di recente ho visto vari film.
(b) Non è un semplice ristorante. **(d)** È una lista delle recensioni recenti di film vari

3.4 The position of multiple adjectives

1 **(a)** guanti neri di pelle/guanti di pelle nera
- **(b)** un golf verde di cachemire/un golf di cachemire verde
- **(c)** una camicetta di cotone bianca e nera
- **(d)** una giacca a quadretti nera, gialla e verde

2 **(a)** una compagnia aerea francese
- **(b)** un sostantivo maschile irregolare
- **(c)** la comunità economica europea
- **(d)** un bracialetto d'oro di valore
- **(e)** un impianto nucleare russo
- **(f)** un vino italiano invecchiato
- **(g)** un problema tecnico abbastanza/piuttosto complicato
- **(h)** un discorso politico geniale

3 **(a)** Sono uscito con dei compagni di scuola simpaticissimi.
- **(b)** Ho visto un documentario storico noioso.
- **(c)** Sono andato a un concerto rock veramente meraviglioso.
- **(d)** Ho incontrato una coppia canadese molto interessante.
- **(e)** Ho comprato un paio di scarpe rosse stupende.

4 Abita in:
- **(a)** un piccolo bungalow moderno.
- **(b)** un vecchio quartiere di Roma.
- **(c)** una bella casa grande.
- **(d)** una stanza affittata piccolina.
- **(e)** uno stupendo attico antico/un attico antico stupendo.
- **(f)** un'enorme villa rinascimentale.

5 (a) Tiziana era bellissima, con lunghi capelli neri e grandi occhi azzurri.
   (b) Stanno cercando una giovane donna dai lunghi capelli neri *or*, **for specification,** una donna giovane, dai capelli lunghi e neri.
   (c) È stata una decisione burocratica assurda.
   (d) Non si può mica accettare quell'assurda decisione burocratica!
   (e) È stato un terribile disastro ecologico inatteso.
   (f) I profughi vivono in condizioni sociali ed economiche molto svantaggiate.

3.5 Expressing 'good' and 'bad': notes on meaning

1 (a) È un bel dipinto, è un dipinto magnifico.
   (b) È un buon vino, è un vino stagionato.
   (c) È un bravo/buon cuoco, è un cuoco geniale.
   (d) È un buon/bel libro di testo, è un libro di testo utile.
   (e) È un bel romanzo, è un romanzo originale.
   (f) Sono dei bravi bambini, sono bambini educati.
   (g) È una brava persona, aiuta sempre gli altri.
   (h) È un bravo studente, che studia tanto.
2 (a) È un brutto quadro.
   (b) È un vino cattivo.
   (c) È un cattivo cuoco.
   (d) È una persona cattiva.
   (e) Il tempo è brutto/cattivo.
   (f) È un brutto libro di testo.
   (g) È un brutto/cattivo romanzo.
   (h) Sono bambini cattivi.
   (i) È un cattivo studente.
   (j) È un brutto saggio.
   (k) È una cattiva madre.
   (l) È un uomo brutto.
3 The film title is: Il Buono, il brutto e il cattivo.

3.6 Further uses of adjectives

1 (a) We did everything possible/everything we could to help him.
   (b) The good thing is that in the end they gave me a discount.
   (c) The worst thing is the banks are closed.
   (d) In old Westerns the goodies always defeat the baddies.
2 (a) Non è il caso di essere scortesi.
   (b) Per rimanere giovani bisogna essere ottimisti.
   (c) Si vive più sani se si pratica uno sport.
   (d) È peggio essere sordi che ciechi.
   (e) L'Internet è sempre utile per tenersi aggiornati.
3 (a) di cemento, d'acciaio, a due corsie, d'atterraggio, di campagna, di viaggi; lunghe, circolari, azzurre, asfaltata, piccola. *'Tabacchi' functions as an adjective but is part of the noun 'un bar tabacchi'.*
   (b) un casone … lungo e grigio, una strada sterrata e piena di buchi
   (c) due lunghe schiere di villette di cemento armato; un grande portico di pietra; quattro misere case di pietra e malta; un bel cartello blu
   (d) a two-lane tarmac road; a dirt road full of holes
   (e) *There is a high proportion of specifying adjectives which makes the description precise and dispassionate.*

4 Adverbs

4.1 The forms of adverbs

1 (a) onestamente (c) cordialmente (e) bene (g) meglio
   (b) brevemente (d) volgarmente (f) male (h) peggio
2 (a) veloce, *fast*
   (b) del tutto, *completely*
   (c) fisso, *fixedly*, i.e. he was staring
   (d) all'improvviso, *unexpectedly*

    (e) così, *so much*

    (f) piano, *slowly*; sano, *healthily*; lontano, *far*. – *'Slow and steady wins the race.'*

3   (a) corre

    (b) inaspettata

    (c) guardava *and the subject of* guardava

    (d) sono partiti

    (e) ti voglio bene

    (f) va.

4   (a) *used as adjectives, not adverbs*: (iv) (città) lontana, (vi) poco (vento), (ix) felici e contenti.

    (b) *not modifying verbs*: (vii) tanto *modifies an adverb* (male),
       (viii) troppo *modifies an adjective* (caro).

4.2 Different types of adverbs and their uses

1   (a) molto   (c) molte   (e) tanto   (g) tanti

    (b) molto   (d) molta   (f) tanto   (h) tanta

2   (a) Giocano bene a calcio.

    (b) Suona molto la chitarra.

    (c) Amava tanto i gatti.

    (d) Mi è piaciuto parecchio quel film.

    (e) Ha sbattuto forte la porta.

    (f) La minestra non è abbastanza calda.

    (g) Mio cugino capisce benissimo i cani.

3   (a) Siamo appena arrivati.

    (b) Ti sento appena.

    (c) Sono appena le due.

    (d) Ho fatto appena in termpo per prendere il treno.

    (e) Gli piace mangiare molto.

    (f) Mi piacerebbe molto mangiare adesso.

4   a volte, qualche volta, raramente, di rado, non … mai, ogni tanto, sempre, spesso

5   (a) Vedo spesso mia sorella

    (b) Qualche volta andiamo al cinema/Andiamo al cinema qualche volta

    (c) Lando esce raramente

    (d) Non bevo mai la birra

    (e) Si alzano sempre presto

    (f) Ogni tanto mangiamo gli spaghetti/Mangiamo ogni tanto gli spaghetti

6   (a) Siamo arrivati tardi

    (b) Hanno mangiato spesso

    (c) Ha nevicato dappertutto

    (d) Devi chiamare spesso

    (e) Ha sempre dimenticato

    (f) Dovresti sempre chiudere

    (g) Sono uscito raramente

    (h) Non ho mai bevuto

7   (a) Faccio sempre io la spesa

    (b) Ogni tanto mangiamo fuori

    (c) A volte/Qualche volta andiamo a teatro/Andiamo qualche volta a teatro

    (d) Vedo raramente la TV.

8   (a) Marco è ancora a Roma. Sta ancora studiando. *Marco is still in Rome. He is still studying.*

    (b) Davide frequenta già l'università? Ha già dato gli esami? *Is Davide already at university?/ Is Davide at university yet? Has he taken any exams yet?*

    (c) Studi sempre in biblioteca? Devi sempre studiare in bibioteca? *Do you always study in the library? Do you always have to study in the library?*

    (d) Suo marito non aiuta mai in casa. Non ha mai aiutato in vita sua. *Her husband never helps at home. He has never helped in his life.*

    (e) Usciamo spesso la sera. Siamo usciti spesso la sera. *We often go out in the evening. We have often gone out/We often went out in the evening.*

9   (a) Hai portato dentro i piatti? Li hai portati dentro?

    (b) Potresti portare indietro I documenti? Li potresti portare indietro?

    (c) Frequentiamo spesso i corsi serali. Abbiamo deciso di frequentarli spesso.

    (d) Aiuta raramente il fratello. Fa male ad aiutarlo raramente

10 **(a)** You must always keep the door shut; You must keep the door shut at all times

(b) I often like playing football; I like to play football often

(c) It isn't always good to tell the truth; It isn't good to always tell the truth

4.3 Other adverbs and their uses

1 **(a)** appunto **(c)** magari **(e)** esatto **(g)** d'accordo

(b) certo **(d)** può darsi **(f)** senz'altro **(h)** come no?

2 **(a)** Purtroppo ha perso la chiave.

(b) Per fortuna non si è fatto male.

(c) Ovviamente/Chiaramente non capiscono niente.

(d) Francamente lo trovo antipatico.

(e) Sinceramente non mi sembra necessario.

3 **(a)** Non ho proprio/davvero capito niente.

(b) È proprio lui!.

(c) È proprio quello che cercavo.

(d) Mi ha perfino prestato dei soldi.

(e) Lo troverai proprio davanti alla porta.

(f) È solo un gioco.

4 **(a)** Mi ha addirittura insultato *He actually insulted me*

(b) Sono proprio matti *They are really/absolutely mad/crazy*

(c) Non è proprio possibile! *It's simply not possible*

(d) È addirittura/proprio assurdo *It's utterly really absurd*

5 **(a)** eccezionalmente **(b)** terribilmente **(c)** eccessivamente **(d)** fortemente

6 **(a)** It's incredibly hot.

(b) He's an exceptionally intelligent boy.

(c) That film is depressingly stupid.

(d) That man is frighteningly ignorant.

(e) The little girl was really sad: she had lost her kitten.

(f) Why are you so terribly offended?

4.4 Further uses of adverbs

1 **(a)** in ritardo

(b) in anticipo

(c) tardi

(d) presto

(e) con un'ora di ritardo/con un ritardo di un'ora

(f) con dieci minuti di anticipo.

2 **(a)** No, non l'ho più visto. **(d)** No, non mi ha ancora scritto.

(b) No, non voglio più provare. **(e)** No, non sono ancora arrivati.

(c) No, non ho ancora rifatto il letto. **(f)** No, finora non ho avuto notizie.

3 **(a)** always **(c)** for ever/always **(e)** still **(g)** always

(b) always **(d)** still **(f)** still **(h)** always/all the time

4 **(a)** Ne vuoi ancora?

(b) Mi dà ancora quattro fette?

(c) Mi fermo/Rimango ancora dieci giorni.

(d) Vorrei fermarmi/rimanere ancora un po'.

5 **(a)** Dorme ancora? (Siempre is also possible)

(b) Paolo è ancora fuori? (Siempre is also possible)

(c) Gianni, Andrai ancora a Milano?

(d) Doveva ancora andare in banca.

6 **(a)** still **(b)** again **(c)** still **(d)** again **(e)** still **(f)** again

7 **(a)** Mi si è di nuovo bloccato il computer!/Mi si è bloccato il computer un'altra volta.

(b) Ho perso le chiavi dell'ufficio un'altra volta./Ho perso di nuovo le chiavi dell'ufficio.

(c) Mi si è rotta la stampante un'altra volta/Mi si è di nuovo rotta la stampante.

8   **(a)** Lo rimando?   **(b)** Dovrà ridare l'esame.   **(c)** Dovrai rifarlo.

9   **(a)** Lo mando un'altra volta?

      (b) Dovrà dare l'esame un'altra volta.

      (c) Dovrai farlo un'altra volta.

10   **(a)** Ne vuoi un altro po'?

      (b) Me ne dai altre quattro fette?

      (c) Mi fermo/Rimango altri dieci giorni

      (d) Vorrei fermarmi/rimanere un altro po'.

11   **(a)** Sono andato a Roma, Milano, Bergamo, Trento e Torino e poi sono anche andato a Bari

      (b) Davvero? Sei andato anche a Bari?

      (c) Marta è intelligente. – Sì, ma anche Marina è intelligente.

      (d) Marina è sensibile. – Sì, ma è anche allegra.

12   **(a)** Abbiamo solo una macchina.

      (b) Oggi studio solo geografia.

      (c) Siamo liberi solo lunedì prossimo, perché dopo partiamo.

      (d) Ieri ho letto solo due capitoli.

      (e) Hai comprato dei panini? – No, ho comprato solo pane.

      (f) Possono solo venire la settimana prossima, non prima.

13   **(a)** inaspettato *unexpectedly*

      (b) addirittura modifies questore: *he asked for the police commissioner, no less*; proprio modifies nella sua vecchia casa: *right there, in that old house of his*

      (c) quando, subito, al più presto

      (d) adverbial phrase: a poco a poco; adverbs: facilmente, troppo spesso, scrupulosamente, forse ancora

      (e) *the possibilities which are perhaps still open to the law*

      (f)   **(i)**   Ha addirittura parlato con il direttore

            (ii)   È morto proprio in quell'albergo

            (iii)   Poco a poco ho cominciato a capire.

5 Comparatives and superlatives

5.1 Regular comparatives

1   **(a)** La luce è più rapida del suono.

      (b) Ada è meno studiosa di sua sorella.

      (c) Mi also più tardi dei miei genitori.

      (d) Carla è più alta di loro.

      (e) Mangiamo la frutta meno spesso di te.

      (f) La casa di Nita è più grande della mia.

      (g) La tua macchina è più vecchia di quella di Giorgio.

      (h) Le tasse italiane sono più basse di quelle svedesi.

2   **(a)** È più facile capire che parlare una lingua.

      (b) Erano più spaventati che arrabbiati.

      (c) I suoi capelli sono più corti dei miei.

      (d) Piera si è vestita più rapidamente del solito.

      (e) Sandra ha meno di dieci anni.

      (f) È stato accoltellato più di trenta volte.

      (g) La strada è più percorribile dell'anno scorso.

      (h) Mara è più sicura di sé che in passato.

3   **(a)** più eleganti di quelle rosse

      (b) più eleganti che comode

      (c) più vino che acqua

      (d) più vino di Pino

      (e) più depresso/a di prima

      (f) più depresso/a che mai

4 *(b), (c) and (f) are comparisons with finite verbs.*
   (a) Guidare a Napoli è più pericoloso che guidare a Londra.
   (b) Guidare a Napoli è più pericolosi di quello che pensi.
   (c) Occuparsi dei bambini è più stressante di quanto pare.
   (d) Occuparsi dei bambini è più stressante che andare al lavoro/lavorare.
   (e) Mangiare in compagnia è più divertente che mangiare da soli.
   (f) Mangiare in compagnia è più costoso di quanto immagini.
5 **(a)** È tornata dalla gara fresca come una rosa.
   (b) Mia nonna è sorda come una campana.
   (c) Mio nonno è sano come un pesce.
   (d) Sei rosso come un peperone!
6 **(a)** così com'era
   (b) così come
   (c) (così) divertente come
   (d) così stupida come
7 **(a)** tanto generosa quanto Lisa/generosa come Lisa
   (b) tanto stupida quanto ingenua
   (c) tanto quanto te/come
   (d) tanto quanto dormono
8 **(a)** Secondo te viaggiare in motocicletta è tanto pericoloso quanto viaggiare in bicicletta? –
       No, in realtà viaggiare in motocicletta è meno pericoloso che viaggiare in bicicletta.
   (b) Sono convinto che prendere l'autobus è altrettanto comodo che prendere la metropolitana.
       – Non credo. Prendere l'autobus è molto più comodo che prendere la metropolitana.

5.2 Irregular comparatives

1 **(a)** migliore   **(b)** più buone   **(c)** peggiore   **(d)** più cattivo
2 **(a)** il più grande/il maggiore; il più piccolo/il minore
   (b) uno sforzo maggiore/più grande
   (c) in chiave minore
   (d) maggiore/più interesse
   (e) minor importanza
3 **(a)** più che durante la settimana
   (b) mangiare meno
   (c) più proteine e meno grassi
   (d) più sete che fame
   (e) meno facilità
4 **(a)** Mi hanno dato trecento euro in più.
   (b) l'anno prossimo ci saranno quattromila posti di lavoro in meno.
   (c) Il 58% delle italiane vuole perdere qualche chilo in meno.
   (d) purtroppo ci sono tante machine in più rispetto a vent'anni fa.
5 **(a)** Ha parlato con meno pazienza di prima.
   (b) Questa volta hanno ascoltato con più attenzione.
   (c) Ho molto meno fretta oggi.
   (d) Adesso ho molta più voglia di aiutarlo.
6 **(a)** meglio di me   **(c)** un posto migliore
   (b) peggio di ieri   **(d)** una macchina peggiore
7 **(a)** peggio/peggiore   **(c)** peggio/peggiore   **(e)** meglio
   (b) meglio/migliore   **(d)** meglio/migiore
8 **(a)** A calcio lui è più bravo/meglio di me.
   (b) Sono più bravi a tennis ma meno bravi a rugby/Sono meglio a tennis ma peggio a rugby.
   (c) La tua squadra è meno brava della mia/è peggio della mia.
9 **(a)** You love me less than (you love) Giorgio.
   (b) You love me less than Giorgio does (love me).
   (c) You understand me better than Maria does.
   (d) You understand me better than you understand Maria.

10   **(a)** Ti voglio più bene che prima.
   (b) Mi fa più male che mai.
   (c) Sto molto meglio adesso.
   (d) Stanno molto peggio di/che ieri.

5.3 Emphatic comparatives

1   **(a)** sempre più difficile, ancora più difficile
   (b) sempre meno probabile, ancora meno probabile
   (c) sempre più spesso, ancora più spesso
   (d) con sempre più attenzione/con ancora più attenzione
   (e) sempre meno freddo, ancora meno freddo
2   **(a)** sempre meno posti, ancora meno posti
   (b) sempre migliori, ancora migliori
   (c) uno sforzo sempre maggiore, uno sforzo ancora maggiore
   (d) mi piace sempre meno, mi piace ancora (di) meno
   (e) sempre di più, ancora di più
3   **(a)** Più legge, meno capisce.
   (b) Più mangio più mi deprimo.
   (c) Meno ci vediamo, meglio è.
   (d) Più mi sforzo, peggio è.

5.4 Regular relative superlatives

1   **(a)** (iii)   **(b)** (i)   **(c)** (iv)   **(d)** (ii)
2   **(b)** Gli Stati Uniti è fra i paesi più ricchi del mondo.
   (c) Stromboli, Lipari e Capri sono alcune delle isole più affascinanti d'Italia.
   (d) Il parmigiano è uno dei formaggi italiani più conosciuti all'estero.
3   **(a)** il cellulare più piccolo disponibile
   (b) parlava il più forte possibile
   (c) il servizio più lento immaginabile
   (d) la più obbiettiva possibile

5.5 Irregular relative superlatives

1   **(a)** il giocatore migliore di tutti tempi
   (b) l'allenatore peggiore del mondo
   (c) la squadra con i più punti fatti
   (d) con meno calorie
   (e) il piatto più buono
2   **(a)** È stata la spesa maggiore/più grande dell'anno.
   (b) Abita in una delle case più grandi del quartiere.
   (c) Sono tra le macchine peggiori di sempre/di tutti i tempi.
   (d) Angelo e Leo sono fra i migliori giocatori della squadra/sono fra i giocatori più bravi della squadra.
3   **(a)** meno energia possibile
   (b) il meno possibile
   (c) il più possibile
   (d) più errori di tutti/il maggior numero di errori. Normalmente ne fa meno di tutti.

5.6 Absolute superlatives

1   biondissimo, felicissimo, larghissimo, antichissimo, comicissimo, vicinissimo, rapidissimamente, benissimo, tardissimo, prestissimo: *the odd ones out are*: terribile (*already a superlative*) and ottimista (*which ends in* -a)
2   **(a)** È una ragazza allegrissima/felicissima.
   (b) È una persona molto egoista.
   (c) È un ottimo/bravissimo artista.
   (d) È un pessimo linguista.
   (e) È una persona veramente eeccezionale.

3   (a) un pessimo lavoro
    (b) il massimo rispetto
    (c) il minimo pretesto
    (d) ottima salute

4   (a) Sì, sono tornati tardissimo/molto tardi, più tardi di tutti.
    (b) Sì, ha lavorato molto veloce/velocissimamente, più veloce di tutti.
    (c) Sì, mi ha scritto molto regolarmente/(*rare:* regolarissimamente), più regolarmente di tutti.

5   (a) Sì, hanno lavorato benissimo, meglio di tutti.
    (b) Sì, ha aiutato pochissimo, ha aiutato meno di tutti.
    (c) Sì, insegna malissimo, insegna peggio di tutti gli altri insegnanti.
    (d) Sì, mi piace moltissimo, mi piace più di tutti.

6   (a) il centro più importante, una delle più ricche della Sicilia, le più antiche, l'isola più complessa del Eolie, le più importanti fumarole; **irregular relative superlative**: l'isola maggiore dell'Archipelago
    (b) il massimo emporio
    (c) le fumarole più importanti
    (d) l'isola più grande; l'emporio più grande di tutti; di altissima/grandissima efficacia
    (e) Lipari è una delle isole più affascinanti della Sicilia.

5.7 Further comparatives and superlatives

1   (a) Certo, ma tu sei altrettanto alto.
    (b) Lo so, ma il mio guadagna altrettanto.
    (c) Bravo, ma ne ho raccolti altrettanti.
    (d) Bene, ho fatto altrettanto.

2   (a) Michele porta la stessa camicia di ieri.
    (b) Giovanna vota per lo stesso partito dei genitori/dei suoi.
    (c) Paolo ha lo stesso parucchiere del fratello.

3   (a) rispetto a gennaio   (b) la stessa che in gennaio   (c) A differenza di suo fratello

4   (a) Preferirei andare a comprare una pizza piuttosto che andare al ristorante.
    (b) Ho intenzione di andare in campeggio piuttosto che dormire in albergo.
    (c) Ho deciso di partire con il treno piuttosto che prendere la macchina.

5   (a) Tu mangi meno di quanto dovresti.
    (b) Era più lontano di quanto (non) pensassimo.
    (c) Sono più anziani di quello che sembrano.
    (d) Mara è più giovanile di come me la ricordo.
    (e) È più ril assato di quando è arrivato.

6   (a) (iii)   (b) (iv)   (c) (ii)   (d) (i)

7   (a) insulti peggiori; migliori amici
    (b) (i)   I conflitti dilagano più rapidamente e sono più violenti che dal vivo
        (ii)   ci si sente più protetti
        (iii) amicizie poco più impegnative di un clic ogni tanto
        (iv) meno rispetto ad altri
        (v)   ha più possibilità di ottenere informazioni … rispetto a chi si chude nei legami familiari
        (vi) serve più a rafforzare relazioni … che a fare nuove conoscenze.

6 Suffixes

6.1 Noun and adjectival suffixes

1   (a) grassoccio, paesino di montagna
    (b) un mesetto, un simpaticona
    (c) deboluccia
    (d) cappellaccio, scarpacce
    (e) dei discorsoni, paroloni

2 **(a)** difettuccio
   (b) problemino
   (c) lavoraccio
   (d) stupidino/stupidello
   (e) Ha fatto un figurone *He made a marvellous impression* Che figuraccia ha fatto! *What a terrible impression he made!* Sembra un figurino *He looks like a model/like a fashion plate.*
3 A 4   B 6   C 11   D 3   E 1   F 13   G 9   H 5   I 7   J 2   K 8   L 10   M 12
4 **(a)** cappellano (*chaplain*), capellone (*hippy/long-haired person*). The others are hats.
   (b) pastello (*pastel crayon*): pastella is *batter*, pastina, *small pasta*, and pasticcio, *a mess*
   (c) cartello (*signpost*) and cartina (*map*). Cartaccia is *waste paper* and cartone *cardboard*.
   (d) bancarella (*stall*) and bancone (*counter*): banchina is *a platform* and banchetto a *banquet*
5 **(a)** F mattone *brick*   **(d)** F mulino *mill*
   (b) F postino *postman*   **(e)** F bagnino *life guard*
   (c) T   **(f)** F rubinetto *tap*

6.2 Adverbial suffixes

1 **(a)** un pochino   **(b)** benino   **(c)** prestino   **(d)** maluccio

6.3 Verb suffixes

1 **(a)** il cagnolino *puppy*, la zampetta *little paw*, il giocherellone *playful character*
   (b) Ha un nasetto adorabile e degli occhioni dolcissimi.

7 Personal pronouns

7.1 Subject pronouns

1 **(a)** Lei   **(b)** tu   **(c)** voi
2 **(a)** lui, lei   **(c)** tu, io   **(e)** tu, io no, loro
   (b) voi, noi   **(d)** Lei, noi due/tutti e due
3 **(a)** Mina e Elena, siete voi? – No, siamo noi, Marta e Lucia.
   (b) Sei tu, Dario? – No, sono io, Giuseppe.
   (c) Chi è che vuole una caramella? – Io no.
   (d) Noi andiamo al cinema, e voi due?
   (e) Chi è che viene domani? – Io e mia sorella.
   (f) Chi è che fa quel rumore? Sei tu? – No, sono loro, i vicini.

7.2 Reflexive and reciprocal pronouns

1 **(a)** mi trucco   **(c)** non ci lacchiamo   **(e)** ti togli
   (b) vi lamentate   **(d)** non si ricorda   **(f)** si trattengono
2 **(a)** si addormenta   **(b)** si lavano, si pettinano   **(c)** ci svegliamo, ci alziamo
3 **(a)** Mi alzo presto.   **(b)** Si lava i capelli.   **(c)** No, si laurea, io mi laureo.
4 **(a)** si incontrano, si salutano, si danno
   (b) ci vediamo, ci sentiamo
   (c) si scrive, scambiarsi
5 **(a)** We're not in the office, we're outside the bar. (reflexive)
   (b) See you tomorrow, then; we'll meet outside the bar. (reciprocal)
   (c) Bye, we'll speak/be in touch tomorrow. (reciprocal)
   (d) Yes, we both feel fine. (reflexive)
   (e) What are your grandchildren called? (reflexive)
   (f) Mariella and Paola often call each other. (reciprocal)

7.3 Direct and indirect object pronouns

1 **(a)** He bought some roses (DO) and gave them (DO) to his wife (IDO).
   (b) He bought her (IDO) some roses (DO).

      (c) Did you ask Francesca (IDO) to leave?

      (d) Did you ask her (IDO)?

2   (a) perché non li compri?   (c) non lo conosco.

      (b) ho intenzione di comprarla.   (d) le conosciamo.

3   (a) ti posso aiutare?   (c) vi ringrazio.

      (b) Arrivederla signore, la richiamerò.   (d) La accompagno io.

4   (a) No, non lo so.

      (b) l'ho detto tante volte.

      (c) Certo, è ovvio che lo sono!

      (d) Sì, ce l'ho.

      (e) Sì, ce li hanno.

5   (a) Sì, la ascolto spesso.   (c) L'aspetto da un'ora.

      (b) Sì, l'ho chiesto.   (d) Le ho pagate 150 euro.

6   (a) gli ho prestato.   (c) gli deve 100 euro.

      (b) Le devi restituire.   (d) le dovrà pagare.

7   (a) Le   (b) Le   (c) vi   (d) ti   (e) vi

8   (a) mi puoi aggiustare   (b) le potresti riparare   (c) ci può cambiare

9   (a) mi ha rotto   (b) gli ha macchiato   (c) gli ha bruciato

10   (a) Gli ho chiesto di comprare il pane.

      (b) Pino, gli hai detto di venire alle dieci?/Hai detto loro di venire alle dieci?

      (c) Dario gli devi rispondere subito. Devi rispondere (a) loro subito.

11   ***Direct object verbs:*** ascoltare, aspettare, disturbare, guardare, invitare, pregare, ringraziare, scusare, sentire. ***Indirect object verbs:*** comprare, impedire, incoraggiare, leggere, mandare, offrire, portare, prestare, spiegare, telefonare, vietare

12   (a) la   (c) lo   (e) lo

      (b) le   (d) gli   (f) gli leggerò/leggerò loro

13   (a) La ringrazio   (c) La disturbo?   (e) vi dispiace?

      (b) Le mando   (d) Le dispiace   (f) La prego

14   (a) Le ho consigliato di partire presto.

      (b) Dobbiamo convincerla ad aiutare.

      (c) Non puoi costringerlo a venire.

      (d) Gli ho permesso di andare alla festa.

15   (a) gli dirò di pagare

      (b) lo convincerò a pagare

      (c) le dovresti incoraggiare a studiare

      (d) le dovresti consigliare di studiare

      (e) li ho invitati

      (f) gli ho offerto la cena

7.4 *Ne*

1   (a) Quante ne prende? – Ne prendo mezzo chilo.

      (b) Quanto ne vuole? – Ne prendo quattro scatole.

      (c) Quanti ne vuole? Ne prendo due.

2   (a) Anch'io ne consumo pochissimi.

      (b) Anch'io ne consumo tanta.

      (c) Anch'io ne compro molto.

3   (a) La minestra è buona, ne vuoi un po'?

      (b) La pasta è fresca, quanta ne vuole?

      (c) Il vino è buono, ne vuole?

      (d) Le salsicce sono eccezionali, ne volete?

4   (a) No, grazie, non ne ho bisogno.

      (b) Ne sono sicuro/a.

      (c) Anche noi ne abbiamo parlato.

      (d) Ma non ne so niente.

      (e) Non lo so, tu cosa ne pensi?

(f) Non ne posso fare a meno

(g) Sì, e ne sono stato/sconvolto/a.

(h) Sì, ne sta uscendo in questo momento/proprio adesso.

7.5 *Ci*

1 **(a)** Sì, ci sono stato/a tante volte.

(b) Sì, ci andiamo fra poco.

(c) Sì, ci sono passato/a stamattina.

(d) Sì, ci sono andato/a ieri.

(e) Ci vado adesso.

2 **(a)** Nel mio appartamento ci sono sei stanze, ma c'è un bagno solo.

(b) Cosa c'è da mangiare? – Ci sono gli spaghetti alle vongole e c'è l'insalata.

(c) C'è Piero? – No, non c'è.

(d) Ci sono Andrea e Massimo? – No, non ci sono.

3 **(a)** Ci metto un'ora

(b) Ci vuole un'ora

(c) quanto ci mettono

(d) ci vogliono tre quarti d'ora

4 **(a)** Sì, ci sono abituato/a.

(b) Sì, ci siamo riusciti.

(c) Sì, (gli) ho risposto.

(d) No, non ci abbiamo pensato.

(e) Sì, li penso spesso/penso spesso a loro.

5 **(a)** There are few trains at this hour (*from* esserci: ci = *there*)

(b) We met by chance. (reciprocal)

(c) We enjoyed ourselves so much. (reflexive)

(d) I often think about the accident; do you think about it too? (ci = *about/of it/them*)

(e) I know you like the cinema; do you often go? (ci = *to there*)

(f) Giancarlo has asked us to help tomorrow. (*indirect object pronoun*)

(g) Our tenant never greets us. (*direct object pronoun*)

7.6 Object pronoun position

1 **(a)** Preferisco vederti più tardi.

(b) Ho intenzione di divertirmi al mare.

(c) Non so se ci vediamo giovedì.

(d) È importante vederci giovedì.

(e) So che Edda ci va domani.

(f) È meglio andarci domani.

(g) Perché non ne compriamo altri?

(h) Ho deciso di comprarne altri.

2 **(a)** Angelica è uscita, lasciandola aperta.

(b) Luigi ha scritto pregandola di rispondere.

(c) È caduto, lasciandoli cadere.

(d) Gli sto leggendo un racconto.

3 **(a)** Gianna, mandala.

(b) Signora, lo spedisca.

(c) Ragazzi, parlatene oggi.

(d) Signore, gli parli domani.

4 **(a)** Sai dirmi se la cena è pronta?

(b) Voglio lavarmi le mani.

(c) Devo finirlo stasera.

(d) Non posso aiutarli.

(e) Non toccarlo.

(f) Non preoccuparti.

5 **(a)** ii   **(b)** iii   **(c)** iv   **(d)** i

7.7 Disjunctive pronouns

1. **(a)** per me, per Lei
   (b) con loro, con lei
   (c) da me, da lui
   (d) secondo noi, secondo voi
2. **(a)** Porti me o lui al cinema?
   (b) Vuoi telefonare a lei o a lui?
   (c) Chiamerò loro e anche Gina.
   (d) Manderò una cartolina a te e anche ai miei.
3. **(a)** di sé   **(b)** di lui   **(c)** di lei   **(d)** a sé   **(e)** da sé   **(f)** per loro
4. **(a)** The actress will get a film made about herself. (D)
   (b) It is her true story told by herself. (D)
   (c) 'Know yourself' is a Greek saying. (D)
   (d) It is useless to blame others: you yourself are the problem. (S)
   (e) I am willing to go myself to pick you up. (S)
   (f) The blog is called 'A letter to myself'. (D)
   (g) The Minister is talking nonsense; he has said so himself. (S)
   (h) Poor thing, after the death of his wife he became a shadow of himself. (D)

7.8 Direct object pronouns and *ne* combined with indirect object or reflexive pronouns

1. **(a)** te lo   **(b)** ve la   **(c)** me ne   **(d)** ce li   **(e)** gliele   **(f)** gliene
2. **(a)** me li   **(b)** te le   **(c)** glielo   **(d)** ve la   **(e)** te ne   **(f)** gliene
3. **(a)** te le stiro   **(b)** gliela imbuco   **(c)** ve lo apro
4. **(a)** gliene scelgo?   **(b)** gliene tolgo?   **(c)** ve ne incarto?
5. **(a)** Chi te l'ha detto?   **(b)** Chi gliel'ha detto?   **(c)** Chi ve l'ha detto?
6. **(a)** Sì, te lo farò sapere senz'altro, te lo prometto!
   (b) Glielo dirò domani, signora, glielo prometto.
   (c) Certo, ve lo racconterò di sicuro, ve lo prometto!
7. **(a)** Se non potete venire, ce lo dite?
   (b) Anna, quando parti, me lo fai sapere?
   (c) Ivo, se vuoi venire, glielo puoi dire?
   (d) Ti aiuterò, Mina, te lo prometto!
8. **(a)** Perché non te li lavi?
   (b) Perché non se lo toglie, signora?
   (c) Ce ne compriamo (un po), allora?
   (d) Certo, me ne occupo io/lo faccio io.
   (e) Non possiamo permettercelo/Non ce lo possiamo permettere.
9. **(a)** È tardi, me ne vado.
   (b) Ma se ne frega!
   (c) Te la senti di venire al cinema?
   (d) Perché te la prendi?
   (e) Me la sono cavata all'esame.

7.9 Other pronoun combinations

1. **(a)** lo si beve come aperitivo!
   (b) la si beve come digestivo!
   (c) lo si vende dappertutto!
2. **(a)** Ti si è bucata la calza.
   (b) Gli si è sporcata la cravatta.
   (c) Le si è strappata la giacca.
   (d) Mi si è staccato il bottone.
3. **(a)** Ci si dorme
   (b) ci si sta

    (c) Non ci si capisce niente

    (d) Ci si riuscirà

4   (a) ci si alza   (b) Ci si veste   (c) i si diverte   (d) ci si abitua

5   (a) Ce ne sono cinque.

    (b) No, non ce n'è.

    (c) No, ce n'è pochissimo.

    (d) È vero, ce ne sono pochissime.

    (e) Bene, quante ce ne sono?

6   (a) È troppo tardi, non ce la faccio stasera.

    (b) È troppo difficile, non ce la fa.

    (c) Dino, perché ce l'hai con me?

    (d) Ti ci vuole molto per arrivare a scuola?

7   (a) In England in the last two years of school you specialise in three or four subjects. (1)

    (b) Flavia is very happy in Naples; she really likes it there a lot. (3)

    (c) It's a brillliant shop, you don't spend much there. (2)

7.10 Agreement of the past participle with object pronouns

1   (a) No, non li hanno ancora scelti.

    (b) No, non le abbiamo ancora innaffiate.

    (c) No, non l'ha ancora mandata.

    (d) No, non li hanno ancora prenotati.

2   (a) Ma te li ho prestati l'altro giorno!

    (b) Ma ve le abbiamo mandate la settimana scorsa!

    (c) Ma te li ho comprati stamattina!

    (d) Ma ve la abbiamo portati ieri!

3   (a) Li hai rotti tutti?

    (b) L'hai rovinata completamente?

    (c) L'hai sfasciata del tutto?

    (d) L'hai distrutto totalmente?

4   (a) Ne ho ordinate molte. Ne ho ordinate quattro.

    (b) Ne ho comprati tanti. Ne ho comprato/i due chili.

    (c) Ne ho ordinato parecchio. Ne ho ordinate/o tre bottiglie.

    (d) Ne ho comprata poca. Ne ho comprato un barattolo.

5   (a) me ne ha dati alcuni

    (b) me ne ha regalate alcune

    (c) me ne ha data qualcuna

    (d) me ne ha offerto qualcuno

    (e) ne ho portate un paio a casa

    (f) ne abbiamo bevuta un po'

6   (a) se l'è slogata   (b) se l'è storto   (c) se le è bruciate   (d) se l'è rotta

7   (a) comando io sola *I alone am in charge*; Devi decidere tu *It's up to you to decide.*

    (b) **Direct object:** ti capisco, la chiamò, lo vuoi? vuoi che lo sposi? **Indirect object:** le disse, mi piace, ti ho detto, ti darebbe. **Reflexive:** farsi avanti, non voglio maritarmi (*repeated*)

    (c) if your father orders you to?;   You will regret it. Think about it.

8 Possessives

8.1 Possessive adjectives and pronouns

1   (a) la tua   (c) il suo   (e) le vostre

    (b) il tuo   (d) i vostri/i loro   (f) il vostro

2   (a) Non ho mai visto la sua casa.

    (b) La sua casa è molto piccola.

    (c) Ti piace la loro nuova casa?

    (d) Il suo appartamento ha un balcone enorme.

(e) Il suo appartamento si trova al secondo piano.
(f) Il loro appartamento è in via Manin.
(g) Non mi piacciono le sue amiche.
(h) Siamo usciti con le loro amiche.
(i) I suoi figli frequentano l'università.
(j) I loro figli vivono tutti all'estero.

3 (a) i miei figli? (b) i nostri nipotini (c) le mie nipoti (d) le nostre figlie
4 (a) mio, nostra (c) la nostra, il suo (e) mia, le nostre
(b) mio, la sua (d) mia, il mio
5 (a) la mia (b) le sue (c) il tuo (d) il mio (e) ai tuoi
6 (a) tuo, mio, il mio (b) sua, mia, la mia (c) sue, sue, mie

8.2 Expressing possession with 's/s' endings

1 (a) La mamma di Leonardo è malata.
(b) La moglie del signor Palladino è in vacanza.
(c) Il gatto dei vicini è nero.
(d) Ho trovato le scarpe di Elisabetta e anche quelle di Antonio.
(e) Ho perso la lettera di Marta e anche quella di sua sorella.
(f) Ti vedrò/Ci vediamo da Giovanni.

8.3 Possessives with other determiners and with *proprio*

1 (a) un mio amico/un amico mio
(b) una sua collega
(c) un loro conoscente
(d) dei nostri amici/amici nostri
(e) dei miei colleghi
2 (a) tre suoi amici/tre amici suoi
(b) alcuni nostri clienti
(c) quei tuoi amici/quegli amici tuoi
3 (a) proprio (b) la propria (c) propria/sua (d) i miei (propri)

8.4 Omission of the possessive in Italian

1 (a) l'ombrello (b) la moglie (c) il golf (d) il piede (e) il cappello

9 Demonstratives

9.1 Demonstrative adjectives and pronouns

1 Ho preso in prestito: questa lampada, queste sedie, questo divano, questi cuscini, quest'armadio, questo scaffale, questi specchi.
2 Mi fa vedere: quella borsetta, quelle cravatte, quel maglione, quei pantaloni, quello specchio, quell'anello, quegli orecchini.
3 (a) quella, quell' (c) quel, quello (e) quei, quegli
(b) quell', quell' (d) quel, quell' (f) quegli, quei
4 (a) quella lì (c) quelli lì, quei tre (e) quello? quell'altro più piccolo
(b) quello lì (d) quelli lì, quelli verdi
5 (a) Questa è la cucina e questo qui è il bagno.
(b) Questa qui è la mia camera e quella là è la tua.
(c) Quanto costa questa? E quella?
(d) Quanto costano queste? E quelle?

9.2 Other ways of expressing 'this' and 'that'

1 (a) Questo/Ciò non mi interessa.
(b) Questo/Ciò non vuol dire che non venga/verrà.
(c) Questo/Ciò non sembra giusto.
(d) Non è vero.

2　(a) Che peccato/È un peccato, non può andare a sciare.
　　(b) Che figura/È imbarazzante, cosa facciamo?
　　(c) Che assurdità/È assurdo!
　　(d) Che seccatura! Hai una chiave di riserva?
　　(e) Grazie, sei molto gentile.
3　(a) È qui che andava a scuola?
　　(b) È là/lì che fa la spesa?
　　(c) È qua/qui che si trova il museo?
　　(d) È lì che lavora sua figlia?
4　(a) Ecco perché/È per questo che sono in ritardo.
　　(b) Ecco perché/È per questo che la macchina non parte!
　　(c) Guarda, ecco come funziona …
　　(d) Mio fratello è un amico di suo marito, ecco come lo so/l'ho saputo.
5　(a) Per avere accesso a Internet, ecco quello che si deve fare …
　　(b) Ecco quello che mi ha detto …
　　(c) Sì, è quello che ho intenzione di fare.
　　(d) Non è quello che voglio/volevo dire.

10 Interrogatives

10.1 Asking questions

1　(a) Partono stasera? *Are they leaving tonight?*
　　(b) Cambiamo discorso? *Shall we change the subject?*
　　(c) Non vengono con noi? *Aren't they coming with us?*
　　(d) È arrivata la posta? *Has the post arrived?*
2　(a) Quando viene l'avvocato?
　　(b) La signorina è polacca?
　　(c) Cosa vuole la dottoressa?
3　(a) La posta è arrivata, (non è) vero?
　　(b) Ti chiami Carla, (non è) vero?
　　(c) È una donna affascinante, non ti sembra?
　　(d) Partono lunedì, (non è) vero?
　　(e) Non hai pagato, vero?
　　(f) La verità/Il fatto è che non vogliono venire, non è così?

10.2 Question words

1　(a) La signora, per quando lo vuole?
　　(b) Voi, di dove siete?
　　(c) Miriam, da quanto tempo sei in Italia?
2　(a) quand'è che devi partire?
　　(b) dov'è che ci troviamo stasera?
　　(c) da quando aspetti?
3　(a) Quando partite?
　　(b) Quando parte il treno?/Il treno, quando parte?
　　(c) Dove andate?
　　(d) Dove vanno I bambini?/I bambini, dove vanno?
　　(e) Perché ridi?
　　(f) Perché ridono, le ragazze?/Le ragazze, perché ridono?
4　(a) Dimmi dove si trova il cinema.
　　(b) Mi sai dire quando torna Maria?
　　(c) Mi dispiace, non so quando apre la banca.
5　(a) Come mai siete in ritardo?
　　(b) Come si fa/faccio per andare in centro?

    (c) Com'è il tuo nuovo lavoro?

    (d) Non voglio uscire. – Perché no?

    (e) Mi dà un bicchiere d'acqua? – Come no!

    (f) Non so come funziona: come devo fare?

6   **(a)** Quando arrivano Pino e Mariella?/P. e M., quando arrivano?

    (b) Quand'è che parte l'aereo?

    (c) Dove abita Susanna?/S. dove abita?

    (d) Dov'è che lavora tua padre?

7   **(a)** Chi è, quell'uomo?

    (b) Di chi è quel libro?

    (c) A chi piace il gelato?

    (d) Di chi parli?

    (e) Di chi è quest'ombrello?

    (f) Che cosa/Cosa hai fatto?

    (g) Di che cosa hai bisogno?

    (h) Di che cosa parli?

8   **(a)** cosa vuole

    (b) a che cosa serve

    (c) di che cosa è fatto

    (d) a chi appartiene or di chi è

    (e) per chi è

    (f) di chi è

    (g) di chi sono/siano

9   **(a)** Che ora è?

    (b) Che lavoro fa?

    (c) Qual è il suo numero di telefono?

    (d) Qual è il suo sport preferito?

    (e) Com'è il suo insegnante? Che tipo è il suo insegnante?

10 In sentence (c): Quali/Che giornali compri?

11 **(a)** v   **(c)** ii   **(e)** iii. The mystery object is: una palla *a ball*

    (b) iv   **(d)** i

12 **(a)** Quanti spaghetti vuoi?

    (b) Quanta salsa vuoi?

    (c) In quanti siete?

    (d) Non so quante uova rimangono.

13 **(a)** Quant'è lontana la tua casa?

    (b) Quanto ci impieghi per arrivarci?

    (c) Quant'è grande la tua cucina?

    (d) Quant'è larga?

    (e) Fra quanto ci possiamo vedere?

10.3 Special uses of *perché?* *che?* and *chi?*

1   **(a)** Perché pagare più del necessario?

    (b) Ma perché aiutarlo?

    (c) Ma perché arrabbiarsi?

    (d) Che lo chiami a fare?

    (e) Che ci vai a fare a Londra?

    (f) Che ci stai a fare qui?

2   **(d)** What on earth are you calling him for? He's never at home.

    (e) What on earth are you going to London for?

    (f) What on earth are you doing here?

3   **(a)** Ma Giulia, chi te lo fa fare? *But Giulia, whatever for?/how/why the hell do you do it?*

    (b) Ma chi ve lo fa fare? But *whatever for?/how/why the hell do you do it?*

10.4 Distinguishing interrogatives from relatives

1
- (a) che cosa
- (b) quello che/ciò che
- (c) chi
- (d) che
- (e) con chi
- (f) con cui
- (g) che
- (h) quale

11 Exclamations

11.1 Exclamations with *che! come! quanto!*

1
- (a) Che delusione! Che peccato!
- (b) Che guaio! Che disastro!
- (c) Che pasticcio! (Che rabbia!)

2
- (a) Che bel giardino!
- (b) Che meraviglia, quella casa!
- (c) Che simpatici quei ragazzi!
- (d) Che amore quella ragazza!
- (e) Che carini questi orecchini!
- (f) Che bellina questa maglietta!

3
- (a) Che stupido/a che sono!
- (b) Che male che suonano!
- (c) Che distratto/a che sei!

4
- (a) Quanto rumore qui dentro!
- (b) Che rumore tremendo!
- (c) Che gente antipatica!
- (d) Quanta gente c'è in giro!

5 (a) Quanto   (b) Quanti   (c) Come   (d) Come/Quanto

6 (a) ii   (b) iii   (c) ii, iii   (d) i, ii, iii

11.2 Other exclamations

1
- (a) accidenti! caspità! or, familiar mannaggia!
- (b) non me lo dire! caspita! mamma mia!
- (c) accipicchia! stupenda!
- (d) bravi!/bravissimi!
- (e) o dio!/dio mio!
- (f) caspità!/ma insomma!
- (g) ma scherzi!/o dio!/mamma mia!
- (h) per carità!

12 Indefinites

12.1 Indefinite pronouns

1
- (a) qualcosa
- (b) qualcuno
- (c) Non c'è niente/nulla
- (d) nessuno
- (e) nessuno
- (f) qualcosa

2
- (a) Vuole qualcosa?
- (b) Non conosco nessuno che si chiama Carlo.
- (c) C'è qualcuno al telefono.
- (d) Non ho bisogno di niente.
- (e) C'è qualcuno alla porta?
- (f) Qualcuno ha visto i miei occhiali?

3
- (a) Sì, qualcuna
- (b) Sì qualcuno
- (c) No, nessuno
- (d) Ce n'è qualcuno sulla scrivania
- (e) Ce n'è qualcuna nel cassetto

4   **(a)** Nessuno dei   **(c)** qualcuno di noi   **(e)** Nessuno di noi
    (b) Qualcuna delle **(d)** qualcuno di voi? **(f)** Qualcuno di loro
5   **(a)** Nessuno dei miei amici vuole fare il medico.
    (b) Non mi piace nessuna delle mie zie.
    (c) Qualcuno dei vostri figli è sposato?
    (d) I miei hanno lavori interessanti ma nessuno dei due ha fatto l'università.
    (e) Mia fratello ha scattato due foto, ma non mi piace nessuna delle due (*or:* né l'una né l'altra).
    (f) Non c'è più posto nella macchina; qualcuno di voi dovrà andare a piedi.
6   **(a)** Può chiederlo a qualcun'altro?
    (b) Prende altro?/qualcos'altro?
    (c) Nessun altro lo sa fare
    (d) Ha qualcos'altro da fare?
    (e) Non ho altro da dire
    (f) Non ha nient'altro?
    (g) Non ha visto nessun altro?
7   **(a)** Ognuno ha diritto/Tutti hanno diritto alla pensione
    (b) In ognuna delle stanze
    (c) Ognuno dei cinque figli
    (d) Ognuno di voi
    (e) in ognuna delle sue parti
8   **(a)** 20 centesimi ciascuna
    (b) tre euro ciascuno
    (c) ciascuno dei soldati
    (d) 200 euro ciascuna
    (e) un computer ciascuno
    (f) Ciascuno di noi
9   **(a)** Ognuno ha bisogno di affetto/Tutti hanno bisogno …
    (b) Ognuna delle sue figlie ha sposato un uomo ricco.
    (c) In ognuno dei quattro ristoranti/In tutti e quattro i ristoranti i camerieri sono antipatici.
    (d) Ognuno di voi deve fare uno sforzo.
    (e) Ciascuno di voi merita un premio.
    (f) I gigli sono cari. Costano 10 euro l'uno/ciascuno.
10 **(a)** 65 euro l'uno/ciascuno
    (b) tutte e due/l'una e l'altra
    (c) o l'uno o l'altro
    (d) né l'una né l'altra/nessuna delle due
11 **(a)** It's nothing: anyone would have done it.
    (b) It's simple: anyone can do it.
    (c) Whoever calls, tell them I'm out.
    (d) Any one of you must be ready to help

12.2 Indefinite adjectives

1   **(a)** ogni   **(c)** ogni   **(e)** ogni
    (b) Qualche **(d)** qualche **(f)** qualche
2   **(a)** ciascun **(c)** Ogni   **(e)** ciascun' **(g)** Ciascun
    (b) ogni   **(d)** ogni   **(f)** Ogni   **(h)** Ogni
3   **(a)** nessun problema
    (b) nessun'alternativa
    (c) nessuno sforzo
    (d) nessuna voglia
4   Non c'è alcun problema
    Non abbiamo alcun'alternativa

5   **(a)** A qualunque qualsiasi ora.

     (b) Qualunque/qualsiasi colore va bene.

     (c) Uno qualsiasi. (*or, without* qualsiasi: quello che vuoi tu)

     (d) Una qualsiasi (*or*: quella che vuoi tu/che vuole lei)

6   **(a)** I'll accept your decision, whatever it may be/whatever it is.

     (b) Elisabetta would do anything for him.

12.3 Indefinite adjectives and pronouns

1   **(a)** tutto   **(e)** tutta la   **(i)** tutta la

     (b) tutti   **(f)** tutte le   **(j)** tutti quanti gli

     (c) tutti   **(g)** tutti quanti

     (d) tutti i   **(h)** tutta quanta

2   **(a)** (iii) is ungrammatical because **diverso** in the singular is used as an adjective, not as a pronoun. In the plural only it can be synonymous with both the adjectives and the pronouns **molti/e** and **parecchi/e.**

     (b) (ii) This means *I have something else to do*.

     (c) He would not use the following: (iii) = *I've made different mistakes*; (v) = *I've made other mistakes*; (vi) = *I've made as many mistakes*.

3   **(c)** is ungrammatical: it should be 'molto poca', as 'molto' is an adverb modifying the adjective 'poca'.

4   **(a)** Ci dev'essere qualche altra soluzione.

     (b) Tutti gli altri posti sono occupati.

     (c) Tutti gli altri sono tornati a casa.

     (d) Puoi prendere tutto il resto.

12.4 Indefinites and quantity

1   **(a)** Tutte e tre le case

     (b) Tutti e cinque gli appartamenti

     (c) Tutte e quattro le mie sorelle

     (d) Tutti e sei giudici

2   **(a)** La maggior parte dei miei parenti abitano in Germania.

     (b) La maggior parte di loro sono dottori.

     (c) Gran parte della penisola sarà coperta di nuvole.

     (d) Ha perso la gran parte della sua fortuna.

3   **(a)** Puoi mettere l'una o l'altra, ti stanno bene tutt'e due/entrambe.

     (b) Puoi chiedere all'uno o all'altro, sono entrambi/tutt'e due degli esperti.

     (c) Vanno bene tutt'e due, sono belli entrambi.

12.5 Indefinites expressing place and time

1   **(a)** I've left my diary somewhere.

     (b) Let's go somewhere else.

     (c) I'm not going anywhere.

     (d) Don't they sell it anywhere else?

     (e) You can find these shoes anywhere/everywhere.

     (f) They have looked everywhere else.

2   **(a)** Lo hai visto da qualche parte?

     (b) Ti ho conosciuto/a da qualche parte.

     (c) Andiamo da qualche altra parte?

     (d) Non voglio andare da nessuna parte.

     (e) Non voglio andare da nessun'altra parte.

     (f) Ho cercato dappertutto.

3   **(a)** With the new software you can find a taxi at any time/at a moments notice.

     (b) You have to be ready to leave at any time.

     (c) You can eat at any time of the day if you have a healthy diet.

4   **(a)** Mangio quando mi pare/voglio, in qualsiasi momento della giornata.

(b) Ogni volta che ne hai voglia, vieni a trovarmi/Vieni a trovarmi quando vuoi.

(c) Ho bisogno di essere in contatto in ogni momento/in qualsiasi momento.

13 Relative pronouns

13.1 Main relative pronouns

1 (a) Marta è un'amica che mi è molto simpatica.
   (b) Eduardo è un lontano cugino che lavora a Parigi.
   (c) I signori Colucci sono i vicini che litigano tanto.
   (d) La Rinascente è un grande magazzino che si trova nelle maggiori città italiane.
   (e) *Roma città aperta* è un film di Rossellini che non ho mai visto.
2 (a) L'appartamento che ho affittato è al primo piano.
   (b) L'uomo che hai conosciuto/incontrato è il marito della padrona di casa, il quale parte oggi.
      L'uomo che hai conosciuto/incontrato è il marito della padrona di casa, la quale parte oggi.
   (c) Hanno aumentato l'affitto, il che non è giusto.
3 (a) che   (b) che   (c) che/la quale   (d) che/il quale
4 (a) Relative – Quello/Ciò che fai è assurdo.
   (b) Relative – Puoi fare quello/ciò che vuoi.
   (c) Relative – Farò quello che posso.
   (d) Relative – Quello/Ciò che non piace è il colore.
   (e) Exclamation – Che colore orribile!
   (f) Interrogative – Che cosa posso fare?
   (g) Interrogative – Non so che cosa fare.
5 *'Quanto' can be used in* (3c): Farò quanto posso

13.2 Relative pronouns with prepositions

1 (a) Il professor Binni è un insegnante per cui/per il quale ho molto rispetto.
   (b) Carlotta è la nipote a cui/alla quale ho regalato una bicicletta.
   (c) Aldo e Stefano sono colleghi con cui/con i quali lavoro da due anni.
   (d) Fiorella è la mia assistente senza la quale non potrei lavorare.
   (e) Il signor Feroni è il nostro capo secondo il quale siamo tutti pigri.
2 (a) Questo è il Duomo accanto al quale si trova il Battistero.
   (b) Qui c'è una bella piazza in centro alla quale c'è un monumento ai caduti.
   (c) Queste sono le due fontane dietro alle quali si vede il museo.
   (d) Qui ci sono i giardini pubblici di fronte ai quali si trova la stazione.
3 (a) Ho due stampanti, di cui/delle quali una non è mia.
   (b) Qui ci sono tre calcolatrici, due delle quali sono rotte.
   (c) Mi ha dato delle cartelle, alcune delle quali sono sparite.
   (d) Abbiamo cenato con degli amici di cui/dei quali uno è deputato.
   (e) Hanno sette figlie ognuna delle quali è bellissima.
4 (a) Il 1905 è l'anno in cui è nato mio nonno.
   (b) Le ragioni per cui è emigrato non sono chiare.
   (c) La casa dove/in cui abitava a Londra è stata bombardata durante la guerra.

13.3 Relatives with special verbs

1 (a) a cui piace; che mi piace
   (b) a cui hanno concesso l'asilo; che hanno richiesto l'asilo
   (c) che mi ha offerto il posto; a cui hanno offerto il lavoro

13.4 'Whose'

1 (a) Ho appena incontrato una signora la cui figlia conosce Anna.
   (b) Mia cugina le cui figlie abitano a Parigi si sente molto sola.
   (c) Il camion i cui freni non funzionavano ha provocato l'incidente.
   (d) È un romanzo di fantascienza di cui non ricordo l'autore.
   (e) Abita in un paesino di cui mi dimentico il nome.

13.5 Other relative pronouns

1   (a) Quello che preferisci.
    (b) Quelle che vuoi.
    (c) Quella che studia medicina.
    (d) Certo/Come no!, prendi quelli che vuoi.
    (e) Chi arriva/Quelli che arrivano in ritardo dovranno tornare domani.
2   (a) tutto quello che
    (b) tutto quello che
    (c) tutti quelli che
    (d) tutti quelli che
3   (a) Sentences (a) and (b).
    (b) *in sentence* (b) tutto quello che *can translate as 'whatever'.*
4   (a) *Relative* – I'm afraid that those who haven't got a student's card can't eat in the canteen.
    (b) *Interrogative* 'chi' *(indirect question)*
    (c) *Relative* – The deadline for those who want to enrol on the course is 3 September.
    (d) *Relative* – It's an ideal place for those who want to have a rest.
    (e) *Relative* – The Miramare Hotel takes care of those who want total relaxation.
    (f) *Relative* – There are those who prefer dogs and those who prefer cats instead.
5   'Quelli che' can replace the relative 'chi', therefore it cannot be used in sentence (b), where chi is interrogative.
6   The key phrases are: (i) Una cosa a cui non rinuncerò mai è … and (ii) Una cosa di cui non posso fare a meno è … You may have followed them with something like: … la vacanza al mare/il vino con la cena/scarpe nuove/un sigaro ogni tanto, ecc.

14 Negatives

14.1 Single negatives

1   (a) No, non mi chiamo Edda, mi chiamo Emma.
    (b) Non credo. – Spero di no!
    (c) Perché vorrei sapere se ha pagato o no/o meno.
    (d) No, mi piace viaggiare in treno, non in aereo.
    (e) No, mi dispiace, niente vino oggi.

14.2 Negatives used without *non*

1   (a) Mica male!   (e) Mai più
    (b) Nient'affatto   (f) Assolutamente/Per niente!
    (c) Niente   (g) Per niente!
    (d) Mai!   (h) Assolutamente no!/Mai!

14.3 Double negatives

1   (a) Non ho visto nessuno.
    (b) Non ha mai visto il Monte Bianco.
    (c) Non è ancora partito.
    (d) Non voglio mangiare niente.
    (e) Non vuole mai aiutare.
    (f) Non voglio più venire.
2   (a) Non mi piace affatto.
    (b) Non lo conosco per niente.
    (c) Non è per niente antipatico.
    (d) Non devi assolutamente andare via.
3   (a) (i) Giacomo has not even called. (ii) Not even Giacomo has called.
    (b) (i) I didn't go either. (ii) I didn't even go.
    (c) (i) I don't even like it. (ii) I don't like it either.

14.4 Further uses of negatives

1 (a) Non ti sei mica dimenticato di imbucare la lettera?
   (b) Non hai mica invitato i vicini?
   (c) Non hai mica lasciato acceso il forno?
2 (a) Non gli ho mica detto che parto.
   (b) Non ho mica intenzione di pagare.
   (c) No! non è mica stata colpa mia.
   (d) lui non capisce mica.
   (e) Non voglio assolutamente aiutare.
3 (a) Non spiega mai niente.
   (b) Non offenderà più nessuno.
   (c) Non è rimasto niente.
   (d) Non ho ancora trovato niente.
   (e) Non ho mica trovato niente.
   (f) Non dirò niente a nessuno.

15 Prepositions

15.1 The use of prepositions: general observations

15.2 The main simple prepositions

1 (a) Abito all'ultimo piano.
   (b) Il ristorante è all'angolo, a destra.
   (c) La libreria è a 200 metri da casa mia.
   (d) Abito in una città/cittadina a sud ovest di Londra.
   (e) C'è un film interessante alla televisione.
   (f) C'è tua madre al telefono./Tua madre è al telefono.
   (g) Ci vediamo a/in dicembre, a Natale.
   (h) A che ora vieni, Ida?
2 (a) Devo andare in Francia.
   (b) Devo telefonare in Italia.
   (c) Vado in aereo.
   (d) Entriamo nel negozio.
   (e) Abiti/a in Inghilterra?
   (f) È nel cassetto.
   (g) Dormo in treno.
3 (a) Devo telefonare a mia cugina in italia – a Roma.
   (b) No, s'impara in pochi mesi.
   (c) Siamo in sei.
   (d) È nato/a in aprile alle 5 di mattina, all'alba.
4 (a) I left London yesterday.
   (b) I left the office at seven.
   (c) The plane is leaving from gate 34.
   (d) We came in through/bythe window.
   (e) Don't look out of the window.
   (f) When I was a student/As a student, I liked travelling.
   (g) I've been here since Saturday.
   (h) Do you want something to drink??
5 (a) dalla   (b) da   (c) di   (d) da
6 (a) in Italia   (e) a Bari   (i) in piscina
   (b) in Sicilia   (f) al supermercato   (j) da Franco
   (c) in Toscana   (g) alla Rinascente   (k) dal parrucchiere
   (d) a Capri   (h) in farmacia   (l) dal medico

    (m) allo zoo   **(o)** a casa
    (n) al mare   **(p)** in campagna

7 **(a)** a casa mia   **(e)** in trattoria   **(i)** dal fruttivendolo
    (b) in biblioteca   **(f)** da mia sorella   **(j)** al ristorante
    (c) da Franca   **(g)** al bar   **(k)** da 'Gigino'
    (d) alla fermata dell'autobus   **(h)** in banca   **(l)** in centro

8 **(a)** a seat/safety belt
    (b) Mauro's house
    (c) A painting by Leonardo
    (d) a 2,000 euro rise
    (e) a two-litre bottle
    (f) a winter's day

9 **(a)** un/un'insegnante di lingue
    (c) la moglie del primo ministro
    (c) un romanzo di Manzoni
    (d) una bambina di dieci anni
    (e) il volo delle otto
    (f) un viaggio di cinque ore
    (g) le otto di sera

10 **(a)** di **(b)** da **(c)** da **(d)** di **(e)** di **(f)** da

11 **(a)** d'oro **(c)** a fiori **(e)** da sole
    (b) da sera **(d)** di paglia **(f)** a quadretti

12 **(a)** dalla **(c)** dalla **(e)** di
    (b) di **(d)** di **(f)** di/da, da

13 **(a)** Lavoro per una compagnia aerea.
    (b) No, sono qui per affari.
    (c) Sono qui per imparare l'italiano. È per il mio lavoro.
    (d) Mi trattengo (per) un mese.
    (e) Mi dispiace, ho molti appuntamenti (per) domani.

14 **(a)** ii The car didn't start this morning because of the cold.
    (b) iii He didn't come to the party out of shyness.
    (c) i My daughter suffers a lot from her fiancé being away.

15 **(a)** per **(b)** per terra **(c)** per strada

16 **(a)** in machina **(c)** da lui **(e)** per un'altra strada
    (b) dal treno **(d)** da/per Milano

17 **(a)** Mirella ha quarant'anni ma ha la voce di una ragazzina.
    (b) Ho visto la camera dei ragazzi.
    (c) È un gioco da bambino.
    (d) La trattano da adulto.
    (e) La ragione del ritardo non è chiara
    (f) La ragione per cui è venuta non è chiara.

18 **(a)** iii **(b)** i **(c)** ii
19 **(a)** ii **(b)** i **(c)** iii
20 **(a)** con la macchina **(c)** con i baffi lunghi
    (b) con il treno **(d)** con i capelli biondi tinti

21 **(a)** I left the documents **on** the desk.
    (b) The cat climbed **onto** the roof.
    (c) *Bridge **over** the River Kwai* is a rather old film.
    (d) It's a film **about** the war in Japan.
    (e) We've been **up** Mont Blanc.
    (f) The journey costs **about** two thousand euros.
    (g) I read the news **in** the paper.
    (h) I left my umbrella **on** the bus.

22 **(a)** I'm arriving between five and six.
    (b) I'm arriving in a week's time.
    (c) Mario is sitting between his cousin and his grandfather.

(d) Out of my cousins I prefer Luciano.

(e) The crossroads is two kilometres ahead.

(f) The new house is between Genoa and Leghorn (Livorno).

(g) You can see the house through the trees.

(h) There is a special understanding between us. *Or:* We really understand each other.

15.3 Other prepositions

1 **di** needed in (b) dopo di me (d) verso di lui (f) fuori dell'Italia (h) senza di te
2 (b) dentro di me (c) dietro (alla) porta (d) dietro di/a te (e) oltre a te (f) oltre ai
3 (a) nel cortile
   (b) accanto alla sua macchina
   (c) di fronte al cinema
   (d) dall'altra parte della strada
   (e) in fondo alla strada
   (f) davanti a casa sua
4 (a) da parte di sconosciuti
   (b) da parte del Comune
   (c) da parte degli alleati
   (d) da parte degli azionisti
5 (a) con sopra una ciliegia
   (b) con accanto un pub
   (c) con fuori un albero enorme
   (d) con di fronte un parco
   (e) con due fontane in mezzo
   (f) con intorno un recinto elettrico

15.4 Adjectives used with prepositions

1 (a) Pina è molto interessata ad imparare il greco.
   (b) Alberta è proprio decisa a cambiare casa.
   (c) Ida è ansiosa di partire, ma Delia non sembra disposta a muoversi.
   (d) Diego è molto soddisfatto del suo lavoro, è responsabile di tutto il reparto.
2 (a) Sono stufo/a del mio lavoro.
   (b) Sono contento/a dei risultati.
   (c) È gentile con me.
   (d) È sposata con un ingegnere.
3 (a) bravo a   (c) costituito di/da   (e) coperto di
   (b) bravo a, in   (d) coperto con   (f) pronta a/ad

15.5 Nouns and prepositions

1 (a) La causa dell'incidente non è chiara.
   (b) Mia sorella è un'esperta dell'Italia medievale.
   (c) Il suo amore per gli animali è noto.
   (d) La sua avversione per i gatti era straordinaria.
2 (1) a casa   (4) in meno   (7) del governo   (10) a
   (2) in viale Tebaldi (5) sulla patente   (8) per   (11) da
   (3) con   (6) nella rete   (9) dalla   (12) di

16 Connectives

16.1 Adding information

1 1 e anche 2 inoltre 3 e 4 oltre a 5 in più
2 (a) Both Emilio and Elisabetta passed the exam.
   (b) Emilio passed the exam, and so did Elisabetta.
   (c) Neither Giorgio nor Giovanna passed the exam.
   (d) After the party Giorgio came back drunk. Not only that, he was stopped by the police.

16.2 Clarifying information

1 (a) cioè (b) o meglio (c) Già (d) Infatti (e) Ecco
2 (a) infatti (b) in effetti (c) anzi

16.3 Expressing alternatives

1 (a) abbiamo la birra o il vino
  (b) possiamo rimanere qui oppure andare al cinema
  (c) altrimenti perderemo il contratto
  (d) invece di mandare un'e-mail.
2 (a) Invece di mangiare caramelle, perché mangia piuttosto della frutta?
  (b) Voglio lavorare con lei anziché/piuttosto che con lui.
  (c) Preferisco andare da solo piuttosto che aspettare.
  (d) Non bere caffè, prendi piuttosto/invece un tè al limone.

16.4 Comparing, contrasting and contradicting

1 (a) ma (c) comunque (e) eppure
  (b) mentre (d) invece (f) d'altra parte
2 (a) invece ho cenato … (b) anzi
  (c) in realtà (d) viceversa/invece

16.5 Expressing reasons, purpose, cause and effect

1 (a) Dal momento che/Dato che/Visto che
  (b) Dato che/Siccome
  (c) Avendo perso la chiave. Siccome avevo perso
2 (a) Dato che/Siccome è il tuo compleanno, possiamo mangiare fuori.
  (b) Non possiamo partire a causa dello sciopero/perché c'è sciopero.
  (c) È per questo che è arrabbiato?
  (d) È merito tuo se/Grazie a te sono stato promosso.
  (e) Sono in ritardo per causa tua/È colpa tua se sono in ritardo.
3 (a) ii The car has broken down, so I have to take it to the garage/mechanic.
  (b) iii He broke his leg, so he couldn't go skiing.
  (c) iv Profits have dropped, so as a result they have closed one factory.
  (d) i I've organised things so as to save more.
4 (a) per (b) perché (c) in modo di/per (d) pur di

16.6 Making exceptions, concessions and conditions

1 (a) meno/tranne/fuorché/eccetto (c) Eccetto/tranne
  (b) a parte (d) fuorché
2 (a) anche se (c) lo stesso/comunque
  (b) malgrado/nonostante (d) comunque
3 (a) Benché (c) Malgrado/nonostante
  (b) Ammesso che (d) Pur essendo
4 (a) Per quanto (c) caso mai (e) Nel caso che
  (b) comunque (d) Ammettendo che
5 (a) Any time is fine for me as long as/provided I know beforehand.
  (b) We'll meet in the library unless it's closed.
  (c) I'll come with you as long as I'm back before ten.
  (d) I'll forgive him only on condition he says sorry to my sister.

16.7 Time sequence

1 (a) *The odd one is*: in questi giorni.
  (b) *The odd one is*: nei giorni scorsi.
  (c) *The odd one is*: nei prossimi giorni.
  (d) *The odd one is*: in quel momento.

2 (a) ii   (b) iv   (c) i   (d) iii   (e) v
3 (a) fino a   (c) finché (non)/fino a quando (non)
  (b) finché   (d) finché/fino a quando

16.8 Initiating, concluding and generalising

1 (a) Dunque/Allora
  (b) prima di tutto
  (c) in linea di massima
  (d) in fondo
  (e) nel complesso
2 (1) actually/on the other hand (2) on the one hand … on the other (3) also (4) basically
  (5) but also (6) on the one hand (7) however (8) since (9) still/also (10) too/as well/also
  (11) as long as/until (12) this is
3 1 non solo 2 ma 3 nonostante si tratti di 4 infatti 5 cioè 6 perciò 7 comunque 8 mentre

17 Numerals and units of measurement

17.1 Cardinal numbers

1 (a) un chilo   (f) quarant'otto ore   (k) mille euro
  (b) una fetta   (g) tre capitoli   (l) diecimila euro
  (c) diciassette libri   (h) ventitré ragazze   (m) un milione di pesetas
  (d) diciannove pagine   (i) cento sterline   (n) cinque milioni di dollari
  (e) trentun(o) studenti   (j) duecento sterline   (o) tre milioni cinquecentomila euro
2 (a) Il dieci per cento degli
  (b) Il cinquantun per cento della
  (c) venticinque euro al litro
  (d) il 2002
  (e) il nove
  (f) zero due trentanove ventiquattro ottantuno, interno settecento cinquanta (*or:* sette, cinque, zero)
3 (a) le dieci   (b) l'una/le tredici   (c) le otto/le venti   (d) le undici/le ventitré

17.2 Ordinal numbers

1 (a) il primo ottobre
  (b) la seconda guerra mondiale
  (c) il Terzo Mondo
  (d) la decima volta
  (e) il ventesimo anniversario
  (f) Elisabetta seconda
  (g) l'ottavo secolo d.C.
2 (a) il Novecento
  (b) il Trecento
  (c) il quindicesimo secolo
  (d) il diciannovesimo secolo

17.3 Other numbers

1 (a) un quarto   (b) un terzo   (c) tre quarti   (d) due terzi
2 (a) mezza bottiglia
  (b) una bottiglia e mezza
  (c) metà del vino
  (d) mezza pagina
  (e) metà (del) libro
  (f) a metà prezzo

3   **(a)** C'era un centinaio di ospiti.
     (b) C'era una ventina di studenti.
     (c) C'è un migliaio di manifestanti.
     (d) Ci sono migliaia di manifestanti.

18 The present indicative tense

18.1 The present indicative tense: regular forms

1	**(a)** abitano	**(c)** scrivete	**(e)** dorme		
	(b) leggono	**(d)** studiate	**(f)** mangia		
2	**(a)** offrire -o *ending*	**(d)** soffrire -o	**(g)** capire -isco		
	(b) preferire -isco	**(e)** seguire -o	**(h)** vestirsi -o		
	(c) partire -o	**(f)** finire -isco			
3	**(a)** mangi	**(b)** paghi	**(c)** cominciamo	**(d)** giochiamo	
4	**(a)** si annoiano	**(b)** si perdono	**(c)** si divertono	**(d)** si stupisce	

18.2 The present tense: irregular forms

1	**(a)** hai, ho	**(b)** stai, sto	**(c)** fai, faccio	**(d)** dai, do	**(e)** vai, vado
2	**(a)** usciamo, uscire		**(e)** traduco, tradurre		
	(b) andiamo, andare		**(f)** sono, essere		
	(c) propongono, proporre		**(g)** sono, essere		
	(d) dite, dire				
3	**(a)** voglio, posso		**(c)** sappiamo, dobbiamo		
	(b) Puoi, devi		**(d)** volete, potete		
4	**(a)** rimani, rimango		**(d)** vengo, vieni		
	(b) rimane, rimangono		**(e)** mi trattengo, si trattengono		
	(c) scegli, scelgo		**(f)** mi siedo, vi sedete		

18.3 Uses of the present tense

1   **(a)** Mi alzo presto e faccio colazione alle sette.
     (b) La Gran Bretagna è un'isola e l'Italia è una penisola.
     (c) Bevete il caffè la mattina/al mattino?
     (d) Pranzano ancora?
     (e) Che lavoro fai?
     (f) Che cosa dice? Non lo sento.
     (g) Non riesco ad aprire la finestra.
2   **(a)** Quando parti per Parigi?
     (b) Domani vado al cinema.
     (c) Ti chiamo la prossima settimana.
     (d) Ci sentiamo presto.
     (e) Stiamo per partire.
3   **(a)** Imparo l'italiano da due anni. *Or:* Sono due anni che/È da due anni che imparo l'italiano.
     (b) Ci conosciamo da tre mesi. *Or:* Sono tre mesi che/È da tre mesi che ci conosciamo.
     (c) Non ci sentiamo dall'anno scorso/È dall'anno scorso che non ci sentiamo.
     (d) Sono in Italia da settembre/È da settembre che sono in Italia.
     (e) Lo aspetto da sabato/È da sabato che lo aspetto.

4	**(a)** Porto	**(c)** ho cambiato	**(e)** scrive		
	(b) Ho portato	**(d)** abito	**(f)** ha scritto		

18.4 The present continuous

1   **(a)** stiamo studiando
     (b) sto leggendo
     (c) sto facendo/faccio
     (d) si stanno divertendo/si divertono
2   (a) and (d) are impossible, as they refer to the future. (b) is possible but unlikely.

19 The future tense

19.1 The simple future

1 (a) scriverò (b) dormirà (c) torneranno
2 (a) giocherò (b) spiegheremo (c) cominceranno (d) festeggerai
3 (a) andrò, farò
   (b) dovrai, potrai
   (c) rimarranno, vedremo
   (d) avrò, sarò
   (e) diremo, verremo
   (f) Tradurrai, darai

19.2 Uses of the future

1 (a) pioverà (b) sarà (c) arriveremo
2 (a) aumenteranno, resteranno
   (b) affolleranno, inquineranno
   (c) diventerà, lavoreranno, otterranno
3 (a) andrò a trovarla (b) prenderemo (c) gli manderò una cartolina di auguri
4 (a) Domani vado a Torino.
   (b) Prendiamo il treno alle cinque.
   (c) Mando dei fiori a mia madre.
5 (a) Avrà almeno sessant'anni.
   (b) Che lavoro farà?/Chissà che lavoro fa.
   (c) Sarà sposato.
   (d) Sarà ricca, ma è proprio stupida.
6 (1) vi spingerà (2) cambierete (3) tenderete (4) toccherà (5) vedrà (6) sarà (7) spegnerà
   (8) riempiranno (9) potrà (10) aiuterà (11) avrete (12) dovrete (13) vorrete
7 (a) Se mi dai una mano, ti compro/comprerò il gelato.
   (b) Se mi impresti la macchina, pago/pagherò io la benzina.
   (c) Se non ti sbrighi, facciamo/faremo tardi.
8 (a) gli insegnanti faranno sciopero.
   (b) la gente morirà di fame.
   (c) il clima della Terra cambierà.
9 (a) Resterò finché resta/resterà lui.
   (b) Resterò finché non arriva.
   (c) Ti telefonerò appena scriverà.
   (d) Quando mi pagheranno, ti comprerò un vestito.

19.3 The future perfect

1 (a) l'avrai dimenticato.
   (b) sarò già partito/a.
   (c) Giovanni sarà tornato.
2 (a) Avrà sbagliato strada?
   (b) Avrà avuto un incidente.
   (c) Sarà un bravo guidatore ma il tempo è brutto.
3 (a) se avrò finito i compiti.
   (b) quando l'avrò letto.
   (c) una volta che avrò sistemato l'appartamento.
   (d) dopo aver fatto la spesa.
4 (a) appena finisco i compiti.
   (b) appena l'ho letto.
   (c) appena ho sistemato l'appartamento.
   (d) appena ho fatto la spesa

5   (a) Vieni a trovarmi quando hai finito.
    (b) Mandagli il libro quando ha pagato.
    (c) Appena divorziato si risposerà subito.

20 The past indicative tenses

20.1 The *passato prossimo*

1   (a) ordinato   (c) capito   (e) caduto/a
    (b) ricevuto   (d) andati/andate   (f) partito/a
2   (a) ho fatto   (c) hai aperto   (e) sono rimasto/a
    (b) ha risposto   (d) sono stato/a   (f) sono venuti/e
3   (a) mi sono alzato/a
    (b) mi sono sentito/a
    (c) mi sono seduto/a
    (d) mi sono messo/a
    (e) mi sono tolto/a
4   (a) *I know Sardinia well. I've been there many times. I've always liked it.*
    (b) *Last year I went to Sardinia. I liked it a lot.*
    (c) Did you fly or did you travel by train? – I took the car, it's more convenient.
    (d) Giulia, I've taken the car. I'll bring it back tonight
5   1 ci siamo alzati 2 siamo andati 3 sono arrivata 4 ho lavorato 5 mi sono annoiata 6 sono
    tornata 7 abbiamo fatto 8 abbiamo camminato 9 siamo tornati 10 abbiamo visto
    11 è piaciuto 12 abbiamo dormito
6   (a) scritto, scritta   (b) letto, letti   (c) parlato, parlato   (d) messo, messa
7   (a) ha intenzione   (c) aveva intenzione
    (b) ha dato   (d) aveva dato
8   (a) Mi ha appena detto che ha prenotato ieri.
    (b) Ieri mi ha detto che non aveva prenotato.
    (c) Mi ha detto che aveva intenzione di prenotare la prossima settimana.
9   (a) mi è servita   (c) mi sono successe
    (b) non mi sono bastati   (d) mi è piaciuta
10 (a) Non ho potuto partire.
    (d) Hai dovuto tornare a casa?
        Sentences (b) and (d) have only one form.
11 (a) Abbiamo dovuto fermarci.
    (b) Elena ha dovuto risposarsi.
    (c) Mi sono potuto/potuta sposare presto.
    (d) Marta non si è voluta fidanzare.
12 (a) ho cambiato   (d) non è migliorata   (g) sono corso
    (b) è molto cambiata   (e) è volata   (h) ho corso
    (c) non ha migliorato (f) ho volato

20.2 The imperfect

1   (a) c'erano pochissime macchine.
    (b) nessuno aveva paura.
    (c) bevevano pochissimo.
    (d) tutti andavano a messa.
2   (a) No, ascoltavo la radio.
    (b) Non so, preparavo la cena in cucina.
    (c) Era buio, ma sì, c'era qualcuno. Portava una giacca a vento e un berretto di lana. L'ho
        visto mentre saliva su un furgoncino bianco.
3   (a) (1) aveva (2) fumava (3) dipingeva (4) Era (5) moriva (6) posava (7) fischiava (8) smetteva
        (9) cominciava (10) faceva (11) chiudeva
    (b) (i) which Maria had never seen before (ii) it was very interesting standing there and
        watching him/to stand there and watch him

4   **(a)** Non riuscivo ad aprire la finestra.

    (b) Era buio: li sentivo ma non li vedevo.

    (c) Li sentivo solo se gridavano forte./Li potevo sentire …/Riuscivo a sentirli …

    (d) Non sapevo ballare, ma sapevo cantare.

5   **(a)** Non la vedevo da dicembre.

    (b) La conoscevo da quando avevo tre anni.

    (c) Aspettava da un'ora.

    (d) Dal 1980 aveva avuto tre mariti.

6   **(a)** da quanto tempo insegnavi a Milano? – Insegnavo da due anni, da quando mi ero sposato.

    (b) Sì, eravamo fidanzati da sei anni.

    (c) non ci vedevamo da tre anni e io non avevo mai visto mia figlia!

7   **(a)** avevano saputo; avevano sentito; non mi ero occupato

    (b) ero da poco nella cucina; da molti anni non esercitavo

    (c) (i) I wouldn't come (ii) I didn't know if I would be capable of being of any help

8   **(a)** che venivano così presto.

    (b) dormiva fuori.

    (c) portava venti ospiti a cena.

    (d) stavano per vendere la casa.

9   **(a)** potevano   **(b)** doveva   **(c)** potevi

10   **(a)** sapevo, venivo   **(b)** dicevi, prestavo   **(c)** spiegavo

20.3 The imperfect and the *passato prossimo*

1   **(a)** Martedì, mentre Anna ascoltava la radio, Pietro ha fatto la cena.

    (b) Mercoledì Anna ha pulito la casa mentre Pietro preparava una lezione.

    (c) Ieri siamo andati a una festa. È stata una serata meravigliosa.

    (d) Ieri siamo abbiamo fatto una passeggiata perché era una bella serata.

    (e) L'anno scorso sono andato/a in Corsica. Mi è piaciuta molto.

    (f) Quando abitavo a Londra, mi piaceva visitare i musei.

2   **(a)** dovevo   **(c)** non ho potuto   **(e)** ho saputo

    (b) ho dovuto   **(d)** non potevo   **(f)** sapevo

20.4 The imperfect continuous

1   **(a)** stavo ascoltando   **(b)** stavo preparando   **(c)** stava salendo

20.5 The pluperfect

1   **(a)** avevo chiesto   **(d)** eravamo nati   **(g)** era uscito

    (b) si era laureato   **(e)** avevo chiesto

    (c) aveva bevuto   **(f)** sono uscito

2   **(a)** Appena uscito/a di casa, mi sono sentito/a male.

    (b) Finiti gli esami, mi sono trovato un lavoro.

    (c) Ero già partito/a quando sono arrivati.

    (d) Una volta uscita dall'ospedale/Quando mia moglie è uscita dall'ospedale, ho potuto tornare al lavoro. *Or:* Dopo che mia moglie era uscita dall'ospedale, ho potuto tornare al lavoro.

20.6 The simple past: *il passato remoto*

1   **(a)** si comprarono   **(b)** ricevette   **(c)** dormì   **(d)** si sedettero

2   **(a)** lessi, leggesti, lesse, leggemmo, leggeste, lessero; scrissi, scrivesti, scrisse, scrivemmo, scriveste, scrissero

    (b) (i) Vennero   (ii) Venisti   (iii) visse   (iv) viveste

3   **(a)** **fu**: essere – fui fosti; **vide**: vedere – vidi vedesti; **pensò**: pensare – pensai pensasti; **aprì**: aprire – aprii apristi; **uscì**: uscire – uscii uscisti; **prese**: prendere – presi prendesti; **avvicinò**: avvicinare – avvicinai avvicinasti; **ritrasse**: ritrarre – ritrassi ritraesti; **seguì**: seguire – seguii seguisti

(b) **È stato** allora che **ho visto** un coniglio in una gabbia. Era un coniglio bianco, di pelo lungo e piumoso … Fuori della gabbia, sul tavolo, c'erano dei resti d'erba e una carota. **Ho pensato** a come doveva essere infelice, chiuso là allo stretto, vedendo quella carota e non potendola mangiare. E gli **ho aperto** lo sportello della gabbia. Il coniglio **non è uscito** … **Ho preso** la carota, **gliel'ho avvicinata**, poi, lentamente l'**ho ritratta** per invitarlo a uscire. Il coniglio mi **ha seguito** …

4   aprì gli vidi, lo prese, ce ne venimmo via, Pietro se lo tolse di spalla, lo posò, lo costrinse, aprì gli occhi, abbandonò una mano, venne avanti , restò nell'orto, venne a pranzo. *Passato prossimo:* I canti, la stanchezza … Me **ne hanno fatto** qualcosa d'irreale …

20.7 The past anterior

1   (a) ebbe finito   (b) aveva finito   (c) sentì   (d) ha sentito
2   (a) aveva cavato, aveva raccolto
     (b) (i) when he was/(had been) satisfied (ii) when all ten were/(had been) cut:
     (c) (i) quando fu soddisfatto: there is no trapassato remoto form of the verb essere; you cannot say 'fu stato soddisfatto'(ii) furono tagliate: there is no passive trapassato remoto form; you cannot say 'furono state tagliate'. (See p. 271)
     (d) These verbs are expressing ongoing actions rather than specific stages in the narrative.
3   (a) (i) arrivò, si radunò, cominciarono, fu chiamato (ii) È finita (iii) gridava, correva, piangevano, non riteneva, pensava, non credeva (iv) era finita, lo aveva saputo, l'aveva saputo, non aveva detto niente
     (b) (i) The war has ended/is over (ii) the was had ended/was over (iii) he had found out
     (c) *the subjunctive,* **fosse,** *is used twice instead of the indicative,* **era,** *and depends on the verbs* **non riteneva** *and* **pensava.**

21 The conditional

21.1 Regular and irregular forms of the conditional

1   (a) laveresti   (b) cerchereste   (c) prenderemmo
2   (a) verrei   (c) rimarresti   (e) faresti
     (b) vorrebbero   (d) potreste   (f) andrei
3   (a) Umberto, mi daresti un bicchiere di vino?
     (b) Anna e Cristina, mi fareste un favore?
     (c) Signora, avrei bisogno di una crema più leggera.
     (d) Signore, me lo preparerebbe per stasera?
4   (a) darei un passaggio   (b) tradurrei   (c) berrei
5   (a) non risponderei.
     (b) proporrei un'altra soluzione.
     (c) si arrabbierebbe.
6   (a) (1) avremmo un clima instabile (2) sarebbe oiù breve (3) potrebbe durare (4) mancherebbe un pezzo (5) non ci sarebbero (6) non potremmo 'volere' la luna' (7) come farebbero gli sposini
     (b) to wish for the moon; honeymoon
7   (a) You should go to the doctor's.
     (b) I am supposed/meant to be leaving at three, but I haven't got my ticket.
     (c) They should already be at home by now.
     (d) Could you come at two?
     (e) You said you could come at two
     (f) He/She could be at auntie's or at granny's.
     (g) Could you tell me if they've come back?
     (h) He/She couldn't/wasn't able to tell me anything.
     (i) Giulia would like to stay in Pisa.
     (j) She would like to stay in Pisa.
8   The sentences (c) and (h) are in the imperfect.

21.2 The past conditional

1 **(a)** Sarei   **(c)** Sarebbero   **(e)** si sarebbe
   (b) Avrei   **(d)** mi sarei   **(f)** ci saremmo

2 **(a)** Avremmo protestato.
   (b) Mi sarei arrabbiato/a.
   (c) Mi sarei lamentato/a.

3 **(a)** Sì, mi sarebbe piaciuto andarci. Mi piacerebbe andarci domani.
   (b) Sì, avrei voluto parlargli. Vorrei parlargli presto.
   (c) Sì, gli sarebbe piaciuto venire. Gli piacerebbe venire la prossima settimana.
   (d) Sì, avrei voluto finire il lavoro. Vorrei finirlo presto.

4 **(a)** Ero convinto che avrebbe telefonato/che telefonava.
   (b) Sapevano che sarebbe partita/che partiva.
   (c) Mi ha detto che sarebbe arrivato/che arrivava alle quattro.

5 **(a)** The minister is apparently not prepared/unwilling to resign.
   (b) The plane is reported to have crashed ten minutes after take-off.
   (c) The robber is reported to have fired/apparently fired twice.

22 The imperative

22.1 The formation of the imperative

1 **(a)** parla/parli/parlate piano
   (b) scendi/scenda/scendete subito
   (c) finisci/finisca/finite il lavoro
   (d) parti/parta/partite subito

2 **(a)** non parlare/non parlate
   (b) non scendere/non scendete
   (c) non finire/non finite
   (d) non partire/non partite

3 **(a)** scegli/scelga una canzone
   (b) rimani/rimanga un po' di più
   (c) tieni/tenga la destra
   (d) vieni/venga dentro
   (e) traduci/traduca il brano

4 **(a)** abbi   **(b)** sta'
   (c) fa'   **(d)** di'
   (e) da'
   voi imperatives (a)–(c) above are abbiate, state, fate

5 **(a)** Fallo subito. Lo faccia subito.
   (b) Dille di venire. Le dica di venire.
   (c) Vacci. Ci vada.

6 Negative imperatives of (a) and (b) are: Non far lo subito. No lo faccia subito.
   (b) Non andarci. No ci vada.

7 **(a)** Svegliati! Svegliatevi!   **(d)** Chiedigli. Chidetegli.
   (b) Finiscilo. Finitelo.   **(e)** Mettiti. Mettetevi.
   (c) Siediti. Sedetevi.   **(f)** Divertiti. Divertitevi.

8 The suggestions are: **mettiamolo gui** and **andiamoci domani** (i.e. the imperative **noi** form).
   (c) is a negative. **tu** imperative; (d) is a voi imperative; (b) and (e) are statements.

22.2 Uses of the imperative

1 **(a)** Si accomodi, Accomodatevi.
   (b) Mi passi il sale.
   (c) Mi dia un po' di pane, per favore.
   (d) Ci faccia un caffè, per favore.
   (e) Ci porti il conto, per favore.

2 (a) Guarda bene prima di attraversare la strada.
   (b) Sta'/Stai attento/a!
   (c) Non toccare niente.
   (d) Non sederti lì!/Non ti sendere lì!
   (e) Esci di qui.
   (f) Sbrigati!
3 (a) (iii)   (c) (iv)
   (b) (i)   (d) (ii) Answers (iii) and (iv) are **noi** imperatives in the form of suggestions
4 (a) Senta!   (b) Non me lo dire!   (c) Senti.
5 (a) (i) Mi porta il conto? (ii) Mi porti il conto.
   (b) (i) Mi faccia un caffè. (ii) Mi fa un caffè?
6 spingi, rallenti, lava, allaccia
7 Eviti … Scelga … Metta… annaffi … tenga … spruzzi
8 Distendete … Legate … Iniettate … praticate … spremete … Trasportate

23 Non-finite verb forms

23.1 The infinitive

1 (a) senza pagare
   (b) prima di partire
   (c) come ringraziarti
   (d) cambiare treni a Milano
   (e) vederti qui
   (f) dove andare
2 (a) Mi piace viaggiare in treno.
   (b) Penso di partire/di andarmene.
   (c) Spero di vederti presto.
   (d) Dubito di poter venire.
3 (a) come migliorare i risultati
   (b) migliorare
   (c) come fai/si fa a migliorare i risultati
4 (a) Mangiarlo? Ma scherzi!
   (b) Fare una passeggiata? No, sono troppo stanco/a.
   (c) Il mio passatempo preferito è giocare a carte.
   (d) Fare la doccia fa risparmiare acqua.
5 (a) comunicare, fare, aprirla, scansionare, consentire, leggerla, spedirla, riciclarla, passarla, distruggerla, archiviare
   (b) comunicare *depends on* **tocca a**; consentire *depends* on **per**; leggerla *depends on* **di**.
   (c) Fare *depends on* **cosa.**
   (d) *The other infinitives have an imperative function: the recipient of the letter has to tell the post office what to do with the letters.*
6 (a) a leggere romanzi.
   (b) a giocare a bridge.
   (c) a riparare la macchina.
   (d) a mangiare cioccolatini.

23.2 The past infinitive

1 (a) aver pagato i debiti
   (b) aver ricevuto il pacco
   (c) essere uscito con te
   (d) essermi divertito
2 (a) aver dovuto partire.
   (b) non aver potuto venire.

3   **(a)** Sono contento di averli comprati.
    (b) È un sollievo averla venduta.
    (c) È un peccato non essere partiti insieme.
    (d) È un peccato non aver viaggiato insieme.

4   **(a)** aver trovato le chiavi.
    (b) non esserci andato.
    (c) di aver capito.
    (d) aver dovuto partire.

5   **(a)** Sono uscito senza fare colazione.
    (b) Sono partiti senza aver pagato.
    (c) Grazie di averci aiutato.
    (d) Verrò a trovarti dopo avergli parlato.

6   **(a)** I think I'm leaving on Monday.
    (b) I think I left last Monday.
    (c) I am happy to see him tomorrow.
    (d) I am happy I saw him yesterday.
    (e) I can't get married before finishing my studies.
    (f) I can't get married before I have finished my studies.

23.3 The gerund

1   **(a)** Lavorando come un matto e risparmiando la metà dello stipendio.
    (b) Bevendo caffè e fumando come un turco!
    (c) Studiando il mercato e offrendo un servizio sempre migliore.

2   **(a)** Andando in città, ho incontrato Giuseppe sull'autobus.
    (b) Attraversando Piazza della Repubblica, ho visto la polizia arrestare/che arrestava due uomini.
    (c) Andando a casa ho visto Letizia che parlava a/con Adriano.

3   **(a)** essendo (stato) malato
    (b) avendo sentito le critiche
    (c) avendo mangiato così male

4   **(a)** Detesto aspettare.
    (b) Erano seduti lì ad aspettarmi.
    (c) È scappata via urlando.
    (d) Urlare non serve a niente.

5   approfittando *taking advantage of*; non essendo pavimentato *since there was no flooring*; evitando *avoiding*

6   **(a)** coming out of; he had seen the two conferring; was clearly thinking; before going off to bed
    (b) Berengario *is not the subject of the sentence.*
    (c) che aveva visto
    (d) I due che confabulavano
    (e) **stava ... pensando** *is a finite verb; the imperfect continuous of* **pensare**.

23.4 The past participle

1   **(a)** Fatta la spesa, Luisa è tornata casa.
    (b) Finite le lezioni, siamo andati in centro.
    (c) Una volta arrivati in albergo, mi dovete chiamare.
    (d) Passati il ponte e la farmacia, troverai la strada a destra.

2   Apart from being smothered in dust.

3   **(a)** Una volta riparata la macchina
    (b) Una volta partita la nave
    (c) Ricevuta la brutta notizia

4   **(a)** Risolto il problema, si sentì più tranquillo
    (b) finiti gli esami partì in vacanza
    (c) Appena ritrovati gli occhiali, sono riuscito a perdere le chiavi!

24 The subjunctive

24.1 The present subjunctive

1   (a) che io gli mandi il pacco?
    (b) che tu gli scriva qualcosa
    (c) che loro dormano subito!
    (d) che lo finisca io?
    (e) che tu lo paghi adesso
    (f) che loro comincino presto

2   (a) che lo faccia io?   (c) che glielo dia io?
    (b) che ci vada io?   (d) che glielo dica io?

3   (a) contenga   (d) produca
    (b) intervenga   (e) opponga
    (c) riesca   (f) attragga

4   (a) È essenziale che tu lo paghi presto.
    (b) È importante che lo spediscano/mandino domani.
    (c) Ma è necessario che io lo sappia oggi.

5   (a) vengano   (b) sia   (c) tornino

6   (a) Mi fa piacere che tu stia meglio.
    (b) Mi dispiace che lei non abbia più tempo.
    (c) Temo che loro vogliano lamentarsi di nuovo.
    (d) Che peccato che loro non possano venire.
    (e) Ho paura che Lucio sia malato.
    (f) Non è giusto che lo facciano loro.

7   (a) beva   (b) mangi   (c) rimangano d) che tradisca

8   (a) faccia   (b) finisca   (c) dia

9   (a) che è infelice
    (b) non dico che lui sia
    (c) Dici che sono?
    (d) Si dice che lui abbia
    (e) che tu tornerai (torni)
    (f) che sia/sarà

10   (a) non possa venire
    (b) riesca a farlo in tempo
    (c) vada via

11   (a) Preferisco farlo.
    (b) Preferisco che tu lo faccia.
    (c) Voglio venire.
    (d) Voglio che loro vengano.
    (e) È importante capire.
    (f) È importante che tu capisca.

12   considerino; concentrino; rallentino; ti dicano

24.2 The past subjunctives

1   (a) sia venuto
    (b) lui non abbia capito
    (c) vogliano venire
    (d) abbiano dimenticato/si siano dimenticati

2   (a) Immagino che sia stato difficile.
    (b) Può darsi che sia già andato via/partito.
    (c) È strano che non abbiano chiamato.
    (d) Pensi che abbia avuto un incidente?

3   (a) tornassi   (c) studiassimo
    (b) potessi   (d) capiste

4 **(a)** fosse   **(c)** stessimo   **(e)** bevessero
  (b) aveste   **(d)** desse   **(f)** traducessi
5 **(a)** fossero tornati
  (b) avessimo studiato
  (c) avessi capito
  (d) fosse uscito presto
6 **(a)** Se venissi a casa mia
  (b) Se fossero arrivati prima
  (c) Se perdessi il posto/il posto
  (d) Se non avesse litigato con il capo
  (e) Se guadagnassi di più
  (f) Se non mi fosse rotto la gamba
7 Sentences (a) and (e) *could also be expressed as:* se dovessi venire; se dovessi predere
8 **(a)** Mi ha detto che se io dovessi cambiare/cambiassi lavoro non mi avrebbe parlato mai più.
  (b) Dissero che avrebbero dato un premio a chiunque avesse risolto il problema.
  (c) Hanno detto che gli avrebbero comprato la macchina quando si fosse sposato.

24.3 The subjunctive sequence of tenses

1 **(a)** We hope they will come soon (F).
  (b) I hoped they would come soon (F).
  (c) I am pleased you are here (C).
  (d) I was pleased they were together (C).
  (e) He/She will think you haven't done anything (P).
  (f) it seemed that no one had seen anything (P).
  (g) It would be absurd for him/her to pay (F).
  (h) You wouldn't think he/she had studied (P).
2 (d) and (e)
3 **(a)** che non ci fosse nessuno
  (b) non avesse risposto nessuno
  (c) venissero
  (d) non fosse venuta
4 **(a)** Mi piacerebbe che tu venissi con noi.
  (b) sarebbe meglio che lo dicesse a loro, non a me.
  (c) Mi farebbe piacere se tu lo facessi subito.
  (d) Vorrei che voi me lo spiegaste.

24.4 Further uses of the subjunctive

1 **(a)** È stanco, sebbene/benché non abbia fatto nessuno sforzo.
  (b) Andremo in piscina a condizione che non faccia freddo.
  (c) Possiamo stare a casa a meno che tu non voglia uscire.
  (d) Uscirò senza che nessuno lo sappia.
  (e) Ti lascio la chiave nel caso che tu ne abbia bisogno.
  (f) Ammesso che sia antipatico, hai fatto male a parlargli in quel modo.
2 **(a)** Che suo figlio non studiasse
  (b) Che io sappia
  (c) non erano disposti ad aiutare
  (d) Che non fossero disposti ad aiutare
3 **(a)** È il posto più bello che ci sia.
  (b) È il posto più bello che io abbia mai visto.
  (c) Era l'unico insegnante che mi avesse mai aiutato.
4 **(a)** sappia   **(b)** sa   **(c)** sta   **(d)** stia
5 **(b)** stiano, chiuda, sia, debbano: *present of* stare, chiudere, essere, dovere
  (c) si chiudessero, levassi, dessi: *imperfect subjunctives of* chiudersi, levare, dare.
  (d) The English equivalents are (i) whoever so desired could go and present himself to the
princess (ii) if the girl was able to find the solution the pretender would immediately have

his head cut off (iii) if, on the other hand, the lady did not succeed in interpreting it, she would marry him.

The town crier's words would have been: (i) 'chiunque vorrà, potrà andare a presentarsi alla principessa' ('whoever so desires can/will be able to go and present himself to the princess'); (ii) 'se la ragazza saprà dare la soluzione, il pretendente avrà subito mozzata la testa' ('if the girl is able to find the solution, the pretender will immediately have his head cut off'); (iii) 'se invece la donna non riuscirà a interpretarlo, lo sposerà ('if, on the other hand, the lady does not succeed in interpreting it, she will marry him').

The pluperfect subjunctives **avesse voluto, avesse saputo, non fosse riuscita** *all refer to the future with respect to the main narrative. They are 'futures in the past' just like the past conditional tenses in these three sentences.*

25 Special verb constructions

25.1 Reflexive constructions

1   (a) Si è lavato.
    (b) Ha lavato la macchina.
    (c) Ho vestito mia figlia.
    (d) Mi sono vestito/a.
    (e) Ci siamo baciati.
    (f) Ci hanno baciato.
    (g) Mi sentivo/Mi sono sentito male.
    (h) Ho sentito un dolore.
2   (a) We're not in the office, we're outside the bar. (*reflexive.*)
    (b) See you tomorrow then; we'll meet outside the bar. (*reciprocal.*)
    (c) 'Bye, we'll be in touch tomorrow. (*reciprocal.*)
    (d) Yes, we both feel fine. (reflexive.)
    (e) What are your grandchildren called? (*reflexive.*)
    (f) Mariella e Paola si chiamano spesso. (*reciprocal.*)

25.2 Causative verbs

1   (a) Show Luigi in
    (b) Why do you make Luigi wait?
    (c) Why don't you make Luigi pay the fine?
    (d) I get my hair cut by Luigi.
2   (a) da   (b) da   (c) al
3   (a) Ho fatto suonare il pianoforte a mia sorella. Le ho fatto suonare il pianoforte.
    (b) Ho fatto fare la spesa a Dino. Gli ho fatto fare la spesa.
    (c) Ho lasciato guidare la macchina a mio fratello. Gli ho lasciato guidare la macchina.
    (d) Ho fatto aggiustare i freni dal meccanico. Gli ho fatto aggiustare i freni.
4   (a) Faccio pulire la casa. La faccio pulire.
    (b) Faccio alzare mio figlio. Lo faccio alzare.
    (c) Lascio mia figlia. La lascio sempre uscire.
5   (a) Fallo studiare di più.
    (b) Fagli studiare medicina.
    (c) Lasciala uscire di più.
    (d) Lasciala/e scegliere le materie che preferisce (*or:* Lascia che scelga …)

25.3 Verbs of perception

1   (a) Dobbiamo ascoltare cantare Pavarotti.
    (b) Ho guardato giocare mio figlio.
    (c) Abbiamo visto passare il corteo.
    (d) Ho sentito il vicino uscire di casa.

2 **(a)** Ha sentito abbaiare il cane?

(b) Ha visto andar via gli uomini?

(c) Li ha sentiti sbattere la porta?

(d) Ha sentito i vicini che gridavano aiuto?

3 **(a)** mi sono avvicinata, si è alzata, si è girata, si è buttata.

(b) *Pronouns are not reflexive: in the phrase* mi ha visto (*she saw me*), mi *is a direct object pronoun; and in the phrase* mi urlava improperi terribili (*she screamed terrible abuse at me*), mi *is an indirect object pronoun.*

(c) ho visto la sua mano stringere il piatto rotto *I saw her hand clutching the broken plate.*

(d) (i) Ho visto l'uomo colpire il ragazzo (ii) Ho visto l'uomo che colpiva il ragazzo.

25.4 *Sapere* and *conoscere*

1 **(a)** so **(b)** conosci **(c)** sa **(d)** conoscete, sappiamo **(e)** sai

25.5 *Piacere*

1 **(a)** Mi piace **(d)** Ti/Le/Vi piace

(b) Ti/Le/Vi piacciono **(e)** Gli piace

(c) Le piace **(f)** Le piacciono

2 **(a)** Do you like travelling? *Or:* Does she like travelling.

(b) Does he like Japanese films? *Or:* Do they like Japanese films?

3 **(a)** Sì, mi piace moltissomo

(b) Sì, mi piacciono molto.

(c) Sì, ci piace moltissimo.

4 **(a)** A tutti piace/Piace a tutti la musica lirica?

(b) Ai tuoi figli piace andare a teatro?

5 **(a)** A me piace il gelato.

(b) A te/Lei/voi non piacciono gli spaghetti?

(c) A lei piace cucinare.

(e) A lui piace l'uva o preferisce le arance?

6 **(a)** ma a lui no

(b) ma a lei sì

(c) Piace anche a loro.

(d) Non piace neanche a me.

7 **(a)** A lui piacciono i pomodori, ma a me no.

(b) A lei piace il caffè ma a me no.

(c) A mio marito piace giocare a tennis e (piace) anche a me.

(d) A me non piacciono le lenticchie ma a mia moglie sì.

8 **(a)** A mia moglie è piaciuto l'albergo di lusso.

(b) A mia suocera sono piaciuti i negozi.

(c) Ai miei figli è piaciuta la piscina.

(d) A me e a mio suocero sono piaciute le passeggiate in montagna.

9 **(a)** Mirella gli è simpatica.

(b) Bruno le è simpatico.

(c) Io non gli sono simpatico/a.

25.6 Other verbs used impersonally

1 **(a)** ti bastano **(d)** vi conviene

(b) ti serve **(e)** basta

(c) Le manca **(f)** bisogna

2 **(a)** Mi è dispiaciuto partire così presto.

(b) Ci sono successe delle cose strane.

(c) Non gli è mai capitato di arrivare in ritardo.

(d) Gli è toccato pagare una multa.

25.7 Further impersonal constructions

1   (a) Come si riavvia il computer/
    (b) Come si archivia un file/
    (c) Come si evidenzia il testo/
    (d) Come si scarica una car tella/
2   (a) ... non si è visto molto
    (b) Non si è capito come avesse fatto.
    (c) ... si è andati prestissimo a votare

25.8 The passive

1   (a) La città è inquinata dalle macchine.
    (b) Il colpevole sarà trovato.
    (c) A giugno gli esami erano corretti dagli insegnanti.
    (d) Queste tasse nuove sarebbero accettate dal pubblico?
    (e) Non è giusto che gli insegnanti siano criticati dal governo.
    (f) La macchina non dev'essere riparata da Carlo.
2   (a) Le finestre vengono pulite.
    (b) I ragazzi venivano spesso puniti.
    (c) La città è rimasta distrutta.
    (d) Siamo rimasti stupiti.
3   (a) Il tetto va riparato.
    (b) La cucina andrebbe rinnovata.
    (c) I soffitti andranno rifatti.
    (d) Le finestre andavano pulite.
4   (a) si spedirà il pacco.
    (b) si mangia il formaggio.
    (c) si è abbandonata la città.
    (d) non si è preso in considerazione il prezzo.
    (e) si dovranno pulire tutte le finestre.
5   (a) *Passives*: sono costretti, vengono impiegati, sono considerati (**present tense**); sono rimasti coinvolti, sono state obbligate (**passato prossimo**); possono essere utilizzati, continuano ad essere arruolati (**present passive infinitives**). *Note also that* **si ritiene** (*impersonal* **si**) *can have a passive meaning*.
    (b) In fact it is claimed/people claim that they are more malleable, more inclined to obey orders and that they have fewer compunction in carrying out savage attacks.
6   (i)   **si passivante**: non si è ancora individuato tutto *not everything has been located yet*
    (ii) *impersonal* **si**: si è incerti *people are unsure/there is uncertainty*
    (iii) *passive:* non sono stati ancora trovati *they have not yet been found*
7   si può arrivare, ci si sente, se si ha un pubblico si diventa, non si sa (**impersonal si**); si dicomo, mai si direbbero (**si passivante**)
8   (a) Aldo è stato chiamato ieri/Hanno chiamato Aldo ieri.
    (b) Hanno telefonato a Patrizia alle nove.
    (c) Antonio è stato derubato del portafoglio.
    (d) La bicicletta di Gemma è stata rubata/A Gemma le hanno rubato la bicicletta.
    (e) Hanno chiesto a Mario di spostare la macchina/A Mario gli hanno chiesto di spostare la macchina.
9   (a) Mi hanno detto di arrivare presto.
    (b) Gli hanno impedito di votare.
    (c) Gli hanno bruciato il negozio.
    (d) Le hanno dato l'orario sbagliato.
    (e) Ci hanno costretto di pagare la multa/Siamo stati costretti a pagare la multa.
10 (a) (i) not very much is known about the most important ones (ii) you ended up in the Kingdom of Hades (iii) the body had to be buried
    (b) **fatta** *is a past participle:* **fatta la conoscenza** *having met. You can also say:* **dopo aver conosciuto**.

(c) (i) not before having made them forget all the horrors of the world (ii) **non prima di avergli fatto dimenticare** ...

(d) **bevendo** *is a gerund which in this context means by drinking.*

(e) *than is expressed first by* **di**, *then by* **che**: **più gaudenti ... degli egizi; le idée più chiare sulla vita che sulla morte.**

(f) the soul would wander

(g) **cagnaccio**: ghastly, vile dog. Cerberus was the many-headed guardian of the underworld.

26 Verbs and prepositions

26.2 Verbs taking *a*

1 (a) Type 2. È venuto a fare ...
   (b) Type 1. È venuto per/a fare ...
   (c) Type 2. Siamo rimasti a vedere ...
   (d) Type 3 Si annoiavano a sentire ...

26.3 Verbs taking *di*

1 (a) Mi sono stufato di aspettare'
   (b) Mi stanco a studiare di sera.
   (c) Non ti vergogni a imbrogliare la gente?
   (d) Mi vergogno di aver imbrogliato Carla.

2 (a) a   (f) di
   (b) a   (g) di
   (c) di   (h) di
   (d) di   (i) a
   (e) a   (j) di

3 (a) Penso di venire presto.
   (b) Spera di ottenere il posto/lavoro.
   (c) Dubito di poter aiutare.
   (d) Temo di essere in ritardo.

26.5 Further uses of *a* and *di*: requests, commands, promises and refusals, etc.

1 (a) a   (b) di   (c) a   (d) di
2 (a) Gli ho proibito di uscire.
   (b) Lo convincerò a uscire.
   (c) Le ho chiesto di rimanere.
   (d) La costringerò a rimanere.
3 (a) Ho detto a Simona di venire più tardi.
   (b) Ho invitato Angela a venire.
   (c) Ho chiesto a Martina di andar via/andarsene.
   (d) Ho ricordato a Susi di telefonare.
   (e) Ha costretto Susi a telefonare
   (f) Ha pregato Fabrizio di scrivere.

26.6 Different preposition, different meaning

1 (a) della   (c) a   (e) a
   (b) di   (d) di   (f) a
2 (a) Puoi credere quello che vuoi.
   (b) Credi a Marina? Le credi?
   (c) Credi in Dio?
   (d) Posso parlarti di Gianni?
   (e) Posso parlare a Gianni?
   (f) Mi ha parlato del suo lavoro.

3 **(a)** comprare a, riuscire a, relegare in, informarsi su

(b) (i) there I was wandering, sighing (ii) or they were consigned/relegated to hidden corners and cupboards under the stairs gathering dust (iii) don't stand there putting down roots into the pavement

(c) (i) from shop to shop (ii) as a child (iii) on modern toys (iv) on that spot (v) in a tiny face

(d) (i) Volevo farmi regalare i giocattoli. (ii) Volevo farmeli regalare.

(e) **che cosa fossero, come potessero, dove … potessero**: *the verbs are subjunctive because they have interrogative antecedents.*

(f) *They are polite imperatives.*

(g) who had popped out of

(h) **Studiava**, *the imperfect, is used after* **da** *and shows the man is still scrutinising him. The pluperfect* **mi ero fermato** *must be used: you cannot say 'who knows how long I was standing on that spot'.*

(i) (i) **angolino, vocetta, botteghino** (*little shop* – **botteghino** is also a ticket/box office), **occhialoni, baffetti, pizzetto** (ii) **sottoscala**

References

Accademia della Crusca (ed.) (1985) *Gli italiani parlati*, Florence: Academia della Crusca.

Bazzanella, Carla (1987) 'I modi dell'imperfetto', *Italiano e oltre* 1, pp. 18–22, Florence: La Nuova Editrice.

_____ (1990)'Il passivo: vario e polifunzionale', *Italiano e oltre* 1, pp. 121–4, Florence: La Nuova Editrice.

Beccaria, Gian Luigi (ed.) (1973) *I linguaggi settoriali in Italia*, Milan: Bompiani.

_____ (1988) *Italiano antico e nuovo*, Milan, Garzanti.

Benincà, Paola (1986) 'Il lato sinistro della frase italiana', *ATI Journal*, pp. 57–85.

Berruto, Gaetano (1987) *Sociolinguistica dell'italiano contemporaneo*, Rome: La Nuova Italia Scientifica.

Bruni, Francesco (1984) *L'italiano. Elementi di storia della lingua e della cultura*, Turin: UTET.

Calboli, Gualtiero, and Moroni, Giuseppe (1989) *Grammatica italiana*, Bologna: Calderini.

Corti, Maria, and Caffi, Claudia (1989) *Per filo e per segno. Grammatica italiana per il biennio*, Milan: Bompiani.

Cresti, Emanuela (1987) 'L'italiano in prima visione', *Italiano e oltre* 2, pp. 60–65, Florence: La Nuova Editrice.

D'Achille, Paolo (1988) 'Un "che" detto da sempre', *Italiano e oltre* 5, pp. 227–31, Florence: La Nuova Editrice.

Dardano, Maurizio, and Trifone, Pietro (1985; 1991) *La lingua italiana*, Bologna: Zanichelli.

De Felice, Emidio, and Duro, Aldo (1993) *Vocabolario italiano*, Turin and Palermo: SEI and GB Palumbo.

De Mauro, Tullio (ed.) (1994) *Come parlano gli italiani*, Florence: La Nuova Italia Editrice.

_____ (ed.) (2000) *Il dizionario della lingua italiana*, Milan: Paravia.

Devoto, Giacomo, and Oli, Giancarlo (2007) *Vocabolario della lingua italiana*, Florence: Le Monnier.

Ferreri, Silvana (1988) 'Gli "aspetti" del gerundio', *Italiano e oltre* 1, pp. 21–2, 31–2, Florence: La Nuova Editrice.

Gianni, D. Angelo, and Satta, Luciano (1988) *Dizionario italiano ragionato*, Florence: G. D'Anna – Sintesi.

Istituto dell'Enciclopedia italiana (1996) *Vocabolario della lingua italiana*, Rome.

Kinder, John, and Savini, Vincenzo (2004) *Using Italian: A Guide to Contemporary Usage*, Cambridge: Cambridge University Press.

Lepschy, Anna Laura, and Lepschy, Giulio (1988) *The Italian Language Today*, London: Hutchinson.

Lo Duca, Maria (1993) 'Tempo imperfetto', *Italiano e oltre* 8, pp. 248–50, Florence: La Nuova Editrice.

_____ (1993) 'Presenti e futuri imperfetti', *Italiano e oltre* 9, pp. 304–6, Florence: La Nuova Editrice.

_____ (1994) '"Aspetti" da considerare', *Italiano e oltre* 10, pp. 53–5, Florence: La Nuova Editrice.

_____ (1994) 'Dare il tempo a tempo', *Italiano e oltre* 11, pp. 122–4, Florence: La Nuova Editrice.

Maiden, Martin, and Robustelli, Cecilia (2007) *A Reference Grammar of Modern Italian*, 2nd edition. London: Hodder Education.

Moss, Howard, and Motta, Vanna (2000) *Using Italian Synonyms*, Cambridge: Cambridge University Press.

Poggi Salani, Teresa (1986) 'Varietà di lingue, evoluzione, norma', in *Per lo studio dell'italiano*, pp. 53–71, Padua: Liviana Editrice.

Pittano, Giuseppe (1987) *Sinonimi e contrari. Dizionario fraseologico*, Bologna: Zanichelli.

Ragazzini, Giuseppe, and Rossi, Gualtiero (1986) *Dizionario inglese italiano italiano inglese*, 2nd edition, Bologna: Zanichelli.

Renzi, Lorenzo, and Cortelazzo, Michele (eds.) (1977) *La lingua Italian oggi. Un problema scolastico e sociale*, Bologna: Il Mulino.

_____ and Salvi, Giampaolo (1988) *Grande grammatical italiana di consultazione*, 3 vols, Bologna: Il Mulino.

Roncoroni, Angelo (1991) *Lexis. Argomentazione e composizione italiana*, Milan: Arcipelago Edizioni.

Rosselli, Renato (1989) *Dizionario. Guida alla scelta dei sinonimi e dei contrari*, Florence: Edizioni Remo Sandron.

Sabatini, Alma (1987) *Raccomandazioni per un uso non sessista della lingua Italia*, Rome: Presidenza del Consiglio dei Ministri.

Sabatini, Francesco (1984) *La comunicazione e gli usi della lingua*, Turin: Loescher.

Scarduelli, T., Achiardi, G., and Barbi, S.(1988) *Lingua e grammatica : analisi e produzione di testi*, Milan: Principato.

Serianni, Luca (1988) *Grammatica italiana. Italiano comune e lingua letteraria*, Turin: UTET.

Simone, Raffaele (1987) 'Specchio delle mie lingue', *Italiano e oltre* 2, pp. 53–9, Florence: La Nuova Editrice.

Sobrero, Alberto (ed.) (1993) *Introduzione all'italiano contemporanea*, vol. 1: *Le strutture*, Rome: Laterza.

Valentini, Ada (1987) 'Il sesso delle parole', *Italiano e oltre* 3, pp. 108–12, Florence: La Nuova Editrice.

Vincent, Nigel (1988) 'Italian', in Martin Harris and Nigel Vincent (eds.), *The Romance Languages*, pp. 279–313, London: Routledge.

Visconti Jacqueline (1996) ' "Deverbal" conditional connectives in English and Italian', *The Italianist* 16, pp. 305–25.

Zingarelli, Nicola (1994) *Vocabolario della lingua italiana*, 12th edition, Bologna: Zanichelli

Index